ANDY STEVES'
EUROPE

CITY-HOPPING ON A BUDGET

FOREWORD

When I wrote my first guidebook 35 years ago, it was a practical manual for a generation of independent travelers taking overnight trains, sleeping in hostels, carrying traveler's checks, and picking up mail at American Express offices.

Times have changed, and today my son Andy has written a new kind of guidebook for Millennial travelers with an entirely new range of options to choose from. They jet between hot spots on the cheap (something inconceivable when I was Andy's age). They find accommodations through social networks like Airbnb and couch surfing. And they leverage digital and online tools that would have been a space age dream in my student vagabond days.

Yet while travel styles and tools may change from generation to generation, the fundamentals of travel remain the same. And today, as much as ever, if you equip yourself with good information and expect yourself to travel smart, you can get the most out of two precious resources: your time and your money.

Another key to good travel is the importance of meeting people. I remember when Andy went on his first solo European trip just out of high school, I laid out all the museums and castles and galleries he should be sure to visit. When he came home he triumphantly declared that he had skipped most of those conventional sights and, instead, made friends in each country.

Andy's right: it's connecting with people that carbonates your travel experience, and he's an expert at that. When you meet people from different cultures face to face, you broaden your perspective. And when your new friends take you out of your comfort zone, the world becomes your playground.

In this guidebook, Andy shares lessons gained from a decade of living on the road while organizing his Weekend Student Adventures tours for tens of thousands of young travelers. In the era of globalization, a complete education includes some foreign travel experience. Andy's advice on sightseeing and practicalities will help any young traveler city-hopping on a budget have an economical and unforgettable adventure in Europe.

A closing note to Andy: This is not your father's guidebook. It fills the needs of young travelers in a way that I never could and it does so brilliantly.

Bravo!

Rick Steves

CONTENTS

Modern travelers have all the technology in the world at their fingertips. Today, thanks to budget airlines and online resources, backpackers have become precision travelers, popping in and out of major destinations all over Europe at the spur of the moment. We're visiting cities rather than countries, and packing incredible adventures into increasingly shorter time slots. This book will help you make the most of your time and money by zeroing in on each destination's must-sees.

TRAVEL PHILOSOPHY

Good travel is really all about two things: bringing the right mind-set to embrace the unexpected, and sorting out the practical logistics. The second part of that equation is what the rest of this book is all about—the logistics of getting from A to B in the most time-efficient and cost-effective way, and having a blast while you're there. I'll be with you every step of the way!

But your mind-set is just as important. We live in a complex world, with many different points of view swirling around us in more media formats and screens than ever before. Technology is accelerating progress around the world, and things are changing at an ever-faster rate. It's never been more important to understand and connect with people from other cultures. The lower to the ground you travel, the more you experience each fascinating destination and achieve life-changing experiences.

Connect With the Culture

If you've never traveled or studied outside the country, being somewhere completely different can be nerve-wracking. People, food, language...even the laws will be different than what you're used to. The resulting anxiety can lead you to trap yourself inside the "American Bubble."

The American Bubble is that safe group of American friends you meet abroad. They listen to the same music as you do, eat the same food, take the same classes, and are therefore quite easy to relate to. Don't get me wrong; I enjoy meeting Americans while traveling. However, if at the end of your time abroad, the only new friends you made are English-speakers, you may need to reevaluate why you came to Europe in the first place.

Don't let the American Bubble prevent you from experiencing Europe to the fullest.

Break free and immerse yourself in something new. Dive into a local festival, sample strange food, flirt with that cute French guy (or girl!). You'll make memories that will ultimately make you a better, more worldly human being.

Say Yes

In my experience, simply saying "yes" to things I haven't tried before is the most direct route to creating unforgettable memories. Of course, some lines should never be crossed, but in general, being a yes man or woman for the day (or night) can be really fun. You have a chance to catch a *fútbol* match in Madrid? Say yes! Never tried smoked herring? Taste it in Amsterdam. Do as the Berliners do and stay out till sunrise. Expose yourself to new experiences. You won't regret it.

Ask Questions

Take every opportunity to learn something new about each place you visit. Ask locals where *they* go on a Saturday night, what their views on European and American politics are, and how they celebrate their holidays. They'll appreciate your interest, and they are sure to have questions for you as well.

When it comes to making conversation, don't ask where someone is from unless you've got a follow-up question ready, or conversation will die shortly afterward. Instead, have a lineup of compelling questions to ask those sitting next to you on the train or at the bar to get people to open up.

Some Suggestions:

- Where are you headed, and what is there to do there?
- Where else should I travel?
- I really like X. Where should I go to experience that?

Maintain Perspective

As this book was nearing completion the headlines were again dominated by terrorist acts. Terrorism is a fact of life in Europe and many other parts of the world, including the U.S., and there's always a chance that another attack will occur in one of the cities covered in this book. If that happens, take a deep breath and try to keep the risk and tragedy of terrorism in perspective. The chance of your being affected directly are astronomically minuscule—you can look it up—and as every European understands, the best way to counter terrorism is by refusing to be terrorized.

ABOUT THIS BOOK

Who is Andy Steves?

I grew up traveling with my father, travel guru Rick Steves. From infancy through high school, I spent my summers learning the ins and outs of budget travel.

My approach to travel fuses my father's love of culture with all the modern tools available today thanks to technology. Through college, I worked as a tour guide for Rick Steves' Europe Through the Back Door. While studying abroad in Rome, I started organizing trips for my friends each weekend, leading groups of 5-10 fellow students. By the end of the semester, these groups numbered over 30.

Upon returning to the United States, I began formulating ideas for tips and trips designed specifically for budget travelers and study abroad students. That led to **Weekend Student Adventures** (wsaeurope.com), which is now the leading student tour company in Europe. Weekend Student Adventures offers an affordable, local experience to budget travelers in Amsterdam, Paris, Barcelona, Berlin, Budapest, Prague, Rome, Krakow, Edinburgh, Dublin and more!

How to Use this Book

I've adapted the tried and tested itineraries I developed for Weekend Student Adventures for the purposes of this book. Each time I visit a city, I try to do it all: visit the most blogged-about restaurants, hit the main museums, pop into the city's churches, relax in the best parks, find the best panorama, grab a beer at the hottest pubs and clubs. Once I tackle the big names, I spend the rest of my time getting off the beaten path and writing about it to share with you. Each chapter gives you the nuts and bolts you need to plan a quick trip to a given city, from tips on calibrating your budget to transportation information to a detailed three-day itinerary that lets you experience that city to its fullest.

BEFORE YOU GO

Think of your trip as one big piece of artwork: Start with the outline first, then get down to the details. Make the outline of your trip by nailing down the following constraints:

- Where you want to go
- How much time you have—and how much of that you're willing to spend in transit
- Budget—daily target and total
- What you want to do (what's your priority—sightseeing, music, culture, architecture, or nightlife?)

Decide Where to Go

If you've got three weeks or less and want to hit a wide range of destinations, like Dublin, London, Edinburgh, Paris, Amsterdam, Berlin, Prague, and Budapest, here's how I would break it down. To split eight cities across 21 days, you'd have a travel day almost every other day, barely giving you a chance to catch your breath. I'd recommend slicing at least two of these destinations from the itinerary. Consider the following factors for each city: inbound and outbound flights, similarity of one city to the next, your own desires and preferences, what exactly you want to do in the destinations, and time and cost to get from one city to the next.

These cities provide a pretty solid range of experiences. Dublin, London, and Edinburgh are of course separated from the continent. While I love Dublin, if it's your first time through Europe, I'd recommend cutting out this city in favor of having a little more time and flexibility.

If you're studying abroad and will be taking multiple trips throughout your school semester, map out when to go based on each destination. Go to the beach cities (like Barcelona) when it's warmer, visit active or pedestrian cities (like Prague) before it gets too cold, and save "museum" cities (like Berlin) for the winter.

Plan Your Route

Now that I've narrowed down my itinerary to a manageable list, it's time to consider how to get from A to B to C. Consider trains, buses, and flights—which are generally the quickest and best option. If you're on a tight budget, book transportation ahead of time, as prices can climb the closer you get to your travel date. For tips on choosing the best mode of transit, along with step-by-step instructions on booking your transportation between cities, see page 350.

Links: Try skyscanner.com, kayak.com, cheapoair.com, momondo.com for flights; sbb.ch for train travel; eurolines.com, orangeways.com, berlinlinienbus.de, renfe.com, and studentagencybus.com for bus travel; carpooling.co.uk for ride-sharing.

Apps: For a list of helpful transportation apps, see page 357.

Decide Where to Sleep

Travelers often ask me whether they should book accommodations ahead of time. To decide, weigh the value of accommodation at potentially cheaper prices against flexibility and spontaneity. If you're on a tight budget or traveling during a famous event, book your hostel as far in advance as possible. For more tips on booking accommodations, see page 355.

If you do book in advance, go the extra mile and find out how to get to your hostel *before* you leave for your trip. Nothing is worse than arriving in a foreign city with a heavy backpack and not knowing where to go. Print out directions or a map, and know which metro line to take and how much it costs.

Links: Use hostelworld.com or airbnb.com. Also check out each site's helpful app.

Calibrate Your Budget

Know roughly how much your trip is going to cost before jumping in headfirst. How much is an individual meal? How expensive is a night out? What's the admission price for that famous art museum? To help you out with this, I've added city-specific tips on calibrating your budget at the beginning of each chapter.

Credit cards are widely accepted across Europe. Visa tends to be more common than Mastercard, and it's difficult to find anyone who takes American Express. For security reasons, the "chip-and-pin" system is ubiquitous in Europe, though swipe cards do still work just about everywhere. It's worth asking your bank to issue a chip-and-pin card ahead of time. **Cash** is often preferred in southern European countries like Italy and Spain. And you may encounter minimums (around €10) set by merchants to use a card.

Apps: Use the XE Currency app to keep track of fluctuating conversion rates and the Mint.com app to balance your budget.

Plan for Precision Sightseeing

Make a list of the top 3-5 things you want to see, and make reservations online to save yourself hours in line. At the beginning of each chapter, you'll find a list of sights that you should reserve in advance. Avoid trying to see too much—travel is a lot more than snapping a selfie in front of a famous monument.

Also consider booking a **local guide.** Doing so costs money, but guides help you get more out of your travels and will reduce the amount of time getting lost.

IF YOU LIKE...

Grand museums:
Paris, London, Berlin, Rome

Culture and live performances:
Dublin, Madrid, Edinburgh

Outdoor recreation:
Edinburgh, Barcelona

Art history:
Paris, Rome, Venice, Florence, Madrid

Cuisine:
Rome, Madrid, Venice

Festivals:
Budapest, Venice, Amsterdam

Cheap thrills:
Madrid, Budapest, Prague

GO TO...

Euro-trash techno discotecas:
Berlin, Barcelona, Rome

Pub life and beer:
Berlin, Prague, Dublin, London

Alternative scene:
Berlin, Budapest, Prague

Casual and social ambience:
Paris, Amsterdam, Prague

Old-world atmosphere:
Prague, Budapest

Late, late nights:
Berlin, Barcelona, Madrid

LGBT nightlife:
Amsterdam, Paris, London, Barcelona

CITY-HOPPING

Group cities geographically so that you don't waste time and money zigzagging across the continent. Each of these itineraries can also be done in the opposite direction, and you can link them together for a longer trip—for example, Best of the North followed by Best of Britain (Amsterdam → Paris → London → Edinburgh → Dublin). Prices are approximate, and tend to be lower the farther in advance you book.

Best of the North
London → Paris → Amsterdam
In as little as one week, you can get a taste of three of Western Europe's major cultural capitals.
- From London's St. Pancras station, take the fast train to Paris (2.5 hours, from €50).
- From Paris, hop a train to Amsterdam (3.5 hours, around €75).

Best of Eastern Europe
Berlin → Prague → Budapest
Explore complex history by day and dive into an alternative nightlife at night. This itinerary is great for history buffs and architecture fiends.
- From Berlin, use studentagencybus.com or orangeways.com to book a bus to Prague (4.5 hours, €40).
- From Prague, consider a Wizz Air or Czech Airlines flight to Budapest (1 hour, from €60), or take a train (7 hours, €75).

Best of Spain
Barcelona → Madrid
Whether you love nightlife, tapas, museums, or simply having a good time, Spain's two most important cities have got you covered.
- Fast trains connect Barcelona and Madrid (3 hours, from €50) several times daily. Buses are also an option. Book at renfe.com.

Best of Italy
Rome → Florence → Venice
This route is a no-brainer for pizza- and gelato-loving foodies. Add in robust art history and architecture, and you'll see why this trip has become a classic.
- From Rome, take a fast train (1.5 hours, from €25, reservations required) or a slow train (3.5 hours, from €20) to Florence. Avoid rush hour for cheaper prices.
- From Florence, take a fast train (2 hours, from €30, reservations required) or a slow train (7.5 hours, €15) to Venice. As with the previous leg of the journey, avoid rush hour for the best price.

Best of Britain
London → Edinburgh → Dublin
Head to the capital cities of the British Isles for pubs, live music, and the ease of connecting with friendly, English-speaking locals.
- From London, hop a cheap flight to Edinburgh (1 hour, €60), or take a train (4.5 hours, €110).
- From Edinburgh, numerous airlines run cheap flights to Dublin (1 hour, from €45) multiple times a day. For the best price, avoid rush hour. Many people commute between these cities for business.

ON-THE-GROUND TRAVEL TIPS

Carry a Map
Getting lost in foreign cities can be fun, but it's always nice to know the way back home. Always carry a map, and take time to look up from it every once in a while to orient yourself. I always take my first morning in town to study up on my favorite sights and mark them on the map. I can then strategically group close-together sights to save commuting time.

Flash Your Student ID
Some cities (like Madrid) offer free or dis-counted admission to students with a valid ID. It's always worth checking when booking ahead or buying tickets.

Customize Your Experience
Whether it's sporting matches, DJs, or architecture, it's worth researching what's on in each city during your visit.

Music, sailing, and cycling races are some of my personal hobbies, so I watch for related events when I travel. If I'm in France in July, I make a point to catch a stage of the Tour de France. On a nice day in May in Berlin, I look up a lake outside of the city and take a friend sailing for an afternoon.

Ready to hit the road? Read on!
Bon voyage, bon viaggio, and gute Fahrt!

Andy Steves

LONDON

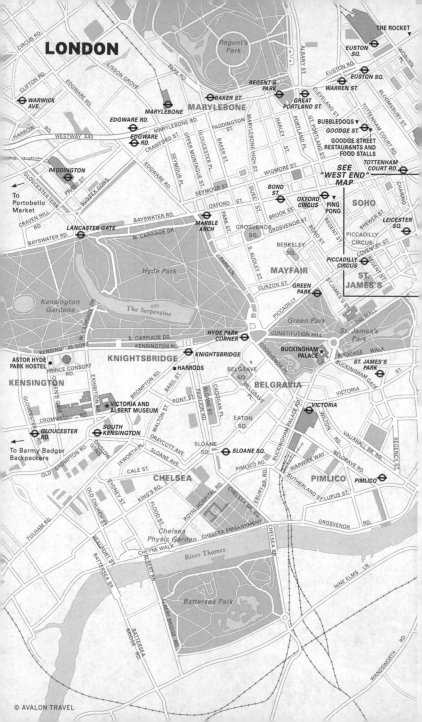

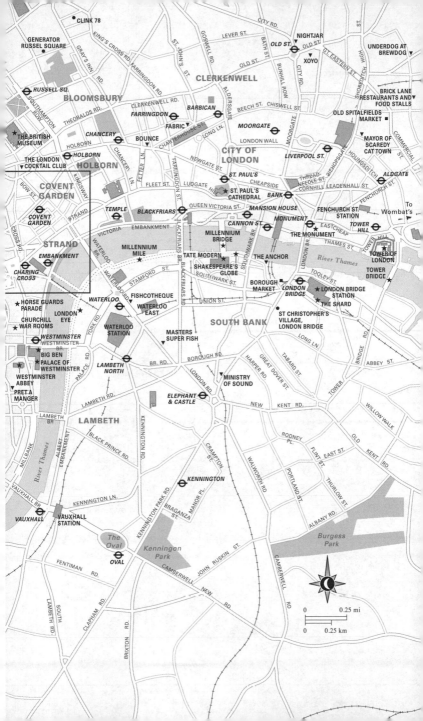

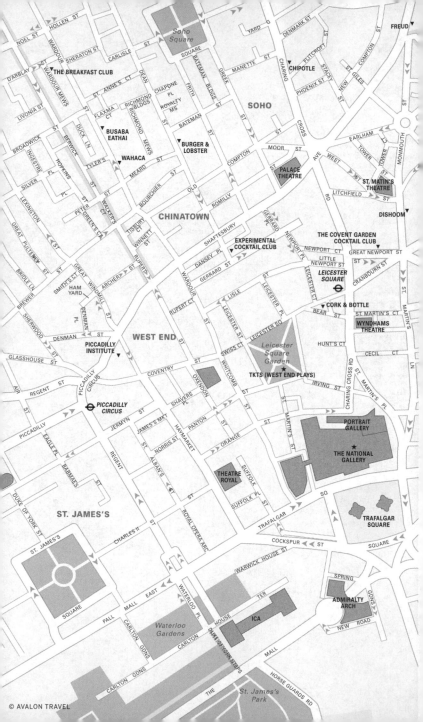

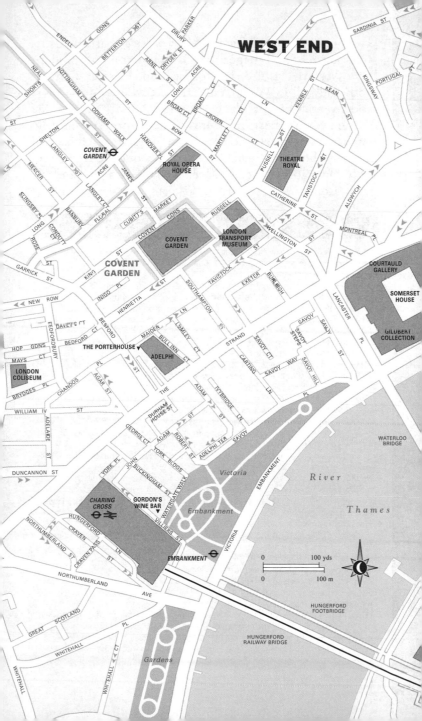

L ondon, a world leader in style, design, art, industry, politics, and pageantry, is the home of modern Western culture. Having rebounded after fighting tooth and nail in World War II, it's now one of the most modern cities on the planet. London proudly offers some of the world's best museums (mostly free!), nightlife that ranges from classic pubs to trend-setting clubs, and probably the best chicken tikka masala outside India. Get ready for a good time, because, as The Clash so famously put it, London's calling.

LONDON 101

London was founded as a far-flung outpost in the Roman Empire nearly 2,000 years ago. The city's strategic location on the Thames put it squarely on the route leading from Britannia to the continent of Europe.

By the Middle Ages, London was a tangle of overcrowded, filthy streets. Disease spread quickly in the dense tenements. In 1350, the bubonic plague rode through on the backs of rats, killing more than 100,000 Londoners in a few short months. Mass graves dating back to these difficult years are often discovered today when city center construction projects break ground.

In spite of the plague, the city continued to grow, but in 1650, tragedy struck again when a three-day blaze now known as the Great Fire of London destroyed nearly 90 percent of the homes in the City of London, displacing tens of thousands of citizens. Numerous plans for rebuilding were submitted but never realized, and many modern streets mirror those of London's haphazard medieval layout.

The Industrial Revolution toward the end of the 18th century transformed London once more. Technologies like the telegraph and industries like the railway propelled wealth and population growth in London as well as Britain's burgeoning global empire. By 1800, London was home to one million inhabitants, becoming the first city to cross that benchmark since the Roman Empire. By this time, British naval prowess had stretched a small island's influence around the globe to the Americas, Africa, and the Far East, concentrating riches never before seen in London.

In 1863, London broke ground on the world's first underground railway, the Underground, aka the Tube. An idea many contemporary skeptics initially laughed at now transports over one billion passengers a year and is the lifeblood of the city, removing a large portion of traffic from the congested streets.

These same tunnels provided shelter when the Germans bombed the city tirelessly during the Battle of Britain in World War II. Winston Churchill conducted the war effort from his own bunker just a few blocks from Westminster Palace. You can visit the Churchill War Rooms today and see them just as they were when the war ended in 1945.

After the war, the city grew even more, as rebuilding efforts focused on reducing density by encouraging residents to move to communities farther from the city center. Former colonies were also allowed open immigration to England, making London one of the most diverse cities in Europe.

Since its early days, the City of London has been the economic capital of England, with prohibitive real estate prices driving many residents out. Each borough beyond the City of London used to be its own independent township, until eventually the borders dissolved and the boroughs combined to become the City of London we know today.

PLAN AHEAD

RESERVATIONS

Reservations are recommended for the following sights:

Tower of London (hrp.org.uk/TowerOfLondon)

London Eye (londoneye.com)

LOCAL HAPPENINGS

Wireless Festival

Founded in 2005, the three-day Wireless Festival (wirelessfestival.co.uk), held annually in late June and early July, offers world-renowned bands and performers from all over the world. Going down each year at Finsbury Park, the Wireless Festival exchanges corporate sponsors often between banks and tech companies. Headliners from recent years included Justin Timberlake, John Legend, Jay Z, and Rihanna.

Bonfire Night

"Remember, remember, the 5th of November." This quote was made famous to Americans through the movie *V for Vendetta*, but it is actually a ditty written about Guy Fawkes Night, now known as Bonfire Night. Fawkes was a Catholic conspirator who organized a group of fellow Catholics to blow up the Houses of Parliament in 1605 (the Gunpowder Plot). Unfortunately for him, his plot was discovered just in time and he was executed for high treason. Today, Brits everywhere celebrate the prevention of this terrorist plot with fireworks, bonfires, and a lot of drinking on November 5. Battersea Park now has a huge bonfire and light show each year.

THREE DAY ITINERARY

A good itinerary of London flanks the south side of the Thames on the first day, and the north side of the Thames on the second day. On your third day, you'll still find plenty to keep you busy.

DAY 1: WELCOME TO LONDON

MORNING

Spend your morning on the South Bank. First, head out for my favorite walk along the water: **Millennium Mile**. It's an enjoyable three-hour stroll. Start with breakfast from a food stall in the **Borough Market**. Continue on to see **Shakespeare's Globe** and the **Tate Modern** (featuring one of the best contemporary art collections in the world). This stroll will orient you and give you a sense of the scale and layout of the city as it wraps around the Thames River.

AFTERNOON

Drop south a couple blocks from the roundabout at Waterloo Station to grab lunch at the best fish-and-chips joint in the city, **Master's Super Fish**.

Head back to the Millennium Mile for a ride in the **London Eye**. Afterward, cross Westminster Bridge to glimpse the famous exterior of **Big Ben** and **Westminster Palace.**

Hop on the Circle Line at the Westminster station over to Bayswater Tube and stop for a bike tour of the Royal Gardens with **Fat Tire Bike Tours** (leaves daily at 15:00 May 15 through September). If you're outside the season, flip today's itinerary to catch their daily morning departure at 11:00. If you prefer to stay seated, take **bus 11** for a ride straight through the heart of the City, connecting Victoria and Liverpool Street stations.

EVENING

Get dinner in the eccentric Covent Garden neighborhood. Choose gastropub grub at **Porterhouse**, authentic Southern Mexican at **Wahaca**, or spicy Thai at **Busaba Eathai**. The nightlife and bars around Covent Garden are sure to keep you busy. **Freud** is an excellent hidden little spot for a nightcap. Or if wine is your thing, head to **Gordon's Wine Bar** right next to the Embankment stop for candlelit glasses within exposed-brick cellar walls.

LATE

Stay in the West End and explore the back streets toward Soho for the night. Consider catching a West End show: Find last-minute discount tickets in **Leicester Square** at the **TKTS** booth.

DAY 2: CHECK OUT THE CITY

MORNING

Spend an hour or so at **Westminster Abbey** (check hours beforehand; the abbey can close for special events), where you'll find all the VIPs of British history: royals, philosophers, and artists like Chaucer and Charles Dickens. Next, pop into a **Pret a Manger** for a quick, cheap lunch along Whitehall Road.

AFTERNOON

From Westminster Abbey, take a slow stroll north and east along Whitehall Road, taking the rest of the day to make your way over to the Tower of London. After Trafalgar Square, Whitehall Road becomes the Strand, London's and Westminster's main boulevard. You'll pass numerous important landmarks along the way, including the traditional parade grounds of the **Horse Guards Parade**, grand **Trafalgar Square**, the **National Gallery,** and **Nelson's Column**. If these sights pique your fancy, be sure to stop in and check them out!

In two miles, you'll come upon the historic but easy-to-miss **Ye Olde Cheshire Cheese** pub (145 Fleet St) and the massive **St Paul's Cathedral**. At this point, you're also crossing the border between Westminster and the City of London. About a mile after St Paul's, keep an eye out on the right for the **Monument** (the tall, singular column), which commemorates the Great Fire of London; you can climb it for only £3.

Finally, arrive at the **Tower of London** and pick up a ticket. Time your visit to catch the wonderfully enthralling Beefeater-guided tour (leaving every half hour from the main gate) and of course see the Crown Jewels! All in all, you'll spend a couple hours here.

EVENING

Take the half-hour walk north from the river to **Brick Lane** for the world's best chicken tikka masala. Soak in all the hipster culture while you're in **Shoreditch**, one of London's trendiest neighborhoods, offering diverse nightlife venues like **Nightjar,** which does just the trick for me.

DAY 3: MUSEUMS & SHOPPING

MORNING

Spend the morning in the **British Museum** and take in everything it has to offer. Then find **Goodge Street** for an early lunch. Choices abound for every type of cuisine you could imagine. Continue up to **Oxford Street** and wander toward **Hyde Park** to enjoy London's main shopping zone. Give yourself the "London look" with a stop in **Selfridges**.

Alternatively, if it's Sunday, spend your morning shopping at **Old Spitalfields Market** (open daily, but best on Sunday). The food's great, but better options are nearby at the weekly **Sunday Upmarket** on Brick Lane. After your fill, wander north on **Brick Lane** through more streets of vintage clothing shops, hipster goods galore, and delicious snacks and food stalls.

AFTERNOON

If you opted for the department store shopping route, drop south from Selfridges through **Soho** and explore the many music stores, market stands, adult shops, cafés, and eccentric people that crowd the winding neighborhood streets.

Make your way west past Hyde Park into **Harrods,** London's iconic department store. If you still have energy, the nearby **Victoria and Albert Museum** boasts the world's largest collection design.

EVENING

Head up to **Camden Market** to explore and check out the alternative scene via the Piccadilly line, transferring to the Northern line. Get ready for a bohemian, eclectic scene with loads of student nights and discount drinks that budget travelers love. Center your efforts around the Camden Market Tube stop and market and north for a few blocks along Chalk Farm road.

TOP NEIGHBORHOODS

The River Thames bisects London west to east, creating a useful navigational aid. The City of London, north of the river, is a mere square mile that was once enclosed within medieval London's walls. Today, **The City,** as it's known, is where you'll find St Paul's Cathedral and the Tower of London, among other sights.

West of The City is London's **West End.** This is *the* entertainment district, with endless restaurants, bars and clubs, and great shopping on Oxford Street. The West End includes the hip neighborhood of Soho (which is the hub of London's LGBT community), the theater district of Leicester (pronounced "Lester") Square, and Covent Garden, known for good food and fun, casual bars.

Westminster, just south of the West End, is the political, royal, and religious hub of Britain. This is where you'll find Buckingham Palace and Westminster Abbey.

South of the river is the **South Bank,** which has famous sights like the London Eye, the Tate Modern museum, and Shakespeare's Globe theater, all conveniently linked by the Millennium Mile riverwalk.

London is big, and there are worthwhile attractions even on its outskirts. Northwest of the City, the **British Museum neighborhood** offers a couple of convenient hostels and awesome budget food options on Goodge Street. **West London** is home to the Victoria and Albert Museum, along with famous Hyde Park. **Shoreditch** (northeast of the City) and **Camden** (about 20 minutes north of the city center on the Tube) are great nightlife districts. These two neighborhoods attract a young, hipster crowd with counterculture bars and shops.

TOP SIGHTS

Tower of London

The Tower of London is a castle right on the banks of the Thames, with foundations dating back to the 11th century. Over the following centuries, the Tower of London was under constant expansion and served as both a defensive fortress and the palace of kings and queens, up until the Tudors in the 1500s.

Besides its defensive and royal purposes, the Tower of London also served as a high-security prison with a long, bloody history of torture and public executions. The lively **Beefeater-guided tours** that depart every half hour (included with admission) provide an enjoyable history of the complex. Inside the tower itself, an exhibit walks you through the 500-year history of royal armor, medieval architectural plans and relics, and full-size replicas of siege weaponry.

Cap your visit with a viewing of the **Crown Jewels,** located just opposite the grounds from the tower. Seeing the jewels is included with admission and definitely worth the wait. Have your camera ready as you get on the moving sidewalk machine to see them. Taking a Beefeater tour, seeing the museum in the tower, and peeking at the Crown Jewels takes around 2.5 hours total.

£24 online, £25 in person, Tues-Sat 09:00-17:30, Sun-Mon 10:00-17:30, closes one hour earlier Nov-Feb, The City, +44 (0)844 482 7777, hrp.org.uk/TowerOfLondon, Tube: Tower Hill

Tower Bridge

After visiting the Tower of London, walk down toward the river and you'll find yourself a great photo op of the Tower Bridge. It's one of the main icons of the city, and tourists commonly mistake this bridge for the London Bridge, which is actually the next, less-exciting bridge upriver. For its 120th anniversary in 2014, Tower Bridge was decked out with a glass walkway that visitors can walk (or crawl) across, taking in the bridge and traffic from a new and impressive angle.

£9, daily 10:00-18:00 in summer, 09:30-17:30 in winter, +44 (0)20 7403 3761, towerbridge.org.uk, The City, Tube: Tower Hill

St Paul's Cathedral

St Paul's Cathedral, originally founded in 604, was rebuilt 1675-1710 after succumbing to the Great Fire of London. (Townsfolk thought that the massive stone cathedral would be a safe refuge, but the structure's wooden scaffolding caught fire, causing great damage inside and out.) The rebuilding was carried out by London's most revered architect of the time, Sir Christopher Wren. Wren drew direct inspiration from St Peter's

Basilica in Rome and strove to use all the formulas of the popular neo-Renaissance style to create his finest masterpiece.

During the German blitzkriegs of World War II, St Paul's Cathedral stood tall and remained unharmed. Many took this as a sign that even in the darkest of times, God would watch over the British people and see them through. During this time, St Paul's dome was actually protected by a crew of brave blokes who lived at the church and would run water buckets at the first sign of danger. Thanks to the success of defying the Germans, and the good fortune it took to escape the flames of war, St Paul's Cathedral became a symbol of British national identity.

Take in beauty of overwhelming magnitude at this Anglican cathedral, located in the middle of the city and on the tallest hill in all of London. With its large, white stone construction, St Paul's is impossible to miss. Inside, you'll discover gilded architectural accents and hundreds of intricate golden mosaics. Climb the 271 steps to the top of this architectural marvel for a beautiful panorama.

£16 online, £18 in person, Mon-Sat 08:30-16:30, Sun worshippers only, The City, +44 (0)20 7246 8350, stpauls. co.uk, Tube: St Paul's

The Monument

The single stone column known simply as the Monument was erected between 1671 and 1666 to commemorate the infamous Great Fire of London, which ravaged the city in 1666. If the column were to fall down toward the east, the end point would mark the exact spot of the start of the fire, in a bakery on Pudding Lane. The column offers a hike of 311 steps and a beautiful panorama of downtown London. A location right in the city of London (a couple blocks from the Tower of London) and an entry price of only £3 make this sight both convenient and cheap!

£4, daily Apr-Sept 09:30-18:00, daily Oct-Mar 09:30-17:30, Fish Street Hill, The City, +44 (0)20 7626 2717, themonument.info, Tube: Tower Hill

Westminster Palace & Big Ben

Westminster Palace was designed and built during the 19th century, when the sun never set on the British Empire. This building was an important project for the architect, Sir Charles Barry. Strategically located just outside of England's capital city, the City of London, Westminster Palace is where the wealthy and powerful had to come to get their voices heard in government. Today, the aggressively neo-gothic building that housed the parliament of the most powerful empire of the world is quite a sight to behold. While England's politics have played out in this governmental center since the palace's completion in 1870, England has been ruled from this neighborhood for even longer—numerous wooden-construction palaces have been lost to fire.

The Elizabeth Clock Tower is the one tourists like to call **Big Ben.** While it's the tallest tower at Westminster Palace, Big Ben is actually the name of the 13-ton bell (which you can't see from the street) that has tolled every hour since 1859. The best angle for selfies is from a few paces down Westminster Bridge. The clock face is a full 23 feet wide,

LONDON'S BEST VIEWPOINTS

Some of London's top sights also offer amazing panoramic city views:

St Paul's Cathedral
Climb the 271 steps to the top of this architectural marvel on the tallest hill in all of London and take in a beautiful panorama of the City.

Tate Modern
The top floor of this museum doubles as a restaurant with a beautiful view of the City. The restaurant is pricey; the view is not.

The Shard
Ride to the top of this London landmark or enjoy a posh cocktail on the 31st floor. Just as at the Eiffel Tower, the best views are seen from halfway up. Otherwise your vantage point is too far removed and the buildings fade into the distance.

London Eye
Take in impressive views from this 450-foot-tall Ferris wheel. Go at dusk for shorter lines and beautiful sunset shots.

and the minute hand moves six feet every five minutes.

While it is possible to visit inside Westminster Palace (see parliament.uk/visiting for information), those on a three-day visit to London are happy with a view from the outside.

Free, open when Parliament is in session, Westminster, Tube: Westminster

Buckingham Palace

You can't leave London without a selfie in front of Buckingham Palace! This is the grand and opulent residence of the royal family, located about a 15-minute walk west of Westminster Abbey. William and Kate shared a kiss on the neoclassical balcony, as did Prince Charles and Lady Diana in years past. Notice the perfect balance of the facade, a classic example of Renaissance-style architectural beauty. Located at the edge of St James's Park, Buckingham Palace contains a total of 775 rooms and has been the official home of British sovereigns since 1837. While today the palace functions as both a residence to the queen and an administrative building, it also serves the grand purpose of being one of the biggest tourist attractions in all of London. Make sure to time your visit during the changing of the guard.

From July through September, it's possible to tour the palace. In this half-mile experience that takes about two hours, you can check out the royal State Rooms (where the royal family entertains guests) and the Royal Mews (the stables), and see dozens of priceless art pieces from greats like Rembrandt, Titian, and Van Dyck in the Queen's Gallery. Tickets for a visit can be purchased all together in the Royal Day Out package (from £20) or in combinations of the various attractions.

Changing of the guards 11:30 every other day (refer to monthly schedule on website), +44 (0)20 7766 7300, Westminster, check full palace information and purchase tickets at royalcollection.org.uk, changing-the-guard.com/dates-times.html, Tube: Victoria

Westminster Abbey

With nearly 1,000 years of coronations, London's premier gothic church, complete with pointed arches, stained glass, and flying buttresses, has played host to the major life events of England's royal family. This Anglican church is still quite active: It was the site of Prince Charles's wedding to Lady Diana (1981), Princess Diana's funeral (1997), and Kate and William's wedding (2011). Many of the United Kingdom's most famous thinkers and national figures are entombed here, including Darwin, Chaucer, and Newton, along with 17 kings and queens of England underneath sequoia-like pillars supporting breathtaking arches and structuring ribbing.

£20, Mon-Fri 09:30-16:30, Wed till 19:00, Sat 09:30-14:30, Sun for worship only, 20 Deans Yard, Westminster, +44 (0)20 7222 5152, westminster-abbey.org, Tube: Westminster

Churchill War Rooms

Can you imagine running a world war in which millions of lives counted on you, coordinating movements of troops by pinning their positions on a wall in a damp, dark bunker deep in the earth? With the help of serious quantities of tobacco and whiskey, that's exactly what Winston Churchill and his military chiefs of staff did for the entirety of World War II, from a series of reinforced concrete rooms located deep beneath the Treasury Building.

Some of these war rooms have been frozen in time to create a museum. Tour each room, seeing the maps, note pads, and communication systems left as they were on VE Day in 1945. You can also walk through a fascinating exhibit on wartime England, which takes you through the daily lives of Londoners during the war, visually presenting everything from ration tickets and propaganda posters to spying technology and what it was like to seek cover from German

bombs in the Tube. This is a fascinating museum—especially for WWII buffs—that fills up an enjoyable two hours.

£18, daily 09:30-18:00, Clive Steps, King Charles St, Westminster, +44 (0)20 7930 6961, iwm.org.uk/visits/churchill-war-rooms, Tube: Westminster

Horse Guards Parade

This graveled parade ground has served as an open space in the heart of the city for events, ceremonies, and practices of the British military and royal family. For the 2012 Olympics, which London hosted, the Horse Guards Parade was transformed into a stage for beach volleyball, and it had a capacity for 15,000 fans surrounding the single court. Today the parade grounds make for a great, quick photo in front of the mounted guards and a chance to see the court through the gates to the back, on Whitehall leading from Big Ben and Westminster Abbey.

Free, guards change daily at 11:00 (10:00 Sun) and dismount at 16:00, Whitehall, Westminster, Tube: Charing Cross

Millennium Mile

The Millennium Mile is an easy-to-stroll riverwalk on the south side of the Thames. Anchored by the **London Bridge** and the **Shard** on one end, and **Big Ben** and the **London Eye** on the other, it's an extremely pleasant and convenient way to see a number of London's most famous sights. Between those major sights, you'll also pass by the **Borough Market, Shakespeare's Globe** theater, the **Tate Modern** museum, and the **Millennium Bridge**.

Free, always open, South Bank, Tube: London Bridge or Waterloo

The Shard

London's newest and most visible landmark is the Shard. Named for its distinctive glass design tearing into the London sky, the skyscraper was completed in 2013. Take the elevator to the 32nd floor, where you can enjoy a coffee in the posh restaurant Oblix. The best views are seen from halfway up; otherwise your vantage point is too far removed and the buildings fade into the distance.

Viewing platform £26 in advance/£31 in person adult over 16, £21 in advance/£26 in person student with valid ID; Apr-Oct daily 10:00-22:00 (last entry 21:30); Nov-Mar Sun-Wed 10:00-19:00 (last entry 17:30) and Thurs-Sat 10:00-22:00; 32 London Bridge St, South Bank, +44 (0)333 456 4000, the-shard.com, Tube: London Bridge

Shakespeare's Globe

While the design of Shakespeare's original theater was innovative, it was not particularly fire safe, and the theater burned down in 1613 after a malfunctioning cannon set the stage on fire. Along with the thatch roof and the stage sets, the architectural plans for this ground-breaking theater went up in flames.

This replica, with the trademark black timber-framed construction and intimate stage, was completed in 1997. It's meant to resemble the original theater as it would have looked in the 17th century. With capacity for about 850 seated nobles and 700 standing peasants, the Globe is an active theater, and viewing a performance here is fascinating. Plays are performed as they would have been in Shakespeare's day, with no voice amplification or artificial lighting. Check showtimes and book online.

It's also possible to **tour the theater** with an excellent guide who speaks about the history of the original building, how plays work in this purpose-built space for live entertainment, and the function of the venue today. Just like Shakespeare's plays, this guided walk appeals to intellectuals as well as potty-humor fans. Tours leave every 30 minutes throughout the day.

Exhibition £6, tour £13.50, price for shows varies, daily 09:00-17:30, Box Office West Piazza, 21 New Globe Walk, South Bank, +44 (0)20 7902 1400, shakespearesglobe.com, Tube: London Bridge

Tate Modern

This imposing remodeled power plant was opened in 2000 to house London's premier modern art museum, featuring one of the best collections of contemporary art in the world. With stark, dark brick construction and wide open gallery spaces, the Tate is packed with works from an all-star roster of artists. You can seek out Andy Warhol's prints, Roy Lichtenstein's large-scale comics, Donald Judd's sculptures of spatial explorations, and pieces by Cézanne. Plan to spend about an hour and a half here. The bookstore alone can keep you enraptured for hours. The top floor doubles as a restaurant with a beautiful view of the City. The restaurant is pricey; the view is free.

Free, Sun-Thurs 10:00-18:00, Fri-Sat 10:00-22:00, South Bank, +44 (0)20 7887 8888, tate.org.uk, Tube: Blackfriars

Millennium Bridge

This beautiful, modern, glass-and-steel pedestrian bridge spans the Thames from directly in front of the Tate Modern on the south side of the river to St Paul's Cathedral on the north side of the river, in the City of London proper. The Millennium Bridge opened in June of 2000, only two months late and £2 million over budget, but the opening day wasn't all applause and champagne. As the first few walked across, the bridge moved, so it became obvious the bridge needed additional support. It was closed back down for two years, and millions more were spent as engineers added support to make the bridge more rigid.

Free, always open, directly between St Paul's Cathedral and the Tate Modern, South Bank, Tube: Blackfriars

London Eye

Hoisted up in 1999 to celebrate the Millennium, this massive observation wheel—*not* Ferris wheel, as the staff and everyone else in London will have you know—is 450 feet tall and the United Kingdom's most popular tourist attraction, with over 3.5 million visitors each year. The 32 air-conditioned glass and steel pods, each holding up to 25 people, rotate around on a wheel on a single, cantilevered arm holding the entire contraption out above the Thames at a constant, crawling speed, completing only two revolutions each hour. Guests hop in and out of the moving pods as they skim the boarding area at the bottom. Insider tip: Sunny days wash out all your pictures. Go at dusk for shorter lines and striking sunset shots.

£20 online, £21.50 in person, daily 10:00-sunset, Riverside Bldg, County Hall, Westminster Bridge Rd, South Bank, +44 (0)871 781 3000, londoneye.com, Tube: Waterloo

British Museum

Opened in 1759, the British Museum was the first national public museum in the world free for all those who want to visit. Showcasing some of the greatest historical treasures the world has ever known, like the Rosetta Stone, the Parthenon Sculptures, and Egyptian artifacts, this well-appointed museum is dedicated to history, art, and culture. It takes about two hours to see the highlights. The museum also offers free 40-minute walking tours in the exhibit of your choice throughout the day. Find the relevant times on the free brochure when you walk in, or check the website.

Free, daily 10:00-17:30, Great Russell St, British Museum Neighborhood, +44 (0)20 7323 8299, britishmuseum.org, Tube: Tottenham Court Road

National Gallery

The National Gallery is a collection of two-dimensional artwork spanning back from the Dark Ages all the way to impressionism. Enjoy the free entry, and ponder 2,000 of the greatest paintings in existence, from Renaissance bosses like Leonardo and Michelangelo to baroque Caravaggio and impressionist Van Gogh.

The National Gallery is right on **Trafalgar Square**, a hub of London's history and public transportation. In the middle of the square, you'll find **Nelson's Column,** dedicated to the valiant Admiral Nelson, who was killed in battle at Cape Trafalgar in 1805 while leading his navy to a crucial victory over the French and Napoleon's navy.

Free, daily 10:00-18:00, Fri until 21:00, Trafalgar Square, West End, nationalgallery.org.uk, Tube: Charing Cross

West End Plays

The business of live entertainment dates back hundreds of years, well before the time of Shakespeare. Theaters began popping up in London on the west side of town, or the West End. Today, the district is home to dozens of theaters—large and small—and it's a popular option to catch a show while you're in town. Some plays, like the classics *Les Miserables* and *Mousetrap,* have been running for decades, while others, like *Wicked* and *The Lion King,* offer a more modern take. Find the **TKTS** booth in Leicester Square for tickets up to half off in the hours and minutes before the show starts.

Theater locations, prices, and show times vary, West End, Tube: Leicester Square, Covent Garden, or Piccadilly Circus

Victoria and Albert Museum

With a collection of more than 4.5 million design and decorative art pieces from all around the world, this massive museum can overwhelm any visitor in both quantity and quality of artifacts dating from the last five millennia. A stop at the information desk is key to organizing your time. Exhibits span religions, centuries, styles, materials, subjects, geography, and media. Beeline toward the subjects that interest you most, because it's easy to get lost in the 145 galleries, which make you feel like you're walking through a life-size encyclopedia. Don't miss my favorite piece, an original, revolutionary "Job" cigarette poster by Alphonse Mucha.

Free, daily 10:00–17:45, Cromwell Rd, West London, +44 (0)20 7942 2000, vam.ac.uk, Tube: South Kensington

TOP EATS

London has undergone a culinary renaissance in the last couple decades. People used to turn up their noses at the thought of British cuisine, but now visitors can find affordable places to eat throughout town. Heads-up: Sit-down lunches can easily run £13 ($20), and dinners will cost past £19 ($30). My suggestions will help you either save or get the best bang for your buck. There is no need to tip at fast food or takeaway shops. If you're sitting down for a meal, take a look over your bill and assess whether cover and service are included. If not, feel free to round up 10 percent or so, based on the service you received.

As **fish-and-chips** is the national dish of England, it would be a crime not to duck into one of the many local establishments that offer it. Master's Super Fish and FishcoTeque are two of my favorite places in town to sample it.

Master's Super Fish

Take a short walk down from Waterloo station and get ready for the city's best tempura goodness! Come for the great fish-and-chips, and don't let the gruff service get to you. This is a no-frills bar that feels more like your grandma's living room than a fast-food joint. The food is sure to make up for any hard feelings.

£5, Mon–Sat 04:30–22:30, 191 Waterloo Rd., South Bank, +44 (0)20 7928 6924, Tube: Waterloo

FishcoTeque

Fish are brought in daily from the Billingsgate market to this street stand restaurant near Waterloo station. The restaurant has recently been renovated to recapture the original 1950s feel it had when it opened. You've got a streamlined menu offering just about anything fried: chips, fish, burgers, and chicken burgers. Eat in or get takeaway to keep your momentum up.

£5.95, daily 11:00–23:00, 79A Waterloo Rd, South Bank, +44 (0)20 7928 1484, Tube: Waterloo

Ping Pong

Modern and fresh both in decor and food, Ping Pong is a stylish Asian fusion joint with delicious steamed dim sum. Ping Pong does spring rolls and beef dumplings especially well. Be sure to try their signature and seasonal Ping Pong cocktail for a tasty treat.

Meals from £10, Mon–Fri 11:00–24:00, Sat 12:00–24:00, Sun 12:00–22:30, 45 Great Marlborough St, West End, +44 (0)20 7851 6969, pingpongdimsum.com, Tube: Oxford Circus

Dishoom

This is my favorite spot for Indian food in the center of London. You pay a little more in this casual and refined atmosphere, but the quality of the naan (go for the garlic!), curries (especially the unique mahi tikka), and grills (I love the lamb roti) is superb. Top it all off with a mango lassi, and you'll remember this meal for sure. I like the open interior, which has a modern cafeteria feeling with wooden chairs and large windows. In addition to the Covent Garden location listed, you'll find three other locations throughout town. These guys don't take reservations, so you might wait up to an hour for your food. Trust me—it's worth it!

From £12, Mon–Thurs 08:00–23:00, Fri 08:00–24:00, Sat 09:00–24:00, Sun 09:00–23:00, 12 Upper Saint Martin's Ln, West End, +44 (0)20 7420 9320, dishoom.com, Tube: Covent Garden

The Breakfast Club

Famous for serving one of the best breakfasts in London, Breakfast Club has lines out the door—sometimes as long as 45 minutes—from opening to closing. Whether you come for the delicious beverages (coffee, cappuccino, or even hot chocolate), the thick-sliced bacon, the pancakes, or the indulgent eggs Benedict, the Breakfast Club may have you coming back every morning of your stay. Slept in? Don't worry, the Breakfast Club serves breakfast until 17:00 daily. Thanks to six locations in town, you're never far from a face full of their cinnamon apple French toast.

Breakfast from £8.50, Mon–Sat 08:00–22:00, Sun 08:00–19:00, 33 D'Arblay St, West End, +44 (0)20 7434 2571, thebreakfastclubcafes.com, Tube: Oxford Circus or Tottenham Court Road

Burger & Lobster

These guys do two things, and they do them well: burgers and lobster. Actually, they do their drinks and desserts (for example, the Lemon Strawberry and Mint cocktail or the chocolate amaretto crunch) exceedingly well, too. Service is friendly, and the menu is simple: choose burger, lobster, or lobster and salad roll (basically a thickly sliced sandwich) and decide on your sides, such as chips (French fries) or a tasty green salad. Deals are offered frequently, at a much better price than you'd expect from anything with "lobster" in the title. Eating a meal here feels like sitting down to a crawfish boil thanks to the long wooden tables and paper tablecloths.

Burger and lobster from £20, Mon–Wed 12:00–22:30, Thurs–Sat 12:00–23:00, Sun 12:00–22:00, 36-38 Dean St, West End, +44 (0)20 7432 4800, burgerandlobster.com, Tube: Leicester Square or Tottenham Court Road

Busaba Eathai

Kick-ass curry and delicious pad thai make this one of my favorite places in London. All of Busaba's locations are done up in a mod, dark Asian-fusion theme, with welcoming service that is happy to make recommendations. Their *tom yam goong*, or spicy and sour prawn soup, will make you feel like you're back in Bangkok. The Songkhla-style red curry is my favorite. In addition to the Soho shop, you'll find many other locations across town.

£8-12, Mon–Thurs 12:00–23:00, Fri–Sat 12:00–23:30, Sun 12:00–22:00, 106-110 Wardour St, West End, +44 (0)20 7255 8686, busaba.com, Tube: Piccadilly Circus

Wahaca

Wahaca offers some of the best tacos, burritos, grilled steak, and *horchata* (a beverage) I've had this side of the Atlantic. I love the fresh ingredients and authentic dishes that remind me of my travels south of the border. Expect colorful decorations, fast and cheerful service, and a casual, welcoming atmosphere. Orders are noted on your big paper tablecloth. There are many locations across town.

£11, Mon–Sat 12:00–23:00, Sun 12:00–22:30, 80 Wardour

St, West End, +44 (0)20 7734 0195, wahaca.co.uk, Tube: Piccadilly Circus

Chipotle

I have to mention this fine delicatessen only because London is one of the few places outside of the US that have this chain eatery. It's fast, it's cheap, and—let's be honest with ourselves—it's delicious. You'll find Chipotle outposts throughout the city.

£8, Mon-Sat 11:00-23:00, Sun 11:00-22:00, 114-116 Charing Cross Rd, Trafalgar Square, West End, +44 (0)20 7836 8491, chipotle.com, Tube: Leicester Square

Pret a Manger

This chain, serving sandwiches that are freshly made daily along with salads and snacks, is a London mainstay—like Starbucks is to Seattle (and just about every other city around the world). Everyone from backpackers to businessmen comes to this functional and clean fast-food chain to enjoy a healthy, cheap lunch. Grab your sandwich from the display rack, order coffee, and pay at the bar. In addition to the Westminster location, you'll find branches of Pret a Manger throughout the city.

£2-5, Mon-Fri 07:30-21:00, Sat 08:00-20:00, Sun 12:00-18:00, 47 Great Peter St, Westminster, +44 (0)20 7932 5401, pret.com, Tube: Westminster or St James's Park

Bubbledogs

Bubbledogs, located near the Goodge Street eateries, is a novelty experience as much as anything else: Get a gourmet hot dog served in a classic red plastic bowl, and wash it down with a glass of champagne. The irony seems to be lost as soon as you walk in the door, because the staff take both their bubbles and their dogs seriously. The Mac Daddy, a brat topped with piping hot mac-n-cheese, fried onions, and bacon bits, is a favorite of everyone except cardiologists. Add a side of tater tots, and enjoy the experience of dining on what you would've had for lunch in the third grade, yet in completely different surroundings, with aproned servers suggesting which champagne to pair with your main.

For a step up, find the hidden Michelin restaurant in the back, called **Kitchen Table**, for an experimental culinary experience that will take both your taste buds and your wallet for a ride. Saddle up to the bar along with 18 other diners, and enjoy the show for the next several hours as the chef and cooks dish up unforgettable meals. Find

more information and make reservations at kitchentablelondon.co.uk.

Dogs from £6, Tues-Thurs 11:30-15:00 and 17:30-22:30, Fri-Sat 11:30-22:30, 70 Charlotte St, British Museum Neighborhood, +44 (0)20 7637 7770, Tube: Goodge Street

Goodge Street Restaurants & Food Stalls

Goodge Street between Tottenham Court Road and Cleveland Street, along with the streets that surround it, offers your highest density of inexpensive, fresh and fast casual restaurants in all of London. At every lunch hour, this street packs out with London's young professionals, who enjoy the span of choice from gourmet hot dogs at **Bubbledogs,** burritos at **Benito's Hat** (56 Goodge St), pad thai at Thai Metro (38 Charlotte St), Greek salads at **Andreas** (40 Charlotte St), and sushi at **Roka** (37 Charlotte St). You'll discover classic British tea at **Yumchaa** (9 Tottenham St), tapas at **Salt Yard** (54 Goodge St), and delicious pizza at **ICCo** (Italian Coffee Company, 46 Goodge St)—all in the space of just a few blocks. All places listed are casual with fast service and are run like serious businesses: If you're there to eat and have the money to pay, you'll be taken care of in cool and quick fashion. One of the more unique restaurants in the district, **Bubbledogs,** is listed separately.

Goodge St between Tottenham Court Rd and Cleveland St, British Museum Neighborhood, Tube: Goodge Street

Brick Lane Restaurants & Food Stalls

Brick Lane between Fashion Street and Bruxton Street is home to many immigrants from the former Southern Asian British colonies. On this meandering street and in the surrounding district, you'll find some of the most authentic Indian food in the world. It's a truly intercultural dining experience, from the moment you're approached by restaurant reps to finally stepping inside your selected restaurant. Do a lap up and down the lane and be prepared to barter for the price and inclusions of your meal! Part of the fun of Brick Lane is the unknown—you never know for sure if you're choosing the right restaurant until after your meal. I usually start my lap at **Brick Lane Clipper** (104 Brick Ln) and **Cinnamon** (134 Brick Ln) restaurants. And I avoid **Saffron** (53 Brick Lane) and **Preem & Prithi** (118-122 Brick Lane), where quality and service vary widely.

Shoreditch, Tube: Aldgate East

London sports one of the hottest nightlife scenes around, with bars, pubs, and clubs to suit just about any interest. When going out, keep some things in mind: The Tube closes at midnight, as do all the pubs in town. Some bars and most clubs stay open late. Always bring valid **photo ID** to get into any bar or club—it puts a damper on the night when you're turned away at the door!

NIGHTLIFE DISTRICTS

London is a massive city, so it's best to plan your nights out based on which neighborhoods you identify best with. Figure out if you're looking for the bright, easy, central, touristy pubs and bars, the posh cocktail lounges, or the serious nightclubs, and go from there.

The West End

This West End is always happening on the weekends and has a ton of nightlife joints that span the spectrum from ale houses to throbbing *discotecas.* **Soho,** one of its hippest neighborhoods, offers numerous music venues, off-the-wall bars, and bohemian cafés. Soho is also the hub for the **LGBT** community and has many gay-friendly bars and clubs to choose from.

West End, Tube: Tottenham Court Road, Piccadilly Circus, Leicester Square, or Covent Garden

Shoreditch

Full of hipsters, artists, and interesting people, this diverse neighborhood on the east side of town feels a bit more off the beaten path. Shoreditch is widely regarded as the trendiest neighborhood in London. You'll find cocktail bars with aproned bartenders who take their craft seriously (**Nightjar**), artisanal beer houses (**Brewdog**), and fun clubs. The nearby **Brick Lane** area also caters to the trendy hipster set with skinny jeans and beards.

Shoreditch, Tube: Old Street

Camden Town

Camden is the heart of London's punk and bohemian scene. Revelers flock here for the underground music, as reflected by residents with their many tattoos, piercings, and dyed hair. While it's sliding toward the mainstream, you can still find excellent live music in venues like **Proud Camden.**

Camden, Tube: Camden Town

Soho

One of the hippest neighborhoods in London, Soho offers numerous music venues, off the wall bars, and bohemian cafes. Soho is also the hub for the LGBT community and has many gay-friendly bars and clubs.

Soho, Tube: Tottenham Court Road

BARS & PUBS

Spend a few days in London and you'll notice the sheer quantity of pubs—one on nearly on every corner throughout the city. And they all have proud, bold signage featuring names that stretch your imagination, like **Shakespeare's Head** (29 Regent St), **Ye Olde Cheshire Cheese** (145 Fleet St), and the **Hung Drawn and Quartered** (26-27 Great Tower St). King Richard II declared in 1393 that pubs must have signs in front of them to mark their location. So pubs sprang up with names that would differentiate them from all the others in town. The signs featured big, bright illustrations that still hang today, because writing the names of the pubs was mostly useless because of the modest literacy rate at the time.

The Anchor

If you're looking for the classic London pub, check out this historic one, located right on the banks of the Thames, on the Millennium Mile between the Borough Market and

---

LGBT LONDON

The gay scene in London is alive and well. All you need to know is **Soho.** In this tangle of streets in central London, you'll find hotels, shopping, bars, restaurants, cafés, dance bars, clubs, lounges, and theaters that cater to the gay community, especially along Old Compton Street. For drinks and good music, try **G-A-Y** (30 Old Compton St, +44 20 7494 2756) or **SheSoho** (23-25 Old Compton St, she-soho.com). **Heaven** (covers around £5, coat check £1, 11 The Arches, +44 (0)20 7930 2020) is the go-to club for a fun night out. They've got a massive dance hall with three bars and a side room for hip-hop—and the drinks are strong! All are welcome for the show. Check the website for events. Find Heaven underneath Charing Cross station.

Shakespeare's Globe. Pint-sized exposed-brick rooms with overstuffed red leather chairs and benches with your classic dark wooden decor make this a favorite pit stop for tourists, locals, and even tour guides.

Pints from £4, daily 11:00-23:00, 34 Park St, South Bank, +44 (0)20 7407 1577, Tube: London Bridge

The London Cocktail Club

For one helluva classy cocktail bar that expertly blends life's simple pleasures with high-society London, check out the London Cocktail Club. With innovative options like Jägerbombs from an oyster shell, martinis featuring fried bacon, and even a sexy love potion that comes complete with a condom (in a wrapper), your mind is sure to be blown. While the unpretentious bartenders are experts at whipping up bizarre concoctions, they don't forget the staples like old-fashioneds and tasty mojitos. In addition to the Covent Garden location, you'll find branches of the London Cocktail Club at 224a Shaftesbury Avenue, 61 Goodge Street, 29 Sclater Street, 6-7 Great Newport Street, and 4 Great Portland Street.

Drinks along with the experience £8-10, Mon-Sat 16:30-23:30, 6-7 Great Newport St, West End, +44 (0)020 7836 9533, londoncocktailclub.co.uk, Tube: Leicester Square

The Rocket

This pub, right next to King's Cross Station, is a great place for students and locals to grab a casual drink or hit the dance floor rocking out to Top 40 on weekends. Imbibers flock here for the fun, casual atmosphere. This is the type of place you can't help but stop into when you walk by. Get there early if you're hoping to not wait in line.

Drinks from £4.50, Mon-Thurs and Sun 08:00-24:00, Fri-Sat 08.00-02:00, 120 Euston Rd, British Museum Neighborhood, +44 (0)20 7388 0021, therocketeustonroad.co.uk, Tube: King's Cross

Freud

With a name like Freud you might expect a bawdier crowd, but this little basement bar is a favorite of the classy hipster set. Come out for some "speed cocktails" (i.e., cocktails you

---

LONDON ALE TRAIL

For a mile-long stretch of London's best ale houses, look no further than the London Ale Trail. It wanders through London's oldest streets in Westminster and into the City. Starting near the Holborn Tube stop and wrapping up at Blackfriars, this route is an excellent way to sip the afternoon away without too many steps in between.

The Princess Louise

(208 High Holborn): Customers have been knocking back the ales since 1891 in this renovated ale house with dark wood Victorian interior. The classic Brit pub offers no music or TV.

Cittie of Yorke

(22 High Holborn): Step back in time in another classic pub serving both ales and hearty fish-and-chips and pies.

The Knights Templar

(95 Chancery Ln): With high ceilings, carpeted floors, and large windows, the Knights Templar feels more like a living room than one of London's more famous pubs.

The Old Bank of England

(194 Fleet St): Power lunchers come here for the stunning interior, and since it's just around the corner from the high courts, you may well see some big shots enjoying a snack and pint before heading back into their legal proceedings next door. You pay for the sumptuous interior; pints break £4, and pies top £9.

Ye Olde Cheshire Cheese

(145 Fleet St): This amusingly named venue is easily one of London's most historic pubs.

The Blackfriar

(174 Queen Victoria St): I love this pub for its charm and beautiful interior, with intricate mosaics and detailed woodwork. You feel like you're stepping into a chapel that serves beer and fish-and-chips.

can make quickly) and enjoy the welcoming scene. Instant gratification, eh?

Drinks from £5, daily 11:00-23:00, till 01:00 on weekends, 198 Shaftesbury Ave, West End, +44 (0)20 7240 1100, freud.eu, Tube: Tottenham Court Road

Porterhouse

Brewing its own collection of beers, the Porterhouse is a dependable sports café. Come out to catch just about any game televised, or descend into the dark basement to enjoy your fresh brew in one of the nooks and crannies spread out across several levels in this creatively constructed pub. In good weather, come early to snag a spot on the partly sunny patio. It packs out once the workday is done!

Pints from £4.50, Mon-Fri 12:00-23:00, Sat 12:00-24:00, Sun 12:00-22:30, 21-22 Maiden Ln, West End, +44 (0)20 7379 7917, theporterhouse.ie, Tube: London Charing Cross, Leicester Square, or Covent Garden

Bounce

Ever spent a night out at a "social Ping Pong club"? Come out to Bounce to experience Europe's first and largest Ping Pong club, featuring the finest tables and paddles around. This place has it all: fun atmosphere, activities like Ping Pong to keep you busy, and delicious pizza upstairs.

Half hour on the table £13, Mon-Thurs 16:00-24:00, Fri-Sun 12:00-01:00, 121 Holborn, The City, +44 (0)20 3657 6525, bouncepingpong.com, Tube: Chancery Lane

SPEAKEASIES

One of London's hottest current trends is the Prohibition-era cocktail bar in a low-lit lounge setting. Sprinkled across town, they're intentionally hard to find, but if you follow my tips on where to look, you'll be having one of the best old-fashioneds in your memory—or why don't you try a nice gimlet?

Nightjar

Step back in time to a speakeasy-esque experience at the Nightjar. Look forward to live music, a cozy atmosphere, and excellent Prohibition-era cocktails in this trendy little bar. Due to its popularity, it can be quite hard to get in. Dress the part to better your chances at the door.

Cocktails £10-12, daily 18:00 till late, 129 City Rd, Shoreditch, +44 (0)20 7253 4101, barnightjar.com, Tube: Old Street

Underdog at Brewdog

For great cocktails and brews, head to Brewdog, a lively bar. Even better, find the canvas sheet at the bottom of the stairs near the main door. Pull it aside and take the stairs down to the clandestine Underdog bar and music venue. Underdog puts on great live music and even DJ sets throughout the week, and the trendy, hipster crowd is less pretentious than what you'll find at similar places elsewhere. After its secret entrance and stairway, the venue is actually much larger than what you'd expect at a "speakeasy," so the party gets that much louder and that much better.

Drinks from £5, Mon-Thurs and Sun 12:00-24:00, Fri-Sat 12:00-01:00, 51-55 Bethnal Green Rd, Shoreditch, +44 (0)20 7729 8476, brewdog.com/bars/uk/shoreditch, Tube: Aldgate East

Mayor of Scaredy Cat Town

At the back of the Spitalfields location of the Breakfast Club, find a secret bar that serves exquisite cocktails like a Peat-nut Butter Cup. You've never had peanuts with a bourbon and Scotch kick like this! Their beautifully presented Bombay Sapphire is to die for. Enter through the refrigerator door by giving the password ("I need to speak with the mayor") to get into this retro, American-style diner and cocktail lounge. Be sure to read and obey the house rules! A full food menu available as well, in all its diner goodness (think burgers and pork sandwiches).

ACT LIKE A LOCAL

Be Trendy

Londoners take keeping up to speed seriously, from fashion and food to neighborhoods and living arrangements. Pick up a *Time Out* magazine to know what I'm talking about. There is something going on every night of the week, which is part of what makes this town so lively and fun. Year after year, the most popular neighborhoods are constantly shifting to different locations, and lots of effort is put into being "indie" or "underground." As soon as that unique flavor becomes mainstream, the trendsetters set off to somewhere new.

Drinks from £10, Mon-Thurs 17:00-24:00, Fri 15:00-24:00, Sat 12:00-24:00, Sun 12:00- 22:30, 12-16 Artillery Ln, Shoreditch, +44 (0)20 7078 9639, themayorofscaredycattown.com, Tube: Aldgate East

Experimental Cocktail Club

If you like classics with a twist, this dimly lit, Roaring '20s-era cocktail lounge is for you. Utilizing proprietary syrups and bitters along with fresh ingredients, these guys have rejuvenated your grandma's vodka tonic. Besides updates on your standard vintage cocktails, the ECC has invented an extensive list of new cocktails featuring exotic liquors, top shelf spirits, and fresh ingredients like homemade ginger syrup and habanero bitters. For a refreshing splurge, try the Watermelon Cooler. They're absolutely capable of making the classic lineup of cocktails, too. All drinks are served in the appropriate vessel, whether that's a lowball or martini glass, which adds to the experience.

Innovative cocktails from £9.50, daily 18:00-03:00, 13a Gerrard St, West End, no phone, chinatownecc.com, reservation@chinatownecc.com, Tube: Leicester Square

CLUBS

Fabric

Of all the clubs in London, Fabric, with an epic reputation on the electronic music scene, is the one that cannot be missed. Located just north of The City, it's famous for its resident DJs and its "bodysonic" room, which shakes you to your core with sound waves. You'll think that half of London is waiting in the queue with you to get in. Fortunately for you, if you stay at one of my suggested hostels, they can make a reservation for you—and drop the cover down to half price.

Tickets online from £7, Fri-Sun 23:00-05:30, sometimes open later, 77A Charterhouse St, The City, +44 (0)20 7336 8898, fabriclondon.com, Tube: Barbican

Piccadilly Institute

Explore this labyrinth of rooms, each decorated according to an insane asylum theme, exploring different shades of craziness. I've had great experience with the service and music choice at this venue with five bars and two clubs, which draws a young, stylish crowd. Dress with nice shoes and collars to get past the bouncers.

£5 cover weekdays, £10 cover weekends, daily 17:00-late, cover charges after 21:00, 1 The London Pavilion, West End, +44 (0)20 7287 8008, piccadillyinstitute.com, Tube: Piccadilly Circus

XOYO

XOYO is a London clubbing classic, well-established on the scene. Any big time DJ coming through is sure to schedule a gig here. Two floors and top-of-the-line sound systems mean you can rock the night away till the sun comes up. Consider avoiding the long lines by getting on the guest list online or hitting the club up on a Monday or Tuesday. Music is of the indie electronic DJ set.

Cover varies up to £20, Mon, Tues, Thurs, Fri, Sat 20:00-03:00, 32-37 Cowper St, Shoreditch, +44 (0)20 7354 9993, xoyo.co.uk, Tube: Old Street

Ministry of Sound

A true institution, Ministry of Sound got so popular and so big that they've created their own recording label. Located on the south side of town (about a 15-minute walk south of the River Thames), the Ministry puts their commitment to music and sound above all else, especially to the beats of house and techno. They're clearly onto something, with a packed house every night since the early '90s. Note that this area can get a bit dodgy later at night.

Pricey covers up to £20, Tues and Fri -Sat 22:00-late, 103 Gaunt St, South Bank, +44 (0)20 7740 8600, ministryofsound.com, Tube: Elephant & Castle

Proud Camden

What was formerly an equestrian hospital is now a massive multipurpose venue hosting everything from private events to drag shows and live music concerts. Former horse stables are now VIP booths, fitting up to 25 parties each. Each has been renovated in a unique style, such as Asian pinup tattoo, the Desert Orchid room, and the gold bedazzled '70s disco room. Enjoy a meal here, or even relax in the sun in their garden and take a dip in their hot tub. When the sun goes down, the party heats up with live music—primarily indie rock bands—taking over the large dance hall. Proud Camden truly is a microcosm of Camden in London, all of the funkiness distilled into one venue.

Check the events listings online ahead of time to see what's going down. The crowd is young, hip, and professional: a well-dressed set that likes to let their hair down.

Show tickets run from £10, drinks from £4, Wed 11:00-01:30, Thurs-Sat 11:00-02:30, The Horse Hospital, The Stables Market, Chalk Farm Rd, Camden, +44 (0)20 7482 3867, reservations through opentable.co.uk, Tube: Camden Town

WINE BARS

Gordon's Wine Bar

Dating back to the 1890s, this place feels like a step back to the Middle Ages. That feeling is due mostly to the candlelit brick cellars you're delving into. On nice days, get a bottle and enjoy the shaded outdoor terrace. The food selection goes well with the wines—from finger food and tapas to meat dishes and Sunday roasts, rest assured you can get both your drink and your eat on at Gordon's.

Reasonable bottle prices from £15, daily 11:00-23:00, 47 Villiers St, West End, +44 (0)20 7930 1408, gordonswinebar.com, Tube: Embankment or London Charing Cross

Cork & Bottle

You may be surprised to find food and wine of this caliber in such a touristy district, just a block off Leicester Square. But at Cork & Bottle, count on an incredible selection of international wines available by the glass or bottle, along with a slew of unforgettable entrées and finger food like Cajun chicken and an impressive ham-and-cheese pie. Cork & Bottle feels like a cozy little slice of France, with hardly a tourist in sight. The servers are happy to walk you through both the wine list and menu.

Sides and salads from £7, mains from £13, daily 11:00-24:00, 44-46 Cranbourn St, West End, +44 (0)20 7734 7807, thecorkandbottle.co.uk, Tube: Leicester Square

PUB CRAWLS

It is still possible to find a sub-£3 pint in central London; it just takes some determination. Pub crawls offer guided parties that run nightly in London and can be a good choice if you're looking to save money and meet travelers. The savings you get from discounted drink deals and what you would have spent on club entry will cover the ticket price.

1 Big Night Out

This pub crawl operates nightly 19:30-21:00 in Leicester Square.

£15, meets nightly at ZOO Bar, 17 Bear Street, +44 20 7836 9995, 1bignightout.com, Tube: Leicester Square

Camden Pub Crawl

As the name suggests, Camden Pub Crawl operates in Camden. Pub crawls run from 19:30 to 21:30.

£14 weekdays, £16 weekends, save £2 by booking online,

meets nightly at Belushi's Camden, 48-50 Camden High Street, undiscoveredlondon.com, info@undiscoveredlondon.com, Tube: Mornington Crescent

London Gone Wild

London Gone Wild is a pub crawl option in Shoreditch.

£13.50, meets Thurs, Fri and Sat between 20:00-21:00 at The Shoreditch, 145 Shoreditch High St, +44 20 7096 0371, nightsgonewild.com, Tube: Aldgate East

TOP SHOPPING & MARKETS

SHOPPING DISTRICTS

Oxford Street

Oxford Street is quite possibly London's single best shopping street and stretches for just about one mile from east to west on the north side of the city. It's here you'll find all the major retailers, along with **Selfridges** (Mon-Sat 09:30-21:00, Sun 11:30-18:15, 400 Oxford St, +44 (0)113 369 8040, Tube: Bond Street), one of London's famous top-end department stores. Be sure to venture southward off of Oxford down **Regents Street** to top off that shopping fix of yours.

West End, Tube: Oxford Circus

MARKETS

Harrods

Visit this massive monument to consumerism to get a taste of what it feels like to be a lowly commoner. Back in the day, London was one of the few cities with enough concentrated wealth to support and kick off what has become the modern department store and mall. Everything—from luxury chocolates to designer lingerie and large-than-life stuffed Paddington Bears to posh home furnishings—is sold across seven full floors of hedonism. Harrods is basically your one-stop shop for everything high end that you could ever want.

Mon-Sat 10:00-20:00, Sun 11:30-18:00, 87-135 Brompton Rd, West London, +44 (0)20 7730 1234, Tube: Knightsbridge

Portobello Market

Every Saturday, one of the world's biggest antiques markets takes over the Notting Hill neighborhood all up and down Portobello Road. If you're actually planning on buying the jewelry, vintage clothing, and other items on offer, be sure to bring enough cash, because the ATMs often run out or have

insane lines. Saturday mornings before 10:00 are best, as you've got the selection without the crowds. Be sure to stop into the famous **Hummingbird Bakery** (cupcakes from £1.50, Mon-Fri 10:00-18:00, Sat 09:00-18:30, Sun 11:00-17:30, 133 Portobello Rd, +44 (0)20 7851 1795) for a cupcake to give you that sugar rush to get you through the day.

Mon-Wed and Fri-Sat 08:00-18:30, Thurs 08:00-13:00, West London, Tube: Notting Hill Gate

Camden Market

London's original craft market dates back to the 1970s. Today, it's a collection of extremely popular street markets, seeing tens of thousands of visitors each weekend. Explore large open-air clothes vendors and thrift shop-type stalls, food shops, and, my favorite, a large shopping complex in a repurposed barn. Save time for food, and stick around for the nightlife, as this is one of London's most intriguing neighborhoods and the center of the alternative fashion scene. The market, open daily, is busiest on weekends.

Daily 10:00-18:00, Camden, Tube: Camden Town

Borough Market

South of the river, this food market is *the* place to challenge your taste buds, with loads of free samples ranging from wild boar to ostrich sandwiches. Conveniently located near the Millennium Mile, Borough Market has permanent shops, restaurants, and cafés built into the ironwork of the awnings, along with farmer stalls that pop up daily to sell fresh goods. Those who just want to nibble can pick up cheeses and meats by the slice. Otherwise, dive into the delicious sandwiches, wraps, and smoothies available throughout the market.

Mon-Wed 10:00-15:00, Thurs 11:00-17:00, Fri 12:00-18:00, Sat 08:00-17:00, 8 Southwark St, South Bank, boroughmarket.org, Tube: London Bridge

Old Spitalfields Market

This grand covered arts-and-crafts market has been located here for the better part of 400 years. Today, find items like graphic tees, hipster shoulder bags, real leather belts, and hand-made art pieces and frames. In the massive barn-like warehouse are both permanent retail stores and semi-permanent stalls. The market makes for great window shopping and even better photos. Skip the overpriced restaurants inside and opt for food at the **Brick Lane Market** nearby.

Daily 08:00-23:00, 16 Horner Square, Shoreditch, Tube: Liverpool Street

Brick Lane Market & Sunday Upmarket

Brick Lane Market is a collection of warehouses and open streets where you can wander and discover untold pop-up shops, custom bike stores, and tons of bars and cafés. Sundays, when street performers and crowds create quite a buzz, are the best day to visit. If vintage is your thing, come here for heaven on earth. Find the **Boiler House** (open Sun, 91 Brick Ln) for yet another international food hall.

Near the Boiler House, what was an old brewery is now the **Sunday Upmarket**, an international food extravaganza. Street food stalls sell everything from Greek to Indonesian, Brazilian to Nepalese. Grab your food at each counter, and find an empty spot on a bench to chow down. You'll leave here with a full belly without hurting your wallet. Between courses, stop at the clothing stalls selling hand-made and designer pieces.

Permanent stores and shops are open throughout the week, best day for the food halls is Sun 10:00-17:00, 91 Brick Ln, Shoreditch, +44 (0)20 7770 6028, bricklanemarket.com, Tube: Algate East

TOP PARKS & RECREATION

St James's Park

St James's Park is right off of Whitehall Street near the Parliament building, conveniently providing a direct path between Buckingham Palace and the Horse Guards Parade. You can walk across this park in barely five minutes. Wander through the gardens and have a sandwich on a bench if you need a break from the hustle and bustle of the city. Enjoy the well-manicured meandering paths wrapping around a beautiful little lake.

Westminster, Tube: St James's Park

Hyde Park

London's "Central Park" is the largest in the city, spanning more than 350 acres. Highlights include the Diana Memorial Fountain, the large Serpentine Lake, and the Speakers' Corner, a place where Londoners can come and speak their minds loudly and proudly on any subject they wish. Take **paddle boats** (£10/30 min, £12/1 hr) out on the lake, or enjoy a drink at any one of the outdoor cafés that line it. Any time there are important sports matches going on, thousands flock to the park to watch on massive projector screens. Music events and festivals take place frequently throughout the year, too.

West London, Tube: Hyde Park Corner

Battersea Park

Well off the beaten track for most tourists, this is my favorite park in town because it offers miles of running trails, waterfront views, and a unique and spectacular 100-foot-tall Buddhist Peace Pagoda monument to reflect on. It's also the site of a huge bonfire and light show held every November 5 to commemorate the thwarting of a terrorist plot to blow up the Houses of Parliament in 1605.

South Bank, Tube: Sloane Square

TOP TOURS

Fat Tire Bike Tours

My favorite way to see the city! Take the **Royal Gardens Bike Tour** and enjoy the musings of a great guide through some of the city's most beautiful scenery. Learn a ton from your funny and informative guide as you cruise through Hyde Park, Kensington Gardens, Green Park, and down the Mall, stopping at each interesting point and photo op along the way. I like how these bike tours avoid street traffic as much as possible, sticking to parks for the most part.

£18, low season Mon and Thurs-Sun 11:00, shoulder season daily 11:00, high season daily 11:00 and 15:00, meets at Queensway Tube Station, West London, fattirebiketours.com/London, Tube: Queensway

Sandeman's New Europe Walking Tours

Take a free walking tour and see some of London's most popular sights with your own personal guide. Satisfied? Tip your guide for a job well done—their earnings are purely gratuity based. You'll learn about some of the top sights in London over this three-hour tour, including Big Ben, Buckingham Palace, Westminster Abbey, and Churchill War Rooms.

Free (tip based), daily 11:00 and 13:00, meets by Wellington Arch, Westminster, neweuropetours.eu, Tube: Hyde Park Corner

TOP HOSTELS

Clink78 Hostel

If buildings could talk, this hostel would certainly have some stories to share. Originally a courthouse, it's made up of dorms that used to be prison cells and an Internet café and movie room that used to be courtrooms. And for those of you who need to brush up on your rock 'n' roll history, this hostel is where the famous punk group The Clash went on trial back in 1978. Today, you'll find a large hostel with comfortable beds and a very social atmosphere with an on-site Clash-themed bar and music. Some complain about the noise and sleep quality, but for those looking for a good time out in London, Clink78 is a great choice.

From £10, £3 Wi-Fi, 24-hour reception, laundry, bar, free breakfast, 78 King's Cross Rd, British Museum Neighborhood, +44 (0)20 7183 9400, clinkhostels.com, reservations@clinkhostels.com, Tube: Kings Cross St Pancras

St Christopher's Village, London Bridge

Get your kicks here if you're looking for your first ever London hangover. London's ultimate party hostel features a basement nightclub, DJs, a bar and restaurant, karaoke nights, a cinema, and a comedy club. Its rooms and bathrooms are clean, and it's next to great sights such as the Tower of London, Tower Bridge, and the famous Tate Modern. Other St Christopher locations in Camden, Greenwich, Hammersmith, and Shepherd's Bush feature similar social scenes and amenities. Check them out and book online at st-christophers.co.uk.

From £15, free Wi-Fi, free breakfast, 24-hour reception, free lockers, 161-165 Borough High St, South Bank, +44 (0)20 7939 9710, st-christophers.co.uk, village@st-christophers.co.uk, Tube: London Bridge

Generator Russell Square

Generator hostels are dotted all over Europe. All of them seem to offer a reliable standard: clean rooms, affordable prices, and more amenities than you know what to do with. Definitely aimed at the younger generation of travelers, this hostel has its own bar, game room with pool tables, free walking tours, a lounge equipped with multiple flat screens, and daily events like karaoke night and drinking games. It's also just a five-minute walk from Euston, St Pancras, and King's Cross Tube stations and train stations.

From £27, free Wi-Fi, laundry, 24-hour reception, lockers, 37 Tavistock Plaza, British Museum Neighborhood, +44 (0)20 7388 7666, generatorhostels.com, info@generatorhostels.com, Tube: Russell Square

Wombat's

One of the Wombat chain's newest locations has opened up to rave reviews. Just outside The City on the edge of East London, Wombat's puts you right where you want to be for sightseeing by day and partying by night. It's a five-minute walk from the Tower of London and Tower Bridge, and ten minutes from the Brick Lane food scene and the nightlife in Shoreditch. Count on a welcoming social atmosphere, a helpful staff that provides good recommendations, and delicious breakfast. It's done up in shabby chic decor with a reception desk that's built from recycled lumber. You'll feel cool from check-in till you're downing drinks under brick arches at the on-site bar. Rooms are clean and bright, featuring a plug and reading lamp at each bunk.

Beds from £24, 24-hour reception, on-site bar, hair dryers, adapters, and towels available, pool table, free Wi-Fi, breakfast extra, 7 Dock St, The City, +44 (0)20 7680 7600, wombats-hostels.com, booklondon@wombats.eu, Tube: Tower Hill

Astor Hyde Park Hostel

The Astor chain is a great option for budget travelers. Set in a 19th-century mansion, this old building has been retrofitted to feature all the modern amenities but retains its authentic wooden soul. Beds are comfortable, the staff is extremely welcoming and helpful, and the location near Hyde Park is spectacular. Simple rooms offer everything from private twins up to 12-bed mixed dorms—bunks are constructed of tubular steel. The Hyde Park branch is my favorite Astor location, but other options include Victoria, Queensway, and near the British Museum.

Bunks from £18, free Wi-Fi, 24-hour reception, laundry facilities, common room with foosball table; towels, hair dryers, and breakfast extra, 191 Queensgate, West London, +44 (0)20 7581 0103, astorhostels.com, hydepark@astorhostels.com, Tube: Gloucester Road

Barmy Badger Backpackers

The Barmy Badger includes everything in your booking. There are no hidden fees, meaning Wi-Fi, continental breakfast, power sockets next to your bed, kitchen use, and "travel advice" are freely offered and included in the price of your bed. Get extras like towels and adapters for a refundable deposit. The owner's two dogs are thrown in for good measure, too. While the bunks are stacked three high in the six-bed dorms, each cubby sports a comfortable mattress, personal light, and charging port, so you get a solid night's sleep. The place feels a bit like your aunt's town home in the posh Earls Court district of London, complete with a large living room and a nice couch to sink into.

Six-bed dorm £24, privates from £65, 24-hour reception, cable TV, free maps, laundry facilities, free Wi-Fi, outdoor terrace, breakfast included, towels with deposit, 17 Longridge Rd, West London, +44 (0)20 7370 5213, barmybadger.com, barmybadger@hotmail.com, Tube: Earls Court

TRANSPORTATION

GETTING THERE & AWAY

Although England is an island, international travel into London has never been easier thanks to the city's efficient infrastructure and extensive public transit system.

Plane

The city of London has five international airports. All have public transportation options into the center.

London City (LCY, londoncityairport.com) is the airport closest to downtown London. Hop on the **DLR** (dlrlondon.co.uk), a commuter train that connects to and uses the same tickets as the Tube, and transfer onto the Tube system at Canning Town to connect into the rest of London. Your journey from the airport to the center will cost £4.80.

From **Heathrow** (LHR, heathrow.com), take the Piccadilly Tube line straight into the center (this takes about an hour, stopping at every station along the way) and connect to your accommodation's Tube stop from there. Single fare runs £5.70. Other connection options are longer, overpriced, and not worth it.

From **Gatwick** (LGW, gatwickairport.com) take the **Southern Train** (southernrailway.

co.uk) service, which runs every 15 minutes, to Victoria station (45 minutes, single fare £15). You'll be tempted to spring for the **Gatwick Express** (30 minutes, single fares from £18, gatwickexpress.com), but the Southern Train saves you cash without sacrificing too much time.

Luton (LTN, london-luton.co.uk) has connections into London every 15 minutes via **EasyBus** (easybus.com); the 80-minute journey puts you at Victoria station. Or take a shuttle to Luton Airport Parkway, which offers different rail services that can get you into the center. For the cheapest fares, visit **Trainline** (thetrainline.com).

From **Stansted** (STN, stanstedairport. com), your best options are either the **Stansted Express** train (£22.50, runs every 15 min, 45-min journey, stanstedexpress.com), which will take you to Liverpool Street station, or **EasyBus** (easybus.com, runs every 20 min, 75-min journey), which will take you to Baker Street station. Visit easybus.com for pricing. Buses can take three hours in rush hour, so be sure to factor that in!

Some budget airlines are also beginning to offer cheaper flights into regional airports well outside of London. Note that flying into these can add considerable time and costs to your travel plans. From London South End, for example, it takes at least 1.5 hours to get to the center.

Train

There are nine major train stations in London. All are connected to the Tube. Rates from Paris—on fast trains taking just under 2.5 hours—range from about £42 (€50) and up, depending on student discount and how far in advance you book your ticket. For more information, visit the **Eurostar** website (eurostar.com).

Bus

There are bus options to London from the rest of the UK as well as Paris, Amsterdam, and Brussels. Rates can be significantly cheaper than your train options, but remember; hours spent on buses can add up quickly. Check out routes and fares at **Eurolines** (eurolines.com), **Megabus** (uk. megabus.com), and **Student Agency** (studentagencybus.com).

Car

By car, London is 460 kilometers (about 5.25 hours) from Paris and 660 kilometers (about 8 hours) from Edinburgh.

GETTING AROUND

London is a massive but very walkable city. **Walking** is a great way to explore one block at a time. Keep an eye out for dark blue neighborhood map signs posted around the city near bus stops. These are a great way to get oriented to the neighborhood immediately surrounding you. To give you a sense of scale, the walk from Big Ben to the Tower of London takes about an hour at a relaxed pace.

Prepare to be amazed, and possibly intimidated, by the London **public transporta-**tion system. Comprising 11 metro lines and over 700 bus routes, it's one of the best and most extensive public transport systems in the world. Buy yourself an **Oyster Card** (£8, includes a £5 deposit) at any Tube station to reduce the cost of your bus and Tube tickets by about half.

Tube

The Underground, also known as the Tube, closes at midnight. (Remember that before getting too deep into your drinking routine!) At the time of writing, 24-hour service was in the works. A single journey costs £4.80 (£2.30 with the Oyster Card). Pick up a free metro map from the desk at any Tube station. Or use the **TubeMap** app, which is just what it sounds like. It also stays up to date, advising you with the latest closures.

Bus

If you ever find yourself lost or disoriented, each little bus stop has a map that shows you where you are and which buses stop there. Do your homework before going out at night to see which night bus can take you back home. Ask the driver when you exit the bus if you are ever in doubt of your return stop. A single journey costs £2.20 (£1.30 with the Oyster Card). Map out your journey beforehand with the **Citymapper** app.

Bus 11 between Liverpool Street station and Victoria offers an excellent cross-section of London with an orientating route leading from The City into Westminster and past the royal parks to Buckingham Palace.

Taxi

The taxi industry in London is highly regulated and quite competitive. It's also quite expensive (about £8.50/12-min ride). If you need to call for a taxi, use only a licensed **Black Cab** or a taxi service recommended by your hostel. A good number to call if you're unable to hail a taxi from the street

is **087 1871 8710,** which gives you access to hundreds of licensed taxis 24 hours a day. Cabbies evaporate when all the bars let out, and they're nearly impossible to wave down. **Uber** is now well-established in London.

Bicycle

Santander Cycles (tfl.gov.uk/modes/cycling/santander-cycles) runs London's public bike-rental system. For £2, you get access to the bikes. Each ride is free as long as you check it back in to a Santander stand within 30 minutes. If you want to keep the bike longer, each subsequent half hour costs £2. Find more information online and in the app store.

DAY TRIPS

LONDON

Leeds Castle

It's easy to get lost in the urban jungle that is London. Thankfully, a two-hour train ride can zip you from the city center to rural England, where you'll find quite a different setting, completely transforming your perspective with a castle fit for a king. From humble medieval beginnings, this castle was rebuilt and rebuilt to now stand as a proud example of Tudor architecture and defenses. The castle played home to six of England's queens and Henry VIII to boot. Today, the castle is a private museum with well-manicured grounds and a hedge maze to get lost in. It's often deemed England's "loveliest" castle.

The castle and grounds are located in Kent. From London, take the Southeastern Rail from Victoria station. In about 1.25 hours, you'll arrive to Bearsted. From Bearsted, it's a 10-minute taxi ride straight to the castle. The whole trip will cost you about £40 round-trip, not including entry into the castle. Tour services like **Golden Tours** (goldentours.com) run from London frequently and offer day trips from £84.

Pricey individual entry at £24, daily 10:30-17:00, +44 (0)1622 765400, leeds-castle.com

Stonehenge

This world-famous prehistoric rock formation is within reach of a day trip from London! The purpose, meaning, and possible construction methods of this monument—carbon dated to before 3000 BC—continue to evade experts. So we are left to use our own imaginations to try to figure out how and why such massive stones (weighing up to four tons each) were hoisted and placed in perfect alignment, all without machinery, modern engineering, or even nylon ropes.

An early morning trip will get you out to Stonehenge in time to enjoy it for a bit. Numerous day-trip options exist; they are worth it because public transportation options can take up to four hours. **London Toolkit** offers a day trip with a stop in Bath (£47, londontoolkit.com). **Premium Tours** has a Stonehenge-only option (from £35, premiumtours.co.uk). **Viator** (viator.com) has curated options available online.

I recommend booking Stonehenge with a tour that also takes you to **Windsor Castle,** a sprawling Tudor and English gothic-style royal castle with foundations dating back to the 10th century, or **Bath,** an old Roman fort town named after the hot springs that bubble out of the ground in the area. Otherwise, it's quite a long time on the bus to see a stack of large rocks, no?

£14.50, £13 with valid student ID, daily 09:30-19:00, closes at 17:00 in winter, last admission 2 hours before closing time, +44 (0)0370 333 1181

HELP!

Tourist Information Centers

London has excellent services for visitors. All the information you'll need for your visit can be found online (cityoflondon.gov.uk and visitlondon.com). For many sights, you can even book tickets through these websites. Keep in mind there are shops throughout London that purport to be unbiased tourist resources but in fact make money selling you shows and tickets. This is London's only impartial tourist information center:

City of London Information Centre, St Paul's Churchyard, +44 (0)20 7332 1456

Pickpockets & Scams

As in the rest of Western European cities, the crime rate in London is pretty low. However, be alert for pickpockets in the larger touristy areas, restaurants, metros, buses, and trains. Teams on scooters have been known to snatch the phone right out of your hand while they drive by. If you need to call for a taxi, you should use only a licensed Black Cab or a taxi service recommended by your hostel.

Emergencies

In an emergency, dial 999.

Hospital

St Thomas' Hospital

Westminster Bridge Rd, Lambeth, SE1 7EH

+44 (0)20 7928 9292

US Embassy

24 Grosvenor Square

+44 (0)20 7499 9000

PARIS

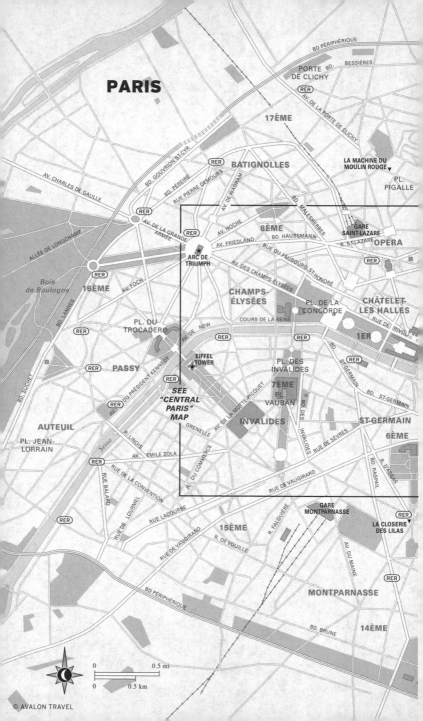

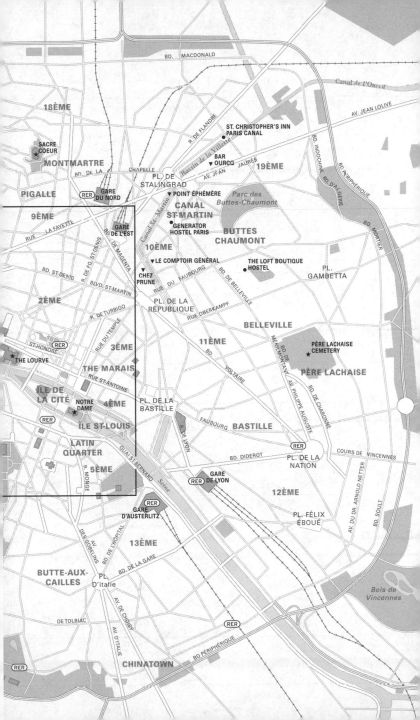

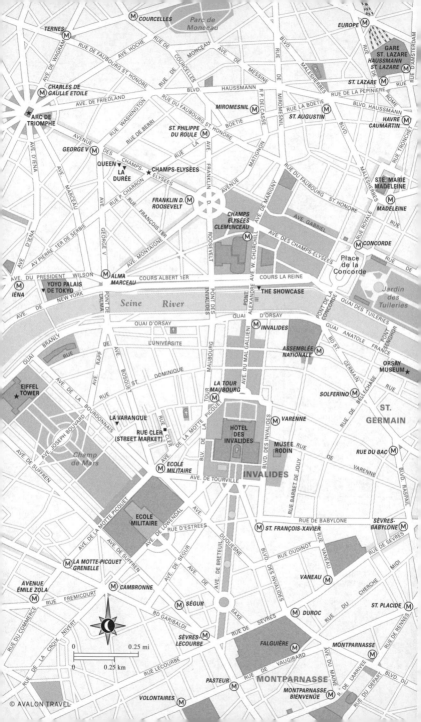

© AVALON TRAVEL

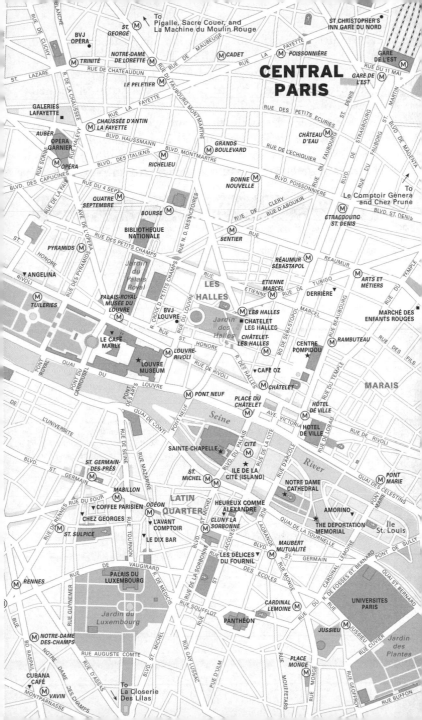

Paris is a treasure trove of art, cathedrals, and magnificent architecture. From the Eiffel Tower to Sacre Coeur, from *Mona Lisa's* coy smile to the gargoyles that guard Notre Dame, Paris is full of refined beauty. But—like a deliciously flaky *pain au chocolat*—the city's real treat lies beneath its surface. Even if you don't fall in love *in* Paris, you will fall in love *with* Paris. Dig deep into the city to discover the people, sights, sounds, tastes, and smells that will make your trip unforgettable.

PARIS 101

Paris's location on a couple islands in the Seine River made the city, founded in 250 BC, a strategic stronghold. By 1200, Paris was one of the most powerful cities in Europe, with a massive castle, cathedrals, trade unions, and all the makings of a major capital. As the city evolved, the French royalty levied untenable taxes on their population to finance wars and opulent palaces like Versailles. Peasants were starving, and a groundswell of anger gave rise to the French Revolution in 1789. Over 10 long years, thousands of nobles were jailed or publicly beheaded by the guillotine.

The revolution was a success in terms of eliminating the ruling class. But it takes more than that. You've got to govern. By 1799, France was struggling to find a leader who could harness their nationalist fervor. A man rose through the ranks (and well beyond his short stature) to become self-proclaimed emperor of France. His name? Napoleon Bonaparte. After conquering much of Western Europe, Napoleon was exiled—twice. He escaped his first exile quickly, suffered tremendous losses at the battle of Waterloo, was exiled again, and lived out his days in disgraced solitude on a small island between Brazil and Africa. But Napoleon did leave his mark on modern society. Our legal and public educational systems and even units of measurement today derive from the developments Napoleon undertook during his reign.

As France entered the modern age, Napoleon III, Napoleon's nephew, was elected in France's first democratic election and reigned nearly 18 years. Napoleon III wanted to beautify his capital city, making it fit for an emperor. The new emperor commissioned his favorite architect and city planner, Georges-Eugène Haussmann, with the immense project of modernizing Paris. Thousands of Parisians were displaced to make room for new wide boulevards and the grand avenues that we see today.

Paris enjoyed a golden age around the turn of the 20th century. An engineer, Gustave Eiffel, completed his tower for the World's Fair, while an eclectic group of outcast artists flocked to the city and developed a new artistic style they called impressionism. The 20th century brought two world wars, but even through the difficult years, Paris continued to attract artists and bohemians. Paris was on its heels after World War II, but thanks to Allied support, the city began the process of reconstruction.

Today, France is liberal and progressive, and the Parisian joie de vivre is as palpable as ever.

PLAN AHEAD

RESERVATIONS

Reservations are recommended for the following sights:
Eiffel Tower (toureiffel.paris/en)
Louvre (louvre.fr/en)

PASSES

Paris Museum Pass

The **Paris Museum Pass** (en.parismuseumpass.com) gives you free entry and line-skipping privileges at some of Paris's major museums, including the Louvre, the Orsay, and Versailles. Choose from two-day (€42), four-day (€56), and six-day (€69) options. The pass is particularly smart if you plan to visit Versailles, which costs €18 on its own. In peak tourism months, the line-skipping privileges are even more valuable than the savings. Purchase the pass online or at any participating museum. Activate it by writing the date of entry to your first sight.

LOCAL HAPPENINGS

Tour de France

The Tour de France, which loops more than 2,000 miles around France each July, is the world's most famous and competitive professional cycling event. Cyclists from all over the world drive themselves to near exhaustion in a three-week-long stage race. The starting point changes yearly (with recent years kicking off in England, Germany, Belgium, and the Netherlands), but the race always ends with eight laps through central Paris, up and down the Champs-Élysées and under the Louvre in a grueling sprint. The festive atmosphere draws tens of thousands of visitors every year. Weathered but exuberant cyclists take a slow victory lap afterward, celebrating the mere feat of completing the world's most punishing race.

Bastille Day

France's national holiday, Bastille Day (July 14), commemorates the day when rebels stormed the Bastille prison and kicked off the French Revolution. On Bastille Day, a grand parade is accompanied by fireworks, musical performances, dances, large communal meals, and, of course, wine and champagne. Expect the entire country—including sights and museums—to shut down. Don't fret; the parties are much more fun anyway!

THREE DAY ITINERARY

It's important to be efficient when making your rounds of Paris's top sights. Get ready to walk—a lot—and get comfortable on the metro to explore the best corners of this beautiful city.

DAY 1: BIENVENUE Á LA GAUCHE

MORNING

Grab breakfast at the hostel or pop into your local *patisserie* (pastry shop) to try your first heavenly croissant or *pain au chocolat* (chocolate croissant).

Head into Île de la Cité and spend a few hours exploring Paris's most quintessential sights: the epically gothic **Notre Dame** cathedral, the compelling and thought-provoking **Deportation Memorial**, and the stunningly beautiful royal chapel of **Sainte-Chapelle**.

Catch a free, three-hour Latin Quarter walking tour with **Discover Walks,** meeting at 11:00 (May 1-Oct 15 daily) at the equestrian statue in front of Notre Dame. This casual, tip-based walking tour will take you to the Left Bank, Paris's student and bohemian quarter. You'll wander through the narrow lanes while enjoying a fun narrative bringing the streets to life.

AFTERNOON

Your walking tour will take a lunch break at a local bakery. If you're on your own, **Les Delices du Fournil** offers fast and dependable lunch options: A baguette sandwich, dessert crêpe, and drink can all be had for around €5, a steal in the touristy Latin Quarter.

After your tour, hop the metro across town up to **Montmartre** (Metro: Blanche, Pigalle, or Abbesses) to explore the artistic and alternative bohemian neighborhood and make a visit to **Sacre Coeur**. If it's a nice day, grab a beverage and snack to tuck into on the steps, taking in the view and enjoying being serenaded by the buskers around you.

EVENING

After freshening up for the night at the hostel, head out to have dinner at **La Varangue** (Metro: Champ de Mars) in the shadow of the Eiffel Tower.

Cap off the evening by heading up the **Eiffel Tower** and taking in the City of Lights at its finest, just as the lights begin to twinkle. Grab a bottle or two of wine afterward to enjoy on **Champ de Mars**. Pick up some cheeses, salami, baguettes, and an extra bottle to share with fellow picnickers and make some friends!

LATE

Sufficiently wined, and dressed right, make your way over to **Showcase** (Metro: Invalides), Paris's glamorous river-front club located underneath the Pont Alexandre III, the same bridge that played the backdrop to Adele's "Someone Like You" music video.

DAY 2: THE ROYAL RIGHT

MORNING

Get a big breakfast to gear up for the **Louvre.** If you've got an EU student card or EU student visa in an American passport, bring it to get free entry! It'll take you about three hours to see the Louvre's destination masterpieces (*Winged Victory, Venus de Milo,* the French Crown Jewels, the large-scale paintings, and of course the *Mona Lisa*). Be sure to pick up a free museum map as you enter to help navigate the endless halls. Afterward, grab a sandwich in the well-appointed cafeteria at the mezzanine level overlooking the ticket lines underneath the main glass pyramid.

AFTERNOON

Hop on the metro, which will zip you uphill to the **Arc de Triomphe** (Metro: Charles de Gaulle-Étoile). Climb the arch for a beautiful panorama of Paris's most exclusive districts. Watch the traffic snake around the busiest intersection in France—and the only roundabout in France where incoming traffic has the right of way.

Spend the rest of the afternoon on the **Champs-Élysées,** shopping till you drop. Get lost wandering all the way down the grandest boulevard in the country.

EVENING

Stop back at the hostel to change for the night and to grab some layers. Head over to the Dupleix metro stop near the Eiffel Tower and catch **Fat Tire**'s amazing three-hour evening bike tour at 18:00. Enjoy the leadership of your fearless guide through the streets of Paris, and cap your ride with a cruise on the River Seine toasting to the good life (untold amounts of wine included!).

Because of the awkward start time, it may be a good idea to pick up a baguette sandwich and snacks on your way to enjoy during the tour. Otherwise, the bars you'll visit next also have kitchens for a later dinner.

LATE

Hop on the metro line from the nearby La Motte-Picquet-Grenelle metro stop over to Place de la République to kick off a crawl up the **Canal Saint-Martin** to experience Paris's trendy hipster nightlife. The funky **Le Comptoir General** (Metro: Goncourt) is just a couple blocks north along the canal and will be bumping by this time in the evening.

DAY 3: CHOICES, CHOICES, CHOICES

If you've got another full day in Paris, consider a day trip to either **Disneyland Paris** or the palace of **Versailles**. Alternatively, enjoy one of Paris's markets and a quiet afternoon at the city's most famous cemetery.

MORNING

Head to the trendy **Marché des Enfants Rouge** (Metro: Filles du Calvaire, closed Mon). Go for coffee on arrival, then take a lap to make the difficult choice of where you're going to want to eat. You'll have to choose between Italian, Korean, Latin American, veggie, sandwiches, and of course French street food: crêpes.

AFTERNOON

Following the market, walk 30 minutes or take the metro to **Parc des Buttes-Chaumont**, a beautiful manicured park that embodies 19th-century French romanticism, or take the metro to **Père Lachaise Cemetery** (Metro: Père-Lachaise) to view some of the most ornate graves around and to pay your respects to greats like Chopin, Jim Morrison, and Oscar Wilde.

TOP NEIGHBORHOODS

Paris is divided into numbered neighborhoods, or *arrondisements*. Each *arrondisement* has its own personality, but it's not all that helpful for visitors to understand the intricacies of each one on a short visit.

The River Seine bisects the city. Two small islands, **Île de la Cité** and **Île Saint-Louis,** rest in the heart of it all. These picturesque islands are home to Notre Dame Cathedral, the Deportation Memorial, and Sainte-Chapelle. To the west of these islands is the **Louvre,** on the north side of the Seine.

The north side of the Seine, known as the Right Bank, has historically been the wealthier part of Paris. The Right Bank is home to the grand shopping boulevard **Champs-Élysées,** which sits at its western edge. The chic **Marais** neighborhood, on the eastern edge of the Right Bank, caters mostly to rich yuppies but offers lively shopping and nightlife. The Marais area is

also Paris's gay district, and is home to the Pompidou Center, a modern art museum. To the north, you'll find trendy nightlife, several recommended hostels, and the pleasant Parc des Buttes-Chaumont along **Canal Saint-Martin.** Finally, the bohemian district of **Montmartre** hovers just north of the city center. Here, you'll find the Moulin Rouge and the lovely hilltop cathedral of Sacre Coeur, with sweeping views of the city.

The south side of the Seine is known as the Left Bank. Traditionally home to starving artists, students, and philosophers, the Left Bank includes the **Eiffel Tower** and nearby Rue Cler market as well as the touristy **Latin Quarter,** just south of Île de la Cité and Île Saint-Louis. **Odéon,** west of the Latin Quarter, is close to Luxembourg Gardens and offers fun nightlife. In **Montparnasse,** find a couple of good restaurants that are worth the jaunt south of the Latin Quarter and Odéon.

TOP SIGHTS

Eiffel Tower

It's not until you gaze upon this iconic building in person that you realize that the photos you've seen come nowhere close to doing it justice. Built in 1889 by Gustave Eiffel for the World's Fair, this 1,063-foot tower was the tallest building in an otherwise strictly height-capped Paris, and still offers the best views of the city. The building comprises three different levels.

The first two are accessible by an elevator and by stairs, and the third level by elevator only. To save yourself some money, hike up the first two levels and then decide if you want to purchase the extra ticket for the ride to the top. I find the view is actually much better from the first two levels, from which you can see the city's landmarks in detail. At a thousand feet, the detail fades and the views are like looking out of a plane. Be sure

EIFFEL TOWER STATS

The Eiffel Tower was built for the World's Fair in 1889. Though it was originally only meant to stand for a few years, this iron monument to industrialization is still breathtaking today. These stats will help you begin to comprehend its scale:

Time to build:
Two years, two months, and five days

Cost to build:
US$36 million in today's money

Original purpose:
Radio tower

Height:
1,063 feet

Mass:
7,300 tons

Area of base:
410 square feet

Shift potential:
7 inches at the top due to warming and expansion of iron in the sun

Metric tons of paint covering the tower:
60

Frequency of repainting:
Every seven years

Number of lights:
20,000 bulbs and 336 lamps

Steps to the top:
1,665

Average daily visitors:
25,000

Distance traveled by one Eiffel Tower elevator in one year:
64,001 miles

Total number of visitors:
250 million, and counting...

to go up the Eiffel Tower, but don't forget to admire it from all parts of the city, up close and from far away. What was initially an eyesore for Parisians is now their dearest icon. After sunset, the tower sparkles with 20,000 computer-controlled strobe lights for five minutes every hour on the hour, drawing a fun crowd of picnicking spectators each night all up and down the Champ de Mars, the open field nearby.

Stairs to 2nd floor €5 for ages 12-24, €7 for 25+, elevator to all levels €14.50 ages 12-24, €17 for 25+; mid-June-early Sept daily 09:00-24:00, rest of the year daily 09:30-23:00; 5 Av Anatole France, Eiffel Tower Neighborhood, +33 (0)8 92 70 12 39, tour-eiffel.fr, Metro: Bir-Hakeim

The Louvre
What was once the French monarchy's decadent city center palace has been converted to the world's most famous and most visited museum, with 8.5 million visitors annually. Before the revolution, the French royalty enjoyed opulence far beyond what the starving people of France could even imagine. Built on the foundations of an old medieval fort, this Renaissance palace is one of the massively expensive projects that helped bring about the climax of resentment of the have-nots toward the haves. Heads rolled, and today we get to enjoy these residences as a public art museum.

The collection of art is so vast that it is said if you spent 30 seconds in front of each piece, you'd spend the better part of a year in here. Pieces span the course of human history, from prehistoric artifacts to cutting-edge modern art. Clearly, it's best to know what kind of art you're interested in before visiting. Definitely hit the key features, as you don't want to go back home saying you missed the *Mona Lisa*, *Nike of Samothrace (Winged Victory)*, *The Raft of the Medusa*, *The Coronation of Napoleon*, *Psyche Revived by Cupid's Kiss*, or *Venus de Milo*. All of these popular pieces are highlighted on the free map you can pick up at the information desk directly underneath the largest glass pyramid.

For those of you retracing the facts blended with the liberal artistic freedoms of the popular book *The Da Vinci Code*, the Louvre hosts numerous stars from the book. Keep your eyes peeled for the meridian rose on the steps leading up to the *Winged Victory*. Stop by Da Vinci's works on display in the Italian Renaissance wing, including the *Virgin of the Rocks*, *Virgin and Child with Saint Anne*, and of course, the lady herself, *Mona Lisa*. And don't leave without finding the inverted glass pyramid, where it all ends, just outside the security in the main entrance wing (follow the hallway out past Starbucks).

Buy your ticket in advance online (ticketnet.fr/index) or enter the Louvre via the metro Palais Royale, where you'll pass through a large food court on your way in (great place to refuel after your visit!).

€12, free with EU student card or EU student visa in American passport, free first Sun of the month, open Mon, Thurs, Sat, and Sun 09:00-18:00, Wed and Fri 09:00-21:45, closed Tues, Louvre Neighborhood, +33 (0)1 40 20 50 50, louvre.fr, Metro: Palais Royale

Île de la Cité & Île Saint-Louis

These two islands, where the city was founded in pre-Roman times, make up the heart of Paris. This tiny patch of real estate in the middle of the Seine River contains several of Paris's most famous sights, but strolling their picturesque lanes is a quintessentially Parisian experience in itself.

Île de la Cité is bustling with tourists. On the north side, you'll find the grand **Palais du Justice,** the judicial center of Paris and former prison, where Marie Antoinette was kept before being guillotined in 1793. Next to it is the beautiful stained-glass private royal chapel, **Sainte-Chapelle**. **Hotel-Dieu,** Paris's oldest and most prestigious hospital, sits in the middle of the island. And on the south side, you can't miss the iconic bell towers of **Notre Dame**. The low profile of Paris's **Deportation Memorial**, behind the cathedral, is more discreet. The metro stop, Cité, is worth a mention for the art nouveau design and style of the signage. Fans of the *Bourne* series will recognize **Pont Neuf**, the bridge on the northernmost point of the island, and the Samaritaine department store (Bourne's meeting point and vantage point), which closed down in 2005 due to safety code issues. The new owners have been navigating French and Paris city bureaucracy ever since.

Île Saint-Louis offers a special quiet zone smack dab in the middle of the city. Cross the bridges here and the noises of the otherwise busy streets fade away, and you'll find yourself in one of Paris's most exclusive residential districts, where the rich and famous (including Johnny Depp) keep their second (or sixth) homes. Find local-feeling *boulangeries* (bread bakeries), and don't miss the **Amorino** gelato shop at 47 Rue Saint-Louis en l'Île.

Free, always open, Île de la Cité and Île Saint-Louis, Metro: Cité

Notre Dame Cathedral

Notre Dame de Paris (Our Lady of Paris) never ceases to amaze me. One of the world's most famous gothic cathedrals is also one of the most visited churches in the world. Construction began in 1163 and continued in fits and starts for 170 years, whenever there was money and the will to build. The next several hundred years weren't so easy for our lady, who endured acts of vandalism, the looting of all her valuables, and the decapitation of her statues. At one point, Notre Dame even served as a stable for livestock, falling into further disrepair. It was in terrible shape when an obscure author, Victor Hugo, inscribed *The Hunchback of Notre Dame,* in 1831, almost single-handedly thrusting the cathedral back into the realm of public interest. A series of renovations, including the addition of the prominent pointy spire, has restored the cathedral to its present grandeur.

Inside, observe the beautiful stained glass of the South Rose Window and imagine the countless hours it took to complete such a grand design. Reflect on the fact that it took generations of builders and artisans to complete the church. After exploring the great halls of this cathedral, climb the stairs to the top of the tower and step outside for a magnificent view of the city. You won't meet the fabled hunchback up here, but you will meet all his creepy gargoyle friends, which line the outer ledges of the building. Note that the tower has separate hours.

Free, climb the towers for €8.50, cathedral open daily 08:00-18:45, Sat-Sun till 19:15, tower open daily 10:00-18:30 Apr-Sept, Fri-Sat 10:00-23:00 July-Aug, Oct-Mar 10:00-17:30, 6 Parvis Notre-Dame-Place Jean-Paul II, Île de la Cité, +33 (0)1 42 34 56 10, notredamedeparis.fr, Metro: St-Michel

Sainte-Chapelle

Dating back to the 13th century, this private chapel was created so the royal family could worship under striking floor-to-ceiling gothic stained-glass windows. The intricate windows tell Bible stories, starting on the left side of the chapel with Genesis and progressing to the right through the New Testament. Thanks to a recent cleaning and restorations, it's never been better—or brighter—to take in the beauty of Sainte-Chapelle.

€8.50 adult, Mar-Oct daily 09:30-18:00, Wed til 21:30 mid-May-mid-Sept, Nov-Feb daily 09:00-17:00, 8 Bd du Palais, Île de la Cité, +33 (0)1 53 40 60 80, sainte-chapelle. monuments-nationaux.fr, Metro: Cité

Deportation Memorial

Situated on the eastern tip of Île de la Cité, this memorial (full name: Memorial to the Martyrs of the Holocaust) commemorates the 200,000 people who were deported from Paris to concentration camps during the Nazi occupation of World War II. The architect who designed it, Georges-Henri Pingusson, wanted to convey the feeling of claustrophobia, which is achieved the moment you descend the narrow staircase. The noise of the street fades away, and each step takes you deeper into an open-topped chamber. Find the corridor with one crystal for each deported Parisian victim. You can watch the clouds and river pass by above and below your feet, but you feel stuck— imprisoned. It's a moving experience.

Free, Tues-Sun 10:00-19:00 Apr-Sept, Tues-Sun 10:00-17:00 Oct-Mar, Square de l'Île de France, Île de la Cité, +33 (0)1 46 33 87 56, Metro: Cité

Champs-Élysées

In French, *champs* means "fields." This entire area used to be the open fields beyond the old walls of medieval Paris. To-day, the grazing fields have been replaced by the world's most famous shopping street. You can find everything here, from Bugattis to brioche, Maseratis to McDonald's, and fashion superstores to nightclubs. To save on energy, start at the top, near the Arc de Triomphe, and enjoy your stroll downhill, popping into any store that suits your fancy. While it's highly recommended for shopping during the day, the boulevard and surrounding streets get touristy and a bit seedy at night.

Free, always open, Champs-Élysées Neighborhood, Metro: Charles de Gaulle-Étoile

Arc de Triomphe

Commissioned by Napoleon and finished in 1833, this 165-foot arch, situated at the top of the Champs-Élysées, honors those who died in the Revolutionary and Napoleonic Wars. When you stand under it, the purpose is clear: It's a pure power move by one of the greatest emperors Europe has ever seen, meant to make you feel small in relation to the size and supremacy of the French Republic.

Underneath the epic nationalist arch, you'll find the eternal flame marking the grave of France's unknown soldier, interred here and guarded constantly since World War I. Climb the 284 stairs for a beautiful panorama of the entire city, where you can look back down the Champs-Élysées and toward the skyscrapers of modern Paris in the opposite direction.

€8, Apr-Sept daily 10:00-23:00, Oct-Mar daily 10:00-22:30, Champs-Élysées Neighborhood, +33 (0)1 55 37 73 77, arcdetriompheparis.com, Metro: Charles de Gaulle-Étoile

Orsay Museum

The Musée d'Orsay was built as a train station and converted into a museum in 1986 to showcase artwork from 1848 to 1914. The museum is most notable for its impressionist and post-impressionist collections, containing artwork from Monet, Manet,

Renoir, and Van Gogh, to name a few. The open floor plan is fun to explore to discover both 2-D and 3-D pieces. The art nouveau furniture upstairs is one of my favorite exhibits around. Find the museum on the Left Bank, a 15-minute walk across the Seine from the Louvre.

€8.50 ages 18-25, €11 over age 25, free first Sun of the month, Tues-Sun 09:30-18:00 (Thurs 09:30-21:00), closed Mon, last tickets sold at 17:00 (21:00 on Thurs), 5 Quai Anatole France, Louvre Neighborhood, +33 (0)1 40 49 48 14, musee-orsay.fr/en, Metro: Solferino

Pigalle

Located in the bohemian neighborhood of Montmartre, the Pigalle quarter, centering around the Pigalle metro stop and the street Rue Jean-Baptiste Pigalle, is Paris's old red light district. While you won't have any ladies grabbing you off the street, if you look up you may notice that buildings have heavily covered windows. Many of these house Paris's porn studios. The famous **Moulin Rouge** (Red Mill, dinner and show €190, show only €105, 82 Bd de Clichy), attributes its fame to the song and movie of the same name. Today, it's a pricey cabaret show with can-canning peacocks strutting their stuff. The **Erotic Museum** (€8, 72 Bd de Cliché, +33 (0)1 42 58 28 73) is worth a gander, and much cheaper.

Free, always open, Montmartre, Metro: Pigalle or Abbesses

Sacre Coeur

The church of the Sacred Heart is a beautiful, all-white modern cathedral located at the top of Montmartre. It was built relatively recently (between 1875 and 1919), during a time of religious resurgence. At the end of World War I, Sacre Coeur was dedicated to those who died in the conflict.

Sacre Coeur is one of my favorite churches in Europe, sporting both a beautiful refined facade and spectacular mosaic interior with the added bonus of one of the best views of the city of Paris. When climbing the Eiffel Tower or the Arc de Triomphe, Sacre Coeur is easily recognizable across the entire city, capping Montmartre hill. The steps leading up to the church appeared in numerous scenes of the fanciful drama *Amélie*. The best part is that both the church and views are free!

Free, daily 06:00-22:30, 35 Rue du Chevalier de la Barre, Montmartre, +33 (0)1 53 41 89 00, sacre-coeur-montmartre.com, Metro: Abbesses

Pompidou Center

The Pompidou's eclectic exterior houses a fabulous collection of modern art on its fourth and fifth floors. The building was an ambitious project by a trio of famous architects from Italy and England. The design puts the guts of the building (like air-conditioning and wiring) on the exterior rather than inside the walls. Inside, the largest modern art museum in Europe takes you through the most comprehensive 20th-century timeline of creative expression, with pieces from cubist Picasso to colorful Warhol and avant-garde Chagall.

The streets surrounding the Pompidou Center are interesting to explore. Local food options abound just to the east in the nearby Jewish district. Otherwise, check out the rooftop restaurant for a midpriced post-museum snack, with sandwiches around €6.

€14 museum entry, free first Sun of the month, Wed-Mon 11:00-22:00, closed Tues, no admissions sold after 20:00,

---

MEANDER THROUGH MONTMARTRE

Historically, the neighborhood of Montmartre existed outside the old city walls of Paris—and therefore outside the city's authority and tax jurisdiction. This was where you would find prostitutes, cheap alcohol, and strip shows...and, eventually, starving artists and students, who could not afford to live elsewhere. Montmartre has been the home to some of the world's most famous artists, including Van Gogh, Matisse, Degas, and Renoir. There are even tales of cafés accepting sketches from these poor struggling artists as payment for their dinners.

Today, Montmartre is a wonderful neighborhood for a hilly stroll. Starting from the Blanche metro stop (and Pigalle and Moulin Rouge), continue uphill toward Montmartre (Hill of the Martyrs) to reach Sacre Coeur. In the streets leading to the church, you'll pass through some of Paris's most fascinating streets, lined with cafés, restaurants, galleries, and textile shops. If you get off the main streets leading to the church, you'll find a neighborhood where today's daily Parisian life is not overshadowed by the thousands of tourists that pass through every day.

19 Rue Beaubourg, Marais and Vicinity, +33 (0)1 44 78 12 33, centrepompidou.fr/en, Metro: Rambuteau

Père Lachaise Cemetery

Populated with everyone from poets and rock stars to political leaders and revolutionaries, Paris's most famous and most beautiful cemetery is toward the northeast part of the city, northeast of the Marais. This cemetery is even more densely populated than Paris's streets. Memorials, tombs, and sculptures practically trip over each other throughout this peaceful park. Must see graves: Jim Morrison, Georges Rodenbach, Frédéric Chopin, Colette, Oscar Wilde, and Victor Noir. The cemetery is quite large, and graves can be difficult to find without the help of a map. Download one ahead of time, or snap a pic of one of the maps posted at each of the entrances of the cemetery to help navigate.

Free, Mon-Fri 08:00-18:00, Sat 08:30-18:00, Sun 09:00-18:00 (17:30 in winter), 16 Rue du Repos, Marais and Vicinity, +33 (0)1 55 25 82 10, pere-lachaise.com, Metro: Gambetta

TOP EATS

You can't talk about France without talking about its famous cuisine. The tastes of Paris should easily be the highlight of your visit, and my recommendations will fit the bill across all budgets and preferences. Stay away from the touristy areas like the Latin Quarter, where restaurants tend to be overpriced. Menus with a *prix fix* sign used to be a good value, but now more often than not, these menus hide cover and service charges and I prefer to steer clear. Tipping is not as assumed as it is in the US. Look over your restaurant bill to see if service is already included. If it is, you'll see the words "*service compris.*" Otherwise, round up to about 10 percent if you liked the service.

For a cheap and tasty way to dine, opt for a **crêpe** (rhymes with "prep"). They're ubiquitous throughout the city, with options found on nearly every street corner, with street stands to boot. Crêpes can be had sweet or savory. Nutella-and-banana is a favorite. For lunch, ham-and-cheese is a classic, and I'm a fan of the tuna with a fried egg option.

La Varangue

Located near the Eiffel Tower in Champ de Mars, La Varangue should really be called Philippe's Restaurant. Philippe is a one-man show who cooks, serves, and entertains in his own funky, Parisian way. If he stops everything and makes you sing happy birthday to a fellow diner, it's best to do what he says. Come to this tiny little restaurant that seats about 18 people and enjoy Philippe's magical duck, beef, escargot, and chicken dishes in a warm and intimate atmosphere. La Varangue will surely be one of your most memorable dining experiences in Paris.

€8-20, daily 12:00-14:00 and 19:30-22:00, often closes down Dec-Jan, 27 Rue Augereau, Eiffel Tower Neighborhood, +33 (0)1 47 05 51 22, Metro: École Militaire

Les Delices du Fournil

Paris is brimming with *boulangeries* and *patisseries* showcasing freshly baked breads and pastries, respectively. Les Delices du

Fournil's excellent location in the Latin Quarter is your best budget option for filling ham, tuna, turkey, and vegetarian baguette sandwiches and sweet, fresh crêpes. Ask about their lunch menu for both sandwich and crêpe with a drink. Be sure to avail yourself of the restroom downstairs at this utilitarian café before striking back out onto the streets!

€7, Mon-Wed 06:00-19:30, Fri-Sat 06:00-19:30, Sun 06:30-12:30, 2 Rue Carmes/49 Bd Saint-Germain, +33 (0)1 43 54 14 47, Latin Quarter, Metro: Maubert-Mutualité

Coffee Parisien

For a deluxe taste of home, head to the Coffee Parisien, a retro American-style diner serving up classics like three-layered club sandwiches, massive bacon cheeseburgers, eggs Benedict, thick pancakes, hash browns, and more. The food and coffee are delicious in this fun, casual eatery, but the service does lag a bit. Make your orders clear, and don't come here if you're tight on time. I like the place mats, which illustrate a history lesson of all past US presidents.

Mains from €8, daily 12:00-24:00, 4 Rue Princesse, Odéon, +33 (0)1 43 54 18 18, coffee-parisien.fr, Metro: Saint-Germain-des-Prés

La Durée

Welcome to the world headquarters of macarons! Consider a stop at La Durée as part of your Parisian pilgrimage. Stop in for a fancy afternoon tea break and sample some of these delightful meringue cookies, a quintessential French treat. La Durée moved into their fanciful Champs-Élysées location in 1997 and they haven't looked back.

Snacks from €5, daily 07:30-23:00, 75 Av Des Champs-Élysées, Champs-Élysées Neighborhood, +33 (0)1 40 75 08 75, laduree.com, Metro: George V

Angelina

Step into this gilded (and a bit pretentious) classic luxury café and into a place seemingly obsessed with achieving the world's finest hot chocolate. Add to that pastries, macarons, and fudge-drowned sugar-coated desserts, and Angelina will floor you (and your wallet). If you're hungry, tuck into the poshest salads, omelets, and eggs Benedicts you've ever tried. Find Angelina on the north side of the Tuileries gardens.

Artfully presented starters from €25, tea from €7, Mon-Fri 07:30-19:00, Sat-Sun 08:30-19:30, 226 Rue de Rivoli, Louvre Neighborhood, +33 (0)1 42 60 82 00, Angelina-paris.fr, Metro: Palais Royal-Musée du Louvre

Le Café Marly

Find this decadent café in the arcade facing the glass pyramids at the Louvre. Breaking just about any budget, it's a welcome glass of white wine after a long day inside the museum. See if you can't convince yourself to splurge on one of their many delectable desserts (from €14). You're paying for the setting and the ambience, and as such are definitely among well-heeled tourists. Reservations are required.

Meals from €30, daily 12:00-23:00, 93 Rue de Rivoli, Louvre Neighborhood, +33 (0)1 49 26 06 60, cafe-marly.com, Metro: Palais Royal-Musée du Louvre

Derrière

Derrière (which translates to "backside" in English) is a trendy and eclectic spot tucked behind the sister 404 Restaurant in a retrofitted mansion in the Marais. Derriere is a unique dining experience from the minute you open up the artistic menu. Enjoy your

meal at the foot of a bed, on a sofa, or even in the kitchen and bathrooms. It's as much about the experience of playing a game of Ping Pong or sneaking through a wardrobe into a hidden room as it is about the food itself—as delicious as it is. The friendly—if French-paced—service is happy to share about their artisanal dishes, like salads made with those multicolored carrots, beef filet, and tuna tartare. The €38 buffet brunch (Sun 12:00-16:00) is a winner. Reservations are required. After dinner consider a drink at the cool 'n' cozy cocktail bar next door,

Andy Wahloo

Mains from €30, daily 12:00–01:30, find the unmarked passageway leading to a courtyard at 69 Rue des Gravilliers, Marais and Vicinity, +33 (0)1 44 61 91 95, derriere-resto. com, Metro: Arts et Metiers

Amorino

If you happen to pass one of these *gelaterie*, stop in and grab some gelato that—when fresh—rivals even the best in Italy. The best part: Ask for as many flavors as you want, and they'll arrange them into an edible bouquet for you. *Speculoos* (graham cracker) is my personal favorite. You'll find several other well-located Amorino branches sprinkled around Paris's most popular neighborhoods.

From €3.50, daily 12:00–24:00, 47 Rue Saint-Louis en l'Île, Île Saint-Louis, +33 (0)1 44 07 48 08, amorino.com/en, Metro: Pont Marie

L'Avant Comptoir

I stumbled upon this gem when I noticed a bunch of locals waiting in line for a spot at the bar. This cozy bar and restaurant pours wine and serves up Spanish-style tapas like *jamón* (ham) and cheese platters, generous sandwiches on rustic bread, and, my favorite, *pimientos de padrón* (fried, salted peppers) by the truckload, all presented with Parisian sophistication. Find the menu and bottles available hanging from the ceiling and enjoy the reasonable prices and a fun, local, in-the-know vibe.

€8-20, daily 12:00–23:00, 9 Carrefour de l'Odéon, Odéon, +33 (0)1 44 27 07 50, Metro: Odéon

Heureux Comme Alexandre

If you're looking for a dinner of fondue, this is my top choice in town. Come for the €16 unlimited salad and potatoes fondue dinner, and stick around for the fun atmosphere and easygoing service. Enjoy the excellent location in the Latin Quarter without the hordes of tourists, leaving you, as the name of the place suggests, "happy as Alexandre." Reservations recommended.

Dinner €16, daily 11:00–24:00, 24 Rue de la Parcheminerie, Latin Quarter, +33 (0)1 43 26 49 66, heureuxcommealexandre.com, Metro: Cluny-La Sorbonne

La Closerie des Lilas

Enjoy a wonderfully Parisian evening on an unforgettable splurge dinner at this Michelin star restaurant just steps from the Luxembourg Gardens. You'll understand why this place was a favorite of Hemingway, Man Ray, and Sartre as soon as you step through the threshold into this Secret Garden-esque experience. You'll dine on a covered patio under flowers and foliage while being serenaded by the pianist inside. If you can stomach the blow to the wallet, the menu spans fish and shellfish to meats to the classic *steak frites* (steak and fries). Make reservations well in advance, and be sure to ask if the pianist will be playing.

Mains from €40, soaring past €50, cocktails from €16, daily 12:00–00:30, 171 Bd du Montparnasse, Montparnasse, +33 (0)1 40 51 34 50, closeriedeslilas.fr, Metro: Vavin

Cubana Café

I prioritize a return to Cubana Café on just about every visit to Paris. Here, you'll get a consistently good meal at a fair price. On the restaurant side, you'll find welcoming staff and a delicious menu complete with shredded pork, beans, and plantains. If it's a cigar you're after, select it with the waiter at the bar and step through the glass doors into the smoking room. This is where you may have the chance to rub elbows with some high rollers in the Paris scene, as well as enjoy some fine Caribbean tobacco with a Havana rum and Coke. Freedom never tasted so good.

Mains from €12, daily 11:00–03:00, 47 Rue Vavin, Montparnasse, +33 (0)1 40 46 80 81, cubanacafe.com, Metro: Vavin

Chez Prune

The quays along Canal Saint-Martin are packed with people chilling and drinking all night, and Chez Prune is a great place to stop for a cappuccino or excellent cheese and meat plates during the day. This cool artsy bar is popular yet seems to escape the tourist eye, drawing a crowd of hip young Parisian professionals. This nondescript café is located right on the canal, so enjoy your drinks outside on nice, sunny days.

Dishes from €13, daily 08:00–02:00, 36 Rue Beaurepaire, Canal Saint-Martin, +33 (0)1 42 41 30 47, Metro: Gare de l'Est or Jacques Bonsergent

PARIS

59

TOP NIGHTLIFE

Parisian nightlife is different than what young Americans may be used to. On an average night out, Parisians may have only a couple of drinks but go through packs of cigarettes. Parisians don't drink to get drunk, unless you somehow find yourself invited to a house party (in which case, bring two bottles of wine for yourself and a third to contribute to the party). Since going out on the town is so expensive, many students prefer to drink with friends in each other's cramped-yet-cozy little apartments to either pregame a night out or spend the entire evening in. By the way, French students take their foosball seriously. So if you've got skills, get yourself to the front of the queue and get ready to school or be schooled—a great way to make friends either way.

Anytime you go out, be sure to bring valid **ID,** as proof of age is required at the door of many bars and clubs. Your best bet is to bring your driver's license and a copy of your passport; leave the real thing at home! It really puts a major damper on the night when you're "bounced" because you left yours at home.

NIGHTLIFE DISTRICTS

Paris is big enough for you to find exactly what you're looking for, but it does come with the typical uptick of pretentiousness— you are in Paris after all. This city is full of districts with distinct personalities catering to all preferences and tastes. The student neighborhoods of Bastille and Oberkampf and the trendy Canal Saint-Martin tend to be the most easygoing and fun, so that's where I go when I'm in town.

Canal Saint-Martin

What used to be a backwater of Paris has now emerged as one of the city's trendiest and most exciting districts. The low rents have attracted bohemian types, and cafés and bars have been popping up in the streets running along the canal, leading north from Place de la République, a mile

north of Bastille. On a nice day, there's nothing better than going for a late afternoon stroll along this 4.5-kilometer canal, stopping at any of the hipster joints that pique your fancy. Start your canal crawl from the north side of Canal Saint-Martin near several recommended hostels, then work your way south.

Canal Saint-Martin, Metro: Gare de l'Est, Goncourt, Jaures, or Louis Blanc

Oberkampf

The narrow, unrefined streets that wind through this hilly neighborhood in northern Paris, near Canal Saint-Martin, create a very Parisian atmosphere, topped off with quaint, locally owned cafés. This neighborhood is popular among students, as it offers some of the cheapest food and drink prices you can find in all of Paris. You'll find most of the ac-

THE MOST FAMOUS NON-SIGHT IN PARIS

The Bastille neighborhood is named after the notorious castle-turned-prison. Built in the 14th century, the castle was converted into a prison by the oppressive monarchs in the 1600s. On July 14, 1789, peasant hordes swarmed the Bastille, thinking it contained hundreds of their imprisoned compatriots. The 600 rebels took over the defenses, but found only a small contingent of opposition, along with just seven degenerate prisoners. It was a glorious success to no real point. Shortly afterward, the Bastille was demolished, as it symbolized the oppression of the revolution's ideals: *liberté, égalité, fraternité* (liberty, equality, fraternity). July 14 is now observed as Bastille Day, an annual holiday.

Though the castle is long gone, you've got to swing through the Bastille neighborhood at some point during your visit. Yes, you may see clueless tourists trying to find the castle, but you'll find only a massive roundabout circling an obelisk (the July Column), with the Opéra Bastille anchoring one side. The canal leading away from the square makes for a wonderful afternoon stroll in good weather, as you check out the boats and munch on fresh baguettes. In the back streets surrounding the grand plaza, you'll find bohemian nightlife, student bars, and a tasteful array of restaurants. Trendy Parisians are now turning their collective nose up at this neighborhood, as it's been well-discovered by tourists, but you can find gems, especially on Rue de Lappe.

tion between the **Avenue de la République** and **Rue Moret.**

Canal Saint-Martin, Metro: Parmentier or Oberkampf

Bastille

East of the Marais, the Bastille district draws a young crowd. It's ideal for a night of pub crawling, as all the action centers on one street: **Rue de Lappe,** just north and east of the Place de la Bastille. This street satisfies the classy and grungy alike, with everything from sports bars and lounges to small, crowded, boutique-style drinkeries. Rue de Lappe used to be a Parisian secret, with tons of places to score cheap drinks, but prices have aligned themselves with the neighborhood's newfound reputation. It's worth taking a lap to evaluate your many options for happy hour or to find the place just right for you.

Marais and Vicinity, Metro: Bastille

The Marais

Bordered on the west by Rue du Renard and the Pompidou Center, and to the east by the grand Boulevard de Beaumarchais and the Bastille district, this is one of Paris's most eclectic and fun neighborhoods. Chic and a bit yuppie, the Marais is known as Paris's gay district.

Marais and Vicinity, Metro: Saint-Paul

Odéon

Once the center of intellectual life, this Left Bank neighborhood was just teeming with philosophers contemplating existentialism, artists toying with surrealism, and musicians exploring the depths of jazz. Now, it's a popular neighborhood with some great restaurants and bars, like **Le Dix Bar,** a cozy sangria bar. The best part is that bars and restaurants center around a single street, **Rue Princesse.** Why is all this goodness so tightly concentrated, you ask? Because it's located just across the street from the

Sorbonne, the University of Paris! Expect to see some revelers out.

Odéon, Metro: Odéon

BARS

Bar Ourcq

Bar Ourcq is a great place to kick off your evening along Canal Saint-Martin. It feels like your comfortable corner bar where you can get cheap drinks, socialize, enjoy some good music, or take your drinks to go and tip them back along the canal. Organic snacks, €1 sandwiches, and the convenient location make for a great start to the night. From the simply decorated café, snag a chair and enjoy your drink overlooking the canal.

Drinks from €3, Wed-Thurs 15:00-24:00, Fri-Sat 15:00-01:45, Sun 15:00-22:00, 68 Quai de la Loire, Canal Saint Martin, +33 (0)1 42 40 12 26, barourcq.free.fr, Metro: Lumière

Point Éphémère

Run by a nonprofit agency charged with converting old and abandoned buildings into lively cultural centers for the arts, this place has it all: great food, art studios and galleries, a concert venue, terrace, cheap drinks for the canal, and a cool crowd without the usual Parisian snob. The Point, having taken over an old canal-side industrial workshop, usually has a number of freshly tagged graffiti pieces scrawled across the exterior. They keep their art and live music shows fresh with a constantly updated calendar of events, drawing a cool and eclectic crowd. Staying true to its name, each visit back to the Point offers something new. Check their website for the upcoming events.

Drinks from €4, book concert tickets online, Mon-Sat 12:00-02:00, Sun 12:00-23:00, 200 Quai de Valmy, Canal Saint-Martin, +33 (0)1 40 34 02 48, pointephemere.org, Metro: Jaures or Louis Blanc

Le Comptoir Général

I love this multifaceted artistic and cultural

LGBT PARIS

The Marais, which overlaps with the Jewish Quarter, is known as Paris' gay district. In this bustling tangle of medieval lanes, you'll find art galleries, design shops, adult stores, high fashion boutiques, florists, cafés, bakeries, and cozy restaurants by day. By night, the fun runs the length of **Rue de la Verrerie,** leading into **Rue de Roi Sicile,** with crowds spilling out onto the surrounding streets. The bears feel at home in the burly **Bear's Den** (6 Rue des Lombards, +33 (0)1 42 71 08 20). If you like beer, stop into **La Caves a Bulles** (45 Rue Quincampoix, +33 (0)1 40 29 03 69), an artisanal brew shop where you get bottles to go and enjoy them on the square in front of the Pompidou Center.

space set back from the canal in an old warehouse—Paris's best equivalent to the popular Budapest-style ruin bars. Begin exploring the complex to discover a serious coffee bar, excellent cocktail bar (of course), space for designers to sell their concepts from pop-up shops, live music acts, and hanging gardens. The crowd and vibe are really as hipster as it gets, but not in a bad way. Enjoy film screenings and concerts, and check their calendar ahead of time to see if tickets are available for hot upcoming events. Heads-up: The line can be long on weekend nights, but that's not the only time to stop by and explore! While the party can ramp up occasionally on their small dance floor, it's much more a quiet and chill place to enjoy a drink while exploring all the rooms in this open and airy garden bar.

Free entry, donation suggested, daily 11:00–02:00, 80 Quai de Jemmapes, Canal Saint-Martin, +33 (0)1 44 88 24 48, lecomptoirgeneral.com/en, Metro: Goncourt

Le Dix Bar

Le Dix Bar is a cool sangria bar with a dark-wood interior in one of my favorite neighborhoods, Odéon. Come out with friends and select your size of pitcher. Give it your best guess, then round up, because the sangria the friendly old man pumps out is delicious and refreshing. Enjoy your fruit-infused wine upstairs or head downstairs to join the social crowd of drinkers.

Pitchers from €12, daily 18:00–late, 10 Rue de l'Odéon, Odéon, +33 (0)01 43 26 66 83, le10bar.com, Metro: Odéon

Chez Georges

For a truly Parisian experience, come to this classic bar with a twist and enjoy some wine with a group of your friends. Or fly solo and sit down at one of the many communal tables to strike up a conversation with your fellow winos. It draws a slightly older crowd. Don't miss the exposed brick arch cellar downstairs, and join the sweaty dancing that kicks off on weekend nights. While it closes at 02:00, it's located near Odéon, which is convenient if you want to keep the night going.

Glasses from €6, Mon–Fri 15:00–late, Sat 12:00–02:00, Sun 19:00–02:00, 11 Rue des Canettes, Odéon, +33 (0)1 43 26 79 15, Metro: Mabillon

Café Oz

Unapologetically touristy and international, this large Aussie sports bar with an open layout also fits the bill for downtown dancing. Pub crawls kick off here, so it gets packed then empties out each night, and you can count on just about every game being televised to be up on the screens—they've got a thing for rugby here. Come out and enjoy the rowdy student crowd dancing to Top 40 and hip-hop spinning after the matches finish up. In town for a holiday? Check out their frequent theme nights for Halloween, Christmas, and more online.

Drinks from €5, Mon–Fri 17:00–late, Sat-Sun 12:00–late, 18 Rue Saint-Denis, Louvre Neighborhood, +33 (0)1 40 39 00 18, cafe-oz.com, Metro: Châtelet

CLUBS

Remember to bring ID with birth date on it, and dress to impress to get past the bouncers. They want you inside having a good time, but they're also picky to keep the party at the level of class they want. Most recommended clubs don't open till 23:00 or so.

Showcase

This posh and cavernous club features an excellent view of the Eiffel Tower from the smoking section from underneath the Pont Alexandre III bridge. Opt for the shots, as the long drinks seem to be watered down. Dress to impress and get past the bouncers, as this colonnaded dance floor is one of the most popular in the city. Get down to the famous resident and visiting DJs spinning electronic and techno and enjoy the energized crowd.

€20 cover, beers and drinks from €8, Fri-Sat 23:00–late, Port des Champs-Élysées underneath Pont Alexandre III, Champs-Élysées Neighborhood, +33 (0)1 45 61 25 43, showcase.fr, Metro: Invalides

YoYo Palais de Tokyo

If you like to dance and have moved beyond the college-dorm party scene, YoYo is a great choice. This large venue in an old theater has plenty of room to get your groove on. Thankfully, the air-conditioning is turned up so you can keep cool without breaking a sweat. Famous DJs visit often to spin house and techno—it's a good idea to purchase entry ahead of time if there's an upcoming gig you like. Be prepared for long, slow lines outside and plenty of security. But once inside, you'll love it! Pregame on the Champ de Mars with some wine before crossing the river and finding this club tucked underneath the Modern Art Museum of Paris.

Covers from €10, Wed-Sat 23:00–late, 13 Av du Président Wilson, Champs-Élysées Neighborhood, +33 (0)1 84 79 11 70, yoyo-paris.com, Metro: Iena or Alma Marceau

La Machine Du Moulin Rouge

This is a massive triple-level dance club with DJs in each room spinning a wide range of music, from house and electronic to dubstep and the more generic Top 40. Don't let the location, right in the middle of the city's famed red light district, unnerve you, as the neighborhood is clean and safe. This place really puts on the party—packed with locals, backpackers, and a fun-loving crowd. Famous acts come through often, so check the program ahead of time to see if there are any names you recognize.

Covers and drinks €10, Fri-Sun 23:00-late, 90 Bd de Clichy, Montmartre, +33 (0)1 53 41 88 89, lamachinedumoulinrouge.com/en, Metro: Blanche

Queen

Champs-Élysées is not the best place to go out, but glitzy Queen is the one exception. It's a popular gay club, featuring costumed male strippers on raised platforms putting on dueling acts throughout the night. Wednesday is ladies night and evens the ratio a bit, but all are welcome any night of the week. Expensive drinks, but shots are passed out to the lucky ones when the managers want to ramp the party up.

€20 cover, daily 23:00-05:00, 102 Av. des Champs-Élysées, Champs-Élysées Neighborhood, +33 (0)1 53 89 08 90, queen fr, Metro: George V

PUB CRAWLS

When it comes to planning a night out in Paris, first consider the way Parisians go out: for one glass of wine and a pack (or three) of cigarettes. If you tend to be thirstier, an organized pub crawl may be a great choice for you.

Sandeman's New Europe Pub Crawl

You know the pub crawl drill: Pay the €25 cover, then get free drinks for an hour at the meeting point. Your itinerary will include about three stops, with a final stop at a club with a free entry. It'll be up to you to get home, but between the opening bell and when "Piano Man" comes on to close the night, you're sure to have a good time with a set of 20-120 new international friends.

€25, Thurs-Sat 20:00, meet at the Bastille metro stop, Marais and Vicinity, newparistours.com, Metro: Bastille

TOP SHOPPING & MARKETS

Stores in Paris close down on Sunday. Stores that do stay open actually pay a fine week after week for keeping their doors open.

SHOPPING DISTRICTS
Champs-Élysées

The most famous shopping street in the world and open every day of the week—despite French law requiring shops to close on Sunday—Champs-Élysées is lined with everything from Louis Vuitton to Gap. Spend a day lost in luxury, making sure to stop for a crêpe or a box of macarons to prevent the "drop" from the famous adage of "shop till you drop."

Champs-Élysées Neighborhood, Metro: Charles de Gaulle-Étoile

The Marais

Paris's gay and Jewish district is also one of its trendiest, with excellent shopping options and delicious restaurants and cafés. You'll find unique boutique stores and the more common high-end designer brands in this neighborhood of winding medieval streets. **Rue de Rivoli** and **Rue Vieille du Temple** are the main intersecting streets in this area, with dozens of lanes turning off them to explore. This neighborhood is a great place to shop on Sunday, as the stores are some of the only ones open in the whole city.

Marais and Vicinity, Metro: Saint Paul

Rue Montorgueil

One of my favorite pedestrian avenues in Paris, **Rue Montorgueil** boasts pastry shops, flower stalls, bistros, and an open-air market that sells the wide variety of meats, cheeses, and other goodies. You'll also find top-notch nightlife, with a large variety of bars that appeal to every person imaginable. Leading north from the Châtelet-Les Halles metro stop, all the way toward Montmartre, Rue Montorgueil offers a casual scene for those who like to spend an evening on a low-key stroll, stopping for snacks, drinks, and gelato on the way.

Louvre Neighborhood, Metro: Étienne Marcel or Sentier

MARKETS

Traditionally, life in Paris centered around the goods purchased at the daily market. Markets are a great way to catch a glimpse of daily Parisian life, with grandmas picking out the freshest fruit and children running home with their daily staple of baguettes. While many cute local markets have been swallowed up by large grocery and department stores, some manage to maintain their charm (no matter how many guidebook-toting tourists plod through). These are some of my favorites, but keep your eyes open for other local neighborhood markets while you wander.

Rue Cler

The market on Rue Cler, a quaint street just east of the Eiffel Tower, is a local market that stubbornly retains its identity. You can see schoolchildren running about, enjoy a crêpe on the street, and pick up some French produce. Though the prices at the restaurants on this street have become a bit outrageous due to its popularity, Rue Cler offers a little slice of picturesque Paris with the cafés, corner markets, and food stands that line these three little blocks.

Eiffel Tower Neighborhood, Metro: École Militaire

Marché des Enfants Rouges

Marché des Enfants is a permanent, semi-covered food market in an old courtyard that has been around since 1628. It's quite popular among trendy Parisians. Pop in for a quick and tasty lunch, from Japanese cuisine to exotic African dishes. Food stalls let you take your food tray to the communal benches and tables around the market.

Tues–Sun 08:30-13:00 and 16:00-19:30, closed Mon, 39 Rue de Bretagne 3e, Marais and Vicinity, Metro: Filles du Calvaire

SHOPPING CENTERS

Galeries Lafayette

Claiming to be one of the oldest shopping malls in the world, this shopping center has an enormous variety of well-known international shops and a spectacular four-level atrium interior under an ornately gilded glass dome. Stop by in December to see their famous 50-foot-tall Christmas tree reaching toward the ceiling.

Mon–Sat 09:30-20:00, 40 Bd Haussmann, Louvre Neighborhood, Metro: Chaussée d'Antin-La Fayette

Forum des Halles

Located right in downtown Paris, Forum des Halles is a massive shopping center dug deep into the ground and sitting right atop the metro. Very popular for Parisians coming in from the *banlouies* (the suburbs of Paris), it's a top choice for blue-collar brands like H&M and Jack Jones.

Mon–Sat 10:00-20:00, Louvre Neighborhood, forumdeshalles.com, Metro: Les Halles

TOP PARKS & RECREATION

Paris has numerous city parks to explore. They're a great option for a cheap picnic and to catch a breather from the bustle of the city.

Luxembourg Gardens

This beautiful 60-acre park is just a few blocks south of the Notre Dame Cathedral, and filled with flower gardens, fountains, ponds, and statues, topped off with an enormous Florentine Renaissance-style palace overlooking it. The manicured lawns and paths make it a favorite among reflective Parisians for an afternoon stroll. Catch a game of *pétanque* (the French game of field bowling) on the southwest side of the park.

Free, daily 07:00-dusk, Odéon, Metro: Odéon, RER: Luxembourg

The Tuileries

The Tuileries are Paris's oldest garden. Be sure to walk through this sprawling park as you're making your way from the Louvre to the Champs-Élysées. Take a moment to relax in the reclining park chairs and enjoy watching little French kids sail model boats in the ponds. Fun fact: *Tuile* means "tile." Paris's tile and ceramics factories were located here until Queen Catherine de Medici family moved them out in 1564 to make room for her royal gardens, which were meant to be reminiscent of those she would have seen in her home town of Florence.

Free, always open, Louvre Neighborhood, Metro: Tuileries

Champ de Mars

The Champ de Mars, or "Field of War," stretches southwest from the Eiffel Tower. This large open space was the parade grounds where officers practiced maneuvering troops. Today, it's a favorite spot for Parisians to picnic on nice summer evenings, watching the glittering Eiffel Tower sparkle for five minutes each hour. When there are important events or sports matches here, large Jumbotrons are brought in for the crowds to watch. It's also just about impossible to find a free square inch here on New Year's Eve, as the fireworks display pops off from the Eiffel Tower.

Free, always open, Eiffel Tower Neighborhood, Metro: École Militaire

Parc des Buttes-Chaumont

This beautiful park in the northeast of Paris features more than a mile of romantic paths and hundreds of trees to make for a wonderful break from the busy city. Typical of 19th-century ingenuity, this ambitious park project with an artificial lake and a peak over 150 feet tall was reclaimed from a garbage dump and stone quarry during the beautification projects under Napoleon III. (This happened during the same era that the boulevards and avenues of Paris were being widened.) I enjoy the rope bridge and short climb to the temple capping the peak for a panoramic view across town. The park is also close to several great hostels and the Canal Saint-Martin nightlife district.

Free, always open, Canal Saint-Martin, Metro: Botzaris

TOP TOURS

Paris is a massive city, and a knowledgeable guide really helps you grasp the complex history and understand better what you're looking at. Fortunately, you've got both walking tours and bike tours to choose from.

Discover Walks

This walking tour company offers some great itineraries through the heart of Paris. Tours are led by fun and engaging locals who are paid only by your generosity in the form of tips at the end of the tour. Their numerous itineraries, organized by theme and neighborhood, could fill up an entire visit to Paris. I recommend their **Latin Quarter Walk,** which will take you through the oldest neighborhoods of the city, including Île de la Cité and Notre Dame Cathedral.

Free, 11:00 and 14:30 daily, meet at the Charlemagne statue in front of Notre Dame, Île de la Cité, discoverwalks.com/paris-walking-tours, Metro: Cité

Fat Tire Bike & Boat Tour

Cruising around by bike is my favorite way to experience the City of Lights. Go for the evening tour and cap your bike adventure with an evening boat cruise! Highlights include Notre Dame, the Louvre, a stop for ice cream, and then a ride down the Seine. With free wine included during the boat tour, this is the perfect way to cap an evening.

Student single €28, day+night €42, tours mid-Feb-Nov, daily mid-Mar-Oct, check website for times and off-season dates, 24 Rue Edgar Faure, Eiffel Tower Neighborhood, fattirebiketours.com/paris, Metro: Dupleix

Paris Noir

Paris Noir (Black Paris) is run by a good friend of mine, Kevi Donat. Kevi leads visitors through the streets of Paris speaking from the perspective of black Parisians, reviewing their oral, musical, and artistic culture. Recognized by French and international media, Kevi does an excellent job of researching and developing new content and delivering these fascinating stories from the turn of the century to today.

Tours on request, blackpariswalks.com

TOP HOSTELS

Paris is woefully lagging in budget accommodations, but those listed are a good value. Use **hostelworld.com** to find the latest hostel ratings, and don't forget to check out **airbnb.com** for private apartment options.

Generator Hostel Paris

The Generator Hostel chain continues to take the continent by storm, and the new Paris location does not disappoint. The Generator team knows exactly what budget travelers are looking for and does an excellent job of providing a fun, chill place to crash after your long days out on the town. Besides the new, clean rooms, mod decor, ubiquitous free Wi-Fi, and plugs and reading lights for each bed, the location, right in the hot spot of Canal Saint-Martin's trendy scene, is a favorite feature of the hostel. In the opposite direction, the beautiful Parc des Buttes-Chaumont is only a few minutes away. Deluxe penthouse and private rooms are available as well, offering views of the neighborhood.

Beds from €22, 24-hour reception, mini grocer, vending machines, free Wi-Fi, terrace, travel options desk, on-site bar and restaurant, laundry facilities, lockers and adapters for rent, 9-11 Place du Colonel Fabien, Canal Saint-Martin, +33 (0)1 70 98 84 00, generatorhostels.com, Metro: Colonel Fabien

St Christopher's Inn Gare du Nord

This hostel, which opened its doors in May 2013, lives up to the St Christopher's brand of large hostels with clean rooms, loads of amenities, and a great location on the north side of Paris, just steps from Paris's northern train station and a couple blocks from the trendy, up-and-coming Canal Saint-Martin district. With over 600 beds, this hostel brings in loads of travelers from all over the world, creating a fun and social atmosphere to meet and connect with other globetrotters.

€24, free breakfast, optional upgrade, free Wi-Fi, bar, café, 24-hour reception, free linens, 5 Rue de Dunkerque, Canal Saint-Martin, +33 (0)1 70 08 52 22, st-christophers.co.uk/paris-hostels/gare-du-nord, paris@st-christophers.co.uk, Metro: Gare du Nord

St Christopher's Inn Canal

This is the original location (and my second choice of the two St Christopher's hostels in town), with a fun vibe and a music bar downstairs featuring acts that even bring in the locals. While it's a half-hour metro ride to sights like the Louvre and the Cathedral of Notre Dame, the comfy beds, helpful yet busy staff, free breakfast, and Wi-Fi make this one of Paris's better budget choices. It's also about a 30-minute walk north of the fun Canal Saint-Martin nightlife district. You can't miss the funky exterior: It looks like a bunch of giant rubber bands wrapped around all six levels of this large hostel overlooking the canal.

€24, daily breakfast, free Wi-Fi, "chill-out room," bag lockers, 24-hour reception, free linens, 159 Rue de Crimée, Canal Saint-Martin, +33 (0)1 40 34 34 40, st-christophers.co.uk/paris-hostels/canal, paris@st-christophers.co.uk, Metro: Crimée

The Loft Boutique Hostel

The Loft tries hard to be Paris's top boutique hostel and is successful in many ways. Highlights include the fun intimate atmosphere in the common rooms, cleanliness (thanks, cleaning staff!), and the included continental breakfast. The outdoor patio and nightly happy hour make for a nice social vibe. The neighborhood feels a bit bohemian and off the beaten path, away from the major tourist sights of Paris, yet right between the Parc des Buttes-Chaumont and Père Lachaise Cemetery.

Beds from €23, 24-hour reception, outdoor terrace, on-site bar, free Wi-Fi, included breakfast, kitchen and laundry facilities available, 70 Rue Julien Lacroix, Canal Saint-Martin, +33 (0)1 42 02 42 02, theloft-paris.com, Metro: Pyrénées

Trendy Hostel

While this hostel southeast of the city center (about 20 minutes away on the metro) suffers in location, backpackers love it for just about everything else: comfortable beds, fun staff, great local restaurants, and a long list of amenities. The value is great, but it may feel like you're commuting into town each time you want to sightsee or go out at night.

Beds from €18 with female dorms available, 24-hour reception, free maps and Wi-Fi, laundry facilities available, linens included, breakfast included, 2B Rue Édouard Vasseur, Greater Paris, +33 (0)982 479 024, trendyhostel.com, Metro: Pierre et Marie Curie

BVJ Louvre

With a title that translates to "Office of Youth Travel," this hostel is painfully institutional, but still worthwhile thanks to the superb location. BVJ Louvre completely misses the mark when it comes to providing what backpackers want these days (i.e., fun, social atmosphere, comfortable mattresses, free Wi-Fi—yes, that's three strikes against BVJ), but you just can't deny how nice it is to roll out of bed straight into the Louvre. If BVJ Louvre is full, you can try their other location, **BVJ Opéra** (1 Rue de la Tour des Dames, +33 (0)1 42 36 88 18, Metro: Trinité d'Estienne d'Orves), offering mostly the same dull experience in another central location.

Beds from €24, towels and breakfast not included, Wi-Fi working sometimes, 20 Rue Jean-Jacques Rousseau, Louvre Neighborhood, +33 (0)1 53 00 90 90, bvjhotel.com, Metro: Louvre-Rivoli

TRANSPORTATION

GETTING THERE & AWAY
Plane

There are three major airports in Paris: **Charles de Gaulle** (CDG), **Orly** (ORY), and **Beauvais** (BVA). Find information for all three at aeroportsdeparis.com. All offer quick and reliable transport into the city.

From **Charles de Gaulle**, take Paris's regional train system, the **RER.** After arrival, follow the signs marked RER leading you to the ticketing area. A one-way ticket will cost you €9.10, with trains departing between 05:00 and 00:15 every 15 minutes. Remember; you need your ticket to exit the RER system, so keep it handy. This is your cheapest and fastest option into the city, with opportunities to connect onto Paris's extensive metro system, including service to Gare du Nord (for St Christopher's Hostels), Châtelet-Les Halles (central Paris), and Luxembourg (south side of Paris) stations. By RER and metro, it takes about an hour to get from Charles de Gaulle into the center of Paris.

Another option is the **Roissybus** express bus (€10). Find it by following the signs marked "Roissybus." Purchase a ticket from an RATP (the name of Paris's public transportation system) vendor, which is clearly marked and located right by the bus stop. Roissybus takes about an hour and a half into the city center.

Lastly, you can hail **taxis** outside the terminal for a €45 one-hour trip into the city.

From **Orly,** take the **Orlybus,** which is a direct route into the center of the city. The bus will drop you at Denfert Rochereau metro station, where you can connect to the metro and ride it to your desired stop. Buses depart every 15 minutes, running from 05:35 to 23:00. The journey costs €7.70 one way and will take you about 25 minutes.

You can also use Air France's **shuttle service** (€9), departing every 15 minutes running to Porte d'Orléans, Montparnasse, and Invalides metro stations. It runs from 06:00 to 23:00, with a journey length of 25 minutes. Or, take a **taxi** into the center for about €25.

From **Beauvais**, catch the Beauvais Airport official **shuttle** (€16), which is a non-stop journey from the airport to the Porte Maillot metro stop in Paris. The journey takes about 75 minutes.

Train

Rates from London—on fast trains taking just under 2.5 hours—range from €50 to €150 and up, depending on student discount and how far in advance you book your ticket. For more information, visit the **Eurostar** website (eurostar.com). Trains to Amsterdam (about €75) run often and take about 3.5 hours.

Six major train stations operate in Paris, so it's important to confirm your departure station when the time comes for you to leave. **Gare du Nord** (in northern Paris) serves connections to London, Amsterdam, and Brussels. **Gare de l'Est** (just east of Gare du Nord) serves Munich, Frankfurt, Luxembourg, and beyond. **Gare de Lyon** (east of the Marais) most likely has your night connections to Nice, Barcelona, and Milan. All train stations are well connected via metro, and it is possible to buy tickets for your departure at any train station for any other station.

Bus

Paris has numerous bus options for France, Germany, Spain, Italy, and even the UK.

For the cheaper price, remember, you're trading time en route and comfort. **Eurolines** (eurolines.fr) is the dominant company. Check their prices and full list of destinations online.

Car

Thanks to Paris's excellent public transportation system, I advise against renting a car for any visit to the city, and caution those who are considering taking a road trip. It's not that it's dangerous or unpleasant, but trains, planes, and buses will all get you to your destination quicker, in more comfort, and most likely at a cheaper price. When budgeting for your trip, don't forget to account for gas (about $10/gallon), parking, and speeding tickets from pesky automated machines all on top of the rental fee, service, and insurance for the car itself.

GETTING AROUND

Take advantage of the fantastic public transportation this city offers, which comprises train, bus, and metro lines. The system is integrated: A single **ticket** costs €1.70. A **carnet** of 10 tickets (€12.70) saves you about 25 percent, and the 10 rides can be shared between multiple people.

Metro

Paris's metro system (ratp.fr) is easily one of the best in the world, and is an extremely useful way to get around. The metro operates Sunday-Thursday 05:30-00:30 and Friday-Saturday 05:30-02:00. You'll rarely walk two blocks without passing a metro stop, and all routes are color-coded and numbered, safe, and easy to navigate. Here's how to use it: On a metro map, find the station you're at and the one you want to get to. Follow the lines stemming from both and see where they meet up to figure out if you need to transfer. You can get nearly anywhere in Paris with one or two transfers between different lines. Once you've figured out which line(s) to take, follow signs to the side of the platform with the final destination indicating the direction toward your stop. The **RATP Lite** app offers a full map of the metro. Be aware that **pickpockets** operate throughout Paris's metro system. Keep your valuables tight and safe.

RER

The RER system, Paris's express regional train, zips straight through the heart of town and to destinations outside the city. It's much speedier than the metro or bus. Keep an eye out for any potential reasons to use it during your stay.

The RER network is lettered A through E. Tickets within the city cost the same as on the metro; remember to hold onto your validated ticket because you need it to exit the system. The RER system also provides fast connections to the airports as well as popular day-trip options outside the city center, like Versailles and Disneyland Paris. Those tickets are more expensive. Numerous easy-to-use ticket kiosks have options in English; you can purchase your tickets with both card and cash.

Bus

Paris has an extensive bus system that offers great views of the city while you ride. The maps at each bus station are helpful for both bus riders and those lost trying to find their way in the neighborhood. While the skinny maps are oriented tightly around the bus routes in the bus stop signage, pedestrians can orient themselves while checking out the maps from the numerous lines. If you buy your ticket on board, you aren't allowed any transfers. If that's an issue for you, consider buying a *carnet* of 10 tickets from any metro station and using them in the integrated system, because each ticket gives you 90 minutes worth of travel with as many transfers as you need—much better!

Taxi

Heads-up: Taxis in Paris have a reputation of scamming tourists. They're a great solution if you're splitting a ride home from the club late at night, but they dry up quickly once all the bars let out. Thankfully, **Uber** works in Paris. Before getting a regular cab, be sure to know your route home. Insist on seeing the meter before you pay. Estimate fare for a cross town ride from the Eiffel Tower to the recommended hostels near Gare du Nord, for example, should run about €25. If you feel your driver is ripping you off, walk into your hostel and ask for help.

Bicycle

Paris is home to the world's most extensive public bike system, **Vélib'** (en.velib.paris.fr). To use it, you need a chip and pin debit or credit card to purchase a 24-hour access pass (€1.70). Users have 30 minutes free to return the bike. After that, subsequent hours cost a euro each. The most popular way to get across town for free on longer rides is to simply check in your old bike and pull a new one.

Before checking out a bike, make sure the tires are full of air, the brakes work, and you can move the seat to the right place. A saddle facing backward signals to the maintenance staff that a bike needs service. Now, with a fully functional bike, you're free to cruise the 400 kilometers of bike paths in the city. But remember to play it safe! There are many Vélib' accidents each year, and drivers don't necessarily yield to bike lanes. Helmets are not provided at the rental stations. If you want to bike but want to do it with a knowledgeable guide and without the stress of trying to navigate, consider **Fat Tire Bike Tours** (24 Rue Edgar Faure, fattirebiketours.com/paris).

DAY TRIPS

Thanks to the RER regional rail system, you've got two excellent day trip options just outside of the city, reachable in an hour or two. With an early start (07:30), you should be able to beat the crowds on just about any day.

Versailles

A visit to Versailles is the perfect way to cap your time in Paris. Constructed under the rule of the Sun King, Louis XIV, this unbelievably extravagant palace, along with its seemingly never-ending gardens, symbolizes absolute monarchy. It's tough to wrap your mind around the sheer scale of this palace, so here are some statistics: 67,000 square feet, 67 staircases, 700 royal rooms, and nearly 2,000 acres of gardens. Tour the palace to see the gilded room where the Sun King slept, the floor-to-ceiling mirrors in the grand Hall of Mirrors (meant to show off royal wealth at a time when hardly anyone could afford a pocket mirror), and much more. After the angry hordes had taken Paris during the revolution, they came out the 24 kilometers to Versailles to drag Marie Antoinette and Louis XVI back to town for a date with the guillotine.

The trip from Paris takes 30 minutes to an hour on the RER-C, depending on the train you catch, and costs €8.20. You will arrive at the Versailles RER train station, with the palace and breathtaking gardens just a few steps away.

€18 for palace and gardens, €15 for palace, daily 09:00–17:30, Place d'Armes, +33 (0)1 30 83 78 00, en.chateauversailles.fr

Disneyland Paris

Can you believe the wonderful world of Disney is just a 32-kilometer train ride away from Paris's city center? Head to this amusement park to live it up with Mickey and Minnie—speaking in French accents—and all the rides you would find at home. If Belle and Aladdin are your thing, budget a full day to visit Europe's happiest kingdom, making kids of all nationalities smile since 1992. Tickets are also sold to the Walt Disney Studios, a theme park that focuses on recent movies like *Toy Story*. These rides, coasters, and experiences take you on inter-active behind-the-scenes trips and are geared toward a slightly older audience.

Ticket prices vary, depending on season and day of week. I recommend purchasing tickets ahead of time online (from about €50 for a single-day, single-park ticket, and €80 for combo tickets for both parks). To get here, take RER A4 (€7.60) toward Marne-la-Vallee Chessy from Châtelet-Les Halles. The last train home leaves shortly after midnight. Trains run every 15 minutes and take about an hour.

Ticket prices vary, daily 09:00–20:00, +33 (0)8 25 30 05 00, disneylandparis.com

HELP!

Tourist Information Centers

Paris has a couple of tourist offices in town. They are great places to stop in and pick up a free map. Get information online at en.parisinfo.com, or find Paris's official tourism office (open daily 10:00-19:00) and info desk at:

25 Rue des Pyramides

+33 (0)1 49 52 42 63

Pickpockets & Scams

As with most European cities, violent crime within the city of Paris is extremely low; however, be on the lookout for pickpockets, as they are numerous. Beware if someone approaches you holding an object and asking if you've dropped it, or if a stranger asks you to take a survey or sign a petition.

Also, a large percentage of pickpockets are children under the age of 16, so be on your guard if a group starts to crowd around you. Lastly, keep a close watch on handbags or purses, and never set them down and walk away, even if it's just for a second.

Emergencies

Dial 112 for emergencies, 17 for English-speaking police, and 15 for an ambulance.

Hospital

Hôpital Américain de Paris

63 Bd Victor Hugo

+33 (0)1 46 41 25 25

US Embassy

4 Av Gabriel

+33 (0)1 43 12 22 22

AMSTERDAM

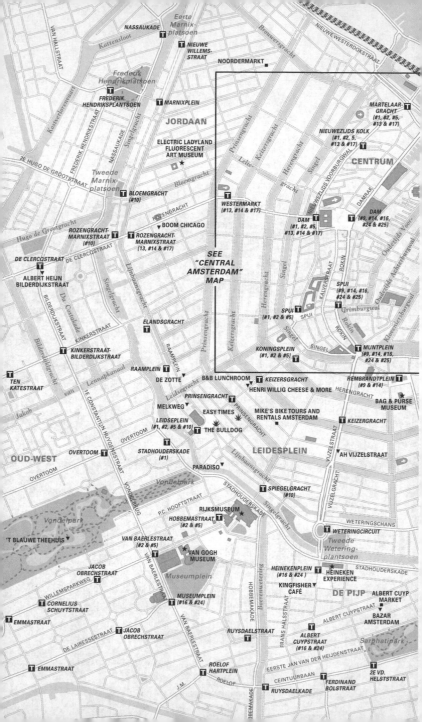

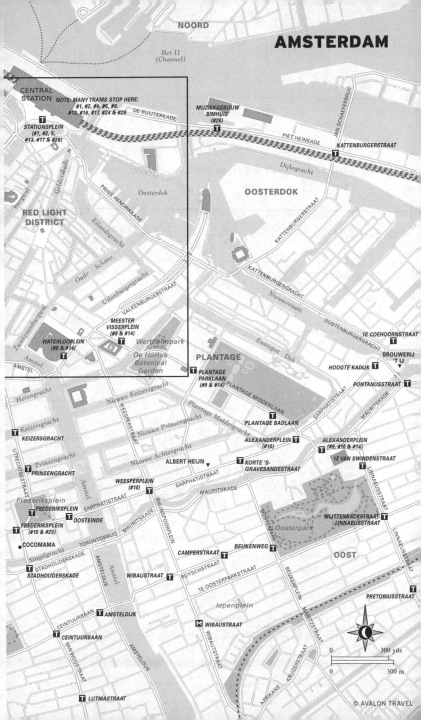

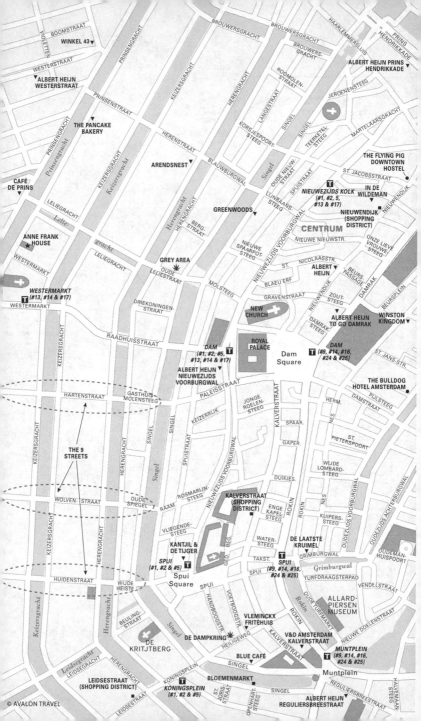

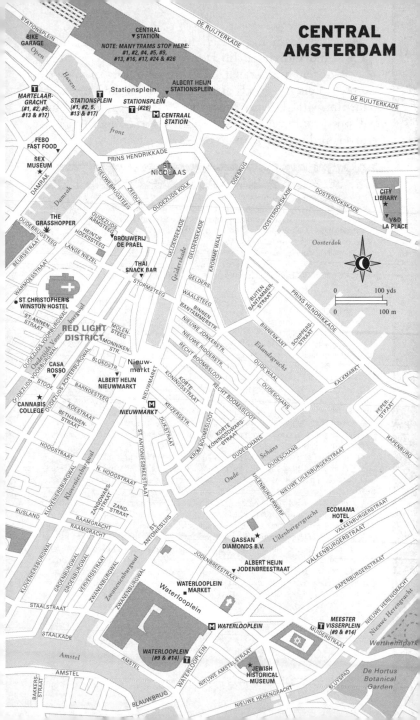

CENTRAL AMSTERDAM

STATIONSPLEIN

DE RUIJTERKADE

BIKE GARAGE
Open

CENTRAL ▼ STATION

NOTE: MANY TRAMS STOP HERE:
#1, #2, #4, #5, #9,
#13, #16, #17, #24 & #26

DE RUIJTERKADE

MARTELAAR-GRACHT
(#1, #2, #5, #13 & #17)

Stationsplein

STATIONSPLEIN
(#1, #2, 5, #13 & #17)

STATIONSPLEIN
(#26)

ALBERT HEIJN STATIONSPLEIN

CENTRAAL STATION

CITY LIBRARY

V&D LA PLACE

Haven

front

FEBO FAST FOOD

SEX MUSEUM ★

PRINS HENDRIKKADE

ST. NICOLAAS

ODEBRUG

OOSTERDOKSKADE

Oosterdok

OOSTERDOKSKADE

DAMRAK

Damrak

THE GRASSHOPPER ★

OUDEBRUGSTEEG

BEURSSTRAAT

WARMOESSTRAAT

NIEUWEBRUGSTEEG

ZEEDIJK

OUDEZIJDS KOLK

OUDEZIJDS ARMSTEEG

HEINTJE HOEKSSTEEG

LANGE NIEZEL

BROUWERIJ DE PRAEL

THAI SNACK BAR

STORMSTEEG

GELDERSEKADE

GELDERSEKADE

KROMME WAAL

PRINS HENDRIKKADE

Oosterdok

0   100 yds
0   100 m

ST CHRISTOPHER'S WINSTON HOSTEL ●

ST. ANNEN STRAAT

OUDEZIJDS VOORBURGWAL

Oudezijds Voor-burgwal

RED LIGHT DISTRICT

MOLEN-STEEG

MONNIKEN-STR.

WAALSTEEG

BINNEN BANTAMMERSTR.

BUITEN BANTAMMER-STRAAT

BINNENKANT

SCHIPPERS-STRAAT

CASA ROSSO ★

OUDEZIJDS VOORBURGWAL

BLOEDSTR.

Nieuw-markt

NIEUWE JONKERSTR.

NIEUWE RIDDERSTR.

RECHT BOOMSSLOOT

Eilandsgracht

OUDE WAAL

KALKMARKT

CANNABIS COLLEGE ★

OUDEZIJDS ACHTERBURGWAL

ALBERT HEIJN NIEUWMARKT ★

BARNDESTEEG

KOESTRAAT

BETHANIEN-STRAAT

NIEUWMARKT

KORTE KONINGSSTRAAT

KEIZERSSTR.

KORTE KONINGSDWARS-STRAAT

KROM BOOMSSLOOT

RECHT BOOM-SSLOOT

OUDESCHANS

OUDESCHANS

PEPER-STRAAT

RAPENBURG

HOOGSTRAAT

KLOVENIERSBURGWAL

N. HOOGSTRAAT

ST. ANTONIESBREESTRAAT

DIJKSTRAAT

OUDESCHANS

Schans

NIEUWE UILENBURGERSTRAAT

ECOMAMA HOTEL

VALKENBURGERSTRAAT

RUSLAND

KLOVENIERSBURGWAL

ZANDDWARS-STRAAT

ZAND-STRAAT

ST. ANTONIESLUIS

Oude

UILENBURGERWERF

Uilenburgergracht

VALKENBURGERSTRAAT

RAAMGRACHT

RAAMGRACHT

GROENBURGWAL

GROENBURGWAL

VERVERSSTRAAT

ZWANENBURGWAL

ZWANENBURGWAL

Zwanenburgwal

GASSAN DIAMONDS B.V. ★

JODENBREESTRAAT

ALBERT HEIJN JODENBREESTRAAT ▼

RAPENBURGERSTRAAT

NIEUWE HERENGRACHT

STAALSTRAAT

Waterlooplein

WATERLOOPLEIN MARKET

Nieuwe Herengracht

STAALKADE

HOOGSTRAAT

Amstel

WATERLOOPLEIN

WATERLOOPLEIN
(#9 & #14)

MEESTER VISSERPLEIN
(#9 & #14)

Wertheimpark

AMSTEL

AMSTEL

BAKKERS-STRAAT

BLAUWBRUG

WATERLOOPLEIN
(#9 & #14)

NIEUWE AMSTELSTRAAT

JEWISH HISTORICAL MUSEUM ★

MUIDERSTRAAT

NIEUWE HERENGRACHT

MUYSPAD

De Hortus Botanical Garden

Amsterdam has a rich history of social inclusion and individual liberty. Spend a few days biking through this canal-laced city, stopping to smell the tulips, sample the goods at the coffeeshops, and tip back a half-pint with the very accepting Dutch. A weekend here will open your eyes to the possibilities of doing things just a little bit differently. So go on—take a taste!

AMSTERDAM 101

The Dutch are a proud lot. It was their ancestors who turned a small, marshy port into the home base for the world's first global corporation. The Dutch East India Company, established in 1602, was the largest company in its time to trade with Asia. It was so successful that private navies were employed to protect its interests halfway around the globe.

The impact of these far-reaching companies made the Dutch language become the first internationally spoken language, and the Dutch guilder was the first internationally traded currency. A small town on the riverbanks of a marshland quickly grew into one of the world's richest cities, sparking a Golden Age of arts, culture, innovation, and a wee bit of gluttony.

Along with its riches, Amsterdam also grew in physical size, but only through the labor-intensive process of driving millions of wooden pilings into the soft marshy surroundings. As you walk through this city, remember that every square inch has been reclaimed from the sea, putting quite a premium on real estate. That's the reason staircases are steep (so as to reduce their footprint) and buildings are built high and essentially stapled together (look for the metal brackets on the older, leaning buildings throughout the city).

In the face of any obstacle, the Dutch have been able to overcome, but not without painful lessons. One such lesson the Dutch learned occurred when speculation over flower bulbs led to the world's first stock market bubble and collapse. "Tulip Mania" saw these plants trading at the price of entire estates, and people were making money hand over fist...until the market realized tulip bulbs just weren't worth that much. Overnight, vast wealth disappeared, shaking the Dutch economy to its core. The small, sea-level country eventually recovered and has now made a triumphant comeback to become the vibrant capital of commerce that it is today.

The Netherlands, as an economic powerhouse, welcomed migrants into its multicultural quilt. This history of integration and tolerance is also reflected in Dutch laws. They've seen few gains in trying to legislate morality. Rather, the business-savvy Dutch have taken a progressive approach in decriminalizing and taxing industries like cannabis and prostitution. Here's the Dutch rule of thumb for determining if an activity should be legal: Does it harm anyone? Is it good for business? Is it discreet?

As long as you answer these correctly, you can safely assume that whatever it is you want to do is legal, or at least decriminalized. This pragmatic approach has done a lot to show how legalization and regulation can undercut gangsters and pimps, and provide needed capital for support and recovery services for those who want out of their respective activities. What better way to experience this fascinating history and rich international culture than in the capital of the Netherlands itself, Amsterdam!

PLAN AHEAD

RESERVATIONS

Reservations are recommended for the following sights:

Anne Frank House (annefrank.org)
Van Gogh Museum (vangoghmuseum.nl)
Rijksmuseum (rijksmuseum.nl)
Heineken Experience (heinekenexperience.com)

LOCAL HAPPENINGS

Keukenhof

Keukenhof (€21, 08:00-19:30, Stationsweg 166A, +31 (0)252 465 555, keukenhof.nl) is the most famous tulip field garden of the Netherlands. It's only open for a few weeks a year during bloom (the last week of March through the second week of May), so it's definitely worth penciling this into your itinerary should you be around at the right time. Make your visit efficient by checking it out on your day of arrival or departure, as the only connection is on bus 58 through Schiphol Airport.

King's Day

April 27 is Amsterdam's biggest celebration of the year, commemorating the king's birthday. The Dutch simply use it as an excuse to 1) sell their junk (the entire city turns into a yard sale) and 2) party hardy with free world-class events and music going on in numerous locations across the entire city. Make your hostel reservations long in advance, and be prepared to pony up a bit more than usual!

Gay Pride Fest

Every first Saturday in August, the historic world capital of tolerance and acceptance turns into one massive party. Club parties, canal parades, and street festivities draw hundreds of thousands and make this one of the most popular weekends of the year to be in Amsterdam.

KNOW BEFORE YOU GO

KEY STATS & FIGURES

Currency:
The Netherlands uses the euro (€); 1 EUR = about 1.06 USD

Population:
820,000

Nationalities Represented:
177

Language:
Dutch

Bicycles:
880,000

Bike paths within the city:
250 miles

Bikes dredged from canals annually:
10,000

Canals:
165

Bridges:
1,281

Houseboats:
2,500

CALIBRATE YOUR BUDGET

TYPICAL PRICES FOR:

Hostel dorm bed:
€30

Two-course dinner and drink:
€15

Pint of beer:
€6

Day bike rental:
€7

Single tram pass:
€2.90

MOVIES TO WATCH
Ocean's Twelve, The Diary of Anne Frank, The Fault in Our Stars
VIDEOS TO WATCH
Holland: The Original Cool

THREE DAY ITINERARY

Amsterdam's touristy center is walkable, but consider renting a bike to get around in a jiffy. Make reservations for the Anne Frank House on the second day ahead of time.

DAY 1: WELCOME TO AMSTERDAM
MORNING

Head to the south end of the heart of Amsterdam for a delicious breakfast at **De Laatste Kruimel.** Come hungry for their delicious pastries and thirsty for some fresh caffeine. Consider picking up a sandwich to go to munch on during your bike tour later. This bustling breakfast joint is just down the way from the University of Amsterdam campus, and a few steps from the floating **Bloemenmarkt** flower market and the **Dampkring** coffeeshop (where the "lost in translation" scene in *Ocean's Twelve* was filmed).

AFTERNOON

Take the better part of the afternoon to get oriented on a bike tour. Rides with **Mike's Bike Tours** kick off daily at 12:00 at Kerkstraat 134 (3 hours), about a 10-minute walk south of De Laatste Kruimel. You'll cover a great deal of ground on the bikes, with plenty of time to enjoy a pit stop at the windmill brewery, **Brouwerij 't Ij.** (Not into bikes? Meet a **Sandeman's New Europe Walking Tours** guide at 11:15 at the National Monument, Dam Square for a three-hour tour.)

After wrapping up back at the shop, consider keeping your bike for your stay at a discounted rate. Walk or hop on tram 2 or 5 south to Museumplein for either the **Van Gogh Museum** or the newly renovated **Rijksmuseum**.

EVENING

Take tram 2 or 5 back north to rest up and relax for a bit at your hostel. When you're ready, hop a tram back to Central Amsterdam, exiting at Dam station, to grab a tasty Thai dinner at **Thai Snack Bar**. Then wander the **Red Light District**, where you'll be navigating some high-density raunch. You're likely to run into plenty of window-shopping creeps among the touristy bars and coffeeshops in the RDL, and you'll have no trouble satisfying the munchies with the plentiful food options around.

LATE

If you're looking to experience Amsterdam's rollicking nightlife scene, drop south to the **Rembrandtplein** entertainment district, where you're sure to find a loud, crowded, sweaty party—Dutch style.

DAY 2: ANNE FRANK HOUSE & JORDAAN
MORNING

Snag breakfast at your hostel, or enjoy some classy English fare at **Greenwoods** before you head to the **Anne Frank House,** a 10-minute walk away. Arrive early to avoid the crowds. Reservations made ahead of time are highly recommended!

AFTERNOON

Grab lunch just down the street at the **Pancake Bakery** (worth calling ahead for a reservation). Save some room for Amsterdam's best apple pie at **Winkel 43** in the **Noordermarkt** just across the canal (you can thank me later). If it's Saturday or a Monday, spend a while exploring the bustling farmers market, taking every sample that's offered to you. Take this opportunity to wander deeper into the **Jordaan** district as well.

Walk about 30 minutes or use tram 14 (exit Waterlooplein) to loop across town to **Gassan Diamonds** for a free diamond-cutting demonstration and factory tour. On the way, stop at the **Cannabis College** after for an education in all things green.

EVENING
Recharge at your hostel for a bit. Then head to dinner at **Kantjil & de Tijger** for an Indonesian meal that's easy on the wallet.

LATE
Head down Leidsestraat to Leidseplein, and catch a comedy show at **Boom Chicago**. Dive into any number of watering holes, or dress to impress to get past the bouncers at clubs **Paradiso** or **Melkweg**. To party like a rock star, catch the **Amsterdam's Ultimate Party pub crawl** kicking off each night with a power hour at 20:30 at Candela Bar.

DAY 3: MUSEUMPLEIN & MORE
MORNING
Starting in Dam Square, stroll down **Kalverstraat,** then **Leidsestraat.** Farther down Leidsestraat, take a lunch to go from the best sandwich spot in the city, **B&B Lunchroom,** and sample local cheeses at **Henri Willig Cheese & More**.

Continue onto **Vondelpark,** a beautiful city park laced with gardens, running paths, and bike trails. Enjoy a snack at **'t Blauwe Theehuis** in the middle of the park or snag a park bench and watch Amsterdam ride by while you munch your sandwich.

AFTERNOON
Exit the park through the south side toward Museumplein and pop into either the **Rijksmuseum** or the **Van Gogh Museum**—whichever you didn't visit on day one. Don't forget your photo op at the I Amsterdam sign on the square! (Insider secret: The front of the sign is always crowded with tourists. Snap your shot from the back, and flip it around in Photoshop afterward to have the sign all to yourself.)

After you get your fill of museums, walk about 15 minutes over to Europe's largest daily market, **Albert Cuyp Market.** Cute *bruin cafés* (brown cafés) line the street, perfect for a coffee or tea. If you're hungry, nearby **Bazar** has delicious ethnic dishes. Drop down to relax in **Sarphatipark,** a block south of Albert Cuyp Market.

You've got a choice: Head to the **Heineken Experience** for a sensational brewery tour, then stick around the **De Pijp** neighborhood, popular among locals for food and nightlife. Or, hop on tram 5 to return to the center. Head to the **City Library** near the train station for a panoramic view of the city at sunset. The **V&D La Place** café on the seventh floor makes for a great early dinner option.

EVENING
Take an hour-long evening canal cruise; they leave hourly from the **Lover's Canal Cruises** stand just across from the train station, opposite the Play In casino. Bring a discreet six-pack to sip on while taking in the city from the canals.

LATE
Take it easy on **Nieuwmarkt,** enjoying some half-pints with the locals at the cafés opening up onto the square.

Amsterdam fans out south of the River Ij. At its heart, historic **Central Amsterdam** is home to the famous Red Light District and the Bloemenmarkt, as well as restaurants, coffeeshops, nightlife venues, and hostels.

West of Central Amsterdam and Singel canal, **West Amsterdam** contains the Anne Frank House, the Nine Streets shopping district, and the beautiful, residential Jordaan neighborhood. Jordaan is unique in Amsterdam in that canals don't cut through the streets, and it's fun to explore, with cafés and cute little shops.

The ring of canals south of Central Amsterdam is home to the **Leidseplein** entertainment district, including recommended restaurants and coffeeshops.

Southeast Amsterdam has a couple of noteworthy attractions (Gassan Diamonds, the Jewish Historical Museum), along with the Rembrandtplein nightlife district. The southwestern corner of the city is Amsterdam's **Museum District,** home to the Rijksmuseum and Van Gogh Museum (which cluster around the square called Museumplein) and Vondelpark, Amsterdam's city park. East of the Museum District is the trendy nightlife neighborhood of **De Pijp** and the Heineken Experience.

TOP SIGHTS

There are dozens of fascinating museums in this city to keep you busy for weeks, but on a short three-day visit, these are the ones worth seeing.

Anne Frank House

The city's most famous historical landmark, this is where Anne Frank and her family hid for more than two years during the Nazi occupation of Amsterdam. It's from this house that she wrote in her diary about the secret annex, growing up, and her personal thoughts. Her diary is now one of the world's most translated books, second only to the Bible. Otto Frank, Anne's father, survived the war, and insisted on keeping the apartment as it was, opting for empty rooms rather than filling them with replica furniture. Today, visitors can walk through the apartment, even passing through the hidden bookcase through which the family entered the secret annex. You'll see photos of the family, their concentration camp registration cards, and the diaries themselves.

€9, Apr-Jun and Sept-Oct daily 09:00-21:00, Sat until

ACT LIKE A LOCAL

Gezellig-What?

The Dutch have an expression, one word that is used for just about everything that makes you feel all warm and fuzzy on the inside: *gezellig* (pronounced GHE-zell-igh, with guttural-sounding Gs). For Americans, bigger and newer is just about always better in my opinion. For the Dutch, *gezellig* is the goal, and it's used to describe just about anything that is warm, inviting, and cozy. Tucked in front of the fire at Christmas is *gezellig*. A good brown pub in Amsterdam is just about always *gezellig*. Use your newfound cultural lingo to strike up a conversation. Where's your favorite *gezellig* place?

Make it a Half-Pint

Prices for a half-pint here in Amsterdam are usually exactly half the price of a pint. So locals prefer to drink a half-pint at a time for a couple reasons: First, their drink stays cooler. Second, Dutch drinking culture tends to be more social—the Dutch often do-si-do between drinks and cigarettes.

22:00; July–Aug daily 09:00–22:00; Nov–Mar daily 09:00–19:00, Sat until 21:00; Prinsengracht 267, West Amsterdam, +31 (0)20 556 7105, annefrank.org, Tram: Westermarkt

Rijksmuseum

Art from the last 800 years of Amsterdam and the Netherlands takes you from the city's humble beginnings through master-pieces of the Dutch Golden Age. The museum features artists such as Rembrandt, Goya, Van Gogh, Cuyp, and Vermeer. The museum is presented across three levels. You'll notice the exterior looks remarkably similar to that of the Centraal Station. The same architect, Pierre Cuypers, designed both buildings.

€17.50, daily 09:00–17:00, last entry 30 minutes before closing, Museumstraat 1, Museum District, +31 (0)900 0745, rijksmuseum.nl, Tram: Rijksmuseum

Van Gogh Museum

Containing all the masterpieces of the most famous and crazed Dutch artist, this museum is wonderfully compact, spreading out over just three floors. Exhibits include Van Gogh's pieces along with those that inspired him and those whom he inspired. Some highlights include: *The Potato Eaters, Sunflowers, The Bedroom,* and *Wheatfield with Crows,* the last painting Van Gogh ever did, which some say was a portrayal of his inner sadness and imminent death.

€17, daily 10:00–17:00, Fri until 22:00, Paulus Potterstraat 7, Museum District, +31 (0)20 570 5200, vangoghmuseum.nl/en, Tram: Rijksmuseum or Van Baerlestraat

Red Light District

Centering around the Old Church (Oude Kerk), this is where Amsterdam grew up from a small fishing village into a world power. The old docks used to line the north side of these streets. So this is where the ladies of the night used to catch sailors on their last night in town or to help lighten their freshly lined pockets upon return. To-day, you'll see the sex trade in action as you stroll by nearly nude prostitutes advertising for themselves behind glass windows. You'll also see touristy cafes and restaurants, coffeeshops, and souvenir stores. In recent years, the city council has made a point to reduce the number of prostitute windows in this district, replacing them with art installations and boutiques. There's a lot to keep you busy, but unfortunately, many tourists don't venture beyond this district to experience the more authentic parts of Amsterdam.

Free, always open, Central Amsterdam, Tram: Dam

Cannabis College

This college in the Red Light District shows you the truth about cannabis and all its potential uses. Pop in for an education in all things green, including information about the plant's medical uses. Ask them where they'd recommend picking up some kush, and they'll bust out a map with their favorite nearby shops. No marijuana is sold here. Pay a few euros to see the college's flower-

ing cannabis garden, a handful of plants in various stages of growth from "babies" to flowering beauties.

Free, donations welcome, daily 11:00-19:00, Oudezijds Achterburgwal 124, Central Amsterdam, +31 (0)20 423 4420, cannabiscollege.com, Metro: Nieuwmarkt

Heineken Experience

This is a top priority for many who come to Amsterdam. Their sensational tour features a virtual reality "bottling experience," two half-pints, and long lines if you don't make reservations ahead of time. For a less mass-produced feel, consider visiting the Brouwerij 't IJ instead.

€18, €16 online; Mon-Thurs 10:30-19:30, last entry at 17:00; Fri-Sun 10:30-21:00, last entry at 19:00; longer hours Jul-Aug; Stadhouderskade 78, De Pijp and Vicinity, +31 (0)20 523 9222, heinekenexperience.com, Tram: Stadhouderskade

Gassan Diamonds

Ever been in the presence of a two-carat diamond? Learn about the craft of diamond cutting from the best with an introductory tour in English through the factory, where you'll see craftspeople going about their business and get an education in the "five C's": cut, color, clarity, carat, and certification. With a free entry and tour, Gassan is a hidden gem, if you know what I mean.

Free guided tour leaves often, daily 09:00-17:00, Nieuwe Uilenburgerstraat 175, Southeast Amsterdam, +31 (0)20 622 5333, gassandiamonds.nl, Tram: Mr. Visserplein

City Library

The last 150 years has seen a complete transformation of Amsterdam's harbor, starting with the construction of Amsterdam Centraal Station, which was completed in 1889. One of the most recent additions to the docklands has been Amsterdam's City Library, a beautiful 10-story modern steel-and-glass structure just northeast of Central

Amsterdam. The top floor offers a magnificent view over the center of Amsterdam. Stop in for lunch and enjoy a wonderfully colorful and affordable spread from a branch of **V&D La Place,** a trendy Dutch self-service cafeteria brand.

Free, daily 10:00-22:00, Oosterdokskade 143, Central Amsterdam, +31 (0)20 523 0900, oba.nl, Tram: Centraal

EXTRA CREDIT

If you've got the time or the desire, check out these options for more ideas beyond the essentials.

Jewish Historical Museum

This in-depth museum takes you through the history and synagogues of this resilient community.

€6, daily 13:00-17:00, Nieuwe Amstelstraat 1, Southeast Amsterdam, jhm.nl, Tram: Mr. Visserplein

Bag & Purse Museum

Come visit this museum, located east of Leidseplein, to enjoy a collection of more than 4,000 different bags, trunks, pouches, and purses, dating all the way back from the Middle Ages to today.

€5, daily 10:00-17:00, Herengracht 573, tassenmuseum.nl, Leidseplein and Vicinity, Tram: Rembrandtplein

Sex Museum

Classic sex museum featuring erotic art and artifacts from the dawn of time through to today. Kinky, eh?

€5, daily 09:30-23:30, Damrak 18, Central Amsterdam, +31 (0)20 622 8376, sexmuseumamsterdam.nl, Tram: Centraal

Electric Ladyland

Made famous through Jimi Hendrix's third album, this experimental museum offers a psychedelic experience, as it's filled with trippy, fluorescent mini-displays and artwork.

€5, Tues-Sat 13:00-18:00, Tweede Leliedwarsstraat 5, West Amsterdam, electric-lady-land.com, Tram: Bloemgracht

TOP EATS

Delicious food may or may not be the first thing on your mind when thinking of Amsterdam, but you might be surprised by the options. True Dutch cuisine is typical of other northern European countries: meat and potatoes. Their most famous dish is an extremely filling one, called **stamppot**: potatoes mashed together with your choice of veggies and a thick bratwurst-style sausage. **Bitterballen** are also a mainstay. Think flash-fried balls of mushy...well, I don't really know. Take it easy on the first bite, though, as they're always steamy on the inside! **Herring** is also a popular lunch dish in this sea-faring culture. Locals stop at any of the dozens of herring stands across the city for a quick lunch of raw herring and veggies.

The **Red Light District** is filled with places to grab a quick bite on the cheap (and satisfy the munchies). Trendy, fresh upscale restaurants can be found around nearly every corner throughout the rest of town. Tipping is not expected, but most locals round up a euro or two. These are some of my favorite budget options.

De Laatste Kruimel

Find this gem just on the south side of the Red Light District, a stone's throw from the University of Amsterdam. Come in for fresh scones, savory and sweet pies, delicious pastries, and hearty sandwiches to get your day off on the right foot. The name means "The Last Crumb" in Dutch, and you'll know why when you're searching your pastry paper for every last morsel.

Pastries and coffee from €3, daily 08:00-20:00, Sun from 10:00, Langebrugsteeg 4, Central Amsterdam, +31 (0)20 423 0499, delaatstekruimel.nl, Tram: Spui Rokin

Greenwoods

Need something more than a continental breakfast? Come here for a classy English breakfast complete with tea or coffee. In nice weather, enjoy your eggs and toast at the outdoor seating right next to the canal. In addition to the one on Singel, find another branch at Keizergracht 465.

Breakfasts from €6 and lunches from €8, daily 09:30-18:00, till 19:00 on weekends, Singel 103, Central Amsterdam, +31 (0)20 623 7071, greenwoods.eu, Tram: Nieuwezijds Kolk

Blue Café

In a glass box on the top floor of the Kalvortoren shopping center, this café offers up close views of Central Amsterdam. Though I love cafés with a view, I come here mostly for the coffee, as the food tends to be a bit overpriced.

Sandwiches from €7.50, Tues-Sat 10:00-18:30, Mon 11:00-18:30, Sun 12:00-18:30, Singel 457, Central Amsterdam, +31 (0)20 427 3901, blue-amsterdam.nl, Tram: Spui (Rokin)

V&D La Place

This is one of those delicious self-service cafeterias where the employees are well-paid and happy, the food is local and delicious, the ingredients are fresh and healthy, and the building is LEED-certified. Did I mention the free Wi-Fi? What else can you ask for? Pop into one of the several locations in town for an affordable, casual lunch at communal tables. All feature a wide range of culinary choices: fresh cooked fish and meats, curries and stir fry, personal pizzas, salads, fresh-pressed juices, and more. In addition to this branch, located on the seventh floor of the City Library just northeast of Central Amsterdam, find another city center location at Kalverstraat 203 in Central Amsterdam.

€10-15 lunches, daily 09:00-20:00, from 11:00 weekend mornings, City Library, Oosterdokskade 143, Central Amsterdam, laplace.com, Tram: Centraal

Thai Snack Bar

Find some of the best Thai food you'll ever taste just steps from the Red Light District in Amsterdam's China Town. This cheap eat-

ery is almost always packed with in-the-know locals stopping by for a quick bite or takeout dinner. If the snack bar is full, consider the sister restaurant across the street with the same great menu. I love the friendly (if curt) service, warm atmosphere, fresh pad thai, and the spicy curries.

Entrées €10, 14:00-21:00, Zeedijk 77, Central Amsterdam, +31 (0)20 420 6289, thai-bird.nl, Metro: Nieuwmarkt

Kantjil & de Tijger

This is Indonesian at its finest. Kantjil has the feel of an Asian fusion restaurant but cranks out Indonesia's most typical delicious dish, *rijsttafel*. Think of it as a culinary experience that comes with a smorgasbord of small bowls of richly spiced rice, meats, and veggies. The poor man's *rijsttafel* is *nasi rames*, which includes many of the same great-tasting samplers as its bigger brother. This sit-down restaurant has a cheap, delicious twin takeaway joint next door. At the takeaway shop, pick your size, noodles, and meat to take advantage of one of the best dinner values in town.

Entrées from €15, takeaway €5-7, daily 12:00-23:00, Nieuwezijds Voorburgwal 342, Central Amsterdam, +31 (0)20 620 0994, kantjil.nl/en, Tram: Spui

Winkel 43

You haven't tried apple pie until you've indulged in this homemade, deep-dish, steaming slice of heaven. Share a piece with a friend because the portions here are generous. (Who am I kidding? Keep it all for yourself!) Winkel also has a decent menu with sandwiches, salads, and appetizers if you don't ruin your appetite on pie, though I always do.

Worlds of steaming crusty pleasure for around €6, daily 08:00-01:00, Noordermarkt 43, West Amsterdam, +31 (0)20 623 0223, winkel43.com, Tram: Marnixplein

Pancake Bakery

Hands down some of the best pancakes you'll ever have. Choose from a traditional variety or take a walk on the wild side and try one of the bakery's international versions, ranging from Hungarian to Thai to Mexican. Those with a sweet tooth should indulge in the *poffertjes*, mini pancakes layered in ice cream, chocolate, and powdered sugar. The staff can seem a bit peeved at all the customers that flock here, so don't expect smiling service.

Pancake plates €12-16, daily 09:00-21:30, Prinsengracht 191, West Amsterdam, +31 (0)20 625 1333, pancake.nl, Tram: Westermarkt

B&B Lunchroom

Stop here along your shopping route for some of the best made-to-order sandwiches you'll ever have, especially considering the price. The options are endless and the staff couldn't be friendlier. Snag a delicious, freshly baked muffin to go for a snack later. In addition to this branch, you'll find other locations around town.

Sandwiches €5, daily 08:00-18:00, Leidsestraat 44, Leidseplein and Vicinity, +31 (0)20 642 1816, onzecatering. nl, Tram: Prinsengracht

Vleminckx Friteshuis

They do one thing, and they do it well! This place is famous for its *frites* (French fries). Crowds flock here for a delicious snack in a cone. The line often wraps out down the street, but it moves quickly, and the fries are well worth the wait.

€3, daily 12:00-19:00, Voetboogstraat 33, Central Amsterdam, +31 (0)20 624 6075, vleminckxdesausmeester. nl, Tram: Spui

Febo Fast Food

Ever bought a burger or fries out of a vending machine? Well here's your chance! Not recommended for the quality of the food, but more so for the prices and the experience. Step into a small shop with floor-to-ceiling cubbies—like the P.O. Box room at your local post office, except that every little door is transparent. Simply drop in a euro or

two, turn the knob, and reach in to grab your snack. Burgermeisters are busy on the inside constantly restocking the popular selections. Febo seems to hit the spot for many a late-night reveler. In addition to this branch, you'll find numerous locations around town.

€3, daily 10:30–02:00, till 04:00 on weekends, Damrak 6, Central Amsterdam, +31 (0)20 638 5318, www.febo.nl, Tram: Centraal

Albert Heijn Grocery Stores
Albert Heijn is to Amsterdam as Starbucks is to Seattle: You've got one on just about every corner. Those on a budget can dive into the aisles of this grocery store for a cheap lunch of anything from pre-made curries to sushi and sandwiches. Don't forget to pick up some of my favorite sweet treats: the *stroopwafel* (syrup-filled waffle). You'll find numerous locations throughout the city, including one inside the train station.

Daily 08:00–22:00, Nieuwezijds Voorburgwal 226, ah.nl, +31 20 421 8344, Tram: Dam

Henri Willig Cheese & More
Thanks to numerous locations across town, you can't spend a few days in Amsterdam without stumbling into at least one Henri Willig cheese shop. Sample typical cheeses like Gouda, goat, sheep's, smoked, and even spicy cheeses, all made in the Netherlands. While it may feel a bit mass-produced and commercialized, a round of cheese makes for a great souvenir...if you can get it home without eating it beforehand, that is.

Pound cheese rounds from €10, daily 09:00–19:00, Leidsestraat 52, Leidseplein and Vicinity, +31 (0)20 620 9030, henriwillig.com, Tram: Kaizergracht

't Blauwe Theehuis
A welcome respite from the bustling city center, this teahouse with a load of outdoor seating is right in the middle of Vondelpark. Considering the idyllic location, prices aren't bad. Pop in for a recharge that won't hurt the wallet.

Simple sandwiches from €5.50, daily 09:00–18:00, Vondelpark 5, Museum District, +31 (0)20 662 0254, blauwetheehuis.nl, Tram: Van Baerlestraat

Bazar
This Amsterdam institution is located right in the Albert Cuyp Market. As soon as you step into the Bazar, you forget you're in Amsterdam and feel like you've traveled to another continent. Come out for fresh kebabs, falafel, sandwiches, and other cuisine from the Middle East. The friendly service is happy to explain dishes that are foreign to you.

Breakfasts and lunches from €6, dinners from €12, Mon-Fri 11:00–24:00, Sat-Sun 09:00–24:00, Albert Cuypstraat 182, De Pijp and Vicinity, +31 (0)20 675 0544, bazaramsterdam.com, Tram: Albert Cuypstraat

TOP COFFEESHOPS

The first question I get from Amsterdam-tourists-to-be: "Where are the best coffeeshops?" First off, if you're looking for coffee, you'll want to head to a café. As all Amsterdammers know, a coffeeshop is a place to buy and smoke the city's famous high-grade marijuana. There really isn't one "best" option in town. I look for friendly staff, fair prices, and a welcoming atmosphere. If the coffeeshop checks those boxes, I'll order a mint tea and make myself at home.

Dampkring
Made famous by the movie *Ocean's Twelve*, Dampkring is a cozy one-roomed rose-colored coffeeshop with a cat named Bowie in permanent residence. The menu is on the pricey side but features an array of award-winning strains. The edibles are also excellent, but quite strong! Order your greens in the back, and drinks at the bar to the left.

Grams from €10, daily 10:00–01:00, Handboogstraat 29, Central Amsterdam, +31 (0)20 638 0705, dampkring-coffeeshop-amsterdam.nl, Tram: Spui

Easy Times
Popular among tourists and locals alike for their space cakes, clean and trendy atmosphere, and friendly service, Easy Times is my pick for the Leidseplein district. Go easy on the cakes, though. They're notoriously strong. On nice days, the canal-side outdoor seating cannot be beat. The interior feels a bit more like a mod hookah lounge than dark coffeeshop.

Grams from €8, daily 09:00–01:00, Prinsengracht 476, Leidseplein and Vicinity, +31 (0)20 626 5709, easytimes-amsterdam.com, Tram: Prisengracht

Grey Area
Grey Area, just west of Central Amsterdam, is a classic in Amsterdam's coffeeshop roster. Pop into this tiny café to stock up, and snag one of the six seats they have in house to roll up

COFFEESHOPS & SMOKING ETIQUETTE

Amsterdam operates by a discreet code: You buy coffee in cafés, marijuana in coffeeshops, and psychedelic mushrooms in "smart shops." Nothing is legal but rather it's "decriminalized." This is why you'll see no advertisements or signs. Coffeeshops can't even have their own website. But they're not hard to find: Just look for a numbered green and white license in the front window of each shop.

Pop into a few shops on your first day to get a sense for the options out there. You're not obligated to buy anything, but it is frowned upon to consume things that weren't purchased there.

The drink bar and marijuana bar are usually separate. Find the menu at the weed bar, and talk to the staff to get exactly what you're looking for. Take your time and don't be afraid to ask questions—if they're rude, walk out and find the next shop. Coffeeshops on the tourist track from the train station to the Red Light District (and inside the canal rings) with Bob Marley and fluorescent lights in the windows cater to tourists and are likely overpriced.

You can no longer smoke tobacco indoors. Hard drugs like heroin and cocaine are strictly illegal, and possession carries stiff penalties. And remember; green-thumbed scientists have been breeding marijuana for years to make it stronger and stronger. It's quite intense, so don't overdo it. Don't mix marijuana with alcohol, as unpleasant side affects like sweating and nausea can arise. Drink something sweet like juice or soda if you're not feeling well. It's good to stick with your friends and have the hostel address handy if you need to make a quick exit.

By the way, per capita, the Dutch smoke less than half as much as compared to Americans. Interesting, eh? Here are some tips to get you started on your coffeeshop experience.

First, some terminology:

- Marijuana = weed.
- Hashish = a small brown brick you rub off into tobacco cigarettes.
- Joint = weed only in a paper wrap.
- Spliff = weed and tobacco (what the Dutch would normally smoke— if they smoked).
- Sativa is the "high" strain (think: high, happy, giggly).
- Indica is the "stoned" strain (think: chill, relaxed, sleepy, heavy).

Here are some other things that are good to know:

- Don't pay more than €11/gram. Any more and you're in a touristy zone!
- A good coffeeshop has helpful staff, a welcoming vibe, nice ambience, and comfy seating.
- After purchasing a gram ask for a few papers for free. Purchase 5 grams and you should get a sleeve of papers included.

- Avoid pre-rolled joints. It's much better to purchase a gram or two of loose weed and buddy up with someone in the shop to help you out. People are usually happy to help, and it's a great way to strike up a conversation with new friends.
- You'll usually get a 10-15 percent discount on purchases of 5 grams (which should be plenty for a few friends over a weekend).
- Take it easy on edibles. Don't drink or smoke more after having eaten them, and wait at least 1.5 hours before taking anything else or anything more. Make sure to ask how many doses are in the edible you're purchasing—some have one, some are good to split across four friends. They usually run €5-15.
- Actually looking for just a coffee? Go to a café!

and meet fellow tokers. The staff is particularly welcoming, and happy to take beginners under their wing to explain the menu.

Grams from €9, daily 12:00-20:00, Oude Leliestraat 2, West Amsterdam, +31 (0)20 4204301, greyarea.nl, Tram: Dam

The Bulldog
I list this place not so much to recommend it, but as a place to pop into to calibrate the kind of scene you're looking for. Here you'll find loud music, a grungy vibe, and touristy prices. It's never far away, thanks to numerous locations in the RLD and Leidseplein.

Grams from €10, daily 09:00-01:00, till 03:00 on weekends, Leidseplein 15, Leidseplein and Vicinity, +31 (0)20 625 9864, thebulldog.com, Tram: Leidseplein

The Grasshopper
While touristy, it's worth popping into this multi-service establishment, where you'll find a steak house upstairs, a bar on the ground floor, and a coffeeshop downstairs. The views of the Centraal Station from the canal-side seating are hard to beat while enjoying a beer and a fresh roll.

Grams from €8, daily 10:00-01:00, Oudebrugsteeg 16, Central Amsterdam, +31 (0)20 626 1259, thegrasshopper. nl, Tram: Dam

TOP NIGHTLIFE

The drinking culture among the Dutch is a very social one and is done over a few beers in the square. Don't be afraid to strike up a conversation with them. Their English is probably better than yours!

Bruin cafés ("brown pubs" or "brown cafés") are a mainstay of Dutch and Amsterdam culture. Affectionately so-called because of their dark wood and tobacco-stained interior, these picturesque spots are perfect for an afternoon tea or snack. Each individual café is rather unremarkable, but they do offer a nice place for a break any time of day: coffee in the mornings, light lunches and snacks throughout the day, and half pints towards the evening. **Café van Zuylen** (snacks and coffee from €5, Torensteeg 8, +31 20 639 1055, cafevanzuylen.nl) inside of Singel canal is one supremely typical *bruin café* with canal-side seating in the summer.

NIGHTLIFE DISTRICTS
Amsterdam's nightlife can be broken down by neighborhood. Each district has its own personality. Match your preferences to my descriptions and get ready for a wild ride!

Red Light District
The Red Light District boasts a rainbow of venues, bars, clubs, street food, peep shows, and more. And it's the most dense, most touristy, and most overpriced part of town. While the RLD is worth an evening out, many tourists unfortunately never get beyond this area in the day or night. Notice the window-shopping tourists change as the day turns to night. At night come obnoxious stag parties and creepers doing more than just window-shopping. Sprinkled with numerous police departments, the neighborhood is actually the safest in town, but keep a close hold on your valuables in the busy and crowded streets. Spend an evening wandering through the canals, bridges, and seductive windows. One redeeming venue in this district is the recommended brewery **Brouwerij de Prael.**

Central Amsterdam, Tram: Dam

Nieuwmarkt
What was once a major gatehouse to enter the city and where Amsterdam's gallows were located is now a popular square lined with bars just on the edge of the Red Light District. You'll find a more subdued, sophisticated vibe with locals sipping half-pints on the east side of the square.

Central Amsterdam, Tram: Dam

Leidseplein
The best entertainment district in Amsterdam is named after a town 20 miles down the road: Leiden. Farmers would bring their milk, produce it, sell it, and then blow all their money before going home. To this day, this area is known for its music venues, concert halls, comedy shows, and restaurants. It's where tourists and locals go out to club. Prices unfortunately reflect its popularity, and you'll often have to pay to use the bathrooms, even in bars where you're drinking. So don't break that seal! Beyond numerous dance bar options on the square, **Melkweg** and **Paradiso** are music venue institutions that have headliners like Lady Gaga and Beyonce pass through often.

Leidseplein and Vicinity, Tram: Leidseplein

LGBT AMSTERDAM

As one of the most inclusive and progressive cities in the world, Amsterdam has long been known to the members of the LGBT community as an excellent place to visit, live, and work. Gay Pride dominates the city each year during the last week of July leading into August. There is no need to specifically seek out gay friendly restaurants and bars in this town, as most options are open to all—and there are many venues with rainbow flags in the windows. You'll find the gay, BDSM and Bear-focused street on Warmoestraat just around the corner from Dam Square to the east. For more information, find the **Pink Point LGBT** information stand on Westermarkt, in the shadow of Westerchurch and just steps from the Anne Frank House, and the **Homomonument** (daily 10:30-18:00, Westermarkt, +31 20 48 1070, facebook.com/PinkPointAmsterdam).

De Pijp

On the south side of town behind the Heineken brewery, you'll find Amsterdam's best-kept secret, where the locals hang out before heading to Leidseplein for the clubs. This is Amsterdam's trendiest and most up-and-coming district. Most of the action centers around a square, **Marien Heinekenplein,** which is lined with a half dozen social bars.

De Pijp and Vicinity, Tram: Stadhouderskade

Rembrandtplein

This square, east of Leidseplein, and the surrounding streets tend to be packed with blue-collar Dutch types and tourists in the know. While a bit pricey, the parties get rowdy here on a nightly basis. You'll find cafés and brown pubs, restaurants, bars, and even Starbucks' flagship location in all of Europe right here on this lively square named after one of the most famous paint-ers to emerge from the Dutch Golden Age. A rock star in life, I think Rembrandt would be happy with the scene that takes over his square on a nightly basis.

Southeast Amsterdam, Tram: Rembrandtplein

BREWERIES

Heineken isn't the only brewery with an Amsterdam connection. Try out these spots as well:

Brouwerij 't IJ

The city has given tax breaks to any com-pany willing to conduct their business in windmills in order to protect the heritage and keep these monuments to Dutch histo-ry alive and well. Thankfully, a local brewery took the city up on the offer, and now you can go in and taste a range of house brews and enjoy a fascinating, quite affordable tour of the hoppy facilities. Brouwerij 't IJ is east of Amsterdam's city center.

Pints from €4.50, pub open daily 14:00-20:00, €4.50 tours Fri-Sun at 15:30 and 16:00 (reservations recommended), Funenkade 7, Greater Amsterdam, +31 (0)20 622 8325, brouwerijhetij.nl, Tram: Hoogte Kadijk

Brouwerij de Prael

Real estate is so hard to come by in Am-sterdam that breweries like this are rare in the center, but this is a wonderful exception to the rule. Step into the Prael brewery and you'll feel at home in the cozy tasting room lined with mugs owned by regulars who frequent this place. Head to the back to see the magic in the making with big fermenta-tion vats, and avail yourself of any one of their 10 house-made brews. Free brewery tours leave on the hour in the afternoons Tuesday-Sunday.

Pints from €5, daily 12:00-01:00, Oudezijds Voorburgwal 30, Central Amsterdam, +31 (0)20 408 4470, deprael.nl, Tram: Centraal

BARS

Unfortunately, many Dutch brews are often overshadowed by another agricultural pro-duction—weed. If artisan beer and unique pubs pique your fancy, follow my **ale trail** (from **In de Wildeman** to **Arendsnest, Café de Prins,** and finally **De Zotte**) for a low-key night of sipping Dutch brews.

In de Wildeman

Famous for its wide selection of beers both in bottles and on tap, this distillery-turned-bar is a great place to start an ale crawl, right in the old town. The cozy setting and helpful staff help you whittle down your hundreds of international brew-tastic choices.

Tastings from €2.40, Mon-Sat 12:00-01:00, Kolksteeg 3, Central Amsterdam, +31 (0)20 638 2348, Tram: Nieuwezijds Kolk

Arendsnest

You may well need guidance by the friendly

bartenders to pick your beer at this spot, which proudly serves Dutch beers only. This is a one-stop shop for you to go on a happy hoppy tour of the Netherlands. Get started with the mini tasting of four beers for €6.

Daily 16:00-12:00, later on weekends, Herengracht 90, West Amsterdam, +31 (0)20 4212057, Tram: Nieuwezijds Kolk

Café de Prins

For your typical little Dutch bar where you can enjoy everything from coffee and snacks to beer and music, Café de Prins checks all the boxes. Across the canal from the Anne Frank House, Café de Prins does a good job of staying under the radar and keeping all its cozy *gezellig* atmosphere.

Soups and sandwiches from €4, daily 10:00-01:00, Prinsengracht 124, West Amsterdam, +31 (0)20 624 9382, Tram: Westermarkt

De Zotte

Drop into De Zotte for its impressive lineup of Belgian brews. A constantly rotating menu offers a new experience for each returning visit. Watch out, the Trappists are coming! Hungry by now? They've got some nice little cheese and meat plates to snack on.

Pints start around €4, daily 16:00-01:00, Raamstraat 29, Leidseplein and Vicinity, +31 (0)20 626 8694, Tram: Raamplein

Winston Bar & Venue

Located in the ground floor of one of my favorite hostels, St Christopher's Winston Hotel, this bar is popular with backpackers who come for the cheap prices, open patio in the back, and smoking lounge. The in-house music venue frequently has rock bands playing. Check the website for the calendar.

Drinks from €4.50, daily 10:00-01:00, till 03:00 on weekends, Warmoesstraat 129, Central Amsterdam, +31 (0)20 623 1380, winston.nl/bar, Tram: Dam

Kingfisher Café

At this comfortable, modern *bruin café*, you'll find locals sipping on beers and nibbling away at cheese plates. Pull up a stool to the bar and strike up a conversation with their friendly bartenders. If you're looking for a quiet local's perspective on a night out, this is a great place to start.

Pints from €6, Mon-Thurs 10:00-01:00, Fri-Sat 10:00-03:00, Sun 12:00-01:00, Ferdinand Bolstraat 24, De Pijp and Vicinity, +31 (0)20 671 2395, kingfishercafe.nl, Tram: Stadhouderskade

CLUBS

Melkweg

Melkweg is a serious live-music Amsterdam institution that draws crowds by the thousands. Be sure to check the program online, and purchase tickets ahead of time if there are acts that you don't want to miss. The venue is expansive: a massive dance floor faces a stage lined with two observation levels above. International DJs, rock bands, rappers, and pop singers all come here to rock out with the enthusiastic young crowds. Plan on lines and cover.

Covers and show tickets from €7, shows generally start 20:00-23:00, Lijnbaansgracht 234A, Leidseplein, +31 (0)20 531 8181, melkweg.nl, Tram: Leidseplein

Paradiso

This famous nightlife venue, housed in an old church, has hosted many big names since opening their doors in the 1960s. Their artist list reads like a who's who of the music and entertainment industry: Amy Winehouse, Lenny Kravitz, the Rolling Stones, James Brown, Daft Punk, Lana del Ray, and

plenty more. The genres of events span a range of tastes.

Covers and show tickets from €10, the party picks up around 23:00 and goes til late every night of the week, Weteringschans 6-8, Leidseplein, +31 (0)20 626 4521, paradise.nl, Tram: Leidseplein

PUB CRAWLS
Amsterdam's Ultimate Party
Take the work out of a night out and join Amsterdam's Ultimate Party pub crawl. You've got two choices: exploring the Red Light District's bars and clubs or hitting the clubbing district of Leidseplein. I'd personally opt for the latter, as it's easy to wander through the RLD and create your own adventure. Show this book for a possible discount.

Pricey at €20, kicks off nightly at 20:30, meets at Candela Bar (Korte Leidsedwarsstraat 85), Leidseplein and Vicinity, +31 (0)20 776 7888, joinultimateparty.com, info@ joinultimateparty.com, Tram: Leidseplein

SEX SHOWS
Nothing is beyond the boundaries in this city, including the option to pay for and witness bored-looking sex performers pound through a series of erotic acrobatics and naughty spectacles.

Casa Rosso
If you're in the market for a sex show, this is Amsterdam's most popular. Pay €40 for entrance, or €50 for two watered down drinks to be included, and you're free to stay for as long or as little as you want. Six erotic shows with solo or more actors perform their scandalous deeds for rotations of about 10 minutes in length, so after an hour you've basically seen it all. For a cheaper alternative, drop two euros into the peep show at **Sex Palace** (#84) next door for some instant gratification.

€40 entry, daily 19:00-02:00, till 03:00 on weekends, Oudezijds Achterburgwal 106-108, Central Amsterdam, +31 (0)20 627 8954, casarosso.nl, Tram: Dam

COMEDY SHOWS
Boom Chicago
Dig comedy shows? This is your place for no-holds-barred English improvisational comedy that artfully blends the quirky Dutch sense of humor with a frank and politically incorrect attitude. Now a mainstay on Amsterdam's cultural scene, Boom Chicago has been putting on critically acclaimed shows since the early '90s.

Seats start at €11, shows run Wed-Sun, doors open at 20:00, show time generally 20:30, Rozengracht 117, West Amsterdam, +31 (0)20 217 0400, boomchicago.nl, Tram: Rozengracht

TOP SHOPPING & MARKETS

SHOPPING DISTRICTS
Nieuwendijk, Kalverstraat & Leidsestraat
This long, semi-unbroken chain of streets leads from the Centraal station, through Dam Square and all the way down to Leidseplein and Vondelpark. You could easily spend an afternoon strolling down these streets, which evolve from kitschy and sleazy by the train station to stylish and trendy as you approach Leidseplein. On this mile-long stretch, you'll find fashion boutiques, chocolate shops, grocery stores, souvenir shops, housewares stores, and more.

Central Amsterdam and Leidseplein, Tram: Dam

The Nine Streets
The Nine Streets neighborhood (theninestreets.com), packed with cute, trendy, and independent shops and eateries, is so called because its three streets (Hartenstraat, Wolvenstraat, and Huidenstraat) cross over

three canals (Herengracht, Keizersgracht, and Prinsengracht). It's just south of Anne Frank's House and Westerkerk and between the Singel and Prinsengracht canals.

West Amsterdam, Tram: Westermarkt

MARKETS
Albert Cuyp Market
Named after a famous Dutch author, the Albert Cuyp Market is Amsterdam's largest and is a main reason for the De Pijp neighborhood's recent popularity. This market features 300 vendors offering everything from chocolate-glazed waffles, fresh fruit, and fish to sparkly pants and leather goods. It's a cultural grab bag that speaks to the diversity of this city.

Free, daily 09:00-17:00, Albert Cuypstraat, albertcuypmarkt.com, De Pijp and Vicinity, Tram: Albert Cuypstraat

Bloemenmarkt
At this famous floating tulip market just

south of the center, flower stalls are parked permanently on houseboats. Vendors are happy to package your bulbs to make sure you get them through customs on your way home.

Free, Mon-Sat 09:00-14:30, Sun 11:00-17:30, Singel near the Mint Tower, Central Amsterdam, Tram: Koningsplein

Noordermarkt

Come here on a Saturday or Monday, and this square will be packed with vendors hawking their fresh produce, meats, cheeses, and more. It's not only a food market, though. Go deeper and you'll find antiques, clothes, jewelry, and pretty much anything else you can imagine.

Sat and Mon 09:00-14:00, West Amsterdam, noordermarkt-amsterdam.nl, Tram: Marnixplein

Royal Delft Experience

Beyond the cliché windmill or phallic souvenirs, Delftware makes a great gift for loved ones back home. Named after a nearby town from where it originates, Delftware is classic blue on white and often depicts typical Dutch scenes. Splurge on hand-painted pieces or find much more affordable, printed versions toward the back of most stores. Find the Royal Delft Experience ceramics shop in the Munt Tower (Mint Tower) just on the south side of the center of town. You can pay to tour the working factory, or just shop.

Experience: Apr-Oct daily 10:00-20:00, Nov-Mar daily 10:00-17:30, €5; shop: Apr-Oct daily 09:30-21:00, Nov-Mar daily 09:30-18:00; Muntplein 12, Central Amsterdam, Tram: Spui

TOP PARKS & RECREATION

Don't leave Amsterdam without exploring at least one of the city's beautiful parks. Each park offers a wonderful respite from the hectic city center.

PARKS

Vondelpark

NYC's Central Park was modeled after Amsterdam's largest and most popular one, located south of Leidseplein. On a sunny day, it's hard to beat this picturesque setting for a relaxing picnic or bike ride. You can spend hours exploring the paths and discovering the small lakes that dot this 120-acre park.

Free, always open, Museum District, Tram: Emmastraat

Sarphatipark

Be sure to stop here while making your trek out to Albert Cuyp Market. This small, beautiful park is skipped by most tourists, so

you'll easily find a great spot to picnic and take a load off after a long day of sightseeing. Manicured lawns and fanciful bridges reflect the Romantic movement of the times from the 19th century. The park is located just south of the city center.

Free, always open, Albert Cuypstraat 2, De Pijp and Vicinity, Tram: Albert Cuypstraat

CANAL CRUISES

Lover's Canal Cruises

Amsterdam's most budget-friendly canal cruises offer day, evening, and dining cruises. Trips are narrated in multiple languages and often come with an entertaining captain. A canal cruise is a relaxing way to change your perspective on the city and take it in from the angle that it was built for. Find the kiosk just in front of Centraal station.

Cruises from €15.50, Stationsplein 10, Central Amsterdam, +31 (0)20 330 1374, lovers.nl, Tram: Centraal

TOP TOURS

Mike's Bike Tours

A tour with Mike's Bike Tours is a great way to see central Amsterdam. It includes a pit stop at a local brewery in a windmill. They'll start you off with a brief story of Amsterdam with some beautiful historical maps, then saddle you up on cruisers to hit the town with a trusty guide. They've also got Dutch countryside tours, where you'll see windmills, tulips, and happy Dutch cows all along the way. You'll take a 30-minute break at a local cheese farm, where you can sample some of their delicious Gouda.

€19, 12:00 daily except Dec 13-Jan 4, 3.5-hour tour, Kerk- straat 123, Leidseplein and Vicinity, +31 (0)20 622 7970, mikesbiketoursamsterdam.com, Tram: Keizersgracht

Sandeman's New Europe Walking Tours

Take a free three-hour walking tour with New Europe to help orient yourself to the city. Your guide will entertain you with Amsterdam's wild history of drugs, prostitution, and Nazi occupation. While your tour group may be a bit large, the guides are skilled at leading you to different parts of the city that you'd never find on your own.

Free (tips required), meets daily at 11:15 and 13:15 at the National Monument, Central Amsterdam, newamsterdam- tours.com, Tram: Dam

TOP HOSTELS

Some of my favorite hostels I've ever stayed at are in Amsterdam. Each has its own identity, and you can generally depend on a cool vibe and fun backpacking atmosphere. All of my recommendations are clean and safe, and all have lockers, towels, and free Wi-Fi available. Many have their own drug policies, so be sure to note and respect them. Generally, you can smoke in a designated area, though harder drugs are never allowed on the premises (or anywhere in the city for that matter). While staying in group dorms, always have your valuables locked whether you're in the room or not, just to play it safe. Real estate is at a premium in Amsterdam, so prices for bunks can climb upward of €30, €40, or even €60 during popular events and weekends.

St Christopher's Winston Hotel

If you're looking to stay in the middle of the action, look no further. Quentin Tarantino camped out here while writing the script for *Pulp Fiction*. Enjoy the fun bar, extensive free breakfast, music venue, smoking lounge, and patio out back, which backs up against the rosy red lights.

Bunks from €35, 24-hour reception, free Wi-Fi, breakfast included, lockers available, full bar, Warmoesstraat 129, Central Amsterdam, +31 (0)20 623 1380, winston.nl, winston@winston.nl, Tram: Dam

Flying Pig Downtown

The downtown branch of the Flying Pig is in one of the oldest parts of town, just minutes from the Red Light District. It's known for its fun atmosphere, which you can also experience at the Flying Pig Uptown (bunks from 16, same amenities, Vossiusstraat 46/47, +31 (0)20 400 4187, flyingpig.nl, uptown@ flyingpig.nl, Tram: Van Baerlestraat), near the mouth of the sprawling Vondelpark, close to the Leidseplein entertainment and party district.

Bunks from €19, 24-hour reception, free Wi-Fi, breakfast included, lockers, café, bar, Nieuwendijk 100, Central Am- sterdam, +31 (0)20 420 6822, flyingpig.nl, downtown@ flyingpig.nl, Tram: Nieuwezijds Kolk

Bulldog Hotel & Hostel

Smack-dab in the center, the Bulldog hostel is a great option to get the most out of your stay. It has a great atmosphere, and a fantastic breakfast is included. Amsterdam is sprinkled with coffeeshops and bars of the same brand, though they don't sport the value of the namesake hostel.

Bunks from €27, 24-hour reception, free Wi-Fi, laundry, lockers, breakfast included, Oudezijds Voorburgwal 220, Central Amsterdam, +31 (0)20 620 3822, bulldoghotel. com, info@bulldoghostel.nl, Tram: Dam

Cocomama

For those who shy away from grungy backpacker hostels, this boutique chain is redefining budget accommodations. While you'll pay a premium for it, you'll find a very different, much more chill vibe. You can relax in the lounge in the common room and sleep easy in comfortable, purpose-built bunks. This hostel east of Leidseplein, run by fun and helpful staff, is non-smoking.

Bunks from €35, 6-bed dorms, free Wi-Fi, 24-hour reception, laundry, lockers, Westeinde 18, Leidseplein and Vicinity, +31 (0)20 627 2454, cocomama.nl, info@cocomama.nl, Tram: Frederiksplein

Ecomama

Run by the same company as Cocomama, Ecomama, just east of Central Amsterdam, has a similar vibe. It's also non-smoking.

Bunks from €32, 5-, 7-, 8-, and 12-bed dorms and private doubles, free Wi-Fi, 24-hour reception, laundry, lockers, Valkenburgerstraat 124, Central Amsterdam, +31 (0)20 770 9529, ecomamahotel.com, ecomamahotel@gmail.com, Tram: Mr. Visserplein

TRANSPORTATION

GETTING THERE & AWAY

The excellent public transportation system in Amsterdam makes getting from the train station or airport to your accommodations easy.

Plane

From **Amsterdam Schiphol Airport** (AMS, schiphol.nl), trains leave for Amsterdam Centraal Station every 10 minutes from platforms one and two, and take about 15 minutes to get to the city center. Grab a snack from the grocery store so you'll have change on hand for the ticket machines. Purchase a ticket (€3.60) there or from the ticket desk. There is an express train called Fyra, but the time saved isn't worth the additional cost. Luggage storage is available in the basement of the airport.

If you're flying into **Eindhoven Airport** (EIN, eindhovenairport.nl), connections are made via bus and take you straight to Amsterdam Centraal Station. Transfers cost €25 each way and take about 90 minutes.

Train

Trains to Paris (about €75) run daily and take about 3.5 hours. For Berlin, trains cost about €50-60 and take 6.5 hours.

The **Amsterdam Centraal Station** is on the northern border of Central Amsterdam.

If your hostel is anywhere in the center, it'll be no more than a half mile away from the train station, so consider walking if you're comfortable with your bags. If your hostel is in the canal rings or farther, opt for the tram. There is a helpful **tourist information center** (look for the blue-and-white VVV logo) just out front of the train station across the tramway. Drop in there to get directions and pick up a map.

Bus

Buses from other destinations in Europe drop off at **Amsterdam Centraal Station.** Check eurolines.com for routes and prices.

Car

Amsterdam is about 500 kilometers (5 hours) north of Paris via the A1 highway. It's about 650 kilometers (6.5 hours) west of Berlin via the A2 highway.

GETTING AROUND

Most of the Dutch speak very good English. Don't be afraid to ask for directions!

Amsterdam is small and walkable. You can get from one side of the historic district to the other in about 45 minutes. I suggest organizing your time by seeing sights close to the center on day one, then renting a bike

or mapping out tram routes for the following days to explore the sights and activities farther from the center. The city center bustles with pedestrians, trams, bicycles, mopeds, and cars all jockeying to get to their respective destinations. It's important to keep your wits about you when on the city streets, especially if there are tram tracks around. As my old football coach used to say, "keep your head on a swivel!"

The **Amsterdam Centraal Station** is the main hub for all local transportation. Many trams and buses start their lines here. The public transit system is integrated. The rates are €2.90/hour, €7.50/day, €12.50/2 days, and €17/3 days.

Metro
While Amsterdam does sport a fast metro, you likely won't need to use it on your visit (though the Nieuwmarkt stop can be useful to access some sights in Central Amsterdam). A new line is supposed to open up in the next few years cutting straight through the center, but it has been delayed by construction and funding difficulties.

Tram
If walking and biking aren't your thing, trams will do just the trick. Purchase your ticket on board. **Trams 2** and **5** are particularly useful to tourists. They run north to south,

connecting Amsterdam Centraal Station with Leidseplein and Museumplein. **Trams 13, 14,** and **17** run east to west from Gassan Diamonds to the Anne Frank House.

Bus
Amsterdam does have a bus system, but it's much less helpful for visitors than trams.

Bicycle
If you like to ride bikes, renting one is a must! Being on two wheels allows you to zip across town to all the popular sites in no time. It's by far the most popular form of transportation for locals, and you'll need to dust up on those riding skills to join the Dutch rush. For those who don't like riding bikes, or are rusty, I'd advise against saddling up, as traffic can get overwhelming occasionally. I love **Mike's Bike Tours** (Kerkstraat 123, Leidseplein and Vicinity, +31 (0)20 622 7970, mikesbiketoursamsterdam. com), and they offer competitive rates for a bike rental (€7/day, €5/half-day). For a bike rental option only, **StarBikes Rental** (Daily 8:00-19:00, De Ruijterkade 143, +31 (0)20 620 3215, starbikesrental.com) is the closest to the train station and has bikes that blend in rather than advertise they're rented (€7/ day). Exit the station, hang left past Mac Bikes and under the bridge, and follow the buildings to the right, down about 100 yards.

DAY TRIPS

North Amsterdam
Modern Amsterdam has expanded north beyond the River Ij. What used to be warehouses and industrial yards are now trendy modern studios, offices, and apartments. It's worth a lunchtime visit out to the **Ij Cantine** (lunch from €6.50, daily 9:00-24:00, Mt. Ondinaweg 15-17, +31 (0)20 633 7162, ijcantine. nl) restaurant. As soon as you step off the ferry, you'll feel like you're in Amsterdam's secret little neighborhood. Studios are tucked away in shipping containers and hipster restaurants open out on the small sandy spots, with collapsing benches abounding. Come out here for urban exploring more than anything else. Free ferries take pedestrians and cyclists every 10 minutes from just

behind the train station to the NDSM Wharf in less than ten minutes. If you're on bike, continue north and cruise through the quiet Dutch suburbs.

Haarlem
If you've got an extra day and want to see what small-town Holland looks like, a visit to the quaint Dutch town of Haarlem is a great way to spend an afternoon. In Haarlem's city center, you'll find shopping, cafés, and a beautiful gothic church right on the main square. To get here, head to Amsterdam Centraal Station and look for departures that leave every 10 minutes for Haarlem, which is just a 30-minute commuter train away. The train station drops you on the edge of town, and it's just a 10-minute walk into the center.

HELP!

Tourist Information
Amsterdam's tourist information offices are good places to stop for information and maps, but they're often crowded.

Pickpockets & Scams
Always have your wits about you, as pickpockets like to target overwhelmed, bewildered tourists in the busy areas of the city. It's very unlikely you'll fall victim to violent crime during your visit, but if you're high out of your mind, you make an easy target. Stick with your friends, have a map with your hostel circled on it, and you'll have no problem at all!

Emergencies
In an emergency, dial 112.

Hospital
VU University Medical Center

De Boelelaan 1118

+31 (0)20 444 4444

US Consulate
Museumplein 19

1071 DJ Amsterdam

+31 (0)20 575 5309

ROME

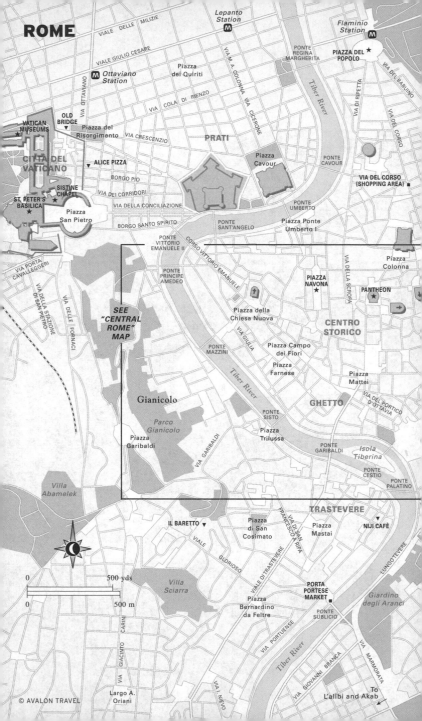

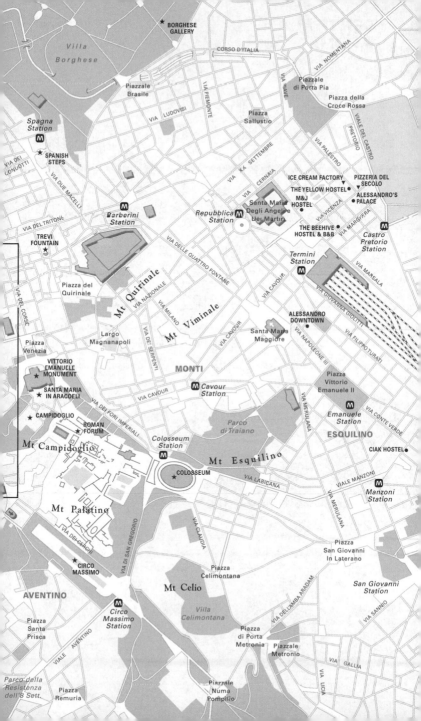

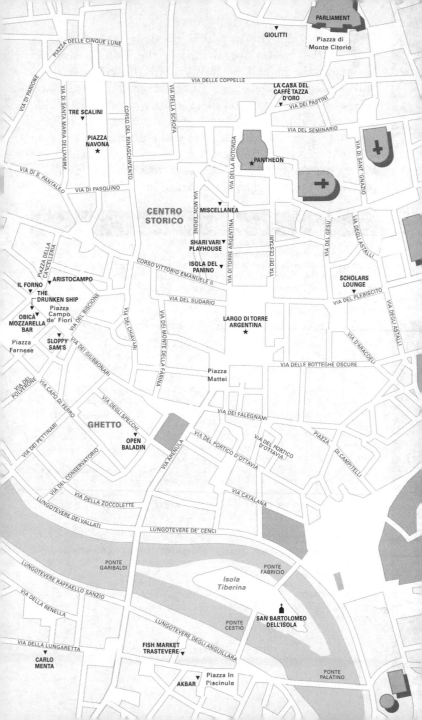

PARLIAMENT

GIOLITTI ▾
Piazza di
Monte Citorio

PIAZZA DELLE CINQUE LUNE

VIA DELLE COPPELLE

LA CASA DEL
CAFFÈ TAZZA
D'ORO
VIA DEI PASTINI

VIA DI PARIONE

VIA DI SANTA MARIA DELL'ANIMA

VIA DELLA SCROFA

VIA DEL SEMINARIO

TRE SCALINI ▾

CORSO DEL RINASCIMENTO

VIA DI SANT IGNAZIO

PIAZZA
NAVONA ★

VIA DELLA ROTONDA

PANTHEON
★

VIA DI S. PANTALEO

VIA DI PASQUINO

VIA DI TORRE ARGENTINA

CENTRO
STORICO

VIA MONTERONE

MISCELLANEA ▾

VIA DEL GESÙ

VIA DEGLI ASTALLI

SHARI VARI ▾
PLAYHOUSE

VIA DEI CESTARI

ISOLA DEL ▾
PANINO

SCHOLARS
LOUNGE

CORSO VITTORIO EMANUELE II

VIA DEL PLEBISCITO

PIAZZA DELLA CANCELLERIA

ARISTOCAMPO ▾

VIA DEGLI ASTALLI

VIA DEL SUDARIO

IL FORNO ▾
THE
▾ DRUNKEN SHIP

VIA DEL BISCIONE

VIA DE' CHIAVARI

VIA D'ARACOELI

Piazza
Campo
de' Fiori

LARGO DI TORRE
ARGENTINA
★

OBICÀ ▾
MOZZARELLA
BAR

VIA DEL MONTE DELLA FARINA

SLOPPY ▾
SAM'S

VIA DEI GIUBBONARI

Piazza
Farnese

VIA DELLE BOTTEGHE OSCURE

Piazza
Mattei

VIA DEL POLVERONE

VIA DI CAPO DI FERRO

VIA DEGLI SPECCHI

VIA DEI FALEGNAMI

PIAZZA DI CAMPITELLI

GHETTO

OPEN ▾
BALADIN

VIA DEL PORTICO D'OTTAVIA

VIA DEL PORTICO
D'OTTAVIA

VIA DEI PETTINARI

VIA ARENULA

VIA DEL CONSERVATORIO

VIA CATALANA

VIA DELLA ZOCCOLETTE

LUNGOTEVERE DEI VALLATI

LUNGOTEVERE DE' CENCI

PONTE
GARIBALDI

PONTE
FABRICIO

LUNGOTEVERE RAFFAELLO SANZIO

Isola
Tiberina

VIA DELLA RENELLA

SAN BARTOLOMEO
DELL'ISOLA

LUNGOTEVERE DEGLI ANGUILLARA

PONTE
CESTIO

VIA DELLA LUNGARETTA

FISH MARKET ▾
TRASTEVERE

CARLO
MENTA

PONTE
PALATINO

AKBAR ▾

Piazza In
Piscinula

Rome is the city to which all roads lead, the center of the known world during the Roman Empire, and the capital of Italy today. The city overflows with ancient, medieval, and Renaissance architecture and art—and also comes complete with romantic little side streets, beautiful panoramas, and unforgettable cuisine. You could spend a lifetime here and still struggle to grasp this modern city with ancient foundations. Set aside time for the sights, but also make sure to pause for espresso, partake in the *passeggiata,* and drink in *la dolce vita.*

ROME 101

Legend has it that Rome was founded in 753 BC by a pair of orphans who were cast off by their human mother on the Tiber River. Their little raft landed in a bend of the river downstream, and they were taken in by a she-wolf and her pack. The fledgling city quickly grew into a regional, then continental powerhouse over the next 1,000 years thanks to technological innovations, incredible engineering feats, and a series of ambitious leaders with a well-organized military to back them up. Rome's population grew to over one million inhabitants and the city was the richest and largest the world had ever seen. Rome exerted its influence across an entire continent thanks to technological developments like the highway (many of today's European freeways follow the path of Roman roads), arches, and water delivery systems like aqueducts and plumbing. Today, you'll see evidence of Ancient Rome's advanced technical prowess at sights like the Colosseum, brilliantly designed to allow tens of thousands of spectators to exit the venue in a mere 15 minutes, and the perfectly domed (and often-imitated) Pantheon.

Rome kept control of far-off territories by installing loyal governors enticed by land grants and plush appointments. Rome also let the inhabitants of newly conquered territories retain a good amount of autonomy—and even their pagan religion—as long as they paid their taxes to Rome. The Roman Empire's decline, which began around AD 300, was the result of overextension as well as weak and corrupt leadership. Leaders were struggling to hold together an empire that stretched across 6.5 million square kilometers without technologies like Skype and Snapchat. Can you imagine?

Rome was finally sacked numerous times by barbarian hordes from the north, driving the entire continent into a period of lawlessness and violence called the Dark Ages. In medieval times, Rome was a dank backwater rife with crime and disease—not a place you'd want to hang out. With a population of only 15,000 after its peak of a million, Rome suffered from constant outside attacks and dealt with outbreaks of disease as mosquitos and pests thrived in the warm, humid climate.

The Vatican City State stepped into this vacuum of power to clean up the city, and inspired the entire continent to come out of the Dark Ages by financing artistic and technical innovations. Eventually, the Catholic church began supporting artists, sculptors, and designers to deck out churches in a beauty and elegance meant to showcase the power of Christianity. The Renaissance sparked artistic and architectural developments, leading to the design and building of ever-greater churches like St Peter's Basilica. Since then, Rome has been a hub of visual and culinary arts, with a contagious love of life and rich Roman personalities to match their city's long history.

PLAN AHEAD

RESERVATIONS

Reservations are required for the **Galleria Borghese** (galleriaborghese.it) and the **papal audience** (papalaudience.org/tickets). When planning, remember that the **Vatican Museums** are closed most Sundays, while the worthwhile (and free) **Porta Portese** market is only open on Sunday.

Reservations are recommended for the following sights:
Colosseum (tickitaly.com/tickets/colosse-um-tickets.php)
Vatican Museums (biglietteriamusei.-vatican.va)

PASSES

Roma Pass
The **Roma Pass** (€36, valid for three days upon validation, romapass.it) offers free entry—and line-skipping privileges—to the first two covered museums of your choice, the most cost-effective being the Colosseum and the Galleria Borghese (reservations are still required for the Galleria), followed by discounted rates to a number of other sights. See the website for a complete list of covered sights. (The Vatican Museums are not covered.) The Roma Pass also earns you free use of all public transportation in Rome during those 72 hours. Pick up the pass at all participating sights and don't validate it until you enter your first sight. Tally up the sights you want to see that are included in the pass to determine if it will be a good value for you.

LOCAL HAPPENINGS

Easter
Easter, which occurs in March or April, is one of the biggest festivals in Rome, with millions of pilgrims coming in from around the world. If you plan to be in Rome during this time, reserve long in advance, and be prepared to pay more for your stay. Christmas and New Year's are also popular times to visit Rome.

HIGH AND LOW SEASON

June, July, and September are Rome's uber-busy months of tourism. August is when all of Italy shuts down for vacation. Don't expect to see much going on in August here. You can still experience all the tourist sites of course, but anyone who can afford to heads to the beach for a month.

KEY STATS & FIGURES

Currency:
Italy uses the euro (€);
1 EUR = about 1.06 USD

Population:
2.7 million

National language:
Italian

National religion:
soccer (football)

Number of metro lines:
2

Kilos of pasta consumed annually per capita:
28 kilos (over 50 pounds!)

Souvenir of choice:
Sexy Wine (try some at Miscellanea), postcards, limoncello liqueur

CALIBRATE YOUR BUDGET

TYPICAL PRICES FOR:

Hostel dorm bed:
€20

Two-course dinner:
€12

Glass of wine:
€4

Metro pass:
€1.50

MOVIES TO WATCH
The Talented Mr. Ripley, Angels & Demons, Eat Pray Love, EuroTrip, Ben Hur, To Rome with Love, Roman Holiday

ROME

THREE DAY ITINERARY

Rome's can't-miss attractions will easily fill three days. Organize your visit chronologically, starting with Ancient Rome on day one and continuing onto Renaissance Rome on day two. Remember that the Vatican Museums are closed on Sunday, so you may need to switch days one and two to avoid missing it, depending on your arrival day.

DAY 1: ANCIENT & MEDIEVAL ROME

MORNING

Catch breakfast at a neighborhood café near your hostel in Termini. Do a lap around the block and pop into any café that has locals inside. Once fortified, grab a bottle of water and catch metro line B down to the **Colosseum** (two stops to Colosseo). I like to tackle the Colosseum before the heat of the day, so make your reservations early to avoid having to stand in line. Download Rick Steves' free podcast and audio tours, which will walk you through the ancient ruins.

Spend at least an hour exploring the ruins, then head to the back of the Colosseum for a quick snack and coffee before your next Ancient Rome experience: the **Roman Forum**. You'll spend about an hour here as well.

AFTERNOON

From the Roman Forum, climb the staircase to Capitoline Hill to look back over the Forum. Continue to the square at the top of the hill, the **Campidoglio**, from which you can look across modern Rome on the other side of the hill. Looking down the steps from the Campidoglio, you'll see the hilltop **Santa Maria in Aracoeli** to your right. Behind that is the **Vittorio Emanuele Monument**, offering both a panorama of the city and an excellent free war museum.

Continue down the stairs and cross the busy street leading to Piazza Venezia and wander through the back streets of Rome toward the **Largo di Torre Argentina**. From the railing tracing the perimeter of the square, look down onto the ruins of three temples dedicated to pagan gods. See any stray cats? You're gazing into Rome's main stray cat sanctuary as well.

Continue to the opposite corner of Largo Argentina toward the Pantheon. After a small block, **Isola del Panino**, my favorite sandwich shop in Rome, will be in an alley on your left. Pop in and order by pointing. Don't forget to say hi to my friend Fabio, who's been cranking out delicious sandwiches for as long as I've been coming to Rome.

Take your sandwich and enjoy it in the shadow of the **Pantheon.** Head inside the open-topped site after and take your time exploring. (If it's Saturday, consider doubling back here later for Mass at 17:00).

Afterward, grab one of my favorite treats in all of Rome: *granita al caffè* at the **Casa del Caffè Tazza d'Oro** coffee shop on the corner to the right as you leave the Pantheon. If you're in the mood for gelato instead, one of Rome's best *gelaterie*, **Giolitti**, is barely two blocks north.

Continue north on the **Via del Corso,** a popular shopping street, toward the **Spanish Steps** and take in the scene there. Relax on the steps or destroy your credit card in the city's top designer fashion stores. Whenever you're ready, catch metro line A from the Spanish Steps back to Termini and the hostel to rest.

EVENING

Take bus H from Termini into Trastevere (get off at the first stop after the bridge over the river, about 15 minutes) to explore Rome's medieval neighborhood. Enjoy a *passeggiata* and take part in the Italian tradition of seeing and being seen. You have some of Rome's best choices for dinner in Trastevere: my favorite pizza in town at **Dar Poeta** or typical Roman dishes at the local favorite, **Carlo Menta.**

LATE

Party it up with the locals in **Trastevere**. There are tons of great venues, like **Niji Café** (classy cocktails) or **Freni e Frizioni** (social drinks), to choose from. So much of Italian nightlife goes down out in the streets, so get a drink and enjoy *la dolce vita* (the sweet life), Roman style.

DAY 2: RENAISSANCE & BAROQUE ROME

MORNING

Do your best to get full from breakfast, and knock back an extra espresso, as you'll be seeing one of the world's largest collections of art, sculptures, and priceless artifacts today at the Vatican Museums!

Catch metro line A to the Ottaviano stop for **Vatican City.** Make reservations online ahead of time to skip the lines. From the metro, follow signs pointing toward Musei Vaticani, walking past the tour hawkers and following the walls and crowds to the entry gate. If you've made reservations ahead of time, continue straight to the entry gate and flash your voucher. Otherwise, be prepared to wait. Once inside, go with the flow through the **Sistine Chapel** and on to **St Peter's Basilica.** Oftentimes, the museum will spit you out a one-way exit, and you'll have to go back through security to enter the basilica. If there's an option to leave from the back right corner of the Sistine Chapel, take it and alight directly in St Peter's Basilica. Otherwise, now's a great time for a lunch break.

AFTERNOON

Find my choice for the best pizza by the slice in this touristy district at **Alice Pizza** on Via delle Grazie. Reward yourself with a visit to **Old Bridge** *gelateria* (ice cream shop) just across the street from the Vatican City walls.

Head back to Piazza San Pietro, the square in front of the massive **St Peter's Basilica,** and get in line for security. While the line may be long, it does move quickly through multiple checkpoints. Once inside, look for Michelangelo's famous *Pietà* immediately to the right as you enter. You can go beneath the basilica into the free crypts, or climb the cupola for beautiful panoramic views.

If you're beat from the day of sightseeing, hop on bus 40 or 64 any time to get back to your hostel in Termini. For superwomen and -men, I highly recommend taking the 30-minute walk/climb up **Gianicolo Hill** for another panorama across the entire city from above Trastevere. With your back to the front of St Peter's Basilica, the hill is to your right beyond the buildings. You should be able to make out the trees behind church administrative buildings. This is where the moped-riding lovers of Rome bring their squeeze after the sun goes down to escape their parents' watchful eyes.

I like to spend the afternoon wandering back into the center of Rome from either St Peter's or Gianicolo Hill, exploring the old side streets of Rome.

Take the bridge directly in front of Castel Sant'Angelo toward Largo di Torre Argentina to catch the bus back up to Termini for a rest. But between the Tiber River and that bus stop, you'll find all sorts of boutique shops, *gelaterie*, cafés, and more beautiful baroque and Renaissance churches.

EVENING

Hop onto metro line A from Termini to the Piazza di Spagna stop, and enjoy an evening *passeggiata* past the **Trevi Fountain** and west toward the **Pantheon.** Grab dinner at **Miscellanea,** right outside the Pantheon, to get the party started with four courses of deliciousness including unlimited wine and water. Mention my name and get unlimited wine with dinner. You're welcome!

LATE

Depending on the breed of nightlife you're looking for, you've got tons of options in front of you. Party with the Americans? Stroll over to **Campo de' Fiori,** a favorite of the study-abroad students in Rome, with staples like **Sloppy Sam's** and **Drunken Ship.** More likely than not, you'll finish your night with a crowd of new friends heading to the Irish bar open late, **Scholar's Lounge.**

Another night out with Italians? Head to **Piazza Navona,** a short walk west of the Pantheon. Keep walking through Piazza Navona and exit the touristy square on the west side, finding an alleyway called Via di Sant'Agnese in Agone, right next to Tre Scalini. This alley leads to some of my favorite nightlife venues, **Bar del Fico** and **Abbey Theater.** (I've dubbed Via di Sant'Agnese in Agone the "Gateway to Hell," because every time I pass through it, a miserable hangover awaits.)

Time to get your clubbing on? Split a cab with friends and head south to the clubs in **Testaccio.**

DAY 3: CHOICES, CHOICES, CHOICES

Shake off that hangover with a *cornetto* pastry. Then consider a day trip to **Via Appia Antica** or the fascist urban development of **EUR,** or stay closer to the city center and visit the Galleria Borghese and/or Porta Portese market.

MORNING

If it's Sunday, leave your valuables at the hostel and take bus H down to Trastevere where you'll find the notorious **Porta Portese** market. It's easy to fill a couple hours strolling the length of the market.

Leaving the market, cross the river and climb the hill up to the **Giardino degli Aranci,** where you'll find the famous viewpoint through the keyhole, showing three sovereign nations in one view.

Wander across the nearby **Circo Massimo,** then north along the river into the **Jewish quarter,** where more restaurants will likely be open—try the kosher gelato!

LATE AFTERNOON

Anyone who appreciates art, especially baroque art and sculpture, should make plans for the **Galleria Borghese.** From Termini accommodations it's a 20-minute walk north, or you can take metro line A to the Piazza di Spagna stop. From there, it's about a 25-minute walk northeast and uphill to the museum. If you've made reservations ahead of time, excellent. Otherwise, head over for a chance to get a last-minute entry. Save time before or afterward for a picnic in **Villa Borghese,** the big park that surrounds the Galleria Borghese. You can rent four-seater bikes and pedal around the park without worrying about the crazy traffic!

TOP NEIGHBORHOODS

Rome straddles a bend in the Tiber River. Most of the tourist sites are on the east side of the river, clustered in the Ancient Rome and Pantheon neighborhoods. This area (along with Vatican City) is sightseeing ground zero. **Ancient Rome** comprises the Colosseum and Roman Forum. Northwest is the **Pantheon neighborhood,** including that famous structure along with Trevi Fountain and Largo di Torre Argentina (often shortened to Largo Argentina). The Pantheon neighborhood also offers romantic alleyways and some good (if touristy) options for food and nightlife, especially near Campo de' Fiori and Piazza Navona.

North of the Pantheon neighborhood, **North Rome** contains the Galleria Borghese, Spanish Steps, Piazza del Popolo, and Rome's most expensive shopping. Restaurants are either upscale or tourist traps, so it's better to eat elsewhere.

On the west side of the river is **Vatican City.** A few worthwhile dining options cluster around this holy city-state, but the sights are your top priority. South of Vatican City,

and west from Ancient Rome, is **Trastevere,** one of my favorite neighborhoods for its authentic, local feel. You'll find winding cobblestone streets, medieval churches, and quaint squares with ivy climbing up the walls. It's easy to blend in with the locals on their nightly stroll to dinner, then gelato, then the bars.

Back on the east side of the river, East Rome is home to the main train station, **Termini,** which gives its name to the surrounding neighborhood. All recommended hostels are located here. While the streets immediately surrounding the station aren't the most interesting, they've recently cleaned up quite a bit. Find student-oriented nightlife in **San Lorenzo,** a 15-minute walk south and east from Termini station. From Termini, it's an easy metro or bus ride into most of the city center sights.

Testaccio, directly south from Circo Massimo, has an excellent neighborhood feel and a daily produce and meat market. You'll find yourself here for one other main reason, though: the club scene.

TOP SIGHTS

Colosseum

Commissioned in AD 70 by Emperor Vespasian, the Colosseum took a mere 10 years to build. This amphitheater (or double theater) packed in 50,000 jeering Romans of all walks of life and castes. It was segregated, of course, with nobles and senators in the lower levels, merchants and soldiers in the mid levels, and slaves and women in the highest rafters. Entry was free with a numbered ceramic fragment. Emperors and campaigning local politicians sponsored events with exotic animal and gladiator fights, food, VIP seating, and more. Hey, I'd

vote for anyone who gave me free tickets to the Seahawks! Thanks to the design, all 50,000 spectators could exit the venue within 15 minutes, something most modern stadiums could only dream of.

Nearly 2,000 years after its construction, the Colosseum is Rome's most popular attraction. Queue along the outer walls, purchase tickets just inside, and continue directly up to the first floor, where you can complete a lap, looking down and imagining the battles that occurred here. Complete your visit with another lap on the ground floor, this time with a close-up view of the

ACT LIKE A LOCAL

Go Take a *Passeggiata!*

Italian culture is all about seeing and being seen—and looking good at
all times. There's even a term for it: keeping *la bella figura,* meaning keeping up
appearances no matter what. That's why clothing labels are so prominent here:
They know people are watching! If you're going to the gym, you'll bring a change
of clothes, as it's not OK for people to see you sweat. If you see someone running
outside, they're either a marathoner or not Italian.

And what better way to display your labels and the cute thing on your arm than to
stroll through town before and after dinner? This aimless little neighborhood walk is
called a *passeggiata,* a nightly ritual that you've got to join at least once. *Passeggiate*
are also taken just to get out of the house. Roman apartments are small, with the
paradoxical result that Italians often have to go out in public to get any sort of privacy
from the family. Sunday afternoons are another popular time to stroll the old streets,
as many close down to be pedestrian only.

Breakfast, the Italian Way

You won't find bacon or hash browns anywhere in Rome! Italian breakfasts are
simple, and they're consumed at the corner café. Step in and observe the scene:
career baristas who are passionate about coffee serving pastries to regulars who
come in five days a week ordering the same thing. Everyone seems like their old
friends. Depending on the café, you might pay for your order first, *then* deliver the
receipt to the barista to redeem your coffee. Otherwise, order at the bar and pay
before leaving—just watch what the locals do. Remember, sitting down at a table
often comes with a small surcharge on each item ordered. The locals often have a
single espresso at the bar to wash down a *cornetto,* a pastry very similar to—but
not quite as good as—the French croissant.

Bread Basics

It's an American invention to dump olive oil and vinegar onto a side plate and sop
it up with bread while you wait for your food. Italians would never do such a thing,
as it kills your appetite and fills you up with carbs. Italians use bread only during
their meal to *fare la scarpetta,* an expression meaning "to make the little shoe"
on—or scoop up—your leftover pasta sauce.

It's Pronounced "Broo-sketta"!

No matter what our friends at the Olive Garden tell you, anytime you see an H
following a C in the Italian language, it turns that letter into a hard C. In other
words, you pronounce the delicious tomato and garlic toast as broo-SKET-a, not
broo-SHET-a. Conversely, *cioccolato,* Italian for chocolate, starts with the same "ch"
sound as our word because it lacks the H after the C.

Street Smarts

Traffic is to Rome as Carrot Top is to just about everything he touches: obnoxious
and overwhelming. Traffic will never stop unless you boldly step out into the
intersection—as long as you're within the zebra stripes!—staring down oncom-
ing drivers. Here's the secret to getting across: Find a local and pair up at the hip
(unbeknownst to them), and cross when they do. Obey any traffic lights if they're
there. If there is no walking signal, wait for a slight break in the traffic. Wave back
at the tourists who are too timid to give it a shot, and once you're an expert, bring
them along!

network of passageways used by gladiators, cages and cells for animals, and trap door loading areas that would have been covered by a wooden floor and sand.

The Colosseum and Roman Forum share a single entry ticket. Consider picking your ticket up at the gate to the Forum if the line at the Colosseum is long. Heads-up: As soon as you arrive to the area, you'll be hounded by promoters offering private tours and ways to skip the line. On days when the line is long, taking an organized tour may be worth it, but be sure to understand what you're getting for your money. Also, take a peek at the line yourself to gauge the value of skipping it. Many tour operators take your money first, then make you wait until they find other customers in order to run a full tour.

€15.50 ticket also covers Roman Forum, free first Sun of the month, daily 08:30 til one hour before sunset, last entry one hour before closing, Ancient Rome, +39 06 3996 7700, get tickets at tickitaly.com, Metro: Colosseo, Bus: Piazza Venezia

Roman Forum

The Roman Forum was the nerve center of the most impressive empire the world has ever seen. It's in this district that daily life went down, with toga-wearing politicians rushing between votes and making impassioned speeches, shopkeepers selling their wares, and triumphant military commanders parading their way back into town in victory processions lasting days on end as they touted their booty, new slaves, and plunder. Over the centuries, much of the Roman Forum disappeared due to urban cannibalism. (It was much easier to come here and take precut stones for your home rather than go to the quarry and cut them from the ground.) Floods carrying river silt and debris also covered the ruins up over time.

Two thousand years later, it is still possible to come here and see many remnants of Ancient Roman society, including the Temple of the Vestal Virgins, the arch of Septimius Severus, and the well-preserved Roman Senate House. When walking on the original Roman cobblestones, note how much lower in the ground you are than street level. This area was right in the floodplain of the Tiber River until the walls were built in the 20th century to prevent the floods.

€15.50 ticket also covers Colosseum, free first Sun of the month, daily 08:30 til one hour before sunset, last entry one hour before closing, Ancient Rome, +39 06 0608, get tickets at tickitaly.com, Metro: Colosseo

Vatican Museums & Sistine Chapel

The Vatican is the center of the global Catholic church. Its public museums offer a glimpse into their awe-inspiring collection of worldly riches amassed over the centuries. The hallways are gilded in baroque embellishments and encrusted with priceless Renaissance masterpieces. Michelangelo's Sistine Chapel is quite literally jaw-dropping, as are the Raphael rooms (*stanze di Rafaello*). Reserve your entry well ahead of time for the Vatican Museums to skip the line. Otherwise, beat the lines by getting up early or going late. Allow at least three hours inside to see everything. You might want to bring a bottle of water and snacks to survive. I highly recommend Rick Steves' audio tours as a way to learn about what you're looking at at your own pace.

€16, additional €4 for online reservation, Mon-Sat 09:00–18:00, last entry at 16:00, closed Sun but open last Sun of the month 09:00–14:00 with free entry before 12:30,

Vatican City Neighborhood, +39 06 6988 3332, biglietteriamusei.vatican.va, Metro: Ottaviano

St Peter's Basilica

Catholicism's proudest cathedral is dedicated to the first pope, Peter. It is said that Peter was crucified between chariot races at the racetrack that used to loop around this neighborhood. After he died, Peter's followers took him down and buried him in a clandestine Christian grave in the hill behind the racetrack. After hundreds of years and multiple chapels and churches, the altar today stands about 60 feet above these catacombs, with Bernini's swirly bronze baldachin rising high above. Designed by an ever-changing team of Renaissance master architects, St Peter's was built to an otherworldly scale that makes visitors feel like ants. Take a look high above at the inscriptions that wrap the interior walls. Those letters are six feet tall. And every image you see in this entire church is not a painting, but rather a mosaic. Paintings fade, so 10,000 square meters of intricate mosaics depict past popes, lessons from the Bible, and all characters you'd expect to see in Catholicism's most important cathedral.

As you enter, immediately to the right is Michelangelo's masterpiece, the **Pietà.** In elongated and exaggerated features, Jesus' body weighs heavy on Mary's lap. Michelangelo completed this piece when he was only 24 years old, and only returned to sign it when he heard rumors that it was being attributed to someone else. In 1972, a crazed Italian man came at Mary's face and arm with a hammer, knocking chunks off the priceless sculpture. Luckily, the Pietà has been restored with marble taken from the back of the piece (raw marble is like a thumbprint—you'll never find two pieces the same coloring, hue, and pattern). Thanks to our disturbed friend, you'll observe the Pietà from 30 feet away and through 2 inches of bulletproof glass.

Visitors can go beneath the basilica into the free crypts or climb the cupola for a beautiful panorama of the entire city (€5 by stairs, €7 by elevator). Papal audiences with Pope Francis take place every Wednesday at 10:30 (arrival recommended at 08:30, free tickets required, papalaudience.org).

Free, daily Apr-Sept 07:00-19:00, Oct-Mar 07:00-18:30, dome open daily from 08:00, last entry to stairs 17:00 (16:00 Oct-Mar), to elevator 18:00 (17:00 Oct-Mar), Piazza San Pietro, Vatican City Neighborhood, +39 800 038 436, vatican.va, Metro: Ottaviano

Pantheon

A revolutionary feat of architecture and engineering, this domed temple has been studied and replicated since its creation. What was a one-stop shop to worship all the gods of the Roman Empire (*pan* = all, *theon* = gods), is now an active Catholic church technically called Church of St Mary and the Martyrs. Raphael, the Renaissance master, is buried in the church, along with the first two kings of Italy and one of their wives, Queen Margherita. (She's the one the popular pizza was named after. The three main ingredients—tomatoes, mozzarella, and basil—represent the three colors of the newly united Italy's flag.)

Two wooden structures burned down on this site before Emperor Hadrian commissioned a stone version and completed it around AD 125. At its base, the walls are nearly 30 feet thick, built with heavy brick and stone. As the walls climb higher and arch into the ceiling, the building materials become lighter. The uppermost portion is made of concrete mixed with light volcanic ash. The ceiling is only three feet thick, and

is recessed both to add decoration and to reduce mass overhead.

The Pantheon is the world's largest and oldest unreinforced concrete dome. It inspired the designs of some of the most famous domes in Rome and the world, including St Peter's Basilica, the Duomo in Florence, Jefferson's Monticello house, and even the American Capitol building in Washington DC.

Today, the Catholic church is active. You can catch Mass here Saturday at 17:00 and Sunday at 10:30. It's a special experience because the noisy tourists are ushered out and the faithful stay in quiet reflection.

Free, Mon-Sat 08:30 19:30, Sun 09:00-18:00, holidays 09:00-13:00, Pantheon Neighborhood, +39 06 6830 0230, Bus: Largo Argentina

Trevi Fountain

Rome's greatest fountain is dedicated to the aqueduct that powered it for more than 400 years. You've got to remember that running water was a luxury (and still is sometimes in modern-day Rome!), and the Romans harnessed this technology to drive population growth beyond one million inhabitants. That's something that didn't happen again until industrialized London nearly 2,000 years later.

The fountain itself dates from the 18th century, when Pope Clement XII commissioned the master, Salvi, to renovate it to today's stature. As you gaze upon the fountain, you'll see Poseidon with two horses, one rearing its head and the other docile. These opposing postures represent the two personalities of the sea: violent and calm. On the reliefs high above, you'll see a girl leading the Roman centurions to the headwaters of the aqueduct that powered this fountain and many others in Rome,

and the cornucopia beneath represents the bounty of the sea. All in all, this fountain is a masterpiece of symbolism and detail—see how many types of flora and fauna you can spot.

And as you take the scene in, look to the right and find the scraggy chunk of rock sticking up out of nowhere. As noisy construction dragged on far beyond the scheduled completion date, a local shopkeeper was complaining about the annoyance. In the end, Salvi graciously left a permanent block of stone just in front the shop to obscure the view of his fountain as a thank-you note for the trouble caused.

Today, the Trevi Fountain is swarmed by tourists, knickknack sellers, and Italian Casanovas looking for love. Reopened in November of 2015 after 16 months of renovation (some of it funded by Fendi design house), it's more pristine than ever. Tradition says that all who wish to return to Rome must come to the fountain and toss a coin in with their right hand over their left shoulder. See if it works for you!

Free, always open, Pantheon Neighborhood, Metro: Barberini

Piazza Navona

Piazza Navona, another of the city's famous squares, used to be a track for chariot racing downtown. If you look closely, the elongated outline of the square is rounded at one end, following the shape of the old track from back in the day. Today, Piazza Navona fills up with artists and trinket vendors and is a prime spot for the *passeggiate* (strolls) that locals take every night. Don't miss the famous chocolate truffles at Tre Scalini and the excellent nightlife in the district just through the alleyway leading toward the river next to the church.

TREVI TRIVIA

Thanks to the tradition of tossing coins into the Trevi Fountain to guarantee a return trip back to Italy, the pool in front of the fountain collects thousands of euros daily. (Apparently, many tourists believe the higher the value of coin, the higher the chance the superstition will actually work.) Well, where does all this money go? For a number of years, it just disappeared. No one knew what was happening...until the police caught a homeless man swimming in the fountain.

They caught him once, then again...and again...and again. He hadn't really committed a real crime, so he couldn't be detained for more than 24 hours. Each time he was caught, he was released. This went on until someone had the brilliant idea to create a waterproof fountain Roomba and donate the money to the Italian Red Cross. Now, several million euros collected from the fountain are donated to the Red Cross each year. *Grazie*, tourists!

Free, always open, Pantheon Neighborhood, Bus: Largo Argentina

Largo di Torre Argentina

One of Rome's busiest squares for bus connections also looks down onto this open-air archeological dig. While the purposes for each are unknown, you'll see the foundations for three Roman temples, which today are called Temple A, Temple B, and Temple C. Rome used to have a serious feral cat problem in the downtown area, and they were able to solve the problem by relegating all stray cats to this one sunken square. On the southwest corner of the square, descend a short staircase to visit Rome's **Cat Sanctuary** (hours vary). Largo Argentina today is more important to know as a reference point for public transportation than anything else, and has conveniently located shops like a bookstore, *tabacchi* (tobacco store), and *gelateria*, as well as many recommended restaurants nearby.

Free, always open, Pantheon Neighborhood, Bus: Largo Argentina

Campidoglio

After climbing out of the Forum, you'll pass through this beautiful, perfectly balanced Renaissance square at the top of Capitoline Hill. Michelangelo was brought in to complete this half-built square in the 16th century. The Campidoglio exemplifies what Renaissance masters held to be most important about architecture: city planning and order. Michelangelo had his work cut out for him, as the pope wanted a square that connected modern Rome with its ancient past; it had to reference the Roman Forum but look forward into the future. Michelangelo's solution was ambitious, but served to unite one of Rome's most important hilltops by reflecting and updating the existing inharmonious medieval palazzi. He

overlaid the square with a geometric pattern, reflecting the advances in math at the time, and squeezed in a mirroring palace (the one closer to the Vittorio Emanuele Monument) to make the square symmetrical.

The equestrian statue in the middle of the square is Marcus Aurelius. Most bronze statues were melted down in medieval times for material, and this statue still exists today only because it was thought to be of Emperor Constantine, the one who turned Rome to the Christian faith—so it was protected by the church. Everyone thought the statue's outstretched arm was meant to be blessing the audience, but instead, Marcus Aurelius is commanding his armies.

Free, always open, Ancient Rome, Metro: Colosseo, Bus: Piazza Venezia

Santa Maria in Aracoeli

As you descend from the Campidoglio down the Renaissance stairway, Santa Maria in Aracoeli is up and to your right. Sitting on the most holy and important hill in Rome, this church rests on ruins dating back to the Roman Empire. In this single church, you can study a wide range of artistic and architectural styles, from Romanesque to gothic and medieval to renaissance and baroque. Thankfully, the church was not destroyed during the construction of the nearby Vittorio Emanuele Monument.

Free, daily 09:00-18:30, Ancient Rome, Metro: Colosseo, Bus: Piazza Venezia

Vittorio Emanuele Monument

The colossal Vittorio Emanuele Monument (aka Altare della Patria) to Italy's first president is located on Piazza Venezia and caps the head of Via del Corso. From the nicknames locals have given it—the Typewriter, Dentures, Wedding Cake—you can guess their sentiments on this neoclassical feat of architecture. An enthralling free military mu-

seum is definitely worth a gander on your way up to the elevators zipping visitors to the roof of the monument. The €7 elevator ride to the top offers the best views of both ancient and modern Rome around.

Free, daily 09:30-18:30, ticket offices close 45 minutes earlier; museum €5, daily 09:30-18:30, Piazza Venezia, Ancient Rome, +39 06 678 0664, Metro: Colosseo, Bus: Piazza Venezia

Circo Massimo

This was Ancient Rome's largest stadium, seating more than 150,000 Romans at once. The sheer scale of the stadium is mind-blowing. It was built over 2,000 years before the Big House, and it's still substantially bigger! The entertainment that attracted these crowds varied: You could come for an afternoon of chariot racing, singing or musical events, gladiator combat, or athletic demonstrations. Located right in the downtown of Ancient Rome, with the Emperor's Palace overlooking the track, the Circo Massimo was near and dear to the empire's heart.

Today, this empty field and long running track are great for a picnic or to get a few laps in. I was here during the 2006 World Cup when Italy faced France and won. You couldn't imagine the melee of happy Italians blaring air horns, shooting bottle rockets off sideways, and riding their mopeds tandem long into the night.

Free, always open, Ancient Rome, Metro: Circo Massimo

Galleria Borghese

This Baroque villa houses possibly my favorite museum on the planet, featuring some of the most incredible baroque paintings and sculptures ever completed, like Caravaggio's dramatically lit *David with the Head of Goliath* and Bernini's spectacular *Apollo and Daphne*. The quality of the exhibition is underrated and missed by the hordes of tour-

ists, but it should be at the top of anyone's list when visiting Rome. Reservations are required; get them at galleriaborghese.it. The Galleria Borghese is about a 15-minute walk from the listed metro stops. From Termini, consider taking bus 910, which will drop you off closer to the museum, or just walk about 20 minutes.

€13, includes mandatory €2 reservation fee, free first Sun of the month, Tues-Sun 09:30-19:00, Piazzale del Museo Borghese 5 (located inside the Villa Borghese park), North Rome, +39 06 841 3979, Metro: Barberini or Flaminio, Bus: Museo Borghese

Spanish Steps

Another example of Roman baroque exuberance, this staircase was built to connect the church and neighborhood high above with the rest of central Rome. Ironically, the name is a misnomer. The steps were paid for by a French diplomat, not the Spanish. We call them the Spanish Steps because the Spanish envoy to the Vatican is just around the corner near the tall freestanding column in front of the nearby McDonald's, and it rolls off the tongue a little nicer, doesn't it? The Spanish Steps are busy throughout the day now—some of the best shopping in Rome is to be had in the streets leading away from the steps. This neighborhood and the steps specifically have always been a meeting place for lovers, romantics, and poets. All it takes is a stop here yourself, and you'll understand why.

Free, always open, North Rome, Metro: Spagna

Piazza del Popolo

This piazza is an excellent example of a Renaissance city planning technique called the *tridente*. See the three grand avenues leading south away from the square into Central Rome? The central one is Via del Corso. To the left, Via del Babuino leads straight to the Spanish Steps, and Via di Ripetta leads off to

the right toward the old medieval center and the bridge that connects the heart of Rome with Vatican City. The streets didn't naturally happen this straight; it was the urban planning of an ambitious pope in the 17th century—any homes in the way were simply demolished in the interest of beautifying the church's capital city.

Today, Piazza del Popolo (People's Square) is a great spot to people-watch and soak in Rome's rich architecture without the bustle of the bigger sites. Demonstrations often use the square to kick off a procession leading into the center of town. Pop into the churches on the square to view some beautiful baroque art, including a piece by Caravaggio.

Free, always open, North Rome, Metro: Flamino

Jewish Quarter

Rome has a rich Jewish history dating back hundreds of years. Though the Jewish community even predates that of the Christians, Pope Paul IV relegated the Jews to this district just outside the bend of the River Tiber in a Papal Bull in 1555. This was a deliberate ploy to place the Jewish community right in the path of the river that floods numerous times each year. The Jewish community persevered through these horrid conditions, then enjoyed a short respite upon the unification of modern Italy toward the end of the 19th century, until the Nazi fervor retook the continent by the 1930s.

Today, the Jewish quarter is well worth a stroll. Keep your eyes open to find inlaid stones with Hebrew inscriptions in buildings throughout the neighborhood. While many other parts of the city close down on Sunday, the Jewish quarter is alive and bustling. Don't forget to look down—you'll notice numerous small bronze cobblestones—aka "stumblestones"—sprinkled throughout the area. They're placed in front of homes from which Jewish victims of the Holocaust were deported in 1939 and on. You'll see the name of each victim inscribed with their birth date, occupation, which camp they were deported to, and last date known to be alive. It started here in Rome, but you'll notice these bronze stumblestones throughout Europe in front of buildings where victims of the Holocaust lived.

Wander through this district and be sure to try and find the following: fried artichoke in the Jewish style (think Bloomin' Onion, *stilo Romano*), kosher gelato, and Bernini's *Fountain of the Turtles* (dedicated to the Jewish community). The turtles represent carrying all your earthly belongings on your back until finding a land to call your own.

Free, always open, Pantheon Neighborhood, Bus: Largo Argentina

EXTRA CREDIT
Churches, Churches, & More Churches

Historically, the church has been the richest patron around, so churches in Rome often house beautiful works of art. (And Rome has more churches than Seattle has Starbucks outlets.) As you explore the city, pop into any church that piques your curiosity to see what treasures you discover. You'd be surprised what masterpieces you can discover by breaking off and exploring on your own. **Santa Maria Maggiore** (Termini, Bus: Equilino-Cavour, bus 70), with its beautiful ceiling and cavernous space; the science-oriented **Santa Maria degli Angeli e degli Martiri** (Termini, Bus: Repubblica, bus 64 or 70); and **San Bartolomeo dell'Isola** (Isola Tiberina, Bus: Sonnino, bus H), uniquely located on the island in the river, are some of my favorites.

Free, open dawn-dusk

Monti District

If you're exhausted from marathoning through the Roman Forum and Vatican City, this quiet neighborhood just north of Ancient Rome might be a welcome change of pace. Monti offers a glimpse into Roman life and is a hive for up-and-coming artisan shops. Wander along **Via Leonina,** which runs parallel to the bigger avenue, **Via Cavour,** to find some of Monti's gems. On Via Leonina alone, you'll find numerous excellent restaurants, **Finnegan's Irish Pub** (Via Leonina 66); **Rome's Ice Bar** (Via della Madonna dei Monti 28), where everything inside is made out of ice, including the cups you drink from; and **MercatoMonti** (Via Leonina 46), an awesome boutique designer minimarket where local jewelry and fashion designers come to sell their one-off handmade goods. MercatoMonti is most popular in the evening hours.

Free, always open, Ancient Rome, Metro: Cavour

TOP EATS

The cuisine is easily one of the highlights of any visit to Rome. There are choices to suit just about any budget. Breakfast is a cheap and simple affair: pastry and espresso. Your target price for each should be about a euro. If you're paying more for that, you're likely in a touristy café. For lunch, I love stopping into any little bakery (*paninoteca*) for delicious freshly made sandwiches. Some of my favorite Roman dishes are **cacio e pepe** (pasta with cheese and pepper), **carbonara** (egg, bacon, pecorino cheese, and pepper over spaghetti), and **amatriciana** (tomato-based sauce over buccatini, a type of thick spaghetti with a hole running through it, reminiscent of a pool noodle). When looking at dinner menus, watch out for "false friends" as we called them in my language classes: *Pepperoni* are bell peppers, *acciughe* are anchovies (not artichokes), and *margherita* refers to the tomato, basil, and cheese pizza—not the tequila-laden drink.

And there's an Italian tradition that you just cannot miss: **aperitivi**. Many bars offer access to an extensive, yet simple buffet included with the price of any drink. You'll find many young professionals heading to their favorite bar after work to take advantage of this incredible deal. The spread often includes things like cold bean and pasta salads, tiny slices of pizza, and tasty focaccia bread. Get your fill for the price of one €6 drink.

Tipping in Italy is not required, but about 10 percent is appreciated. Look at your receipt to determine whether or not *"servizio incluso"* appears, which means a service charge was included.

Miscellanea

Frisky Mikki runs this popular lunch and dinner spot located just at the back corner of the Pantheon. Pumping out pasta dishes, meat, salad, and delicious bruschetta, Miscellanea is a favorite of all who come here, from Italian senators and the Swiss Guard to poor study-abroad students and tourists like you. All are attracted to the fun and quick service and the welcoming atmosphere. Immensely popular among students is a menu I designed with these guys a few years ago: For €15 you get bruschetta, pizza, two types of pasta, dolce, water, red and/or white wine, and of course, Mikki's famous Sexy Wine. Be sure to tell him *"ciao bello"* for me!

THE ORDER—AND THE ORDERING—OF FOOD

In Italy, food is like a religion: You do things a certain way because that's the way it has always been done, and who are you to question it?

Aperitivo: Kick off your meal with a drink to toast with. This can often be a flute of Prosecco or Spumante.

Antipasti: Begin your feast with cold cuts (*salumi*) and a selection of cheeses. Prosciutto, salami, and savory cheeses are quite typical.

Primo: This is typically a pasta or otherwise carb-focused course, like a risotto. Don't overload on this course, because you've still got several more on the way!

Secondo: This is your meat course. Don't ask for chicken pesto pasta because Italians don't mix pasta and meat. It's sacrilege. So enjoy your pasta course, and then dig into something like pork chops, steak, or chicken breast with potatoes and veggies on the side.

Insalata: While we start with a salad, the Italians finish with it. Expect it to be light and leafy.

Formaggi/frutta/dolce: What better way to finish your meal than with a selection of cheese or fruit? These will come before any sort of *dolce* (sweet), which may well be gelato, tiramisu, pannecotta, or cake.

Caffè/digestivo: To keep you going into the night, cap everything off with a single espresso. At this time, many also have a round of whiskey or a typical grappa, *limoncello* (lemon liqueur), or *sciacchetrà* (Italian sweet wine).

Plates and sandwiches from €8, feast for €15, daily 11:00-late, Via Della Palombella 34/35, Pantheon Neighborhood, +39 06 6813 5318, Facebook: Miscellanea Pub, Bus: Largo Argentina

Isola del Panino

Between Largo Argentina and the Pantheon, you'll find one of the best values in the heart of Rome. This one-man show, run by friendly Fabio, attracts power lunchers and budget backpackers alike. Fabio doesn't speak much English, so order your sandwich fillings by pointing to the fresh ingredients (chicken, beef, ham, turkey, salads, cheeses, other toppings, and sauces) in the glass case. They'll toast the sandwich and wrap it in a way you can eat while on the go; there's no seating here, just a skinny bar on the sidewalk.

From €3.50, Mon–Sat 11:00-14:00, Via Monterone 19, Pantheon Neighborhood, +39 06 6830 7769, +39 328 785 8717, Bus: Largo Argentina

Obicà Mozzarella Bar

I love the experience of eating at Obicà: tour Italy through the prism of fresh mozzarella cheese. Your place mat is a map of Italy that explains where your locally and regionally sourced ingredients are coming from. The restaurant has a mod, sophisticated decor, and I like how the servers are clearly passionate about their ingredients.

Dinners from €12, daily 06:30-02:00, Piazza Campo de' Fiori 16, Pantheon Neighborhood, obica.com, Bus: Largo Argentina

Il Forno

Not a restaurant, but an excellent spot to drop in and get a bready snack at any time day or night—I love their salty focaccia bread. Il Forno (The Oven) has an excellent location right on the corner of Campo de' Fiori, making it a convenient stop whenever the mood strikes.

Snacks from €1.50, Mon–Sat 07:30-14:30 and 16:40-20:00, Piazza Campo de' Fiori, Pantheon Neighborhood, +39 06 6880 2366, Bus: Largo Argentina

Tre Scalini

Tre Scalini, with their outdoor seating spilling out onto Piazza Navona, is famous for their to-die-for chocolate-ice cream truffles. Imagine dark, white, and milk chocolate rolled into a ball then dusted with chocolate powder and sprinkles and you're almost there. The only other thing you've got to do is shovel it down! When you're ready for nightlife, some of my favorite joints are just down the alley leading away from the square toward Piazza del Fico.

From €6, daily 12:30-15:50 and 19:00-24:00, Piazza Navona 30, Pantheon Neighborhood +39 06 687 9148, ristorante-3scalini.com, Bus: Largo Argentina

Casa del Café Tazza d'Oro

This café still offers one of my favorite frozen treats in Rome: their famous *granita al café*, or coffee granita. Pay at the counter in the back first, *then* bring your receipt to the front to claim your prize. Personally, I like to ask for more granita, less whipped cream: "*Per favore, piu granita, meno crema.*"

From €1.50, Mon–Sat 07:00–20:00, Sun 10:30–19:30, Via degli Orfani 84, Pantheon Neighborhood, +39 06 678 9792, tazzadorocoffeeshop.com, Bus: Largo Argentina

Alice Pizza

Alice Pizza near the Vatican offers my favorite pizza by the slice. You know it must be good when old nuns elbow you out of the way to order. Head into either of the doors, and get to the front of the line. Don't hesitate when it's your turn to order or you'll miss your chance, and don't be afraid to ask for more *or* less! The ladies at this place serve delicious pizza, but don't expect any smiles.

From €4, Mon–Sat 11:00–18:00, Via delle Grazie 9, Vatican City Neighborhood, +39 06 687 5746, Metro: Ottaviano

Dar Poeta

Rome's best pizzeria is tucked away in a small alley in Trastevere. Run by three friends, this place pumps out an incredible menu of wood-fired pizzas for a great price. If you're in a spicy mood, go for the *lingua del fuoco*. Hungry? Ask for *"pizza alto"* to get a double crust. Be sure to save some room for their famous *calzone cioccolatto* (chocolate calzone), big enough to split amongst friends... Or don't share and keep it all for yourself. I won't tell.

Pizzas from €8, daily 12:00–15:00, 19:00–late, Vicolo del Bologna 45, Trastevere, +39 06 588 0516, darpoeta.com, Bus: Sonnino/Piazza Belli

Carlo Menta

Carlo Menta is a Trastevere institution that packs out with locals for fresh pasta, artichokes, and lasagna. If you lived in Rome, this is where you might come for Sunday afternoon brunch with your family and grandparents. I love it for the cheap prices (pizza from €3.50!). Don't expect any niceties from the busy staff, but you can count on solid value even with the €1.50 cover charge. Split the liter of table wine with friends for a reasonable €8.

Dinners from €5, daily 12:00–24:00, Via della Lungarina 101, Trastevere, +39 06 580 3733, Bus: Sonnino/Piazza Belli

Hostaria del Moro (aka Tony's)

A favorite of the study-abroad students in Rome, this is your go-to feast for €15 on the west side of the Tiber. Tony and the boys have boiled the experience down to a science: fast service, great food—pastas, pizzas, meats, fish, and desserts—at fair prices. Your best bet is to sit down and go with the flow, enjoying whatever comes your way—seriously, Tony will dictate the menu to you, and I always go for whatever is recommended. It's up to you to engage with the waiters. When they're busy, you may need to request the check a few times.

Dinners from €11, daily 19:00–late, Vicolo del Cinque 36, Trastevere, +39 06 580 9165, Bus: Sonnino/Piazza Belli

ITALIAN COFFEE

Italians love their espresso almost as much as their Vespas. It can seem a bit intimidating to join in on the tradition, but you've got to do it at least once. Italians consider coffee a digestive, not to be consumed *with* food, only *after* food. Expect to pay about €1 per espresso, €2 per cappuccino, and double that if you'd like to sit down rather than take it at the bar.

Here's a breakdown of your options at any normal Roman *caffè*:

Caffè: Your standard single shot of espresso, consumed in one toss back.

Doppio: A double espresso.

Macchiato: Espresso "stained" with just a touch of hot, steamed milk. This is my favorite one to try.

Cappuccino: Your standard espresso and steamed milk mix, though it's smaller than the Starbucks counterpart you may be used to. *Never* to be ordered or consumed after the clock strikes noon. Italians believe that milk must not be consumed anytime after breakfast, so keep this in mind while preparing to order.

Caffè Americano: American-style coffee, as interpreted by Italians, meaning espresso diluted with hot water.

Caffè Corretto: An espresso "corrected" with a shot of liquor. Italians enjoy mixing coffee with grappa. My favorite is to have it with a splash of Baileys, the perfect blend of liquor and cream.

Caffè Ristretto: An even denser, more intense shot of espresso.

Fish Market Trastevere

For fresh seafood at a great price, head to Trastevere's best fast seafood joint, Fish Market. The jovial, welcoming staff squeezes you like sardines into tables packed with locals, handing you a paper menu and pencil. Order à la carte oysters, prawns, fish, salads, and more, checking off all the various samplings you want, then take your order up to the register and pay. With all the *frittura* (fried food), it can be a heavy meal, but oh so good! Don't forget a nice bottle of white wine to wash down your selections!

Plates from €5, Mon–Fri 19:30–01:00, Sat–Sun 13:00–16:00, Vicolo della Luce 2, Trastevere, +39 366 914 4157, fishmarket-roma.com, Bus: Sonnino/Piazza Belli

Pizzeria del Secolo

When I'm in the mood for a snack in the Termini neighborhood, this is where I come. Friendly pizza maestros keep the ovens hot all day, creating steaming pizza masterpieces like *caprese* (Capri style), sausage, potato, and eggplant. Order and pay by weight, and wait as they heat up your selection before chowing down at their high-top tables. This is Italian fast food at its finest.

From €3, daily 11:00–23:00, Via Vicenza 46, Termini, +39 041 0298 0580, Metro: Termini

TOP GELATO

Gelato is not just a treat for tourists. At just about any time of year, you'll see locals of all ages frequenting their favorite *gelateria* (ice cream shop). Zeroing in on the places where you hear the most Italian is a surefire way to get good gelato in your cone. There are tons of knock-your-socks-off *gelaterie* across Rome. For tips on finding the best, see page 142.

Giolitti

Pay for your order as you step in the door, then take your receipt over to the overflowing supply of chillingly good flavors. Giolitti is located a three-minute walk away from the Pantheon, so can you really *not* go to this place every day? I don't think so.

From €2.50, daily 07:00–01:30, Via degli Uffici del Vicario 40, Pantheon Neighborhood, +39 06 699 1243, Bus: Largo Argentina

Gelateria del Teatro

I like this place because you can watch your gelato being made right in front of your eyes. Pop in here and ask what's being made, and what is the freshest off the press.

I tend to go for the coffee and pistachio flavors.

From €2, daily 12:00–24:00, Via dei Coronari 65, Pantheon Neighborhood, +39 06 4547 4880, Bus: Largo Argentina

Old Bridge

This famous *gelateria* is perfectly situated to fortify you for (or help you recover from) the daunting Vatican experience. There's always a line halfway around the block for Old Bridge, but don't be scared; just roll up your sleeves and dive into the crowd. Get up to the front and place your order, paying as you do so. This business has thankfully opened up another location in Trastevere (Via della Scala 70), making for another perfect post-dinner stop.

From €2.50, Mon–Sat 09:00–02:00, Sun 14:30–02:00, Viale Bastioni di Michelangelo 5, Vatican City Neighborhood, +39 06 4559 9961, gelateriaoldbridge.com, Metro: Ottaviano

Ice Cream Factory

I was skeptical at first, but was pleasantly surprised that this new entry into the gelato scene adheres wonderfully to the traditional processes. Don't be afraid to ask for a sampler from the friendly staff: "*Posso assaggiare?*" (POSS-so assad-JAH-ray).

From €2, daily 10:00–24:00, Via Palestro 47, Termini, Metro: Termini

TOP NIGHTLIFE

While some Americans are always about the next shot or moving on to the next bar, their Italian counterparts much prefer getting lost in the moment and catching up with friends in the streets. Italian students also work with a rather tighter budget generally—so it's easier to enjoy a beer on the square rather than pay for a mixed drink at the bar. That's why you may notice mostly internationals inside the bars, with the locals hanging out outside.

Unfortunately, creepers abound at nightlife venues. That's not to say that ladies can't have a good time out. But to my surprise, there seem to be plenty of men grabbing ass at the clubs. It's also important to keep an eye on your drink, as roofies are unfortunately not all that rare in the discos in town. There are just as many creepers in Testaccio as there are at your local Phi Delta Theta chapter. Don't let this get in the way of your fun, but do be smart and keep your wits about you.

NIGHTLIFE DISTRICTS

Nightlife varies by neighborhood in Rome. The cheap student bars tend to bunch together, with the glitzy clubs sprinkled here and there throughout the city. These are my favorite neighborhoods.

Trastevere

Local students like to drink beers on the steps of **Piazza Trilussa,** located right at the end of the Ponte Sisto bridge crossing the Tiber River. American study-abroad students love to hang out around **G Bar** and **Almalu Shot Bar**. And I like to explore and get lost in Trastevere's windy streets. You're sure to stumble upon some great hole-in-the-wall bars or cafés where you could have experiences absolutely unique to Rome.

Trastevere, Bus: Sonnino/Piazza Belli

Campo de' Fiori

Overrun with grungy locals and American students, this "field of flowers" morphs from a daytime market to a happening nightspot after the sun goes down. Do a lap of the square to pick out the vibe you like most. Its proximity to Largo Argentina bus stop is great for taking the night bus home or catching a taxi. Hungry later? **Aristocampo** *paninoteca* (Piazza della Cancelleria 93) makes excellent sandwiches fresh to go from €3.50!

Pantheon Neighborhood, Bus: Largo Argentina

Piazza Navona

Classy—if touristy—cafés line this square. Just off the square to the west you can find excellent and affordable local pubs, like **Bar del Fico,** offering great drinks and an extensive *aperitivo*, with no Americans in sight.

Pantheon Neighborhood, Bus: Largo Argentina

San Lorenzo

With dark streets full of mingling Italians and not a tourist in sight, this is one of the most authentic nightlife districts in Rome. East of Termini, San Lorenzo bars offer €4 drinks and there is *pizza al taglio* (by the slice) on just about every corner. The action centers on two main streets, **Via Tiburtina** and **Via dei Sardi,** from which you can turn in just about any direction and discover your own tangle of bars and cafés. Some travelers may associate the dark streets and people milling about with a bad vibe, but this is just what makes San Lorenzo that much more authentic. Start your night at the dependable **La Piazetta** (Largo Degli Osci 15-19) for cheap beers, *aperitivo*, and pizza by the slice.

San Lorenzo, Metro: Termini

Testaccio

Rome's ancient garbage dump for used clay containers has decomposed into a hill into which some of Rome's trendiest clubs have burrowed. (Look closely, and you'll see the entire hill is made of broken down

LGBT ROME

Italy is generally very accepting of the LGBT community, and LGBT travelers will have no trouble experiencing Rome. The streets directly behind the Colosseum, following Via San Giovanni in Laterano, have come to be known as Rome's gay district. Here, you'll find great lunch spots, cafés, restaurants, and bars. **L'Alibi** (€10 cover, Via di Monte Testaccio 44, +39 06 574 3448), in Testaccio, is one of Rome's most popular gay clubs. For more information and listings, head to **Arcigay,** Italy's LGBT association (Via Goito 35b, +39 06 645 011 02, arcigay.it).

and stacked ceramics). For the clubs, dress up and play the part, as this is definitely Rome's top neighborhood and draws a posh crowd. I recommend doing a lap around the district and selecting the club that looks best to you—do your best to get a sense of the ratio of ladies and gents inside before you pay, as you'll often find the ratio leaning far to the guys. Ask at your hostel for best transportation connections. You'll probably be cabbing it back at the end of the night. Remember, Uber works in Rome!

Testaccio, Metro: Piramide

BARS
Niji Café
Easily my favorite cocktail bar in Rome, this speakeasy-style lounge kicks ass. Sometimes you step into a place staffed by wannabe hipsters. Niji only employs real ones, complete with aprons and, if you're lucky, handlebar mustaches. Rather than fumbling through complex, Prohibition-era drinks, they know them like the back of their hand, and the drinks they throw together are made with tender loving care, all in a refined and cozy faux-reading room setting. Order an old-fashioned and sip on the good life.

Drinks from €7, daily 18:00–02:00, Via dei Vascellari 35, Trastevere, +39 06 581 9520, Bus: Sonnino/Piazza Belli

Almalu Shot Bar
This teensy tiny little bar back in the alleys of Trastevere is famous for its creative shots. Known for varieties such as the Harry Potter shot and the Blowjob shot, Almalu features drink specials throughout the week and was the innovator that brought the €1 shot night onto the scene. This bar is often standing room only, with customers spilling out and socializing on the nearby streets.

Shots from €1, Mon-Sat 18:00–late, Via Della Scala 77, Trastevere, +39 06 5833 3558, Bus: Sonnino/Piazza Belli

Vendita Libri, Cioccolata e Vino
I suppose every bar needs a gimmick here in Trastevere. Some pull it off quite well and others struggle, but this spot, the name of which translates to the Book, Chocolate, and Wine Store, takes the cake. Each shot is served in a shot glass made of chocolate. More of a curiosity than anything else because it feels like you're drinking in your local bookstore, this place is worth popping into for a quick one and then moving on.

Shots from €2, Mon-Fri 18:30–02:00, Sun 14:00–02:00, Vicolo del Cinque 11a, Trastevere, +39 065 830 1868, Bus: Sonnino/Piazza Belli

G Bar
Gilded in ostentatious gold, G Bar draws the crowd that loves rocking out to Lady Gaga and Nicki Minaj. Getting a drink upstairs takes patience, and you'll be lucky if you can breathe downstairs. (This dance bar does not enforce a max capacity.) Nonetheless, this bar is very popular with the study-abroad crowd and local observers. The drinks are cheap and strong!

Shots from €2, daily 15:00–late, Vicolo Dei Cinque 60, Trastevere, +39 347 994 1825, g-bar.it, Bus: Sonnino/Piazza Belli

Q's Rummeria Rum Bar Trastevere
This place takes sugar cane-derived alcohol seriously. With an entire wall full of more shades of amber than you can shake a sugar stick at, the Rum Bar serves just what you'd think: shots and concoctions made with rum as the base ingredient. Be sure to give the freshly casked honey rum a try! Once you get your sipper, climb the stairs to get lost in their stash of games, like Connect Four and Pick Up Sticks. Don't miss the retro *Playboy* magazine covers in the stairwell, either.

Drinks from €3, daily 19:30–02:00, Vicolo Moroni 53, Trastevere, +39 331 996 6996, qsrummeria.it, Bus: Sonnino/Piazza Belli

Akbar
Akbar is Roman shabby chic on steroids. Come out to this bar for coffee in the morning, an extensive *aperitivo*, or drinks late into the night. I love the funky decoration, unique seating, and cool crowd that packs this place out late every night.

Drinks from €5, Mon-Thurs 08:30–02:00, Fri-Sat 08:30–03:00, Sun 10:00–02:00, Piazza in Piscinula, Trastevere, +39 06 580 0681, Bus: Sonnino/Piazza Belli

Freni e Frizioni
This trendy *aperitivo* bar has taken over what used to be a mechanics garage with a name that fits: Brakes and Transmissions. Chow down on their extensive nightly buffet and get stuffed for the price of a drink. In warm weather, the cool crowd spills out onto an intimate little square. Come out to this place and feel like a local.

Aperitivi from €6, daily 06:30–02:00, Via del Poloteama 4/6, Trastevere, +39 064 549 7499, Bus: Sonnino/Piazza Belli

Il Baretto
If you can find and get into this place, located about a 15-minute walk from the Sonnino/Piazza Belli bus stop, you'll think you've discovered an oasis of Italian trendi-

ness unspoiled by the tourist hordes. It's bordering on pretentious, so dress nice and act the part to enjoy an excellent happy hour and an *aperitivo* that suits any budget. At sunset, enjoy the outdoor patio overlooking the city with a crowd that smugly knows it is indeed in the know.

Drinks from €8, Mon–Sat 07:00–02:00, Via G. Garibaldi 27, Trastevere +39 06 589 6055, Bus: Sonnino/Piazza Belli

Sloppy Sam's

With seating spilling out onto Campo de' Fiori, Sloppy Sam's is an excellent choice for unpretentious—if touristy—drinks and people-watching. Frequent specials throughout the week draw budget-oriented booze-hounds and students. The bar inside is like any other dark dive bar, but the international bartenders seem to do just fine passing out drinks with a smile.

Drinks from €5, daily 09:00–03:00, Piazza Campo de' Fiori 10, Pantheon Neighborhood, +39 06 6688 02746, sloppysamsrome.com, Bus: Largo Argentina

Drunken Ship

Drunken Ship is a fave with the expat crew looking to down shots and play some beer pong. Don't come looking for especially cheap drinks or for an authentic local experience. Do come for an enjoyable time getting drunk with fellow international backpackers. Somehow the guys at Drunken Ship have figured out the impossible: convincing cheap students to buy expensive drinks every night of the week!

Drinks from €5.50, daily 15:00–03:00, Piazza Campo de' Fiori 20, Pantheon Neighborhood, +39 06 6830 0535, drunkenship.com, Bus: Largo Argentina

Caffè Peru

Caffè Peru is possibly the cheapest pregame bar open late in Rome. If the Giordano Bruno statue walked forward, turned left and exited Piazza Campo de' Fiori, turned right after a block and continued north one block, it would arrive at the brightly lit Café Peru. Don't come here for the decor, but this is a great place to enjoy beers with friends in an unassuming, mostly empty bar that no one seems to know about.

Drinks from €3, Mon–Sat 06:30–02:00, Sun 09:00–21:00, Via di Monserrato 46, Pantheon Neighborhood, +39 06 687 9548, Bus: Largo Argentina

Bar del Fico

Named after the piazza outside, Bar del Fico is a popular and casual spot to grab a drink with friends. It's best known for its all-you-can-eat *aperitivo* buffet, from which I'm guilty many times over of getting my dinner fill, at the price of my rum and Coke.

Drinks from €5, daily 08:00–02:00, Piazza del Fico 26, Piazza Navona, Pantheon Neighborhood, +39 066 880 8413, bardelfico.com, Bus: Largo Argentina

Abbey Theater

This Irish pub just around the corner from Piazza Navona is a great spot to catch a game on one of its 14 TVs. It also boasts free Wi-Fi, excellent happy hours, and live Irish music on the weekends! But did you really come all the way to Rome for €12 burgers and Guinness? Who knows, maybe you did!

Drinks from €5.50, daily 12:00–02:00, from 11:00 on weekends, Via del Governo Vecchio 51, Piazza Navona, Pantheon Neighborhood, +39 06 686 1341, abbey-rome.com, Bus: Largo Argentina

Scholar's Lounge

Located between Largo Argentina and Piazza Venezia, Scholar's is a cornerstone to almost every semester-abroad experience in Rome. They're open late, with karaoke nights twice a week and excellent cover bands on the weekends. Game on? They'll be playing it no matter the hour.

Drinks from €5, daily 11:00–03:30, Via del Plebiscito 101, Pantheon Neighborhood, +39 06 6920 2208, scholarsloungerome.com, Bus: Largo Argentina or Piazza Venezia

Bar Open Baladin

Beer buffs will notice it's difficult—and expensive—to find a nice cold pint in Rome. IPAs are just about impossible to find in Italy, but Baladin will get you as close as possible with their wide selection of beers both on tap and by the bottle. This bar serves artisan beer with a full menu of massive burgers, from the standard bacon cheeseburger to more creative versions topped with mozzarella and basil mayonnaise. Their hand-cut fries are delicious, too!

Pints from €5.50, daily 12:00–01:00, Via degli Specchi 6, Pantheon Neighborhood, +39 06 683 8989, openbaladin-roma.it, Bus: Largo Argentina

CLUBS

If you're trying to club, Testaccio is the place to go. More than a dozen clubs and bars encircle this mound that rises up near the Piramide metro stop, and your best bet is to dress to the nines, pregame hard (drinking at the clubs is expensive), and split a cab home with friends. Do your best to pick a place close to midnight, and plan on sticking around—once the club goers show up, lines get long!

Akab

Akab is Testaccio's most famous and longest-running dance club, spinning a wide mix of music from house and dance music to even "Straight Outta Compton" hip-hop and R&B. Check the website for upcoming events that take over this club, which has two floors and a massive dance floor, and be sure to dress well to get through the door.

€10 cover, Thurs-Sat 23:30-05:00, Via di Monte Testaccio 69, Testaccio, +39 06 5725 0585, akabclub.com, Metro: Piramide

L'Alibi

L'Alibi is a popular gay-and-straight-friendly club featuring drag shows during breaks in the house techno and dance music. Check out the website for details and shows. Recently, Friday has been deemed "Hetero Night," but all are welcome throughout the weekend. Rock out over two dark levels with low-slung arches, plus an open patio and terrace during the hot summer months.

€10 cover, Thurs-Sun 23.30-05.00, Via di Monte Testaccio 44, Testaccio, +39 06 574 3448, lalibi.it, Metro: Piramide

Shari Vari Playhouse

Shari Vari, a posh and ultra-pretentious nightclub, comes with discerning doormen and velvet ropes to keep you out, as well as sexy bartenders and great DJs to keep the party going once you get in. It's popular among Rome's young professionals and jet-set elite; those who come here can afford the €12 drinks, and they dress like it too. You can stop in here for coffee and breakfast and even *aperitivo* before the venue transforms into its trendy, swanky house and techno-spinning self. Themed nights go down often. Consider reserving a table with friends ahead of time to skip the fuss at the door—as long as the budget permits.

Cover and drinks from €10, daily 08:00-04:00, Via di Torre Argentina 78, Pantheon Neighborhood, +39 06 680 6936, sharivari.it, Bus: Largo Argentina

PUB CRAWLS

Since the city enacted an ordinance outlawing pub crawls, these moving parties have taken a direct hit. Recently, they've reincarnated as parties that start in one place then go to their last stop at a club, which renders them technically legal but of questionable value.

Rome's Ultimate Party (aka Spanish Steps Pub Crawl)

These guys have dominated the Roman party scene for the last decade and have adapted their itinerary to the new laws laid out by the city council. While the route may struggle as far as quantity of stops, the party definitely does not.

€25, free wine, beer, and mixed drinks until 22:00, pizza and drink specials included, +39 06 4544 7204, pubcrawlrome.com

TOP SHOPPING & MARKETS

Many know Italy to be the world capital of fashion and fine living. You can find everything in this city, from €1,200 purses and €5,000 suits all the way down to wares and goods for us mere peasants. Enjoy the window-shopping, find some great deals if you time your visit with the semi-annual sales, or *saldi* (July-mid-August and January-mid-February), and get even better deals at the outdoor markets.

SHOPPING DISTRICTS

Via del Corso

Translating directly to "Way of the Race," Via del Corso was once just that: a horse-racing track. Horse racing here was a popular spectator sport until a noblewoman saw a gruesome accident right underneath her VIP window. After that, the city council outlawed horse racing in Rome. Today, Via del Corso, extending south from Piazza del Popolo toward Piazza Venezia, is a bustling modern avenue with tons of recognizable Italian brands and shops, including Diesel, H&M, and Zara. It's relatively more "blue collar" than the district immediately toward the Spanish Steps.

North Rome, Metro: Flaminio or Spagna, Bus: Piazza Venezia

Shopping Triangle of Death

Leave Via del Corso toward the Spanish Steps and you'll enter the area I've affectionately dubbed the Shopping Triangle of Death, home to high fashion stores Zegna, Gucci, Prada, Yves Saint Laurent, and Louis Vuitton. The district is near the Piazza di Spagna, with the streets of Via del Corso, Via del Babuino, and Via del Tritone forming the triangle. This is where fashion-conscious Italians come to spend their inheritance. This high-end fashion district is designed for deep pockets...and big-brand window-shopping for the rest of us.

North Rome, Metro: Spagna

MARKETS
Porta Portese

This Sunday morning market is fundamental for a true Roman experience. Throughout history, cheap vendors have hung out just outside city walls to avoid paying city taxes.

While the walls of Rome have fallen, the tradition survives today. Go early on Sunday morning, and leave everything but a little bit of spending cash: Porta Portese is notorious for pickpockets who prey on bewildered tourists lost in the throngs of shoppers. I would also think twice before biting into one of the pork sandwiches for sale on the street... Just speaking from personal experience.

Sun 06:30-13:30, Trastevere, Bus: Sonnino/Piazza Belli

TOP PARKS & RECREATION

Giardino degli Aranci

Located on the south side of town, across the river from Trastevere and just north of Testaccio, this picturesque little garden of orange trees faces north and west. It's a quiet and welcome respite from the busy streets of Rome. With Testaccio's daily bustling farmers market nearby, this place makes an excellent picnic spot. Enjoy the view from the square, and before descending back into Rome's screaming traffic, check out **Il Buco di Roma** (The Mouth of Rome) nearby. Il Buco di Roma is a keyhole through which you can peer to see the sovereign Priory of the Knights of Malta in the foreground, Roman buildings in the distance, and the dome of St Peter's far off on the horizon. It's a fascinating visual effect with three independent states in a single view.

To get here, take metro line B to Circo Massimo and head north along the track of the Circo Massimo. From there hang a left and go up the hill after about 300 meters.

Free, 07:00-sunset, Testaccio, Metro: Circo Massimo

Gianicolo Hill

Gianicolo (jah-KNEE-koh-lo), rising behind Trastevere and south of the Vatican, offers a beautiful panoramic view of the heart of Rome. See if you can't pick out the domed roof of the Pantheon, green Palatine hill, the crest of the Colosseum, and even Termini train station way off in the distance. The impressive building off to your left is the old Palace of Justice. For local teenagers, and even older *mammoni*, this is the place to sneak away to for a necking session at sunset. This hike is a good way to cap a visit to the Vatican and St Peter's Basilica.

Free, always open, Vatican City Neighborhood, Metro: Ottaviano

---

MAMMONI: DECONSTRUCTING THE MAMA'S BOY

Everyone loves a mama's boy—and in Italy, you've got about 10 million of them. Italian mothers put their sons on pedestals and smother them with love, food, clothes, and just about anything else you can imagine. With life so good, why would you ever move out? Add that to the prohibitive costs of buying an apartment or condo in town, and you've got a dilemma that is facing nearly all men in Italy: Should I stay or should I go?

Though it feels a bit like the plot of *Step Brothers*, in Rome, it's not unusual for Italian men to live at home until they break the ripe age of 40. Even then, the economic prospects are difficult when it comes to buying property. So you've got half the population with more than enough to live on at their parents' house, but nowhere near enough capital to buy a place. So where does their expendable income go? Food, fashion, and nightlife. Party!

This also introduces a dilemma: Where do you take a hot date? Well, if you get a feeling that Italian men are content with a grope and making out on the dance floor, it's because they really don't have a place to take a date home. You'll notice that viewpoints like the one on Gianicolo Hill are populated with couples who, ironically, go out in public to find a little privacy.

Villa Borghese

This tree-lined park, just to the north and east of town above Piazza del Popolo, was once a noble family's private gardens. Today, it's Rome's largest public playground, with manicured paths, a full-scale replica of Shakespeare's Globe Theatre, thousands of trees, the Galleria Borghese, and even Rome's zoo. It's a beautiful place for a picnic on a sunny day. Rent fun four-person **pedal carts** (€15/hour) or **bikes** (€6/hour) to explore the far corners of the park.

North Rome, Metro: Barberini

TOP TOURS

If you're on a tight budget, a high-quality tour in Rome may be beyond the means. But for history buffs, a tour guide's inside knowledge is well worth the price.

Walks of Italy

Walks of Italy connects you with excellent local guides who bring the ancient, confusing, and overwhelming history of Rome to vivid life. I appreciate Walks of Italy's attentive booking service and their passionate guides, who adapt to their audience depending on the balance of heavy history vs comedic relief preferred.

Walking tours starting at €29, museum tours from €49, +39 069 480 4888, walksofitaly.com/rome-tours

Eating Italy Food Tours

Gastro food tours have taken the world by storm, and Kenny and his team have developed an excellent walking tour through one of Rome's richest neighborhoods, Testaccio. Sample the fruits, sweets, pastries, *salumi* (cold cuts, including but not limited to salami), cheeses, pastas, coffees, and gelati of daily Roman life, all on this three-hour neighborhood walk. Eating Italy tours kicked off a craze that has been replicated many times over now by companies seeing just how successful these experiences are.

Testaccio Food Tour €75, +39 391 358 3117, eatingeuropetours.com

TOP HOSTELS

Hostels cluster around the Termini train station. This neighborhood has really cleaned up its act, and it gives you the best value for your money by far. What was a seedy set of streets is now welcoming and brighter, with some restaurant options nearby. Find more hostel options at **hostelworld.com.**

The Yellow Hostel

The Yellow just finished their subterranean micro-club, meaning that it finally lives up to its claim as a party hostel, and it has actually developed a following for its nightly specials. The rooms are clean, and the staff is welcoming and helpful. Private budget rooms and hotel rooms are also available. The on-site café and bar churns out great breakfast sandwiches and coffee to get the day started.

Dorms from €25, privates at €120, free Wi-Fi, iPad rentals, Via Palestro 44, Termini, +39 06 49 382 682, the-yellow.com, Metro: Termini

Alessandro's Palace

Alessandro's Palace, located near Termini, is fun, safe, clean, and bright, with an in-house bar downstairs, air-conditioning in all rooms, and a new rooftop terrace. Alessandro Palace's sister location, **Alessandro Downtown** (Via Carlo Cattaneo 23) is another solid budget option, located opposite Termini train station.

Dorms from €22, privates at €90, free Wi-Fi, sheets included, showers, towels for rent, Via Vicenza 42, Termini, +39 06 4461 958, hostelsalessandro.com, Metro: Termini

The Beehive Hostel & B&B

The Beehive has been helping budget travelers feel at home in Rome for years. With recent updates like an organic, on-site vegetarian café and welcoming outdoor garden, it's now more popular than ever. Choose from either a handful of dorm beds or a private room (reasonable €40/night). Check out their website for current rates and more details. If these guys don't have availability, they have a network to fall back on that will get you sorted.

Dorms from €25, privates from €40, check-in 07:00–23:00, check-ins outside this window for a fee, free Wi-Fi, sheets, showers, towels for rent, non-smoking, Via Marghera 8, Termini, +39 064 470 4553, the-beehive.com, Metro: Termini

ROME

Ciak Hostel

This is a smaller, more intimate option near the Termini neighborhood. I like this place as it feels more like home than a big commercial hostel. With only about 35 beds in funkily decorated, comfortable rooms (like a Madonna picture frame set over classic car wallpaper), you'll feel like you're hanging out at a friend's house rather than a hostel. Deluxe private rooms with double beds are worth inquiring about.

Beds from €19, free Wi-Fi, sheets, showers, towels for rent, Viale Manzoni 55, Termini, +39 06 7707 6703, ciakhostel. com, Metro: Termini

M&J Hostel

This recently renovated hostel is fun, laid-back, and staffed with helpful people at the reception desk. It's in a great location, just steps from Termini station, but consider yourself warned: The building is quite old; the hot water cuts out at times, and the sewage system seems like it needs to be improved. The smell can get unfortunate sometimes.

Dorms from €18, posh privates at €90, free Wi-Fi, bar venue downstairs, Via Solferino 9, Termini, +39 06 446 2802, mejplacehostel.com, Metro: Termini

TRANSPORTATION

Rome is well-connected by all modes of transportation. Just remember that not everything works the way you may think it should. Strikes frequently mess up travelers' plans; be sure to ask at the hostel if any may be coming up. Usually, public transport sectors try not to strike simultaneously, so as to avoid really messing the city up...but sometimes they do. Just do your best to roll with Italy's punches and you'll do just fine.

GETTING THERE & AWAY

Trains and buses arrive at Rome's main train station, **Termini,** located in the Termini neighborhood east of the city center. From Termini you can catch local buses, metro connections, and taxis to anywhere you need in Rome. All of my recommended hostels are within walking distance of the train station.

Plane

Rome has two airports: **Da Vinci-Fiumicino** (FCO, adr.it) and **Ciampino** (CIA, adr. it). Both airports take roughly the same amount of time and money to get to and from Termini.

The **Da Vinci Express Train** departs every 30 minutes from Da Vinci-Fiumicino and will get you to Termini in 30 minutes (€15). This is the fastest and most comfortable option connecting to Termini, but it's also more expensive than the buses or slower train.

Both airports are serviced by **Terravision** (terravision.eu) buses, your simplest and cheapest option at €8 single and €13 round-trip. Departures are frequent throughout the day and take about one hour. Check timetables and get more details online. On your departure day, it's worthwhile to go to the Terravision office well ahead of time to ensure you get on the bus you need to go on. On busy days, buses can fill up and you'll be stuck waiting for the next one or shelling out for a taxi.

Taxis now charge a flat rate from anywhere

within Roman city walls to both airports (and vice versa). The rate to and from FCO is €48. To and from CIA is €30.

Train

Though most trains arrive at **Termini** station, remember that Rome has other major train stations, including **Trastevere** and **Tiburtina**. Be sure to confirm your station if connecting out of Rome via train. From Florence, Rome is 1.5 hours via the fast train (from €25, reservation required) and 3.5 hours via the slow train (from €20). It's about 3.5 hours (€70) from Venice. You can find overnight options on slow trains as well.

Pickpockets take advantage of the commotion at train stations to snag tourists' wallets. Take the time on travel days to arrange your valuables securely into one safe place, either on you or in your bag that you know will not go anywhere. Be wary of distractions staged by pickpocketing teams in an effort to take your attention off your pockets. If you need cash, find the Bancomat (ATM) in the least trafficked area of the station.

Bus

All buses connect into Termini station, but most of the travel across Italy is done via train. You can find cheap domestic connections through **Eurolines** (eurolines.it) and their affiliates.

Car

I don't recommend driving in Italy. It

comes with just too much headache: traffic, parking, hidden speed trap cameras, etc. To rent a car, you'll need a passport and an international driver's license (purchase for US$20 from AAA before leaving home). Overall costs run high when you factor in everything that you'll be paying for: rental, insurance, gas, highway tolls, and any tickets you accidentally rack up.

GETTING AROUND

Navigating the streets is your first mission to accomplish, but with frequent *caffè* and gelato stops, I know you'll do just fine! The **bus, tram, and metro systems** use the same **ticket** (€1.50).

Metro

Rome's two metro lines intersect under the main train station, Termini. The red line, **line A,** will get you to the Spanish Steps (stop: Piazza di Spagna) and the Vatican (stop: Ottaviano). The blue line, **line B,** zips you over to the Colosseum (stop: Colosseo) and the Testaccio neighborhood farther south (stop: Piramide). There's a fabled line C under construction, and I'm hoping it will be completed at some point during my lifetime.

Bus

Buses in Rome work well but operate without timetables. Purchase a *biglietto* (ticket) at any *tabacchi* (tobacco shop). Once you're on the bus, be sure to validate it in the yellow boxes. Non-validated tickets can earn you a €50 fine. If an inspector catches you without a validated ticket, he or she may insist on taking you to an ATM so you can pay the fine on the spot. Ask for the written ticket instead to ensure these inspectors are legitimate, and whatever you do, don't hand over your passport or ID.

Orient yourself by getting familiar with the main bus points in the city: **Termini** (near most hostels), **Largo Argentina** (Pantheon,

historic center, nightlife), and **Piazza Venezia** (Vittorio Emanuele Monument, Via del Corso, Colosseum, and Scholar's Lounge). There are a few major bus routes you might find yourself using a lot. **Bus H** is the express bus from Termini to Trastevere, a neighborhood untouched by the two metro lines. For Trastevere, get off at **Sonnino/Piazza Belli,** just after you cross the river. **Buses 40** and **64** connect Termini and Vatican City, hitting the major Largo Argentina and Piazza Venezia bus stops along the way.

Tram

Rome has a limited tram network. **Tram 8** connects Piazza Venezia in central Rome with the Trastevere neighborhood. You may see other lines in town. As they don't intersect, riding them is really quite simple. Validate your ticket on the tram just as you would on the bus or metro.

Taxi

Taxis are a good way to get home at the end of the night and affordable if you split with friends. Make sure that the meter reads Tariffa 1 and that it starts at no more than €5 when you get in. The Tariffa 1 zone covers all of Rome inside the old city walls. As soon as you go outside of that, you'll jump to Tariffa 2. At night, taxis start their meters at €6.50. While higher in initial cost, I find Rome's taxi rates to climb relatively more slowly than taxis in other cities.

Bicycle

Rome isn't bicycle-friendly at all, so getting around on two wheels is not recommended. There are rental options in Villa Borghese, where you've got a few kilometers of trails without a car in sight. Via Appia Antica, the old Roman highway leading south to Naples and Sicily, is another place that's great to explore by bike, and you can stop at cafés and catacombs along the way.

DAY TRIPS

Touring Rome's major sights will easily fill three days and more. But if you've got more time, there are excellent options for day trips outside the city center.

Via Appia Antica

The Ancient Appian Way was one of the most important roads leading to Rome during the Roman Empire. It connected all settlements and territories south of Rome to the capital. And this several-kilometer section just outside of the modern city of Rome can still be seen today. Numerous crumbling churches, catacombs, tombs, and ancient ruins are sprinkled along the road, making taking a bike out here to explore very worthwhile. You'll also get a nice glimpse of the Italian countryside.

Allow just about all day for this excursion from the city center. Take bus 118 (leaves often) heading south toward the Via Appia Antica. Get off at Appia Pignatello—Erode Attico and follow signs to the "Via Appia Antica." From there, it's a three-kilometer walk back into the city center, where you can hop on the metro line B at Circo Massimo.

Free, always open, Greater Rome

EUR

Find Mussolini's best attempt at blending Ancient Roman architecture with stark and imposing fascist architecture just south of Rome at the development called EUR—a massive planned district complete with offices, residential buildings, a church, reflecting pools, and a massive sports stadium. It feels a bit like a college campus, without the life or soul. The EUR was supposed to embody the legacy of Ancient Rome while showing how advanced and perfect Italian culture and life was, but a walk through this inhabited ghost town that didn't quite realize its dream of becoming the New Rome gives you an eerie post-apocalyptic feeling. Accessible by metro, it's easy to spend a few hours exploring these streets. Three metro stops will put you at EUR: EUR Magliana, EUR Palasport, and EUR Fermi.

Free, always open, Greater Rome

HELP!

Tourist Information Centers

Many tourist information centers purport to be unbiased, but in fact only promote a limited number of tours. Pop in for a quick run-down of the city and a free map, but remember this when being offered tour options.

Pickpockets & Scams

Ladies should expect plenty of attention from locals. Keep your wits about you, whether you're in a cab or enjoying a night out. Italian men can be persistent and aggressive. It's nothing to worry about, but good to be aware of.

Rome does have a pickpocketing problem. Pickpockets usually work in teams and hang out in the most touristy areas: metros, bus 64, Spanish Steps, Termini train station, Campo de' Fiori, the Colosseum, and even inside the Vatican Museums. Try to identify pickpockets by sight, especially the ones

swaddling "babies," as the extra clothing often conceals a sly, quick hand. If there is any commotion around you first make sure your valuables are secure. Oftentimes the teams create a distraction on the bus or in the metro, and while everybody's attention is turned one way, there's a guy making off with purses and wallets in the opposite end of the bus.

Emergencies

Dial 118 for an ambulance, or 113 for police.

Hospital

Policlinico Umberto I

Via del Policlinico 155

+39 06 499 71

US Embassy

Via Vittorio Veneto 119

+39 06 467 41

FLORENCE

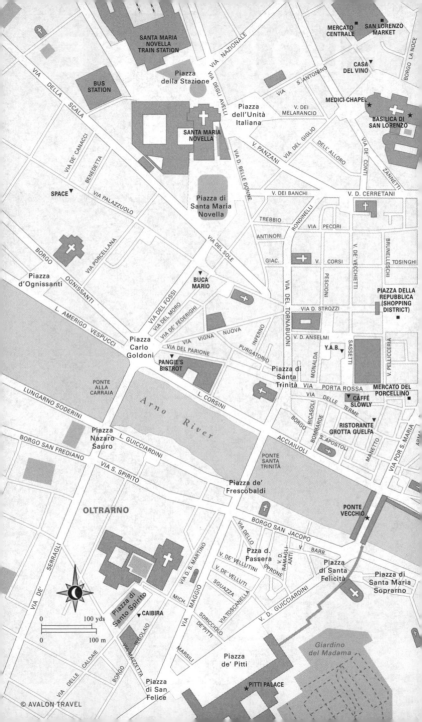

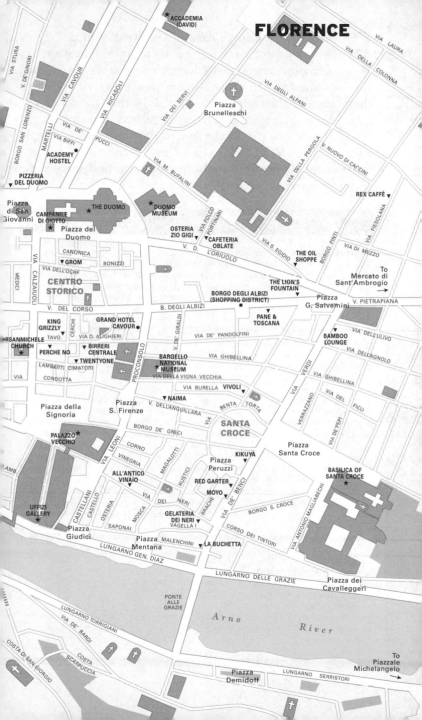

Florence is the birthplace of the Renaissance. You're sure to catch a whiff of inspiration yourself as you glimpse the city's iconic dome, gaze up at the *David* statue, and imagine Michelangelo himself walking these regal cobblestone streets. Luckily, this Tuscan city's larger-than-life reputation hasn't tarnished its charm. As a study-abroad hot spot and a key stop on the international backpacking circuit, Florence offers modern attractions, too—from fun student nightlife to cheap and tasty eats and unforgettable gelato.

FLORENCE 101

Founded as an important Roman outpost in AD 59, Florence sat on an important trade route from Rome leading north to the rest of the continent. With the fall of the Roman Empire, all of Europe fell into chaos. The Florence region was one of the first to bounce back economically from the turmoil of the Dark Ages after several hundred years. Traded back and forth between warring rivals, Florence finally emerged independent around AD 1100. The city extended its influence through banking and trade around the subcontinent and beyond as it grew into the medieval age.

By the 14th century, a quarter of Florence's population was supported by the wool and textile industries. With this trade, one family, the Medicis, rose to immense riches and power—it didn't hurt that the Medicis were the bankers to the pope, either. Cosimo de Medici (1389-1464) was the first of the family to hold significant influence over the city from behind the scenes. The wealthy Florentines had the luxury of splurging on the finer things in life, like art and architecture, which helped Cosimo kick off a wave of artistic, literary, and architectural innovation.

Lorenzo de Medici, Cosimo's grandson, was the family's biggest patron of the arts and devoted vast sums to a handful of promising artists. Some of his personal friends (Michelangelo, Leonardo da Vinci, Botticelli) changed the course of history with their contributions thanks to the support of Cosimo. This enlightenment of the human spirit and intellect—known as the Renaissance, or rebirth—ushered in developments at an accelerating rate, slowly wrenching the rest of Europe from the grip of feudalism. During the Renaissance, buildings became taller, windows bigger, and decoration more exuberant. Paintings were brighter and more lifelike. Artists came to be paid in relation to their skill, not as a function of the costs of their raw art materials. Technical developments like sewage disposal allowed for population growth and healthier, longer lives. It may seem like a stretch, but one wealthy family's investment in the arts revolutionized the world and continues to have a lasting impact today.

Florence was annexed as part of the Holy Roman Empire in the 18th century. Population growth and modernization efforts like cutting new boulevards for traffic and commerce continued into the 20th century. In World War II, Florence rested under Nazi occupation for a year before Allied troops chased them out. The departing Nazis destroyed as many river crossings as they could but spared the Ponte Vecchio, thanks to a rare consideration by Hitler of the historic importance of the bridge.

Today, Florence's lifeblood is tourism, tourism, and more tourism. This historic city sees millions of visitors every year, but with my suggestions, you'll be able to find your own little corner of this fascinating Renaissance town.

PLAN AHEAD

RESERVATIONS

Note that most museums in Florence, including the Uffizi and Accademia, are **closed on Monday.**

Reservations are recommended for the following sights:
Accademia (firenzemusei.it)
Uffizi Gallery (firenzemusei.it)

PASSES

Firenze Card

Serious sightseers should consider the **Firenze Card** (€72, valid for 72 hours, firenzecard.it), which provides free entry (and line-skipping privileges—just go to the head of each line and flash the card) to Florence's major museums. Your three days of exhaustive sightseeing kick off the moment you validate the pass, so be sure to line up your visits within this window. Before purchasing the card, add up the entry fees for all the sights you plan to see, then see how that total compares to the cost of the Firenze Card. The card includes the Uffizi, Accademia, Palazzo Vecchio, Medici Chapels, Bargello Museum, the Duomo (including the Baptistry and dome climb), Pitti Palace, the archaeological site of Fiesole, and over 50 other sights. Purchase the pass or find the full list of covered sights online, at the ticket offices of these museums, or at either of the tourist information centers in town. If you're planning on seeing each of the sights I've listed, this pass will just barely cover the cost—as you see, you've got to be quite busy (and up early) to get your money's worth. The Firenze Card also includes your public transportation for the three days of validity.

Duomo Sights

The Duomo itself is free, and a single ticket (€15) covers entry to all Duomo-related sights (Baptistry, dome climb, belltower climb, and the museum). The ticket, which you can buy at the ticket office (7 Piazza San Giovanni), is valid for six days after purchase. You must enter all the specified sights within 24 hours after your first entry.

THREE DAY ITINERARY

As the de facto capital of the Renaissance, Florence is packed to the rafters with famous museums displaying priceless artwork. Any short visit here is a mad dash mostly on foot to take in top sights. For the Uffizi and Accademia, I highly recommend making reservations well ahead of time to skip lines and avoid hours of waiting. Otherwise, opt for the pricey but effective Firenze Card as another way to skip the lines.

DAY 1: BENVENUTO A FIRENZE!

MORNING

Grab a hearty breakfast at your hotel before striking out to join the free walking tour. Consider today your chance to get acquainted with the city.

At 11:00, meet up with your fun local guide just in front of Santa Maria Novella for a free two-hour walking tour with **Florence Free Tour** to learn the basics about the history and culture of the city. You'll stroll past the **Duomo,** numerous famous piazze, and the **Uffizi,** and will learn some background info on the Ponte Vecchio.

AFTERNOON

Depending on where you end up, try out **Oil Shoppe** or **All'Antico Viniao** for fresh and cheap sandwiches to keep you going.

Continue on toward the iconic **Ponte Vecchio** for a beautiful view of the river. Cross the bridge into the **Oltrarno** neighborhood and stop at the **Piazza Santo Spirito** for an afternoon spritz cocktail.

LATE AFTERNOON

Stop to pick up a bottle of wine and maybe a snack to enjoy later, and climb up to the **Piazzale Michelangelo** for an awe-inspiring late afternoon panorama of the entire city of Florence. Bust out your picnic supplies and take in the scene. You can see the Duomo and San Lorenzo, along with the spine of Santa Croce and spire of the Palazzo Vecchio. Selfie with David, anyone? There's a replica of the famous statue up here in this square.

EVENING

Hungry? Start walking back the way you came, but hang a right on Via dei Benci and cross the Ponte alle Grazie to my favorite spot in the Santa Croce neighborhood for *aperitivi,* **Moyo.** Stop in here for a drink and access to an impressive buffet of simple local dishes while listening to the cool grooves from the DJ.

It's still early, so go back to your hostel to rest up, shower, and get ready for a crazy night out!

LATE

Return to the Santa Croce neighborhood to kick your night off right at some of my favorite spots, including **Naima, The Lion's Fountain**, and **Kikuya**, and go late at **Red Garter**.

DAY 2: UFFIZI & ACCADEMIA

MORNING

Overachiever? Get in line by 07:30 (yes, AM) at the **Uffizi** to avoid the lines that stretch through the rest of the day. Or better, sleep in and pat yourself on the back for making reservations ahead of time! You'll spend about two hours exploring this world-class museum.

AFTERNOON

Walk north about 10 minutes to the Piazza del Duomo for pizza by the slice at **Pizzeria del Duomo**, or stroll down Via dell'Oriuolo to the east of the Duomo to **Caffetteria Oblate** for a tasty lunch at a hidden yet beautiful library. If you saved room, some of my favorite *gelaterie,* **Grom** and **Perché No!,** are just a couple blocks away.

Spend the rest of the afternoon **climbing the dome** of the Duomo to get a better grasp on the scale of the engineering feat that truly kicked off the Renaissance. Can you imagine construction starting on the church's foundations before the technology existed to build a dome big enough to cap the church?

And if you're on your game, catch your afternoon **Accademia** reservations around 16:00 today and enjoy the one-floor museum to see the original of Michelangelo's masterpiece, *David.* Walk back to the hostel to rest up a bit and put those feet up.

Make sure you've got reservations for dinner if you're picking a popular spot like Buca Mario.

EVENING

On the way to dinner, pop into **Casa del Vino** for a sampling with my friend Gianni. Admire the old-school pictures hanging up on the wall as you sample some of Tuscany's best vintages. Then enjoy authentic Florentine fare at one of my favorite restaurants, like **Osteria Zio Gigi's**, **Buca Mario,** or **Osteria Brincello.**

LATE

Get classy at **Hotel Cavour's rooftop bar** and enjoy a cocktail with a beautiful view of central Florence. Afterward, join the party at my favorite downtown club, **Club TwentyOne,** just around the corner. Good night!

DAY 3: DAY TRIP OR SHOPPING

If you have the whole day, consider a day trip to **Fiesole** or a **Tuscan hill town,** just a short trip away. Otherwise, spend the morning shopping for leather goods and delicious local produce at the **San Lorenzo Market**. More time? Walk over to another one of Florence's world-class museums, the **Bargello**, in the afternoon.

TOP NEIGHBORHOODS

Florence's compact medieval center is called the **Centro Storico.** You can trace the old walls, tight medieval streets, and expansion beyond the walls on any city map. With the Duomo in the middle, the Centro Storico contains most of the sights tourists will want to see on a short visit. Here, you'll find the Accademia, the Uffizi Gallery, and the famous Ponte Vecchio, along with recommended restaurants, hostels, and nightlife venues.

Santa Croce, a few blocks east of the Duomo on the eastern edge of the historical center, is one of my favorite neighborhoods. This is where you'll find some of Florence's best nightlife, from trendy *aperitivo* bars to lounges and student favorites like Kikuya and Red Garter.

Crossing the Arno River, you enter into **Oltrarno,** translating roughly to "the other side of the Arno." This district is quieter, with more upscale restaurants and a fun local scene centered around Piazza Santo Spirito. It's also home to the Pitti Palace and the access point to the Piazzale Michelangelo viewpoint.

TOP SIGHTS

Uffizi Gallery

This extensive art museum fills out what were the offices of the astronomically wealthy Medici family. Today, you can tour these long hallways and corridors packed with priceless medieval and Renaissance works of art. The Uffizi museum takes you through their collection in chronological order, so you can see the transition from flat, gold-encrusted medieval triptychs to the voluminous and dimensional Michelangelo masterpieces. Find Botticelli's *Birth of Venus*, as well as paintings by da Vinci, Raphael, and Titian. Lines can be long. Reserve ahead, or go early or late to avoid the crowds.

€12.50, free first Sun of the month, Tues-Sun 08:15-18:35, closed Mon, Piazzale degli Uffizi, Centro Storico, +39 055 975 7007, uffizi.firenze.it

Accademia

Thankfully occupying only a single floor, this museum is the permanent home of Michelangelo's colossal little squirt, **David.** This magnificent example of sculptural *contraposto* (a stance where the weight is placed on one foot, with the corresponding hip jutting out slightly, adding tension and movement in otherwise static paintings and sculptures) captures the moment just before the underdog slew the giant in the biblical story of David and Goliath. Catch his gaze, and notice exaggerated features like furrowed eyebrows and large, veiny, oversized hands. The posture and embellishments go a long ways in bringing this stone to life. Monitors nearby allow visitors to get a close-up view on a high definition 3-D scan of the sculpture.

As you walk down the hallway from the entryway, toward the larger-than-life sculpture, you're flanked by Michelangelo's "prisoners," pieces that he never quite finished. Michelangelo believed he simply freed shapes from the confines of each block of marble. He could visualize the finished piece inside the stone before he ever took his first whack.

€12.50, additional €4 for reservation, free first Sun of the month, Tues-Sun 08:15-18:50, closed Mon, via Ricasoli 66, Centro Storico, +39 055 215449, accademia.firenze.it

The Duomo

Many say that the Cattedrale di Santa Maria del Fiore, or Duomo for short, is the building that kicked off the Renaissance. Brunelleschi, an engineer and architect, won the contract to dream up what was to be the greatest church around. He designed the floor plan

FLORENCE

and began construction on the cathedral before the technology to build a dome big enough to cap it even existed. A perfect example of form and function, the beautiful cathedral now dominates the Florentine sky line. Just about every large modern dome, from the Vatican to the Capitol building in Washington DC, can point to this structure for its inspiration. Even today, the scale and beauty of the Duomo is captivating as you **climb the dome,** moving through the space between the double-domed structure to get to the top. The inside, lighter dome provides the ceiling to the church. The tiled outer dome supports the lantern at the top and protects the church from the elements, a design that greatly diminished the weight of this structure. You can also **climb the bell-tower** for views over Florence. A heads-up for the claustrophobic: Both stair-stepping hikes gets quite tight and darker the higher up you go.

Back in the day, you were not allowed to enter a Catholic church without having been baptized. As such, the **Baptistry** of the Duomo was separated, and new converts were baptized there so they could then enter the church holy and cleansed. This famous octagonal baptistry sports three sets of large bronze double doors. These outward facing doors were a prime place to introduce the unbaptized and the illiterate to Christianity. The world-famous eastward-facing set recounts 10 stories from the Old Testament. Lorenzo Ghiberti's bronze doors were ground-breaking works of art, vividly depicting three-dimensional scenes on flat bronze panels. The doors you see are replicas. To see the originals, head to the interesting and worthwhile Duomo Museum.

Duomo free, €15 ticket covers dome climb, belltower, Baptistry, and Duomo Museum (you must enter all sights within 24 hours of first entry), Mon–Fri 10:00–17:00, Thu until 16:00 May and Oct, until 16:30 Nov–Apr; Sat 10:00–16:45, Sun 13:30–16:45, Piazza del Duomo, Centro Storico, +39 055 230 2885

Duomo Museum
If you're anything like your dear author, you love geeking out about how revolutionary structures like the Duomo are built. The Museo dell'Opera del Duomo is located just behind Brunelleschi's dome. This museum showcases Ghiberti's original Baptistry doors, along with historical drawings and images of Florence's main cathedral.

€15 ticket also covers Duomo dome climb, belltower, and Baptistry (must enter all sights within 24 hours after your first entry), Mon–Sat 09:00–19:00, Sun 09:00–13:45, last entry 45 minutes before closing, Piazza del Duomo 9, Centro Storico, +39 055 230 2885, museumflorence.com

Basilica di Santa Croce
The imposing facade of the main Franciscan church in Florence is a Renaissance veneer over a more modest 14th-century beginning. Famous for its permanently interred residents—Galileo Galilei, Lorenzo Ghiberti, Niccolo Machiavelli, Michelangelo Buonaroti, and Dante are all buried here—the church now costs €6 to go inside, but it's worth it for those really interested in Tuscan-style Renaissance churches. Just behind the church and through a garden, you'll find the **Leather School of Santa Croce** (free, observe students' ongoing work Mon-Fri 10:00-17:30, entrance at Via San Giuseppe 5R, +39 055 244 533, scuoladelcuoio.com), a workshop that carries on the long tradition of leather working.

€6, Mon–Sat 09:30–17:30, Sun 14:00–17:30, Piazza Santa Croce 16, Santa Croce, +39 055 246 6105, santacroceopera.it

Bargello Museum
Among the great museums of Florence, this one tends to be overlooked, but by no fault of its own. I actually prefer it as the poor man's option to see great sculptures by Renaissance masters, such as Donatello's *David*, a much more subtle representation of the Bible character than that of his rival Michelangelo. Another one of Donatello's works, the armored *St George* statue representing the armorers guild, was taken from its original exterior niche at the Orsanmichele church and placed here to keep it out

of the elements and for better protection. The museum is housed in a 13-century palace, which has also served as a prison and even police barracks; this is one of the oldest and grandest buildings in Florence— and half of my reason for visiting is the chance to see the inner courtyard, staircase, and large halls.

€7, free first Sun of the month, Tues-Sat 08:15-17:00, 08:15-13:50 if there are no special exhibits, also open on the second and fourth Mon and the first, third, and fifth Sun of each month, Via del Proconsolo 4, Centro Storico, +39 055 238 8606, polomuseale.firenze.it

Palazzo Vecchio

This is Florence's old fortified Town Hall. It was built like a fortress because of the turmoil enveloping Florence in the 16th century: Both internal politics and external city-state were threatening the city, which made defensive features necessary. In fact, when a physical fight broke out between Florentine politicians in 1567, a chair was thrown from the window, striking the *David* in the Piazza della Signoria far below. The statue's left arm broke into three pieces, prompting the move of the statue to safe cover in the Accademia museum.

Today, it takes visitors about two hours to wander through a tangle of more than 20 rooms extensively decorated with more Renaissance artwork. Keep an eye out for interesting temporary exhibits, as the museum has a strong rotation of them. Climbing the tower costs extra but proffers excellent downtown Florence views with the Duomo in the frame.

Courtyard free, museum €10, tower climb €10, museum and tower €14, Apr-Sept Fri-Wed 9:00-24:00, Thurs 9:00-14:00, Oct-March Fri-Wed 9:00-19:00, Thurs 9:00-14:00, tower has shorter hours, last entry to either one hour before closing, Piazza della Signoria, Centro Storico, +39 055 276 8325, commune.fi.it

Basilica di San Lorenzo & Medici Chapels

San Lorenzo is where the noble Medici family went to church, and as such, it's one of the grandest churches in town. The exterior is imposing (yet dwarfed by the Duomo nearby), but the interior displays the true treasure: the Medici family tombs. Just about every important member of the noble family is buried here under grand tombs, giving the viewer no doubt what a big deal these guys actually were.

Basilica €4.50, chapels €8, free on first Sun of the month,

basilica: Mon-Sat 10:00-17:30, Sun 13:30-17:30, chapels: Apr-Oct Tues-Sat 08:15-16:50, Nov-March Tues-Sat 08:15-13:50, Piazza di San Lorenzo, Centro Storico, +39 055 238 8602, polomuseale.firenze.it

Orsanmichele Church

Possibly more famous for its exterior than the interior, this church visually demonstrates just how important trade was in Renaissance Florence. The church auctioned off niches around the facades of the building to the networks of professional guilds in Florence at the time. Wanting to outdo each other, the guilds hired master sculptors to artfully represent their sponsors. See if you can't pick out the niches representing the wood- and stoneworkers, the bankers, the wool producers, the shoemakers, and the doctors. Ghiberti, Donatello, and Brunelleschi all gave their best shot at their respective guilds' patron saints. Donatello's *St George* (with the large shield), designed and sculpted for the armorers guild, is my personal favorite. Remember that making a statue out of bronze was 10 times more expensive than creating the same thing out of stone. So to display their success, wealthy guilds like the merchants of Florence created theirs from bronze. Most original statues are now distributed around town for permanent protection and have been replaced with copies.

Inside the church, check out the beautiful and ornate tabernacle, off center due to the fact it was a repurposed monastery kitchen before it became a church. Ever-practical Florence used the upstairs as grain storage. Just inside the entrance to the left, you'll see the hole in the ceiling that was used to feed grain down to ground level.

Free, daily 10:00-17:00, Via dell'Arte della Lana, Centro Storico, +39 055 23885

Ponte Vecchio

Right up there with the Duomo as a key icon of the city, this is the oldest bridge in town and the most important crossing point of the Arno River in Florence. To avoid the common Florentine people, the Medici family constructed a long passageway connecting their private residences in Oltrarno to their offices, the Uffizi. A stretch of this passageway, called the Vasari Corridor, actually runs along the spine of the Ponte Vecchio. Historically, the bridge was populated by butchers and fishmongers. But they were deemed too smelly by the Medici above, so they banned them and replaced them with goldsmiths and jewelers. Ahhh, much better.

Today, the bridge is still full of jewelers, shops, and tourists snapping selfies. My favorite photo op of the bridge itself is from half a block north and west along the river, where you can look back to see the shops stacked haphazardly like Jenga blocks along the length of the bridge.

Free, always open, Centro Storico

Piazzale Michelangelo
Offering the best viewpoint of the whole city, Piazzale Michelangelo is worth the hike (and sweat) up and out of town, especially if you bring a bottle or two to enjoy at sunset. What's actually a glorified parking lot is capped with a replica of Michelangelo's *David*. Also in the square, you'll sometimes find a company called **TestDriveFirenze** (+39 331 20 55 888, testdrivefirenze.com, info@ testdrivefirenze.com), which lets you drive a Ferrari in chunks of 15 minutes for €60. Bucket list, anyone?

Free, always open, Oltrarno

EXTRA CREDIT
Pitti Palace
It's impossible to miss the outside of this dominating and imposing palace containing dozens of richly decorated rooms and tens of thousands of pieces of art. If you're big into late-Renaissance artwork, this is a great museum for the likes of Caravaggio, Titian, Rembrandt, and Raphael.

€13, Tues-Sun 08:15-18:50, Piazza de Pitti 1, Oltrarno, +39 055 294 883

TOP EATS

Here you are, in the middle of Tuscany, a region world-famous for its rustic and delicious cuisine! Take every opportunity to indulge in the extra-virgin olive oil, fresh produce, and wine the region is so well-known for.

Like many northern Italian towns, Florence has a culture of *aperitivi*, an extensive buffet of pastas and salads all for the price of a glass of wine—or even better, the popular spritz, a refreshing drink made with sparkling Prosecco and a dash of sweet Aperol or bitter Campari. I prefer the Aperol version myself.

Examine your bill before paying to determine whether or not service is built into the final price. Many restaurants include either a mandatory or optional tip, but it's up to you to determine it. Additionally, *coperto* (a "cover fee" for sitting down at a table) should also be considered before simply rounding up your bill about 10 percent for service.

Pangie's Bistrot
Pangie's makes great focaccia sandwiches for €5 and also has a full menu of delicious *primi*, *secondo*, and platters with bruschetta, meats, and cheese. This casual, welcoming shop is small, with a handful of tables. The sweet owners, Mario and Francesca, are happy to make made-to-order sandwiches to keep you going between visits to museums and sites. They are open for lunch and dinner daily except for the second and third Sundays each month.

Sandwiches from €5, Tues-Sun 12:00-15:30 and 19:00-24:00, Via del Parione 43-45r, Centro Storico, +39 055 295 439, pangies2010@gmail.com

DINING TIPS
Keep these factors in mind when dining in touristy Florence:

Coperto: Many restaurants charge a "cover fee" (usually €1-2) for sitting down at their tables. It's meant to cover the bread brought out to you and will be added to your final bill. You'll find *coperto* listed in fine print at the bottom of the menus out front of most restaurants. If the charge is any more than €2, keep looking.

Servizio: Check your bill closely to see whether service is included. If it is, you don't need to tip beyond that. If service was not included in the bill, feel free to round up to add about 10 percent.

Tap water: Most restaurants do not offer free tap water. If you order water, they will ask you "Still or sparkling?" and then deliver a nice bottle of water (which you'll pay for) to your table. Be sure to check the price in the menu. Interestingly enough, table wine is often cheaper, and bottles of water can run past €6!

Osteria Brincello

Osteria Brincello offers what is easily one of the most solid values and authentic experiences in town. Run by a jovial crew of friends and family, Brincello has a limited, constantly refreshing menu of delicious and ultra-typical Tuscan pastas, like tagliatelle with meat sauce, and Florentine steaks. Count on fresh ingredients on every visit. The location of this sit-down and easygoing restaurant is another plus—not far from the train station, and close to many of the hostels in town.

Plates from €12, Fri-Wed 12:00-15:00, 19:00-23:00, Via Nazionale 10, Centro Storico, +39 055 282 645

Caffetteria delle Oblate

Stop by the Oblate library for a spectacular and unique close-up view of the Duomo while enjoying a budget snack served cafeteria-style on the top floor of a historic library. The open-air loggia in the upper floor of the library is my favorite little getaway in central Florence. The atmosphere and people-watching are endlessly interesting: This is your chance to observe the Italian version of your local library.

Free entry, eats from €4.50, Mon 14:00-19:00, Tues-Sat 09:00-24:00, Sun 11:00-18:00, Via dell'Oriuolo 26, Centro Storico, +39 055 263 9685, lospaziochesperavi.it

Trattoria Nerone Pizzeria

Imagine an Italian take on the American Buca di Beppo chain, and you've got this casual sit-down pizzeria, Nerone. The restaurant is done up in a gregarious fashion, but the service and pizza are thankfully less obnoxious. As soon as you step in, you're greeted straightaway with the warmth of their firewood stove, cranking out fresh and delicious pizza left and right.

Pizzas from €7, daily 11:30-23:00, Via Faenza 95r, Centro Storico, +39 055 291 217

Mercato Centrale

Florence's bustling main market is great spot to pick up picnic supplies for a hike up to Piazzale Michelangelo. Drop by vendors selling everything from pigs' feet to fresh veggies and fruit. I love asking *"puo fare un panino?"* ("will you make a sandwich?") and getting a fresh sandwich made right before my eyes. Just pick the places that have bread, meat, and cheese visible and order by pointing. For a quick, casual, and cheap eat, find **Nerbone** inside the market and sharpen your elbows to grab a plate of their delicious Tuscan fare. Pastas, sandwiches, pork meat, and other dishes all go for around €5 each.

Eats from €4, daily 07:00-14:00, Piazza San Lorenzo, Centro Storico

Casa del Vino

If sampling wine is your thing, I highly recommend stopping in to say *"ciao"* to Gianni, who's the latest in a family line of sommeliers. This shop has been in the family for over 70 years. Admire the old school photos on the wall, and get an education in local and regional Tuscan wines. Pick up a bottle for the road if you're in the mood!

Tasting platters from €8, Mon-Sat 09:30-20:00, Via dell'Ariento 16r, Centro Storico, +39 055 215 609, casadelvino.it

Pizzeria del Duomo

Imagine biting into a slice of thick-cut, freshly made pizza while taking in one of the best views of the Renaissance (the Duomo and Baptistry) in the warm Tuscan sun. That's exactly what's offered at my favorite *pizza al taglio* (pizza by the cut, or slice) spot in Florence! Order your pieces in the display windows, and grab a spot either outside on the square or downstairs in their cellar. To find this place, look for the Pizzeria al Taglio awning at 5 Piazza di San Giovanni behind

the Baptistry. You'll enjoy the best pizza and cheapest view around. I'm just praying they don't get spoiled by the tourist popularity.

Slices from €2, daily 11:00-24:00, Piazza di San Giovanni 21r, Centro Storico, +39 055 210 719

Oil Shoppe
This fast and casual sandwich shop is famous for their generously appointed sandwiches filled with local meats called *salumi* (prosciutto, ham, salami), veggies (eggplant, tomato), and cheeses (pecorino and mozzarella). It's a favorite among the study-abroad students in Florence. Stop in for a bite to take away or eat in along the bar on the wall. Don't let the name of the place throw you off: Vegetarian and healthy options are plentiful!

Overflowing sandwiches from €3.50, Mon-Sat 10:00-19:00, Via Sant-Egidio 22r, Centro Storico, +39 055 386 0091, facebook.com/theoilshoppe.it

Pane & Toscana
Another excellent choice for a fast and easy city-center lunch, Pane & Toscana tops their menu with two dozen typical Florentine sandwiches incorporating ingredients like artichokes, mushrooms, smoked tuna, and a wide array of sauces. Select your fillings and have them on either salty focaccia or a healthy wrap. Tourists and locals enjoy the fast service and tasty sandwiches. Try to grab a spot on the bench outside.

Sandwiches €3, Tues-Sun 09:00-22:00, Borgo degli Albizi 31, Centro Storico, +39 345 173 3604

Osteria Zio Gigi's
Zio Gigi's offers surprising quality and value for a sit-down restaurant this close to the Duomo. I love the comfortable, welcoming atmosphere and the set menu for large portions without the large price tag. Pop in here for simple and hearty Tuscan fare, like pasta with meatballs, salad with prawns, and Florentine steaks. Gigi is a load of fun and will take good care of you for both lunch and dinner.

Dinners from €12, daily 12:00-15:00 and 19:00-23:00, Via Portinari Folco 7r, Centro Storico, +39 055 215 584

Moyo
I love this place for an *aperitivo* that will tide you over but still leave room for drinks and gelato later—very important! Step in and grab a spot, and a waitress will take your order for a drink—I always opt for the spritz with Aperol. Then, head to the buffet table—free as long as you have a drink—and enjoy an eclectic yet tasty spread of everything from salad and cheese pizza to hummus, risotto, and French fries. Good food, well-poured drinks, suave mod atmosphere, and a spinning DJ all make this place a favorite of mine.

Aperitivo €7, daily 08:00-02:00, Via dei Benci 23r, Santa Croce, +39 055 247 9738, moyo.it

Buca Mario
If you like steaks, this is your place to splurge. Buca Mario is possibly Florence's best steakhouse. Wash your meal down with typical Chianti from the region based on recommendations from the suited-up servers. Reservations recommended due to its popularity, and be sure to dress your nicest!

Steaks from €28, daily 12:00-23:30, Piazza degli Ottaviani 16r, Centro Storico, +39 055 214 179, bucamario.com

La Buchetta
Famous for its typical Florentine beef stew (*peposo*), the clean and refined La Buchetta doesn't disappoint with their steaks, pastas, or beautifully presented desserts. This splurge-worthy and somewhat formal restaurant will set you back a bit, with meals running around €40 or €50 a head, but the superb steaks, immaculate pasta carbonara, crunchy bruschetta with mozzarella, and unforgettable cheese plate have me itching to come back year-round.

Peposo €15, daily 09:00-02:00, Via de Benci 3, Santa Croce, +39 055 217 833, labuchetta.com

All'Antico Viniao
One of my favorite little holes in the wall churns out meaty sandwiches and wine by the glass. Enjoy your stand-up meal in the alley, and return the glasses once finished to the rack on the side of the door. This is a perfect protein pit stop during those long days of sightseeing.

Sandwiches from €3, Tues-Sun 12:00-16:00 and Tues-Sat 19:00-24:00, Via dei Neri 74r, Centro Storico, +39 055 238 2723, allanticoviniao.com

Ristorante Grotta Guelfa
I love this place for the varied menu, especially for their bubbling pizzas, Florentine steaks, and perfectly sharable meat and cheese platters. Find this sit-down restaurant with white tablecloths and limited outdoor seating tucked away just a couple blocks down Via Pellicceria toward the river from Piazza della Repubblica.

Get your fill from €16, daily 11:00-22:30, Via Pellicceria 5r, Centro Storico, +39 055 210 042, grottaguelfa.it

Birreria Centrale

Need a break from *vino*? Pop in here for some delicious craft *birra*. Their menu is surprisingly varied and tasty menu for a beer hall, but who's complaining? Enjoy their steaks, pastas, gnocchi, and salads un-derneath exposed brick cellar arches, in an authentic and casual old-time atmosphere. In nice weather, enjoy their outdoor patio.

Beers from €4.50, Mon-Sat 11:00-24:00, Piazza de Cimatori 1r, Centro Storico, +39 055 211 915, birreriacentrale.com

TOP GELATO

Gelato will be a staple in your diet during your visit to Florence whether you like it or like it more. Challenge yourself to never try the same flavor, or *gusto*, twice. Many are tempted to get the XL after trying their first taste, but exercise a bit of restraint and go for the small. This not only gives you an excuse to get another one soon, but also helps you enjoy the rich flavor.

Perché No!

It's considered by many to be the top *gelateria* in town, so you can't visit Florence without dropping into this place just off the main shopping drag of Via del Calzaiuoli. With the convenient location, I also ask, why not?

From €1.50, daily 11:00-22:30, until 23:30 on Sat, Via dei Tavolini 19, Centro Storico, +39 055 239 8969, perchno. firenze.it

Vivoli

They say this is the oldest and most famous *gelateria* in Florence, and by many accounts, also the best. This is a classic spot for some of the best flavors around, like tiramisu, melon, and Nutella.

From €2, Tues-Sat 07:30-24:00, Sun 09:00-21:00, Via dell'Isola delle Stinche 7, Centro Storico, +39 055 292 334

Grom

This quality chain is sweeping Italy by storm. Their flavors feature locally sourced ingredi-ents and a menu that is constantly updated based on the season. While it's still a chain, the quality and value are right on par with the other independent options in town.

From €1.50, daily 10:30-24:00, corner of Via del Campanile and Via delle Oche, Centro Storico, +39 055 216 158

Gelateria dei Neri

Gelateria dei Neri is another heavyweight in the Florentine gelato scene. Their colorful piles of goodness are mouthwatering just to look at!

From €2, daily 10:00-24:00, Via dei Neri, 9/11, Centro Storico, +39 055 210 034

FINDING GREAT GELATO

Not all gelato is created the same! Here are my tips on what you have to look for when selecting your *gelateria*:

Look for natural colors. Check out the banana and pistachio flavors, and make sure they're the right color. What's the right color, you ask? The natural one, of course! For banana, that's a grayish white. Pistachio should be earthy green, not neon or lime green. If the banana flavor is bright yellow, keep looking.

Walk away from artificial flavors. Don't ask me why, but some *gelaterie* stack their artificial flavoring in plain sight for all to see. If you see stacks of burlap sacks of arti-ficial flavoring behind the counter, keep on walking!

Say no to flair. Touristy places attract customers by piling their gelato high and stacking it with all sorts of beautiful memorabilia. Although this is a treat for the eyes, keep on moving! The right temperature for gelato puts the mixture at a nearly liquid state that allows for the flavors to be that much more pronounced and vivid. If the bins are piled high, that means there's a chemical stabilizer in the gelato.

Go for the metal. Metal bins, which are reused, are a good indicator that the gelato they contain is made on-site. Plastic bins have likely been transported to the *gelateria* from somewhere else, so gelato in your cone will not be as fresh. Also keep in mind that half-full bins are usually a good sign that the owners keep their batches fresh— but look closely for a layer of ice or hardened gelato crust, which indicates that the gelato is old and has been frozen for a while.

NIGHTLIFE DISTRICTS

Centro Storico

Thanks to Florence's compact size, you'll find a good number of nightlife venues popular with locals, students, and tourists within walking distance in the Centro Storico. As a general rule, prices will be higher the closer you are to the Duomo.

Centro

Santa Croce

The secret's out: Santa Croce is probably the best neighborhood for those who want to party hardy in Florence. Especially in the **Piazza Santa Croce,** you'll find endless options for food, *aperitivi*, snacks, bars, lounges, clubs, and more. Many of my recommended venues are located in this district.

Santa Croce

Piazza Santo Spirito

Head to the square in front of the Santo Spirito church in the Oltrarno to see what the locals' style of nightlife is. Enjoy a couple beers on the steps, and join the tradition of the *passeggiata*, or evening stroll, through town. Santo Spirito feels like it's the start and finish point for many on their walk, and you'll find everything from cheap sandwich bars to upscale restaurants. **Caibira,** at #4 on the square, is an ideal spot for an evening spritz, especially if you can sit out on their outdoor patio.

Oltrarno

BARS

Hotel Cavour's Rooftop Bar

Find this bar on the rooftop terrace of the palatial Hotel Cavour. The quiet and classy bar offers a rare vantage point from the center of Florence. Standing on the terrace, turn in a circle to see Santa Croce, Piazza della Repubblica, Bargello, Palazzo Vecchio, and one of the most spectacular views of the Duomo in the entire city. A drink up here, while a bit pricey, is a much more affordable option to experience the luxury of the hotel than splurging for a full night's stay.

Drinks from €10, Via del Proconsolo 3, Centro Storico, +39 055 266 271, albergocavour.it

King Grizzly

For the beer drinker lost in a world of Tuscan wines, King Grizzly is your refuge. A welcoming staff is happy to help you work through their extensive selection of hoppy remedies. Find some of the best local beers on tap, in town with a central location between Piazza Signoria and Piazza del Duomo. The dark wooden paneling inside and friendly, unpretentious crowd create a fun atmosphere and guarantee a great time, just about every time.

Beers from €4, daily 18:00-02:00, Piazza de Cimatori 5, Centro

REX Caffe

REX Caffe is one of the oldest jazz clubs in Tuscany. The intimate, standing-room-only space is a shade gaudy with a bohemian, bearded atmosphere. Consistent, top-quality live music and DJs spinning house keep the

LGBT FLORENCE

Italians—especially younger ones—are progressive and welcoming, and Tuscany was the first Italian state to pass legislation in 2004 protecting gays and rights for gay couples. Holding hands, sharing a room, or going out for food and drinks won't elicit a second glance, making Florence fun and enjoyable for everyone. **Piccolo Café** (Borgo Santa Croce 23r, +39 055 241 704) is a favorite for its welcoming atmosphere, friendly crowd, great music, and fun bartenders in downtown Florence. **YAG Bar** (Via dei Macci 8r, +39 055 246 9022) is another super-social choice, a mod and trendy café/bar popular among the young and expat crowd; it's a great place to kick off the night. For more information and tips, check out Florence's two resource offices during normal business hours: **Service Center for the Queer Community** (IREOS, Via de Serragli 3, ireos.org, +39 055 216 907) offers event schedules, maps, and information for the LGBT community. **Arcigay** (60 Via del Leone, +39 055 051 6574, Firenze@arcigay.it) is Italy's national gay association, which frequently sponsors events in Florence.

well-dressed crowd coming back for more of their fantastic cocktails.

Drinks from €5, daily 18:00–03:00, Via Fiesolana 25, Santa Croce, +39 055 248 0331

Rari Ristoro sull'Acqua

The best things about Rari are the location and beautiful view across the river. While the service and food may leave a little to be desired, you really can't complain as you sip a spritz watching the sun set over the Arno. They also have frequent live music that justifies the 15-minute walk upriver.

Aperitivi from €10, daily 09:30–01:00, Lungarno Francesco Ferrucci 24, Oltrarno, +39 055 680 979

Naima

My friend Sergio heads up this fun sports bar, which runs frequent student discounts and hosts game watches all the time. This is a solid spot to begin your night, and it's well located for nearby bars and clubs.

Beers from €2, daily 18:00–late, Via dell'Anguillara 54r, Centro Storico, +39 055 265 4098, facebook.com/naimaflorence

The Lion's Fountain

Every city in the world has to have an Irish pub, right? The Lion's Fountain is just that. Count on a fun, casual scene focused on beer and shots for the study-abroad population.

Drinks from €4, daily 10:00–03:00, Borgo degli Albizi 34, Santa Croce, +39 055 234 4412, thelionsfountain.com

Kikuya

This English-style pub is just steps away from Piazza Santa Croce, where the Santa Croce neighborhood's nightlife is concentrated. The relaxed atmosphere is great for a draft beer from the UK and a local soccer game on the TV.

Drinks from €5, daily 18:00–late, Via dei Benci 43, Santa Croce, +39 055 234 4879

Red Garter

Red Garter is a sports bar and steakhouse in the heart of Florence nightlife. It's probably the best place to catch an American football game during the fall. Many American students are sure to be trying their luck at beer pong or belting it out for karaoke inside the large bar rooms.

Drinks from €5, daily 16:00–04:00, Via de' Benci 33, Santa Croce, +39 055 248 0909

Caffe Slowly

This bar is famous for its *aperitivo* bar and cocktail lounge. Slowly is a great place for a light dinner and drink before going out to a bar or club. It's just a couple blocks from Piazza della Repubblica; buy a drink and hit the buffet of appetizers and finger foods.

Aperitivi from €7, daily *aperitivi* 19:00–23:00, Via Porta Rossa 63, Centro Storico, +39 055 035 1335, slowlycafe.com

CLUBS

Florentines enjoy their nights out, and their home city offers plenty of options. Remember, Florence is stylish, and the selective bouncers don't hesitate to turn away would-be partiers on the basis of appearance or level of inebriation. Be on your best behavior while waiting in line.

Heads-up: In several clubs around town, you'll receive a punch card upon entry. This is the drink ticket you'll be racking up your tab on with each drink ordered. At the end of the night, turn in your card to settle up your bill based on the number of punches. Don't lose it, or you'll be charged for a full card (€100+!) before you're permitted to leave.

Otel Varieté Restaurant

Otel is just outside of the main city center but easily accessible by taxi. This club is the gold standard in Florence, flooded with the most stylish and high-profile locals. Dress your very best and arrive early to make sure you get in. Expect incredible music, dancing, drinks, and, very possibly, the best night of your life.

Check website for covers and events, Fri–Sun 20:00–04:00,

Viale Generale Dalla Chiesa 9, Greater Florence, +39 055 650 791, otelvariete.com

Bamboo Lounge

Even if you're new to the club scene, Bamboo is a great place to get down to Top 40, hip-hop, and R&B. Dress to impress and be prepared to dance and drink the night away in this intimate venue popular with the younger crowd and students. Check out their Facebook page for theme nights and upcoming events.

€10 cover usually includes a drink, lounge, and *aperitivi* Thurs-Sat 19:00-22:00, club Thurs-Sun 23:00-04:00, Via Giuseppe Verdi 57r, Santa Croce, +39 335 434 484, bamboologneclub.com

Space

Space is a go-to nightclub for anyone visiting Florence. Packed out with both Americans and Italians, this large, double-level club boasts an awesome sound system and light show. Bring some extra cash for the cover charge.

Covers from €10, daily 22:00-04:00, Via Palazzuolo 37, Centro Storico, +39 055 293 082, spaceclubfirenze.com

Y.A.B.

Known as a glamour club in the heart of the city, "You Are Beautiful" is both loved and hated. Keep your drink card with you at all times to avoid the €60 exit fee. There's a €10 cover, but it includes a drink. If hip-hop and Top 40 are your thing, this is the place to go. Have fun but stick with your friends and keep an eye on your drinks to be safe.

€10 cover, Mon and Wed-Sat 19:00-04:00, Via de' Sassetti 5, Centro Storico, +39 055 215 160, yab.it

Club TwentyOne

Small and rowdy, Club TwentyOne gets straight down to it: good music, fun vibe, central location, and light-up disco floor. It's small, but the upside is that everyone in the house is basically forced to party together by virtue of proximity.

No cover on Wed, otherwise €5-10, shots from €3, Wed, Fri, Sat 23:30-04:00, Via Cimatori 13r, Centro Storico, +39 055 295 262, facebook.com/Club21Florence

PUB CRAWLS

Italians don't go drink to get drunk, so pub crawls don't score too high on the "local experience" scale, though they can be a fun way to meet fellow travelers in this compact town. Recently, cities like Florence and Rome have taken a hard line against the raucous mobile parties due to a string of fatal accidents, pushing crawls to change their style or go underground. The best option is to find out if your hostel organizes any nightlife outings, or check out my friends at **Tuscany on a Budget** tours and their evening walking tour of Florence with *aperitivi* included (€22, Mon, Wed, Fri, italyonabudgettours.com).

TOP SHOPPING & MARKETS

SHOPPING DISTRICTS

Florence has shopping options just about everywhere in the historic center. Whatever you're looking for, don't spring for the first one you find. Shop around to calibrate your pricing, and figure out what it's worth to you. When it comes to things like leather goods (which Florence is known for), never hesitate to haggle. Beginning to walk away will often illicit the best price you'll get from the shop-keeper, so don't be afraid to do just that.

Piazza della Repubblica

If Italy is the fashion center of the world, Florence could arguably be considered its capital, with many fashion houses based here or in Milan. You'll find all the high fashion brands in the streets surround Piazza della Repubblica, including Gucci, Fendi, Dolce & Gabbana, and Prada. If you're serious about picking up some new looks at any of these stores, dress the part to get attention from the often-snooty staff. This experience is definitely not budget friendly.

Centro

Borgo degli Albizi

I often find better prices for just as good of quality on this street leading east from the Centro Storico. Storekeepers are eager to rope you into their shops. Go willingly, but also don't be afraid to step on out and continue your mission to find the best prices and fit!

Centro

MARKETS

With its foundation as a trading city, I love exploring Florence's many markets. Observe your fellow shoppers to determine what kind of zone you're in. All touristy? Or are you lucky enough to have found a place where the locals shop?

San Lorenzo Market & Mercato Centrale

The daily open-air San Lorenzo Market is where you'll find rows upon rows of vendors selling leather goods, souvenirs, and typical food products of the region. Many of the stalls are parked in front of storefronts of the same brand all up and down the streets of Via dell'Airento, Via Sant'Antonino, and Via del Canto dei Nelli. Once you betray even a little interest, many salespeople will take you back into the store for the full selection. Always haggle your prices and do a couple laps to decide where you want to make your purchase.

San Lorenzo Market surrounds **Mercato Centrale,** the covered, permanent food market on Via dell'Airento and Via Sant'Antonino. You'll find food stalls and tons of local produce, including olive oil, meats, veggies, and *limoncello* galore.

Free, Mon-Sat 09:00-18:00, Via dell'Arento, next to the San Lorenzo church, Centro

Mercato di Sant'Ambrogio

Just a 15-minute walk east of the Duomo, the Sant'Ambrogio market feels more distinctive and authentic than the other tourist-flooded markets in town. Here you'll find a market both covered and uncovered, permanent and less-permanent, with stalls selling everything from fresh produce and meats to clothes and shoes. If you're here around lunchtime, seek out a spot that looks like they get their food from the market.

Free, Mon-Sat 07:00-14:00, Piazza Ghiberti, Santa Croce, mercatosantambrogio.it

Mercato del Porcellino (aka Mercato Nuovo)

Packed with touristy knickknacks, this is a great place to find leather purses, colorful scarves, and the like. You might find better prices elsewhere, but this market's central location makes for a convenient stop between major sights.

Besides the shops there are two minor sights in the Mercato Nuovo. The circular **Stone of Scandal** is where poor saps who ran up tabs they couldn't pay had to sit naked while being beaten with stones. Pay those bills! Don't miss the fabled **bronze boar** either, just on the south side of the portico. As legend has it, if you take a coin, put it on the boar's tongue, release it, and it falls into the grate below, you'll have good luck and a guaranteed return visit to Florence. Well worth a dime, I'd say!

Free, daily 09:00-18:30, Piazza del Mercato Nuovo, Centro

TOP TOURS

Florence Free Tour

Florence Free Tour leads free daily walks around town. They're a fun and informative way to get oriented with the city and its long history. The morning walk focuses on the Renaissance history of the city; the daily afternoon walk digs into the intrigue and secrets of the family that kicked it all off, the Medicis. For the full introduction, you can fit both two-hour tours in one historical day by doubling back to the starting point by 14:00.

Free, tip-based, Renaissance Tour 11:00, Medici Tour 14:00, both tours start in front of Santa Maria Novella church (near the train station), Centro Storico, florencefreetour.com, info@florencefreetour.com

Tuscany on a Budget Day Tours

My friends at Tuscany on a Budget are the answer for those who can't quite afford private drivers and crates of limited production vintage. ToaB has a lineup of fun experiences to get you out of the city and into the countryside, including day trips for wine tasting, jaunts out to the Cinque Terre and Pisa, food tours hosted at typical farm houses, and more. They've also got longer weekend excursions for students and budget travelers to destinations like Naples and the Amalfi Coast. Check out their website for all details and trip information.

Experiences starting from €22, Via Nazionale 149R, Centro Storico, +39 055 05 03517, tuscanyonabudget.com, info@italyonabudgettours.com

Tuscany Cycle

Tuscany Cycle puts on fun, casual rides in the countryside after a short car ride out from their office in downtown Florence. Bilingual tour guide, bike rental, lunch, wine tasting, and round-trip transportation are included. Extend your bike rental for a discounted rate after the trip if you want.

Day tours from €75, performance road bike rentals from €35/day, Via Ghibellina 133r, Centro Storico, +39 328 071 4849 or +39 055 289 681, tuscanycycle.com, tuscanycycle@gmail.com

TOP HOSTELS

Hostels in Florence are improving. You used to have extremely limited budget options unless you wanted to crash in a convent with a curfew and a long list of house rules—these are still available by the way, and probably the only €10 bed in town (sanctuarybbfirenze.com). Still, the number of good hostels remains limited. In addition to my recommendations, find more listings on **hostelworld.com.** The private apartments available on **airbnb.com** for short-term stays provide another excellent budget solution.

Plus Florence Hostel

Located just down the street from the main train station, Plus Florence is my favorite in town and offers comfortable dorm and private rooms and a rooftop terrace. It's a large hostel that comes with the feel of a large hostel (brisk, efficient check-in, mediocre opt-in breakfast, and six floors of dorms), but it manages to maintain a fun social atmosphere thanks to the common areas and the on-site bar downstairs. Although they advertise a pool, it's probably closed during your visit.

Beds from €15, free Wi-Fi, breakfast optional, 24-hour reception, free lockers, Via Santa Caterina D'Alessandria 15, north of Stazione Santa Maria Novella, Greater Florence, +39 055 628 6347, plushostels.com

Academy Hostel

This hostel tries to be boutique, but don't come in with overbearing expectations. The dorm rooms are converted large rooms; temporary dividers between beds provide some privacy. The location—right between the Duomo and the Accademia, meaning it's stumbling distance from the bars—couldn't be better. The helpful staff is happy to make recommendations for sights and activities during your stay.

Dorms from €15, free Wi-Fi, free lockers, breakfast optional, 24-hour reception, Via Ricasoli 9, Centro Storico, +39 055 265 4581, academyhostel.eu

Hotel Il Bargellino

I find this spot, run by an expat Bostonian and her husband, a quiet respite from the bustle of the city. Rooms are simple and comfortable. The rooftop terrace is a major plus for afternoon drinks, picnics, and conversation.

Private rooms from €45, free Wi-Fi, no breakfast, Via Guelfa 87, near Stazione Santa Maria Novella, Centro Storico, +39 055 238 2658, ilbargellino.com, carmel@ilbargellino.com

TRANSPORTATION

GETTING THERE & AWAY

Plane

Flight prices should help you make the decision about which of the six airports to fly into the region.

It's most convenient to fly into Florence's relatively small **Peretola** (FLR, aeroporto.firenze.it) airport, just a 20-minute shuttle bus from the city center, running every half hour. Look for the **Vola in Bus** shuttle, and purchase your ticket on board from the driver (€6 each way to connect into the city center main train station).

It's a one-hour commute from Pisa's **Galileo Galilei Airport** (PSA, pisa-airport.com), the largest airport in Tuscany, to Florence. Because of gnarly traffic on the highways to Florence, it's better to get there via train from Pisa's central station. The airport and station are connected by the **PisaMover**, a free automated connection open since December of 2015 that runs every 10 minutes.

Pick up your train ticket (€10) at the Pisa train station. Departures run often.

Budget airlines also use the **Bologna** (BLQ, bologna-air.it) airport. The **Appenino Shuttle Bus** service connects to Florence's main train station for €20. Follow signs at the airport and catch one of the frequent departures (takes about 1.5 hours).

It's also possible to fly into one of Rome's airports, **Da Vinci-Fiumicino** (FCO, adr.it) and **Ciampino** (CIA, adr.it), or into Milan's **Malpensa** (MXP, milanomalpensa-airport.com) and take a train into Florence (1.5+ hours, tickets €30+ each way).

Train

The main train station, **Santa Maria Novella**, is on the western edge of the historic center. From this station, it's about a 15-minute walk to each of my recommended accommodations. Train tickets from Rome run about €30 each way and the ride can take about 1.5 hours. To Milan, it takes two hours on the

CALCIO STORICO

Roughly translating to the "old kicking game" or "historical kick," *calcio storico* is a game that was first created to keep Roman soldiers in fighting shape. Today, it's played on a rectangular, sandy field in front of the Santa Croce church. Fifty-four players line up and enter into what looks like mortal combat for 50 grueling minutes. In any given game, 10-15 players are carried off in stretchers from the brawl without even a pause in the action, and teams finish the game with no replacements. With no replacements, players are incentivized to try to injure or otherwise incapacitate each other with kicks and flurries of punches and swings, and moving the ball across the field often appears to be an afterthought.

With elements of boxing, rugby, soccer, and American football combined into one open-field bare-fisted gang fight, *calcio storico* seems a touch gruesome and medieval—barbaric even. The fact that there's a ball involved, and that the players are trying to get it into the net on either side of the field, is easily lost amid the violence. The players identify by colors and come from four districts of the city; they practice all year for their annual competition on June 24. Enjoy the fireworks from the Piazzale Michelangelo following the finals.

fast train and costs €40. Trains to Venice run often, also cost around €40, and take about three hours.

When booking your tickets, be aware of the difference between the slow and local trains vs the faster regional trains—it can make the difference between a one- or four-hour ride to the same location. Also, if you're traveling with an open ticket (without a specific time and date of validity stamped on it) you must validate it before departure or immediately find a conductor to validate it. Nonvalidated tickets can result in heavy fines or even being thrown off of a train.

Bus

Eurolines.com offers your best options for international bus connections into Florence. Connections from cities like Prague, Paris, and Barcelona push 15 hours each way, but at €50-100, they may be your cheapest options. Arrivals will drop you off at Florence's main train station, **Santa Maria Novella.**

Car

Florence is about three hours north of Rome via the A1 highway.

GETTING AROUND

Florence is a pedestrian city; just about all sights can be enjoyed on foot thanks to the compact size of the town. Buses are the public transit option of choice, as there is no metro and tram lines are limited.

Bus

Santa Maria Novella train station is also Florence's main bus station, and is the hub of both local and regional bus connections.

Validate your **ticket** (€1.20) once you step on the bus to avoid hefty fines 200 times the cost of a normal ticket. Remember, playing the "stupid tourist" card just doesn't work here anymore! It is possible to purchase tickets on board, but they often run out. Your best bet is to purchase tickets before boarding at any *tabacchi* (tobacco store) in town.

Car

Within Florence, parking can be quite difficult, and there are strict traffic restrictions. Watch for the **Zona a Traffico Limitato** sign, which you'll see throughout central Florence, meaning that traffic is restricted to buses, taxis, and local traffic only. If you cross this sign, an automatic camera will snap a picture of your license plate and you'll be sent a nasty fine.

Renting a car does open up the countryside to you, and may be a good option if you want to spend time in the Tuscan region outside of Florence. A GPS system is a must to navigate the confusing terrain outside of Florence.

Taxi

You cannot wave down taxis in Florence. Instead, catch the registered white cabs at designated taxi stands. Taxis are normally parked outside of the Santa Maria Novella train station, Piazza Santa Croce, Piazza del Duomo, and Piazza della Repubblica. Once in the car, take a look over the rate information card and make sure the meter is set correctly. Daytime rates begin at €3.20, and evenings start at twice that (€6.40). Women traveling alone can ask for a 10 percent discount between 21:00 and 02:00, so ask for it! Call taxis at +39 055 4242, +39 055 4390, or +39 055 4499.

Bicycle
Cycling is a great way to see more of Florence. Make sure you lock your bike up when parking, inside or out. Also, keep your eyes on the road and pathways, because pedestrians, bikers, cars, horses, and potholes are just about everywhere. It is particularly beautiful and easy to ride up and down the river on bike paths. Rent bikes from tour company **Tuscany Cycle** (Via Ghibellina 133r, from €35/day) in the city center.

DAY TRIPS

Fiesole
Only a half hour north of Florence via public bus is Fiesole. This small town perched on a hill is your best shot at experiencing true Tuscany without the long and involved day trip to the farther out hill towns. (You can actually see Fiesole from high viewpoints in Florence like Piazzale Michelangelo—it's the town far off in the distance, on the opposite side of the valley up on the hill.) If you've got four days in town, spend the fourth visiting Fiesole to get away from the crowds of Florence. The main draw of this town is to experience a quieter Tuscan town without the hordes of tourists. Explore the quaint little square, and don't miss the Roman amphitheater and relatively minor **Ancient Roman ruins archeological site** (€7, generally daily 10:00-17:00, check website for current hours, +39 055 59118, museidifiesole.it) just behind the **Cathedral of Fiesole.** In summer, you'll also find a weekly **Sunday market** selling souvenirs, handmade goods, and local produce.

Take in the panoramic views of Florence and the surrounding valley, and enjoy a meal at my favorite restaurant in town, **Ristorante La Reggia** (Via S. Francesco 18, +39 055 59 385, lareggiadeglietruschi.com).

To get to Fiesole, take bus 7 from Piazza San Marco to the last stop at the top of the hill (about 30 minutes, €2 each way).

Tuscan Hill Towns
Florence is in the heart of Tuscany, a region famous for beautiful, isolated hilltop towns with medieval foundations. They sprang up along Roman trade routes and persevered through the challenging medieval ages. Today, these hill towns transport visitors back in time as they wander the cobblestoned streets, taste the local products, and chase their romantic dreams. It's hard to choose between them, but none will disappoint. Check out **Tuscany on a Budget Tours** (+39 055 0503 517, tuscanyonabudget.com) for their lineup of day trips to these towns just a short drive away. Siena is one popular option; it's just a couple of hours away by train.

HELP!

Tourist Information Centers
Get information online at firenzeturismo.it, or pick up maps and information on sights at Florence's two TI locations (open Mon-Sat 09:00-19:00, Sun 09:00-14:00). The first is near the train station, the second near the Duomo.

Piazza Stazione 4

+39 055 212 245

Piazza del Duomo (west corner of Via Calzaiuoli, inside the Bigallo Museum)

+39 055 288 496

Pickpockets & Scams
Though you'll find many beggars in Florence, pickpocketing isn't as aggressive as in other cities like Rome and Paris. That said, never leave your drink or belongings unattended, especially while out at the bars and clubs. Always keep your wits about you and keep your valuables locked at the hostel.

Emergencies
Dial 113 for English-speaking police, or 118 for an ambulance.

Hospital
Ospedale di S. Maria Nuova

Piazza S. Maria Nuova 1

+39 055 69 381

US Consulate General
38 Lung'arno Vespucci

+39 055 266 951

VENICE

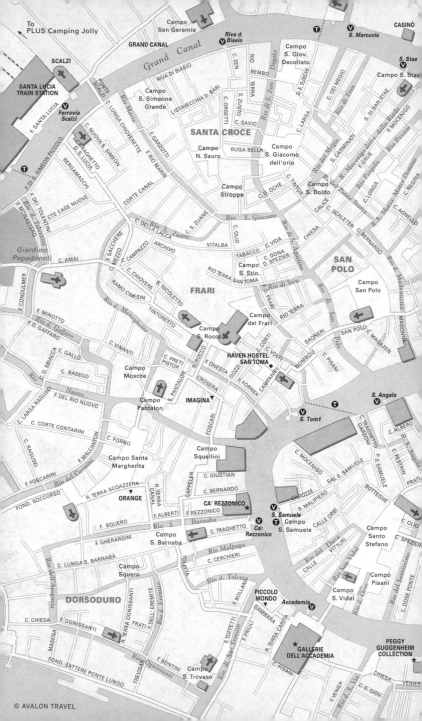

To PLUS Camping Jolly

CASINÒ

S. Marcuola

S. Stae

Campo S. Stae

GRAND CANAL

Campo San Geremia

Riva d. Biasio

Campo S. Giov. Decollato

SCALZI

Grand Canal

GRAND CANAL

RIVA DI BIASIO

SANTA LUCIA TRAIN STATION

Ferrovia Scalzi

Campo S. Simeone Grande

LISTAVECCHIA D. BARI

RUGA BELLA

SANTA CROCE

Campo N. Sauro

Campo S. Giacomo dell'orio

Campo S. Boldo

Campo Stroppe

Rio S. Giacomo

Giardino Papadopoli

VITALBA

TABACCO

Campo S. Stin

SAN POLO

Campo San Polo

FRARI

Campo del Frari

Campo S. Rocco

HAVEN HOSTEL SAN TOMA

S. Angelo

Campo Mosche

Campo Pantalon

IMAGINA

S. Tom‡

Campo Squellini

Campo Santa Margherita

ORANGE

CA' REZZONICO

Ca' Rezzonico

S. Samuele

Campo S. Samuele

Campo Santo Stefano

Campo S. Barnaba

Campo Squero

Campo Pisani

DORSODURO

PICCOLO MONDO

Accademia

Campo S. Vidal

Campo S. Trovaso

GALLERIE DELL'ACCADEMIA

PEGGY GUGGENHEIM COLLECTION

© AVALON TRAVEL

Known as La Serenissima—the most serene—
Venice is famously sinking into elegant decay.
Glide through the lagoon on a gondola, make
your pilgrimage to St Mark's Basilica, catch a glassblowing demonstration, and sample delicious seafood
and delectable *cichetti* (tapas-like snacks). But also take
time to wander its backstreets, alleyways, and magical
canals. In Venice, getting lost is the dreamiest part of
the experience.

VENICE 101

Ingenuity, trade, and plundering hordes all contributed to the creation of one of the world's
most distinctive cities: Venice. The name of the city derives from the fishing tribes that
lived on the shores of the marshy Venetian lagoon. With the decline of the Roman Empire,
the inhabitants of the surrounding area sought shelter in the difficult-to-navigate estuaries,
creating small man-made islands for refuge. Venetians began pounding wooden pilings
into the ground, reclaiming land from the sea inch by inch to expand their living space.
They traded fish for basic needs like wood, wool, and grains while staying out of the way of
the barbarian tribes roaming the Italian peninsula.

Before long, Venice grew into a powerhouse of trans-Mediterranean trade, sparking a
golden period that lasted for nearly 1,000 years. Venice thrived as a hub of commerce,
riches, and excess while the rest of Europe struggled through the Dark Ages. Immense
treasures flowed through this port connecting the East to West, and the influence in its
architecture is evident in the unique "Venetian gothic" style, a hybrid of the golden domes
and decoration from the East with the gothic arches and spires of Western Europe.

By AD 700, the leaders of Venice recognized that internal threats were just as much a
hazard to the city as external ones. To protect against corruption and violent interfamilial
feuds, Venice developed a process of electing their leader, or doge, so complex it just
about guaranteed against the possibility of purchasing that seat of power. With this stable
process of non-hereditary succession in place, Venice continued pursuing riches through
expansion of trade routes.

In 828, Venetian merchants made off with the bones of St Mark from the coastal Egyptian
city of Alexandria and brought them back to Venice. With these religious relics under "protection," Venice became not only an important economic destination but also a religious
one. In fact, the doges decreed that it was every Venetian's obligation to go out into the
world and bring back treasures to beautify their hometown. Venice was the kick-off point for
the Crusades, and also the first port of entry on their return, and the city benefitted from
the riches attained by the armies passing through.

When Columbus put the New World on the map, attention gradually turned from East to
West, and Venice slid into decline after being battered by the plague. Contemporaries considered this to be God's punishment for Venice's excesses, having grown fat and lazy from
generations of success. The final debilitating straw was Napoleon's focus on quashing the
island empire once and for all to take its riches and to eliminate it as a threat to his power.
Today, tourism is the city's strongest trade, with visitors flocking to take in the elegant
buildings and architecture left over from Venice's heyday.

PLAN AHEAD

RESERVATIONS

In such a compact city, real estate is limited and so are hotel rooms. Make hostel reservations well ahead of time to avoid exorbitant prices or no vacancy upon arrival.

PASSES

Venezia Museum Pass

The **Venezia Museum Pass** (€24 adults, €18 students) offers entry into 11 city museums, including the Doge's Palace, Correr Museum, Ca' Rezzonico, the Glass Museum on Murano, and the Lace Museum on Burano. With this pass, you can skip lines, but it's worthwhile only if you plan on visiting most of the museums included. Find more information at visitmuve.it; click into the sight that you're most interested in.

LOCAL HAPPENINGS

Carnevale

Carnevale is Venice's Mardi Gras, happening annually during the two weeks leading up to Ash Wednesday, the start of Lent. The festivities are packed with people dressed in ornate, traditional costumes from throughout the ages. There are frequent parades and marches through St Mark's Square, so you'll have to jockey with the crowd to get a good spot for viewing. The second weekend of the party is the climax of the multiday string of events. Remember: Early February is cold and damp in Venice. Bring waterproof boots and wool socks.

VENICE

THREE DAY ITINERARY

The #1 thing to do in Venice is wander…and wander… and wander some more. If you feel lost, take a deep breath and relax, because you're probably never more than half a mile from where you started. Don't cross that long bridge back onto the mainland and you'll be just fine. Beyond the city, which makes up one of the world's best outdoor museums itself, Venice has dozens of world-class museums and sights to check out. You'll hit the highlights with this itinerary.

DAY 1: WELCOME TO VENICE

MORNING

Take your first plunge into **St Mark's Square** and steel yourself for your first Venetian breakfast—take it standing at the classic **I Quadri**. Don't sit unless you want to drop €20 on an espresso!

After breakfast, stand in front of the flag poles in front of **St Mark's Basilica.** In a single clockwise-turning panorama, you can see the **Doge's Palace**; the island of **San Giorgio Maggiore** across the canal, through the famous **Columns of Venice** (with both the winged Lion of St Mark and Venice's original patron saint, St Theodore, on top), and the Venetian Lagoon behind; the **Campanile**; thousands of pigeons; some of the most expensive cafés you've ever encountered (which have live music after sunset); and the famous **Torre dell'Orologio**, a clock tower with one of the world's oldest digital faces. If the line is short at St Mark's, pop in! If the line is long, and you have a backpack with you, find the free bag check in the alleyway leading away from the square on the left side of the basilica and you'll get a skip-the-line pass at no cost. This is also your chance to climb the **Campanile** (bell tower).

AFTERNOON

Head to the streets a couple blocks behind the Doge's Palace to find **Panini Row,** and pick a spot for lunch. Then double back for a free **glassblowing demonstration** at **Galleria San Marco** (181A San Marco, on the main square). They'll usually have a sales rep standing in the square just in front of the archway between Café Lavena and the clock tower. Ask him if any demonstrations are happening soon, and you'll be escorted through an alleyway and up the stairs into the shop. If you time your visit with a well-heeled tour group, you'll be treated to an extended demonstration (and aggressive sales pitch).

Follow signs toward Ponte Rialto and wander toward the **Rialto Bridge,** enjoying the shops and bustle along the way.

EVENING

The neighborhood just beyond the Rialto Bridge is a great place to begin a *cichetti* crawl, snacking at the various bars all along the way. For the price of a drink, avail yourself of a delightful Venetian tapas tradition, sampling some fresh harvest of the sea. Stay on the north side of the bridge to see what the locals are getting into around **Campo Cesare Battisti**.

DAY 2: THE DOGE'S VENICE

MORNING

If you're an early riser, explore and get lost in another district of Venice. Off the main track, Cannaregio has some excellent hole-in-the-wall cafés to start your day, my favorite being the popular **Café Filermo**. Then catch your reservation at the **Doge's Palace**, and don't miss the **Bridge of Sighs**!

AFTERNOON

Hop over to the **San Giorgio Maggiore Island** on *vaporetto 2* and climb the bell tower there for a magnificent view of the entire lagoon. Heads-up: It gets loud at the top of each hour!

Head back to the San Marco neighborhood and enjoy a **gondola ride** with budget traveler friends before 19:00 to avoid the price hike. Pick an area of town you like first, then find a gondola in that area, because your tour is a 40-minute loop of the nearby canals. I like the area northwest of St Mark's Square, bordering the Grand Canal. If you're trying to save some cash, hop on a *traghetto* instead for only €0.50!

EVENING

Catch dinner and spend a night out in **Campo Santa Margherita** enjoying the selection of restaurants and bars.

DAY 3: CIAO VENEZIA, CIAO, CIAO!

MORNING

There are still plenty of things to see if you've got the time, but you'll have to prioritize! If you need some more art and history, the **Accademia** and **Peggy Guggenheim Venice** museums fit the bill. Endless shopping awaits you on the **Mercerie**. Beyond Venice, you've got the sleepy cemetery island, **San Michele**; **Murano**, the glassblowers' island; and **Burano**, the quieter lace-making island with cute little pastel houses to consider.

AFTERNOON

Don't dilly-dally if you've got a train or flight later in the day. It's easy to be delayed on your way out by getting lost or missing a *vaporetto* departure. Give yourself some extra time just to be safe. Happy travels!

TOP NEIGHBORHOODS

The main island of Venice is shaped like a large fish. It comprises six districts, but learning the major landmarks of the city is the best way to orient yourself. Most of the major sights are located toward the middle and south side of the fish shape, with the main train station, bus terminal, and cruise ports in the northwest.

San Marco is the bull's-eye for most tourists, making it the most touristy district in an extremely touristy town. This is where you'll find the Campanile, St Mark's Basilica, the Doge's Palace, Correr Museum, and many popular shops. A footbridge crosses from San Marco south to the district of **Dorsoduro,** where you'll find the Accademia and the Peggy Guggenheim Venice museum. Smack dab in the middle of the main canal is the famous Rialto Bridge. In the surrounding neighborhood, also known as **Rialto,** you'll find a number of recommended restaurants as well as the famous fish market.

A few districts offer nice opportunities to escape the tourist mobs. **Cannaregio** is where most Venetians live, and also the ghetto to which Jews were once restricted.

Going deep into this district yields off-the-beaten-path cafés and local hangouts. **Castello,** home to shipbuilding yards and the massive arsenal complex, was once Europe's biggest ship building operation. Today, it's a quiet residential district with plenty of streets slightly larger than what you'll find in San Marco and a number of churches to explore. **Giudecca,** across the Grand Canal and south of Dorsoduro, is quiet and residential. It's a nice place to escape the crowds in the main island. It's also where my favorite hostel in town is located.

Outside the main island of Venice, you have the islands of **Murano,** famous for glassblowing, and **Burano,** known for it's lace-making. Both offer a close-up view of their respective historical industries. The walled **San Michele Island** is a beautiful cemetery island, where people have been buried since the early 19th century. **Lido** is the long and skinny island with beaches, cars, and larger resort-like hotels. **San Giorgio Maggiore Island** offers the church bell tower to climb for beautiful panoramic views looking back onto St Mark's Square.

TOP SIGHTS

St Mark's Square

One of the most famous squares in all of Europe, Piazza San Marco embodies the image of Venetian elegance that comes to mind when daydreaming about this remarkable city. Originally set out in the 800s, and built up in the 12th century, this square is named after the patron saint of Venice, Saint Mark, and serves as the city's beating heart. Today, it's the epicenter of Venice's Disneyland-style experience. Lined with Venetian gothic colonnades and enlivened by live music and hundreds of pigeons, it's really quite idyllic on a nice day.

The square also contains some of Venice's top attractions, including the **St Mark's Basilica,** the **Campanile,** and the **Doge's Palace.** It also contains the **Torre dell'Orologio,** a clock tower that caps the high arched gateway leading to Venice's merchant district, the Mercerie. Dating back to the 15th century, this tower is loaded with Venetian symbolism (notice the winged lion of St Mark at the top). It also displays one of the world's oldest digital clocks clicking away

on five-minute intervals, and tolls out the hours with two bell-hammering figures.

Free, always open, San Marco

St Mark's Basilica

By the 9th century, Venice had become a regional power but was lacking a spiritual connection. Venetians believed they had a claim on St Mark because of a local legend. The story goes that St Mark was blown off course into the Venetian lagoon and had a vision in which an angel told him he would be laid to rest there. In the medieval world, relics brought substantial revenue from visiting pilgrims, and Venetians were all about getting that business. So in 828, two Venetian merchants snuck into a church in Alexandria, Egypt, stole St Mark's bones, hid them under cuts of ham and pork to deter the Muslim guards, and smuggled them back to Venice.

The basilica we see today was completed in the 11th century after only 30 years and dedicated to St Mark. **Basilica di San Marco** is one of the most richly decorated churches in Europe, with strong Byzantine influences clearly visible in the domes, decorated spires, and ornate, pointed arches. The golden mosaics on the facade cannot be missed and depict the return of the relics of St Mark into the Venetian Lagoon. The inside holds over 4,000 square meters of intricately detailed mosaics. In a nod to the power of the doge, there are two pulpits inside the basilica: one for the priest and the other for public announcements from the doge.

After the basilica was built, the winged lion of St Mark became the symbol of Venice. Also at this time, the doge declared it the duty of all Venetians to capture and bring back treasures from overseas. Before long, Basilica di San Marco was one massive robber's den, with huge quantities of gold and jewels deposited into the treasury inside the church. Even the equestrian statues in the facade of the church over the entrance (which are now replicas) were stolen from modern-day Istanbul. While the original structure of the basilica hasn't been altered much, adornment with newly attained treasures went on for hundreds of years.

Free general entry (€2 online reservation), €5 to go upstairs to see the horses up close, €3 to go into the treasury (both recommended!), general entry Mon-Sat 09:45 17:00, Sun 14:00-17:00 (until 16:00 Nov-Easter), St Mark's Square, San Marco, group reservations +39 041 241 3817, basilicasanmarco.it

Doge's Palace

This palace-turned-museum is an unforgettable example of Venice's typical marriage of Eastern and Western architecture. In a time when everyone else hid out in cold, dark castles, Venice's doge and government met and lived in a grand structure that was continuously rebuilt and added upon, even after numerous fires. The first palace was built in 810, and each new version became the center of political life in Venice. The Palazzo Ducale turned into a state-run museum in 1923 and is packed with Renaissance artwork and furniture. Your visit will take you through the institutional chambers, the royal apartments, an old, dank armory, and once-bug-infested prisons where troublemakers were kept. While touring these vast halls, keep an eye out for the little mailboxes decorated with scary faces. These were slots in which you could place letters accusing anyone of foul play or corruption. Holy Mother Mary is depicted in paintings in the palace galleries. Her presence is a nod to the power of the doge and his near-god-like influence upon the 2,500 representatives of Venice.

Crossing from the palace's chambers into the prison, you'll traverse the **Bridge of Sighs**, so named because it was the last glimpse of the beautiful canals that the imprisoned would have for quite some time. For a good view of this enclosed bridge, find the pedestrian bridge on the first bridge past it on the lagoon side of the palace.

The Doge's Palace ticket also covers the Correr Museum. If you plan to visit both sights, buy your ticket at the less crowded Correr Museum, so you can skip the line at Doge's Palace.

€18 adults, €11 students, ticket also covers entry to Correr Museum, Museo Archeologico Nazionale, and Sale Monumentali della Biblioteca Nazionale Marciana, also covered by Venezia Museum Pass, Apr-Oct daily 08:30-19:00, Nov-Mar daily 08:30-17:30, last entries an hour before closing, closed on Christmas and New Year's Day, St Mark's Square, San Marco, +39 041 271 5911, palazzoducale.visitmuve.it

Correr Museum

I've always found the Correr Museum to be one of the most interesting in town. Bequeathed by a wealthy collector, the art went on display in 1836 and features daily life and culture of Venice in the 16th and 17th centuries. Find the works of famous Venetian art-

ists, painters, and sculptors from its earliest days through the golden period of trade and wealth. Enter in the passageway on the far end of St Mark's Square and turn right up the grand staircase. Plan to spend about two hours in this museum, which spans a floor the length of St Mark's Square.

€18 adults, €11 students, ticket also covers entry to Doge's Palace, Museo Archeologico Nazionale, and Sale Monumentali della Biblioteca Nazionale Marciana, also covered by Venezia Museum Pass, daily Apr-Oct 10:00-19:00, Nov-Mar 10:00-17:00, last entry one hour before closing, St Mark's Square, San Marco, +39 041 240 5211, correr.visitmuve.it

The Campanile

The Campanile is Venice's bell tower, located in St Mark's Square. It's the tallest building in town, and you can ride an elevator to its top. Naturally, it provides the best panoramic views of the city—and even a view of the Alps far off in the distance on clear days—from 91 meters high. Originally built as a lighthouse to assist navigation through the lagoon, it achieved the look we see today in 1514. After a dramatic collapse in 1902 (where, fortunately, no one was hurt), it was rebuilt in time for the 1,000-year anniversary of the laying of the original tower's founda-

tions. To avoid the crowds, visit as early as possible. (And remember that San Giorgio Maggiore Island, just across the canal, provides a much less crowded panorama option.)

€8, daily Easter-June and Oct 09:00-19:00, July-Sept 09:00-21:00, Nov-Easter 9:30-15:45, St Mark's Square, San Marco

Columns of Venice

Without GPS, the first glimpse of home must have been a welcome sight for sailors returning from long voyages. As such, the Campanile and the two Columns of Venice bore significant sentimental value to Venetian merchants. Both monolithic marble columns stand more than 40 feet tall, with a Doric cap. **St Theodore,** the original patron saint of Venice and a Roman soldier who refused to conform to pagan religions, crowns one column. With his Byzantine origins, St Theodore became politically inconvenient, and Venetians eventually ousted him in favor of **St Mark,** whose symbol of the winged bronze lion with a paw resting on a book stands proudly on the second column.

Free, always open, St Mark's Square, San Marco

SO YOU WANT TO BE A DOGE...

Being a doge—the ruler of medieval Venice—was a big deal, and with it came power and riches. So Venice wanted to ensure that the right people were elected in the right way. Here are the 10 easy steps to the process of selecting a doge in the 1200s.

1. A *ballottino*, a boy chosen at random, draws 30 names by plucking balls out of a vase, beginning the entire selection process by chance.
2. From the group of 30, 9 are randomly chosen.
3. These 9 vote up 40 names, each of which needs at least 7 of the 9 possible votes to be considered.
4. The 40 are then cut down to 12 by random draw.
5. Those 12 vote up another 25.
6. Those 25 are reduced to 9 again.
7. Those 9 choose 45, each of which needs at least 7 votes once more.
8. From those 45, 11 are then randomly selected.
9. Those 11 choose 41, who must not have been included in any of the reduced groups that named candidates in earlier steps.
10. Those 41 then choose the doge by a vote.

The doge was carefully monitored by the nobles and not allowed to speak to foreign emissaries without direct supervision. All letters and communications coming in and out of the doge's palace were monitored, and appropriate gifts for the doge were limited to items of relatively low value, like flowers and herbs. All these precautions, while they may seem overbearing, went a long way toward minimizing corruption at the pinnacle of Venice's power, allowing the city-state to spend its energy expanding trade routes and the treasury rather than funneling it off to line the pockets of a few in power.

Glassblowing Demonstration

Due to fire hazard, glass factories are no longer permitted on the main island, but you can catch a professional glassblowing demonstration at **Galleria San Marco.** The welcoming team ushers you through a back alley just off St Mark's Square on the north side (just to the left of the clock tower), up the stairs, and directly into the workshop. There, an artisan grabs a slag of molten glass, then goes through a series of puffs, pinches, reheating, rolling, kneading, and adding other pieces of glass for color and texture, until there's a little vase or tiny horse statue. An English-speaking narrator explains the process as it happens before your eyes. Your 20-minute demonstration ends with your glassblower tossing the just-finished glass piece back into the oven to recycle for the next show, then an enthusiastic 15-minute sales pitch. Take another 10 minutes to shop around, and make use of the free restrooms. See if you can't pair up with a well-heeled tour group—you'll piggyback onto the extended presentation and showcasing of more expensive pieces.

Free, souvenirs from €20, daily 10:00–17:00, demonstrations running whenever there's an audience, 81A San Marco, San Marco, +39 041 277 0365

Grand Canal

If the canals of Venice are its arteries, the Grand Canal is Venice's aorta. All of Venetian life passes through this man-made waterway, through the dozens of islands that make up this city. You'll see everything pass through here that you'd see on a highway on land, but here, they're boats: taxis, buses, ambulances, private boats, construction boats, grocery delivery services, police and firefighting, and more—all aquatic versions of their four-wheeled, landlocked counterparts. This waterway slices the city into almost two equal halves, meaning that sooner or later, all visitors will cross its path.

Ca' Rezzonico

This collection of furniture and artwork focusing on Venice in the 1700s is housed in a merchant family's elaborate palace, built in Venetian baroque style with large windows and ornate balconies spread across three glamorous floors. The exterior's elegance matches that of the art on inside. Find masterpieces of Venetian baroque artwork, including pieces by Canaletto, Longhi, and Tiepolo.

€10, covered by Venezia Museum Pass, Wed–Mon 10:00–18:00, Nov–March until 17:00, closed Tues, ticket office closes one hour before museum, Fondamenta Rezzonico, Dorsoduro, +39 041 241 0100, carezzonico.visitmuve.it

Accademia

Venice's most famous art museum, the Galleria dell'Accademia, features a wide range of pieces from 1300 through the 1700s. You'll find pieces from greats like Tintoretto, Titian, Bellini, and Veronese. My favorite highlight is da Vinci's *Vitruvian Man*—that's the guy in a circle with his arms and legs outstretched (also called *Perfect Man*) that we see on T-shirts and TV shows about da Vinci.

€9, free first Sun of the month, Tues–Sun 08:15–19:15, Mon 08:15–14:00, last entry 45 minutes before closing, Campo della Carita, Dorsoduro, +39 041 520 0345, gallerieaccademia.org

Rialto Bridge

The Rialto Bridge (Ponte Rialto) is the grand, gleaming white stone bridge you see in all the pictures of Venice. It's possibly the most famous bridge in the world. From the time of its construction in 1181 until the 1800s, when two more bridges were built, it was the only permanent bridge crossing the Grand Canal. If you remember that bridges are the only way for pedestrians to cross a river without a boat, it makes sense that the Rialto district became the economic and commercial heart of the city. The stone version we see today was completed in 1551.

VENICE

It's lined with shops where you can pick up touristy knickknacks, watches, and jewelry.

Free, always open, Rialto

Peggy Guggenheim Venice

Housed in the Venetian palace that belonged to American heiress Peggy Guggenheim, this collection makes up Venice's premier modern art museum, housing an array of American and Italian pieces from the 20th century. You've got all the funky styles here, including futurism, cubism, and surrealism, and pieces by artists ranging from Picasso to Dalí and Pollock.

€16.50, Wed-Mon 10:00-18:00, closed Tues, Dorsoduro 701, Dorsoduro, +39 041 240 5411, guggenheim-venice.it

San Giorgio Maggiore

Directly across the Grand Canal from St Mark's Square, through the Columns of Venice, proudly stands the island of San Giorgio Maggiore. A short *vaporetto* hop zips you over to this tiny, one-sight island, which is dominated by the grand, gleaming white **San Giorgio church** (free, climb bell tower for €6, daily 09:00-19:00, Nov-Mar closes at dusk, +39 041 522 7827). Take the lift to the top for stunning views of the main islands of Venice and the entire lagoon. (Note that the lift stops running 30 minutes before the church closes and is not accessible Sundays during services.) On the island, you may also find occasional modern art installations on the *vaporetto* landing.

Connect to San Giorgio Maggiore with *vaporetto 2* from a stand on St Mark's Square. The ride takes about five minutes.

Murano

This island was a commercial center as far back as the 17th century, but in 1291 the Venetian Republic ordered that all glassmaking operations move off of Venice due to continued threat of fire, so the entire industry was restricted to Murano. Glassmaking grew into such an important industry that artisans were awarded exceptional privileges, like high social status, immunity, and the right to wear swords, and their daughters were able to marry into royal families. However, glassmakers were not allowed to leave the republic under the penalty of death. They were the only artisans who knew who to make mirrors as well as glassware.

If you're into the art of glassmaking, the **Glass Museum** (Museo Vetrario, €8, covered by Venezia Museum Pass,

daily 10:00-18:00, Nov-Mar until 17:00, Fondamenta Giustinian, +39 041 739 586, museicivicivenezianti.it) is a worthwhile visit. The dusty displays (a bit dated) take you all the way back to 1,900-year-old Roman glass through the techniques and artifacts from Venice's golden age. Time your visit for a live demonstration and tour (Tues and Thurs at 14:30) that goes in-depth about the glassmaking process.

Actual factories are generally closed to the public, but there are a number of opportunities to watch a basic piece get made in front of your eyes, followed by a sales pitch. As you get off the boat platform, follow signs for Fornace Glass. Workshops tend to close down around lunchtime (13:00-15:00), with the best time to visit being in the morning.

Getting to Murano is easy enough. From the Piazzale Roma car parking area or from the Santa Lucia train station, take the direct *DM vaporetto*, getting you there in 19 minutes. *Vaporetto 42* also works, but it takes 40 minutes.

Burano

Burano, known for its lace-making industry, is well worth the trip for some window-shopping. Burano's pastel-colored houses and quiet lanes make for an exceptionally peaceful afternoon just a short *vaporetto* ride away from the bustle of the main islands. On the main square, Piazza Galuppi, you'll find the small and well-done **lace museum** (€5, Apr-Oct daily 10:00-18:00, until 17:00 Nov-Mar, Piazza Galuppi 187, museomerletto. visitmuve.it, +39 041 730 034) demonstrating the island's typical trade. Loads of items on display take you through the centuries all the way back to the 1500s. You can even catch local grannies carrying on the tradition in person who are happy to show you what they're working on.

Vaporetto 14 connects San Marco with Burano in about an hour.

Isola San Michele

St Michael Island is Venice's cemetery. With real estate at such a premium, Venetians couldn't take up valuable space with cemeteries, nor was it very sanitary. San Michele—an entire island of the dead—is a unique sight to behold. You'll also find Venice's first Renaissance church, **Chiesa di San Michele.**

Hop out here on a quick seven-minute ride. Take *vaporetti 4.1* or *4.2* from Fondamente Nova B, on the north side of the main island, just north of Ospedale (Hospital) San Giovane e Paolo.

Lido
Lido is the long and skinny island that separates the Venetian Lagoon from the Adriatic Sea. As it's built on actual land, Lido feels like more of a city—complete with buses and resorts—than Venice does. Come out here on a hot day to relax on the beaches and get away from the crowds.

Take the *rossa* (red) *vaporetto* from the San Marco Giardinetti stop, for a fast 12-minute ride across the lagoon. Buses take you up and down the island for €1.50. The best beaches are toward the middle of the east side of the island.

TOP EATS

Venice has a history of fresh seafood and pasta. But it also has more than its fair share of tourist traps. Do your best to recognize them: menus in a dozen languages, neon lights, food out on display, recruiters holding menus out in the streets, and locations right on main tourist thoroughfares. The local places are usually a couple blocks off the busy streets. **Campo Santa Margherita,** between the Dorsoduro district and Rialto Bridge, is a great stop for relatively cheap food options. It's also easy to make a *cichetti* crawl of the restaurants lining the intimate **Campo Cesare Battisti**, famous for nightlife.

A few food terms will help you find what you're looking for. **Cichetti** (pronounced "chee-khetti") are Venetian snacks like tapas. You'll find spreads of cod, anchovies, octopus, and other bite-sized morsels, making for an excellent way to turn a booze tour slightly more classy, and to keep from getting a little too lubricated. Many snacks also come like an open-faced sandwich: a slice of bread topped with a little olive oil and whatever the fishers caught that day. **Tramezzini** remind me of the sandwiches my grandma used to spoil me with when my mom was away: soft white bread with the crust cut off. Smothered in mayonnaise, these not-quite-filling sandwiches are quite typically Venetian and are downed on a daily basis by its residents. **Ombra** refers to a glass of wine, and **tiramisu** was invented in Venice, so save room for some.

There's no need to tip while on your *cichetti* crawl. At restaurants, be sure to look closely for whether or not service is included already (*servizio incluso*), and check for *coperto* as well, or a cover charge. If you see either of these, there's no need to tip. If not, consider rounding up to the next even euro.

Cantina Do Mori
This is your classic old-school Venetian wine and tapas bar. Walking into this place, with its wooden paneling and tin pots and pans hanging from the ceiling, is like a step back in time. The tapas are simple, but not too filling, but the wine is tasty and easy to knock back in the tourist-friendly social bar.

CICHETTI CRAWL

Make a fun *cichetti* crawl of the restaurants lining the intimate **Campo Cesare Battisti** near the west side of the Rialto bridge, branching off later toward Cantina Do Spade and Cantina Do Moro. Take 20 minutes to take a peek at each of the listings to see which is best for your taste and budget. Order your food and drinks one at a time to gauge service and value before committing to sit down at a restaurant.

Muro Venezia Rialto (Sestiere San Polo 222): Very trendy.

Al Merca (Fondamenta Riva Olio): Sandwiches and glasses of wine to go.

Ancora Piano Bar (Sestiere San Polo 120): A sit-down musical experience; amazing seafood salads.

Al Pesador Osteria (Sestiere San Polo 125): Upscale food bar that tries a little too hard.

Osteria Bancogiro (Campo San Giacometto 122): Classy bar serving hearty Venetian fare—seafood, pastas, and bruschetta.

Naranzaria (Sestiere San Polo 130): Nice little tapas and wine bar; serves pizza on their terrace out back.

Finger food from €2, glasses of wine from €3.50, Mon–Sat 08:00–23:30, Sestiere San Polo 429, Rialto, +39 041 522 5401

Cantina Do Spade

This family-run cantina isn't so much about the smiles, but the typical Venetian food is lovely. Try their *cichetti* at the front of the bar, or sit down in back and go for the unique *pasta al nero di seppia* (squid ink pasta). They have excellent *frittura*, fried fresh seafood. The meatballs in tomato sauce are also a highlight.

Dishes from €14, daily 10:00–15:00 and 18:00–22:00, San Polo 859, Rialto, +39 041 521 0583, cantinadospade.com

Poste Vecie Ristorante

If you can fit it into the budget, splurge for this classic restaurant—supposedly the oldest in Venice. Converted from a 16th-century post office, the building was redone in the 1800s as a nice restaurant popular among the elite of Venice for its typical and fresh cuisine. It was at this stage that the frescoes were added inside. You can still appreciate fine dining beneath them and next to a grand fireplace today.

Unforgettable menus from €35, Wed–Mon 12:00–15:00 and 19:00–22:30, Rialto Pescheria, Rialto, +39 041 721 822, postevecie.com

Antico Forno

Step off the main drag into this takeaway joint cranking out steaming hot slices of pizza all day long. While quality and freshness can vary, the Antico Forno, or "Old Oven," checks my boxes for clutch pizza by the slice in downtown Venice. I usually go for the thick-crust spicy pepperoni.

Marinara focaccia from €2, daily 11:30–21:30, Ruga Ravano 973, Rialto, +39 041 520 4110, anticofornovenezia.com

Rialto Fish Market

The Rialto Fish Market (Pescheria) is a great place to come for lunch, when dozens of bars and stalls serve up the freshest seafood you'll find anywhere in Italy. A favorite of mine is **Muro**, a stall that serves heaping plates of their dish of the day for €7-10 (glass of wine included). Always fresh, always delicious.

Free entry, Tues–Sat 07:00–14:00, Campo Bella Vienna 222, Rialto

Panini Row

The small street known as Panini Row is your best budget option closest to St Mark's Square. Facing the facade of the St Mark's Basilica, head down the left side of it and hang a right at the bridge so you cross the bridge to your right. After another block or so, you'll find Calle degli Albanesi and Calle le Rasse, both of which have a good number of budget eating options.

Calle degli Albanesi and Calle le Rasse, San Marco

Harry's Bar

Don't let the casual name deceive you: This place is posh, with a price tag to match. Harry's is renowned for the famous patrons who've saddled themselves on these bar stools since it opened in the 1930s. Kings and queens, famous writers and artists, and common tourists like you and I have all enjoyed knocking back cocktails at this corner bar. You can get food here, but it's brutally expensive. The cheapest food on the menu: bean soup (€19). But hey, this was Ernest Hemingway's favorite watering hole in Venice.

Drinks from €15, daily 10:30–23:00, Calle Vallaresso 1323, San Marco, +39 041 528 5777, harrysbarvenezia.com

I Quadri

Sample the elegance of Venice at I Quadri, one of the institutional cafés on St Mark's Square. Be forewarned: A sit-down espresso runs you in the neighborhood of €20. To save a little, take your breakfast and coffee at the bar inside. I Quadri, which has hosted the likes of Mikhail Gorbachëv and Woody Allen, is a worthy splurge. Be sure to observe the frescoes by Tintoretto and Canaletto. If you're in after hours, try the typical Vov liqueur, made with egg whites, along with a Baicoli biscuit to dip in it. It doesn't get much more Venetian than that!

Meals easily climb past €50, daily 09:00–24:00, St Mark's Square 121, San Marco, +39 041 522 2105

Rosticceria San Bartolomeo

Come here for some great comfort food at an incredible price. At this self-service cafeteria, choose from over a dozen tasty pasta dishes, seafood entrées, and meat options for €6-10. Eat your food on the lower level; prices are 20-30 percent higher upstairs. For an even better deal, order your food to go and you'll get a discount.

Bites from €4, daily 09:00–21:30, Sottoportego della Bissa 5424/A, San Marco, +39 041 522 3569

Arte della Pizza

This is my favorite pizza by the slice in Venice. Grab a slice for €1.50, or get a whole pizza for €6. Order at the glass case and take it away or eat at the bar along the wall. Most get takeaway to eat along the canal nearby.

Pizza from €6, Tues–Sun 11:00–21:00, Calle Dell'Aseo 1861/A, Cannaregio, +39 041 524 6520

Café Filermo

The owner, Rafael, sets the welcoming tone in this fun bar. It's an excellent place to start the day with real espresso and pastry, or to unwind with a glass of wine after conquering the Doge's Palace and St Mark's Basilica. While located on the main pedestrian circuit from the Santa Lucia train station toward St Mark's Square, Café Filermo doesn't lose the authentic feel or fun atmosphere. Look for the Brazilian flag out front, and enjoy your drinks and meal on the handful of chairs and stools while socializing with the owner and fellow guests.

Coffee from €2, daily 08:00–20:00, around the corner and bridge from Campo della Magdalena church, Cannaregio, +39 041 524 4946

Orange

Probably the hippest bar in Venice, Orange offers a buffet *aperitivo* (Mon–Thurs 18:30–21:00), where pasta dishes, *tramezzini* sandwiches, fruit, and desserts await. Hang around and grab drinks here: The atmosphere really livens up in the evening hours.

Aperitivo from €7, daily 09:00–02:00, Campo Santa Margherita 3054, Dorsoduro, +39 041 523 4740

Coop

Find this welcome grocery store just toward St Mark's Square from Campo Santa Maria Formosa. Pop in here to pick up heaping sandwiches (€3.50) and fresh pizza by the slice (€3), along with all the other usual groceries. Many budget travelers have the same idea, so it gets busy at lunchtime.

Daily 08:30–20:30, Salisada San Lio, San Marco, +39 041 241 2273

TOP NIGHTLIFE

Don't expect late nights and ridiculous parties in this town. Venice's social venues are limited to just a couple squares. Your best grouping of spritz-serving bars is a stone's throw away from the Rialto Bridge. Just follow the noise off the north side of the bridge to **Campo Cesare Battisti**. Once there, it's easy to do a fun crawl down the line of pubs trying their different specialty drinks. **Campo Santa Margherita** is a popular square for socializing. Follow the crowds later on to the nightlife spots.

Generally, Venetians eat around 20:00 and head to the bars at 21:00 until late-ish but nowhere near as late as the Romans, Milanese, or Florentines. Venetian nightlife is low-key and laid-back.

BARS

Imagina

This place is a quadruple threat, serving cappuccinos and pastries in the morning, tasty panini and salads at lunchtime, and cocktails at night. It even comes complete with a photography gallery with ever-changing exhibitions. At night this place gets packed with party-goers ready to take on the night.

Drinks and snacks from €8, Mon–Thurs 07:00–21:00, Fri–Sat 07:00–24:00, Sun 08:00–21:00, Ponte dei Pugni 3126, Dorsoduro +39 041 241 0625

Piccolo Mondo

"This Little World" is the closest thing I've found to an actual club in Venice. It fills up with the only people on the island who seem to want to party, and who don't mind paying €10 for a bottle of beer. Be sure to count your money both before and after you pay for your drinks. Good luck finding your hostel at the end of the night!

Drinks from €10, daily 22:30–04:00, Dorsoduro 1056a, Dorsoduro, +39 041 520 0371

LGBT VENICE

While Italy as a whole is generally conservative, members of the LGBT community will have no problem visiting Venice. But the nightlife scene in Venice is spotty to begin with, and the LGBT nightlife scene is even spottier. In fact I can't recommend a single place on the main island. It's full of friendly cafes, restaurants, and tapas bars, but you may just have to surf the mainstream wave on your time in Venice.

TOP SHOPPING & MARKETS

SHOPPING DISTRICTS
Rialto
There are dozens of shops on the Rialto
Bridge itself, as well as in the surrounding
area. You'll find the cliché touristy souvenirs:
postcards, Venetian masks, snow globes,
and little gondola figurines. Come here to
get ideas, but make your purchases farther
off the tourist circuit, where you may be able
to find them for a bit less.

Rialto

Mercerie
The Mercerie (Merchants' Streets) is made
up of a series of narrow streets—Mercerie
dell'Orologio, Mercerie San Zulian, Mercerie
del Capitello, and Mercerie San Salvador—
linking the political and religious hub of Venice (San Marco) with the just-as-important
commercial heart of the city (Rialto). Take
your time to stroll these tight lanes, where
you can pick up everything from trinkets to
lingerie to Carnevale masks.

San Marco to Rialto

MARKETS
Rialto Market
This market just north of the Rialto Bridge
provides an excellent chance to catch daily
Venetian life with vendors selling fruit, fresh
seafood, and vegetables. Read the origin
information closely for the produce, as some
is imported from Asia or South America. Of
course, opt for the produce originating in
"Italia."

Free, produce and goods market daily 07:00-20:00, fish
market Tues-Sat 07:00-14:00, Rialto

TOP PARKS & RECREATION

Gondola Rides
There's nothing more quintessentially Venetian than cruising through the canals with
your very own gondolier. In recent years, the
gondolieri have unionized and standardized
their prices, taking the stressful negotiation
out of the experience. Now you can count
on steady—if lofty—prices. You can fit up to
five people on one gondola, and the price
doesn't change whether you've got one or
the max load. Your best bet is to link up
with fellow budget travelers and go in on
a ride together. Note: With Venice in all its
hyper-commercialized glory, the romance
of the experience sometimes gets lost, with
gondolieri busy texting the entire time and
shorting you on cruising time. Try to look
past his catcalls and the winks at your girl-
friend. Temper your expectations, and find
the beauty in the small things around you.
If you're not willing to drop the wad of cash,
hop on a **traghetto** (ferry), which shuttles
visitors across the Grand Canal at numerous
points along the Grand Canal—there's one
from the Rialto Fish Market. It's the poor
man's gondola and costs only €0.50! Tipping
gondolieri or *vaporetto* drivers isn't expected.

Numerous starting points throughout the city, 40-minute

GONDOLA TRIVIA
Venetian gondolas are a touristy cliché today, but they evolved over hundreds of
years, developing tons of traditions. Gondolas are slightly asymmetrical, allowing the boat to be steered and powered from one side and still move forward in
a straight line. Each boat is handmade with about 280 pieces from eight different
kinds of wood, and they cost €25,000-50,000 to purchase new. *Gondolieri* licenses
number only 425, are highly coveted, and are often passed down from generation
to generation, keeping them in the family. Today, there is currently only one licensed
female gondolier. The curved metal prow of the gondola represents the S-shape of
the Grand Canal, with the crest representing the funny-shaped cap that the doge
used to wear. The six forward-facing teeth represent the six *sestieri* (subdivisions) of
Venice, and the one facing back represents Giudecca Island. The prow is weighted
in front so as to counterbalance the weight of the gondolier in back. As you can see,
there's actually quite a lot going on in a seemingly simple little boat. Now all you've
got to do is ride one! *O sole mio...*

ride €80 before 19:00, €100 after 19:00, last rides depart around 23:00

Palace Gardens

Located just around the corner from San Marco, toward the *vaporetti* stops, these small gardens are a welcome respite from the massive crowds, who don't seem to notice this square. I like to come here for a quiet moment to enjoy an icy *granita* or ice cream. If you've got picnic supplies, the benches are a nice place to enjoy them.

Free, daily dawn-dusk

TOP TOURS

Touring Venice with a professional guide provides an excellent introduction to the layout of the city and its complex history. Free tours are available as well as private and semi-private options with the companies below.

Walks of Italy

My friends at Walks of Italy offer excellent guided walks with licensed guides, canal tours, *cichetti* crawls, and private entries into the top sights of Venice throughout the year. Check out their website for tour itineraries and pricing.

Day tours from €70 per person, +39 069 380 4888, walksofitaly.com/venice-tours, info@walksofitaly.com

Discovering Venice

I love these small group tours led by local, licensed guides taking you through the popular sights in Venice. You'll learn all about St Mark's Square and the Rialto Bridge, but you'll also go inside the basilica (free ticket included) and get into the back streets and canals often glossed-over by ordinary tourists. Antonella, Eugenia, and Frederica also offer options beyond the standard walk in Venice, like boat tours out into the canals and other islands. Find dates and schedules on their website.

€50 adults, €35 students under 25, discoveringvenice.com, info@discoveringvenice.com

Free Tour Venice

These daily walking tours follow the same format as other tip-based walking tours across Europe. They're informative, fun, and casual, and provide a great introduction to the city. Tours cover the foundations of Venice, the rise in trade, Napoleonic influences, World War II, and more recent history. Quality of guides can vary, and the turnover is high due to the fact guides subsist on what they generate in tips.

Free and tip-based, daily departures at 10:45 and 16:30, meet at Campo Dan Geremia, freetourvenice.com

TOP HOSTELS

Unfortunately, Venice's accommodations are expensive, limited, and oftentimes disappointing. When making reservations, take note of where your place is actually located. Lido di Venezia is Venice's beach island, but you'll have to take a 20-minute ferry every time you want to go into the main center. Same thing with Venice Mestre—this is the last town on the mainland before the bridge connecting into Venice proper. It's not the end of the world, just a pain to have to transfer between your accommodations and the main island of Venice. Make reservations in advance: Hostels book up quickly.

Generator Venice

Generator Venice is easily the best and most comfortable hostel in town. It's hard to even recommend any others, considering the comfortable beds, new interior, friendly staff, and slew of amenities. It's across the way in Giudecca, but worth the trek for general comfort and experience.

Beds from €25, 24-hour reception, free Wi-Fi, on-site bar, hair dryers and lockers available, towels for rent, laundry facilities, breakfast options, Fondamenta Zitelle 86, Giudecca, +39 041 877 8288, generatorhostels.com/en/destinations/venice

Sunny Terrace Hostel

Also located on Giudecca, this institutional hostel seems like it was converted from student housing. It's an acceptable alternative if the Generator is full.

July-Sept only, beds from €22, terrace, spotty free Wi-Fi, Ramo della Palada, Giudecca, +39 347 026 8037, book on hostelvenezia.com

Venice Gold

Check out this B&B option, but steel yourself for your typical abrupt Venetian service and long list of rules. To me, it's a solid upgrade that won't break the bank. They've got five-bed dorms, single rooms, and double rooms. The location is great, just a few minutes from St Mark's Square. This is the kind of place that insists on cash only for payment when you arrive, but they will not hesitate to charge the card you used for booking if you're a no-show or have to cancel within five days of your arrival time.

Dorm beds from €35.50, daily lockout for cleaning, reception 09:00-21:00, latest check-in at 21:00, free Wi-Fi when working, paid luggage storage, Castello, +39 328 209 4718, book on hostelbookers.com

Haven Hostel San Toma

This is my backup hostel. If the other options are full, head to Hostel San Toma for a comfortable-enough stay. The location, right on Campo San Toma in the San Polo district

near the Rialto Bridge, is great, and the Wi-Fi works more often than not.

May-Aug only, 4-bed dorms from €24, Campo San Toma, Rialto, +39 347 026 8037, venezia@havenhostel.com, havenhostel.com

PLUS Camping Jolly

This is the Italian version of "glamping." Opt for PLUS Camping Jolly for a fun stay in either rented tents, bungalows, or parked camper vans. I enjoy the on-site pool, bar, extensive optional breakfast, Wi-Fi, friendly staff, and genial backpacker scene. I don't like the commute into town (about 45 minutes to an hour, with last connections around 23:00), though shuttles are organized often in high season.

Bungalows from €30, Via Giuseppe de Marchi 7, on the mainland, free Wi-Fi, optional breakfast, towels for hire, +39 041 920 312, book on plushostels.com/pluscampingjolly

TRANSPORTATION

GETTING THERE & AWAY

The **Santa Croce** district is dominated by infrastructure that facilitates tourists' arrival by train, cruise ship, ferry, bus, and car.

Plane

Two major airports serve the city. **Marco Polo** (VCE, veniceairport.it) is the closest option. **Treviso** (TSF, trevisoairport.it) is popular with budget airlines. From both, your best connection into town is by bus.

From Marco Polo airport, the **ATVO shuttle bus** will get you into the center in about 20 minutes for €3. Purchase your ticket at the ATVO ticket window in the arrivals hall. If you're on a budget, you can take the local ACTV bus for €1.20, taking about 30 minutes. Both options drop you off at the same terminal station, Piazzale Roma. Skip the water taxi option, as it will easily run you €100 or more.

From Treviso, purchase your **ATVO bus** ticket (€5) in the arrivals hall at the ATVO ticket window. The journey into Venice takes about 70 minutes.

Train

Trains to Florence run often, cost €40, and take a little over two hours. Trains to Rome take almost four hours and cost €55 (you can find overnight options on slow trains as well, about €70).

Venezia-Santa Lucia is the train station

on the island, located in Santa Croce. Don't get off at Venezia-Mestre, as this is the last city on the mainland before the bridge to the island! From Santa Lucia, you'll exit the train station directly toward the famous Grand Canal, busy with *vaporetti*, gondolas, and private boats. From here, it's possible to walk anywhere you need to go, though it takes about 30 minutes to reach San Marco. There two docks in front of the train station both have ferries that will get you to St Mark's Square. Purchase your ticket (€7) from the clearly marked booth and hop on either the *vaporetto* 1 (slow local ferry, excellent for your first intro to the city) or the *vaporetto* 2 (express boat that makes fewer stops along the way).

Bus

Eurolines (eurolines.com) deposits international connections either at the **Venice Mestre Station** (on the mainland across from Venice Island) or at the main bus terminal, **Piazzale Roma**, in the Santa Croce district of Venice proper. Be sure to check which location is your final destination. Mestre is just a short connection into Venice proper via train. Your bus driver will be able to point the way.

Car

It is possible to drive into Venice, but you'll need to leave your car at the parking lot on Tronchetto Island on the edge of the city, about a 20-minute walk to the train station and beyond into the canals of Venice. Rates go from €21 per day. Cheaper options exist on the mainland in Mestre and Marghera, giving you the option to connect into town via train.

GETTING AROUND

Walking is your primary way to get around town—so be sure to wear comfortable shoes! You'll be tired after long crowded days, but *vaporetto* rides cost €7 a pop, so think twice before taking the option to put your feet up. Rather than trying to memorize districts and the city plan, orient yourself by the major **landmarks** of the city. (A map is also a smart investment.) Signs posted above eye level on just about every corner around town point the way to the major sights. Use them like bread crumbs to find your way around:

Alla Ferrovia: To the train station
Piazzale Rome: To the bus terminal
Per Rialto: To the main and most famous bridge in town
Per S. Marco: To the beautiful St Mark's Square and church

Vaporetto

Vaporetti (bus-boats) give you a chance to see the city from the vantage point for which it was built: the canals. An extensive network of *vaporetti* connects stops around the island in both directions at the floating docks. Check signs to know where to catch the *vaporetto* you want. Boats going in opposite directions will stop near each other, but often not at the same dock. Look for diagrams and route numbers to know where to catch yours. A **single ride** costs €7, so **day and multi-day passes** (€16/12 hours, €18/24 hours, €23/36 hours, €28/48 hours, €33/72 hours, €50/7 days) quickly pay for themselves. Strategize to make a 12-hour pass worth the cost by consolidating all of your cross-lagoon sightseeing and *vaporetto* rides into one busy day. Purchase tickets at the transport kiosks or at tobacco shops. Remember to validate your ticket at the yellow machines before you board your boat! Routes generally run from 05:00, with last runs around 23:30. See actv.it/en/hellovenezia for more information.

HELP!

Tourist Information Centers

Stop into one of Venice's information offices (both open daily 10:00-18:00, turismovenezia.it) for information and directions to your accommodations:

Marco Polo Airport

+39 041 529 87 11

Santa Lucia Train Station

+39 041 529 87 11

Pickpockets & Scams

The crime rate throughout Italy is moderate but generally only involves petty street theft such as pickpocketing and purse snatching. Thieves generally work in groups, so be mindful if a stranger comes up and starts talking to you out of nowhere. A common trick they use is to have one guy "accidentally" spill something on you, and while he helps you clean yourself off, his accomplice empties your pockets. Also, be mindful of

groups of children encroaching on you, as they aren't as innocent as they appear.

Venetian merchants are also notorious for taking your €50 note and claiming you only gave them a €20. To protect yourself, say the denomination loud and clear as you hand it over. This way, you'll remember it better, and they'll have a harder time trying to deny it.

Emergencies

Dial 118 for an ambulance, or 113 for English-speaking police.

Hospital

Ospedale San Giovanni e Paolo

Castello 6777

+39 041 529 4111

US Consulate

Venice Marco Polo Airport, General Aviation Terminal

Viale Galileo Galilei 30

MADRID

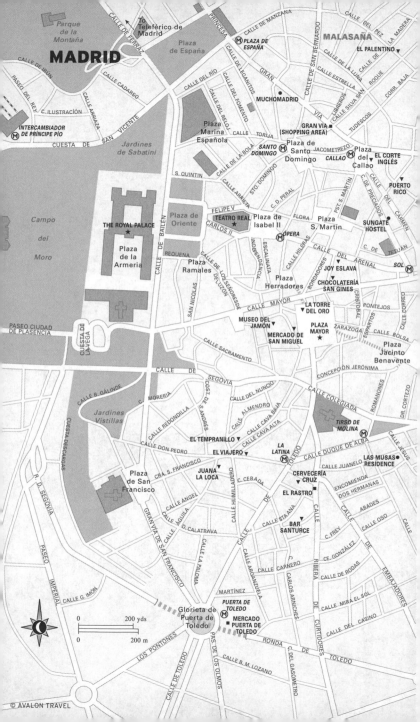

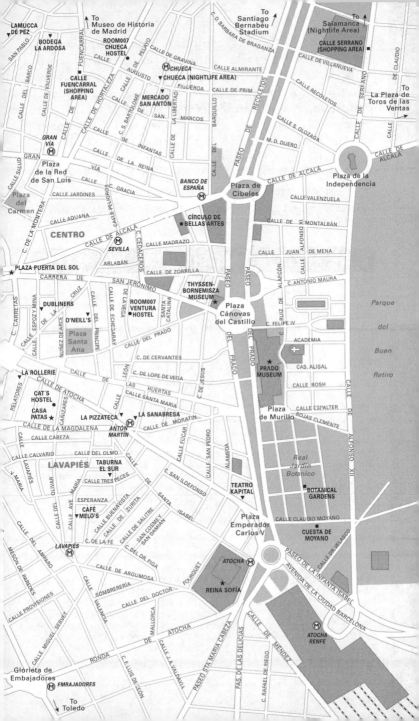

Madrid, Spain's capital, is packed with world-famous parks and museums—but it really comes to life when the sun goes down. Hit the town for some tasty tapas, catch a flamenco performance, and stroll diverse neighborhoods, from hipster Malasaña to Plaza Puerto del Sol, Spain's version of Times Square. After dark, massive clubs rage till sunrise. Barcelona might lure more international tourists, but Madrid is my favorite for a rich, authentic Spanish experience. This energetic city provides one of the best bang-for-your-buck experiences in all of Europe.

MADRID 101

Madrid was founded in the 9th century as a Muslim stronghold among a strategic network of forts sprinkled throughout Spain. Madrid's name stems from the Arabic word for "waterway," and its prime location was hotly contested between Christian and Muslim armies vying for control over the Iberian Peninsula. Eventually, Alfonso VI conquered Madrid in 1083, and the main mosque was converted into a Catholic church. As time went on, the Muslims who stayed in the city were isolated and eventually expelled.

By the 1700s, Madrid began taking shape into the city we know today through a series of ambitious construction projects that put the Royal Palace, Royal Theatre, the city gates of Puerto de Toledo, and the Botanical Gardens on the map. In 1807, the Spanish king, Carlos IV, and Napoleon signed a contract that allowed French forces entry through Spain to fight Portugal. Napoleon wound up violating the original treaty and began conquering and occupying Spanish cities along the way to Portugal. This led to a revolt on May 2, 1808, and a war that lasted for five years until the French forces were finally rebuffed.

Spain had a complex and bloody 20th century, replete with economic collapse in 1929. Political instability ensued, with a fascist military dictatorship headed up by Francisco Franco taking control of the country—all before the start of World War II. During the war, German planes bombed cities across Spain, including Madrid. But it was the inconsequential town of Guernica that they used to practice their intense blitzkrieg bombing runs and surveillance operations before the outbreak of all-out war a couple years later. Picasso's infamous *Guernica*, now on display at the Reina Sofia museum, depicts the horrific strafing and bombing unleashed on the town on the busy market day. This run killed nearly 1,000 people during more than two hours and leveled most of the town. All the while, Spain remained neutral during World War II.

Franco ruled an isolationist Spain for nearly 40 years until his death in 1975. Franco was convinced that things would remain status quo by returning power back to the king upon his death, but the king began setting up a constitutional monarchy as soon as Franco passed, ending over three decades of oppressive military rule.

With the veil of fascism lifted, Spain burst onto the world stage as a nation that had a lot of living and celebration to catch up on, and Madrid is where it all went down. Today, while the economic situation in Spain remains challenging—with a nearly 50 percent unemployment rate for young adults—the mood is generally optimistic. Madrid's urban progress has accelerated, and it is one of Europe's most beautiful capital cities, pleasing for its intense animated spirit, welcoming people, and compelling blend of modern and proud classic culture.

PLAN AHEAD

RESERVATIONS

Reservations are recommended for the following sights and activities:

Prado Museum (entradasprado.com)
Real Madrid matches (realmadrid.com)

FREE ENTRY TIMES

A number of Madrid museums are free to enter at certain times of day or certain days of the week or month, like these three:

Prado Museum (free Mon-Sat 18:00-20:00, Sun 17:00-19:00, always free for those under 18 and students 18-25)

Reina Sofía (free Mon and Wed-Sat 19:00-21:00, Sunday 15:00-19:00, always free for those under age 18 and students 25 and under with ID)

Museo Thyssen-Bornemisza (free Mon)

LOCAL HAPPENINGS

Just like their siestas, Spaniards take their festivals seriously. If a public holiday falls on a Thursday (or even a Wednesday in some cases) people get their weekend started early. It's great for them, but it can be a hassle for tourists. Assume most businesses will be closed during these national holidays:

January 1, New Year's Day

March 29, Good Friday

May 1, Labor Day

August 15, the Assumption

October 12, National Holiday of Spain

November 1, All Saints' Day

December 6, Spanish Constitution Day

December 25, Christmas Day

KNOW BEFORE YOU GO

KEY STATS & FIGURES

Currency:
Spain uses the euro (€);
1 EUR = about 1.06 USD

Population:
3.2 million (double that of Barcelona, and 1 million more than Paris)

Language:
Spanish

Days of sun per year:
300+

Elevation:
650 meters (the highest capital city in Europe)

Dinner time for Madrileños:
21:00

Time to hit the clubs:
02:00

CALIBRATE YOUR BUDGET

TYPICAL PRICES FOR:

Hostel dorm bed:
€18

Two-course dinner:
€10

Pint of beer:
€2.50

Metro pass:
€1.50

MOVIES TO WATCH
Abre Los Ojos (Open Your Eyes), El Día de la Bestía (Day of the Beast), La Flor de Mi Secreto (The Flower of My Secret)

THREE DAY ITINERARY

Madrid is packed with beautiful architecture, massive museums, sprawling parks, and photogenic boulevards. It's a challenge to balance all the sightseeing options with the Madrileño love of life and just having a darn good time. But with these tips, you can walk that line that's just right for you.

DAY 1: WELCOME TO MADRID

MORNING

Get your visit off to a sweet start with a breakfast of churros and chocolate at the famous **Chocolatería San Ginés** just around the corner from **Plaza Puerta del Sol**.

At 10:00, catch the three-hour walk with **Sandeman's New Europe Walking Tours** in **Plaza Mayor** for an efficient introduction to Madrid's top sights, including the **Royal Palace** and some historic Moorish ruins dating back to Madrid's early days.

AFTERNOON

Satisfy your appetite at **Taberna El Sur** on the way toward the museum quarter of Madrid. After lunch, continue downhill south and east a few blocks and power through your siesta time in the **Reina Sofía**. Spend at least a couple hours soaking in an extensive collection of 20th-century artwork in all media—from experimental film to sculpture.

Afterward, walk about a mile slightly uphill along the grand tree-lined boulevard of Paseo del Prado to the rooftop café at **Círculo de Bellas Artes** for a stunning panorama of downtown Madrid. Trace the thousands of steps you took today in one view and reward yourself with a cold beer or iced coffee.

EVENING

Rest up back at the hostel before heading out for dinner. Around 21:00, strike out for an authentic tapas crawl in the Malasaña District, one of the liveliest neighborhoods in town. **Bodega La Ardosa** is a good place to start your crawl. Explore this dense network of lanes and streets, and concentrate your imbibing efforts around **Plaza del 2 de Mayo** and the bars on **Plaza de Carlos Cambronero.**

LATE

In the clubbing mood? **Joy Eslava**—just around the corner from Chocolatería San Ginés, where your day began—is just a 15-minute walk downhill from the Malasaña neighborhood, between the Teatro Real and Plaza Puerto del Sol. If you queue up before 01:30, the €10 cover usually includes one drink.

DAY 2: YOUR BIG MUSEUM DAY

MORNING

Get yourself up at an appropriate hour considering how "Madrileño" you really got last night. Splurge on breakfast and coffee at **La Rollerie,** then walk a few minutes southeast to Madrid's top museum: the **Prado.** (If you made reservations in advance online, you can skip the line.) You'll want to spend a couple hours here.

AFTERNOON

After the museum, pick up some food to take to nearby **Retiro Park** to rest your feet over a relaxing picnic in the shade for a couple hours. Retiro gives you a chance to get away from the crowds, and you've got plenty of outdoor activities to choose from. Rent a paddle boat or bike and explore Retiro's 350 acres. Extra credit: Find the *Statue of the Fallen Angel,* the only statue dedicated to the devil in all of Europe, somewhere in the park.

Return the bikes, then cut across town on the metro from the Retiro stop on the north side of the park to the Ópera stop on the red line (line 2) to explore the **Royal Palace** (open daily until 20:00).

EVENING

Regroup at your hostel for a short siesta. Then head out to bond with other backpackers at **O'Neill's** bar in Sol. For a quieter scene, grab a bottle of wine and people-watch at nearby **Plaza Santa Ana.**

Fancy catching a show? The nightly **Flamenco Show at Casa Patas,** just a few minutes on foot south of O'Neill's and Plaza Santa Ana, kicks off in the 21:00 and 23:00 hours. This show features the best dancers and singers in town.

LATE

Dressed to the nines and wallet still too heavy? Make your way toward the Atocha train station (just east of the Lavapies district) and find **Teatro Kapital**'s seven floors of throbbing hedonism.

DAY 3: OPTIONS
MORNING

If it's Sunday, head straight to the bustling **El Rastro**, Madrid's largest flea market, where you can find everything from playing cards and antiques to electrical equipment and trading cards. Stop for lunch along the way at my favorite spot in the neighborhood: **Bar Santurce**.

AFTERNOON

If you want to continue on the shopping theme, hop on the metro to get to **Calle Serrano**.

If you prefer museums, take a 20-minute walk from El Rastro to spend the afternoon at **Museo Thyssen-Bornemisza**.

If you (like me) love finding fresh air and views over the city, head west of Malasaña to the **Teleférico de Madrid** to catch your last panorama of this awesome city.

Finally, if soccer is your thing, make your pilgrimage outside the city center to **Estadio Santiago Bernabéu** for a tour.

TOP NEIGHBORHOODS

Madrid is a massive, modern metropolis. The **Sol** (Centro) district, with Plaza Puerta del Sol at its center, is the heart of the city and the most touristy part of town. This is where you'll find major sights like Plaza Mayor, along with restaurants, bars, hotels, commercial nightlife, and Joy Eslava, a *discoteca* institution.

The city spreads out to the north and south from Sol. About five blocks north of Plaza Puerto del Sol are two of my favorite districts: Chueca and Malasaña. **Chueca,** known as the gay district, has excellent shopping, food, and nightlife. This is one of Madrid's top up-and-coming neighborhoods. To the west is **Malasaña,** which, for me, is what Madrid is all about: a community vibe, unforgettable tapas, lively nightlife, and indie shopping. Malasaña is bordered by Calle San Bernardo to the west and Calle Horteleza and Chueca to the east.

In the **Museum District,** sandwiched between Sol and Retiro Park (Madrid's

Central Park), you'll find the world-famous Prado, the Reina Sofia, and Museo Thyssen Bornemisza. North of Retiro and east of Chueca, **Salamanca** is your spot for high-end shopping and nightlife. This is the nice part of town, where the glitterati go about their flashy lifestyles.

South of Sol, neighborhoods huddle around the La Latina and Lavapies metro stops. **La Latina** is where the young, in-the-know professionals of Madrid like to go out—especially along two parallel streets: Calle Cava Baja and Calle Cava Alta, which offer classy little bars and cafés. **Lavapies,** just to the east, is home to El Rastro market. This is Madrid's gritty underground district. It's too dark for many tourists, and feels a touch run-down, but I love wandering the narrow lanes to find a cheap *cañas* (half-pints of beer). This area is also the heart of Madrid's ethnic community. You'll find some delicious, cheap food, and a chance to get away from the tourist hordes.

TOP SIGHTS

The great thing about Madrid's museums is that most are free at certain times or on certain days of the week or month—and, even better, some are *always* free if you're a student and/or under the age of 18. For example, the Prado is always free for those under 18 and students age 18-25 who bring a valid student ID; the Reina Sofia is free with a student ID as well. If you can take advantage of these youth and student discounts, you might want to avoid the times when these sights are free to the entire public, as that's when they tend to pack out. If you can't take advantage of the youth and student deals, go early or during siesta time and pay the entrance fee if there's a particular artist or exhibit that you're all about—it's worth it to have it all to yourself!

Prado Museum

One of Europe's finest art museums, the Prado houses collections from famous Spanish artists such as Goya, El Greco, Ribera, and Velázquez, as well as international artists like Rembrandt, Raphael, and Orly. The museum is absolutely massive, so go in with an idea of what you want to see.

Find the medieval works of art dovetailing into early Renaissance pieces on the ground floor, from masters hailing from across the entire continent. As you climb upstairs, you enter into the high Renaissance and baroque masters from about 1600 on.

For those short on attention span, the museum's highlights include *Las Meninas* by Velázquez, *The Nobleman with His Hand*

on His Chest by El Greco, *The Three Graces* by Rubens, and *Jacob's Dream* by Ribera. It's a good indoor activity to hit in tandem with a visit to Retiro Park, as they're just minutes from each other.

Free entry Monday-Saturday 18:00-20:00 and Sunday 17:00-19:00 is great on the budget, but understandably the museum is packed with visitors jumping on the great deal.

€14 adult, additional fee for temporary exhibits, free Mon-Sat 18:00-20:00 and Sun 17:00-19:00, always free under 18 and students 18-25, Mon-Sat 10:00-20:00, Sun and holidays 10:00-19:00, last entry 30 minutes before closing, closed Jan 1, May 1, and Dec 25, Calle Ruiz de Alarcón 23, Museum District, +34 913 302 800, museodelprado.es, Metro: Atocha

Reina Sofia

This imposing museum, housed in a former convent and hospital done up with a multimillion-dollar refurbishment, features Spain's biggest collection of 20th-century art. Enjoy original work from Spain's two most famous artists: Pablo Picasso and Salvador Dalí. This is where you can view Picasso's most famous piece, *Guernica*, commemorating the abhorrent bombing of the town of Guernica by the Germans in World War II. The Reina Sofia has free entrance Monday and Wednesday-Saturday 19:00-21:00, Sunday 15:00-19:00, and is always free with a valid student ID.

€8 adult, €3 under 18, free Mon and Wed-Sat 19:00 21:00, Sun 15:00-19:00, always free with valid student ID, Mon and Wed-Sat 10:00-21:00, Sun 10:00-19:00 (fourth floor not accessible Sun after 15:00), closed Tues, Calle de Santa Isabel 52, Museum District, +34 917 741 000, museoreinasofia.es, Metro: Atocha

The Royal Palace
(Palacio Real de Madrid)

Though it's officially the residence of the king of Spain, the king actually resides in the Palacio de la Zarzuela outside of the city. It may also come as a surprise that the Royal Palace in Madrid is the largest palace ever built in Western Europe (even bigger than Versailles!). It's also arguably Madrid's most beautiful building, constructed in the baroque style and bursting with ornate architectural accents in white stone, reminiscent of Buckingham Palace in London. The interior, done up in high baroque fashion, will blow you away as well. You'll find detailed frescos and gilded detailing, along with royal furnishings and paintings throughout the private apartments upstairs.

The palace is definitely worth the price of admission, as it holds artifacts and works from Velázquez, Goya, and Giordano; the Royal Armory; and the world's only complete Stradivarius string quintet.

€11 adult, €5 ages 5-16 and students up to age 25 with ID, free under age 5, Oct-Mar daily 10:00-18:00, Apr-Sept daily 10:00-20:00, Calle Bailén, Sol, +34 914 548 700, patrimonionacional.es, Metro: Ópera

Plaza Mayor

The principal square in Madrid, the Plaza Mayor is a great place for people-watching, as it boasts many cafés serving all sorts of tapas and drinks, and is the home to many street artists. Come for the people-watching, but avoid the touristy restaurants that line the square. If the square doesn't look particularly Spanish to you, it's because it's not. The square was constructed during the Austrian rule of the Habsburgs in 1617, and is known in Madrid as "Madrid de los Austrias."

Free, always open, Plaza Mayor, Sol, Metro: Ópera

Plaza Puerta del Sol

All of Madrid seems to converge on this large, sunny square in the heart of town. It's truly the heart of both the capital and the country as a whole—as evidenced by the **KM 0** monument in the middle of the square. This is the point from which all the road signs in the country measure their distance to the capital. Bustling with activity and tourists in the day, the square is also lively at night with touristy bars just to the south of it and tons of shopping, cafés, and restaurants in the surrounding streets. Sol is also a major metro station, and you'll often be connecting through or getting off here.

Free, always open, Puerta del Sol, Sol, Metro: Sol

Teatro Real

Madrid's majestic neoclassical opera house was newly remodeled and opened with 1,750 seats in 1997 after being closed for nearly 75 years. It's come a long ways since serving as munitions storage during the Spanish Civil War. Today, you can enjoy a slice of high society at a show while taking in the wraparound seating and excellent acoustics. Find tickets online from just €9 for the cheap seats.

If you're not interested in catching a show, the theater has numerous general, technical, and artistic-focused tours going off daily. The €8 general tours kick off every 30 minutes daily 10:30-13:00 and last about an hour. The tour focusing on the artistic production of an opera runs twice daily at 09:30 and 09:45, costs €12, and runs about 1.25 hours. The technical tour (twice daily, 09:30 and 12:00, €16) explains what it takes logistically to take an opera from concept to stage, all about changing and constructing sets, lighting, and even acoustics.

All tickets can be purchased on arrival at the box office opening at 09:15 daily.

Ticket prices vary, shows often, Plaza Isabel II, Sol, +34 915 160 660, teatro-real.com, Metro: Ópera

Flamenco Show at Casa Patas

While flamenco isn't technically native to Madrid (it comes from the southern cities like Seville and Granada), this show is a blast and has the best dancers and singers in town. Grab a seat toward the stage of this intimate black box venue serving both drinks and food. Once the lights go down for show time, you'll be treated to a dramatic show of gesticulating vocalists, stomping dancers, and impressive musicians playing guitar, drum box, and even violin.

Tickets from €36, includes first drink, dinner options available, shows nightly at 22:30 (check online to confirm times and specials, as they change often), Calle de los Cañizares 10, Sol, +34 913 690 496, casapatas.com, Metro: Antón Martín

Teleférico de Madrid

Take a ride in the *teleférico*, a cable-car that is suspended in the air, and catch some of Madrid's top sights from above! During your ride you'll fly by the Royal Palace and La Plaza de España, across the Manzanares River, and over a large beautiful park, the Casa de Campo. The *teleférico* is located west of Malasaña.

€4 one-way ticket, daily 12:00-21:00 (weekends only in winter), station just off of Paseo Pintor Rosales, just south of the intersection with Calle del Marqués de Urquijo, Greater Madrid, +34 902 345 002, teleferico.com, Metro: Argüelles

Museo Thyssen-Bornemisza

A much quieter experience than you'll get at the Prado, which is always overrun by tourists, the Museo Thyssen-Bornemisza offers a quiet atmosphere with an amazing impressionist and post-impressionist collection that could keep you busy for hours. Come enjoy the works of greats like Van Gogh, Renoir, Monet, Manet, Gauguin, and more.

€10 adult, €6 student, additional fees for special exhibits, free on Mon, Mon 12:00-16:00, Tues-Sun 10:00-19:00, Sat until 21:00 in the summer (exhibits only), last entry 45 minutes before closing, Paseo Prado 8, Museum District, +34 902 760 511, museothyssen.org, Metro: Banco de España

Estadio Santiago Bernabéu

In Spain, soccer is a religion, and Estadio Santiago Bernabéu is its cathedral. This gargantuan 80,000-seat stadium north of central Madrid is home to the soccer world's most winningest team: Real Madrid. But you should know that already. Real Madrid is kind of the Yankees of the soccer world—it's the richest team, so it can afford the most expensive players, so it keeps winning and making even more money. It's a nice upward spiral. If you're in town for a game, the tickets can get pricey but are absolutely worth it for fans. It's an experience you won't soon forget. Otherwise, you can take a tour of the facilities, check out the locker room, see the posh company boxes, get down to field level, learn about the history of the club, and pick up some sweet Real swag in the gift shop.

Game tickets can be hard to come by, and priority goes to season ticket and pass holders, with tourists holding up the rear. Purchase your tickets online at realmadrid.com, call into +34 902 324 324, or pick them up from the box office itself at the stadium or at most Caixa Bank branches in Madrid. You'll likely need to purchase tickets at least two weeks out for a good chance of getting them.

Cheap seats at the game from €50, unguided tours €19, Concha Espina 1, Greater Madrid, +34 913 984 300, realmadrid.com, Metro: Santiago Bernabéu

Bullfights at Plaza de Toros de las Venta

Each Sunday throughout the year, the bullfight stadium in Madrid packs out with tourists and locals alike to watch the spectacle of Spanish bullfighting. It's here that you'll see the best in the business do their thing: disorient, tease, stab, and ultimately kill bulls one after the other for a stretch of three-plus hours. I was taken aback by the timed, mechanical nature of the fight ritual, but something so famous and integral to Spanish history and culture warrants at least a short visit. It's possible to scalp tickets, but it is illegal and you risk losing your tickets if caught. You can't miss Plaza de Toros, about 25 minutes north of town via metro.

€5-150, cheaper shows feature novice bullfighters and messier bullfights, days and times vary, Calle de Alcalá 237, Greater Madrid, +34 913 562 200, las-ventas.com, Metro: Ventas

EXTRA CREDIT
City History Museum (Museo de los Orígenes)

If you're anything like your dear author, you dig learning about the history of any modern city with medieval foundations. In this modest and free museum you can check out a model of the old town and begin to visualize the old streets that have otherwise been cleaned up and straightened out.

Free, Sept-July Tues-Sun 09:30-20:00, Aug Tues-Fri 09:30-14:30, Sat-Sun 09:30-20:00, Plaza de San Andrés 2, La Latina, +34 913 667 415, madrid.es, Metro: La Latina

TOP EATS

Madrileño cuisine consists of succulent meats, dried *jamón* (ham) served in paper-thin slices, delicious cheeses like Manchego, potato- and chickpea-based stews, and many deliciously fried treats like churros, *patatas bravas* (fried potatoes with a spicy ketchup sauce), and *tortilla española* (potato omelet). The dishes can be a touch heavy, but they're well-portioned, and the fresh ingredients used don't make you regret it. Tapas, a favorite of locals and tourists alike, give you a chance to sample a number of dishes every time you sit down for a meal. Madrid offers a wide array of food beyond the typical Madrileño cuisine, too. The city is a magnet for people from all around the world, and with them they bring their own cuisine.

Malasaña is my favorite district in town for food, as there seems to be a popular local spot around just about every corner. The action tends to center around these squares: **Plaza del 2 de Mayo, Plaza Juan Pujol,** and **Plaza de San Ildefonso,** and you can find the local favorites in the streets between. For a real neighborhood feel, head to Malasaña's **Plaza de Carlos** to choose between the welcoming cafés and bars, like Lamucca de Pez and El Palentino, with outdoor seating spilling out onto this cute little square.

The streets around **Lavapies** are home to Madrid's ethnic (especially Indian) population. This neighborhood also has an underground, gritty feel, and you can find bargain food and drinks at every turn. You'll likely notice that the streets are darker here, but you're not in the danger you'd be in on a similarly poorly lit street in any city back in the States. Just stick with your friends and keep your wits about you—you're sure to have an awesome time. You can also find some fast-food gems in the streets around **El Rastro market** (Calle de Ribera de Curtidores).

Tipping is not expected, but rounding up to the next euro mark is appreciated. Be sure to check whether or not your bill says *"servicio incluido,"* as many touristy restaurants sneak this 10-15 percent charge in there.

Bodega La Ardosa

Bodega La Ardosa, in the Malasaña district, is one of my favorite old-time tapas restaurants in all of Madrid. Pop in for a cup of gazpacho and *patatas bravas,* and huddle with locals around upended kegs doubling as table tops. A snack in here feels like a step into old-world Spain, and the dusty bottles of spirits and liquors lining the walls add a bit of history to the place. There is standing-room only, which makes it easy to meet the friendly locals. Order only a dish or two to start, then wait to see what looks good coming out of the kitchen. La Ardosa is an excellent place to kick off a wander through Malasaña.

€11-20, Mon-Fri 08:30-02:00, Sat-Sun 11:45-02:30, Calle Colón 13, Malasaña, +34 915 214 979, laardosa.es, Metro: Tribunal

Lamucca de Pez

On the uphill side of Plaza de Carlos is Lamucca de Pez, a bright, posh cocktail and tapas bar with friendly service, exposed brick

EATING ON THE CHEAP

Here are some basic tips on how to stay on that budget while eating out in Madrid.

- *Bocadillos* are simple (i.e., one topping), delicious, handmade sandwiches put on a small baguette and made to order. They're my top choice for budget eats just about anywhere in Spain because nearly every café and bar can make them on demand. Your only challenge is to figure out your favorite fillings: chorizo, *jamón* (ham), *tortilla de patata* (Spanish potato omelet), and even *calamares*, fried calamari rings. And the best part? Getting your *pan con tomate* or having a tomato puree ladled onto your bread to make it extra juicy. The Brits have butter, Americans use mayonnaise, Italians olive oil, but Spaniards—*tomate*. And it's *so* good! *Bocadillos* normally run about €3, and are a filling snack to power you through the day.

- Most restaurants charge a small cover for sit-down table service. Skip the charge by standing up and eating at the bar.

- You'll often be charged for the bread at your table. Before digging in, ask, "*¿gratis?*"

- If you ask for water without specifying which kind, restaurant staff will bring out a bottle for which you've gotta pay. Ask for tap water by saying "*agua del grifo, por favor.*"

- Avoid restaurants with pictures in the windows in place of menus. More often than not, pictures are used to cater to tourists rather than locals. Much better: Find the hole-in-the-wall restaurants without a menu that serve up delicious, fresh, and typical cuisine to loyal returning customers.

- Keep your eyes open for the menu of the day, or *menu del día*. These are often a great value, and you'll find that for Madrileños, lunch is the biggest meal of the day, just before siesta—no wonder they've gotta sleep it off!

interior, and an extensive wine selection. They take pride in both their Italian-style pizzas and expertly mixed alcoholic concoctions.

Bocadillos from €3, pizzas from €12, Tues-Sat 12:00-24:00, Sun 19:00-24:00, Plaza de Carlos Cambronero, Malasaña, +34 910 210 000, lamucca.es, Metro: Tribunal or Noviciado

El Palentino

Across from Lamucca de Pez is El Palentino, your classic nondescript neighborhood pub and bar that pumps out fresh *bocadillos* (sandwiches) all day and *cañas* (half-pints of beer) to wash them down. Come here to get a true glimpse into the jovial Madrileño lifestyle.

Bocadillos from €3, pizzas from €12, Tues-Sat 12:00-24:00, Sun 19:00-24:00, Plaza de Carlos Cambronero, Malasaña, +34 915 323 058, Metro: Tribunal or Noviciado

Bar Santurce

My favorite spot around El Rastro market is this little anchovy shop that cranks out platefuls of the salty snack. It's near the top of the hill on Calle de las Amazonas. An order of *pimientos de padrón* (fried peppers), fried anchovies, a bread bowl, and two *cañas* makes for an excellent afternoon stop

if you're in the area. The place is busy with locals and tourists alike. Step in, work your way to the front of the line, and be ready to order when you wave your bartender down. If you haven't worked up the guts to try anchovies, Bar Santurce is the perfect place to do it! There's a pickle shop next door that hits the spot too.

Plates from €3, Tues-Sat 12:00-16:00, Sun 09:00-16:00, Plaza General Vara del Rey 14, La Latina, +34 646 238 303, barsanturce.com, Metro: La Latina

Cervecería Cruz

This is your classic Madrileño beer hall: brightly lit, with steel countertops, grandpas playing cards, and a food bar serving classics like *pimientos de padrón* and calamari on order. Its location at the top of El Rastro market makes it a popular place on Sunday.

Dishes from €3.50, daily 08:00-23:00, Calle de las Maldonadas 1, La Latina, +34 913 663 738, Metro: La Latina

Puerto Rico

This is one of my favorite and affordable restaurants in the center. Come out to Puerto Rico for simple, filling cuisine like typical Madrileño stews, roast chicken, and your whole array of tapas. Thanks to its location

and casual atmosphere, Puerto Rico fills up daily with power lunchers at lunch. Tourists love the place for its great value. Go for their menu of the day for a three-course lunch for under €12, which should easily last you through dinner. Don't miss their rice pudding and flan if you've got room for dessert!

Lunches and dinners under €10, daily 13:00-16:30 and 20:30-23:30, Calle de Chinchilla 2, Sol, +34 915 219 834, Metro: Callao or Gran Vía

Mercado San Antón

I love this polished, multilevel indoor market for collecting fresh ingredients for a picnic and snacks. Find the baker for a fresh baguette, and pick up 100 grams each of *jamón Serrano* and *queso Manchego* (ham and cheese) from the butcher for a delicious sandwich that should last you till the next day. Climb to the top level for prepared food options like *Salmorejo* and surprisingly tasty burgers.

Create your own adventure for around €5, daily 10:00-24:00, Calle de Augusto Figueroa 24, Chueca, +34 913 300 730, mercadosananton.com, Metro: Chueca

Museo del Jamón

This chain does one thing and it does it well: It serves fresh slices of some of the world's best cured ham. We Westerners may lack a developed palate for *jamón*, but that's all the more reason to pop into one of their downtown locations and order a smattering of different types to sample. Spring for a taste of *jamón ibérico de bellota* (pig raised on a diet of acorns), as it's widely regarded as the best type of this thin-sliced ham in the world. Don't let them get carried away

when slicing! Prices are paid by weight. Take in the view of hundreds of ham legs hanging from the walls and ceiling—these guys take their selection seriously. Find other locations at Calle Gran Vía 72 and Calle de Atocha 54.

From €5, daily 09:00-24:00, Plaza Mayor 18, Sol, +34 913 692 204, museodeljamon.es, Metro: Ópera

Chocolatería San Ginés

Like chocolate? Go here. You can't pass through Spain without enjoying one of the country's top treats: fried doughy sticks (churros) dunked in hot chocolate (which is more like concentrated melted chocolate than something you could actually drink), and Chocolatería San Ginés offers some of the best of both in the city. Enjoy your thick and rich cup of chocolate in a classic, warm setting that is exactly what you'd think an old-school café should be: prominent espresso bar, outdoor seating, wooden interior with large mirrors, and old-time locals enjoying their favorite snack. The café is tucked in a back street behind the Iglesia San Ginés de Arles, just a couple blocks west from Plaza Puerta del Sol.

Churros and chocolate from €4, daily 24 hours, Pasadizo San Ginés 5, Sol, +34 913 656 546, chocolateriasangines. com, Metro: Sol

Torre del Oro

Located right on Plaza Mayor, Torre del Oro is widely known as the best bullfight bar in town. As long as you don't lose your appetite when seeing bull heads mounted on the walls, you'll enjoy their typical Madrileño dishes, like fried anchovies and ham sandwiches. The restaurant itself is the main attraction, with dozens of framed pictures of bullfighters, including some gory shots of when the matadors must have taken their eye off the ball...er, bull.

Bites from €3, daily 11:00–02:00, Plaza Mayor 26, Sol, +34 913 665 016, torredeloro.sellsoc.org, Metro: Ópera

Café Melos

Stroll downhill from Sol to find the bright (and a bit sterile) Café Melos, famous for its inexpensive fare ideal for students and travelers on tight budgets. Try their *zapatilla*—a huge stuffed sandwich overflowing with ham and cheese, easily splittable between two people, or enough to put you into hibernation just in time for siesta. If you've still got room, don't miss their flash-fried croquettes either. The picture-based menu makes selection easy.

Snacks from €3.50, Tues–Sun 08:00–02:00, Calle del Ave María 44, Lavapiés, +34 915 275 054, Metro: Lavapiés

El Corte Inglés

In the basement of this massive department store just a couple blocks from Sol, you'll find a modern grocery store where you can stock up on extensive options for picnic supplies. They've also got an affordable café upstairs that's very popular among locals for power lunches during the work week.

Cheap, daily 10:00–22:00, Plaza de Callao 2, Sol, +34 913 798 000, elcorteingles.es, Metro: Callao

La Sanabresa

La Sanabresa is your best choice near the Antón Martín metro stop for sit-down value. Their lunch and dinner *menus del día* offer astounding value even though they're located in the heart of touristy Madrid: €10-16 will get you three courses (starter, main, and dessert) with a drink, bread, and little taste of liquor to cap it all off. Mains range from grilled meats and fish like chicken, pork, beef, and salmon to stews and roast veg-

gies. And it all goes down in a casual setting with white tablecloths, efficient service, and bright and inviting atmosphere.

Mains from €8, Mon–Sat 13:00–16:30 and 20:30–23:30, Calle Amor de Dios 12, Lavapiés, +34 914 290 338, Metro: Antón Martín

Taberna El Sur

I love El Sur's excellent selection, which ranges from light (Cobb salad) all the way to classic and heavy (fried egg topped with bacon over fried potatoes). Either way you go, dishes come with impressive presentation. Delicious drinks, like salted margaritas and sangria complete with cinnamon sticks, are available, too. Enjoy an afternoon or evening meal in this welcoming yet refined restaurant with somewhat mod decor, tucked away in an authentic neighborhood just a couple blocks south of the Antón Martín metro stop.

Excellent-value meals from €10, Sun–Thurs 12:00–01:30, Fri–Sat 12:00–02:00, Calle de Torrevilla del Leal 12, Lavapiés, +34 915 278 340, Metro: Antón Martín

La Pizzateca

La Pizzateca is your classic pizza-by-the-slice fast food joint, but they do it well, and at good prices. Don't come for the fancy atmosphere, but do stop by to choose from their racks of pizza made with fresh ingredients like peppers, zucchini, sausage, spinach, and potatoes. They'll warm your slices up for you while you wait. Eat in at their simple wooden bar, or take it outside to enjoy in the square.

Slices from €2.50, Tues–Sun 13:00–16:30 and 19:00–24:00, Calle Lean 35, Sol, +34 913 693 210, lapizzateca.com, Metro: Antón Martín

La Rollerie

La Rollerie is my favorite breakfast choice in town. While Spaniards generally eat a light breakfast, La Rollerie has just about anything to suit my fancy no matter what I'm

craving, from cinnamon rolls and pastries to bacon-and-egg bagel sandwiches. They try a little too hard to mimic a French bakery, but, thankfully, they are on point when it comes to what matters: carrot cake, Andalucian breakfast (toast with tomato puree), and of course, coffee. The Rollerie is a touch posh, and draws the locals and tourists who can spend €10 or more on a delicious breakfast.

Coffee from €3, daily 08:00–22:30, Calle de Atocha 20, Sol, +34 914 204 675, larollerie.com, Metro: Sol or Tirso de Molina

TOP NIGHTLIFE

Like all Mediterranean cultures, nightlife in Madrid starts late. Ask around your hostel to get a feel, but the real party doesn't start until after 01:00 or later. Pace yourself, and make sure your hostel windows can block out the sun in the morning!

Madrid's neighborhoods have distinct vibes and different sorts of venues. Rather than aiming for a specific venue, it's most fun to pick the district that appeals to you, then set out to discover your own favorites. Many of Madrid's top eateries also double as fun nightlife venues.

NIGHTLIFE DISTRICTS

Malasaña
My favorite neighborhood in town has a slightly hipsterish and trendy feel without really trying. It's a popular spot to meet up with friends for drinks. The streets are narrow and tangled, so it's fun to wander and see what gems you discover.

Malasaña, Metro: Noviciado

Chueca
Chueca is Madrid's gay district, with fun bars and tasty food options centered around **Chueca Square.**

Chueca, Metro: Chueca

Sol
The area around Puerta del Sol is understandably touristy. Bars catering to the international crowd are sprinkled throughout Sol but are concentrated just south of Madrid's central plaza. It's here you can find Irish bars and study-abroad students by the hundreds. If you keep your eyes open, you can still discover winners in the area.

So much of Madrid's nightlife is pedal to the metal, so if you prefer a more low-key evening, grab a bottle of wine and head down to **Plaza de Santa Ana,** southeast of Puerta del Sol, for a night of relaxing and people-watching from the benches that line the square. It's an endlessly entertaining plaza filled with a mix of tourists and locals passing through on their way to more shenanigans.

Sol, Metro: Sol

Lavapies
In Madrid's grungy, too-gritty-for-some underground district, Lavapies, you can find some hidden theaters and great music venues. Of course, the money saved by finding off-the-beaten-path watering holes is a plus, too!

Lavapies, Metro: Lavapies

La Latina
La Latina is the trendy upscale neighbor-

LGBT MADRID

LGBTQ travelers will find Spain welcome and progressive. Spain was the first country in the EU to legalize gay marriage, and as such is considered a very progressive and liberal country with respects to equal rights for gay couples. Gay visitors should expect to enjoy safety and no unwanted attention during their time in Madrid.

All of my recommended nightlife venues are gay-friendly, but **Chueca** is your neighborhood for partying while in town for the gay scene. Your best bet is to head to the main square and take a stroll around the neighborhood branching off from there. In the surrounding streets you'll find happy, welcoming people, an excited buzz, and numerous cafés, restaurants, delis and grocery stores, bars, lounges and dance bars, and clubs. Stores run the whole gamut from high street fashion to drag suits and more, suiting just about all tastes. **El Bulldog** (San Bartolomé 16, +34 915 991 260) draws the bear crowd, **Griffin's** (Calle Marqués de Valdeiglesias 6, +34 915 22 20 79) is your dominating drag spot, and **La Kama** (Calle Gravina 4, +34 915 22 32 26) is a fun go-go bar serving cocktails in a lounge setting.

hood in downtown with tapas bars, classy restaurants, and a fun vibe. The action centers around two streets: **Calle Cava Baja** and **Calle Cava Alta,** which turns into **Calle Grafal** farther north. These two parallel streets running just northwest of the La Latina metro stop have a fun little world of classy bars, shops, cafés, and *jamón* shops. It's easy to make an evening starting at the top of one street and looping around, popping into any tapas bars that strike your fancy. The district is a bit of a tourist trap and is notorious for wildly varying service and food quality. So rather than order a slew of dishes, I spring for one at a time to ensure the experience is up to par before ordering more.

El Tempranillo (Calle Cava Baja 38, +34 913 64 15 32), which sports an impressive wine selection and *pintxo* menu, and **El Viajero** (Plaza de la Cebada 11, +34 913 66 90 64), a contemporary, simple-fare bar with a delightful terrace and offerings like beef sliders and ribs, are two places to start your crawl, though you can run up a tab quite quickly at both venues. **Juana la Loca** (Plaza Puerta de Moros 4, +34 913 640 525) is where all the in-the-know locals flock after work. With excellent cocktails, a delectable dessert menu, and a chill lounge vibe, this one of my first stops when I'm in town.

La Latina, Metro: La Latina

Salamanca

You may see Spanish celebrities at the numerous cocktail bars and posh clubs in glitterati-populated Salamanca. With the hot vibes come the highest prices and most pretentiousness you'll find in the city. Bars and clubs in this neighborhood tend to open and close frequently. Jersey chaser? Come here for the chance of a glimpse at the Real Madrid crew, who often show up to celebrate a win.

Salamanca, Metro: Serrano or Velazquez

BARS & PUBS
Dubliners Pub
There are a few of your standard fake Irish pubs in the heart of Madrid, offering mediocre drinks and food, but they're dependable at least for that and for a wide selection of sports being played. Don't expect sharp service or any sort of local experience at this touristy bar, but it's a good place to bond with fellow backpackers.

Daily 11:00–03:00, Calle de Espoz y Mina 7, Sol, +34 915 22 75 09, irishpubdubliners.com, Metro: Sol

O'Neill's
O'Neill's is a favorite for its large beer hall feel, pool table, drink and shot specials, and comfortable living room-style ambience. You can count on a sloppy, sticky-floor-good-time backpacking experience here. You'll likely cross paths with the American students "living" in Madrid on their study-abroad experience.

Mon–Wed 17:00–01:00, Thurs 17:00–02:00, Fri 17:00–03:30, Sat 13:00–03:30, Sun 13:00–01:00, Calle del Príncipe 12, +34 915 212 030, facebook.com/ONeillsMadrid, Metro: Sol

CLUBS
Clubs open and close often in Madrid. It's a raging scene that continues till the sun comes up nearly every day of the week. I've listed the nightlife institutions of Madrid,

ACT LIKE A LOCAL

Party Like a Madrileño

Madrileños eat around 20:00 or 21:00, enjoy friends and socializing for the next few hours, then begin heading out around 01:00 or later. To draw revelers in earlier, many clubs have free cover or extra drinks included in the price of the cover fee before 01:30. While you'll get more by showing up early, oftentimes you'll need to wait until the party shows up around 02:00. *Cervecerías* (beer halls) are a great way to get some food to keep you going and enjoy the Spanish tradition of *cañas*—half-pints served cheap and easy from bright, steel-topped bars.

If you're in a *cervecería* or tapas place packed with locals and want to order food, you'll need to sharpen your elbows and work your way up to the bar. If you're passive, you'll likely lose your place in line. Keep your ears open, take a look at what everyone else is ordering, and practice your order in your head while trying to make eye contact with the bartender. Ordering by pointing (and smiling) works, too!

but be sure to ask at your hostel to see what new and hot venues have opened up.

Joy Eslava

A massive, horseshoe-shaped nightclub in central Madrid, Joy has been converted from a 1950s theater, meaning this place was practically built for the impressive light shows and loud music that partiers drown in every night of the week. Music is heavy on the techno but also mixes in local and international hits. Drinks can be pricey, so pregame well before showing up, but not so well you turn off the picky bouncers!

Covers around €12 (sometimes negotiable), pricey drinks and beers from €10, Sun–Thurs 12:00–05:30, Sat–Sun 12:00–18:00, Calle Arenal 11, Sol, +34 913 663 733, joy-eslava.com, Metro: Ópera

Teatro Kapital

This is a club on steroids with everything from the floor count (seven) and the light system (spectacular and nearly blinding) to the cover and drink charges (€20+ and

€12+, respectively) and dance shows (inspiring). If you're trying to have the euro-club experience, see if you can't get in here for their standard cover, which should include a drink at €20. Dress smart, though: The bouncers have been known to try and charge €50 at the door.

€20 cover with drink, Thurs–Sat 12.00–06.00, Calle de Atocha 125, Museum District, +34 914 202 906, grupo-kapital.com, Metro: Atocha

PUB CRAWLS

Sandeman's New Madrid Pub Crawl

Sandeman's New Madrid offers a nightly pub crawl if you want to pass off the responsibility for charting your night out. Cheaper than their pub crawls in other European cities, this Sandeman's crawl is fun and social, stops in three bars, and finishes in one of Madrid's famous clubs.

€12, nightly at 22:00, meet at Plaza Mayor, Sol, newmadrid-tours.com, Metro: Ópera

TOP SHOPPING & MARKETS

Madrid has the whole range of shopping, from cheap flea markets to high fashion and prices.

SHOPPING DISTRICTS

Gran Vía

In Sol and **Gran Vía**, Madrid's downtown and most central shopping district, a slew of retail shops sell everything from touristy trinkets to shoes, hats, and clothes. This is your Champs-Élysées, Piccadilly Circus, and Piazza Venezia of Madrid.

Sol, Metro: Plaza de Santo Domingo, Plaza del Callao, or Gran Vía

Calle Fuencarral

This charming pedestrian boulevard runs north-south through the heart of Malasaña. It features pop-up fashion shops and hidden gems like boutique clothing and shoe shops, where you'll uncover finds that'll make your friends jealous. The main attraction is the people-watching you'll enjoy on a stroll up and down the street. There are some great options for food and brunch on **Calle de Augusto Figueroa.**

Malasaña, Metro: Chueca or Gran Vía

Calle Serrano

On Calle Serrano, a long street in the Salamanca district that runs north and south, you'll find high-fashion shopping from the Plaza de la Independencia all the way north to Calle Juan Bravo. It's here you can expect to find brands like D&G and Gucci.

Salamanca, Metro: Retiro, Serrano, or Ruben Dario

MARKETS

El Rastro

You'll find everything from trinkets and antiques to clothing and fabric stores at what is probably the biggest flea market in Madrid. On Sunday during outdoor market hours, the atmosphere here is insane. The avenue turns into one massive garage sale that makes the *Antiques Roadshow* look like child's play. Each little side-street branch has vendors that focus around some similar good, like "bird street" or the "painting street" and another selling collectibles like trading cards. So cruise the main boulevard, but don't forget to wander off!

It's easy to get distracted with all the energy, but keep a hand on your wallet at all times. If you're going to get pickpocketed, it'll happen here.

Free, Sun 09:00-15:00, Plaza de Cascorro, La Latina, Metro: La Latina

Mercado San Miguel

Mercado San Miguel is Spain's answer to markets like Whole Foods and Trader Joe's. This food market has all sorts of unforgettable cuisine that you can buy to take home, and many shops will cook up your ingredients right in front of you. San Miguel is worth the trip no matter where you're staying in town.

Free, Sun-Wed 10:00-24:00, Thurs-Sat 10:00-02:00, Plaza de San Miguel, Sol, Metro: Ópera

Mercado Puerta de Toledo

What used to be a bustling fish market is now a shopper's paradise, as the Mercado Puerta de Toledo is chock full of galleries, fashion retailers, and shops, along with many trendy cafés, pubs, and restaurants.

Free, 10:30-20:30 daily, Sun til 14:30, Ronda de Toledo 1, La Latina, Metro: Puerta de Toledo

Cuesta de Moyano

If you're into old books, this is the market to hit up. Book collectors from all over the world come to barter in this collection of over 30 outdoor stalls.

Free, open daily (hours vary stall to stall), Calle Claudio Moyano, Museum District, Metro: Atocha

TOP PARKS & RECREATION

PARKS

Retiro Park

This park, directly east of the Museum District, is full of beautiful gardens, sculptures, buildings, and a man-made lake. It's a great place to take a break during your busy day of sightseeing. A highlight is the Crystal Palace, a massive steel and glass greenhouse in the industrial style so popular at the turn of the 20th century. Don't miss the dramatic *Statue of the Fallen Angel* either—it's the only public statue in Europe dedicated to the devil.

Free, daily 06:00-22:00, Plaza de la Independencia, Metro: Ibiza

Botanical Gardens

Bordering the Prado and Retiro Park, the affordable Botanical Gardens are worth popping into for a stroll away from the hustle and bustle of the capital. With over 30,000 plants and 1,500 trees, the noise and stress of the city fades away and you can find numerous prime locations for a little picnic to rest and recharge.

€3, Mon-Sat 09:30-14:00 and 15:30-18:00, Plaza de Murillo 2, Museum District, +34 914 203 017, rjb.csic.es, Metro: Atocha

Madrid Río

On the west side of town, Madrid's river walk is an excellent way to get away from the crowds, as it doesn't seem to be on the tourist radar quite yet. Head over to the governmental and office district of Príncipe Pío, just behind the Royal Palace and Jardines de Sabatini, for a peaceful walk along the river. You can also rent bikes and cruise farther on the newly laid meandering paths, which stretch for miles.

Free, always open, Greater Madrid, Metro: Intercambiador de Príncipe Pío

VIEWPOINTS

In addition to the **Teleférico Madrid,** a couple of other venues in Madrid offer sweeping views of the city.

El Corte Inglés

This large shopping center doubles as one of the best viewpoints in Madrid. Ride the escalators up to the ninth floor and relax in the café that overlooks the city skyline.

Free, Mon-Sat 10:00-22:00, 11:00-21:00, Sun Plaza de Callao 2, Sol, +34 913 79 80 00, elcorteingles.es, Metro: Santo Domingo or Gran Vía

Circulo de Bellas Artes Terraza

Find a classy terrace with bar and café at the top of Madrid's Fine Arts Association building. The view from this city-center location is one of my favorites, and it doubles as a popular nightlife venue after the sun goes down.

€4, Mon-Thurs 09:00-02:00, Fri 09:00-02:30, Sat-Sun 11:00-02:30, Alcalá 42, Sol, +34 913 892 500, circulobellasartes.com/azotea, Metro: Sol

TOP TOURS

Sandeman's New Europe Walking Tours

After years of battling the Spanish tourist authorities, Sandeman's walking tours have finally restarted in Spain with gusto. Hop on any of their free and fun but scripted and tip-based walking tours. They leave daily at 10:00, 11:00, and 14:00 from Plaza Mayor. You can count on a several-hour stroll picking up tons of entertaining fun facts and trivia, along with frequent plugs for their other paid tours. Pub crawls are also available.

Free, daily, tours leave from Plaza Mayor, Sol, newmadridtours.com, info@neweuropetours.eu, Metro: Ópera

Spanish Cooking Classes: Paella, Gazpacho, & Sangria

I always say the best way to experience a new culture is through the stomach! If you enjoy hands-on cooking experiences, this is your top option in town. Come out for a crash course in some of Spain's favorite dishes. Choose from their selection of classes, from paella to tapas and even wine-tasting. Kick off your experience with a visit to the local market to pick up ingredients. Your friendly chef teacher can help even the clumsiest feel right at home in their modern kitchen facilities. These guys have their act together, and you get a fun recipe book as a keepsake from your visit. Classes take about four hours and start at 10:00. Book online ahead of time.

Options from €70, Mon-Sat, Calle de Moratin 11, Sol, +34 910 115 154, cookingpoint.es/classes, info@cookingpoint.es, Metro: Antón Martín

Letango Tours

Carlos and Jenn, a husband and wife couple, run this upscale, custom tour operations outfit. While their price points set them beyond most backpackers' budgets, they're definitely worth a look for families, or for a group of friends for excursions beyond the city of Madrid. Letango offers options for multiday excursions all around the Iberian Peninsula, with options to focus on history, culture, and food.

Multi-day trips from €300, +34 661 752 458, letango.com, tours@letango.com

TOP HOSTELS

You've got a wide selection of well-located budget accommodations around Madrid. It's good to search by the district you identify best with. Personally, I love to drill down to **Malasaña** for its proximity to the trendy, fun, and casual restaurants and nightlife. Others may prefer the hustle and bustle of **Sol**, and still others may enjoy the extensive food and nightlife options in **Chueca**.

For more hostel choices, visit **hostelworld.com** to find the best deals. With the economic situation in Spain these days, many locals are turning to sites like **airbnb.com** to generate a little extra income by renting out their spare rooms. Private apartment options are also worth considering. Three-star hotels in Madrid range €80-120 per night.

Las Musas Residence

The simple and spartan Las Musas Residence is in the heart of the Lavapies neighborhood, where you'll find recommended restaurants, cafés, and nightlife. The hostel has big rooms for about €20 per night and sports all your basic amenities, including a kitchen. The free sangria and drinking game nights turn the party up and draw backpackers like moths to light.

€18, 24-hour reception, laundry facilities, free Wi-Fi, common room, lockers, Calle Jesús y María 12, Sol, +34 915 394 984, lasmusasresidence.com, info@lasmusasresidence. com, Metro: Tirso de Molina

Sungate Hostel

Sungate is loved by all who stay for the awesome atmosphere that the staff creates. They give this clean, centrally located hostel that extra little something that makes it feel like home away from home rather than just a place to crash. The 24-hour reception means you can check in any time of the day, and there will always be people to recommend nearby restaurants and to organize activities. It's just up the hill from Plaza Puerta del Sol, so you're right in the thick of it whether you're looking for churros or *chupitos* (shots).

Private twins from €30, 6-bed dorms from €18, Calle de Carmen 16, Sol, +34 910 236 806, sungatehostel.com, Metro: Sol

MuchoMadrid

Offering only twins, triples, and quads, these budget accommodations are for those who appreciate both their fun and their sleep. Done up in a clean-yet-funky design, the bright rooms are comfortable and quiet. There's a well-appointed kitchen, but the hostel lacks a social area, so if meeting other cute backpackers is your goal, you may want to consider other options.

4 bed dorms from €20, Gran Vía 59, Malasaña, +34 915 592 350, muchomadrid.com, Metro: Santo Domingo

Cat's Hostel

A hostel with marble pillars, ornate arches, and colorful patterned walls, Cat's Hostel is a uniquely wonderful place to stay. It also offers a party atmosphere with its own bar that's open late, along with a free breakfast to help fuel you the next morning.

€14-18, 24-hour reception, free Wi-Fi, laundry facilities, bar, free breakfast, lockers, computer access, Calle Cañizares 6, Sol, +34 913 692 807, catshostel.com, info@catshostel. com, Metro: Antón Martín

Room007 Hostel: Chueca

This is a large hostel with a couple hundred beds and good-value on-site bar and restaurant. Social events often include music nights and bar crawls. The rooftop terrace is a favorite too. This is one branch of a multi-location hostel chain in Madrid that has it down to a science. You'll find Wi-Fi everywhere (though weaker in the rooms), good-value breakfast, great city-center locations, and helpful staff facilitating a social environment. Hostels are done up in a sort of shabby chic decor that makes you feel like you're in a magazine shoot from time to time.

11-bed dorm from €18, Calle Hortaleza 74, Chueca, +34 913 688 111, room007.com/es, Metro: Chueca

Room007 Hostel: Ventura

This branch of Room007, centrally located directly between the Prado Museum and Plaza Puerta del Sol, shares many of the same attributes as the chain's Chueca hostel. This location is smaller and more personal, with more than 100 beds split across four- and eight-bed dorms. The reception will help you make the most of your time with a ton of sightseeing and activity recommendations.

4- and 8-bed dorms from €19, Ventura de la Vega 5, Sol, +34 914 204 481, room007.com/es, Metro: Sol

GETTING THERE & AWAY

Luggage storage facilities are available at all major train stations and at the airport.

Plane

The massive **Madrid-Barajas Airport** (MAD, aeropuertomadrid-barajas.com) is the main international airport serving the city, and is your only option if you decide to arrive by air. (You may find options for Barcelona and Girona, but remember, those are more than four hours away!). You can connect into the center from the airport via metro, bus, or train.

Metro trains leave every 5 minutes 06:00–02:00 and depart from Terminal T2 and Terminal T4. Take **line 8**, which you will probably want to ride to the end stop, Nuevos Ministerios. The approximately 15-minute trip will cost you €5. Consider purchasing a multiday metro pass at the machines just before you enter the metro so it will include this first trip into town.

The **Exprés Aeropuerto** (Airport Express) is a 24-hour bus service that has only three stops: O'Donnell, Plaza de Cibeles, and Atocha (this last stop only 06:00-23:30). Check the location of your hostel for your most practical hop-off point. The buses leave every 15 minutes from Terminals T1, T2, and T3, with a journey time of about 40 minutes. Purchase your ticket (€5) on board.

The **C1 train line** departs from Terminal T4 for a 10-minute journey into Madrid (€2.40). This train line has connections to Chamartin, Nuevos Ministerios, Atocha, and Príncipe Pío stations.

Train

Trains between Barcelona and Madrid run often and take about three hours. If you purchase in advance through **renfe.com,** tickets can be as cheap as €50, but they climb past €150 closer to the date and during peak travel times. For the cheapest options, avoid peak commuter times (early morning, late afternoon).

Madrid has two main train stations: **Atocha,** near the Reina Sofia, and **Chamartin,** about eight kilometers north of Puerta del Sol. Both main stations are well connected with the local metro system. You should have no trouble getting to your hostel. There

are secondary stations as well, so always double-check your departure station before heading to catch your train. Other train stations include **Nuevos Ministerios, Príncipe Pío, Delicias, Pirámides,** and **Méndez Alvaro**. There is also the **Recoletos** station, though it is not connected with the metro. Trains run generally 06:00-23:00 and depart frequently for both national and international destinations. If you need to book in person, allow at least an hour and a half, as lines can be long and slow.

Bus

Spain has an extensive network of bus lines that can get you across the country. Of the main bus companies, I recommend **Alsa** (alsa.es/en) and **Eurolines** (eurolines.es/en). Remember, though; it's a big country! So you'll have to weigh the cheaper price you'll usually get against the additional time spent en route. If arriving by bus, you will be dropped off at **Méndez Alvaro** (Estación del Sur) bus station, Madrid's main bus station, or **Avenida de América** bus station. Both are very well connected, making it easy to get to anywhere you need to go in the city.

Car

It's a serious six-hour drive from Barcelona, going on the EU-funded and toll-supported E-90 freeway to Madrid. Having a car does give you the flexibility to stop along the way or drive along the coast. Madrid itself is a car city, but it has some intense traffic. There isn't any sort of park-and-ride system, so your best bet is to park on the outskirts of the city within a few blocks of a metro stop and take the metro in to avoid hefty parking fees during your visit. Of course, lock your doors, and leave nothing of value in the car.

GETTING AROUND

Madrid's excellent **public transportation** network makes it easy to get across this sprawling city. Be sure to consider the great-value short-term **day passes,** which get you onto the integrated bus and metro network and can save money if you plan on using the metro even just a few times a day. Spring for the one-day (€8.40) two-day (€14.20), three-day (€18.40), or five-day (€26.80) multiday pass at the entrance to the metro from the airport, as the local pass covers all of downtown Madrid, including your first transfer into town.

Metro

Madrid's **metro system** (metromadrid.es/en) comprises over 238 stations and 13 lines, making connections across town fast and easy. The metro runs 06:00-01:30, with trains coming every few minutes during rush hour (07:30-09:00) and every five minutes during regular hours. A single metro ticket costs €1.50.

Bus

Madrid has a new line of hydrogen-fueled (and air-conditioned!) buses. Buses run every 5-15 minutes 06:00-02:00. And for you late-nighters, night buses operate 23:45-06:00, with buses coming every 15-30 minutes.

Car

Madrid is much better for cars than most other European cities. Its wide, modern boulevards make getting around much easier than topsy-turvy medieval streets do. If you'll only be visiting Madrid, there's no need to rent a car thanks to the extensive local transportation networks. Even connecting between major cities is easy with trains and buses. Consider renting a car only if you want to get farther out into the countryside, where bus and train connections are more difficult.

Taxi

With more than 15,000 taxis serving the city, you won't have a problem flagging one down. Look for the white taxis with a diagonal red band on the side door with the city's emblem, featuring a bear, tree, and crown just above the stripe. With such a great public transportation system in place, only use these if you need to get across town in a jiffy or are coming back from the clubs before the next morning's rush hour. At the time of writing, Uber had not yet made inroads into Madrid.

Bicycle

With the big streets and fast-driving cars, Madrid is notoriously unfriendly for cycling, and biking around town is not recommended. The one exception is Retiro Park, a great place to ride around and explore. Find several bike shops on the east side of the park.

DAY TRIPS

Toledo

Toledo was Spain's capital for nearly 1,000 years. Today, it's a beautifully preserved stone town perched on top of a rocky outcropping. It's touristy and kitschy but also wonderful to explore for an afternoon. One highlight is the **Cathedral of Toledo** (€8, Mon-Sat 10:00-18:00, Sun 14:00-18:00, Calle Cardenal Cisneros 1, +34 925 22 22 41, catedralprimada.es). Stepping into this church, exquisitely executed in high gothic style and dripping in golden accents with baroque embellishments, is truly a spiritual experience. The **Mirador del Valle** is a breathtaking vista overlooking the horseshoe bend in the river from which the rock that Toledo sits on rises. Time your visit on a clear day and hop the river via the bridge on the east side of town, then continue south to climb the hill to the viewpoint. You'll know it when you see it. For your museum fix, don't miss the **Alcázar of Toledo** (€5, Thurs-Tues 11:00-17:00, Calle Unión, +34 925 23 88 00, museo.ejercito.es), the palace that dominates the city's skyline. Originally built as a fort and Roman palace, the Alcázar of Toledo served as a major standoff point in the Spanish Civil War between the loyalists and republicans. Today, it's a fascinating military history museum. It's interesting to tour this grand structure, which dates back hundreds of years. Trains leave from Atocha station more often than hourly and take about 40 minutes. Fares are about €13 one-way. Purchase tickets from the machines at the station.

HELP!

Tourist Information Centers
Find Madrid's TI conveniently located steps from Puerto del Sol (daily 09:30-20:30, Plaza Mayor 27).

Pickpockets & Scams
Madrid has a relatively low crime rate; however, always keep a close watch over your bags and other items, as pickpocketing and street theft can occur. Be especially wary of crowded areas such as train stations and crowded tourist attractions. In Spain, it's better to carry only what you need for the day rather than carrying all your cards and cash with you. Leave what you don't need in the safe at the hostel. The area just south of La Latina is known to have a higher density of pickpockets and thieves. Avoid going there alone at night, and keep your wits about you during the day, too.

Emergencies
In an emergency, dial 112. You can also dial 091 for police.

Hospital
Hospital Ruber Internacional

Calle de la Masó 38

+34 913 875 000

US Embassy
Calle Serrano 75

+34 915 872 240

BARCELONA

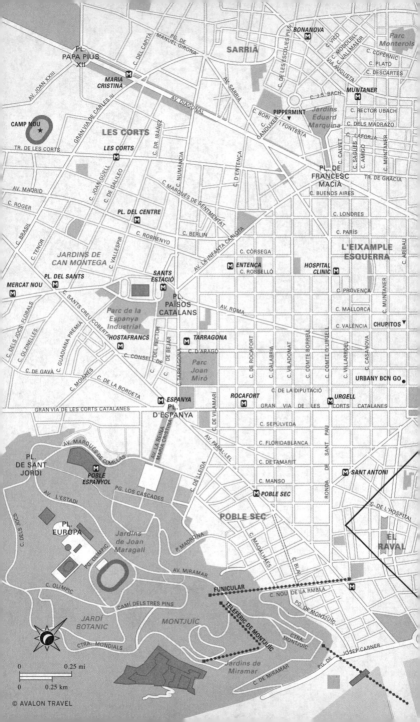

© AVALON TRAVEL

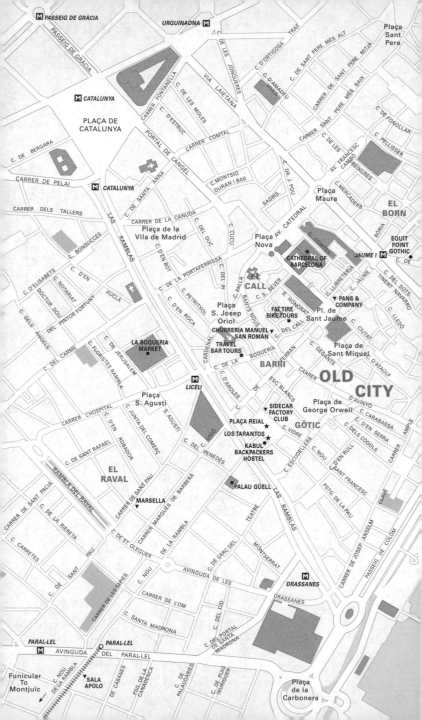

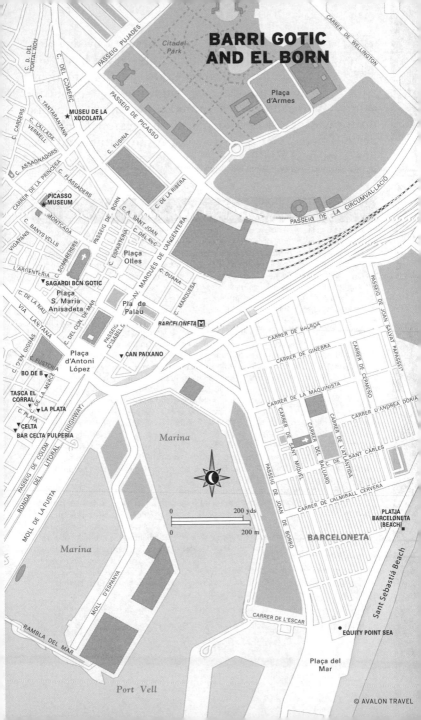

BARRI GOTIC
AND EL BORN

Citadel Park

Plaça d'Armes

CARRER DE WELLINGTON

PASSEIG PUJADES

C. DEL PORTAL NOU

C. D. DEL COMERÇ

PASSEIG DE PICASSO

C. TANTARANTANA

★ MUSEU DE LA XOCOLATA

C. CARRERS

C. L'ALLADA VERMELL

C. FUSINA

C. ASSAONADORS

CARRER DE LA PRINCESA

C. FLASSADERS

C. DE LA RIBERA

PICASSO MUSEUM

MONTCADA

C. BANYS VELLS

PASSEIG DE BORN

C. A. SANT JOAN

C. DE LA ARGENTERIA

VIGAYANS

C. SOMBRERERS

C. DEL REC

C. ESPARTERIA

Plaça Olles

C. DUANA

L'ARGENTERIA G

AV. MARQUÈS DE L'ARGENTERIA

▼ SAGARDI BCN GOTIC

Plaça S. Maria Anisadeta

Pla de Palàu

C. MARQUESA

C. DE LA NAU

VIA LAIETANA

C. DEL COLL DEL MAR

Pla de Palàu

BARCELONETA Ⓜ

C. D'EN GIGNAS

PASSEIG D'ISABEL II

▼ CAN PAIXANO

C. FUSTERIA

Plaça d'Antoni López

CARRER DE BALBOA

CARRER DE GINEBRA

PASSEIG DE JOAN SALVAT PAPASSEIT

BO DE B ▼

C. DE LA MERCÈ

CARRER DE LA MAQUINISTA

CARRER DE CERMEÑO

TASCA EL CORRAL ▼

C. PLATA

▼ LA PLATA

▼ CELTA

BAR CELTA PULPERIA

PASSEIG DE COLOM

RONDA DEL LITORAL (HIGHWAY)

Marina

CARRER DE SANT MIGUEL

CARRER DEL BALUARD

CARRER DE L'ATLANTIDA

SANT CARLES

CARRER D'ANDREA DORIA

C. DE L'ATLANTIDA

MOLL DE LA FUSTA

MOLL D'ESPANYA

Marina

CARRER DE L'ALMIRALL CERVERA

PASSEIG DE JOAN DE BORBO

PLATJA BARCELONETA (BEACH) ■

0   200 yds

0   200 m

BARCELONETA

Sant Sebastià Beach

RAMBLA DEL MAR

CARRER DE L'ESCAR

EQUITY POINT SEA ●

Plaça del Mar

Port Vell

© AVALON TRAVEL

Barcelona offers white sandy beaches by day and glitzy dance clubs by night. This town has it all: surreal modernist architecture, bustling markets with fresh local produce, and nightlife that pops till sunrise. Barcelona is the capital of Catalonia, Spain's northeasternmost territory, and the regional cultural pride is fierce. Get ready to soak in the culture and live like a local by finding your own perfect siesta to fiesta ratio.

BARCELONA 101

Founded as a military encampment and then an ancient Roman walled port town with—count 'em—72 towers, Barcino, as it was known, was handed back and forth between numerous conquering powers throughout the centuries. As a result, citizens developed a unique cultural identity that reflected the amalgamation of the cultures that controlled the city over the years. Catalonia was consolidated under one crown in the 12th century and grew wealthy from its rich sea trade. When Ferdinand (king of Catalonia) and Isabella (queen of Castile, aka the rest of Spain), famous for the Spanish Inquisition and for sponsoring Columbus, married in 1496, political power gradually shifted to Madrid. Buffeted by war and plagues over the next several hundred years, Barcelona endured a slow decline.

The 20th century kicked off with an ambitious city-planning project epitomized by a unique architectural style: modernism, also known as Catalan art nouveau. It left a significant mark on the city you see today. From palaces to private residences (Block of Discord), and light posts (Plaça Reial) to the grandest, most ambitious cathedral project in the world (Sagrada Familia), Barcelona was architect Antoni Gaudí's canvas, over which he enthusiastically spread his nationalist pride. Simultaneously, the bloody and tragic Spanish Civil War followed. Many civilians fled to France as fascist dictator Franco came to power in 1939 and began actively suppressing the Catalan language, traditions, and culture. The only way to express regional patriotism was by cheering for the soccer club, FC Barcelona, which at least partly explains the passion of the team's modern fan base. For Catalans, *fútbol* was an opportunity to keep their quieted culture alive. After 36 long years, Franco reinstated the Spanish monarchy, putting King Juan Carlos I, who promised to continue Franco's dictatorial style, on the throne. But upon Franco's death, the king returned the country to a democratic system.

In 1992, Barcelona hosted the Olympics and found itself back on the international stage. The city was revitalized with a brand-new metro system, beautiful parks, a cleaned-up medieval center, and four kilometers of brand-new white-sand beaches. (Fun facts: The sand was imported from Egypt, and the metro map mirrors the colors of the Olympic rings.)

Today, Barcelona is Spain's second largest city after Madrid and is the capital of Spain's richest region, Catalonia. Children here learn Catalan first and Castilian Spanish second. The pride and identity of Catalonia is as strong as ever. This pride has fostered both energy and tension, as the people of Catalonia decide which future they want for their children: an independent state, or one that continues to pay into the system to support the rest of Spain.

PLAN AHEAD

RESERVATIONS

Reservations are recommended for the following sights:

Sagrada Familia (sagradafamilia.cat)

Picasso Museum (museupicasso.bcn.cat/en, free on Sun afternoon!)

LOCAL HAPPENINGS

Gay Pride

Pride Barcelona festivities take place around the third weekend of June each year. Expect a full two weeks of music, parades, parties, debates, and lectures. Find the agenda and more at pridebarcelona.org. Book ahead for accommodations—they'll sell out.

Siestas

Siestas are real, people! Barcelona has four rush hour times every day: not only in the morning and evening but also at siesta time, when all the shops close and everyone runs home for their two- to four-hour-long siesta after lunch. This means that most places close around 14:00 and reopen around 18:30. If you need to purchase something, remember to keep this in mind.

Holidays

If a public holiday falls on a Thursday—or sometimes, even a Wednesday—people here bridge the holiday into the weekend, giving themselves more days off. It's great for them, but not so great for tourists. On these public national holidays, all businesses will be closed:

January 1, New Year's Day

March 29, Good Friday

May 1, Labor Day

August 15, the Assumption

October 12, National Holiday of Spain

November 1, All Saints' Day

December 6, Spanish Constitution Day

December 25, Christmas Day

KNOW BEFORE YOU GO

KEY STATS & FIGURES

Currency:
Spain uses the euro (€);
1 EUR = about 1.06 USD

Population:
1,620,943

Language:
Catalan and Spanish

Kilometers of beaches:
4.2

Nightclubs:
enough to keep you busy for years

CALIBRATE YOUR BUDGET

TYPICAL PRICES FOR:

Hostel dorm bed: .
€14

Two-course dinner and drink:
€12

Pint of beer:
€3.50

Bicycle rental:
€10/half day

Single metro pass:
€2

MOVIES TO WATCH
*Vicky Cristina Barcelona,
Barcelona, The Passenger*

THREE DAY ITINERARY

Organize your visit to Barcelona chronologically. On your first day focus on the Old Town: the Barri Gotic and El Born. Then explore the Eixample, with its many beautiful examples of modernism, on day two. Save your third day for hiking or lounging on the beach.

DAY 1: WELCOME TO BARCINO

MORNING

Grab breakfast at your hostel or head to one of my favorite *churrerías* (churro bakeries), **Churreria Manuel San Román,** located right in the Old Town, near the kick-off point for your free walking tour.

After breakfast, walk over to **Travel Bar** to catch a free three-hour walking tour for a casual introduction to the layout and history of the city. The tour begins at 11:00. You'll explore the **Barri Gotic, La Rambla,** and the **Cathedral of Barcelona** just to get started. Two important tips: Always watch your pockets in the tourist center, and remember to tip your tour guide!

Your guide will give you free time inside the famous **La Boqueria,** a market where you can grab a quick snack. Saddle up at any one of the countertop bars inside the market. Try out something that looks strange and foreign—you might surprise yourself with what you like!

AFTERNOON

After your tour, walk about 15 minutes to the **Picasso Museum** in El Born and spend a couple hours exploring. El Born is also home to the enticing **Chocolate Museum** and some tasty tapas at **Sagardi BCN Gotic.**

EVENING

Take a minute back at the hostel to freshen up, then head out to catch Travel Bar's three-hour **Paella & Sangria Cooking Class,** which meets daily 17:45 at Travel Bar. Make your reservations earlier in the day to confirm your spot. Dress to stay out because the class goes late.

LATE

Remember, Spaniards don't really kick off the night until the wee hours of the morning. Spend the time after your paella class in the nearby **Plaça Reial,** where you'll find some of my favorite nightlife attractions: **Los Tarantos Flamenco Show** and **Sidecar Factory Club.**

DAY 2: THE EIXAMPLE & BEYOND

MORNING

Get ready for a day of modernism with a large breakfast at your local **Pans and Company.** A tortilla sandwich with a *café con leche* is a filling start to your day.

After breakfast, meet up for another free walking tour, this time with **Discover Walks** on the Passeig de Gràcia, in front of **Casa Batllo**. Their Modernism Walk, which meets at 10:30 Friday, Saturday, Sunday, and Monday, covers the **Block of Discord,** comprising a number of bizarre and noteworthy houses.

Your walk, which lasts three hours, will continue on through Barcelona's modern expansion—or "Eixample"—and finish at Gaudí's unfinished masterpiece, the **Sagrada Familia**. Pop in to any café that looks good along the way and ask for a *bocadillo*, or sandwich. My go-to sandwich is a *chorizo con queso* (sausage and cheese) or *jamón con queso* (ham and cheese). Ask your guide for a good spot.

AFTERNOON

After ogling the Sagrada Familia for a couple hours, take bus 92 up to Gaudí's famous, beautifully failed development, **Parc Güell.** Alternatively, take bus V21 from the north side of the open square adjacent the Sagrada Familia downhill to the **beach** for some Vitamin D! In the late afternoon, head back to your hostel for a quick siesta.

EVENING

Leave your hostel to crawl some of the best tapas bars in the city, along **Carrer de la Mercè.** Formerly a gritty street paced by Barcelona's prostitutes and sailors, it is now known for its authentic tapas flavor and scene.

LATE

From Carrer de la Mercè, split a cab with friends into the Eixample to **Chupitos**—the famous shot bar—and **Dow Jones** a stock market-esque bar—for a pair of fun and shamelessly touristy experiences.

Now fully loaded, head to the **Puerto Olimpico** for the glitzy nightlife that Barcelona is so famous for. Flag another cab back to the famous venues on the beach, including disco **Shoko** and its posher sister, **Opium Mar**. Rage till late and watch the sunrise the next morning.

DAY 3: CHOICES, CHOICES, CHOICES

Later flight on your last day? If it's Sunday, head to the **Cathedral of Barcelona** to catch the traditional **Sardana dances**.

Much later flight? Pack a lunch and head for a hike up **Montjuic** to take in the panoramic views of the city and Mediterranean Sea. Or enjoy a lazy day soaking in the sun on **Platja Barceloneta** or **Platja Nova Mar Bella,** two of Barcelona's best beaches.

If you've got the entire day and are spending a fourth night, consider a **day trip to Montserrat** for a strenuous and rewarding day of hiking outside the city.

TOP NEIGHBORHOODS

Barcelona's Old Town is built on Roman foundations with narrow, winding streets. The Old Town comprises two main districts: the Barri Gotic and El Born. The **Barri Gotic** (Gothic Quarter), with Plaça Catalonia at the top and the famous street of La Rambla running through the middle, filled the old medieval walls of the town. This neighborhood manages to balance its touristy nature with some excellent finds for food, culture, and entertainment. This is where you'll find the Cathedral of Barcelona, along with Plaça Reial, the town's central square. Just north of the Barri Gotic is trendy **El Born,** with classy restaurants and posh cocktail bars to suit the young professional set (and in-the-know tourists). El Born is home to the Picasso Museum as well as some tasty tapas.

Surrounding the Old Town up the slightly inclined landscape is the **Eixample**, or expansion, so named because it's the world's best-executed example of true city planning, with a modern grid layout. You'll find a number of key sights here, particularly those that relate to modernist architecture, including the Sagrada Familia and the Block of Discord.

Barceloneta is on the east side of town, with El Born just inland, the marina to the south, and Barcelona's long stretch of beaches and boardwalk leading north along the water line. Here you'll find surf shops, local bars and cafés, and pricier restaurants along the boardwalk. Along the north end is **Puerto Olimpico,** the town's port, which is the center of Barcelona's clubbing scene.

TOP SIGHTS

La Rambla

Take a downhill stroll from Plaça de Catalonia (Barcelona's proud, most central square) down La Rambla, Barcelona's most popular and busiest series of contiguous streets. This experience is at the heart of any tourist's visit to Barcelona. In one kilometer you've got vendors selling birds, flower stalls, a world-famous market (La Boqueria), beautiful baroque churches, works by Gaudí and other famous architects, dozens of street performers, a square populated by the wealthiest traders from Barcelona's golden age, and churros galore. The street referred to as La Rambla actually comprises four streets, all following what used to be a spring coming from the surrounding hills: Rambla de Canaletes, Rambla dels Estudis, Rambla de Sant Josep, Rambla dels Caputxins, Rambla de Santa Mònica. Most of these portions of La Rambla are named after buildings or sites that don't exist any more, but that's the order starting from Plaça Catalonia and down.

Explore the winding streets leading off from La Rambla on either side and soak in the dense history of the old Roman town that is the Barri Gotic. A walking tour is a great way to get your bearings of this neighborhood.

Always keep your wits about you and watch out for scam games and pickpockets who rove the entire length of the Rambla, preying on bewildered tourists at all hours of the day and night. It can get a bit seedy late into the night after 03:00.

Free, always open, Barri Gotic, Metro: Catalunya

Picasso Museum

Besides Gaudí, another famous artist hails from Barcelona: the painter, Pablo Picasso. A museum dedicated to this revolutionary artist resides in Barcelona's trendy El Born district. The great modern artist called Barcelona home, and the impressive museum is juxtaposed against the backdrop of some classical Barcelona palaces. The museum features an extensive collection of works progressing through his various stages in chronological order. They say that Picasso, when a child, painted as a master in photorealistic pieces, and when an adult, he painted as a child, with geometric shapes, disagreeable coloring—in the opinion of contemporaries—and stark outlines. A survey of the rooms will take visitors about 90 minutes.

€11-14, €7 students, free all day first Sun of the month and other Sun afternoon, Tues-Sun 09:00-19:00, till 21:30 on Thurs, closed Mon, Carrer Montcada 15-23, El Born, +34 93 256 30 00, museupicasso.bcn.cat/en, Metro: Jaume I

Sagrada Familia

This church, designed by Gaudí, is my favorite sight in all of Europe. If you see nothing

ACT LIKE A LOCAL

Getting on Barcelona Time

To fully enjoy Barcelona, it's important to adapt to the timeline that Spaniards live by here. If you try to follow the schedule you keep back home, you'll likely only get frustrated and miss out on incredible experiences and opportunities. This is a timeline of when Spaniards eat, sleep, and go out:

08:30: Grab a light breakfast of a croissant and *café con leche* (coffee with milk).

09:00-12:30: Locals head to work! For visitors, this is a good time to hit the sights.

13:00-17:00: Stores close down for lunch and siesta. A side effect: double the traffic in a major city where everyone commutes twice a day. You wouldn't be missing much in the streets if you decided to take a siesta after a large Spanish lunch.

19:00-21:00: Evening stroll time. The city is still sleepy as stores are opening back up, and people are roaming the streets.

21:00-23:00: Dinnertime. Take your time to enjoy it. Spaniards take their dinner slowly and socially.

23:00-01:00: Pregaming with friends, either in parks or back at the flat.

01:00-03:00: Time for the bars. Get the drinks and pound the vodka energies to get ready for the club.

03:00 till you can't keep your eyes open: Club like there's no tomorrow. Stumble out of the *discotecas* at Puerto Olimpico onto the beach and watch the sunrise.

else on your visit to Barcelona, you've got to see the Sagrada Familia, an ongoing construction site since the late 19th century. Gaudí laid the foundations, began living in one of the towers, and did his best to recruit donors and patrons to support his colossal project from 1882 onward.

The church has grown in fits and starts because it is all publicly funded: They build when they have money. When they run out, they take collections again. Construction is slated to be completed by 2025. Let's cross our fingers! Because it's an ongoing construction project that has lasted over 120 years, it's worth going back to again and again to see the progress local builders have made since Gaudí's death in 1924.

Both the exterior and interior are finally taking shape. Two completed facades face north—where you'll find the Nativity facade—and south—where the geometric Passion facade dominates. These facades communicate the phases of Jesus' life. Look closely at the Nativity facade, with the Holy Family in the center and the farm animals surrounding in adoration. Don't miss the turtles at the base of the columns. This is the side Gaudí toiled on during his life. The more modern Passion facade walks viewers through the 13 stages of the cross, from

flagellation at the pillar to crucifixion to rising from the dead.

Step into the church, and it feels like you've stepped into a giant rainforest complete with a canopy. The coloring is miraculous thanks to the detailed stained glasswork throughout. Gaudí never got to see the church at this stage, but one moment in here, and you can begin to contemplate the scale of his dreams. Don't miss the workshop to the side of the church or the small architectural museum downstairs in the crypt.

Plan to send about 90 minutes exploring, with more time if you choose to go up the towers. Ticket sales end 15 minutes before closing time.

€15 adult, €13 student, entry to the towers €4.50 extra, Apr-Sept daily 09:00-20:00, daily Oct-Mar 09:00-19:00, Carrer de Mallorca 401, Eixample, +34 935 13 20 60, sagradafamilia.org, Metro: Sagrada Familia

Block of Discord

This single block of ostentatious homes on Passeig de Gràcia, featuring **Casa Amatller, Casa Lleo Morera,** and **Casa Batllo**, is a perfect example of modernist architects attempting to outdo one another. Each house has a distinct personality. The name of the city block reflects the jarring appearance of each of these homes when lined up next to each other. Paid entry into these modernist houses is possible, but casual observers are often content with checking out the exterior for free.

Free, always open, Passeig de Gràcia, Eixample, Metro: Passeig de Gràcia

Casa Batllo

Known as the dragon house, this fanciful house built for the Batllo family depicts the story of George and the Dragon, and it's loaded with symbolism. The columns on the exterior represent the past victims of the dragon, with the balconies made of skulls. The tiles of the roof are clearly the scales of the back of the dragon, with the spire of the turret representing the sword plunged into the serpent's back. The interior is just as detailed, with beautifully carved wooden door frames, styled light fixtures, and even an atrium paneled with darker tiles at the top, cooling to lighter tiles near the ground floor to help distribute natural light across all rooms evenly. Gaudí was an architectural master and also possibly the world's most intense micro-manager to achieve such detail across all of his projects.

€21.50, €18.50 students, daily 09:00–21:00, Passeig de Gràcia 43, Eixample, +34 932 16 03 06, casabatllo.es, Metro: Passeig de Gràcia

Casa Amatller

Josep Puig i Cadafalch designed and built the stepped, Minecraft-style facade of Casa Amatller along the row of competing houses for the Amatller family. They made it rich off the chocolate trade, and the ground floor door is sometimes open for visitors to pop

in and view the interior. Go all the way back to find the chocolate shop.

Free, €15 for guided tour, daily 11:00–18:00, English tours at 11:00 and 15:00, Passeig de Gràcia 41, Eixample, Metro: Passeig de Gràcia

Casa Lleo Morera

Bursting with modernist decoration, this corner building is really a collaboration between a number of artists and architects. Their various styles can be seen in the ornate balconies, numerous arches, and diverse architectural accents. See if you can't pick out some of the high-tech inventions that were just coming to light at the time this building was erected in 1906. And don't miss the mulberry tree (*morera*), this family's namesake.

€15 for 70-minute English tour, €12 for 45-minute tour, Tues-Sun, check website for tour times, purchase tickets online or in person at the cultural center Palau de la Virreina, Passeig de Gràcia 35, Eixample, Metro: Passeig de Gràcia

Casa Milá

Casa Milá is also known as La Pedrera (Stone Quarry), so named because of the striking similarity of its shape with that of a quarry. This, another masterpiece of Antoni Gaudí's unique and innovative modernist architecture, appears like a sculpted layer cake on the corner of Passeig de Gràcia and Carrer de Provença. Peer up at the rooftop, where you'll notice a series of twisted chimneys, sculpted in such a way that they look like the storm troopers from *Star Wars*.

€20.50, €16.50 students, daily Mar-Oct 09:00–20:00, daily Nov-Feb 9:00–18:30, last entry 30 minutes before closing, Provença, 261-265, Eixample, +34 902 20 21 38, lapedrera. com, Metro: Diagonal

GAGA FOR GAUDÍ

Antoni Gaudí is easily one of Barcelona's most famous denizens. His profession: architecture. You'll see his thumbprint on almost every block across the city, in the form of churches, private residences and palaces, sidewalks, benches, parks, urban planning, and even light posts. As is clear from the **Sagrada Familia,** the most incredible church ever (being) built, down to minute details on the facades of his projects and even street tiles, Gaudí was truly an architectural prodigy who was well ahead of his time. The **Block of Discord** (which includes **Casa Batllo** and **Casa Milá**) and **Parc Güell** are some of his most famous sights in the city. He also designed the **lampposts in Placa Reial.**

Plaça Reial

This picturesque, renaissance-style city center square harkens back to Barcelona's explosive architectural period in the late 19th century. Entitled the Royal Square, this is where Barcelona's elite would come for a stroll and to admire each other's palatial city homes. Today, us lowlifes can enjoy the scene at any time of day or night. During the day, enjoy *café con leche* at one of the many cafés that line the square. Note the lampposts, which were designed by Gaudí. Perhaps join a pickup *fútbol* game with the kids running around, but be warned: They may school you! Each Sunday a stamp and coin market takes over the square. When the sun goes down numerous bars, clubs, and shows line the square and the streets.

Free, always open, Barri Gotic, Metro: Liceu

Los Tarantos Flamenco Show

A typical dance originating in the south of Spain, flamenco drips with passion and culture. Los Tarantos captures this Spanish tradition in a perfectly succinct and varied show featuring tap dancers, box-drummers, guitarists, and vocalists who belt out songs ranging from upbeat to morose melancholy. You'll definitely walk out of this show saying "wow." Even with three shows a night, the quality and energy of each show are impressively consistent, and I love the venue for its intimate and casual atmosphere.

€15, 30-minute shows daily 20:30, 21:30, 22:30, Plaça Reial 17, Barri Gotic, +34 933 01 77 56, flamencotickets. com/los-tarantos-barcelona, Metro: Liceu

Cathedral of Barcelona

Not to be confused with the much more modern Sagrada Familia, the Cathedral of Barcelona is located right against what would have been the main entry gate into the old Roman town. Construction began in the 1200s and was completed in 1448 with a rather austere facade. In the 1800s, a much

more boisterous neo-gothic facade, a style popular at the time, was added. That's what we take in today when we see the cathedral, facing proudly out onto the Placita de la Seu. Take a lap around the exterior to take in the funky gargoyles, which are both decorative and functional. Try to find the grasshopper and the unicorn.

The cathedral is dedicated to Barcelona's original patron saint, Saint Eulalia, who met a gruesome end from the occupying Romans for not recanting her Christian faith. As a result, the centurions inflicted 13 different kinds of torture on her, including rolling her downhill in a barrel stuffed with sharp objects and knives. This was followed by both crucifixion and decapitation. Saint Eulalia is buried in the crypt underneath the cathedral.

The interior is rather dark thanks to the thick walls that hold up the impressive gothic arch work. Inside you'll find richly decorated chapels, the crypt of Saint Eulalia, and a cloister with 13 white geese, remembering Saint Eulalia's age at the time of her martyrdom. Entry is usually free, but visits to the cloister and roof cost a few euros.

Free entry Mon-Fri 08:00-12:45 and 17:15-19:30, free entry Sat 08:00-12:45 and 17:15-20:00, free entry Sun and holidays 08:00-13:45 and 17:15-20:00; during free times museum is €3, terrace is €3, and choir is €3; entry with €7 donation Mon-Fri 13:00-17:00, Sat 13:00-17:30, and Sun 14:00-17:00, Pla de la Seu, Barri Gotic, +34 933 428 262, catedralbcn.org, Metro: Jaume I

Sardana Dances

Every Sunday, Sardana dances take over the square in front of Barcelona's cathedral. The dance is a Catalan tradition that celebrates community in the region. Dancers put their belongings in the middle and hold hands while dancing in circles to the beat of a beautiful and traditional series of tunes.

Free, Sun 12:00, sometimes Sat at 18:00, no dances in Aug, in front of the Cathedral of Barcelona, Pla de la Seu, Barri Gotic, Metro: Jaume I

Chocolate Museum (Museu de la Xocolata)

A favorite of those with a sweet tooth, this small museum explains the process of chocolate making with displays of sweet artwork. The museum also features activities, such as wine tasting and "blind" chocolate tasting, but you must book ahead online for these. Your €5 entry ticket is actually a chocolate bar. The museum can be tackled in about 45 minutes.

€5, Mon-Sat 10:00-19:00, summer till 20:00, Sun 10:00-15:00, Carrer del Comerc 36, El Born, +34 932 68 78 78, museuxocolata.cat, Metro: Arc de Triomf or Jaume I

Camp Nou Stadium

If soccer were a religion, the Camp Nou soccer stadium would be one of the world's greatest cathedrals. Barcelona rooted for the home team, FC Barcelona, throughout Francisco Franco's oppressive dictatorship. During the later half of the 20th century, supporting the team was one of the few legal ways to wear your Catalan colors and express your Catalan pride. Today, Barcelona essentially shuts down every time the FC Barcelona takes the field, whether they're home or away. You can take a self-led audio tour of the stadium and museum to see vast amount of memorabilia and the trophies amassed over the years by this dynasty.

€23, mid-Apr-early Oct Mon-Sat 10:00-20:00 (off-season until 18:30), Sun 10:00-14:30, shorter hours on and before game days, Carrer d'Aristides Maillol 12, Greater Barcelona, +34 902 18 99 00, fcbarcelona.com, Metro: L3 Palau Reial or Les Corts, L5 Collblanc or Badal

EXTRA CREDIT

Palau Güell

Palau Güell, one of Antoni Gaudí's early projects, is worth going inside if you're a huge modernism buff. You can tell this is the work of a budding master, but one who has not quite yet matured. For most, it's sufficient to peer in through the entryway to get a glimpse into another Gaudí interior. This palace was designed for the same patron family as Parc Güell, built uphill and farther out of town.

€12 adult, €8 students, Tues-Sun 10:15-17:30, Carrer Nou de la Rambla 3-5, Barri Gotic, +34 934 72 57 75, palauguell.cat, Metro: Liceu

TOP EATS

Eating in Barcelona is easily one of the highlights of any visitor's experience. My favorite element is the tapas tradition. When you order tapas, your food arrives on sharable platters, or you pick and choose from a bar with preportioned, open-faced sandwich-style bites. Ingredients are primarily fresh tomatoes, seafood, bread, a little garlic, and fried treats like calamari, *tortilla española* omelets, and *piementos de padrón* peppers.

You'll catch some of Barcelona's most authentic Spanish tapas on **Carrer de la Mercè.** Do a lap up and back down this street, popping into a few places along the way. No menus necessary, just point at whatever you want, and you'll be dished up heaping plates that are great for family-style tapas.

Tipping is not expected, but rounding up to the next euro mark is appreciated. Be sure to check whether or not your bill says *"servei inclòs,"* as many touristy restaurants sneak this 10-15 percent charge in there.

Tasca el Corral

This little hole in the wall on Carrer de la Mercè is a winner—and it's also a one-man show. On this stop, you've got three things to try: fresh *manchego, chorizo al diablo* (flaming sausage), and cider poured from on high. Watch the boss take the cider jug and pour over his shoulder into cups held far below. Order a round of these winners to kick off any crawl right.

€8 and up, Sun-Thurs 13:00-02:00, Fri-Sat 13:00-03:00, Carrer de la Mercè 17, Barri Gotic, +34 93 315 20 59, Metro: Jaume I or Barceloneta

La Plata

This is your place to toss back anchovies like popcorn at the movie theater. Get over your aversion and try some of these deliciously savory snacks. Get some *vino tinto* (red wine) to wash it all back, enjoying the casual, social scene. The simple decor makes it clear this joint caters to the locals.

€8-20, Mon-Sat 09:00-15:30 and 18:30-23:00, Carrer de la Mercè 28, Barri Gotic, +34 933 15 10 09, Metro: Jaume I or Barceloneta

Celta

Celta is the anchor of any tapas crawl down Carrer de la Mercè. Stop in for a feast of

TAPAS CHECKLIST

Major treats for any visitor coming to Barcelona are the tapas—snack-sized, finger food dishes allowing for a wide range of tastes in any one dinner. Tapas also allow diners to have a few dishes in one place before continuing their crawl elsewhere. Just like there are can't-miss sights for Europe's top cities, there are can't-miss flavors that every visitor must try once their first time in Barcelona. Consider this your delectable hit list:

Piementos de padrón: A plate of steaming, salted peppers that's made to order. Ordering these is like playing culinary Russian roulette: Most peppers aren't hot, but there's one per plate that will knock your socks off.

Polpo: Freshly cooked spiced octopus, usually presented on a wooden platter. If it's on the menu, look down the bar and find the heaping plate of tentacles that the chefs are dicing and slicing to order.

Tortilla española: Spain's delicious potato and egg omelet. Additional ingredients are often tossed in, along with salt and pepper, but it's just as good plain for breakfast, lunch, or a quick bite on the run. Get it in a *bocadilla* (Spanish sandwich) for the best way to get full on €2.

Patatas bravas: Hot, freshly fried potato wedges doused in a slightly spicy ketchup-mayonnaise sauce. If you're trying to add some starch to round out the meal, this is a no-brainer.

Pa amb tomàquet: Toasted bread rubbed down with fresh garlic and tomato. This is my personal favorite side order.

Anchoa: Fresh anchovies with nothing but a slice of lemon on the side. Get over your inhibitions and order a plate to share between friends, and pop 'em like popcorn at the movies. Salty, crunchy, and washed down with a glass of *tinto* (red wine)—what more could you want?

Jamón ibérico: Cured ham. Spain has delicious cured ham, some of the best in the world. You've got to try some while you're here. They come in different grades and prices based on the pigs they come from, their processing, their location, and their diet. Go for 100 grams of this, 100 grams of *queso manchego,* and a baguette and you've got lunches for days.

Queso manchego: Spain's dry, salty cheese goes along with basically anything. Order 100 grams at the supermarket when you see some you like for a perfect afternoon snack. Don't be afraid to try (say *"probar"*) a few different selections before purchasing. They also contribute to some wonderful cheese plates.

Salmorejo: Creamy tomato soup, topped with diced *jamón* (delicious) and generally consumed for breakfast. (I'll take it any time of day, though.)

Gazpacho: Tomato soup that tends to be a savory side dish to your lunch or dinner. Fresh tomatoes are tossed in with garlic, salt, spices, and a little bit of vinegar for the perfect zing. You really can't go wrong. Gazpacho is served cold, mainly during hot summer months. Gazpacho and *salmorejo* are my favorite tomato soups in the world.

pan con tomate (bread with pureed tomato and olive oil), fresh *polpo* (octopus), *patatas bravas* (fried potatoes with a spicy ketchup sauce), and even *gambas* (meaty jumbo prawns). This place and the waiters are always busy, so pop in, scope around a bit to see the dishes that look good to you, and have your order ready when you finally make eye contact with a member of the crew. Tables in the back are great for groups of friends.

€4 and up, Tues-Sun 12:00-24:00, Carrer de la Mercè 9, Barri Gotic, +34 933 150 006, barcelta.com, Metro: Jaume I or Barceloneta

Bar Celta Pulperia

Pop into the new sister restaurant to Celta, across the street, for tapas sitting down at tables with your friends in a bright and clean setting. This place is newer, and as such feels slightly more done up than the others on your crawl.

€5 and up, daily 08:30-24:00, Carrer de Simó Oller 3, Barri Gotic, +34 933 15 00 06, barcelta.com, Metro: Jaume I or Barceloneta

Sagardi BCN Gotic

The Grupo Sagardi chain has numerous locations across Spain, with several in Barcelona alone, and all for a good reason: their incredible finger-lickin'-good tapas. Ask for a plate to start, and move down the line and pick whatever looks good to you on the bar. Go slow! Dishes are refreshed periodically, and hot dishes are paraded through every 15 minutes or so. Settle up your bill by turning in your toothpicks at the end of your meal. Their summer wine, *tinto de verano*, is delicious. Get a similar experience at any of Grupo Sagardi's other operations, including **Basca Irati** (Carrer del Cardenal Casanas 17) and **Euskal Etxea** (Placeta de Montcada 1).

€4-20, daily 13:00-16:00 and 20:00-24:00, Carrer de l'Argenteria 62, El Born, +34 933 199 993, sagardi.com, Metro: Jaume I

Bo de' Be

Bo de' Be is famous among the student population in Barcelona for their overflowing sandwiches, delivered quickly at unbelievably cheap prices (only €3 or €4!). Grab one to go on your way to the beach, as it's right at the bottom of Via Laietana. Lines can be long, but the service is quick. Because there isn't much room to eat inside, most take their sandwiches to go.

€3-4, Mon-Fri 11:00-24:00, Sat-Sun 13:00-16:00, Carrer de la Fusteria 14, Barri Gotic, +34 936 674 945, Metro: Jaume I

Pans and Company

This Spanish-owned and -operated chain store makes for a quick and tasty lunch stop any time you see a branch. This is where everyone drops in on the daily grind for a fresh sandwich on the way to work. Grab a *café con leche* and do what the locals do! The information given is for the convenient Barri Gotic location, but you'll find multiple locations throughout the city.

Sandwiches from €4, generally daily 07:00-24:00, Plaça Sant Jaume 6, Barri Gotic, +34 933 15 16 06, pansandcompany.com, Metro: Jaume I

Can Paixano

If you're looking for an authentic local experience, look no further. Come out for some delicious Barcelona-style burgers, cheese sticks, chorizo, french fries, and more. Located in Barceloneta, one block from Barceloneta Metro, this eat-on-your-feet fast-food joint offers a glass o' *cava* (Spanish champagne) with every order. Sharpen your elbows, as this boisterous place gets packed to the gills with hangry customers ready to chow down.

€4-12, Mon-Sat 09:30-22:30, Carrer de la Reina Cristina 7, Barceloneta, canpaixano.com, Metro: Barceloneta

Churreria Manuel San Román

This spot is one of my favorites for churros in town. No website, no frills, nothing fancy, just delicious churros and chocolate. The chocolate is so rich that you'll either wish you could drown in it, or you'll need to split it with friends. You won't likely fall in between the two camps.

€4, Mon-Fri 07:00-01:30, Sat-Sun 07:00-14:00 and 16:00-20:30, Carrer dels Banys Nous 8, Barri Gotic, +34 933 187 691, Metro: Liceu

TOP NIGHTLIFE

Barcelona's nightlife rages just about every night of the week. The most important thing is to adjust to the local timeline for going out. Eat dinner 21:00-23:00 or so, then start having your drinks. Head to the bars around 01:00 and then to the clubs around 03:00 and party till the sun comes up. Fast drinks (think two ingredients: rum and coke, gin and tonic, vodka and lime, etc) are generally the poison of choice in this town.

NIGHTLIFE DISTRICTS

Eixample has tons of choices for bars, lounges, and cafés, but because it's so big, it's best if you know exactly where you want to go.

Barri Gotic

This district has bars centering mostly around Plaça Reial. The touristy spots are numerous there.

Barri Gotic, Metro: Liceu

El Born

El Born offers a series of classier, young professional-type trendy lounges and bars.

El Born, Metro: Jaume I

Puerto Olimpico

Puerto Olimpico is the main marina in town. Nearby, you'll find a stretch of clubs all with dancers and electronic music to boggle the mind.

Puerto Olimpico, Metro: Ciutadella/Vila Olímpica

BARS

Dow Jones

Famous for its constantly inflating and "crashing" drink prices, this otherwise non-descript bar—a favorite among the American study abroad crowd—makes drinking and consuming an interactive game. Every time you order a drink, the price of that drink rises with "demand." As the night goes on, there are sporadic "crashes," sending the prices tumbling and sparking another rush to the bar. All of the information is projected on screens so you can keep your finger on the pulse of the action.

Mon-Thurs 19:30-02:30, Fri 19:30-03:00, Sat-Sun 12:00-03:00, Carrer del Bruc 97, +34 934 76 38 31, bardowjones.com, Metro: Girona

Chupitos

Chupitos is a fave among students abroad in Barcy due to its selection of 550-plus different types of shots. Adventurous? Try the Monica Lewinsky. The Boy Scout never disappoints. Feeling brave? Go for the Viking Shot. Chupitos is a relatively small place, and it's either dead or flush with shooters who are making a short stop before the clubs. It does get a bit sweaty once the party arrives.

Daily 22:30-02:30, Carrer d'Aribau 77, Eixample, +34 697 81 44 61, espitchupitos.com, Metro: Universitat

Pippermint

This bar is overridden by study abroad students who come here for the massive cocktails poured into 1, 5 and even 10-liter cups—or should I say goblets? Come here for a quick and cheap way to get the night—and your buzz—started. Keep walking if you're looking for anything resembling an

LGBT BARCELONA

Spain rates first in the Pew Research Center's most recent survey of acceptance of homosexuality, at 88 percent. The LGBT community is welcome in Barcelona, and you'll find numerous options for gay-friendly cafés, bars, restaurants, and clubs throughout town—both in the Old Town and in the Eixample. Gay pride festivities in Barcelona take place around the third weekend of June each year. Book ahead for accommodations because the city sells out. Check out **Osbar** (Carrer de la Diputació 225, +34 934 53 46 42) for the bear scene. (*Os* means bear in Catalan.) All are welcome and have a good time!

authentic or redeeming experience. This place is shamelessly for those looking to get their drink on before the clubs.

Liters of cocktails from €12, Mon 08:15-01:30, Tues-Thurs 08:15-02:30, Fri 08:15-03:30, Sat 10:15-03:30, Sun 16:30-01:30, Carrer de Bori I Fontesta 20, Eixample, +34 932 010 008, pippermintbcn.com, Metro: Maria Cristina

Marsella

Two hundred absinthe-laden years since it opened, this dusty bar is still at the top of the game. Do your absinthe right with the fancy spoon and sugar cube—if you need help, just ask! The service is friendly and welcoming. Order your drinks at the bar, then take your supplies to any of the open cafeteria-style low-slung tables to get the party started. While still just a few steps from La Rambla, this district was notorious for petty crime and prostitution up until a few years ago. Keep your wallets and purses tight.

Daily 22:00-02:30, Carrer de Sant Pau 65, Barri Gotic, +34 934 42 72 63, Metro: Liceu

Sidecar Factory Club

Descend into this subterranean rock bar located right on Plaça Reial. Touristy because of its location, this club is still a good time, featuring frequent live acts and colorful cocktails. Find show information on the website.

€8-12 cover with drink, Mon-Sat 19:00-05:00, Plaça Reial 7, Barri Gotic, +34 933 02 15 86, sidecarfactoryclub.com, Metro: Liceu

CLUBS

If glitzy clubbing is your thing, look no farther than Barcelona. Covers generally run about €15, with your first drink included. Each drink after that tends to run €8-10. So it's worthwhile to get your party started before heading to the club. It's also worthwhile to Google or search Facebook to find out about planned events and what type of music will be playing. Follow the four major promoters in Barcelona on Facebook (Aashi

Guest List, Michael Jordan, Kyke Navarro, and Kike Barcelona/De Lis Group) to see what their events are during the time you're planning on visiting. Call ahead to the clubs or join events to get yourself on the list, saving you time and hassle at the door. Most of the clubs listed are near **Puerto Olimpico.**

Opium Mar

This is a swanky spot with notorious bouncers enforcing a strict dress code. Dress to impress, as this is a favorite among FB Barcelona team members, along with other glitterati and celebrities. It's a posh scene, so expect all the wonderful things that come with that: pricey cover, expensive drinks, big bouncers, and great DJs. Close this place out to view the sunrise over the Mediterranean. It's worthwhile to get your name on the guest list online ahead of time.

€20 cover including drink, drinks about €12, daily 24:00-06:00, Passeig Marítimo de la Barceloneta 34, Puerto Olimpico, opiummar.com, Metro: Ciutadella/Vila Olímpica

Shoko

Shoko is your best and most consistent bet for the clubs on the beach strip. The crowd is classy, but not over the top. The music is well-balanced, and they pull off the Asian fusion quite well, from the decor all the way to the food available throughout the day. Dance the night away in a faux-bamboo forest, and enjoy the flushed, low lighting. This is a place where you want your name on the list, so call ahead or click online. Dress to get past the picky bouncers!

Drinks around €10, daily 12:00-06:00, Passeig Marítimo de la Barceloneta 36, Puerto Olimpico, +34 932 25 92 00, shoko.biz, Metro: Ciutadella/Vila Olímpica

Carpe Diem

This pricey and posh lounge restaurant/club has a Moroccan-Asian twist. You'll find a decidedly well-heeled, older crowd downing top-class sushi and washing it back with

Dom Perignon while lounging out on day beds. Reserve ahead for both the dinner and nightclub entry.

Drinks and dinners start at €20, daily 13:00-04:00, Passeig Marítimo de la Barceloneta 32, Puerto Olimpico, +34 932 24 04 70, cdlcbarcelona.com, Metro: Ciutadella/Vila Olímpica

Catwalk

I think of Catwalk as the grungy little brother with a chip on his shoulder to the classier disco clubs opening up onto the beach. And likewise, it attracts the types who wouldn't necessarily get into the flashier clubs nearby. Stay downstairs for techno, or head upstairs for R&B and hip-hop. If you prefer to leave the pretentiousness at the door, you'll like Catwalk. This club does depend on promoters certain nights to fill the place out, so don't let them get too pushy on you. Feel comfortable to negotiate cover and included drinks at a place like this.

€10 cover including drink, Thurs-Sun 23:30-18:00, Carrer de Ramon Trias Fargas 2, Puerto Olimpico, +34 932 240 740, clubcatwalk.net, Metro: Ciutadella/Vila Olímpica

Razzmatazz

This is a popular club for students and locals alike. You're guaranteed a great time in this labyrinth of five rocking dance floors.

It's heavy on the electro-sound scene, but if that's not your thing, you'll likely find something else in this complex of music. Check out the agenda online for upcoming events and DJs.

€10-12 cover including drink, drinks about €7, daily 23:00-05:00, Carrer Almogàvers 122, Greater Barcelona, +34 933 20 82 00, salarazzmatazz.com, Metro: Marina

Sala Apolo

This is your alternative to the techno-ridden club scene in Barcelona. Sala Apolo is a medium-sized club that also features live music and parties throughout the week. Sala Apolo is most famous for its Nasty Monday parties, where it seems that all of Barcelona's punks and rockers come out to rage. The crowd tends to be young and tattooed, but the venue is in a rustic old theater with the seats removed from the ground floor and the booths taken out from the wraparound balconies. This is a favorite of the study abroad demographic as well. Come pre-gamed, as the drinks aren't cheap. Check the website to stay up on events and performances.

€8 cover and drinks, Mon 20:00-05:00, Thurs 20:00-05:00, Fri-Sat 19:00-06:00, Sun 21:00-05:00, Carrer Nou de la Rambla 113, Greater Barcelona, +34 934 41 40 01, sala-apolo.com, Metro: Paral-lel

TOP SHOPPING & MARKETS

SHOPPING DISTRICTS
La Rambla

The shopping district in Barcelona runs from the top of La Rambla through Plaça de Catalonia to Passeig de Gràcia and up Avinguda Diagonal. You'll find everything from high-end fashion like Burberry, Versace, and Armani to your everyday stores like H&M.

Barri Gotic, Metro: Catalunya, Liceu, or Drassanes

WISHING YOU A CRAPPY CHRISTMAS!

Caga Tió or "Crap Log" is a character in Catalan Christmas tradition that is observed in the Spanish region of Catalonia. Caga Tió is a small log with a smiley face painted on one end, with twigs for arms to support it. Oftentimes the tió sports a fun Santa hat. Beginning in early December, children give the tió little bites to eat (as Americans leave cookies for Santa). They feed him every night over the span of a couple weeks, and cover him with a blanket so that he will not be cold. On Christmas Eve, kids put the tió partly into the fireplace and order him to, well, dump out all the presents. To encourage him to take this generous defecation, the kids beat him with sticks while singing selections of typical Catalan Christmas songs. This fun little tradition originally symbolized the fertilization of the fields for an abundant crop in the upcoming year, but perhaps something was lost in translation...

You'll see small tió figurines in souvenir shops across town caught in the middle of this act. They always make for a funny—if somewhat odd—gift for loved ones back home.

MARKETS

La Boqueria

This is one of the most eccentric public markets I've ever been to. You can find everything from entire pig heads to fresh smoothies. Challenge yourself to try one thing you've never dreamed of! Then, grab a glass of sangria before rambling the rest of the way down La Rambla. Their iced fruit drinks are a tasty, touristy treat.

Mon-Sat 08.00-20:30, La Rambla 91, Barri Gotic, boqueria. info, Metro: Liceu

TOP PARKS & RECREATION

PARKS

Parc Güell

Gaudí's Parc Güell is a beautiful failure. It was one of the world's first gated and planned communities, built at the turn of the 20th century, but the neighborhood never quite took off as planned. Always attentive to detail, Gaudí touched everything from the park benches to the street tiles in this whimsical park at the top of the city.

Today, Gaudí's planned development functions as a park. Come to explore the curvy paths, the photogenic *plaça*, and the famous breaking-surf passageway and to check out another panorama over the city, all the way down to the beaches miles away.

€7 online, €8 in person, daily 08:30-18:00, Carrer d'Olot, Greater Barcelona, +34 902 20 03 02, parkguell.org, Metro: Vallarca via L3

HIKING

Montjuic

Montjuic is the big mountain south of town, to the right as you face out toward the Mediterranean. It was home to a 19th-

THE HUMAN CASTLES OF CATALONIA

So you think you're tough? Let's see how you stack up against the *casteller* teams that put their strength, balance, coordination, and teamwork on full display in main squares across this region. *Castellers* erect free-standing, self-supporting human castles up to seven or eight levels tall of people standing on one another's shoulders. *Casteller* teams come together and, in one massive orchestrated effort, lay the foundation (burly, large men), pile on the next layer (young, lean strong-men), and continue climbing ever higher into the sky. Groups of three scramble up the growing tower like monkeys up a banana tree, as the whole human tower goes up and comes down in minutes. Watch closely, though, because the tower isn't complete without one last team member (usually a small child sporting a riding helmet), who must go to the very top and raise one hand in the air to "cap" the castle. Teams are composed of men, women, and youngsters, who climb to the highest levels. It's a beautiful teamwork tradition that has brought communities together for friendly competition for hundreds of years.

As if this weren't enough of a show, there's also a soundtrack. A small band playing typical Catalan instruments, led by a wilting reed instrument, belts out a tune as if to narrate the whole operation. It climaxes as the little one who makes it to the top raises his or her hand 40 feet above in the air. As soon as those at the lower levels hear the final crescendo, they know the end of their effort is near. The tune changes as the *castellers* at the top shimmy down their teammates like firefighters sliding down a pole as quickly as possible. The men at the bottom are usually dripping in sweat and trembling uncontrollably after holding everyone up. In 2010, UNESCO declared the *castellers* an Intangible Heritage of Humanity. For dates and details of the next public events, follow the link castellersdebarcelona.cat. You can also find incredible feats of human castle-building on YouTube.

century military fort and, later, the 1992 Olympics. Take the steep hour-long hike up Montjuic and soak in the best views of Barcelona and the beautiful coastline. Bring a water bottle and explore the star-fort castle (free, daily 10:00-20:00, €5 paid museums inside) while you're at it. For decades, this fort represented the oppression of Franco rule from Madrid. The fort was the military's way of keeping control over the surrounding city. Now it's a place where Catalan families come to picnic on weekend afternoons.

From the top of the mountain, see the Sagrada Familia rising in the distance and the cruise ships entering and departing through the harbor opposite, just to the south. To get to the base of the hill, head to Barcelona's marina and follow the pathway south. After about a kilometer, you'll see options leading uphill. You can't miss it.

Free, always open, Greater Barcelona, Metro: Plaça Espanya

BEACHES
Platja Barceloneta
Due to its proximity to the tourist center, this is Barcelona's most popular stretch of sand. This beach is filled with tanned locals and pale tourists, with both groups having the same goal: to soak in the sun. The people-watching is the best in Barcelona and could make for an entertaining afternoon, but don't go if you're looking for a tranquil, solitary experience.

Free, always open, Barceloneta, Metro: Ciutadella or Barceloneta

Platja Nova Mar Bella
This is the favorite beach among students and the younger crowd coming from the city. Much less touristy then Platja Barceloneta because of its location far north of the center, yet still easily accessible by metro, this beach is the best of both worlds, offering you an authentic local experience at a manageable distance.

Free, always open, Greater Barcelona, Metro: Selva del Mar or Poblenou

TOP TOURS

Fat Tire Bike Tours
Fat Tire's expert guides bring their cities to life on two wheels. The Barcelona City Tour lines up all the top sights, including the Cathedral of Barcelona and the Sagrada Familia, in a four-hour ride around town. Cap your cruise with sangria on the beach before riding back to the shop. While the pace is relaxed, you won't have the time to go into each sight along the way, so you may want to double back to some later.

€24, students €22, Jan-mid-Apr daily 11:00, mid-Apr-mid-Oct daily 11:00 and 16:00, mid-Oct-Dec daily 11:00, meets at Plaça Sant Jaume—just look for the Fat Tire sign, Barri Gotic, +34 933 429 275, barcelona.fattirebiketours.com, Metro: Jaume I

Discover Walks' Modernism Walk
Run by young, passionate local guides, Discover Walks is a fresh European response to the free walking tour craze, offering consistently good quality and a unique flavor. I prefer this tour company for the Modernism Walk, which takes you from Casa Batllo on the Block of Discord and finishes at Gaudí's unfinished masterpiece, the Sagrada Familia. Multiple tours, including a Las Ramblas & Barri Gotic Walk, are offered throughout the week; just watch for the guides' trademark bright pink vests, or check the website for details.

Free, 10:30 Fri-Mon, meets at Casa Batllo, Eixample, +34 649 60 99 41, discoverwalks.com/barcelona-walking-tours, Metro: Passeig de Gràcia

Travel Bar's Barcelona Old Town Tour
Travel Bar (Carrer Boqueria 27, daily 10:00-23:00, travelbar.com) has it all: coffee in the morning, a bar at night, cooking classes throughout the week and daily walking tours venturing out into the city. TB's introductory walk to Barcelona's Old Town is just what any visitor needs to get comfortable with the city. You'll retrace the Roman foundations of the city, discuss the numerous high and low points of the city's history, and wrap up with a lunch just steps from Barcelona's marina. The tour lasts about 2.5 hours.

Free, daily 11:00, 13:00, and 15:00, meets at Travel Bar, Carrer Boqueria 27, Barri Gotic, travelbar.com, Metro: Liceu

Travel Bar's Paella & Sangria Cooking Class
Let a professional *paellador* walk you through the art of preparing the typical seafood rice platter with perfectly spiced prawns, mussels, and calamari. You'll meet at the Travel Bar and then head to La Boqueria for a guided walk through the dozens of market stalls and to pick up fresh ingredients. From there, you'll head to the

cooking location, where you'll dive into your bags of seafood and spices. The class, which lasts about three hours, is capped off with a delicious dinner and unlimited drinks. A discounted after-party at the bar is available. This is truly a great value.

€28, meets daily 17:45 at Travel Bar, Carrer Boqueria 27, Barri Gotic, travelbar.com, Metro: Liceu

TOP HOSTELS

Hostels have done so well in this socially oriented city that you'll find most worthwhile ones have multiple locations in town. While they're technically chains, they don't sacrifice the intimate feel and service of one-off hostels. In fact, they manage to combine the energy of their many locations through nightly pub crawls and meet-ups between their locations to amp up the party.

One of my favorite chains is **Sant Jordi** (santjordihostels.com), which offers fun, social party hostels with great locations throughout town. Their baby dragon logo is a nod to the patron saint of Barcelona, Saint George. Another great chain, **Urbany Hostels** (urbanyhostels.com), focuses on the mod backpacker who wants all the amenities at a great price. Slightly more institutional **Equity Point** (equity-point.com) really competes on price. Generally, stays here are quieter and less social. You'll likely get a bit better sleep but are less likely to have wild nights at their three locations. My favorite branches of all three hostels are listed.

Kabul Backpackers Hostel

This is your best bet for a raging party. Kabul's is a party hostel through and through, and its great location smack dab on the Plaça Reial at the bottom of La Rambla makes it easy to hit the clubs at night and the top sights and beaches during the day. And their free breakfast in the morning is key to starting the day (or ending the night) right.

Beds from €13, 24-hour reception, laundry facilities, breakfast included, common room, terrace, Plaça Reial 17, Barri Gotic, +34 933 18 51 90, kabul.es, info@kabul.es, Metro: Liceu

Sant Jordi Gràcia

I love this hostel for both its clean, modern build-out and its location. The Gràcia district is just a short metro ride from the busy streets of the Old Town, but it feels distinctly more local and authentically Catalan. Street events happen often here but are missed out on by many tourists. The hostel has a fun social room with bean bags, comfortable modern bunks, and clean basic rooms. The shared bathrooms are clean, and the staff is welcoming and helpful.

Eight-bed mixed dorm from €14, free Wi-Fi, 24-hour reception, laundry facilities, breakfast extra, free maps and walking tours, pub crawl organized often, kitchen, towels extra, Carrer de Terol 35, Greater Barcelona, +34 93 342 41 61, santjordihostels.com, gracia@santjordi.org, Metro: Fontana or Gràcia

Equity Point Gothic

A superbly located hostel right in El Born, Equity Point Gothic is in one of the oldest parts of Barcelona. The bohemian atmosphere of the neighborhood, with trendy plazas and cafés, puts you right in the middle of young Barcelona. The proximity to the Picasso Museum and La Rambla makes this hostel a great option for serious sightseers. Heads up: They really pack in the bunks in their larger dorms, up to three or four levels high.

Beds from €11.90, free Wi-Fi, breakfast included, basic kitchen, laundry, 24-hour reception, Carrer Vigatans 5, El Born, +34 932 31 20 45, equity-point.com, infogothic@equity-point.com, Metro: Jaume I

Equity Point Sea

The hostel itself isn't the cleanest, and the beds aren't all that comfortable, and the scene isn't all that fun. But the location is to die for—right on the tip of the Barceloneta, near excellent cafés, restaurants, tapas bars, and—most importantly—the beach!

Dorms from €10, 24-hour reception, breakfast included, a/c when it works, social common room, on-site bar, free Internet, laundry facilities, Plaça del Mar 1-4, Barceloneta, +34 932 24 70 75, equity-point.com, infosea@equity-point.com, Metro: Barceloneta

Equity Point Centric

The largest of the Equity Point hostels, this one is right on Passeig de Gràcia, mere steps from the main square of Barcelona and all of Catalonia, Plaça Catalonia. The price is right in this massive hostel with everything from single and twin rooms to large 14-bed dorms. The rooftop terrace and its location are the major highlights.

Dorms from €9, 24-hour reception, breakfast extra, on-site bar, lockers, laundry facilities, free Wi-Fi, common room, towels extra, Passeig de Gràcia 33, Eixample,

+34 932 15 65 38, equity-point.com, infocentric@equity-point.com, Metro: Passeig de Gràcia

Sant Jordi Rock Palace

This large hostel (150-plus beds), one of Sant Jordi's newer entries, features an on-site bar, social room, bright reception with helpful staff, large dorms, and comfortable chilled-out vibe. The rooftop terrace and pool make it a favorite. The decor is well executed: funky retro posh.

Ten-bed dorms from €16, free Wi-Fi, 24-hour reception, breakfast extra, towel for rent, Balmes 75, Eixample, +34 934 53 32 81, santjordihostels.com, rockpalace@santjordi.org, Metro: Passeig de Gràcia

Sant Jordi Alberg

This local hostel chain really understands what makes a great hostel. Awesome staff, value, atmosphere, and free nightly pub crawls pack this place out year-round, so be sure to reserve long in advance.

Beds from €13, 24-hour reception, free lockers, laundry facilities, common room, Internet access, Calle de Roger de Llúria 40, first floor, apartment 2, Eixample, +34 933 42 41 61, santjordihostels.com, lluria@santjordi.org, Metro: Passeig de Gràcia

Sant Jordi Apartment Sagrada Familia

Sagrada Familia Apartments offers single, double, triple, and quad rooms in a private apartment setting. The rooms are modestly decorated, clean, and modern. The slick design follows the smooth concrete mod skateboard-inspired culture.

Basic singles from €30, free Wi-Fi, breakfast optional, towels included, laundry facilities, 24-hour reception, Carrer del Freser 5, Eixample, +34 934 46 05 17, santjordihostels.com, sagradafamilia@santjordi.org, Metro: St Pau-Dos de Maig

Urbany BCN GO

Sporting a rooftop terrace, all new facilities, a Jacuzzi, and comfortable, bright rooms, this is isn't your papa's dingy hostel. Enjoy the perfect blend of comfort and great social atmosphere at one of this chain's newest and most popular locations.

Beds from €14, 24-hour reception, laundry service, breakfast available, mini pool and Jacuzzi, free Wi-Fi, luggage storage, Corts Catalanes 563, Eixample, +34 937 37 96 18, urbany-hostels.com, info@urbanybcngo.com, Metro: Universitat

Urbany Barcelona

If BCN Go is full, try Urbany Barcelona nearby. The welcoming receptionists can recommend activities for your stay. The pool table, rooftop terrace, and social setting will be your favorite parts of the hostel. The beds are nothing to write home about, but the price is right.

Dorms from €10, 24-hour reception, laundry facilities, breakfast extra, rooftop terrace, free Wi-Fi, luggage storage available, Avinguda Meridiana 97, Eixample, +34 932 45 84 14, urbanyhostels.com, Metro: Clot or Encants

TRANSPORTATION

GETTING THERE & AWAY

Barcelona is well connected and offers numerous public transportation options from the transport hubs into the center and your accommodations.

Plane

Two airports serve Barcelona. From **El Prat** (BCN, barcelona-airport.com), take the **AeroBus,** which leaves every 20 minutes, directly into the center (40 minutes, €5.65 one-way, free Wi-Fi and charging plugs on board). Stay on till the end of the line, Plaça de Catalonia (Barcelona's main square), and make your connection from there by foot, metro, or bus.

If you're flying into **Girona** (GRO, girona-airport.net) simply hop on the **Barcelona Bus** into the city center (about 1.5 hours, €15 one way). You'll get dropped off at **Estacio d'Autobus Barcelona Nord,** from which you can head into the metro. Google "Barcelona bus from Girona" for the latest timetables.

Train

The train system is excellent in Spain. Trains between Barcelona and Madrid run often and take just about three hours. If you purchase in advance through **Renfe** (renfe.com), tickets can be as cheap as €50, but prices climb past €150 closer to the date and during peak travel times. Since there's quite a bit of business traffic between these cities, avoid the times that commuters would want (early morning, late afternoon) to find the cheapest options. The trip from Paris is about 7 hours (€130). Train websites are notoriously difficult to navigate. For that reason, research timetables online, and then book in person at your closest international train station. Barcelona has two major train stations: **Estacio de Sants,** west of the Old Town,

and **Estacio de Franca,** located between El Born and Barceloneta. Both stations have integrated metro stops.

Bus

Barcelona has two major bus stations: **Estacio de Sants,** west of the Old Town, and **Estacio de Nord,** north of El Born. Check out **Eurolines** (eurolines.com) for your best national and international connections. While bus tickets may be cheaper than train tickets, don't forget to value the extra time you'll be spending en route.

Car

By car, Barcelona is about three hours west of Madrid and about 10 hours south of Paris.

GETTING AROUND

Barcelona is a wonderful city to walk, but factor its large size into your planning. The heart of Barcelona, the medieval city called Barri Gotic, is a 20-minute walk from one side to the other. The Eixample is the modern expansion beyond the Old Town and is much bigger, with block after block of traffic and modern buildings.

The **bus and metro systems** in Barcelona are integrated with each other, meaning that you can use the same passes for both a bus ride and a metro ride. Buy the **T10 pass** (€9.95), which is one ticket that can be used by one person for ten rides, by ten people once, or by two friends all weekend for five rides each. With this pass, you save almost 50 percent of the **individual ticket rate** (€2) and will take care of your transportation needs while in town. You can buy your T10 passes from the automated machines in the metro. Use change, as paying with a big

bill will give you a pocket full of heavy coins in return.

Metro

The metro is a fast and efficient way across town if you don't mind missing the views along the way. You'll notice the metro-line colors reflect those of the Olympic rings—the entire metro was revamped for the 1992 Olympics. The metro closes at midnight during the week, at 02:00 on Friday, and goes all night on Saturday.

Barcelona has a serious **pickpocketing** problem. Pickpockets work the busy areas in the touristy metro stops like Plaça de Catalonia, so always have your wits about you.

Bus

Barcelona boasts an extensive network of buses. Routes and numbers are easy to read at each bus stop. Look for the arrow pointing toward the Mediterranean Sea to get yourself oriented, as the maps won't be oriented north-south but along the bus line itself. Buy tickets before boarding or from the driver.

Taxi

Official licensed Barcelona cabs are painted black, with yellow doors. There are fleets of them across the city, and you can wave them down. Rest assured that the meter will be in the right setting. There are four tariff rates: T1 (€2.10 + €1.07/km) is weekdays 08:00-20:00, T2 (€2.10 + €1.30/km) is weekdays 20:00-08:00, T3 (€2.30 + €1.40/km) is weekends and holidays 20:00-06:00, and T4 is fixed rate. At the time of writing, **Uber** had not yet made inroads into Barcelona.

Bicycle

Barcelona has a **public bike rental** (bicing.cat)

system for registered users. I recommend renting a bike through **One Car Less** (Calle Esparteria 3, +34 932 682 105, biketoursbarcelona.com) in El Born. For €10 for the half day, you can hire a bike to ride the length of the beaches, finding just your perfect spot. There's not much of a reason to venture into the Eixample on a bike. I prefer to avoid the heavy traffic of the modern town, though there is a network of bike paths.

DAY TRIPS

Montserrat

For beautiful views of the surrounding countryside and coastline far off in the distance and challenging hiking outside the city, look no further than Montserrat. Montserrat (Serrated Mountain) has a monastery, **Santa Maria de Montserrat** (free, daily 07:00-19:30 with masses often, +34 938 77 77 77, montserratvisita.com) tucked into the armpit of the rocky crag. Explore the gilded gothic monastery and the ramparts looking out over Cataluña, then make a pit stop at the cafeteria and gift shop. To cap it off, take the funicular (€3.70, runs every twenty minutes until about 17:00 in the low season, and 18:00 in summer months, cremalleradementserrat.cat) straight up the mountain to the peak.

Located on the R5 line, in the direction of Manresa, the station is just an hour away from downtown Barcelona. On arrival to the train station, take the Aeri cable car for a beautiful view as you transfer up into the monastery location. From this location you can wander around or choose between two different funiculars that lead you to separate areas.

Trains depart hourly from Plaça Espanya to Monistrol de Montserrat. Tickets run about €30 all told. Allow a full day for the trip.

HELP!

Tourist Information Centers

The tourist information center (Mon-Thurs 09:00-14:30 and 15:30-18:30, Fri 09:00-15:00), just beneath the Plaça Catalonia at the top of La Rambla, is easy to find. Pop in for sightseeing tips, sight reservations, maps, and help finding accommodations. You can also get information at barcelonaturisme.com.

Plaça de Catalonia 17

+34 932 85 38 34

Pickpockets & Scams

Barcelona has a serious pickpocketing problem. Tourists are often targeted on busy boulevards, where they're easily distracted. Busy metro stations are also a prime pickpocketing zone. Wear your backpacks on your front, use a money belt, and keep your valuables close in busy touristy areas. More often than not, you won't notice you've been pickpocketed until it's too late.

Gambling in public is illegal, and you should avoid the games on La Rambla, where gamblers work in teams to lure unsuspecting tourists. You'll win fast—then lose it all in the blink of an eye.

Emergencies

For emergencies, dial 112. You can also reach fire service (061) or city police (092), or dial 061 for medical emergencies.

Hospital

Hospital Clinic Barcelona

Emergency entrance: Casanova 143, 08036 Barcelona

+34 93 227 5400

US Consulate

Paseo Reina Elisenda de Montcada

+34 93 280 22 27

BERLIN

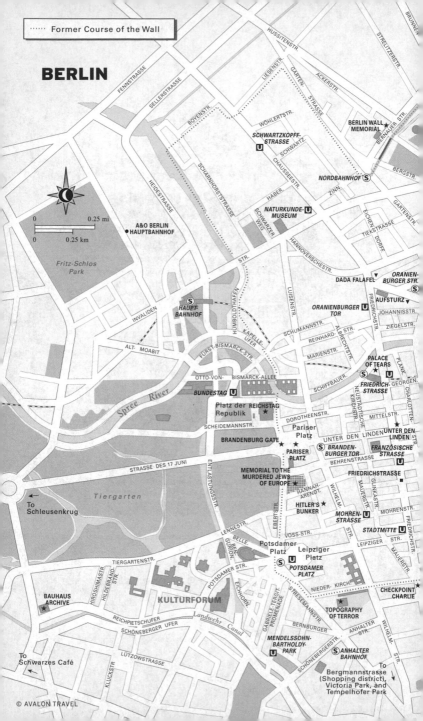

Willkommen, *bienvenue,* and welcome to Berlin! Once divided by the post-WWII powers, Berlin's east and west parts have since reunited and blossomed into a thriving, vibrant metropolis. Germany's capital is teeming with history and culture, including an alternative nightlife scene that will either turn you on or freak you out. So embrace your will to be weird, along with the zeitgeist that awaits!

BERLIN 101

Berlin experienced a difficult 20th century. Following Germany's defeat in World War I, inflation soared as a result of the reparations laid out in the Treaty of Versailles. By the early 1920s, 4.2 trillion German marks were equal to less than one US dollar, and it cost a wheelbarrow full of bills to purchase a single loaf of bread. This situation improved through renegotiation with the Allied forces in 1924, and Berlin prospered toward the later half of the decade. With residents such as Albert Einstein breaking boundaries in science and artists like George Grosz making headway in the Dada movement, Berlin became the cultural haven of Europe. It also boasted the wildest cocaine-fueled nightlife the world had ever seen.

The good times ended as Hitler finagled his way into power. Hitler reenergized the country, but in a terrible direction, and embarked on a vicious genocide against Jews and other minorities, whom he blamed for problems like corruption and inflation. After systematic deportations and executions, only 1,200 of Berlin's 160,000 Jews were left in the city after the Holocaust. As for the city itself, over 80 percent of Berlin was flattened by bombs during World War II.

Following the war, Germany as a country was divided in two, East and West. The city of Berlin, located smack dab in the middle of East Germany, was divided into four sectors: British, French, American, and Russian. The former three created an island of capitalism in a sea of Soviet East Germany. To maintain a foothold in Berlin, the Western Allies put huge effort into sustaining the citizens of West Berlin. The quality of life was better in West Berlin and West Germany, so the East German population—including many intellectuals and professionals—started slowly bleeding west.

Refusing to accept the exodus, the Soviets decided to build a wall north-south through East Germany and all around West Berlin. In the middle of the night on August 13, 1961, the East German government laid the foundations for what they called the "anti-fascist protection wall." The existence of the Berlin Wall implicitly admitted that nobody wanted to live in this supposed communist paradise. The Berlin Wall remained in place until 1989, when a miscommunication during a routine TV announcement kicked off a surge of East Berliners to the handful of gates, pushing to cross into West Berlin. Overwhelmed, the bewildered guards permitted families to reunite across the wall, and the celebratory dismantling of the wall began as quickly as it went up almost 30 years before. The wall's collapse sparked the collapse of the entire Soviet Union. East and West Germany were reunited, and the city of Berlin once again became the capital city of Germany.

Today, East Berlin is the world's largest construction project, and is transforming once more to reflect the vibrant energy of the unmistakable Berliner culture.

PLAN AHEAD

RESERVATIONS

Reservations are required for the **Reichstag** (bundestag.de/htdocs_e/visits).

PASSES

WelcomeCard

Berlin's **WelcomeCard** (visitberlin.de) covers public transportation within the city and offers discounted entry into sights, including the TV Tower and DDR Museum. The 48-hour version costs €19.50. See the website for 72-hour or five-day options, or options that cover transit to Potsdam.

LOCAL HAPPENINGS

Unity Day

Unity Day is a public national holiday in Germany that is celebrated on October 3, commemorating the day when East and West Germany were reunited. People celebrate with festivals, fireworks, concerts, communal meals, and speeches by politicians or other prominent figures.

Christmas Markets

If you find yourself in Berlin around Christmastime, enjoy a mug of mulled wine and sausages at one of the many Christmas markets that pop up every year toward the end of November and run until the New Year. The scene really puts you in the Christmas spirit, with decorated Christmas trees, warming huts, stalls selling ornaments and other trinkets, and jolly musicians playing all the Christmas classics.

KNOW BEFORE YOU GO

KEY STATS & FIGURES

Currency:
Germany uses the euro (€);
1 EUR = about 1.06 USD

Population:
3,500,000

Internationals:
30 percent

Language:
German

Number of bridges:
1,700 (triple that of Venice)

Number of museums:
175 (5 on Museum Island alone)

Favorite dish:
currywurst

Annual tax to own a dog:
€150

CALIBRATE YOUR BUDGET

TYPICAL PRICES FOR:

Hostel dorm bed:
€12

Two-course dinner and drink:
€12

Pint of beer:
€4

Currywurst and potatoes:
€4

Day bike rental:
€14

Single S-Bahn & U-Bahn pass:
€2.40

MOVIES TO WATCH

The Lives of Others, Good Bye Lenin!, Cabaret

THREE DAY ITINERARY

It's a tall order to soak in the history, experience the complex modern culture, and visit all the must-see sights that Berlin has to offer in three short days. But you'll cover a lot of ground if you stick to this itinerary and make reservations well ahead of time for entry into the Reichstag, Germany's parliament building.

DAY 1: WELCOME TO BERLIN

MORNING

Grab a breakfast to go like all the Berliners at your closest **Back-Factory,** then begin a free three-hour walking tour with **Alternative Berlin** or a 4.5-hour bike tour with **Fat Tire Bike Tours.** Both meet at 11:00 daily at Alexanderplatz just on the north side of the TV Tower. Both introductory tours take you past sights like **Checkpoint Charlie**, the **Brandenburg Gate**, the **Memorial to the Murdered Jews of Europe**, **Hitler's Bunker**, and some still-standing remnants of the **Berlin Wall**. Note any interesting sights you may want to double back to later in your stay.

AFTERNOON

Your tour will stop for lunch along the way and finish up midafternoon. Now that you know your way around the city, opt to keep your bike from Fat Tire for another couple days.

Get some Mitte shopping time in on **Unter den Linden** and on the streets surrounding the Weinmeisterstrasse U-Bahn stop. Otherwise, grab a snack to go and rest the legs for about 45 minutes on historic bus route 100, listening to **Jimbo's Cheap Man's Bus Tour,** available for free download online. This route will take you over to West Berlin and show you the scale of the city. Notice how the streets become more residential the farther west you go? For a snack at the turnaround point, try **Schwarzes Café** just a long block down Kantstrasse from the Zoologischer bus stop. If you plan to visit the **Bauhaus Archives** museum during your visit, now is the most efficient time to do it (stop: Lutzowplatz on bus 100). Then return to the hostel to freshen up.

EVENING

Head to Oranienburger Strasse for pre-dinner beers at **Aufsturz**. Then cross the street to my favorite Turkish joint on this side of town: **Dada Falafel**. Pop in for the kebabs and stay for the fresh juice and smoothies—and a peek at **Tacheles** across the street, Berlin's most famous ex-squatting complex.

LATE

In a jazzy mood? You're not far from **Zosch**, a famous Berliner jazz bar. Descend into their WWII bomb shelter cellar to enjoy a foot-tapping great time. If it's a Wednesday night, you'll be treated to some of the best live jazz in the city. Order your beer by the liter.

You've had a long day, so stay close and take the 10-minute walk over to **Rosenthaler Platz** for a wonderful slice of fun, hipster nightlife. Be sure to have a round at my favorite bar in the city, **Mein Haus am See**.

DAY 2: IRON CURTAIN & MORE

MORNING

If your hostel is anywhere near the Rosa-Luxemburg-Platz U-Bahn stop (both Wombat's and St Christopher's hostels are), you've got to try my favorite coffee shop in town, **Kaschk,** with some of the best beans this side of the Alps. Then take a stroll through Mitte to the **Palace of Tears.** What was the main exchange point between the two halves of the split city is now a free and heavy-hitting exhibit.

AFTERNOON

From the Palace of Tears, take S1, S2, or S25 north to Nordbahnhof to transfer onto the M10 tram to the **Berlin Wall Memorial** to see a full-scale remnant of the Berlin Wall. Climb the nearby observation tower to look out over the walls and across the entire city. Afterward, your super typical Berliner lunch lies just a 10-minute walk away at **Altberliner Kaffeestube** on Arkonaplatz.

Loop on tram M10 toward Warschauer Strasse, over to the **East Side Gallery**, the Berlin Wall's longest remaining intact section. Today, it's the world's largest outdoor mural, with hundreds of famous artists having returned to recently retouch their original work from nearly 25 years ago.

Being in this part of town puts you in perfect position to explore the **Kreuzberg** neighborhood, Berlin's most ethic neighborhood, centering around Oranienstrasse.

EVENING

For dinner, stick around Kreuzberg for amazing Italian at **Il Casolare** or authentic Turkish at **Hasir**, or head to Mitte for the classic German beer hall meat-and-potatoes dishes at **Georgbrau**.

LATE

Return to the hostel to change and down a couple shots at the hostel bar to get ready for your night out in **Friedrichshain**, Berlin's famous entertainment district. Stop at the numerous bars in the neighborhood to get amped up for the nearby famous clubs of **Berghain** and **Tresor**.

DAY 3: SHOPPING, DAY TRIP, & REICHSTAG

MORNING

If it's Sunday, head north to the **Mauerpark Flea Market**, my favorite of Berlin's outdoor markets. You'll find everything from antiques to handmade crafts. Street food options abound: pizza, bratwurst, and typical stews.

AFTERNOON

Take the hour-long trip north to see **Sachsenhausen**, the closest Nazi concentration camp to the Berlin city center (take the M10 tram to Nordbanhof, connect onto the S1 north to Oranienburg station, and catch bus 804 to the camp). This is where the Nazis developed their concentration camp layout and instruments of mass torture and murder to be used later at camps like Dachau and Auschwitz.

EVENING

Return to town for an evening entry into the **Reichstag** (reservations required), Germany's parliament. Notice the striking architectural symbolism of the transparent glass, meant to illustrate the transparency of the German democratic system.

LATE

Return to your hostel neighborhood and pop into the unique bars along **Schönhauser Allee**, a prime spot to toast to an amazing three days in Berlin.

Massive Berlin is divided into East and West sections. East Berlin is where you'll spend the vast majority of your time. At its center, **Mitte** contains most of the top sights, from the Reichstag, Brandenburg Gate, and Unter den Linden on its west end to the TV Tower on the east end, with a cluster of museums on Museum Island.

Northeast of Mitte, yuppie **Prenzlauer Berg** (P'berg, for short) is your chance to see what tattooed ex-punks look like 15 years down the road and offers low-key, mature restaurants and nightlife. South of the Spree River is the **Kreuzberg** neighborhood, Berlin's most ethnic district, made

up of a sizable Turkish population. Come here to experience a Turkish flea market and enjoy rich and tasty kebabs. East of Mitte on the north side of the river, **Friedrichshain** offers the impressive East Side Gallery and some of the city's richest unique nightlife.

Central Berlin is home to Tiergarten park and the Bauhaus Archives. West and south of Tiergarten is **West Berlin**, the quieter residential side of town. Lacking the heavy sightseeing punch of East Berlin, West Berlin isn't worth the valuable time on a short visit. Don't stress if you don't make it out there.

The Topography of Terror

On the site of the old Gestapo headquarters, the Topography of Terror is an intense exhibit taking you chronologically through the downward slope of Germany in the 1930s toward full-on fascism. Detailing the early power grabs of the Nazi party through to the segregation of Jews and minorities and the atrocities that followed, this museum doesn't shy away from the difficult history that the country is still coming to terms with. The museum is thankfully on a single floor, and heavy-hitting displays create a maze of suspended text and images. A café and lockers are available toward the right as you enter, and toilets are downstairs.

Outside the museum, you'll find a stretch of the Berlin Wall with exposed foundations just beneath. These were the cells where political prisoners were held, interrogated, and tortured by the Nazis.

Free, daily 10:00-20:00, outdoor exhibit closes at dusk, Niederkirchnerstrasse 8, Mitte, +49 (0)30 254 50 90, topographie.de/en, U-Bahn: Kochstrasse

Checkpoint Charlie

When thinking of the Berlin Wall, most Americans remember Checkpoint Charlie. Not named after Charlie Chaplin, rather this checkpoint was the third checkpoint after Alpha and Bravo. This was the checkpoint that the Americans controlled. Today, you can snap pictures with fake guardsmen during the day. Rumor has it these guards moonlight at the local Chippendales.

Nearby, the interesting **Checkpoint Charlie**

Museum (€12.50 adult/€9.50 student, daily 09:00-22:00, Friedrichstrasse 43-45, Mitte, +49 (0)30 253 72 50, mauermuseum.de, U-Bahn: Kochstrasse) focuses on creative and successful escapes from East Berlin into West Berlin over the years. The museum is full of ingenious inventions for getting over the wall or disguising oneself to get through the checkpoints. To make escapes more difficult, rope and other implements that could be used to scale walls were sold with very tight restrictions.

Free, always open, Mitte, intersection of Zimmerstrasse and Friedrichstrasse, U-Bahn: Kochstrasse

TV Tower

Standing 368 meters tall, the TV Tower is the tallest structure in Germany. It was built by the communists in 1969 to show off their engineering prowess (though they secretly imported Swedish engineers to finish the job). In an ironic twist, the textured ball toward the top of the tower reflects light from the sun in the shape of a cross, creating the largest one around in this secular communist territory. It's possible to head to the top of the TV Tower via speedy elevator for a beautiful 360-degree panorama over downtown Berlin.

Nearby **Alexanderplatz** is a famous downtown square that played the backdrop to an exciting scene from the *Bourne Supremacy*. It's also a main public transportation hub through which you're sure to connect during your visit.

€13 entry, daily 09:00-24:00, Panoramastrasse 1A, Mitte, +49 (0)30 247 57 58 75, tv-turm.de, S+U-Bahn: Alexanderplatz

BERLIN

ACT LIKE A LOCAL

Embrace Your Inner Hipster

Berlin—with its young population, many artists and musicians, bohemian lifestyle, and cheap rent—has been a magnet for counterculture types and has been the capital of "hipsterness" since before the term existed. Up until the last few years, squatting in abandoned houses and buildings was actually a protected right held by the citizens of the city. While you're here, hit up a thrift market, revel in great nightlife, and imagine a time when taking up residence in an abandoned building was a perfectly acceptable housing option.

Love the Ampelmann

There were quite a number of aspects of daily life to hate while under communist rule: food shortages, only getting oranges once a year for Christmas, and the fact it took more than 10 years on a waiting list to get even a basic car made from epoxy and heavy cardboard, just to name a few. But there was one part of East Berliner life that the comrades eventually held near and dear: the Ampelmann.

While you walk the streets of Berlin, notice the cute little green walking man and red no-go man lights at each crosswalk. This is the Ampelmann! After the fall of the wall, the crosswalk lights were undergoing a standardization process until local protests caught such momentum that the city council canceled their efforts and even replaced the ones they had taken down. The Ampelmann had become an endearing, nostalgic symbol of East Berliner life. Today, there are Ampelmann stores where you can get everything from mugs to messenger bags decked out in the familiar symbol.

Brandenburg Gate & Pariser Platz

Built during the Prussian monarchy in 1791, the Brandenburg Gate once served as the grand passageway to Unter den Linden, the beautiful tree-lined boulevard that led straight to the city palace. During the Cold War the gate was closed off and isolated in no-man's-land, going from a symbol of passage and unity to a persistent symbol of separation. It wasn't until the fall of the Berlin Wall in 1989 that the gate was once more made accessible.

Today, the clean, white Brandenburg Gate stands as a symbol of a unified Germany and is an iconic landmark of the city, capping one of the most important squares: **Pariser Platz.** Here you'll find the famous Hotel Adlon (yes, the five-star hotel from which Michael Jackson infamously dangled his baby), the fortress-like US Embassy, the French Embassy, and hundreds of tourists. When designing the embassy in a post-9/11 world, the Americans wanted an extra few feet in the security perimeter than the existing Brandenburg Gate would allow, and they even asked to shift the historic gate by a couple meters. They were denied, but it's easy to note the stiff security all the way around the building between Pariser Platz and the Memorial to the Murdered Jews of Europe.

Free, always open, Pariser Platz, Mitte, S-Bahn: Brandenburger Tor

Palace of Tears

The Palace of Tears occupies an old checkpoint station where East Berliners were permitted to cross into West Berlin, but only after serious interrogation by strict border guards. Those leaving East Berlin didn't know if they'd ever see their families and loved ones again. Today, through multimedia and interactive displays, a single-floor exhibit depicts life behind the Iron Curtain, the moments during the fall of the wall, and the long process of reunifying a great nation. You'll learn about the ingenious ways that East Berliners coped with the challenge of living under communism.

Free, Tues-Fri 09:00-19:00, Sat-Sun 10:00-18:00, Reichstagufer 17, Mitte, +49 (0)30 46777790, hdg.de/berlin/traenenpalast, S+U-Bahn: Friedrichstrasse

Reichstag

The Reichstag, built in 1894 and remodeled in the 1990s, is the traditional seat of Germany's parliament. Its magnificent glass dome, which represents the government's commitment to transparency, offers a stunning view of the Berlin skyline, but don't forget to look down. Visitors can keep an eye on what the elected officials are doing below, with a clear view over their shoulders. Take your time listening to the well-done audio guide as it loops you up and back down the spiraling track inside the glass dome. You'll enter through a security check to the right of the main entrance as you look at the facade. While the entry is free, reservations are required. Don't be late for your appointment, as these Germans really stick to the clock! You can also enjoy a restaurant at the roof level of the building, serving breakfast, lunch, and dinner.

Free, reservations required, daily 08:00-24:00, last entry at 22:00, Platz der Republik 1, Mitte, +49 (0)30 227 32152, bundestag.de, S-Bahn: Brandenburger Tor, U-Bahn: Bundestag

Berlin Wall Memorial

Head up to Bernauer Strasse on the northern edge of Mitte to see a small, yet fully preserved section of the Berlin Wall. You'll see the double layer of defense, the combed and mine-strewn sand in no-man's-land, and the trespassing detection systems, all of which make one think that when a government has to work so hard to keep their people inside their borders, there must be something wrong with the system. This was a unique stretch of the wall because it incorporated existing buildings into the wall to save on building materials. People lived in these buildings, and several escaped through the westward-facing windows. It wasn't until a tug-of-war between police and an escaping old lady hanging halfway out the window occurred that they bricked up all opportunities for escape.

Climb the stairs in the tower across the street for a free panorama of the neighborhood and a view into the section of the Berlin Wall.

Free, always open, Mitte, +49 (0)30 467 98 66 66, S-Bahn: Nordbahnhof

Memorial to the Murdered Jews of Europe

This Holocaust memorial, completed in 2005, consists of 2,700 different-sized stone slabs positioned on a rolling plane. It evokes powerful feelings of instability, claustrophobia, and disorientation as you remember those deported and killed during the war. As you step deeper into this memorial, the sounds of the city fade away and are replaced by silence and an eerie sense of isolation, even among the many people viewing the memorial with you. To prevent graffiti, the blocks were covered with a protective coating, which has actually worked quite well. Ironically, the company that provided this protective chemical was distantly affiliated with the company that developed Zyklon B, the gassing chemical used by the Nazis in their extermination camps. When this came to light, the company provided the service and products free of charge.

Free, always open, Cora-Berliner-Strasse 1, Mitte, +49 (0)30 2639 4336, holocaust-mahnmal.de/en, S-Bahn: Brandenburger Tor, U-Bahn: Potsdamer Platz

Hitler's Bunker

In the last days of World War II, Hitler and his inner circle retreated to a complex deep in the ground with 10-foot-thick reinforced concrete walls and ceilings to coordinate their last stand. Dark and damp, it wasn't a comfortable or particularly pleasant place to be hanging out. The bunker was destroyed and dismantled after the war, and the remains are still buried underneath this nondescript parking lot. The parking lot is left

"I AM A JELLY DONUT"

In 1963, during a speech at the site of the Berlin Wall, President John F. Kennedy announced to the world that the United States would stand by West Berlin in this time of conflict with Russia, while also saying that East Berlin was officially not ours to control. *"Ich bin ein Berliner,"* stated Kennedy in solidarity. While the phrase literally translates to "I am a Berliner," in German the use of the indefinite article *ein* with this phrase is unnecessary, and gives the phrase the alternative meaning of "I am a jelly donut." Needless to say, cartoonists all over the world had a field day, and jokes about talking pastries were scattered all over the press. Though he probably regretted his mistake, Kennedy's declaration really only endeared him to the German people.

deliberately empty to avoid drawing any sort of attention or pilgrimage from extremists, but you can find a small sign board sharing information about what was below.

Free, always open, just southeast from the Memorial to the Murdered Jews of Europe at Wilhelmstrasse 77, Mitte, U-Bahn: Mohrenstrasse

East Side Gallery

The largest open-air gallery in the world, the East Side Gallery is a preserved mile-long section of the Berlin Wall that has been since painted over by hundreds of artists from all over the world. This once gray, bleak, soulless piece of concrete is now a multicolored work of art, bearing messages of peace and hope. Farther down the wall, there is an exhibit about all the walls around the world, from the Gaza Strip to Belfast in Northern Ireland.

Free, always open, Mühlenstrasse 45-80, Friedrichshain, +49 (0)172 391 87 26, eastsidegallery-berlin.com, U-Bahn: Schlesisches Tor

German History Museum

This extensive museum takes you from the early medieval ages of kings and serfs to the tumultuous 20th century through displays, paintings, artifacts, full suits of armor, weapons, and more. It's easy to spend several hours in just the permanent exhibition taking up the two large floors of this building. Check out the website ahead of time to see if any of their innovative temporary exhibits sound interesting as well.

Free up to 18 years, €8 for adults, daily 10:00-18:00, Unter den Linden 2, Mitte, +49 (0)30 2030 4444, dhm.de, U-Bahn: Hausvogteiplatz

Unter den Linden

Take a stroll down Berlin's grand downtown boulevard, which connects the Brandenburg Gate and Tiergarten with Alexanderplatz and the TV Tower. You'll pass by beautiful historic buildings like the Berlin

Opera, the State Library, the German History Museum, the Neue Wache (Memorial to the Victims of War), Bebelplatz (the site where the Nazis emptied out banned books from nearby libraries to be burned), and Humboldt University, where Albert Einstein taught.

Free, always open, Mitte, S-Bahn: Brandenburger Tor (Brandenburger Gate end) or S+U-Bahn: Alexanderplatz (TV Tower end)

DDR Museum

Enjoy this unique museum through interactive experiences that reveal the daily life of those living under the communist regime. Exhibits are fully hands-on. See what East Berliner denim looks like, sit in a communist-era car, and wash your brain with some communist propaganda.

€7 adult, tickets online from €5, daily 10:00-20:00, Sat. until 22:00, Karl-Liebknecht-Strasse 1, Mitte, +49 (0)30 847 12 37 31, ddr-museum.de, S-Bahn: Hackescher Markt or S+U-Bahn: Alexanderplatz

Berliner Dom

Climb to the top of Berlin's oldest church for an amazing view of the city. It's well worth the effort climbing up the stairs but up to you and your budget.

€7 adult/€5 student, Mon-Sat 09:00-20:00, Sun 12:00-20:00, until 19:00 Oct-Mar, closes around 17:30 on concert days, interior closed but dome open during services, Am Lustgarten, Mitte, +49 (0)30 20269136, berlinerdom.de, S-Bahn: Hackescher Markt

Bauhaus Archives Museum

It's impossible to overstate the impact of the Bauhaus School (founded 1919) on modern design. A ragtag group of professors and students experimented with avant-garde shapes and designs in both two and three dimensions, pushing the boundaries of aestheticism and function. Unfortunately, colors and performances irritated the Nazis, and the school was shut down in 1933. But in even those few years, Bauhaus left an impact that can still be seen in everything from President Obama's campaign posters to just about every corporate brand today. Many of the students' drawings, posters, watercolors, and models are on display in this purpose-built museum toward the west side of town, just south of Tiergarten. For any industrial or graphic design major, this is an obligatory pilgrimage.

€7 Wed-Fri, €8 Sat-Mon, open Wed-Mon 10:00–17:00, closed Tues, Klingelhöferstrasse 14, Central Berlin, +49 (0)30 254 00 20, U-Bahn: Nollendorfplatz

Berlin's Jewish Museum
This museum will send chills through your body, not just from the personal stories of Jewish history and culture, but from the stark and jagged architecture of the building, reflecting the cold abuse of the Holocaust. Designed by Daniel Libeskind, the building is defined by its zigzag hallways, skewed windows, and great "voids," leaving you with a feelings of unease and apprehension. Plan on spending about half a day here following the worthwhile audio guide through over 1,000 years of German-Jewish culture.

€8, Mon 10:00–22:00, Tues-Sun 10:00–20:00, last entry one hour before closing, closed on Jewish holidays, Linden-strasse 9-14, Kreuzberg, +49 (0)30 2599 3300, jmberlin.de/en, U-Bahn: Hallesches Tor or Kochstrasse

TOP EATS

The cuisine in Berlin is diverse. You'll definitely see the influence of its multicultural—particularly Italian and Turkish—makeup. Traditional German cuisine is often based on meat and potatoes, and flattened and fried pork steak, called **schnitzel**, is a common choice. **Currywurst** (a sausage with ketchup and curry) is a Berlin staple that's best eaten with a side of fries.

Tips of 5-10 percent of restaurant bills are appreciated. When paying, round up to the next couple euros. Remember that the water and any bread or pretzels that are waiting for you at the table are not generally included and will be added to your bill if you touch them.

Back-Factory
Back-Factory is a simple cafeteria with mass-produced pastries and self-service coffee machines. It's not a super special place, but it's a convenient place to grab a quick break-fast pastry or sandwich on the go. There are multiple locations throughout town.

Pastries from €1.50, Mon-Fri 06:00–20:00, Sat 06:00–18:30, Sun 06:00–19:00, Rosenthaler Platz at Brunnenstrasse 1, +49 (0)30 40056105, back-factory.de, U-Bahn: Rosenthaler Platz

Georgbrau
If you're looking for classic German fare and fine beer in a beer hall, look no further. Located right in the middle of Berlin's old medieval town (you won't be able to tell), this beer hall proudly serves piping hot racks of ribs, duck, and brats with sizable salads, potatoes done just right, and delicious house brews. Just a few steps from Unter den Linden, Georgbrau is a great nearby option if you find yourself in Mitte around dinnertime.

Mains from €8, daily 12:00–24:00, Spreeufer 4, Mitte, +49 (0)30 242 42 44, brauhaus-georgbraeu.de, U-Bahn: Klosterstrasse

Kaschk
Kaschk gets my vote for best coffee in town. Round that out with beers after the sun goes down and a shuffleboard table to boot, and what more could you ask for? This is your quintessential hipster brew house—of both grains and beans—with bearded baristas and one long common wooden table, yet without the pretentiousness that comes along with coffee snobbery. Ask the friendly staff about their best beans at the moment, and have them brew you something unforgettable.

From €2.50, Mon-Fri 08:00–02:00, Sat-Sun 10:00-late, Linienstrasse 40, Prenzlauer Berg, +49 (0)1578 197 99 70, instagram.com/kaschk, U-Bahn: Rosenthaler Platz or Weinmeisterstrasse

Dada Falafel
If you're in Mitte and feeling in the mood for a Turkish dish, head to Dada Falafel, where the boys crank out fried chickpea balls sunup to sundown. Their freshly squeezed orange juice is wonderful. As you leave, take a close look at the rundown **Tacheles** across the street, Berlin's most famous ex-squatting complex (it may not be around for long, as developers are already salivating at the real estate value).

From €6, daily 10:00–02:00, Linienstrasse 132, Mitte, +49 (0)30 2759 6927, dadafalafel.de, U-Bahn: Oranienburger Tor

Konnopke Imbiss
If you've never tried currywurst before, Konnopke Imbiss is *the* place to do it. Find this

inconspicuous takeaway joint underneath the elevated U2 rails and post up next to everyday Berliners enjoying their everyday meal.

€2-4, Mon-Fri 05:30-19:00, Sat 11:30-19:00, Schönhauser Allee 44B, under U-Bahn tracks, Prenzlauer Berg, konnopke-imbiss.de, U-Bahn: Eberswalder Strasse

Aufsturz

Aufsturz is famous more for their endless beer list than their food. But the menu still isn't bad and features varied Berliner dishes that are easy on the budget. Ask the friendly staff to help you translate, and try a beer you haven't heard of before. Aufsturz is a great place to pre-game before a night out. A side note: This street is known to be where many prostitutes work, so don't be swayed by any overly friendly women as you stumble out of the bar.

Beers from €3, dishes from €6, Mon-Thurs 12:00-01:00, Fri-Sat 12:00-02:00, Sun 12:00-01:00, Oranienburger Strasse 67, Mitte, +49 (0)30 2804 7407, S-Bahn: Oranienburger Strasse, U-Bahn: Oranienburger Tor

Prater

A beautifully renovated swing-era bar, Prater serves up enormous portions of meat and vegetables, topped off with frothy mugs of delicious German lager. During the summer, it's easy to spend the better part of the afternoon in the shaded beer garden, enjoying the buzz of Berliner beer and life.

€6-15, Mon-Sat 18:00-24:00, Sun 12:00-24:00, Kastanienallee 7-9, Prenzlauer Berg, +49 (0)30 448 56 88, pratergarten.de, U-Bahn: Eberswalder Strasse

Altberliner Kaffeestube

This is an excellent choice for your typical Berliner meal: meat-based dishes with sauerkraut, potatoes, and salads. While a staple for

those who live in Prenzlauer Berg, Altberliner does come with inflated P'berg prices.

Mains from €10, daily 12:00-24:00, till 01:00 on weekends, Fürstenberger Strasse 1, Prenzlauer Berg, +49 (0)30 449 51 51, altberliner-restaurant.de, U-Bahn: Bernauer Strasse

Taisu

Located just around the corner from Checkpoint Charlie, Taisu is said to have some of the best sushi in Berlin, and the location makes for a convenient pit stop. Pop into this clean and mod yet casual restaurant during lunch and enjoy their 2-for-1 sushi roll lunch special.

€2-6, daily 12:00-23:00, Rudi-Dutschke-Strasse 28, Kreuzberg, sushiwok.de, U-Bahn: Kochstrasse

Hasir

Give Berlin's best Turkish food a try in this classy, upscale kebab shop with guaranteed fresh ingredients and delicious plates like *kofta* (meatballs), pita, and fresh baklava. Find a second location in Mitte just north of the Hackescher Markt S-Bahn station (Oranienburgerstrasse 4).

Dishes from €8.50, daily 24 hours, Adalbertstrasse 10, Kreuzberg, +49 (0)30 614 23 73, U-Bahn: Kottbusser Tor

Il Ritrovo

Tired of sausage and curry? This family of restaurants gives you a dose of punk and pizza rolled and kneaded to perfection. Work your way to a free table and get ready for the most authentic and arguably best pizza in town, topped with your favorite ingredients. Il Ritrovo is well-located for after-dinner drinks in the bumping district of Friedrichshain.

Pizzas from €7, daily 12:00-24:00, Gabriel-Max-Strasse 2, Friedrichshain, +49 (0)30 2936 4130, S-Bahn: Warschauer Strasse

IF YOU ARE RACIST, SEXIST, HOMOPHOBIC, OR AN ASSHOLE ...DON'T COME IN.

Il Casolare

Il Casolare is easily one of my favorite Italian restaurants in town. They pride themselves on their authentic pizza and pasta. Sit in the cozy interior, or enjoy their outdoor seating on nice days. Go for a pitcher of their house wine to split with friends.

Pizzas from €6, daily 12:00–24:00, Grimmstrasse 30, Kreuzberg, +49 (0)30 6950 6610, U-Bahn: Kottbusser Tor

La Pausa

One step into this place and it feels like you've been transported to another country, with the smells of fresh pizza in the oven and the commotion of happy eaters to boot. Order pizza by the slice as you would in Italy, sprinkle with red pepper, and you've got a great late-night snack after a night out on Rosenthaler Platz.

Slices from €2, daily 11:00–02:30, Torstrasse 125, Prenzlauer Berg, +49 (0)30 2408 3108, U-Bahn: Rosenthaler Platz

Curry Mitte

If you're in the mood for Berlin's most famous snack, jump on this opportunity. Go for the currywurst and chips to keep you going late in the night.

Mon-Sat 11:00–24:00, till 06:00 on Fri and Sat, Torstrasse 122, Prenzlauer Berg, +49 (0)1520 106 95 59, currymitte.de, U-Bahn: Rosenthaler Platz

Schwarzes Café

This 24-hour café is a great option in the heart of residential West Berlin. I recommend it as a pit stop at the turnaround point of the recommended bus 100 audio tour. Step into this typically eclectic café, which like so many other places in Berlin somehow pulls off being great at just about everything, from coffee to beer and tasty plates of fruit, omelets, and salads.

Plates from €8, daily 24 hours, Kantstrasse 148, West Berlin, +49 (0)30 313 80 38, schwarzescafe-berlin.de, S+U-Bahn: Zoologischer Garten

International Restaurant Row

Why some of the most interesting restaurants in town decided to huddle on a half block on Weinbergsweg, I don't know, but I'm not complaining either! A lunch at these sit-down restaurants will run around €15, dinners €20-25. Find your bargains at the takeaway shops. On a single block, cafés and restaurants take you from Moscow to Mexico and from Chinese pork dumplings to French pastries in just a few meters. Beyond restaurants, you'll find a bakery selling cheap sandwiches, pastries, and coffee; the recommended **Circus Hostel**; and a **convenience shop** (Weinbergsweg 26-27) that sells beer and has chairs to relax on out front while consuming. (Why isn't this anywhere else in the world? Because I love it!)

Some of my favorite spots include **Gorki Park** (Weinbergsweg 25), which serves very good burgers and Russian staples like goulash; **Yumcha Heroes** (Weinbergsweg 8) offering tasty—if slightly overpriced—Chinese dim sum; **Café Fleury** (Weinbergsweg 20), a cozy and classic French bakery and café, with pastries, salads, sandwiches, and limited outdoor seating; **Soup 'n' Roll** (Torstrasse 117, around the corner from Weinbergsweg), serving a cheap and quick noodle; **Bagel Company Berlin** (Rosenthaler Strasse 69), serving breakfast bagels and sandwiches, and **My Smart Break** (Rosenthaler Strasse 67), with fresh and healthy sandwiches and coffee to go. Also check out **St. Oberholz Bar and Cafe** (Rosenthaler Strasse 72), a classic Berliner hipster café and bar, with yuppies on laptops and a classy drinking crowd at night. If they're open, spring for the lifeguard high chairs outside to take in the view from a new perspective.

Prenzlauer Berg, U-Bahn: Rosenthaler Platz

TOP BEER GARDENS

While Munich is famous for its Oktoberfest, the world's biggest beer-drinking festival, Berlin will not be left out. In typical Berliner form, these biergartens each come with a little something unique to make them some of my favorites in town.

Prater Garten

Established in 1837, Prater Garten is Berlin's oldest beer garden. It seats over 600 in a beautiful, outdoor area shaded by chestnut trees. If the weather is bad, step inside the indoor beer hall, where you can enjoy some of the best sausages and wienerschnitzel Berlin has to offer.

Pints from €4, Kastanienallee 7-9, Prenzlauer Berg, +49 (0)30 448 56 88, pratergarten.de, U-Bahn: Eberswalder Strasse

Schleusenkrug

Berlin's most idyllic beer garden, Schleusenkrug is in Tiergarten park, just north of the zoo. On a sunny day, there's nothing better than a crisp German lager and the cool breeze through the trees here. The food is of so-so value, so I recommend getting your fill on the liquid bread in your stein. The recommended Fat Tire Bike Tour takes its pit stop here to refuel.

Pints from €3.50, daily 10:00–24:00, Müller-Breslau-Strasse, Central Berlin, schleusenkrug.de, S+U-Bahn: Berlin Zoologischer Garten

Bierhof Rüdersdorf

I stumbled across this unique, mod beer garden on my way out to Friedrichshain for the night, and I quickly understood why it's one of Berlin's favorites. Tucked behind the famous techno-club Berghain, this small beer garden and posh one-floor patio bar is easy to miss, but a beer here is a great way to while away an afternoon, or to enjoy while eyeing the line to get into the big club next door. Check online ahead of time because the Bierhof is open seasonally (closed in the winter), and dates change often.

Snacks from €2, burgers from €6, Rüdersdorfer Strasse 70, Friedrichshain, +49 (0)30 2936 0215, bierhof.info, S-Bahn: Ostbahnhof

TOP NIGHTLIFE

NIGHTLIFE DISTRICTS

In this sprawling city, nightlife centers around several districts. All are slightly grittier than what you might find in London or Paris, but what my favorite spots may lack in cleanliness, they more than make up for in party mode and attitude.

Prenzlauer Berg

Prenzlauer Berg is known as the yuppie district, filled with young professionals getting their family life started. Look forward to seeing heavily tatted ex-punks pushing strollers down the street. **Kastanienallee** is an entire street full of bars and clubs.

Conveniently located near most of the recommended hostels, **Schönhauser Allee** leads uphill from Rosa-Luxemburg-Platz. In the first couple blocks from Torstrasse, you'll find some interesting and alternative venues. The kitschy goth-punk **Last Cathedral** (Schönhauser Allee 5) puts on frequent specials and events. **White Trash Food** (Schönhauser Allee 6-7) is a funky, American diner/Chinese shop/British pub hybrid with frequent live music shows. It's a great spot for huge burgers and fries, drinks, and a casual night out.

Prenzlauer Berg, U-Bahn: Rosenthaler Platz (Kastanienallee), U-Bahn: Rosa-Luxemburg-Platz (for Schönhauser Allee)

Rosenthaler Platz

This five-point intersection of everything Berliner has all the essentials for a night out—including proximity to good eats at the recommended **La Pausa** and **Curry Mitte**—and a hair of the dog recovery the next morning.

Mitte, U-Bahn: Rosenthaler Platz

Friedrichshain

Friedrichshain, a dense tangle of nightlife complexes, bars, and restaurants, is edgy Berlin at its best. Though the district is beginning to show the wear of normalization and mass tourism, everyone knows this is Berlin's best nightlife. Of the range of options in this area, **Hops & Barley** (Wühlischstrasse 22/23) and **Szimpla** (Gärtnerstrasse 15) are two of my favorite, more authentic bar choices. Start there and wander south toward the major clubs straddling the Spree River, like **Watergate** and **Tresor.**

Friedrichshain, S+U-Bahn: Warschauer Strasse

BARS

Bars in Berlin are fun and always a bit alternative to keep you on your toes. Each featuring its own little twist, Berliner bars reflect the city's eclectic makeup: Cocktail lounges give way to Ping Pong bars and authentic jazz cafés to keep the masses entertained.

Dr. Pong

This bar's all about one thing: Ping-Pong. And beer. Drop a five-euro deposit on a paddle and buy a ticket for a beer at the door, then get started running around the table in a game of group Ping-Pong. In this game of elimination, hit the ball from each side in turn and be the last person standing.

Drinks from €5, Mon-Sat 19:00–06:00, Sun 18:00–06:00, Eberswalder Strasse 21, Prenzlauer Berg, drpong.net, U-Bahn: Eberswalder Strasse

Mein Haus am See

This is a quintessential Berlin bar: warm atmosphere, hipster clientele, full bar with a few different options, smoking room, stadium seating in the back to look out over your fellow imbibers, and a bumping club downstairs with some enjoyably funky features. It's open 24/7, so you can get your drink or coffee on any time of day. At this

LGBT BERLIN

Berlin is known by many as Europe's gay capital. With prominent public figures, celebrities, and everyday people openly gay, the LGBT scene hardly raises an eyebrow in this city that's seen it all, and Germany has strict and extensive anti-discriminatory laws. Check out the website of **Out In Berlin** (out-in-berlin.com) for recommendations on cafés, restaurants, clubs, bars, nightlife districts, hotels, and more. Europe's biggest gay parade each year toward the end of June draws parties by the thousands.

spot, near Rosenthaler Platz, it feels like you're hanging out at your friend's place more than the local bar. As their tagline goes, "It's not a bar, it's not a club... it's something sexier in between."

Drinks from €4.50, daily 24 hours, Torstrasse 125, Prenzlauer Berg, +49 (0)163 555 80 33, mein-haus-am-see.blogspot.com, U-Bahn: Rosenthaler Platz

Die Weinerei

This bar is based completely on the honor system: You simply pay €2 to rent a glass and drink as much wine as you want, paying only as much as you think you owe in the tip jar when you leave. It sounds crazy, and seems like something that could be easily abused; however, with the charming atmosphere and trusting group mentality, imbibers just about always adequately pay for their consumption.

€2 to get started, Mon–Fri 13:00–20:00, Sat 11:00–20:00, Veteranenstrasse 14, Mitte, +49 (0)30 440 69 83, weinerei.com, M: Rosenthaler Platz

Luzia

Complete with an outdoor terrace overlooking the street, Luzia is one of the most popular bars in the Kreuzberg area. Inside you'll find old velvet armchairs, peeling vintage wallpaper revealing chipped red bricks, mismatched tables, and dim lamps that create a warm, laid-back atmosphere.

Coffee and beers from €4, daily 12:00–24:00, Oranienstrasse 34, Kreuzberg, +49 (0)30 8179 9958, luzia.tc, U-Bahn: Moritzplatz

Zosch

This bar churns out mediocre food, excellent beer throughout the week, and life-changing jazz sessions every Wednesday. Even for non-believers, these jazz sessions in the WWII bomb shelter downstairs are magical. The crew jams in front of regulars and in-the-know tourists alike. Grab a stein and join the communal tables. Be respectful to those who are there for the music, and keep your conversations hushed. Notice the three tiers

of brick candle holders sticking out from the wall. The candles at each height (knee, waist and chest) indicated gas seeping in and displacing oxygen, telling those seeking shelter "It's time to pick up the kiddies from the floor and give them piggyback rides." I much prefer today's less menacing atmosphere.

Liters from €7.50, daily 16:00–late, Tucholskystrasse 30, Mitte, +49 (0)30 280 76 64, zosch-berlin.de, S-Bahn: Oranienburger Strasse, U-Bahn: Oranienburger Tor

CLUBS

Berghain

Even if you're not a fan of techno, Berghain is the place to go if you want the real Berlin disco experience. Once a working power plant, the place is absolutely massive, with the cavernous main room blasting minimalist techno and the upstairs Panorama bar rocking purely house music. Though notoriously hard to get into, Berghain is the epitome of what you would expect a no-holds-barred European dance club to be and is worth it even with the chance of being turned away at the door. Be cool in the line, wear dark clothes, look like you're there to party hardy, don't take out your phone, and avoid speaking English. The nightly rave goes well into the next day, with Saturday-Monday events being the most popular.

€15 cover, open 24 hours Fri–Mon, Am Wriezener Bahnhof, Friedrichshain, +49 (0)30 2936 0210, berghain.de, S-Bahn: Ostbahnhof, U-Bahn: Weberweise

Tresor

Tresor is hailed as the godfather among the clubbing crowd, taking techno beats to an industrial scale in a massive abandoned power plant just across the river in the alternative neighborhood of Kreuzberg. This labyrinthine club comprises three dance floors, with long, dark graffitied hallways, dimly lit corners, and strobe lights pulsing throughout. Every inch of Tresor's 230,000 square feet is filled with an incredible sound system, top-tier DJs, ear-shattering bass, and a friendly mixed crowd that will dance well past midmorning. If you are looking for a staple of Berlin's nightlife (and don't feel like waiting in the endless line at Berghain), give Tresor a shot. Get your buttoned-up hipster mode on for best chances at the door.

€10-15 cover, parties rock out every Mon, Wed, Thurs, Fri, and Sat, Köpenicker Strasse 70, Kreuzberg, +49 (0)30 6953 7721, tresorberlin.com, U-Bahn: Heinrich-Heine Strasse

Watergate

Dance the night away at this midsized, double-floor nightclub spinning a solid blend of house music and techno, putting it on *DJ Mag*'s Top 100 Clubs list several years in a row. It's loved for its waterfront location, an open-air glass-bottomed patio that seems to float on the water (great to catch your breath on between beat drops), and an innovative LED-lighted ceiling upstairs that throbs with the music. Party-goers are happy they waited through the sometimes-long (but fast-moving) line. It's casual, but dress slightly smart to avoid any hassle with the bouncers.

€15 cover, 21+ age policy, Wed, Fri, and Sat 24:00-07:00, Falckensteinstrasse 49, just east of Oberbaumbrucke bridge, Kreuzberg, +49 (0)30 6128 0394, water-gate.de, U-Bahn: Schlesisches Tor

KitKat Club

KitKat Club is a legendary Berlin nightclub where fetishes, debauchery, hedonism, and the LGBT community are all welcome. This is an eclectic dance venue spinning EDM and house. Inspired by the free-love beach parties of Goa in the '80s, this is where freaks step out of their shells and into their leathers and glitter costumes—the more fabulous and edgy, the better. Friday, Saturday, and Sunday are their big nights, with CarneBall being their trademark event each Saturday night; bartenders do their own cabaret show to the glee of party-goers. The doors at this part exhibitionist party, part erotica club usually open at 23:00, but the party doesn't really kick off till around 03:00, going until the sun comes up. Show up wearing too much clothing and you'll have to leave some at coat check to hit the sweaty, neon-lighted dance floor sans shirt.

While the club is safe, friendly, and welcoming, it's much better to party with friends than solo on a first visit to KitKat Club. It's important to check out the website both for dress code guidelines—you won't be allowed in with street clothes—and also to really understand what you're getting yourself into. Find the entrance to the club

inside the U-Bahn station.

Cover €7-10, parties run Fri-Mon usually but vary according to the program on the website, Köpenicker Strasse 76, Kreuzberg, kitkatclub.org, U-Bahn: Heinrich-Heine Strasse

PUB CRAWLS

New Berlin Pub Crawl

Sandeman's, the folks who run daily walking tours, also organize nightly pub crawls to show you the fun part of town. €12 gets you a juicy welcome shot, a handful of bars, a fun crowd, and drink deals throughout the night. Picking up at the old post office on Oranienburger Strasse, this crawl shows you the best of the central Mitte district, ranging from grungy bars to hipster lounges, and is within walking distance for centrally located hostels. These groups get rowdy and frequently climb past 80 party-goers, funneled to this party from the walking tours in the day.

€12, daily 20:00, meet in front of the old post office at the corner of the Oranienburger Strasse S-Bahn station, Mitte, newberlintours.com, S-Bahn: Oranienburger Strasse

Alternative Berlin Pub Crawl

Thankfully, Berlin has an alternative to your standard rowdy pub crawl, rightly called Alternative Berlin Pub Crawl. Come out to enjoy interesting stories, classy drinks, and unique spots that may be a highlight of your trip. The crawl includes free entry to five bars and clubs and is capped at 15 or so people, so the experience is much more intimate than the one offered by Sandeman's.

€10, daily 21:00, meet outside Starbucks at the TV Tower, Mitte, alternativeberlin.com, S+U-Bahn: Alexanderplatz

BERLIN

SHOPPING DISTRICTS

Friedrichstrasse

Comparable to Oxford Street in London, Friedrichstrasse between the namesake station and Checkpoint Charlie is your standard downtown commercial zone with clothing brands like All Saints, Gucci, and Gap.

Friedrichstrasse, Mitte, S+U-Bahn: Friedrichstrasse

Hackescher Höfe Courtyards & Hackescher Markt

The area surrounding Hackescher Markt (+49 (0)30 2809 8010) is a trendy little downtown neighborhood offering a wide selection of boutiques, designer shops, and big international brands like Urban Outfitters and American Apparel. Find Rosenthaler Strasse to find the courtyards and wander through this maze of shops, cafés, and boutiques to get your shopping fix. Built as a housing project, this entire area has now developed as a great place to pick up unique finds. Keep your eyes open for deals! On Thursday and Saturday 09:00-18:00, there's a funky outdoor market selling handmade goods, snacks, and trinkets.

Rosenthaler Strasse 40-41, Mitte, S-Bahn: Hackescher Markt, U-Bahn: U Weinmeisterstrasse

Oranienstrasse & Bergmannstrasse

Located in the district of Kreuzberg, these two shopping streets are geared toward people who are interested in vintage clothing, old records, books, and secondhand shops. These streets also have a vibrant café culture and make for a pleasant afternoon of window-shopping and people-watching. **Oranienstrasse** is most interesting between Oranienplatz and the Gorlitzer Bahnhof U-Bahn station. On **Bergmannstrasse,** find charming cafés, shops, and restaurants between Mehringdamm Street to the Marheineke Markthalle. Bergmannstrasse is a 20-minute bike ride south from Mitte, so time a visit here with a casual cruise through the nearby recommended Tempelhofer and Victoria parks.

Kreuzberg, U-Bahn: Gorlitzer Bahnhof (for Oranienstrasse), U-Bahn: Gneisenaustrasse (for Bergmannstrasse)

MARKETS

Berlin is a flea market paradise. Macklemore would think he died and went to thrift-shopping heaven. Even the permanent stores often feel like they have a unique edge, so you're sure to find some great styles and whatever else you may be looking for.

Nowkoelln Flowmarkt

One of Berlin's newest and trendiest flea markets, Nowkoelln Flowmarkt caters to hip Berliners and tourists in the know. Located alongside the Landwehrkanal canal, the market sells funky vintage clothing and home goods and is complete with some top-notch food stalls. The market tends to run every other Sunday, but check the website to confirm dates, as they can vary during winter break.

10:00-17:30 every other Sun, Nowkoelln Flowmarkt, Maybachufer 31, Kreuzberg, nowkoelln.de, U-Bahn: Schönleinstrasse

Türkischer Markt

The Türkischer Markt is the closest you'll get to Istanbul's Grand Bazaar in Germany. This market serves the needs of the large local Turkish community and offers some of the best Turkish food around. The market also sells clothes and fabrics and is becoming very popular with Berlin's younger demographic, who like to make their own styles.

Tues and Fri 11:30-18:30, Türkischer Markt, located around Maybachufer 7, Kreuzberg, tuerkenmarkt.de, U-Bahn: Schönleinstrasse

Mauerpark Flea Market

What was once a part of the "death strip" of the Berlin Wall has now become one of my favorite outdoor markets in Europe. ("Death strip" refers to the no man's land between the Berlin Wall's double walls.) Brace yourself: The throngs flocking to this popular flea market can be overwhelming. Follow the smell of fresh sauerkraut, currywurst, and waffles until you find a great street food stand to tide you over. Bands and magicians gather in the amphitheater-like bowl, creating a jovial atmosphere. Be careful, or you may never leave this magical place.

Sun 09:00-18:00, Bernauer Strasse 63-64, Prenzlauer Berg, U-Bahn: Eberswalderstrasse

TOP PARKS & RECREATION

Tiergarten

What was once the official hunting ground of the Prussian king was converted into a public park in the late 18th century. Spend an afternoon enjoying the many ponds, trees, and open-air cafés this sprawling piece of land has to offer. This leafy park, which takes about 45 minutes to walk across, is ideal to explore on a bike.

Find the **Victory Column** (€2.20 adult, Apr-Oct Mon-Fri 09:30-18:30 and Sat-Sun 09:30-19:00, Nov-Mar Mon-Fri 10:00-17:00 and Sat-Sun 10:00-17:30, Grosser Stern), located in the park's center. The column represents Prussia's victory over France in 1871. The golden statue at the top is of the goddess Victoria, often referred to as Goldelse (Golden Elsi) by the locals. Climb the 285 steps to the top to get a spectacular view of the Tiergarten and Berlin.

Thirsty? Head to **Schleusenkrug** beer garden (Muller-Breslau-Strasse, daily 10:00-24:00) on the far west side of the park, just north of the zoo, for a pint and grub.

Central Berlin, S-Bahn: Tiergarten, U-Bahn: Hansaplatz

Tempelhofer Park & Victoria Park

The old Templehof airport was used by the Americans during the Berlin Air Lift (June 24, 1948-May 12, 1949), the epic effort of flying in tons of food and supplies every 30 minutes around the clock to support the people of West Berlin for 46 straight weeks when the communists shut down the land access routes to West Germany. This was the only way food, medicine, and other supplies were delivered to help an entire city survive. Seeing the futility of the situation, the DDR

SPREEPARK

What do an ex-communist theme park, a cocaine smuggling bust, and an unbeliev-able family drama have in common? Answer: Berlin's abandoned amusement park, Spreepark. Get ready to have your mind blown.

In 1969, the communists opened Kulturpark Plänterwald in East Berlin and oper-ated the amusement park continuously until the wall fell. At that point, a family business headed up by Norbert Witte took over, changing the name to Spreepark. Spreepark's first few years went well. The owners added new rides, and visitors to the park climbed to 1.5 million per year. But the Witte family soon got into hot water. The forest that the park was located in was rezoned, and the park was not permitted to add the parking spaces it needed. Ticket sales declined, and Witte slid deeper and deeper into debt.

At this point, Mr. Witte got desperate and started looking for ways to move the park, sell the rides, and wash his hands of this whole ordeal. In 2002 he found an opportunity in Peru. He shipped six attractions to South America and moved there himself with his family. But Witte just couldn't make it work, and with debts topping 10 million euros, Witte relied on "friends" to help pay off his debts, but of course they wanted something in return. And we're only just getting started.

By 2004, things weren't looking good for the family. They owed a lot of money to people you just don't want to owe money to. With his back against the wall, Witte decided to ship his rides back to Germany...with over 400 pounds of cocaine hidden inside them. Witte, along with his son, was busted before leaving Peru. He was caught with enough drugs to put him away for four years. Even worse, his son—who had been kept in the dark about the entire mission—was busted with even more drugs and is currently serving a 20-year sentence.

Nearly 15 years since Spreepark officially closed its gates, the rides are overcome by weeds and the entire park seems stopped in time. Adventurers often climb or crawl under the fences for a glimpse of the eerie park grounds. Ferris wheels blow slowly in the wind, play houses lean sideways, and swan boats sit lonely in the pond. The site was taken over by the city in 2014 and remains closed to the public. Hopping the fence is certainly against the law, yet many still get through and leave with pictures of a fascinating, post-apocalyptic world. If you decide to see for yourself, take the S-Bahn to Triptower Park or Plänterwald and walk in to Spreepark from there.

finally reopened the land access as the United States demonstrated its commitment to not leaving West Berlin behind. Today, Tempelhofer is an expansive park where Berliners come to relax. And rather than sending planes into the sky, the airstrips are enjoyed by cyclists, joggers, and kite skaters—yes, kite skaters. Nearby, the man-made waterfall in **Victoria Park** offers a spectacular view of Berlin from above one of the city's hipper districts. From Mitte, Tempelhofer, Victoria Park, and the Bergmannstrasse shopping street are about a 20-minute bike ride south, so it's best to lump these sights together.

Kreuzberg, M: Platz der Luftbrücke

BERLIN

TOP TOURS

Tours in this city go a long ways toward bringing to life the complex history, monuments, and memorials of Berlin. Remember, there are a number of different perspectives by which you can examine Berlin: medieval, Roaring '20s, Nazi Berlin, postwar Berlin, communist Berlin, and eclectic modern Berlin. For first-time visitors, the best tours combine a mixture of all the above in a casual and introductory format, but history buffs can also go on deep dives specific to any of these subjects through more specific tours offered by all of the operators below.

Fat Tire Bike Tours

I like bike tours as a way to quickly get a handle on the layout and size of a city. Fat Tire's enthusiastic guides help visitors begin to grasp Berliner culture and history on two wheels over about 4.5 hours. Highlights along the route include the Berlin Wall, Hitler's Bunker, Museum Island, Checkpoint Charlie, Brandenburg Gate, Victory Column, and the compelling Holocaust Memorial. Log on to the website for details on all their tours, prices, and meeting points. Smart travelers will note the sights they see along the way and remember them so they're not doubling back during the rest of their visit. Tours meet at varying hours and days throughout the year just on the north side of the TV Tower. Ask about their discounted rate to extend your bike rental for an extra couple days from €10 per day.

€26 adult/€24 student, Panoramastrasse 1a, Mitte, +49

(0)30 2404 7991, fattirebiketours.com/berlin, S+U-Bahn: Alexanderplatz

Brewer's Walks Berlin

The Brewer's team takes professional tour guiding to the next level. Come out for a history buff's enthralling all-day walking tour of the highlights of central Berlin or enjoy the free 3.5-hour walking tour each afternoon. Local experts, off-script and passionate about their hometown, take you on a deep dive into the numerous events that put Berlin on the world stage over and over again. Choose from the **Free Berlin Tour** (free, tip-based, daily 13:00, 3.5 hours), the **Best of Berlin Tour** (€15, daily 10:30, 6 hours), or the **Local Beer & Breweries Tour** (€30, Thurs, Fri, and Sat 19:00, 3 hours).

All tours meet in front of Friedrichstrasse station at the corner of Friedrichstrasse and Georgenstrasse, Mitte, brewersberlintours.com, S+U-Bahn: Friedrichstrasse

Alternative Berlin

Focusing on the fascinating subcultures that make up this diverse city, Alternative Berlin is a great choice for those more interested in street art and hidden neighborhoods that most tourists miss out on. Choose a **free tour** (daily 11:00 and 13:00, 3 hours), the **Street Art Workshop** (€15, Mon, Wed, and Fri-Sat 12:00, 3.5 hours), the **Real Berlin Experience** (€12, Tues, Thurs, and Fri-Sat 12:00, 4.5 hours), or their innovative and intimate small-group **Pub Crawl** (€10, daily 21:00, free entry to five bars and clubs).

All tours meet outside Starbucks at the TV Tower, Mitte, alternativeberlin.com, S+U-Bahn: Alexanderplatz

Jimbo's Cheap Man's Bus Tour

Bus 100 cuts straight through the center of Berlin, taking you on a double-decker ride past most major tourist sights. Create your very own hop-on, hop-off bus tour by listening to this free audio tour. Just google "Circus Hostel Jimbo's Cheap Man's Bus Tour" and follow the link to the download. Thanks, Jimbo!

Tour free, bus ticket €2.40, bus runs every few minutes

throughout the day, bus 100 running between Alexanderplatz (Mitte) and Zoologischer Garten, S+U-Bahn: Alexanderplatz

Sandeman's New Europe Walking Tours

Sandeman came to Europe and shook up the tourism industry by offering mass-produced, scripted walking tours led by expats and English-speakers for free—yes, free! How can you beat that price? They only ask for you to tip what you think the tour deserves. Each day crowds gather to go on these entertaining 2.5-hour introductory tours of Berlin's center. During the tour you'll be informed about the company's other paid tours on offer, including a day trip to **Sachsenhausen Concentration Camp** (€15, daily 11:00, 5+ hours), **Red (Communist) Berlin** (€12, Tues, Thurs, and Sat 14:00, 3.5 hours), a day trip to **Potsdam** (€14, Wed, Fri, and Sun 11:00, 5+ hours), and of course the backpacker pub crawl.

Free tours daily at 11:00 and 14:00, meet at the Starbucks in front of Brandenburg Gate, Mitte, newberlintours.com, S-Bahn: Brandenburger Tor

TOP HOSTELS

You've got a ton of options for a fun social stay in Berlin. For a time, real estate was cheap so owners bought up properties and converted old buildings into fresh new hostels. While real estate prices have skyrocketed, hostel bed prices have thankfully not followed suit...yet.

St Christopher's Inns

Another solid addition to the St Christopher's hostel chain, this hostel has it all: bar, lounge room, free showers, great location near Rosa-Luxemburg-Platz, and cool staff. Free walking tours leave from the hostel daily and the cheap drinks give you a great way to kick off the evening.

Beds from €10, 24-hour reception, free Wi-Fi, bar with happy hour, continental breakfast included, restaurant, Rosa-Luxemburg-Strasse 41, Mitte, +49 (0)30 8145 3960, st-christophers.co.uk/berlin-hostels, U-Bahn: Rosa-Luxemburg-Platz

Wombat's City Hostel Berlin

Wombat's Berlin puts you right in the middle of Mitte, with options for food, nightlife, and shopping abounding just meters away in nearly every direction. The on-site bar (with frequent happy hours) and rooftop patio (offering panoramic views of downtown) are great places to kick off your night. And you've got spacious, modern, and clean rooms to look forward to at the

end of it. Being just a 10-minute walk from Alexanderplatz, Rosenthaler Platz, and the Hackescher Hof means anything you're looking for is close at hand.

Beds from €10, 24-hour reception, free Wi-Fi, bar, breakfast, rooftop patio, kitchen access, Alte Schonhauser Strasse 2, Mitte, +49 (0)30 8471 0820, wombats-hostels.com/berlin, U-Bahn: Rosa-Luxemburg-Platz

Circus Hostel

This classic Berliner hostel is different from the others in its personal touch. Enjoy the bar downstairs and some very tasty breakfast each morning. This bar is on the same street as International Restaurant Row. I love the bars and venues nearby, which offer food and entertainment at all hours. The hostel staff leads free daily tours to far-flung corners of the city. If you're interested in private accommodations, check out their hotel and comfortable apartment listings online.

Beds from €8, 24-hour reception, free Wi-Fi, bar, breakfast, Weinbergsweg 1A, Prenzlauer Berg, +49 (0)30 2000 3939, circus-berlin.de, U-Bahn: Rosenthaler Platz

BERLIN'S SQUATTING CULTURE

Until recently, squatting in abandoned buildings was a legally protected right in Berlin. How did this whole culture come about? When the Berlin Wall fell, a large exodus of people fled to the more prosperous west, and East Berlin was left with hundreds of abandoned buildings. Simultaneously, there was a movement of people seeking studio space, cheap rent, and a chance to create a new artistic community to the east. Squatters moved to East Berlin and treated the place like home. This was accepted at the time because having people live in empty buildings was the best way to maintain them. Due to a German law preventing landowners from kicking out those living on their properties, individuals taking over abandoned buildings were actually given a degree of legal protection.

The 1990s were the golden years for squatting. Neighborhoods developed their own identities spanning the rainbow of the counter-culture set: hippies, punks, and activists.

Then, all of a sudden, real estate was worth something in Berlin. Fifteen years into the squatting trend, police began to boot squatters from buildings that owners wanted back. But, rather than being snuffed out, squatting culture continues to evolve, as groups band together to purchase property titles to the buildings they're living in. In this way, squats are morphing into communes.

To see a remnant of Berlin's squatting culture, head to Oranienburger Strasse for Berlin's most famous ex-squat: **Tacheles.** *Tacheles* is Yiddish for "straight talk." The building got its pre-WWI start as a massive department store, small factory, and even Nazi SS office. By the '90s, Tacheles was abandoned and had fallen into disrepair. Squatters moved in, forging a creative community with art studios, movie theater, shops, a bar, and frequent live performances. Tacheles was shut down a few years ago, and today, all you'll see is a rundown building. Use your imagination to recreate the dreads, musical instruments, and spray-paint cans of its heyday.

Generator Hostel Berlin East

Generator Hostel Berlin East offers clean facilities, loads of amenities, and all the pre-game entertainment you could ask for. The Generator has its own bar and lounge, where you can mingle with other travelers, and is located in trendy Prenzlauer Berg, putting you right next to some good shopping, convenient trains, and Berlin's relatively more sophisticated nightlife.

From €9, 24-hour reception, free Wi-Fi, bar, restaurant, lockers, laundry facilities, mini supermarket, Storkower Strasse 160, Prenzlauer Berg, +49 (0)30 417 24 00, generatorhostels.com, berlin@generatorhostels.com, S-Bahn: Landsberger Allee

Pfefferbett Hostels

This hostel in a massive old retrofitted brewery is an affordable option for larger groups. Guests appreciate the clean rooms and retro-chic, exposed-brick-arches vibe of the place. I like to relax in the backyard patio when the weather is nice, and the proximity to the Schönhauser Allee and Rosenthaler Platz nightlife makes for an easy stumble home. The team is working hard to install routers to get Wi-Fi to reach all rooms, but for now Wi-Fi only reaches the common room in the reception because of the thick brick walls.

Beds from €8, 24-hour reception, free Wi-Fi in lounge, breakfast, Christinenstrasse 18-19, Prenzlauer Berg, +49 (0)30 9393 5858, pfefferbett.de/en, U-Bahn: Senefelderplatz

A&O Berlin Hauptbahnhof

Located just 10 minutes from Berlin's main train station and a stone's throw away from major sights like the Reichstag, the Victory Column in Tiergarten park, and the Brandenburg Gate, the A&O Hauptbahnhof hostel is a convenient place to stay. The staff is very friendly and helpful, and the rooms are modern and clean.

Beds from €9, 24-hour reception, free Wi-Fi, bar, laundry facilities, lounge, Lehrter Strasse 12-15, Central Berlin, +49 (0)30 322 920 42 00, aohostels.com, S-Bahn: Berlin Hauptbahnhof

A&O Berlin Mitte

The conveniently located A&O Mitte is situated just on the southern edge of downtown, bordering Kreuzberg not far from Alexanderplatz. The rooms are cheap and clean, and the bar offers a variety of drinks, karaoke, billiards, and dart-tossing fun.

Beds from €8, 24-hour reception, free Wi-Fi, beer garden

(summer), bar, laundry facilities, lounge, bar, Köpenicker Strasse 127-129, Mitte, +49 (0)3 080 947 52 00, aohostels. com, S-Bahn: Ostbahnhof, U-Bahn: Henrich-Heine-Strasse

TRANSPORTATION

GETTING THERE & AWAY
Plane
Berlin is served by two airports: **Schoenfeld** (SXF) and **Tegel** (TXL). Find information on both at berlin-airport.de. The **Berlin Brandenburg Airport** (BER) is scheduled to be completed in 2017.

Schoenfeld is about 15 miles south of the city center. From the airport, take Airport Express train **RE7** or **RB14** into the center and connect to the city's S- and U-Bahn systems. Connections leave every half hour, cost €3.30, and take about 40 minutes.

If you're flying with the major airlines, you're more likely to arrive at the **Tegel** airport. Take bus **TXL** into the city center. It stops at all three key transportation hubs: Zoologischer Garten, Hauptbahnhof, and Alexanderplatz. Leaving every 10 minutes, this bus takes about 30 minutes and costs €2.70.

Train
Trains from Prague run eight times daily and cost €40, taking 4.5 hours. Trains take about 6 hours and cost €90 to Munich.

Just about all international arrivals show up at the massive, four-level **Hauptbahnhof,** on the western edge of Mitte. Berlin's other major stations are **Ostbahnhof,** in Friedrichshain; **Spandau,** on the far western edge of Berlin; and **Zoologischer Garten,** in Central

Berlin, just on the edge of Tiergarten park. All stations have transfer connections with the S-Bahn public transportation network, which can get you anywhere you need to go in the city.

Bus
The main bus station is **Zentraler Omnibus-Bahnhof** in West Berlin. From here, you have connections with both the S-Bahn and the U-Bahn, making connecting into the center easy. When connecting out of town leave at least an hour to get there—figuring on about 45 minutes to the bus station from Mitte and allowing 15 minutes to hit the bathroom, grab a snack, and find your bus.

Car
Berlin is about 650 kilometers (6.5 hours) east of Amsterdam via the A2 highway. It's about 350 kilometers (3.5 hours) north of Prague via the A13 highway.

GETTING AROUND
Walking is a great way to discover Berlin, but remember, the city is massive, and it would take hours to walk from one end to the other. Try to gauge the distance ahead of time and organize your strolls by neighborhood, hopping on trams or the metro to save time and energy.

Berlin has an excellent **public transportation system,** but the city is so big

the system can be overwhelming at first. Once you get used to it, you'll be zipping around Berlin on the trams, buses, and underground in no time. Find a city map that includes tram and metro lines to keep with you during your visit. This really helps before you know the names of the primary landmarks around town.

S-Bahn, U-Bahn, buses, and trams all use the same ticket. A single **ticket** costs €2.40 for zones A and B (which cover the city of Berlin itself but not the airport or outlying cities) and allows as many transfers as you wish for a total of two hours. The **day ticket** (€7) pays for itself by the third ride in one day.

S-Bahn & U-Bahn

The city is crisscrossed by Berlin's integrated metro system consisting of both underground (U-Bahn) and overground (S-Bahn) lines. Purchase your ticket from one of the ticket machines at each station. You must validate it before your journey by sticking the end into one of the validation machines located either on the platform or on the entry to the station—ticket checkers will ask to see validated tickets and fine those who aren't able to show one (watch the locals and learn). While the S- and U-Bahns close down around 01:00 during the week, they run throughout the night on Friday and Saturday.

Bus

Follow the same rules as you would for the metro and you will be good to go when riding the bus. Visit bvg.de for information on night bus schedules. For a quick and cheap introduction to the city and its layout, jump on **bus 100**, a double-decker bus that cuts straight through the center of Berlin, connecting most major tourist sights, including the Reichstag and Brandenburg Gate, and ending at Alexanderplatz. Bus 100 departs "Zoo Station" on the west side of town about every five minutes.

Tram

More than 20 lines make up Berlin's tram network, extending the reach of the S- and U-Bahns to the street level. The trams are new and quite comfortable, linking famous sights like Alexanderplatz to the Bernauer Strasse section of the Berlin Wall and neighborhoods like Mitte and Prenzlauer Berg.

Bike

Renting a bike for the weekend is a great way to open this big city up. Berlin has focused much energy and capital on making itself a more bike-friendly city, and the bike paths are a welcome sign of these efforts. Heads-up: There are many intersections in Berlin's Mitte that do not have street signs or lights, so it's up to traffic to yield to each other. Consider a tour with **Fat Tire Bike Tours** to see Berlin's highlights and its more alternative neighborhoods.

Taxi

Taxis charge a flat rate of €3.20 plus €1.65 for each kilometer. Taxis are ideally split among friends for late-night partying on the far side of town. I prefer **Taxi Berlin** (+49 (0)3020 2020, taxi-berlin.de).

DAY TRIPS

Sachsenhausen Concentration Camp

As one of the first Nazi concentration camps, Sachsenhausen was utilized to test the most efficient layout of detention camps for Jews and political prisoners, which numbered in the thousands by the time the war ended. It's located in the suburbs, and it's disturbing to think that the Nazi vision extended practically to their front door and capital city of Berlin. About 200,000 prisoners were held here throughout the course of the war, and 10,000 victims succumbed to the harsh conditions, starvation, torture, and execution.

For those who want to see a concentration camp or remember the victims of the Holocaust, Sachsenhausen is the best nearby option. A visit to Sachsenhausen offers an introduction to the scientific process that the Nazis used to develop and refine their sadistic detention and systems of mass murder as displayed in the on-site museum, barracks, and chilling execution trench.

The camp is free to enter, with paid and donation-based tours running daily. The paid tours are well worth the cost to understand the horrors that took place in the living areas and dank cells you'll see at Sachsenhausen. Official **tours** (€14) of the camp are offered on Tuesday, Thursday, and Saturday at 11:45 and 14:30 at the visitors center at the south corner of the camp. The first tour has an optional meeting time in Berlin in Mitte:

Potsdamer Platz by the historic traffic light tower at 10:20. Transportation is not included in the price. **Sandeman's New Berlin Tours** also offers day trips to Sachsenhausen from Berlin (€15, daily 11:00, 5+ hours).

To get there on your own from central Berlin, take the S1 or regional trains RE5 or RB12 to the end of the line: Oranienburg station. From the station, you've got a mile walk north following signs to "Gedenkestatte Sachsenhausen," or bus 821 takes visitors to the camp hourly in four stops. Or opt for a short taxi ride from Oranienburg station to the camp; it should cost no more than €8. The whole journey takes about an hour each way via public transport.

Free, mid-Mar-mid-Oct daily 08:30-18:00, mid-Oct-mid-Mar daily 08:30-16:30, Strasse der Nationen 22, Oranienburg, +49 (0)3301 200 0, stiftung-bg.de/gums/en

Potsdam & Frederick the Great's Palaces

Forty kilometers southwest of Berlin is the town of Potsdam, where you'll find a gigantic park sprinkled with awe-inspiring 18th-century Prussian palaces built by Frederick the Great. Germany's equivalent to Versailles, these gargantuan palaces seem to try to outdo each other. The gardens can be exhausting, and really go on forever. You may visit one palace with hundreds of rooms only to gaze down a corridor of beautiful hedges, trees, and finely groomed walkways to yet another palace absolutely dripping in rococo decoration.

The most famous and popular palaces to see are **Sanssouci** (€12, Nov-Mar Tues-Sun 10:00-17:00, Apr-Oct Tues-Sun 10:00-18:00, closed Mon) and the **New Palace** (€8, Apr-Oct Wed-Mon 10:00-18:00, Nov-Mar Wed-Mon 10:00-17:00, closed Tues). If you plan to visit both, buy the **sanssouci+ ticket** (€19), which covers a single visit to all the Potsdam palaces in one day. Find more information on the palaces at spsg.de/en or by calling +49 (0)331 96 94 200. **Sandeman's New Berlin Tours** also offers day trips to Potsdam from Berlin (€14, Wed, Fri, and Sun 11:00, 5+ hours).

Connections to Potsdam are easy. Simply connect to the S7 in central Berlin and take it out to Potsdam Hauptbahnhof. The trip takes just under an hour each way.

HELP!

Tourist Information Centers
Berlin's tourist information centers are for-profit institutions. Find one at Hauptbahnhof train station and one at Brandenburg Gate.

Pickpockets & Scams
Violent crime is virtually nonexistent for tourists in Berlin. Still, keep a close watch over your valuables while in train stations, crowded areas, etc, and always be on your guard if someone approaches you with questions. Do not accept any discount train tickets from street sellers, as they are counterfeit and against the law.

Emergencies
In an emergency, dial 112.

Hospital
Campus Mitte, Humboldt-Universität Faculty
Charitéplatz 1
+49 (0)30 450 50

US Embassy
Pariser Platz 2
+49 (0)30 83050

PRAGUE

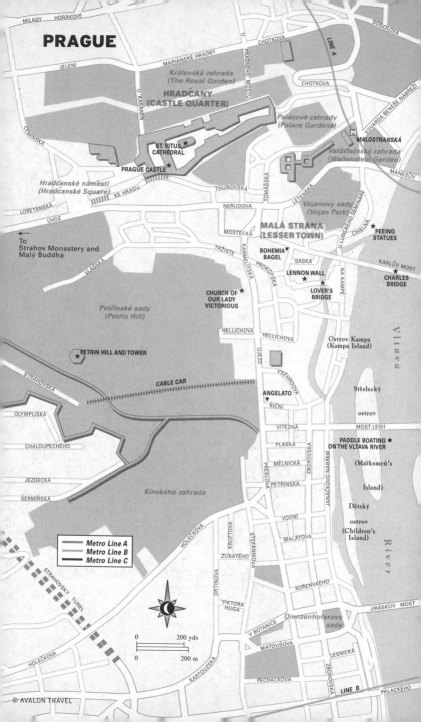

PRAGUE

MILADY HORÁKOVÉ

GOGOLOVA

JELENÍ

MARIÁNSKÉ HRADBY

U PRÁSNÉHO MOSTU

CHOTKOVA

LINE A

Královská zahrada
(The Royal Garden)

CHOTKOVA

U KASÁREN

**HRADČANY
(CASTLE QUARTER)**

EDVARDA BENEŠE NÁBŘEŽÍ

Palácové zahrady
(Palace Gardens)

★ ST. VITUS
CATHEDRAL

M **MALOSTRANSKÁ**

ČERNÍNSKÁ

Valdštejnská zahrada
(Wallenstein Garden)

★ PRAGUE CASTLE

MÁNESÚV

Hradčanské náměstí
(Hradcanské Square)

KE HRADU

THUNOVSKÁ

LORETÁNSKÁ

ÚVOZ

NERUDOVA

TOMÁŠSKÁ

LETENSKÁ

Vojanovy sady
(Vojan Park)

CIHELNÁ

★ PEEING
STATUES

MOSTECKÁ

**MALÁ STRANA
(LESSER TOWN)**

U LUŽICKÉHO SEMINÁŘE

To
Strahov Monastery and
Malý Buddha →

VLAŠSKÁ

TRŽIŠTE

PROKOPSKÁ

KARMELITSKÁ

**BOHEMIA
BAGEL** ▼

SASKÁ

NA KAMPĚ

KARLÚV MOST

LENNON WALL ★

★ **CHARLES
BRIDGE**

Petřinské sady
(Petřín Hill)

★ CHURCH OF
OUR LADY
VICTORIOUS

★ **LOVER'S
BRIDGE**

HELLICHOVA

HELLICHOVA

Ostrov Kampa
(Kampa Island)

★ PETŘIN HILL AND TOWER

ÚJEZD

V l t a v a

STRAHOVSKÁ

CABLE CAR

VŠEHRDOVA

Střelecký

OLYMPIJSKÁ

ANGELATO ▼

ostrov

ŘÍČNÍ

CHALOUPECHÉHO

VÍTEZNÁ

MOST LEGIÍ

JEZDECKÁ

PLASKÁ

ZBOROVSKÁ

PADDLE BOATING ▪
ON THE VLTAVA RIVER

ŠERMÍŘSKÁ

MĚLNICKÁ

(Mařksmeň's

Kinského zahrada

PŘESLOVA

PETŘÍNSKÁ

JANÁČKOVO NÁBŘEŽÍ

Island)

Dětský

HOLEČKOVA

VODNÍ

ostrov

KROFTOVA

ŠTEFÁNIKOVA

MALÁTOVA

(Children's
Island)

Metro Line A
Metro Line B
Metro Line C

ZUBATÉHO

DRTINOVA

KOŘENSKÉHO

R i v e r

STRAHOVSKÝ TUNEL

VIKTORA
HUGA

JIRÁSKÚV MOST

0   200 yds

Dienzenhoferovy
sady

0   200 m

V BOTANICE

MATOUSOVA

LESNICKÁ

HOLEČKOVA

KARTOUZSKÁ

PECHACKOVA

ZBOROVSKÁ

LINE B

PALACKÉHO

© AVALON TRAVEL

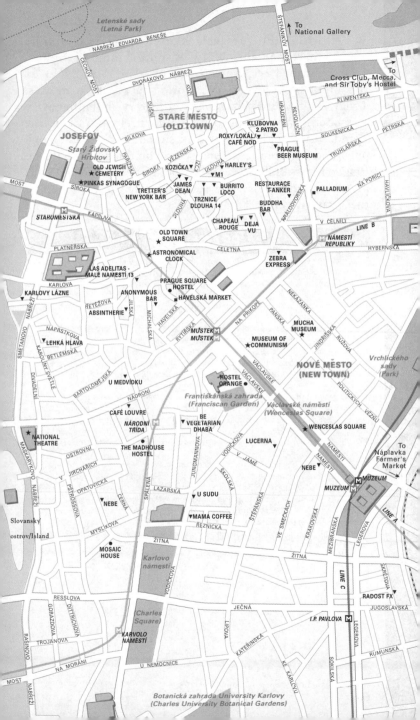

PRAGUE

V isiting Prague feels like stepping into a time machine. The "City of One Hundred Spires" escaped widespread bombing in World War II and often provides an "old world" backdrop in movies. Today, the traces of Czech-Soviet history are fading away as modern-day capitalism integrates itself into daily life. Wander the cobblestone streets, sip cheap beers in smoky pubs, and explore the timeless castle on the hill. You'll love Prague for its bohemian and baroque architecture, raucous nightlife, and picturesque setting, tucked into a bend in the Vltava River.

PRAGUE 101

Prague and the Czech Republic were very different places until the late 1980s. Because of the liberation of Czechoslovakia from Nazi Germany in 1945 by the Russians, the majority of Czech people were pro-Russia, and strong ties were formed with the USSR and its ideals of a communist state. In 1948, the communist party seized control of the majority of votes, and Czechoslovakia joined the ranks of other Central European countries in the Soviet Bloc.

With the support of Moscow and a highly oppressive government, the Czech economy saw a dramatic improvement. Yet with this growth also came the price of pursuing that "improved" communist state: mass imprisonment, corruption, and rigged trials. Once the boundaries and laws became clear to the people, the government eased up a bit, and a new way of thinking began to emerge. Greater freedom was granted in the media, the arts, and citizens' right to travel during this period, which became known as the Prague Spring.

These new ideas were seen as a threat to communism, as they resembled the West and its "bourgeois" take on life. So Russia, along with other members of the Warsaw Pact, invaded Czechoslovakia on August 21, 1968, forcibly ending this progressive trend. Over the next 20 years, a period of "normalization," which emphasized censorship, spying, and police brutality, ensued. This led to the stagnation of the Czech economy, as well as the arrests and abductions of more than 250,000 people who were seen as threats to the communist state.

By the late 1980s, the people had finally had enough. From November 17 to December 29, 1989, hundreds of thousands of Prague's citizens gathered in Wenceslas Square in the peaceful protest known as the Velvet Revolution. These protests led to the end of the single-party communist state and played a large role in the collapse of the Soviet sphere of influence as a whole in Central Europe. Czechoslovakia's first president, Václav Havel, was voted into office on December 29, 1989. A few years later, on January 1, 1993, Czechoslovakia peacefully dissolved into two different countries, forming what we now know as the Czech Republic and Slovakia.

PLAN AHEAD

RESERVATIONS

Because Prague lacks major sightseeing attractions like Paris and Rome, visiting its sights doesn't require all that much forethought. The Czechs do, however, love to make reservations for everything from dinner to tea. So if there's a restaurant you know you want to enjoy, call and reserve a few days ahead of time.

LOCAL HAPPENINGS

One World Film Festival

Movie lovers should plan their visit around mid-March for the annual One World Film Festival (Lucerna Cinema, Štěpánská 61, oneworld.cz). Each year the festival offers a new set of thought-provoking documentaries that emphasize human rights and issues around the world.

Velvet Revolution Anniversary

A public holiday on November 17 celebrates the end of communism in the Czech Republic by means of peaceful demonstration in Wenceslas Square back in 1989. Revelers take to the streets in a mix of pride and a bit of nostalgia. Time has healed the wounds of police brutality and oppression, and massive stages set up across town turn the entire city into one big party.

KNOW BEFORE YOU GO

KEY STATS & FIGURES

Currency:
The Czech Republic uses the Czech koruna (Kč); 26Kč = about 1 USD

Population:
1,250,000

Language:
Czech

Number of metro lines:
3

Amount of beer consumed annually per capita:
132 liters

National drink:
slivovice (a moonshine liquor made from plums)

Souvenir of choice:
puppets

Favorite TV show among Czechs:
How I Met Your Mother or *Friends* (heavily debated)

CALIBRATE YOUR BUDGET

TYPICAL PRICES FOR:

Hostel dorm bed:
180Kč

Two-course dinner:
250Kč

Pint of beer:
39Kč

Metro pass:
24Kč

MOVIES TO WATCH
EuroTrip, Mission: Impossible, Kafka, A Knight's Tale

THREE DAY ITINERARY

It's easy to experience Prague entirely on foot. Wear comfortable walking shoes for this tour of the city.

DAY 1: OLD TOWN

MORNING

Kick off your visit right with a hearty, classy breakfast at Prague's best café, **Café Louvre** in the Old Town. Climb the stairs and step into a world harkening back to the golden age of Viennese cafés.

Meander on toward **Old Town Square** and get a feeling for the city and its beautiful baroque architecture. While you're in the area, hang around and watch the **Astronomical Clock** chime and click away at the top of every hour. Take notice of the **Jan Hus statue** in the center, along with the **Týn Church** and **St Nicholas Church**.

Join a free three-hour walking tour with **Sandeman's New Europe Walking Tours**, meeting daily at 10:45 at the Astronomical Clock. These guys will break down the history of the tower and the Old Town and take you through the **Jewish Quarter**, **Wenceslas Square,** and the **Charles Bridge** for some great Kodak moments.

AFTERNOON

Grab a quick and healthy lunch just inside the Jewish Quarter at the posh grocery store **Tržnice Dlouhá 14**. Return back to the river to take in the late afternoon sun. Find a vantage point downriver from the **Charles Bridge** to take in the view or do it from the river on a **paddle boat ride** from Slovanský Island on the Vltava.

Return back into town toward Café Louvre (where you started the day) to my favorite brewhouse, **U Medvídků,** for your first foray into the famous Czech goulash culinary experience and some of the most delicious beer you've ever tasted. Enjoy a few rounds here, and then go on a short jaunt north for a pre-party drink at **Anonymous Bar**, an excellent speakeasy-style cocktail lounge.

EVENING

If you're trying to go out, an organized pub crawl is a great way to get oriented in town. **Drunken Monkey Pub Crawl** is my favorite. Just look for the team in blue underneath the Astronomical Clock in the Old Town Square nightly 21:00-23:00. Otherwise, get cultured at one of the numerous live concerts that go on often in beautiful old-world settings, like theaters, baroque churches, and opera houses. Find more information in the music office located in the passage leading to Týn Church just off the Old Town Square.

LATE

Either way you go—cultured or otherwise—late-night munchies are unavoidable. The *klobasa* sausages sold at the street stands are tasty, but the burritos rolling out of **Burrito Loco** really hit the spot at 02:00, 03:00, or 05:00.

DAY 2: LESSER QUARTER & CASTLE DISTRICT

MORNING

Shake off that hangover with a hefty breakfast sandwich at **Bohemia Bagel** across Charles Bridge in the **Lesser Quarter**. When I come through town, I'm nearly always bacon-deficient, so that's what I opt for in my breakfast bagel!

From Bohemia Bagel, loop around the corner for the **Church of Our Lady Victorious**, **John Lennon Wall**, the **Lover's Bridge**, and the **peeing statues**, all within a 20-minute walk.

Begin the hike uphill to the **Prague Castle** and **St Vitus Cathedral**. Visiting the first section of the cathedral is free, but to go in farther you'll have to purchase tickets from the castle ticket office opposite the church entrance.

AFTERNOON

In summer months, there is a beer and wine garden open at the castle's downhill exit next to the viewpoint. But you should double back beyond the uphill end of the castle to find the **Strahov Monastery**, my favorite place for a filling afternoon meal in a classic beer hall setting.

From the Strahov Monastery, **Petřín Hill** is just south of the walls. Find it and descend through the steep grade of the park into the city, stopping at the **Memorial to the Victims of Communism** (the abstract statues walking on the staircase). Just across the street at the bottom of the steps, you'll find my favorite gelato in town, **Angelato**. About time for a taste, don't you think?

EVENING

Head out to Prague's most famous party street, Dlouhá, where you can start the night at the **Prague Beer Museum**, and tuck into **Lokál** for hearty Czech cuisine when the mood strikes. Also on this street, and nearby: **Klubovna 2. Patro**, **M1**, **James Dean**, **Harley's**, **Café Nod**, and **Roxy**.

DAY 3: DELVE DEEPER

MORNING

Begin your detox at my favorite coffee shop and vegetarian café in town: **Mama Coffee**.

If Jewish history is important to you, visit the Jewish Quarter and get lost in **Pinkas Synagogue** and the **Old Jewish Cemetery**.

Otherwise, art nouveau lovers should check out the **Mucha Museum**, or for a bit of a history lesson, stop by the **Museum of Communism**. These museums are both wonderfully small, near each other, and can be tackled in about 45 minutes each. Both are just north of Wenceslas Square.

AFTERNOON

Grab a bite of lunch at Kozička in the town center for some good food and warm atmosphere.

Pick up a *trdelník* and stroll south along the Vltava, soaking in the beauty of Prague on your last afternoon, then climb the steps to the **Vyšehrad Castle**. In summertime, there are outdoor bars and grills vending brats and beer.

EVENING

All Czeched out? Grab some margaritas and a bite to eat at **Las Adelitas**, my favorite Mexican spot in Prague, just steps from the Old Town Square.

LATE

Take your pick at the many clubs and bars Prague has to offer. If you haven't tried absinthe yet, tonight's the night—the **Absintherie** will give you a rundown on the proper way to prepare and down it!

TOP NEIGHBORHOODS

The city of Prague straddles a bend of the Vltava River. The river makes for a great navigation aid, as long as you remember that it turns around the Old Town at nearly 90 degrees near Prague Castle and Letná Park. Most of the tourist sights are situated on the east side of the bend. The **Old Town** (Staré Město) is where you'll find the famous Old Town Square and Astronomical Clock, as well as the **Jewish Quarter** (Josefov), which is arguably the best collection of Jewish sights in Europe and a must-see for all visitors. In addition to its sights, the Jewish Quarter is now the nicest district in Prague, with fine dining, fancy cafés, and high-fashion outlets like Dolce & Gabbana and Prada. Also on the east side of the river, south of the Old Town, is the **New Town**

(Nové Město), which includes Wenceslas Square.

From Old Town, cross the iconic Charles Bridge to discover the quieter and more-upscale **Lesser Quarter** (Malá Strana), tucked between the Castle District, Petřín Hill, and the Vltava River. In the Lesser Quarter, check out a series of unique, free, and superbly Czech sights, like the John Lennon Wall. In close proximity, you've got the **Castle District** (Hradčany); **Petřín Hill** (capped by the Petřín Tower); and **Letná Park** (with the giant, ticking red metronome).

Prague's trendy up-and-coming district, **Prague 7** (Holešovice), is home to hot clubs and backpacker hostels and is just north of Letná Park.

TOP SIGHTS

Old Town Square
(Staroměstské Náměstí)

Dating back to the late 12th century, the Old Town Square was the central marketplace and hub of commerce of medieval Prague. Over the following few centuries, many buildings went up around the market in Romanesque, baroque, and gothic styles.

While you're waiting for the Astronomical Clock to work its mechanical wonderment, check out all the sights in Old Town Square. Step inside the beautifully baroque **St Nicholas Church** or the gothic **Týn Church** (Church of Our Lady Before Týn), which is accessed through a passage in the building extending from the church's facade. Be sure to pop in to the **music event vendor** right next to the front door of the church, where you can book cheap tickets to beautiful (and succinct) string and symphony concerts in stunning venues across town. Get the cheap seats—which aren't all that bad in these small venues—and you're set for a culturally enlightening evening.

The **Jan Hus statue** in the center of the square is a testament to the man who stood up against the papal tyranny of the Catholic church in the 15th century. The 27 crosses in the cobblestones next to the tower are a tribute to the 27 Protestant nobles who were executed in 1620 after a failed rebellion against Ferdinand II of the Holy Roman Empire, a Catholic.

Free, square always open, churches open generally dawn to dusk, Old Town, Metro: Staroměstská

Astronomical Clock

Take a moment and try to decipher this complex time-telling machine. Find it difficult? Imagine gazing upon this marvel of clock-making engineering back when it was first constructed in the early 1400s. Designed by Mikulus of Kadan in 1410, the two outer circles of the clock show us Bohemian time (represented by the numbers 1-24) and modern time (represented by two sets of Roman numerals I-XII). The blue area of the clock face represents daylight hours, the orange and brown represent dawn and dusk, and the black represents night. The sun attached to the big hand signifies the sun's position in the sky (it'll be over the black at night), and the small hand represents the moon's position. The inner offset circle displays the signs of the zodiac.

The smaller circle beneath the clock was added in the late 19th century, depicting the date, zodiac sign, and different pictures of everyday peasant life. If you look closely, you will also notice that every day of the year is inscribed around the circle with its patron saint, with an indicator showing which day of the year it is.

The four statuettes on either side of the clock represent the four despised traits of the day manifested through a series of unapologetic stereotypes: Vanity looking into the mirror, Greed represented through the caricature of a Jew holding moneybags, a guilty Turk succumbing to pleasures of the flesh, and a skeleton warning these hedonists of the imminent arrival of their final judgment day. (Political correctness is clearly a 21st-century invention.)

At the top of each hour, tourists and pickpockets alike gather to watch the 12 apostles parade through the two window openings. Though it's a show without 3-D glasses and special effects, you can't help but smile at this charming performance, which has been going on hourly for over 600 years. The performance is capped by a caped trumpeter beckoning you to climb the stairs of the **Old Town Hall Tower** for spectacular views of the city.

110Kč adult; 70Kč student, Mon 11:00–22:00, Tues-Sun 09:00–22:00, Old Town Square, Old Town, +420 236 002 629, staromestskaradnicepraha.cz, Metro: Staroměstská

Pinkas Synagogue

This synagogue in the Jewish Quarter has been converted into a memorial for the 80,000 Jewish victims of the Holocaust from this region. On its walls are inscribed the names of all the victims, delineated by family name, listing, and the known dates of birth and death. In a room upstairs, you can also find chilling crayon drawings by young children sequestered into the Ghetto before their deportation by the occupying Nazis.

One ticket gets you into the grouping of all the Jewish Quarter's six sights. Avoid the queue and pop into any corner shop in the neighborhood that has the pass picture in the window. This will save you half an hour of standing in line at the popular sights.

Tickets that cover all Jewish Quarter sights from 300Kč, Jan–Mar 09:00–16:30, Apr–Oct 09:00–18:00, Nov–Dec 09:00–16:30, closed Sat and Jewish holidays, Široká 23/3, Jewish Quarter, +420 222 749 211, jewishmuseum.cz, Metro: Staroměstská

Old Jewish Cemetery

In this cemetery, which is the oldest surviving Jewish cemetery in Europe, the dead had to be buried on top of each other due to lack of space. There are approximately 12 burial layers, over 12,000 gravestones, and an estimated 100,000 people buried here. A walk through this cemetery is like stepping into the set of a Tim Burton movie—the cognitive dissonance is striking and eerie. You expect cemeteries to be orderly and pristine, but the tombstones here, which date back two-to-five hundred years, appear to be sag under the weight of the difficult circumstances that those interred here faced during their lifetimes.

Tickets that cover all Jewish Quarter sights from 300Kč, Jan–Mar 09:00–16:30, Apr–Oct 09:00–18:00, Nov–Dec 09:00–16:30, closed Sat and Jewish holidays, Široká, Jewish Quarter, jewishmuseum.cz, Metro: Staroměstská

Charles Bridge (Karlův Most)

Named after King Charles IV, who reigned during Prague's Golden Age, this bridge connects Old Town Prague with its Castle Quarter and Lesser Quarter. The keystone was laid at 5:31 on July 9, 1357, an interesting

numerical palindrome (1357.9.7.531) that's a deliberate nod to the astrological powers. Many believe this to be the reason the bridge has withstood both natural and human disasters since its construction nearly 700 years ago. During the day, this wide pedestrian bridge is packed with tourists and trinket vendors and caricature artists. At night, it's practically deserted. Take a detour after sunset across the bridge on the way back to your hostel and gaze out over the Vltava toward the illuminated castle shrouded in Bohemian fog.

Notice that the twin towers on the Lesser Quarter side of the bridge are not mirror images of each other—one predates the other by a couple hundred years. The gashes in the gateway between these two towers happened when Godzilla passed through and sharpened his talons. Actually, they're just the sharpening marks of mercenaries as they prepared their weapons for battle over the years.

Free, always open, Metro: Staroměstská

Prague Castle (Pražský Hrad) & St Vitus Cathedral

Prague Castle is the dominating feature of the cityscape, holding the Guinness world record as the "largest ancient castle in the world"—but don't expect the crenellations and turrets of classic medieval castles. This castle appears in its Renaissance rendition today. This has always been the seat of Czech power as well as the official residence of those in power. Constructed in the 9th century by Prince Bořivoj, the castle has since been transformed from a wooden fortress sur-rounded by earthen bulwarks to the imposing stone fortress it is today. Each ruler extended the castle to some degree, so there's a great mix of styles on display. Modern palaces and buildings obscure the profile of your cliché castle, but it is a castle nonetheless.

Don't miss the breathtaking **St Vitus Cathedral** (Mon-Sat Apr-Oct 09:00-17:00, Nov-Mar 09:00-16:00, Sun from 12:00, last entrance at 15:40), located within the castle walls. Constructed with both church and state funds, the cathedral now charges entrance for all visitors, though you can enter and take a peek with the crowds from the narthex. Go all the way up to the corner of the roped-off area and peer left to catch a glimpse of the window by Alphonse Mucha, making out his of rich use of colors, floral patterns, and metaphorical use of subjects. This window is not stained glass, but rather painted glass, allowing for more freedom in shading and blending of colors.

Find the underwhelming **Golden Lane** by turning left on Zlatá Ulička u Daliborky. It's not worth paying to get into, but the cutesy street with dwarf-sized houses is free for visitors from an hour before closing (Apr-Oct daily after 16:00, Nov-Mar daily after 15:00).

Adult tickets from 250Kč, student tickets from 125Kč to go inside the castle, the churches, and Golden Lane; castle open daily 05:00-24:00, historical buildings open daily 09:00-17:00 Apr-Oct, until 16:00 Nov-Mar, last entrance at 15:40; Pražský Hrad, Castle District, +420 224 37 3368, hrad.cz/en/prague-castle, Tram: Pražský Hrad, Metro: Malostranská

DAVID ČERNÝ'S CHARMING LOVE OF THE ABSURD

The Czechs have developed a unique and intriguing sense of self-deprecating humor that is evidenced in various forms throughout the city. There's no other more active and current artist than Prague's own David Černý, who is responsible for just about all of the slightly subversive statues and installations around the city. Černý takes a light-hearted approach to his work but clearly doesn't shy away from political and controversial issues.

The **peeing statues** in the Lesser Quarter are actually relieving themselves into a reservoir with the outline of the Czech Republic. Inside the Lucerna building just off Wenceslas Square, there's a statue of an **upside down horse with St Wenceslas** riding bare...belly...?

Just off of Betlémské Square, you'll spot a **man hanging by one arm** high above the street looking down, reminding us that there's always someone watching. The massive **TV tower** in the Žižkov neighborhood can be seen from all over town, with especially great views from Letná Park and the castle. You'll notice funny bumps sprinkled all over the tower. If you look closer, you'll see those are actually giant **baby statues** crawling up and down its vertical walls.

Just a minute or two from the Old Town Square toward Dlouhá street, you'll see a proud pixelated and massive **pregnant lady** on her knees, made from reflective metal material. The meaning? No one really knows. Finally, tucked behind the shopping center at Národní Třída, and in front of the recommended vegetarian Indian restaurant, you'll see a large **rotating metal sculpture** in the shape of the head of Franz Kafka. Černý's latest work displays this head through topographical lines like those of a map taking a 3-D shape. It goes through patterns of churning faster and slower to make the face appear and disappear.

David Černý also owns a club about 20 minutes south of town called **Meet Factory** (meetfactory.cz), where DJs and artists come out to spin the night away.

John Lennon Wall

After John Lennon was killed in the 1980s, young Czechs created an unofficial memorial out of a large wall located in Lesser Quarter, covering it in graffiti messages that inspired hope, freedom, and peace. The communist government considered phrases like "Imagine" and "All You Need Is Love" a threat to society and had them painted over immediately. Naturally, rebellious teens saw this as an opportunity to stick it to the man. Night after night, they arrived to repaint the wall with Beatles' lyrics and John Lennon portraits. When the officials finally gave up, they legalized graffiti in this one place in town only and stopped painting over the tags. Today, the wall represents a vision of hope. You'll see everything from sloppy scrawls and notes tacked to the wall with chewing gum to more artistic portraits and messages.

Free, always open, Velkopřevorské Náměstí, Lesser Quarter, Tram: Malostranské Náměstí, Metro: Malostranská

Peeing Statues

Take a walk to see these two urinating gentlemen while wandering through Lesser Quarter. Created by the famous homegrown artist David Černý, these mechanical statues up until recently would use their stream to spell out any text you sent to a number posted nearby. That practice stopped back in 2012, and now they spell out lines from popular Czech literary works and poems. If you look closely, the pool into which they're contributing is actually the outline of the country, and the two figures represent Nazi and Communist invaders, one angling from the West and the other from the East. Černý is famous for pointed projects like this one and has numerous slightly subversive installations throughout town.

Free, always open, Cihelná 2b, Lesser Quarter, Tram: Malostranské Náměstí, Metro: Malostranská

Church of Our Lady Victorious

This baroque church is famous for its life-size wax figurine of infant Jesus. The icon just over a foot and a half tall is revered around the world and numerous outfits have been donated showcasing international styles, making this one of the best-dressed dolls I've ever seen. It's free to go in, and also to climb the stairs in the back right of the church to see a sampling of the rest of the outfits on display. A crew of nuns has the important responsibility of changing the baby into a new outfit from time to time!

Services often, open to the public in daylight hours, Karmelitská 9, Lesser Quarter, +420 257 533 646, pragjesu. info, Tram: Hellichova, Metro: Malostranská

Lover's Bridge

Adjacent to the Lennon Wall, a short bridge connects the street to an underwhelming district known as Prague's "Little Venice." The grate on this bridge has become the place for lovers to attach a lock representing their love to any available space. They then toss the key into the canal to show that their love will never be undone.

Free, always open, Lesser Quarter, Tram: Malostranské Náměstí, Metro: Malostranská

Petřín Hill & Tower

Petřín Hill rises on the west side of the river, just south of the Castle District and Lesser Quarter. The observation tower atop the forested hill—clearly modeled after the Eiffel Tower in Paris—was built in 1891 as part of the Jubilee Exhibition, an event showcasing national pride and achievements similar to the World Fair. An additional 299 steps above Petřín Hill, the tower's vantage point allows you to see the entire city of Prague and beyond into Bohemia.

At the bottom of the hill, you'll pass by a morbid series of tall abstract human figures climbing a staircase. This is Prague's **Memorial to the Victims of Communism,** commemorating those who were put on fake trials and killed during the years under control of Moscow.

Park free and always open, tower 105Kč adult, 65Kč student, tower open Apr-Sept daily 10:00-22:00, Oct and Mar daily 10:00-20:00, Nov-Feb daily 10:00-22:00, Petřín Hill, petrinska-rozhledna.cz, Tram: Újezd

Wenceslas Square

This long, modern square was the site of the peaceful overthrow of the communist government in 1989, an event that turned the tide and brought about the fall of the Soviet Empire and an end to the Cold War. The square is capped by the National Museum (free), which is rather dull and not worth your time on a short visit, though you'll recognize the beautiful interior as the backdrop for the scene where Ethan's target was marked with a special spritz visible only with those spy glasses in *Mission: Impos-*

sible. Wenceslas Square is traditionally where important events kick off and demonstrations end, and it is now the heart of modern Prague, complete with casinos, clubs, and seedier types later at night.

Free, always open, New Town, Metro: Můstek

Museum of Communism

This throwback museum walks you through the lead-up to the Cold War and depicts daily life behind the Iron Curtain. The Museum of Communism contains a collection of artifacts from daily life under communist rule, from propaganda posters and leader busts to the depressing selection of food available at the market at the time; milk, canned beans, and lard. When stores began to sell more than one kind of butter and the hot new Western clothing styles came out, people were keen to update their look, and an enterprising expat American gathered up these goods and created this museum, lending it a slightly tacky yet authentic insight into what life was like leading up to the 1990s in Czechoslovakia.

Be sure to stay for the entirety of the emotional film playing on a loop toward the end of the exhibit; it helps to underline your experience at the museum.

190Kč adult, 150Kč student, daily 09:00-21:00, Na Příkopě 10 (just north of Wenceslas Square, next to McDonald's), New Town, +420 224 212 966, muzeumkomunismu.cz, Metro: Můstek

Mucha Museum

For those fascinated by art nouveau, a visit to Prague isn't complete without stepping into the Mucha Museum, a one-floor extravaganza of the master's best original works. Alphonse Mucha (1860-1939) pioneered this genre of art and design, which came around as a response to the rigid forms of the industrial revolution. Art nouveau is characterized by organic shapes and the blending of a wide range of materials, including ceramics, metal, glass, and wood, to convey the harmony of nature. This museum, still run by Mucha's grandson, displays paintings, photographs, drawings, and memorabilia. Beyond the museum, Prague itself is home to some of the most beautiful art nouveau architecture and art in the world. Keep your eyes open when passing by the Municipal House (Náměstí Republiky 5), Hotel Europa on Wenceslas Square, and even the dome of the main train station, Hlavní Nádraží.

Adult ticket 240Kč, student ticket 160Kč, daily 10:00-18:00,

Panska 7, New Town, +420 224 216 415, mucha.cz, Metro: Můstek

National Theatre (Národní Divadlo)

From the outside, it's easy to identify the National Theatre, with its remarkable Louis Vuitton-like pattern across the tiled roof. But the real treat is to go inside and catch an opera, and they frequently offer discount tickets to students with ID cards for only 50Kč—an incredible deal. Just show up 30 minutes before the show and see if they have any available.

Refer to website for ticket prices/showtimes, Ostrovní 1, New Town, +420 224 901 448, narodni-divadlo.cz, Tram: Národní Divadlo, Metro: Národní Třída

The Slav Epic at the National Gallery (Veletržní Palác)

Alphonse Mucha was a proud Czech nationalist, and he spent over 15 years working on this dreamy and strikingly beautiful series of 20 massive-scale paintings depicting the legends and history of the Slavic people. At the height of his artistic prowess, Mucha mastered depth of field, contrast, and use of color and composition for what really is an epic collection of paintings, some measuring 20 feet tall. For Mucha fans, it's a no-brainer—you've just gotta see it. For others, it's still worth the short tram ride on #6 or #12 to get to the museum in Holešovice.

Adult ticket 180Kč, Tues-Sun 10:00-18:00, Dukelských

Hrdinů 530/47, Prague 7 (Holešovice), +420 224 301 111, ngprague.cz, Tram: Veletržní Palác, Metro: Vltavská

EXTRA CREDIT
Churches

As you wander, don't miss the opportunity to soak in some baroque beauty in a few of the many churches in Prague. Most feature decadent architecture and some real gems in the form of paintings. You'll see an over-the-top exuberance not seen in the more austere Renaissance style. Architectural restraint is thrown out the window and replaced by glittering gold statues, radiant stained glass, and over-decorated pulpits.

Vyšehrad Castle

A seldom visited and beautiful sight, Dracula-esque Vyšehrad Castle is a fun afternoon jaunt about half an hour's walk along the river south of town. This is the area where experts think the first settlements in the region occurred, expanding into the city of Prague as we know it today. I love exploring the well-preserved modern star fort's two-kilometer-long ramparts, looking out from the numerous vantage points to the suburbs of Prague, and reflecting on a walk through the cemetery just behind the church, where Alphonse Mucha is buried.

Free, Apr-Oct daily 10:00-18.00, Nov-Mar daily 10:00-16:00, V Pevnosti 159, Greater Prague, praha-vysehrad.cz, Tram: Albertov, Metro: Vyšehrad

TOP EATS

With dishes generally consisting of some kind of meat, potatoes, dumplings, and gravy, classic Czech cuisine is not for the faint at heart (seriously—these dishes are heart-stopping). But while you're here, you've got to duck into one of the many Czech pubs and at least try a bowl of their famous goulash.

Up until recently, there weren't many options beyond the heavy local food, but you'll find that a culinary renaissance has taken Prague by storm. Selection and variety have grown substantially, and ingredients much improved. It used to be hard to find vegetarian or eco-friendly options, but now they're all over the place.

Tipping is not expected but is appreciated. Be aware of some subtleties: Locals take a look at the bill, then hand their cash to the waiter, who makes change right there at the table out of a large wallet. If your service and food were good, round up to the nearest 10 percent, and ask for the change that you want back. For example, if your meal was 450Kč (about US$20), hand him your 1000Kč, and ask for 500Kč back. Saying "thank you" while handing over the cash effectively means, "keep the change." So wait until you have your change in hand before thanking the waiter for his service.

Lokál

To experience authentic Czech food at an amazing price, look no further than Lokál. Upon entering, you'll feel as if you've stepped back in time into an old communist beer cellar—the scribbles on the walls and naughty bathrooms are a nod to what you'd see at real beer halls in the countryside. The menu is thankfully short and sweet, and the servers are happy to get you an English

SPIRALLY, SUGARY GOODNESS: THE *TRDELNÍK*

Typical to the region is a delicious pastry that's baked on top of glowing coals: *trdelník* (pronounced ter-DEL-neek). The bakers take a roll of dough and wrap it around a wooden cylinder to cook and toast into a golden-brown chewy dessert. When they're ready, the doughy spirals are tapped off the log and rolled in sugar, spice, and everything nice. Prices are climbing to 60Kč each, but it's well worth it to keep the blood sugar levels up on those long days of sightseeing. Enterprising vendors have been popping up everywhere, but that doesn't mean the quality is always the same. Some places will try to hawk cold, stale *trdelníks* at you. Have patience and wait until you pass a stall that's passing out steaming hot fresh rolls. The stall on Malostranské Námĕstí has been consistently tasty for the last several years, and I tend to skip the ones in the Old Town Square area.

menu on request. Service is brisk. The *svíčková* (beef sirloin in cream sauce) and goulash never disappoint.

About 120Kč, Mon–Fri 11:00–01:00, Sat 12:00– 01:00, Sun 12:00–22:00, Dlouhá 33, Old Town, +420 222 316 265, ambi.cz, Metro: Staroměstská

Kozička

Come enjoy a meal inside this cozy, brick cellar of a place for some incredible Czech food at lovely prices. Because of its nondescript entrance, most tourists miss it, so it's a favorite among locals, who can look past the service with attitude and come back for the cheap drinks, great atmosphere, and delicious $10 steaks.

Dishes from 160Kč, Mon–Fri 12:00–04:00, Sat 18:00–04:00, Sun 19:00–03:00, Kozí 1, Old Town, +420 224 818 308, kozicka.cz, Metro: Staroměstská

U Medvídků

Have a meal here for a selection of great local food and enjoy the warm atmosphere. U Medvídků could practically have its own section in a Prague history book—they've been serving house-brewed pints and delicious Czech goulash since 1466! Check out their open-top brew barrels by going all the

way to the back and up the stairs. You can sit up here and eat if you want to try their extra special house pilsner.

Dishes from 140Kč, Mon–Fri 11:00–23:00, Sat 11:30–23:00, Sun 11:30–22:00, Na Perštýně 7, Old Town +420 224 211 916, umedvidku.cz, Metro: Můstek

Malý Buddha

For vegetarian food, Malý Buddha ("Little Buddha") is among the best in the city. This Thai fusion restaurant offers stir-fried and roasted veggie and tofu dishes in a quiet, warm ambience. This healthy option may be a welcome break for those tired of heavier Czech cuisine.

Dishes around 120–240Kč, Tues–Sun 12:00–22:30, Úvoz 46, Castle District, +420 220 513 894, malybuddha.cz, Tram: Pohořelec

Strahov Monastery

Find some of the best beer in town in a wonderful, bright beer hall setting in the old Strahov Monastery, which dates back to the 12th century. The old monastery is just at the top side of the Prague Castle, making it a perfect pit stop for a pint and a meal. The goulash in a bread bowl is a personal favorite, but their cheese plate and duck dishes don't disappoint either.

Dishes from 100Kč, daily 10:00–22:00, Strahovské Nádvoří 1/132, Castle District, +420 233 107 704, strahovskyklaster.cz, Tram: Pohořelec

Café Louvre

This is Prague's classiest and most classic Bohemian café, set one floor above street level. Having served classy brunches, lunches, and dinners for over 100 years, Café Louvre follows the lead of the coffee culture in nearby Vienna. It's a must for anyone who agrees with my mother that breakfast is the most important meal of the day. Dine under tall ceilings on delicious omelets served by waiters in smart dress. The carrot cakes are quite fortifying as well.

Omelets from 140Kč, Mon–Fri 08:00–23:30, Sat–Sun 09:00–23:30, Národní 22 (upstairs), Old Town, +420 224 930 949, cafelouvre.cz, Metro: Národní Třída

Mama Coffee

Mama Coffee is a favorite among local coffee snobs (like me) and vegetarians. And if you need to tackle a day of work while on vacation, this is your place for ear plugs, Wi-Fi, and strong coffee. I can while away the hours with a good book upstairs by the window enjoying their delicious fresh ginger tea. Toss in their tasty pastries and a hummus lunch, and I'm fat—er, lean—and happy all day without racking up much of a tab at all.

Coffee and tea from 60Kč, daily 08:00–22:00, Vodičkova 674/6, Old Town, +420 773 337 309, mamacoffee.cz, Tram: Vodičkova, Metro: Národní Třída

Buddha Bar

This is the kind of place you'd splurge on for a birthday dinner (it's where I've spent two of mine!). Buddha Bar is an Asian fusion chain restaurant with locations around the world. It features a creative menu with fresh salads, innovative sushi rolls, numerous other main options, an extensive wine menu, and delicious expertly mixed cocktails. The service is impeccable, and the ambience is breathtaking. Start upstairs with a cocktail at the bar, and descend once your table's ready to your religious culinary experience at the foot of a giant Buddha. Stay late for an after party among the young, well-heeled professionals of Prague.

Dishes from 350Kč, Tues–Sat 18:00–03:00, Jakubská 8, Old Town, +420 221 776 400, buddha-bar.cz, Metro: Náměstí Republiky

Zebra Express

If Buddha Bar can't fit into your budget, Zebra can—and it's nearby, just inside the Powder Gate and around the corner from the Municipal House. Zebra offers excellent pad thai along with curries and sushi in a casual setting, with fast and friendly service. You can even banter with the chefs, who really appreciate your compliments and clearly enjoy what they're doing. The second location in town, Zebra Asian (Melantrichova 5), is right on the corner of the Havelská Market, a block south from the Old Town Square.

Dishes from 150Kč, daily 11:00–24:00, Celetná 988/38, Old Town, +420 774 727 611, zebranoodlebar.cz, Metro: Náměstí Republiky

Burrito Loco

Stop into this fast food, almost-as-good-as-Chipotle burrito shop for a cheap Tex-Mex fix 24 hours a day. Numerous locations, including at Národní Třída and near numerous nightlife venues on Dlouhá, make it hard to say no when the munchies strike late. Post up in the

limited seating, or take your rolls to go and find a bench nearby. Find a second Old Town location at Spálená 104/43.

Burritos from 120Kč, daily 24 hours, Masná 620/2, Old Town, +420 606 039 333, burritoloco.cz, Metro: Staroměstská

Bohemia Bagel

If you're anything like me, you're really missing a bagel sandwich right about now. Head to Bohemia Bagel—a favorite among the study abroad students in Prague for the taste of home it offers—for freshly made bagel sandwiches throughout the day. It's owned by the same enterprising entrepreneur who started Burrito Loco and the Museum of Communism. He picked up a warehouse full of old Bohemian tiles in the early '90s, which decorate the walls of and are sold at the Bagel. Order at the cashier and take a seat with your number—they've capitalized on our love of bagels, and they're not letting go anytime soon!

Bagels from 100Kč, daily 07:30-18:00, Lázeňská 19, Lesser Quarter, +420 257 218 192, bohemiabagel.cz, Tram: Malostranské Náměstí, Metro: Malostranská

Lehká Hlava

True to Prague's culinary revival, this celestial little abode has visitors raving about their delicious vegetarian, vegan, and gluten-free dishes. Creative dishes like cucumber spaghetti and beetroot burger make this a popular spot for those seeking an alternative to the ubiquitous heavy fare throughout the rest of town. If you love cheap, fast, casual, and healthy food like this, be sure to look up its sister location, Maitrea, just behind the Týn Church and steps from the Old Town Square.

Mains from 150Kč, daily 11:30-23:30, Boršov 180/2, Old Town, +420 222 220 665, lehkahlava.cz, Tram: Karlovy Lázně, Metro: Národní Třída

Restaurace T. Anker

What's better than good food? Good food with a panoramic view over downtown Prague. Find T. Anker at the top of the funky octagonal-shaped department store directly across from the city-center shopping mall, Palladium. Grilled options like duck, chicken, burgers, and fish go well with their homemade brews on tap.

Mains from 180Kč, daily 11:00-20:00, till 18:00 on Sun, Náměstí Republiky 656/8, 5th floor, Old Town, +420 722 445 474, t-anker.cz, Metro: Náměstí Republiky

Beas Vegetarian Dhaba

Your dear author couldn't be any further from a vegetarian, but there is something amazing about a light lunch or evening snack of Indian curries and salads. This place is by far the quickest, easiest, and tastiest vegetarian option I've found in Prague. Their Národní Třída location makes for an easy pit stop during the day, but you may see other locations around town. Pop in, grab a tray (plastic, if you want it to go) and start filling it with all sorts of rice dishes, grilled veggies, and more. Their lassi isn't the best I've ever had, but it does the trick if you've got a hankering.

Pay by weight, Mon-Fri 11:00-21:00, Sat-Sun 12:00-18:00, Vladislavova 158/24, Old Town, +420 777 551 256, Metro: Národní Třída

Las Adelitas

Difficult to find, and tucked inside a passageway and downstairs, this is one of Prague's hidden gem Mexican restaurants. Head downstairs and you'll forget you're in central Europe, half expecting to hear the waves of Puerto Vallarta as you sip your perfectly concocted margarita. Enjoy the toasty salted chips and wide selection of appetizers and entrées—I loved the steak burrito—and take it at the bar.

100-200Kč, daily 11:00-01:00, Malé Náměstí 457/13, Old Town, +420 222 233 247, lasadelitas.cz, Metro: Staroměstská

Tržnice Dlouhá 14

This Whole Foods-with-a-twist-style grocery and deli is an excellent stop for both breakfast and lunch, and very nearby the Old Town Square. Their thick sandwiches with generous fillings and deep-dish pizza are made from the high-quality ingredients found in-store. Come back for dinner and throw together a charcuterie plate and a bottle of wine from their cellar downstairs for a classy, easily made picnic dinner.

Sandwiches from 80Kč, Mon-Fri 08:00-21:00, Dlouhá 14, Old Town, +420 224 815 719, dlouha14.cz, Tram: Dlouhá Třída, Metro: Staroměstská

Angelato

Angelato whips up Prague's best authentic Italian gelato, with flavors that are a taste-powered travel machine with a one-way ticket to Italy. The location makes for an excellent reward after a long day of sightseeing in the Lesser Quarter. It's not far from the rental location for the paddle boats, either!

Cups of love from 80Kč, daily 11:00-20:00, Újezd 425/24, Lesser Quarter, +420 777 787 344, angelato.cz, Tram: Újezd

TOP NIGHTLIFE

Prague is notorious for its nightlife. You can find everything from smoky dive bars and grungy clubs to classy lounges and cocktail bars. Pay attention to flyers and posters around the city, and keep your ears open at the hostel to get a feel of what's happening each night—there are often events throughout the week at various venues. The pubs are cheap, the clubs are nuts, and dance bars (my favorite) are numerous. When there's a dance floor, you can expect to pay 100-200K, or less than US$10, to get into the party.

NIGHTLIFE DISTRICTS

The Old Town of Prague is where the hopping nightlife is for both tourists and locals. Once you get out of the dense streets of the Old Town into the New Town, Wenceslas Square area, and Prague 7, clubs are bigger and more intense, and generally more Czech, but fewer and farther between. It's nice to jump on an organized pub crawl your first night in town to get a sampling of what Prague has to offer.

Dlouhá

You'll find nightlife throughout Prague's Old Town, especially on Dlouhá, the city's well-known party street. Several of my favorite venues are located on this street.

Old Town, Tram: Dlouhá Třída

Náplavka

Two bridges south of Charles Bridge is the bridge known as Jiráskův most. Beginning just south of Jiráskův most and extending about five blocks is a strip of street bars and pubs that open up in the summer. This riverside street, known as Náplavka, is on the east side of the river. It's hugely popular with locals on weekends and sunny afternoons, and hardly known by tourists. It's a great way to spend an afternoon after your paddle boat ride on the river, meeting locals

and making friends over cheap pints while overlooking the river. Beers start around 30Kč. Most beer gardens stay out as long as it's warm enough to enjoy a pint outside.

Greater Prague, Tram: Paleckého Náměstí, Metro: Karlovo Náměstí

BARS & PUBS

U Sudu

U Sudu is a Prague institution. Upon entry, it seems to be just another ordinary Czech pub, but head to the back and down the stairs and you'll find a labyrinth of exposed medieval brick cellars and lounge rooms with foosball tables and numerous bars where you can drink, chill, and be merry. Try not to get lost on the way back to your seat!

Daily 09:00-05:00, Vodičkova 677/10, Old Town, +420 222 232 207, usudu.cz, Tram: Lazarská, Metro: Národní Třída

Anonymous Bar

Anonymous is a welcome non-smoking alternative to the smoky beer pubs throughout the city. Head to the back of a dimly lit, quiet courtyard and step into a classy low-key speakeasy-themed bar, with the Anonymous mask face pasted everywhere across the interior. Enjoy one of the many experimental cocktails described by the helpful staff, or go for one of the classics—the bartenders excel at both.

LGBT PRAGUE

When it comes to entertainment for the LGBT community, Prague has a lot to offer, including dance clubs with go-go dancers, such as **Factory** (Vinohradská 63, factoryclub.cz) or **Escape Club** (V Jámě 1371/8, escapeclub.xxx). **Střelec Pub** (Anglická 2, facebook.com/clubstrelec) is for guys who prefer good beer. **Club Termix** (Třebízského 1514/4a, club-termix.cz) is a smaller, more intimate dance club that packs out throughout the week, and its big brother, **Termax Club,** is the biggest gay club in Prague, so sometimes the big rooms look rather empty. Both these clubs have the same owner, and prices are similar and reasonable across the two. These clubs attract bigger DJs, so in case of special events, there is often a cover. **Friends Club** (Bartolomějská 11, friendsclub.cz) is open seven days a week and is very popular among the tourist crowd, with programs like karaoke, partying, meeting, talking, chilling, and even cabaret across different nights. And keep an eye on **Mecca**'s program (mecca.cz); they organize their famous OMG Party every two months with a house and techno set.

ACT LIKE A LOCAL

Pivo, Prosím?

Thanks to its clean water, fresh hops and barley, and a longtime monastic brewing culture, the Czech Republic has some of the best beer in the world. The beer coming from the Bohemia-Moravian region has been imitated many times, yet nobody does it quite like the Czech. Order one by saying to the waiter *"pivo, prosím?"* or "beer, please?" As it's by far the most popular beverage in any restaurant, even just holding up a finger will land a pint of frothy goodness on your table in short order.

Today, beer culture is alive and well in Prague. Bars and restaurants generally have two taps—light and dark—of the same beer brand. "Light" doesn't necessarily mean lower-calorie; rather, this is the lighter-colored, crisp pilsner-style beer, the predecessor to the American perversion of Budweiser and Coors. "Dark" tends to be heavier and a touch sweeter, with a slightly higher alcohol content. This beer goes well with the meat-and-potatoes Czech cuisine. Goulash is oftentimes even made with a splash of beer. So toast to the brewers and knock back a few of what many consider the best brew around. Here are some common brands you'll see:

Pilsner Urquell: Deliciously light and bitter. Quenches a thirst at the end of a long day of sightseeing and widely recognized as the best beer in the world.

Budvar: The precursor to the Budweiser brand we all know in the States. The two brands are in constant legal battles over who owns the rights to the brand Budweiser.

Staropramen: The runner up to the better brands of Urquell and Budvar. Also a lighter, crisper, cheaper beer.

Proprietary brews at Strahov Monastery and U Medvídků: Delicious small-batch brews coming in both lighter and darker manifestations. A swig of these and you'll understand what "good beer" actually means.

Daily 17:00–02:00, till 03:00 on weekends, Michalská 432/12, Old Town, +420 608 280 069, Metro: Můstek

Prague Beer Museum

Located on Prague's party street, Dlouhá, the beer museum is much more than museum, but who's complaining? Pick up a menu in this dark, smoking bar and you'll realize it may as well be an exhaustive library of all the tasty beers from around the world. I challenge you to find a beer that's not on the list! If you can't choose, go for the sampler paddle to taste a number of different beers on tap, and take your tray out to the patio in the back if the weather is good. The servers are sometimes in the mood to make recommendations, but other times, they're just not. Don't take it personally.

Daily 12:00–03:00, Dlouhá 720/46, Old Town, praguebeer-museum.com, +420 732 330 912, Tram: Dlouhá Třída

Café Nod

Another classy spot on the party street, Dlouhá. This one is the sister bar to the Roxy club. Pop in here, next door to the recommended Lokál restaurant, and climb the stairs to a spacious bar/café/lounge

that's perfect for anything from afternoon tea to late-night drinks. The space in the back doubles as an art gallery with frequent exhibits. Nod draws the young professional set who work downtown, creating a chill and unpretentious vibe.

Drinks from 60Kč, Mon–Fri 10:00–01:00, Sat-Sun 14:00–04:00, Dlouhá 33, Old Town, nod.roxy.cz, +420 604 790 921, Tram: Dlouhá Třída

Tretter's New York Bar

Tretter's is your classic Roaring '20s cocktail bar, complete with professional bartenders; an extensive list of wine, short and long drinks, and cigars; and even a gentleman's guide integrated into your menu. This place is now "discovered" and packs out later in the evening, but the old-fashioned I had was well worth the stop and a great start to the night.

Daily 19:00–03:00, V Kolkovně 3, Jewish Quarter, +420 224 811 165, tretters.cz, Metro: Staroměstská

Absintherie

Prague is famous for the drink that supposedly made imbibers hallucinate and enjoy extra creative powers thanks to the

wormwood soaked in this liquor derived from anise, the licorice-flavored root. The hallucinogenic ingredients have gone by the wayside, as products made or sold within the EU cannot contain wormwood. But it's still fun to pop into this green-hued bar and decide between the cool French preparation or the fiery Czech one. The former entails dripping water over a sugar cube sitting on a fancy spoon with holes in it with the shot of absinth below, both watering it down and making it sweeter. The Czech preparation is made by soaking the sugar cube in absinthe, lighting it on fire, and caramelizing it as it falls into the drink. Better yet, get both and share with your friends!

Prepared drinks from 100Kč, daily 12:00–24:00, Jilská 7, Old Town, +420 224 251 999, absintherie.cz, Metro: Můstek

DANCE BARS

I love how dance bars blend the line between sit-and-drink pubs and deafening clubs. These bars make for the perfect place to sow those seeds of fascinating conversation and bring your dude or damsel to the floor when your jam comes on.

Klubovna 2. Patro

This is probably my favorite spot—and best-kept secret—in Prague. The name translates to "2nd floor club," and this spot frequented by the classy hipster set is a cross between a speakeasy, lounge, bar, and club. It's quite popular with young, friendly Czechs who love the throbbing techno put on nightly throughout the week. You've got a coat check as you enter, affordable drinks, a dance floor, a large bar, and then a back room where you can chill out and catch your breath. The proximity to many other popular venues on the same block makes this a great place to continue or cap the night.

Covers 100–200Kč, Mon–Thurs 17:00–02:00, Fri–Sat 17:00–04:00, pass through the discreet entrance in the back of a parking lot at Dlouhá 729/37, Old Town, so hipster they don't even have a phone or website, Tram: Dlouhá Třída

M1

A small club that's popular with Erasmus students, M1 is a chic but not-too-snobby single-room dance bar that plays a good mix of popular hip-hop and R&B. Check out the website before you go out, as they often have daily specials and promos. And bring a thick skin for the bouncers, who can be a bit moody. It's generally not worth paying the cover, so if they're pushing for it, skip it for the numerous nearby options.

100Kč cover sometimes applies, daily 21:00–late, Masná 1, Old Town, +420 227 195 235, m1lounge.com, Metro: Staroměstská

Chapeau Rouge

Chapeau Rouge is notorious for being a head trip—the good kind. While the upstairs is (relatively) quieter and more straight-laced, descend the stairs into the low-ceilinged smoky cavern, where you'll rock out to intense dubstep where just about anything goes... As they say, what happens in Chapeau stays in Chapeau. Not a good place for those who don't like being around drugs.

Mon–Fri 12:00–04:00, Sat–Sun 16:00–late, Jakubská 2, Old Town, +420 222 316 328, chapeaurouge.cz, Metro: Náměstí Republiky

Nebe

With three locations in town, Nebe has the clubbing vibe down to a science. The crowd here dresses well but comes without the pretentious flavor that fills so many clubs in other cities. Their different locations have slightly different characteristics, but each is enjoyable in its own right for great music, drinks that go down easy, prices that won't break the bank, and a sexy crowd ready to dance the night away. Each location features a long bar and a separate dance floor to get down on. In addition to the Wenceslas

Square location below, find other locations at Náměstí Republiky (V Celnici 1036/4) and Karlovo Náměstí (Křemencova 10).

Cover on weekends 100Kč, Mon 16:00-03:00, Tues-Thurs 16:00-04:00, Fri-Sat 16:00-05:00, Sun 18:00-03:00, Václavské Nám. 802/56, Wenceslas Square, New Town, +420 608 644 784, nebepraha.cz, Metro: Muzeum

James Dean

I skipped out on this bar for years until I realized that this is actually where the locals go. Thanks to its '50s-diner theme, you wouldn't be blamed for thinking this is a tourist trap, but pop in and descend the stairs in the back to a raging party that goes until 6 or 7 in the morning. With the relatively lax door policy, the ratio does get a bit unbalanced at times toward the guys who just gawk for hours at the dancers on stage.

Daily 08:00-late, V Kolkovně 922/1, Old Town, +420 606 979 797, jamesdean.cz, Metro: Staroměstská

Harley's

Widely recognized as Prague's pickup joint, this dive bar and club is the after-party location for all the clubbers in town. While busy around midnight and 01:00, it really notches up around 03:00 till closing around dawn. The rowdy downstairs party features a small stage, to which bachelors on their stag parties are drawn like flies.

Daily 19:00-late, Dlouhá 18, Old Town, +420 602 419 111, harleys.cz, Metro: Staroměstská

Deja Vu

Get your drink on upstairs and your dance on down below. The music here can be hit or miss, so head downstairs and listen to a groove before throwing down for a drink. Sharable large drinks are popular at the upstairs bar, where you can lounge around some mean-looking garden lion statues.

Daily 18:00-late, Jakubská 648/6, Old Town, +420 222 311 743, dejavuclub.cz, Metro: Náměstí Republiky

CLUBS

Many of the clubs in town focus on one genre rather than featuring a mix and usually charge a 100Kč or 200Kč cover. Nightclubs come along with a more serious sound system, generally a larger venue and bigger crowds, and higher drink prices than what you'd find at dance bars. So it's a good idea to look up the programs online ahead of time to determine the music you'll listen to as well as the crowd that will be showing up to party. This way, you can avoid genres that just don't get you going, like house techno for me.

Karlovy Lázně

This is the famous five-floor club everyone has heard about. It's the largest in Central Europe and boasts two floors of techno, one pumping '80s beats, one for hip-hop, and a dark, chill level at the top with couches and giant bean bags that I usually try to stay away from. This club is good as long as you've imbibed plenty, but the hordes of high-schoolers and the male creepers they attract make a second visit unlikely for most.

There's a bar next door on the river side of Karlovy Lázně where many people get their cheap drinks fix before heading to the club. The happy hour 10:00-24:00 features 60Kč shots, wine, and beer.

Daily 21:00-06:00, Smetanovo Nábřeží 198/1, Old Town, +420 222 220 502, karlovylazne.cz, Metro: Staroměstská

Radost FX

Locals and tourists alike highly recommend this spot out past the top of Wenceslas Square, which is both the city's best vegetarian restaurant by day and a bumping hip-hop club by night. Rihanna even filmed a music video here—the one where they went behind a secret refrigerator in the back of a convenience store and resurfaced in Prague's biggest club featuring R&B and rap.

Daily 11:00-02:00, Bělehradská 234/120, New Town, +420 224 254 776, radostfx.cz, Metro: I.P. Pavlova

Roxy

Taking over a massive and recently renovated subterranean concert hall, Roxy gives off a slightly alternative, grungy warehouse feel with music ranging anywhere from techno and reggae to house and hip-hop. This casual club—yes, sneakers and jeans are fine—is free sometimes but often charges cover on weekends (100Kč), but it's generally a great party. I recommend taking a look at the website for event schedules and genres of music to be played.

Daily 19:00-05:00, Dlouhá 33, +420 602 691 015, roxy.cz, Metro: Staroměstská, Trram: Dlouhá Třída

Lucerna

This is one of my favorite unpretentious dance clubs in town. Enjoy the music of the '80s and '90s on weekend nights while rocking out to the music videos your mom never let you watch on the enormous projector screens. And when your favorite '90s song comes on, don't feel ashamed knowing all the words—everyone here does (or thinks they do at least). You may find younger, more attractive crowds elsewhere, but Lucerna is always a safe bet for

A SORE BUTT ON EASTER

Your Easter traditions might include Easter egg hunts, church, rocking the pastels, and so on. But the Czechs have their own set of traditions, with one in particular that I found hard to believe.

Every Easter Monday, all the boys and men of the Czech Republic take decorated sticks called *pomlázka* (or thin wooden whips) to the streets, going door to door smacking women's butts in exchange for candy and chocolate eggs for the youngsters and shots of liquor or alcohol for the older boys and men. Additionally, at each stop along the way, the little girls tie colored ribbons on the ends of the boys' sticks. So a busy little guy will come home with a stick decked out in all sorts of pieces of flair. This naughty tradition is supposed to bring good luck to both genders and is also meant to preserve the beauty of the women for the next year. The act itself is supposed to symbolize health, fertility, and the coming springtime.

a popping good time. Continue into the gallery from the entry hallway to see an upside-down horse statue by David Černý mocking the one that sits prominently and correctly at the top of the Wenceslas Square.

Doors usually open around 20:00 or 21:00, and the party turns up around 22:30, Štěpánská 61, Wenceslas Square, New Town, +420 224 225 440, lucerna.musicbar.cz, Metro: Muzeum

Cross Club

This primarily dubstep club features one of the funkiest and most futuristic interiors I've ever experienced, with servos spinning on the walls and a half-level above the bar where you can bear-crawl to your own little cove to overlook the scene below. Taking over a nondescript house in Holešovice, Cross Club is a favorite among those who love drum and bass. The eclectic lineup of performers and DJs spans a wide range of tastes.

Cover usually around 100Kč, daily 14:00 till way late, Plynární 1096/23, Prague 7, (Holešovice), +420 736 535 053, crossclub.cz, Tram: Ortenovo Náměstí, Metro: Nádraží Holešovice

Mecca

For an all-out central European clubbing experience, take the hike out to Mecca, where you'll descend into a world of laser shows, smoke machines, go-go dancers, and throbbing house and futuristic techno every

Friday and Saturday. The music lineup varies occasionally on Saturday, so check their program for the schedule. Dress to impress to avoid any trouble at the door.

Cover usually around 200Kč , more when special events are on, Fri-Sat 22:00-05:00, U Průhonu 799/3, Prague 7, (Holešovice), +420 734 155 300, mecca.cz, Tram: U Průhonu, Metro: Nádraží Holešovice

PUB CRAWLS
Drunken Monkey Pub Crawl

This team puts on a rowdy party every night of the week. Check out their website for special upcoming events. Their parties for New Year's, the Super Bowl, Halloween, and Fourth of July are always worth booking ahead. Their standard nights kick off with a double power hour—two hours of unlimited sugary shooters, wine, and beer. They then take you on a tour of 4-5 top nightlife venues across town. Jump onto the backpacker crawl at 21:30 for the full crawl experience for 350Kč, or tag along the more local-student-oriented power hour plus club entry kicking off at 23:30 for 250Kč. Crawls start at their own bar, Drunken Monkey, and are a great option on weekend nights. Catch one of their flyers from their reps in blue in the Old Town Square for more info.

Pub crawl open bar 20:30-23:00, U Milosrdných 848/4, Jewish Quarter, +420 775 477 983, drunkenmonkey.cz, Metro: Staroměstská

TOP SHOPPING & MARKETS

SHOPPING DISTRICTS

Pařížská

Get your high-end shopping fix by strolling down Pařížská—"Paris Street"—Prague's own Champs-Élysées, offering stores like Prada, Louis Vuitton, and Gucci.

Jewish Quarter, Metro: Staroměstská

Wenceslas Square

If Pařížská is out of your budget, check out the stores lining **Národní** and quarter-mile-long **Wenceslas Square**, which has basically every brand you've ever heard of back in the States.

New Town, Metro: Můstek or Muzeum

MARKETS

Náplavka Farmers Market

Every Saturday, this exciting farmers market takes over a stretch of the walkway along the Vltava River. Shoppers come out to see what's on offer, from baked goods and pastries to meat, dairy, and sandwiches, and from food trucks to handmade goods and more. The beautiful setting makes for an excellent place for a lunch and break from a busy day of sightseeing.

Sat 08:00–14:00, Náplavka street, just south of Jiráskův most, Greater Prague, Tram: Paleckeho Náměstí, Metro: Karlovo Náměstí

Havelská Market

This touristy market has descended into selling tchotchkes and souvenirs. But the most kitschy thing about this market is that every single vendor seems to have dozens of clap-activated cackling witches on brooms hanging from their stalls, so you'll hear this street market long before actually seeing it. It's worth a stop if you've got loved ones to pick up souvenirs for, but don't expect anything that isn't mass-produced.

Apr-Sept daily 07:00–19:00, Oct-Mar daily 07:00–18:30, Havelská, Old Town, Metro: Můstek

SHOPPING CENTERS

Palladium

Palladium is Prague's best city center mall. You'll find all the standard brands, like Puma and H&M, along with Starbucks and a food court.

Daily 09:00–21:00, Náměstí Republiky 1, Old Town, Metro: Náměstí Republiky

TOP PARKS & RECREATION

Letná Park offers beautiful views, and the Vltava islands, just minutes from Charles Bridge, offer a chance to escape the crowds and busy streets of the city.

Letná Park (Letenské Sady)

For a stunning view of the entire city, climb the hill up to Letenské Sady park. Here you will find a giant ticking metronome (before it stood a colossal statue of Stalin leading the people of Czechoslovakia to the bright future of communism), which symbolizes the time ticking away until the end of all tyranny around the world. On nice days, this is where Prague citizens get their sweat on, going on jogs and roller blading around the large, flat park. There's a beer garden about a quarter mile

north from the metronome. Music events and concerts are put on often, and in the winter, they create an ice track to skate on.

Free, always open, Letná Park, Tram: Čechův most

Střelecký Island

Cross on the bridge known as Most Legií to get down to this island, perfect for enjoying a picnic lunch on the benches overlooking the river, with an uninterrupted view toward Charles Bridge. Enjoy a pint of Pilsner at the beer boat that pulls up to the island in summer.

Free, always open, between Lesser Quarter and Old Town, south of Charles Bridge, Tram: Národní Divadlo, Metro: Národní Třída

Slovanský Island

Winter in Prague can be freezing, but in the summer it's great to get out on the river for some time away from the crowds and to cool down a bit. From Slovanský Island, you can rent **paddle boats** for up to four people for about 200Kč an hour. Bring some snacks, beer, and wine to make an afternoon of it! To get to Slovanský Island, cross the short footbridge just south of Národní divadlo.

Daily, closing an hour before sunset, just south of the National Theater and Legií bridge, Tram: Národní Divadlo, Metro: Národní Třída

Žluté Lázně

Consider Žluté Lázně Prague's beach. With volleyball and tennis courts, numerous beer gardens, cafés and restaurants, pizzerias, and a generally chill and fun-loving atmosphere, this outdoor adult playground is where the city comes out to enjoy nice weather any chance they get. Once the sun goes down, freshly tanned Czechs stick around for dinner and the party to follow at their on-site dance hall. To get here, take the 20-minute tram ride south on tram #17 from any stop along the east side of the river.

Cheap entrance fee of 80Kč, daily 09:00-02:00, Podolské Nábřeží 3/1184, Greater Prague, +420 244 462 193, zlutelazne.cz, Tram: Dvorce

TOP TOURS

Sandeman's New Europe Walking Tour

These free tours took Europe by storm a few years ago, and you can count on them for cheap, entertaining, entry-level history and culture about a city. They leave daily from the Astronomical Clock at 10:00, 10:45 and 14:00. Sandeman's Castle Quarter Tours depart from the Czech Tourism Center on the Old Town Square at 14:00, and pick up

LOST IN TRANSLATION?

In the Czech Republic, not only are American movies dubbed, but also their titles are often changed drastically. The reasons for this vary. Sometimes, American movie titles just don't sound right in direct translation, or they may even have a completely different meaning when translated to Czech. Regardless of the reason, the results can range from confusing to hilarious. Here are some of my favorites translated back into English:

English	Czech	English	Czech
The Hangover	Party in Las Vegas	The Amityville Horror	You Will Die at 3:15
Wicker Park	Love Me Please		
Freaky Friday	Between Us Girls	Meet the Parents	The Father is a Ruffian
Bad Santa	Santa Is a Pervert		
Hurt Locker	Death Waits Everywhere	Bourne Identity	Agent Without a Past
A Beautiful Mind	A Pure Soul	Any Given Sunday	Winners and Losers
Full Metal Jacket	Lead Vest		
Cool Runnings	Coconuts in the Snow	Hot Fuzz	Overly Rapid Deployment Unit
Beverly Hills Ninja	Fatty from Beverly Hills	Van Wilder	Sexy Party

others on Jan Palach Square just in front of Rudolfinum at 14:30 before continuing across the river and up the hill to the castle.

Tip-based and paid tours, pub crawl option, newprague-tours.com

Biko Prague Bike Tours

Filippo, from Italy, met his wife in the Czech Republic, quit the corporate tobacco industry world, moved here, and started this adventurous bike tour company. You can choose between numerous offerings to suit any fitness and skill level. I love these tours because they let you see a different side of Prague in the hills beyond the city, all with friendly guiding and coaching throughout.

Tours including bikes from 1,300Kč, Vratislavova 58/3, +420 733 750 990, bikoadventures.com

TOP HOSTELS

Mosaic House

Recently renovated and consistently blowing away backpackers with its value and mod decor, Mosaic House is my favorite hostel in town. This hybrid boutique hotel and designer hostel is a 12-minute walk from the Old Town Square, putting you close to all the main attractions in the city. The showers, with their rainforest drizzle, are a favorite. They keep it happening at the bar with frequent live acts, creating a fun and inviting atmosphere. Daily free walking tours (at 11:00) and the hostel's own nightly pub crawl (at 20:00) meet in the lounge.

190-350Kč, free Wi-Fi, laundry facilities, 24-hour reception, breakfast 150Kč (optional), Odborů 4, Old Town, +420 221 595 364, mosaichouse.com, Metro: Karlovo Náměstí

The MadHouse Hostel

If you, like me, are bemoaning the slow death of the social atmosphere in hostels around Europe due to mobile tech and "social networking," hit up the MadHouse Party Hostel for the hostel with the best social vibe in town. This is Prague's most legit backpacker hostel, and these guys put on events every night of the week. While your sleeping pattern will take a hit, it's for a noble reason: experiencing the true nightlife of this city.

Beds from 160Kč, free Wi-Fi, city maps, parties and events organized throughout the week, Spalena 39, Old Town, +420 222 240 009, themadhouseprague.cz, Metro: Národní Třída

Hostel Orange

This is a favorite among backpackers for the chill atmosphere and excellent location right on Wenceslas Square. They have a hard time keeping their locks working, so don't head here if you're carrying the crown jewels with you. Without a common room, the Orange isn't as social as my other recommendations, but the value and location make up for it.

Beds from 155Kč, laundry available, free Wi-Fi, towels included, hair dryers available, 24-hour check-in, Václavské Náměstí 781/20, New Town, +420 775 112 625, Metro: Můstek

Prague Square Hostel

This hostel is in the heart of it all—you just can't beat the accessibility of this hostel, not only to sights but to the nightlife as well. Places like Chapeau Rouge, Roxy, and James Dean are just a five-minute walk away, with Wenceslas Square not much farther in the opposite direction. The staff are welcoming and happy to help you make the most of your stay in town. As the hostel is in an older building, don't expect too many modern amenities (like plugs by every bed), but what it lacks slightly in features, it makes up for in location right on the Old Town Square.

Beds from 300Kč, free Wi-Fi, free towels, 24-hour reception, free breakfast, Melantrichova 10, Old Town, +420 224 240 859, praguesquarehostel.com, Metro: Můstek

Sir Toby's

Located in the trendy area of Holešovice (Prague 7), this hostel gives you an opportunity to get away from the touristy streets of Old Town and to see a more local flavor of Prague. Though it's a 10- to 15-minute tram ride to the center, the location puts you right next to the some interesting sights, like Alphonse Mucha's Slav Epic in the National Gallery, Stromovka (largest green space in Prague), and some of the most popular clubs in the city, like Cross Club and Mecca. This hostel offers you an attractive pub downstairs with live music, a nice outdoor area, and a friendly staff.

Beds from 225Kč, free Wi-Fi, 24-hour reception, optional breakfast, Dělnická 24, Prague 7 (Holešovice), +420 246 032 610, new.sirtobys.com, Tram: Dělnická

PRAGUE

GETTING THERE & AWAY

Prague is well-served by all modes of ground and air transportation.

Plane

Prague's main airport, **Václav Havel International Airport** (PRG, prg.aero/en), is served by all the major and budget airlines. Connections are easy and cheap into the city center. Get cash from an ATM in the airport and break your big bills at a convenience shop so you can purchase your local transportation connection into town.

You've got two options to connect into the city center: The **Airport Express** bus stops at Náměstí Republiky and Hlavní Nádraží, the main train station, for 120Kč, taking about 25 minutes to get to central Prague. A cheaper option is to take **bus 119** to Praha-Veleslavín (the last stop) and connect to the metro. From the airport, stride out confidently past the row of taxis and catch bus 119 waiting for you at the next row. Hop on and take it to the Veleslavín stop, where you'll connect directly onto the metro, following the crowds down into the station. Don't worry about which direction to take the metro—you're boarding at the end point and it only goes one direction from here. Your 32Kč ticket is valid through your metro ride, so just hop on and you'll be on your way. The entire journey will take you about 45 minutes. From this metro line, you can connect to any others as well as exit for local trams.

Remember to validate your ticket by plugging it into any of the yellow boxes on board the bus and metro, as plainclothes ticket controllers are quite common.

Train

Prague's main train station, **Hlavní Nádraží**, has numerous daily connections for both national and international destinations. Its location just on the edge of the Old Town makes it easy to connect to your accommodations. Connections run often to Budapest (7 hours), Krakow (8 hours), Vienna (4.5 hours), and Berlin (4.5 hours). Check timetables, find prices, and make reservations online (czech-transport.com).

The station also boasts a convenience store and fast food joints in case you need something for the road.

Bus

International connections into Prague arrive at **Prague Florenc Station,** east of the Old Town. Central Europe has a wide range of bus options. My favorite sites to find connections are Student Agency (studentagencybus.com), Orange Ways (orangeways.com), Berlin Linien Bus (berlinlinienbus.de), and Eurolines (eurolines.com). Florenc has both tram stops and a metro station nearby for local connections.

Car

The Czech Republic has an extensive freeway network. Drives to nearby cities like Budapest (5 hours), Berlin (4 hours), and Vienna (4 hours) are easy.

GETTING AROUND

Prague's relatively compact center is easily walked across in about half an hour. Oftentimes walking is faster than taking a car through the tight, one-way streets of the downtown.

While the communist system didn't work out so well in many ways, it did leave an excellent public transit system of trams, metro lines, and city buses. The **public transportation system** is integrated so the same ticket can be used across all modes of transport. Purchase a **ticket** (24Kč valid for 30 min, 32Kč/90 min) at one of the machines (with coins only!) inside any metro station or at the convenience stores around town and validate it at the top of each escalator. If you'll be zipping across town quite a lot, consider a **day pass** (110Kč) or a **three-day pass** (310Kč). Note that you'll need to use the system at least five times a day to save on those longer passes. Look up routes, delays, and more information at dpp.cz/en.

The public transportation system operates on the honor system, and there are ticket checkers all over the place! Always buy a ticket, and remember to validate it. You may wonder why nobody else is validating theirs: That's because locals have monthly passes that don't need the validations required for single-use tickets.

Metro

The three-line metro system zips you across town in a jiffy. Connections are clearly marked on every landing area with both simplified and full maps on display, making it easy to know where you need to go.

Tram

Trams are an easy way to get across town—and enjoy the views en route. Pick up tickets and validate them on the machines to avoid a hefty fine. Ticket checkers are quite active on the popular and touristy tramlines.

Tram 22 is a great line to take to get oriented to the city, taking you from Královský Letohrádek (near Prague Castle) through Malostranské Náměstí (Lesser Town Square), across the Vltava River, past Národní Divadlo (National Theatre), and down to Národní Třída, which puts you right near the shopping district and Wenceslas Square.

Familiarize yourself with the major landmarks near your accommodations so you can recognize them in the destination list at each tram stop. Each tram has maps inside that highlight your route and allow you to figure out where the heck you're going, but stops only have a list of stop names.

Bus

Unless you're trying to get outside of the city for the day, most tourists generally don't use buses. Thanks to superior city-center tram and metro systems, the bus system mostly offers connections to the suburbs.

Taxi

Prague is definitely a city where you want to call ahead for your taxis. Don't hail taxis on the street. **Nejlevnější Taxi** (+420 226 000 226) is my favorite. Don't even try to pronounce the name; just call the number and be thankful they speak English. This is the cheapest and most reliable company in town. If they're full, call **TickTack** (+420 721 300 300), who provide free water and accept credit cards. If you ever feel you're being ripped off (which happens all the time to tourists), pay a maximum of 300Kč (for a city-center ride), get out of the cab, and pop into your hostel to ask for help. A trip within downtown shouldn't run any more than that. **Uber** and a similar Czech company/app called **HaloTaxi** (+420 244 114 411) are also active in Prague.

Car

With a trusty TomTom, Prague is easy enough to navigate. Do your best to stay away from the Old Town center, where streets were designed for horse and cart and are clogged with modern cars. The city has numerous parking garages throughout. They get cheaper the farther out you stay, so find a parking lot near a far-off metro station for cheaper daily rates. The garage near the Chodov shopping center is right on the red metro line and is staffed, offering rates for around 200Kč per day. There are also numerous park-and-ride (P&R) lots on the outer metro stops that charge only about 25Kč per day but are unguarded.

Bicycle

With its cobblestones and crowds, I don't recommend cycling in downtown Prague. If you love staying active, a tour with **Biko Prague Bike Tours** takes you into hills around Prague for beautiful views of the surrounding countryside.

DAY TRIPS

Český Krumlov

Český Krumlov is a picturesque medieval Czech town in southern Bohemia. If you see a postcard from the Czech Republic and Prague isn't on it, you're probably looking at a shot of Český Krumlov, famous for its quaint small-town atmosphere in a hairpin turn of the river with a picturesque castle looking over it high up on a ridge. This town is worth the 3.5-hour trip out from Prague for an overnight visit to explore the castle and old town, only four blocks across. Remember, a visit is much more pleasant in nice weather—it gets *cold* in January and February, and most of the town's tourist shops and restaurants shut down. Visitors come to enjoy the atmosphere and get away from the big city.

To get there, opt for **Student Agency** buses (studentagencybus.com), which leave from Florenc station. Tickets (210Kč one way) do sell out in advance, so reserve ahead of time.

Trains take about 4.5 hours (around 550Kč) including a transfer in České Budějovice. While more comfortable, this option does take more time, and the train station is a ways from the center of Český Krumlov, so pack light or hail a taxi on arrival.

HELP!

Travel Tips

It is required to have identification on you at all times. If you are a victim of any crime or have lost any of your travel documents (passport, etc), contact the US Embassy and they will sort you out. More and more places accept credit cards these days, but it's good to carry some cash to avoid getting caught in a bind.

Important: Respect local authorities, and don't draw negative attention to yourself. Their English may be limited, and you don't necessarily have the same rights as you may have in the US, so it's best to just fly under the radar and have a nice, jail-free experience. Prague is a safe city, but you can find yourself in trouble when seeking out brothels and drugs.

Tourist Information Center

Find Prague's tourist information center (daily 09:00-21:00, prague-information.eu) just into the Lesser Quarter from Charles Bridge on Mostecká street. Pop in here for help on everything from finding accommodations to booking concerts, bus tours, local guides, and even renting cars.

Mostecká 4, Lesser Quarter

+420 257 213 420

Pickpockets & Scams

Though Prague is a safe city with a low violent crime rate, there are still scams and situations to be mindful of when touring the city, particularly pickpockets. Always keep a close eye on all your valuables, especially in crowded areas such as the city center, public transportation, and nightclubs. If possible, avoid using the taxi service altogether, as many cabbies like to overcharge naïve tourists.

Beware of the sketchy men trying to lure you into the many strip clubs off of Wenceslas Square. Most of these clubs are rip-offs, selling watery cocktails and leaving you broke by the end of the night.

Emergencies

In an emergency, dial 112. Dial 158 for police.

Hospital

Nemocnice Na Františku

Na Františku 8

+420 224 810 502

US Embassy

Tržiště 15

+420 257 022 000

BUDAPEST

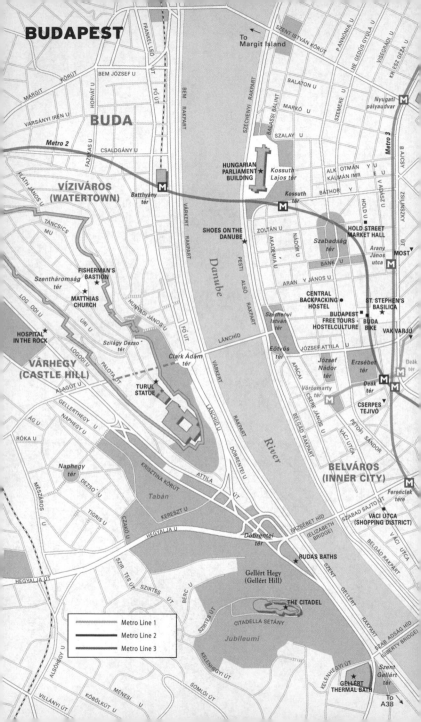

Budapest, with stunning baroque architecture, magnificent bathhouses, and rocking ruin pubs, is unlike any other city you'll visit. Rather than traditional sightseeing, offbeat experiences—from subterranean caving expeditions to escape games to partying on a boat on the Danube—will be the highlight of your trip. But keep your eyes peeled as you wander Budapest's wide boulevards. There's plenty to see. And with lots of fun, social hostels, Budapest fits quite nicely into even the tightest of budgets.

BUDAPEST 101

The Carpathian Basin was settled by Celtic tribes, who were attracted to the area's fertile land and abundant thermal hot springs. Around AD 100, the Romans arrived and established a military encampment, calling it Aquincum in a nod to the region's healing springs. The Romans built roads, baths, and amphitheaters, the foundations of which are still sprinkled around town today.

In 896, the legendary Hungarian—or Magyar—tribes arrived from the east and found the place to their liking. The fabled seven tribes and their brave leader, Arpad, followed their legendary *turul* bird, who carried the sword of the Hungarian people. The bird dropped the sword, and the tribes settled where it landed.

By the early 19th century, Hungary had become a part of the Habsburg Empire, ruling out of Vienna. In 1848, revolution burned through the continent and Hungary followed suit. The Habsburgs made an example of crushing this revolt. Curiously enough, the Hungarians were granted semi-autonomy about 20 years later when the Austrians realized they needed a friendly capital in Hungary. This deal was cemented in the Austro-Hungarian Compromise of 1867, laying the foundations of the Austro-Hungarian Empire, a complicated powder keg of clandestine transcontinental alliances. The assassination of Archduke Franz Ferdinand, heir to the Austro-Hungarian throne, triggered a violent domino effect that ignited World War I.

As a loser, Hungary was sliced up after the war and lost 70 percent of its territories and two-thirds of its population. A couple decades later, World War II brought widespread destruction along with executions and deportations of Budapest's Jews. Hungary was "liberated" by the Russians, but the Soviets hung around for the next few decades. Hungarians rebelled against communist rule by 1956. Thousands fled the country, and it took a massive effort to put down the rebellion.

Hungary, considered the "bread basket" of the Soviet Empire because it produced food that was distributed across the Soviet Bloc, enjoyed a rather privileged position and relatively high standard of living under Soviet rule. Hungarians were even able to leave the country occasionally. That's not to say the populace wasn't policed. The Hungarian secret police (the State Protection Authority, or AVH), were responsible for torture, detentions, and executions that mirrored those of the Nazi SS. By the 1980s, communism was crumbling around the Eastern Bloc, and Hungary was among those celebrating the fall of the Berlin Wall.

In the last 25 years, Budapest has undergone a transformation, but it remains culturally distinct from just about every other European city. You'll see posh shopping boulevards like those in Paris, nightlife a little like Berlin's, a city layout similar to that of Prague (with a river down the middle and a castle on a hill), and a cool vibe like that of East London. There's no other city that rolls all of this into one—and cheaply, at that!

PLAN AHEAD

RESERVATIONS

Reservations are required for the **Hungarian Parliament Building** (parlament.hu/en).

Reservations are recommended for the following activities:

Caving (barlangaszat.hu; tickets can often be bought at your hostel)

Spa parties (bathsbudapest.com/budapest-bath-parties; tickets can often be bought at your hostel)

Budapest Boat Party (facebook.com/BudapestpartyHostels)

LOCAL HAPPENINGS

Sziget Music Festival

Sziget Music Festival (szigetfestival.com), a world-famous, week-long electronic music and dance festival, kicks off each year around August 10, taking over an entire island (Obudai-sziget) 45 minutes north by bus of Budapest. If you want to attend, buy tickets well in advance. My friends and I loved the atmosphere, food options, plentiful porta-potties, and, above all, the always-hot music lineup.

St Stephen's Day

August 20, the country's biggest national holiday, is the Hungarian equivalent of Fourth of July. Named in honor of Hungary's first king, Stephen I, it commemorates the foundation of the Hungarian state. Visitors are welcomed into events like fireworks and general festivities that take place all over the city.

October 23

October 23 marks two important events in Hungarian history: the Revolution of 1956, when the Hungarians rose up against the Soviet Union, and the Day of the Republic, the day in 1989 when communism officially fell and Hungary was declared a republic. The mood is jubilant, but thoughtful, as Hungarians remember those who gave their lives so that Hungary could break away from the Soviet Bloc.

KNOW BEFORE YOU GO
KEY STATS & FIGURES

Currency:
Hungary uses the forint (Ft);
285 Ft = about 1 USD

Population:
9,971,000

Language:
Hungarian

Size of Hungary:
93,000 square kilometers
(about the size of Michigan)

National dish:
goulash and anything spiced with paprika

Number of hot-water springs:
123 in greater Budapest

Famous inventions you never knew were Hungarian:
Rubik's Cube, the ballpoint pen, binoculars, color TV, Microsoft Word and Microsoft Excel, the hydrogen bomb

CALIBRATE YOUR BUDGET
TYPICAL PRICES FOR:

Hostel dorm bed:
4,000Ft

Two-course dinner:
2,000Ft

Pint of beer:
600Ft

Bicycle rental:
3,500Ft

Metro pass:
340Ft

MOVIES TO WATCH
Mission: Impossible—Ghost Protocol, I Spy, 8MM 2, Transporter 3, Munich
VIDEOS TO WATCH
Katy Perry's *Firework*

THREE DAY ITINERARY

Budapest is one of my favorite cities, not just for the culture, affordable prices, food, and nightlife but also because the sights are different from those in most other major cities. Rather than just going from museum to museum, you'll be jumping from one unforgettable activity to the next.

DAY ONE: TO THE BATHHOUSE!

MORNING

Before leaving your hostel, throw a swimsuit in your bag—you'll be visiting the baths later this afternoon. Pop into **Mozsar Kavezo** for breakfast.

From Mozsar Kavezo, it's a five-minute walk to catch a tour with **Yellow Zebra Bike Tour** for an excellent four-hour introduction to the city departing at 11:00 daily (Apr-Oct) from their office just behind the **Hungarian State Opera House**.

AFTERNOON

Finish the bike tour back at the Yellow Zebra office and get a sandwich en route to **Széchenyi Fürdő,** the bathhouse located in the **City Park**. To get to the baths, either take the peaceful 40-minute walk all the way down Andrássy Út or take the yellow metro line toward Mexico and get off at Széchenyi Fürdő.

Spend the afternoon soaking in the baths. Be sure to explore the entire complex, hopping from cold dunk baths to piping hot saunas again and again until you feel rejuvenated! Get a traditional *lángos* (deep-fried flatbread with toppings) at the stand outside the baths on your way out.

EVENING

Head back to the hostel to freshen up, then to a fun Hungarian dinner at one of my favorite spots in town: **Vak Varju**.

LATE

Dinner at Vak Varju puts you in the perfect place to explore the **Gozsdu Court & Passage** and bars in the Jewish Quarter. Or catch back up at the hostel's bar to head out with them on the night's crawl around the city. Lineups for nightly parties change often; Thursday is boat party night!

DAY 2: CAVING & RUIN PUBS

MORNING

Dress comfortably and wear shoes that you can get dirty—you'll be exploring caves later. Purchase tickets from your hostel staff, and confirm meeting place and time before leaving. Shake off your hangover with a bite at the famous **Great Market Hall.** Find shopping and food on the ground floor; fast food, cafés, and lace vendors upstairs; and a real-world standard grocery store downstairs. Stock up a bit for afternoon snacks.

Take a 15-minute walk north along **Váci Utca,** Budapest's main medieval avenue and a touristy shopping street that's parallel to the Danube, till you reach

Vörösmarty Tér, the main town square in Pest. From Vörösmarty Tér, catch tram 2 and ride it a couple stops north toward the **Hungarian Parliament Building**. On a short five-minute ride, you'll see the Danube River, **Castle District**, **Fisherman's Bastion**, the **Shoes on the Danube Memorial** (keep your eyes peeled, they're easy to miss!), and **Gellért Hill** all from the windows of the tram.

If you're interested in going inside the **Hungarian Parliament Building**, make an appointment online ahead of time (tours run at 10:00, 12:00, and 14:00 and take about 1.5 hours, so factor that in with caving)!

AFTERNOON

Catch up with the group meeting for the four-hour **Barlangaszat Caving Tour** at Nyugati station, a 10-minute walk from the Hungarian Parliament Building. Tours occur Monday, Wednesday, Friday, and Saturday afternoons, so purchase tickets and confirm ahead of time through your hostel. The meeting point is at the bus 206 stop, near the cement staircase leading up to the overpass. These guys will take you up to the cave via two buses, so you'll need four metro tickets per person going caving. Enjoy your adventure! Heads up: Your shoes will get dirty with clay, but you'll have coveralls for everything else.

If you're claustrophobic, enjoy another one of Budapest's many thermal baths instead of the caves. For the most authentic, old-school Turkish bath experience, I recommend **Rudas**.

EVENING

Refresh at the hostel, and head to an eclectic dinner at **Most**, not far from the Opera house.

LATE

Head out for a ruin pub crawl of your own, starting at **Instant**, right around the corner from Most, then checking out **Fogashaz** and **Szimpla**. If you're ready to rock 'n' roll, walk the 15 minutes to **Corvinteto**, one of Budapest's rooftop clubs.

DAY 3: JEWISH QUARTER SIGHTS & MARGIT ISLAND

MORNING

Is it Sunday? If so, dive into **Szimpla's farmers market** and get lost in the delicious organic cheeses, pastries, coffees, salami, greens, soups, and more. If it's not Sunday, settle for **Sugar!** and grab a coffee and something sweet.

Szimpla and the farmers market are located in the **Jewish Quarter**, so it's a convenient time to make your way to see the **Dohány Street Synagogue** and the **Raoul Wallenberg Holocaust Memorial Park**.

AFTERNOON

Make your way out to **Margit Island** to explore and rent bikes. On a nice day, it's a perfect place for a picnic alongside the river. Tram 6 will zip you there; get off at the stop at the middle of the bridge directly over the island.

Are you a history buff with energy left? Pick between the **House of Terror** or the **Hospital in the Rock** for mind-blowing historical lessons.

EVENING

When your appetite comes back, head to **Belvarosi Disznotoros** for a cheap, filling meal made in front of your eyes.

LATE

Take part in Budapest's latest craze: **escape games**. A drink or three with dinner makes the games that much more enthralling.

TOP NEIGHBORHOODS

Budapest is large but relatively easy to navigate. The majestic Danube River runs down its center. On the west side is hilly, residential Buda. Pest, on the east side, is flat and sprawling.

Just about all the action happens in Pest, within three major concentric ring roads. Inside the first ring (Karoly/Muzeum/Vámház Körút) is the heart of the medieval town, including the districts of **Leopold Town** (home to the Hungarian Parliament Building and St Stephen's Basilica) and **Pest Town Center,** where the Váci Utca shopping street connects Vörösmarty Tér (Pest's town center) with the Great Market Hall.

The second, larger ring (Szent Istvan/Terez/Josef/Ferenc Körút) encircles **Andrássy Út,** a major boulevard where you'll find the Hungarian State Opera House and House of Terror. Also inside this second ring is the **Jewish Quarter (District VII),** site of the Dohány Street Synagogue and the center of Budapest's raging nightlife scene. East of this second ring road, **City Park** houses the famous Széchenyi baths.

In Buda, the **Castle District** is home to Fisherman's Bastion and Matthias Church. Today, you won't see an actual castle, but this district remains the political heart of historic Budapest. It's full of worthwhile sights, though I rarely pay to enter them, finding their exteriors beautiful enough. To the south, prominent **Gellért Hill** is capped by the Citadel, with Gellért and Rudas baths at the base.

TOP SIGHTS

Hungarian Parliament Building

Budapest's most famous and recognizable landmark, this spectacular building was built in 1896 to commemorate the millennial celebration of Hungary's 896 founding. Topped with 1,896 spires, this massive bicameral structure faces the Castle District and sits right on the Danube. Inspired by Westminster Palace in London, the Parliament building is built in proud and pointy neo-gothic architecture.

The Parliament cost 38 million gold crowns—equal to a sizable chunk of Hungary's GDP—to build. That's nearly US$1.5 billion in today's currency. People were appalled at the price, which could support an entire small city in the countryside. The spire atop the dome is 96 meters tall, of even height with St Stephen's Basilica. During Soviet times, this spire was topped with a massive red star, reminding Hungarians that their rulers in Moscow lorded over all, in both the terrestrial and spiritual worlds. Fun fact: The first ever air-conditioning system was developed and installed in this building. Air is blown over massive ice blocks in the basement and routed up into the large parliament rooms above.

It's possible to take guided tours, but reservations must be made in advance. Free tours run at 10:00, 12:00, 13:00, 14:00, and 15:00 and take about 1.5 hours.

THE NUMBERS GAME

The numbers **7** (the original number of Magyar tribes that settled in the Carpathian Basin), **896** and **1896** (the dates of Hungary's foundation and millennial celebration), and (by extrapolation) **96** are basically all you need to know for just about anything in town. How many points does the Fisherman's Bastion have? 7. How many spires on the Parliament building? 1,896. How tall is St Stephen's Basilica? 96 meters tall. Keep these numbers in mind if you find yourself playing trivia anywhere in town!

5,000Ft, half-price for EU citizens with passport, on Mon when Parliament is in session (usually Sept-May) the only English tour is usually at 10:00, Kossuth Lajos Tér 1-3, Leopold Town, +36 1 441 4000, parlament.hu, Metro: Kossuth Tér

Shoes on the Danube Memorial

Nazi atrocities were carried out across Hungary, and during the winter of 1944 and 1945, the Arrow Cross, or fascist Hungarian puppet police, rounded up Jews from the ghetto, lined them up along the banks of the river, and shot them at close range so they would fall into the river and get washed away. Today, 60 iron pairs of period-accurate men's, women's, and children's shoes are fused to the concrete in the place where these murders occurred. This discreet memorial serves as a reminder about the importance of remaining vigilant against bigotry and ignorance. Use caution when crossing the street and tram tracks to get to the memorial.

Free, always open, two blocks south along the river from the Parliament building, Leopold Town, Metro: Kossuth Tér

St Stephen's Basilica

St Stephen's bold neoclassical architecture, with twin bell towers and prominent dome and spire, is recognizable from anywhere in town. On entry, you may be hassled by someone requiring donations, but the church is free to enter. You can find the famous shriveled hand of Saint Stephen in the back of the church toward the left of the altar. It is possible to climb the dome for less than US$2, but the views aren't particularly amazing.

Interior free, 500Ft for observation deck, Mon 09:00-16:30, Tues-Fri 09:00-17:00, Sat 09:00-13:00, Sun 13:00-17:00, Szent István Tér 1, Leopold Town, +36 1 311 0839, bazilika.biz, Metro: Bajcsy-Zsilinszky Út

House of Terror

The House of Terror occupies what used to be the headquarters of both the Nazi SS and the Communist Party Police, Arrow Cross. It's best for those who are very interested in WWII and communist history. The interactive exhibits walk you through daily life under communism, including a stomach-turning room stacked floor to ceiling with lard, the most common cooking ingredient at the time due to lack of butter and olive oil. Descend into the basement via a slow elevator while listening to the chilling tales of an executioner who worked his trade here. While it's famous and well-done, I do get the sense it's a bit commercial and made for mass market school groups.

2,000Ft, Tues-Sun 10:00-18:00, last entry 30 minutes before closing, Andrássy Út 60, Andrássy Út, +36 1 374 2600, terrorhaza.hu, Metro: Vörösmarty Utca

Turul Bird Statue

Legend has it that the Hungarian tribes would settle and flourish in the place where the *turul* (the mythical bird of Hungarian folklore) dropped its Magyar sword. Commonly thought to be a falcon, the *turul* is often represented in statues and on coins throughout Budapest. The most majestic statue in town is perched, sword-in-claws, in the Castle District, looking out to Pest. Don't miss the selfie-op with the Hungarian National Guard standing at attention nearby.

Free, always open, Castle District, Metro: Szell Kálmán Tér

Matthias Church

The majestic neo-gothic Matthias Church is famous for its beautiful white stone architecture and colorful roof tiling typical in Hungary, which comes from the town of Pecs. Though its foundations date back to 1015, the church appears brand-new thanks to recent renovations. The relatively steep entry fee (US$5) keeps many content with the exterior, but those who go inside are treated to a holy Technicolor kaleidoscope of decorations on nearly every square inch of the columns, arches, ribs, altar, stained glass, and pulpit.

1,400Ft, Mon-Fri 09:00-17:00, Sat 09:00-13:00, Sun 13:00-17:00, possibly open later in summer, Szentháromság Tér 2,

Castle District, +36 1 355 5657, Metro: Szell Kálmán Tér

Fisherman's Bastion

With a name like Fisherman's Bastion, not many people know what to expect. Don't look for it on the river. The gleaming white ramparts with seven pointed turrets are perched high on the hill and afford stunning panoramas across the Danube and over the Parliament building and into Pest. Constructed in 1896 to commemorate the millennial celebration of Hungary, the decorative bastion symbolically represents the seven Hungarian tribes. Climb the stairs for a small fee and slightly better view, or come after sunset and go for free! From the Fisherman's Bastion you can see all of Pest and a beautiful-yet-distant view of the Parliament building. If you cross back through the Castle District to the other side, you can peer out across the hills of Buda as well.

700Ft, mid-Mar-mid-Oct daily 09:00-19:30, open and free to enter after closing time or off season, Szentháromság Tér 5, Castle District, +36 1 458 3030, fishermansbastion.com, Metro: Szell Kálmán Tér

Hospital in the Rock

This cave network underneath the Budapest castle originated as a storage space but was widened to become a hospital during World War II, and it served hundreds of patients. Later on, it was used as a nuclear bunker during the Cold War. With some impressive engineering, the hospital was designed to withstand nuclear attack and provide emergency medical assistance. This bunker also acted as the control center of the commanding elite for continuing the war effort in the case of nuclear war. Today, you can take a fascinating guided tour of these tunnels—well worth it for history buffs!

4,000Ft, daily 10:00-20:00, last tour departs at 19:00, Lovas Way 4/c, Castle District, +36 70 701 0101, sziklakorhaz.eu, Metro: Szell Kálmán Tér

Hungarian State Opera House

The Hungarian State Opera House was constructed during the height of the Austro-Hungarian Empire in 1884. As the second capital of the great Hapsburg Empire, Budapest simply had to have an opera house, and license was granted to build one—as long as it wasn't bigger than the one in Vienna. Playing within the rules, the architects sought to make this opera house grander—not bigger—than the one in their rival sister city. Through their proud neo-Renaissance architecture and gilded golden concert hall comfortably seating over 1,400 in three levels of balconies and a large main audience floor, I'd say they achieved their goals! Both the exterior and interior are breathtaking with opulent baroque decorations.

Free to pop in to the lobby, Mon-Sat 11:00 until show time, usually 19:00, or until 17:00 if there's no performance, Sun open 3 hours before performance, usually 16:00-19:00, or 10:00-13:00 if there's a matinee, English tours daily at 15:00 during high season (June-Oct) for 2,900Ft, mini concerts often for the screaming deal of 600Ft, check show calendar and prices online, Andrássy Út 22, Andrássy District, +36 1 814 7100, opera.hu, Metro: Opera

Dohány Street Synagogue

With the capacity to seat nearly 3,000 worshippers, the Dohány Street Synagogue (also known as the Great Synagogue) is the second largest synagogue in the world. The architects deliberately toned down the structure to blend in with the surrounding architecture, so the structure's massive size isn't evident from the outset. While Budapest's Jewish population still hasn't recovered from the deportation of 600,000 Hungarian Jews during the Holocaust, the synagogue stands proud and serves the 100,000 Jews living in Budapest today. Your ticket also includes entry to the modest **National Jewish Museum,** showcasing artifacts of daily life and culture like Torah scrolls, artwork, sculpture, and menorahs from traditional to modern, along with a room about the atrocities of the Holocaust.

If you don't want to pay to enter the synagogue, you can still appreciate the beautiful facade and cemetery, visible from Wesselenyi Utca. The striking **Raoul Wallenberg Holocaust Memorial Park** is in the back garden of the Dohány Street Synagogue but is also visible from the street. It's designed in the shape of a weeping willow, which also bears resemblance to an overturned menorah. Each of the thousands of shimmering leaves bears the name of a Hungarian victim of Nazi hate crimes. The space is named after Raoul Wallenberg, a Swedish world traveler, son of a wealthy diplomat, and playboy turned unlikely hero. Wallenberg secretly helped to rush emergency (read: official yet fake) Swedish passports to thousands of Jewish families, protecting them from deportation during the Nazi occupation. Exhibiting both bravery and cunning in the face of danger, Wallenberg saved the lives of thousands of Hungarian Jews.

3,000Ft, Mar-Oct Sun-Thurs 10:00-17:30, Fri 10:00-16:30, closed Sat, closes at 15:30 Fri in Mar; Nov-Feb Sun-Thurs 10:00-15:30, Fri 10:00-13:30, closed Sat; refer to website for the annual list of days closed, Dohány Utca 2, Jewish Quarter, greatsynagogue.hu, Metro: Astoria

The Citadel

This decommissioned military fort now offers the best viewpoint to see both the castle and Pest, but it's a hike to get to the top. Start the climb after crossing either Erzsebet Bridge or Szabadsag Bridge. Allow about three hours total to get up, check out the views, and get back down again.

Free, daily 11:00-23:00, Citadella Sétány 1, Gellért Hill, Metro: Ferenciek Tere or Kálvin Tér

TOP HUNGARIAN BATHHOUSES

A visit to Budapest is simply not complete without a dunk in at least one of the city's invigorating aquatic wonderlands. This is the most popular activity (and my personal favorite thing to do) in Budapest. Water in this region comes out of the ground nearly boiling at 170 degrees Fahrenheit. It's just a matter of how much they cool the water before channeling it into the beautiful public bathhouses and pool complexes. While you have numerous choices in this city, these are a few of my favorites.

Széchenyi Fürdő

This is the most famous bathhouse, and the best one for first-timers in Budapest. Széchenyi is a delightful jumble of steam rooms, saunas, pools, and baths both outside and inside this grand yellow baroque complex. While away the hours wandering through this labyrinth, trying each room and pool along the way, enjoying the rejuvenating qualities of this special water. Purchase your wristband upon entry, go downstairs to claim a locker, change and shower, then hit the large outdoor pools open year-round (two lounging pools and one lap pool, swim cap required). Look for small stone plaques denoting the temperature of each bath or room, with 20°C being as cold as you can stand, and 40°C being as hot as you'd want. I recommend going in the entrance closest to the permanent circus toward the back, the side facing away from downtown.

4,500Ft, for locker, 500Ft more for personal changing cabin, cheaper after 19:00 and more expensive on weekends, daily 06:00-22:00, thermal bath open 6:00-19:00, may be open later on summer weekends, last entry one hour before closing, inside the City Park (on the Pest side of the capital, just beyond Hero's Square), City Park, szechenyibath.com, Metro: Széchenyi Fürdő

Rudas

Rudas is your legit Turkish bath, with low lights, burning hot steam rooms, and *ice-cold* dunk baths. With no frills and only six pools, as compared to Széchenyi's 18, Rudas still features a wider range of temperatures (18-42°C), perfect for those who want the real experience. This is the only bath in Budapest that still offers gender-segregated days during the week (during which suits are optional) and mixed-gender bathing from Friday evening through Sunday (bathing suits required).

3,000Ft, men only Mon, Wed, Thurs, Fri 06:00-20:00; women only Tues 06:00-20:00; gender mixed Fri 22:00-04:00, Sat 06:00-20:00 and 22.00-04:00, Sun 06:00-20:00, Rudas Gyógyfürdő és Uszoda, Gellért Hill, +36 1 356 1010, rudasbaths.com, Metro: Szent Gellért Tér, Tram: Döbrentei Tér

Gellért

Widely regarded as the most posh bathhouse in Budapest, Gellért is also part of a five-star hotel by the same name. Gellért features an outdoor wave pool (generally open in the summer) that toes a dangerous line. A handful of interior rooms are gender separated so you can really let it hang out. Gellért is located on the southern part of the city center, on the Buda side, adjacent to Liberty Bridge.

4,900Ft for locker, 400Ft more for personal changing cabin, cheaper after 17:00, last entry one hour before closing, daily 06:00-20:00, Kelenhegyi Út 4, Gellért Hill, +36 1 466 6166, gellertbath.com, Metro: Szent Gellért Tér

ACT LIKE A LOCAL

Splish, Splash: Hungarian Bathhouse Etiquette

Here are some general rules and tips so you can skip that confused feeling when heading into Budapest's *fürdő* (baths):

Don't show up on the wrong day. Certain baths have days for men (*férfi*), days for women (*noi*), and gender-combined days, though most have shifted toward being open for everyone every day of the week.

Go for privacy, or let it all hang out. Private changing closets, which you can share with friends, are available but a little more expensive than the standard communal (gender-segregated) changing areas and lockers.

Consider a massage. You can opt for massages by speaking with the women just inside the paid entryway. They'll be holding a clipboard with information, and relatively good deals can be had in these bathhouses for a nice massage.

Skip the medical treatments. Thermal and mineral spas are recognized in Hungary to have serious health benefits. Doctors actually prescribe a whole host of treatments. You may see a list of such treatments, which can be confusing. Just make it clear you want the basic entry.

Your wristband is your entry ticket, your locker access, and your exit ticket. This is what you receive when you pay your entry fee. Put your wristband on and hold it up to the button on your locker to lock and unlock it. That's also how you "claim" an empty locker—by placing and pushing your wristband against it. You can open and close your locker as many times as you want. If you forget your locker number, find the little box with a screen mounted on the wall in the locker room. Hold your wristband up to it and it will light up with your locker number.

Bring your own suit and towels to save $$$. Towels and swimsuits are generally available for rent from the service desk inside the complex.

Consider bringing flip-flops. They're nice to have in the showers and for getting around the various pools, but not required.

Don't be afraid to ask for help. It may seem like everyone knows what they're doing, but don't worry, they don't! Locker room attendants are there to assist with any questions you may have. They usually answer you in English, or at least they can find someone who does speak English.

TOP EATS

Traditional Hungarian food is simple and based mostly on meat and potatoes. Classic dishes like **goulash** (spiced beef stew ladled over dumplings or gnocchi-like noodles) are cheap—so cheap that nicer restaurants are shifting away from authentic Hungarian food in order to justify a higher price point!

Budapest's cuisine reflects its reputation as Europe's most diverse city. One street in particular overflows with all sorts of international cuisine: **Kazinczy Utca,** located in the Jewish Quarter. Beyond the fast food joints on this street, you also have food options inside the ruin pubs Szimpla and Ellato Kert, and a new food garden just opened up in an empty space two doors down from Szimpla. **Gozsdu Court & Passage,** located between Dob Utca 16 and Király Utca 13 in the Jewish Quarter (a couple blocks west of Kazinczy Utca) is a great nightlife district, but you'll also find restaurant after great restaurant, including an amazing burger joint, authentic Italian and pizza, Asian, and more.

Tipping is not expected, but it is appreciated. Touristy restaurants have come to expect tips, and some will automatically put an "optional" tip on your bill. So be sure to read each line item to understand how you got to your total and to avoid tipping twice. If you loved your service, round your bill up about 10 percent.

Kiado Kocsma

I stumbled upon this gem and found myself going back again and again for a hearty plate of ham and eggs for only about US$3! Couldn't ask for anything more to start off your day. Come back in the afternoon for the goulash soup or to split their heaping meat dish with your travel buddy. If you've got to catch up on emails, Kiado Kocsma is a great place to post up and pound through a little work, sharing the cozy space with other young locals with the same idea.

700-1,500Ft, Mon-Fri 10:00-01:00, Sat-Sun 11:00-01:00, Jokai Tér 3, Andrássy District, +36 1 331 1955, facebook. com/kiadokocsma, Metro: Oktogon

Mozsar Kavezo

Mozsar Kavezo has all the necessities in a modish café: fresh pastries, good coffee, hot breakfast menu, and fast Wi-Fi. What's not to love? Located near a number of recommended hostels, just off Andrássy Út and near the opera house, it's a great place to grab breakfast. On a hot day, the large windows turn the place into a stuffy greenhouse, so I take my breakfast to go.

Pastries from 300Ft, daily 09:00-23:00, Nagymező Utca 21, Andrássy District, +36 1 898 1115, facebook.com/ mozsarkavezo, Metro: Opera

Vak Varju

If you're looking for a bit of traditional Hungarian at an affordable price, this is the place for you. Try their goulash or duck entrée and you won't be disappointed. Vak Varju was started by a group of enterprising friends, and I like the modern yet subtly irreverent decor. Eat under the watchful eyes of your Hungarian grandma and grandpa leaning over the balcony railing, and discover surprises in both bathrooms. If you're thirsty or sitting with friends, the 3.5-liter beer tower comes with your own tap and is a great way to start the night. Their pizza bread is delicious as well.

900-2,000Ft, daily 11:00-24:00, Paulay Ede Utca 7, Andrássy District, +36 1 268 0888, vakvarju.com, Metro: Bajcsy-Zsilinszky Út

Most

This candlelit restaurant offers a little bit of everything—from the most decadent chocolate chip pancake brunch to chicken tikka masala and pad thai dinners. The atmosphere is great, and the menu caters to everyone. The service, unfortunately, is consistently disappointing.

Moderate prices, daily 10:00-05:00, Zichy Jeno Ucta 17, Andrássy District, +36 70 248 3322, mostjelen.hu, Metro: Arany János Utca

Leves

Hungarians are a straightforward bunch, so it's no surprise that they appreciate the literal the name of this quick lunch stop: Leves means soup in Hungarian. And man, they make some delicious soup! Choose from four daily specials, fill up a small or large bowl to go, and deck it out with chunky croutons. This makes for a great quick lunch, and it's just down the way from the Great Market Hall.

Soups from 700Ft, daily 11:00-19:00, 14 Vámház Körút, Pest Town Center, +36 30 241 7760, facebook.com/levespont, Metro: Kalvin Tér

Cserpes Tejivo Milk Bar

Milk bars—bars that sold subsidized milk to comrades to ensure everyone was fit and healthy—were a communist institution. In perfect Budapest hipster fashion, Cserpes Tejivo has taken this concept and infused it with a modern twist. With great sandwiches, delicious sweets, and, of course, fresh milk (of the normal, chocolate, and butterscotch varieties) in the middle of downtown, this is an excellent stop for brunch or lunch.

Sandwiches from 700Ft, Mon-Sat 07:30-22:00, 2 Suto Utca, Pest Town Center, cserpestejivo.hu, Metro: Deak Ferenc Tér

Sugar!

Designed and owned by the daughter of a big café family in town, Sugar! is your typical sugar shack, yet amped up another level with handmade cupcakes and desserts, plus coffee. My go-to is the sweet rice pudding with a dash of cinnamon sugar on top. One order is plenty to share between two or three people.

Sweets from 600Ft, Mon 12:00-22:00, Tues-Sun 10:00-22:00, 48 Paulay Ede Utca, Andrássy District, +36 1 321 6672, sugarshop.hu, Metro: Opera

FOR THE LOVE OF *LÁNGOS*

Lángos (LON-gohsh) is a favorite local savory or sweet treat. Think of it as a deep-fried elephant ear from the carnival covered in all sorts of ingredients of your choice, such as sour cream, cheese, and garlic, or even sugar and almonds and peanuts. *Lángos* are sold from street stands and kiosks throughout the city, so if you see one, go for it! They're rich and heavy enough to be split by at least two if not three or four people—and only after your trip to the baths.

Belvarosi Disznotoros

Pop in here for fresh grilled meat and veggies. Think of it like a Hungarian food court, where you point to your choice to the attendant, and they flash-grill it right in front of you and you then take your tray upstairs to enjoy a piping hot meal. The name translates to "downtown pork," and it's a meat lover's paradise with steaks, ribs, sausages, bacon, and more to enjoy. It's right next to the Gozsdu Court & Passage.

Pay by weight, so don't let those eyes get too big! Mon-Sat 07:00-22:00, Karolyi Utca 17, Pest Town Center, +36 1 267 3795, Metro: Ferenciek Tere

Bors GasztroBar

A welcome player on the Kazinczy Utca restaurant lineup, Bors makes excellent sandwiches and innovative soups (like red cabbage and sour cherry), and it packs out with locals day in and day out. Pop in here if you need a break from the Szimpla hubbub.

Sandwiches from 900Ft, Mon-Sat 11:30-21:00, 10 Kazinczy Utca, Jewish Quarter, +36 70 935 3263, Metro: Astoria

Abszolut Pho

With functional, takeaway-style decor, this is a great choice for a light meal of super fresh pho. I appreciate the classy sister bar next door and the restaurant seating upstairs above it.

Dishes from 900Ft, Tues-Sun 18:00-22:00, 52/C Kazinczy Utca, Jewish Quarter, +36 70 551 7630, Metro: Opera

Kis Parazs Thai

I've got to recommend a hot Thai place in just about every city, and this is my favorite in Budapest, located just across the street from the famous Szimpla ruin pub. The curries and pad thai are just killer! If you ask for spicy, they make it kick-ass Thai spicy (read: bleary eyes, running nose, sweating buckets, pure heaven).

Mains from 1,700Ft, Mon-Sat 12:00-22:00, 7 Kazinczy Utca, Jewish Quarter, +36 30 733 7760, parazspresszo.com, Metro: Astoria

El Rapido

I love a good Tex-Mex joint, and you can't beat these prices for a tasty freshly made burrito at just about any hour of the day. The ingredients, service, beer selection, and ambience are all winners. But the food consistently takes forever. Do they need to turn up their grills? If you're good to suck down a beer while waiting, it's well worth it. And don't miss the thousands of retro blast-from-the-past games and toys downstairs, like Connect Four and Hungry Hungry Hippos.

Burritos from 1,000Ft, Mon-Fri 10:30-late, Sat 12:00-late, Sun 17:00-02:00, 10 Kazinczy Utca, Jewish Quarter, +36 30 279 2861, elrapido.hu, Metro: Astoria

TOP NIGHTLIFE

You can have an incredible time out on the town in Budapest—especially in the Jewish Quarter (District VII). Drinks are cheap, and the experiences are as eclectic as it gets. Most hostels in town do a great job of arranging party nights out just about every night of the week. Get ready for a wild ride!

NIGHTLIFE DISTRICTS

Nagymező Utca, Király Utca & Kazinczy Utca

Nightlife centers on Király Utca and Kazinczy Utca, two intersecting streets in the Jewish Quarter, and Nagymező Utca, not far from Andrássy Út. On these streets, you'll find some of Budapest's best ruin bars, including **Ellato Kert, Kurplung,** and **Szimpla.** Along with nearby Gozsdu Court,

these venues really define the vibe of the Jewish Quarter.

Jewish Quarter, Metro: Opera

Gozsdu Court & Passage

There's no stretch of the city that is more quintessentially Budapest than Gozsdu Court & Passage, located between Dob Utca and Király Utca. Just a few years ago, this passage was just another dark alleyway.

Now there are dozens of bars, restaurants, pop-up shops, and more. Head toward the action, and to your left and to your right bar after bar and restaurant after restaurant are packed out with Budapest's young, sexy, in-the-know crowd. In one block, you've got **Epic Winebar,** a chill British-style pub called **The Pointer,** and **Kolor,** an upscale lounge and restaurant. In good weather, find the **Gozsdu Sky Terrace** for rooftop views across downtown Budapest. This district is a bit posh, so prices will be rather "Western."

Jewish Quarter, Metro: Deak Ferenc Tér

RUIN PUBS

After World War II, many bombed-out buildings were never fully restored and rested empty for decades. Eventually, pubs started moving in to these old tenement houses and run-down factories, transforming them into a cornerstone of BP's nightlife. Cool, eh? These pubs incorporate salvaged furniture, items from old community centers, cinemas, boats, and even donations from older residents of Budapest. The mismatching trinkets and knickknacks lying around only add to the peculiar ambience these pubs emanate. I've listed some of my favorites below, but don't be afraid to pop into any scene that looks intriguing.

You'll notice *kert* (garden) in the titles of most of the bars, meaning there's an outdoor space somewhere in the complex— great to enjoy the warm summer evenings. In winter, bars often cover the gardens with heavy tarps so you can still take in the fresh air without freezing your bum off.

Szimpla

Budapest's most famous ruin bar, Szimpla, is a can't-miss on your BP pub crawl. With everything from swinging gnomes to ski racks and umbrellas hanging on the walls, the place is packed out year-round with a hipster crowd, minus the pretentiousness that usually comes with it. Grab a beer and get lost in this multi-floor labyrinth of rooms, hallways, and balconies. Hookahs are a great way to make friends, so put in your order to the left as you enter, and find a comfy place to chill. Don't be surprised if someone comes up to you selling carrots out of a basket—just embrace the eclectic vibe and enjoy. And don't miss the local organic farmers market inside the bar each Sunday morning (09:00-14:00).

Daily 12:00-04:00, Kazinczy Utca 14, Jewish Quarter, +36 20 261 8669, szimpla.hu, Metro: Astoria

Instant (aka Enchanted Forest)

This mainstay of Budapest's famous ruin bars is a labyrinth of cubbies and rooms sprinkled across several floors. Everything centers around one massive owl mounted on the wall chasing dozens of styrofoam bunnies suspended in a net.

Daily 16:00-late, Nagymező Utca 38, Andrássy District, +36 1 311 0704, instant.co.hu/en, Metro: Oktogon

Fogashaz & Fogashaz Kert

Recently given a face-lift, these are two adjacent bars, with the Kert being the outdoor garden pub. *Fogas* translates to "teeth," and *haz* means "house"; welcome to the Teeth-house. Enjoy excellent music in both bars, fast service, and a chill crowd keeping the party going till late.

Daily 14:00-late, Akácfa Utca 51, Jewish Quarter, +36 1 783 8820, fogashaz.hu, Metro: Opera

Kuplung

A recent entry into the ruin bar scene, Kuplung has taken over a former mechanic's shop, letting you chill out, drink up, play some Ping Pong, and get your dance on all in one go. The music changes often, with skilled DJs spinning away nightly and a dance floor just big enough to let loose with your friends.

Daily 17:00-late, Király Utca 46, Jewish Quarter, +36 30 755 3527, kuplung.net, Metro: Opera

Ellato Kert

While this is one of the more low-key ruin pubs, the crowds keep coming back for the foosball tables and the amazing tacos sold just inside to the left. While the other ruin pubs have clearly seen the money to be made off the tourist obsession with edgy-yet-clean-and-bright ruin bars, Ellato hasn't quite got the memo, making me think it's one of the more authentic ruin bars on Kazinczy.

Mon-Wed 17:00-02:00, Thurs-Fri 17:00-late, Sat 18:00-late, Sun 18:00-02:00, 48 Kazinczy Utca, Jewish Quarter, +36 20 527 3018, Metro: Opera

Anker't

Anker't is a new bar and club that reminds me more of the Meatpacking District, NYC: exposed brick, warehouse feel, large bars, and an excited the-night-is-young vibe. The wide open layout makes socializing easy. This is my pick for a fun place to pregame the busier ruin pubs and clubs just around the corner, like Fogashaz and Szimpla.

Mon-Sun 16:00-03:00, 33 Paulay Ede Utca, Andrássy District, +36 30 360 3389, ankerklub.hu, Metro: Opera

NIGHTCLUBS

A night out in Budapest starts early at the bars and ruin pubs and runs late at the clubs. My favorites will leave you looking forward to soaking away your hangover in the spas the next day.

Corvinteto

Corvinteto feels like a '90s life-is-plastic rooftop dance bar in an old, gray communist-style building just outside the Jewish Quarter. Finding the place is a bit tricky, because it's hidden down a side street and up a cargo elevator, but it's well worth the trip if you can figure it out. The guys/gals ratio often skews toward gentleman-heavy, but if the scenery inside doesn't match your tastes, at least you've got a panorama of the city outside to enjoy.

Cover varies, beers from 500Ft, Blaha Lujza Tér 1-2, Jewish Quarter, corvinteto.hu, Metro: Blaha Lujza Tér

360 Bar

This rooftop club is on Andrássy between Oktogon and the opera house. While the staff and cocktails come with a bit of an attitude, the views over all of downtown Budapest are the best in town, and there's an unobstructed view of the Parliament dome. Go on a warm summer afternoon or for the sunset and enjoy a beer or cocktail. By wintertime, it gets too cold to enjoy.

No cover, cocktails from 1,750Ft, beer from 500Ft, Sun-Wed 14:00-24:00, Thurs-Sat 14:00-03:00, Andrássy Út 39, Andrássy District, 360bar.hu, Metro: Oktogon

A38

Always wanted to party on a boat? Step onto this Soviet Ukrainian ship-turned-nightclub that's docked on the Danube, just south of Gellért Hill, and rock the night away on their three different dance floors. Heralded by guidebooks as the best club in the world in 2012, A38 is well worth a visit.

Entry usually free, beers from 450Ft, Buda side of Petofi Bridge, Gellért Hill, a38.hu

PARTIES YOU'LL ONLY FIND IN BUDAPEST

Spa Parties

Someone once had the brilliant idea of bringing in strobe lights, lasers, a DJ, sound system, wet bar, and smoke machines into the bathhouses of Budapest for a massive, raging spa party, and "sparties" were born. They took off in popularity, and each sparty is a guaranteed wild time. To look past the rampant hooking up and floating condoms, you'll need to be well lubricated yourself with as much Jägermeister as you can keep down. If that doesn't sound like your thing, steer clear! Sparties happen often during high season and at different bathhouses, so be sure to ask at your hostel about your

options. Book tickets online at sites like Széchenyispabaths.com/sparties, at the ticket office on Szabadsag Tér, or through your hostel when you arrive. Tickets run about €35 or 10,000Ft.

Shipwrecked Boat Party

My friends at Budapest Boat Party put on an aquatic rager every Monday, Thursday, and Friday. Rock out on a 2.5-hour cruise up and down the Danube with drink specials and a full-on maritime dance floor underneath the floodlit Hungarian Parliament Building and Fisherman's Bastion of the Castle District. The folks at Budapest Party Hostels take guests at all five of their locations on the Thursday cruise weekly. Book tickets online.

5,000-7,500Ft (additional 1,500Ft for optional bottle of champagne—everyone does it), meeting points vary, confirm online, embarking at 22:00 on Mon, 22:30 on Thurs, and 23:00 Fri, +36 30 908 7598, budapestboatparty.com

PUB CRAWLS

Many hostels in Budapest organize their own pub crawls. The **Budapest Party Hostels** network will never leave you lacking on your desired nightlife endeavors. Organized pub crawls help to get you oriented in the maze of streets that make up District VII.

HostelCulture Backpacker Pub Crawl

My friends at HostelCulture put together a nightly party that takes you to the hottest spots across town. Join their free daytime walking tour, get a free welcome beer and welcome shots along the way, and cap the night off in a club with the nightly pub crawl.

Every night 20:00-21:00 at the first bar, meets at Akvarium Club, Erzebet Tér 12, Leopold Town, +36 70 424 05 69, backpackerpubcrawl.com/Budapest, Metro: Vörösmarty Tér

TOP SHOPPING & MARKETS

Budapest is a paradise for those looking for retro clothes and nostalgic memorabilia. And the Great Market Hall and shopping streets are can't-miss attractions. Typical Hungarian souvenirs are hand-made woven goods, ceramics, woodcarving, and pottery. Don't be afraid to haggle, and be sure to decide what the piece is worth to you before you start negotiations!

SHOPPING DISTRICTS
Váci Utca

Starting at Pest's central square, Vörösmarty Tér, and continuing down to the Great Market Hall, Váci Utca is medieval Budapest's main street. Find kitschy touristy restaurants and all the cliché goods like postcards, traditional clothing, and souvenirs in this popular pedestrian shopping district. You'll pay for the convenience and bright lights with higher prices. Look for Hungary's famous herbal liqueur, **Unicum.** And the beautiful handmade lace makes for an excellent present for loved ones back home.

Pest Town Center, Metro: Vörösmarty Tér or Fővám Tér

MARKETS
Szimpla Farmers Market

One of the coolest markets you'll ever see is the farmers market in the Szimpla ruin pub on Sunday mornings. It's a surreal experience to party late in the bar, then return the next morning and see farmers who have just brought in their harvest to sell at the market, probably arriving just minutes after you called it a night.

Free, Sun 09:00-14:00, Kazinczy Utca 14, Jewish Quarter, szimpla.hu, Metro: Astoria

Great Market Hall

Yet another beautiful building from the Hungarian millennial anniversary of 1896. Find produce and meat on the ground floor; souvenirs, a café, and cheap eats upstairs; and a large modern supermarket downstairs. Great Market Hall is on the southern border of Pest Town Center.

Free, Mon-Fri 06:00-18:00, Sat 06:00-15:00; Vámház Körút 1-3, Pest Town Center, Metro: Fővám Tér or Kálvin Tér

Hold Street Market Hall (Hold Utcai Piac)

For a more off-the-beaten-path market experience, drop into the Hold Street Market Hall. Located just behind the US Embassy, it was built in 1897 and has nearly 400 stalls for vendors selling everything from cheeses and breads to salami and paprika. The Great Market Hall may have a wider selection, but I like this market for its yet-undiscovered ambience.

Free, Mon 06:30-17:00, Tues-Fri 06:30-18:00, Sat 06:30-14:00, Hold Utca 13, Leopold Town, +36 1 353 1110, Metro: Arany János Utca

BUDAPEST

PARKS

City Park

The largest green space in the city is northeast of town. In the park, you'll find the **Vajdahunyad Castle** (free, always open), built in—you guessed it—1896 to show off the various architectural styles found throughout the country. The original was built out of wood and canvas but was so popular that a permanent version soon took its place. You'll see styles reminiscent of Romanesque, gothic, Renaissance, and baroque periods in this one funky structure. Deeper into the park are the **Széchenyi baths** and a circus. Get to City Park by hopping on the yellow (line 1) metro and riding it to the Széchenyi Fürdő stop.

Free, always open, City Park, Metro: Széchenyi Fürdő

Margit Island

This island in the Danube River is long and skinny. In the summertime and shoulder season, you'll find tons of bars, pools, and spas open to enjoy. Renting a four-seater pedal bike (about 2,500Ft/hour) is always a favorite—especially of Italian tourists. Toss a liter or three of beer into your caddy and you're ready to cruise!

Margit Island is accessible via Margit Bridge on the south side and Arpad Bridge on the north side. Both bridges are open to pedestrians.

Free, always open, Margit Island, Metro: Nyugati Pályaudvar

CAVING

Barlangaszat Caving Tour

Under the hills of Buda lies a vast network of limestone caves both discovered and undiscovered. Get ready to get down and dirty as you explore them—you need to be flexible and able to crawl through tight spaces. You'll follow your professional English-speaking caving guides several chambers deep into the earth, crawling on your hands and knees in the passageways between each stop. The casual guides like to share stories and break down the geology of how caves occur. They also watch their group to determine the difficulty of the route.

These tight tunnels are not for the faint of heart, and definitely are not for the claustrophobic, but they're highly recommended!

Wear comfortable shoes and clothes. Jeans get tight when crawling around, so stretchy shorts or athletic pants are your best bet. The provided coveralls protect your clothes, but shoes will get some Hungarian clay souvenirs.

Barlangaszat is currently the only operation that has a license to take visitors down into the caves. Availability is limited and often sells out in advance. Reserve ahead via email or through your hostel on your arrival day. Do the tours run during the rain? Yes, caves are unaffected by rain outside, and the temperature stays at about 55°F year-round.

Tours meet at the bus 206 stop at Nyugati station, near the funky low-cover staircase leading up to the overpass. Guides will take you up to the caving via two buses, so you'll need four metro tickets per person. Or get there yourself by taking bus 65, which leaves from Kolosy square. Step off at the fifth bus stop, named Pál-völgyi.

5,500Ft, four-hour tours Mon, Wed, Fri, and Sat afternoons, Tues and Thurs mornings, barlangaszat.hu, info@barlangaszat.hu, Metro: Nyugati Pályaudvar

ESCAPE GAMES

I was skeptical when my friend wanted to bring me to the escape games that are taking Budapest by storm, but I've become a fan. Here's how the games work: After a briefing laced with hints, you and your friends are locked into a room. These rooms are monitored by your "puzzle master," whom you can ask for hints if you run into a roadblock during the challenge. You get about 60 minutes to solve the series of challenges and escape...or be lost forever.

Go for the themes that intrigue you the most. Prices are generally set per game, getting cheaper for each person you add. The abundant decrepit buildings across town have lent a natural setting to these exciting puzzles. Some hints from yours truly to get your head in the right place: Embrace the challenge enthusiastically; try every idea that comes up; don't stop communicating with your teammates; look everywhere in the room—up, down, over, behind, etc; be on the lookout for time-wasting decoys; and, finally, don't take it all too seriously. Have fun!

I picked the top three based on friendliness of the staff, price, value, location (all in the Jewish Quarter, near the bars), and the success of their themes—they can get pretty creative. In addition to these recommendations, I also enjoyed **Mystique Room** (Egyptian and Cathedral themes, mystique-room.hu), **Escape Zone** (Rescue the Captive theme, escapezone.hu), **PANIQROOM** (Saw and Lost themes, paniqszoba.hu), and **Exit Point** (Mirror House, Madness, and Rabbit Hole themes, exitpointgames.hu). There are so many popping up throughout the city that these may change in time and new ones may become more popular.

Emergency Exit Escape Games
Descend a few steps into this nondescript little complex. The friendly staff sits you around a table and preps you for the challenge to come. Read the details of their hint sheet, and do your best to get out in 60 minutes. I found both their themes—1984 Apocalypse and Scary Circus—both fun and challenging. And I can't wait to see the third game they're building out.

Two people 8,000Ft/game, up to six people 11,000Ft/game, multiple time slots available daily, online reservations required ahead of time, Nyár Utca 27, Jewish Quarter, +36 30 889 3633, e-exit.hu, Metro: Blaha Lujza Tér

Team Escape
Team Escape offers a fun, low-pressure entry-level escape game. Its single Hollywood theme is great for those who don't want to be in the dark or scared (although, what's the point of that?). The staff is welcoming and helpful, and the records for escape times are posted online. The best team got out in 41 minutes flat. See if you can beat that!

Two players 8,900Ft, 3-4 players 9,900Ft, book online ahead of time, Nagy Diófa 3, doorbell 15, Jewish Quarter, +36 20 420 5750, teamescape.hu, Metro: Blaha Lujza Tér

Time Trap Escape Games
You've got two themes to choose from: Psychopath Killer and Prison Trap. The first one is better for beginners, but it pushes your boundaries with fake blood and bones, like the *Saw* movie series. With Prison Trap, two or four friends are blindfolded and handcuffed together and taken deep into a wine cellar. This one is much more challenging.

12,500Ft/game for 2-5 people, daily 10:00-24:00, reservations required ahead of time by phone or online, Kazinczy Utca 10, Jewish Quarter, +36 20 311 9471, idocsapda.hu/en, Metro: Astoria

TOP TOURS

Yellow Zebra Bike Tours
This is an entertaining and relaxing way to get oriented with the city and see all of Budapest's top sights. Pop into the office on one of your first days to hang out in their fun office/library/tourist zone. The friendly staff is happy to hook you up with any of their walks and rides, along with a slew of other activities. Take the day tour and you'll even get a coffee and pastry break! Book online to save yourself a little cash.

5,600Ft adult/5,000Ft student , Apr-Oct daily 11:00 daytime ride, June-Aug daily 17:00 evening ride, Nov and Mar Fri-Sun daytime ride 11:00, Lázár Utca 16, Andrássy District, yellowzebrabikes.com, Metro: Opera

Buda Bike
I love the rides put together by the Buda Bike team. They have everything you might expect from a well-organized bike tour company, including an engaging Highlights tour, along with more in-depth city rides and more extensive rides in the countryside. Several

members of the team and a good friend of mine keep up an excellent blog with all sorts of tips and tricks about making the most of your visit to Budapest (bebudapest.hu).

6,200Ft , group discounts available, 10:30 and 15:00 in front of St Stephen's Basilica (look for the stairs leading down to a parking garage), Szent István Tér 1, Leopold Town, confirm season and availability ahead of time, budabike@ymail.com, budabike.com, Metro: Bajcsy-Zsilinszky Út

HostelCulture
HostelCulture has put together some

exciting itineraries designed specifically for backpackers, to get you familiar with the city. Come out for their free city tour of Budapest, covering highlights like Matthias Church, the Hungarian State Opera House, and more. If you dig it, check out their more specific tours about communist history and the Jewish Legacy walk. In for a party? Join their nightly pub crawl.

Free tip-based tour meets daily 10:30 and 14:00 in front of St Stephen's Basilica, Szent István Tér 1, Leopold Town, hostelculture.com/budapest-tours, Metro: Bajcsy-Zsilinszky Út

TOP HOSTELS

I love Budapest for its strong and healthy backpacking hostel culture. There are a ton of excellent accommodation choices at very competitive prices. If **Airbnb** is your thing, remember how affordable accommodations *should* be here in Budapest, and don't spend more than about €25, or 7,800Ft, per person. It's best to stay around District VII. You may first think that the area around the Parliament and the embassies would be the most central location, but it gets rather quiet and boring at night.

Budapest Party Hostels is a group of awesome accommodations (Grandio Party Hostel, Retox Hostel, Carpe Noctem VITAE, Carpe Noctem, and Penthouse Privates), each with a unique vibe and personality. Prepare yourself for a PG-13 welcome briefing that doesn't concern itself with any sort of political correctness.

Grandio Party Hostel
For serious partiers only! Come to this hostel if you're looking for some "interesting" life experiences, which you'll want to both brag about to your friends and hide from your parents. There are beds upstairs, a social garden bar on the ground floor, and a sloppy late-night karaoke bar in the cellars beneath.

3,000-5,000Ft, free Wi-Fi, computers, 24-hour reception, common room, bar, bicycle rental, Nagy Diófa Utca 8, Jewish Quarter, +36 20 350 7441, grandiopartyhostel.com, info@grandiopartyhostel.com, Metro: Blaha Lujza Tér

Retox Hostel
Retox is a solid all-around bet if you're into partying late into the night. You'll get some rest here as long as your sleep schedule is on par with the other guests: falling to sleep at 06:00 and waking up at 14:00. They've done an excellent job updating the bar on the ground floor, and the sister hostels come out for a good time here most nights of the week. They host a Jägerbomb train party every Sunday night, delivering a domino effect of drinking shenanigans. I don't know how they pull it off, but I'm blown away by how clean the hostel is every morning, even after the most hard-core late-night festivities.

3,500-4,000Ft, free Wi-Fi, 24-hour reception, bar, hookah, computers, Ó Utca 41, Andrássy District, +36 70 6700 386, budapestpartyhostels.com, info@retoxpartyhostel.com, Metro: Oktogon

Carpe Noctem VITAE
For those who like to have a great time, but also want the option to chill, this hostel offers a lot of different common spaces with different vibes. Head up the stairs to a multi-floor hostel with a small rooftop patio and friendly staff. Comfortable private rooms with views are available for those who appreciate their own room but don't want to miss out on the party.

3,000-4,500Ft, free Wi-Fi, computers, 24-hour reception, bar, hookah bar, free locker/lock, Erzsébet Körút 50, Jewish Quarter, +36 70 6700 382, carpenoctempenthouse.com, info@carpenoctemvitae.com, Metro: Oktogon

Carpe Noctem
The most low-key and comfy Budapest Party Hostels option boasts orthopedic beds, spacious rooms, and a quiet place to retreat to after a night on the town. It's much smaller than the other hostels, and hostel guests appreciate the more intimate ambience.

4,000Ft, free Wi-Fi, computers, 24-hour reception, free lockers/locks, common room, Szobi Utca 5, Andrássy District, +36 70 6700 384, carpenoctemoriginal.com, info@carpenoctemoriginal.com, Metro: Nyugati Pályaudvar

Penthouse Privates
Budapest Party Hostels' newest member, Penthouse Privates is a collection of five private double rooms for travelers who

want accommodations to feel more like home. Relax in their comfortable common room, enjoy full access to a kitchen, and sleep well at the top of a six-floor building (no elevator). With those stairs, you'll be working off each meal and beer every time you go home!

8,500Ft, two-night minimum stay, free Wi-Fi, computer for use, on-site staff that comes and goes, Király Utca 56, Jewish Quarter, +36 70 671 2723, facebook.com/ penthouseprivates, penthouseprivates@gmail.com, Metro: Opera or Oktogon

Wombats Hostel

This Austrian hostel chain has great hostels down to a science and knows exactly what every American backpacker wants: bright rooms, free Wi-Fi throughout the hostel, breakfasts included, an on-site bar, and frequent free tours and pub crawls. The BP

Wombats has an excellent location, around the corner from Kazinczy Utca and across the street from the Gozsdu Court & Passage.

Beds from 3,500Ft, 24-hour reception, free Wi-Fi, 20 Király Utca, Jewish Quarter, +36 1 883 5005, wombats-hostels.com/Budapest, office@wombats-budapest.hu, Metro: Bajcsy-Zsilinszky

Central Backpacking Hostel

Located just down the way from the US Embassy and Parliament building, this hostel sits right in the middle of all the downtown sights. It's far enough from the nightlife, making it relatively quiet, but I still appreciate the hostel's fun vibe, welcoming staff, and comfortable rooms.

Beds from 3,300Ft, 24-hour reception, kitchen access, lockers and towels available for rent, hair dryers available, 15 Oktober 6 Utca, Leopold Town, +36 30 200 7184, centralbackpackking.hostel.com, Metro: Bajcsy-Zsilinszky

TRANSPORTATION

GETTING THERE & AWAY

Budget airlines make frequent connections into Budapest, making this city an attractive stop on a longer trip. Overnight bus and train options also make for good connections to Vienna and Prague. Train and bus connections from Krakow can be a little more involved, often connecting through Bratislava.

Plane

Plenty of budget airlines fly into Budapest's sole airport: **Ferenc Liszt International Airport** (BUD, bud.hu). Find cheap flights by using skyscanner.net, cheapoair.com, and kayak.com. Don't buy your tickets without checking WizzAir.com, a competitive Hungarian budget airline. It is important to note that some budget airlines like RyanAir may count the Balaton regional airport as their main "Budapest" airport. Be sure to look closely to see if this is the case while researching your options. Connections from Balaton are a two-hour train connection into Budapest. This airport is on a beautiful lake but is hours away from the city you need to get to.

Connect from Ferenc Liszt International Airport into Budapest by taking **bus 200E** to the Kobanya-Kispest Metro stop. Hop on the metro and into town to find your hostel from there, validating a new metro ticket each time you transfer. Change to the red or yellow metro line at Deak Ferenc Tér if necessary. The whole journey will take about an

hour and cost between two and three metro tickets, running about 900Ft total.

Train

Connections run often between Prague and Budapest (7 hours, €75 or 23,000Ft).

Budapest is served by two main train stations: **Nyugati,** in Pest, north of Leopold Town, and **Keleti,** also in Pest, south of City Park. Both have metro, tram, and bus connections immediately outside the station. From both, it's a safe 20-minute walk into the general center, where you'll find your accommodations.

Bus

There are dirt-cheap bus options in Central and Eastern Europe. To begin shopping, take a look at orangeways.com and eurolines.com for timetables and prices. A ride to Prague may take up to ten hours, and cost at least €11 (4,000Ft). What you save in money, you may pay for in time and comfort, though modern buses often have onboard Wi-Fi and comfortable leather seats. Also note if there is a required transfer for longer connections.

If leaving from Budapest by bus, *triple* check your bus station because there are several in town. The bus terminals are located on the southeast side of town, at metro stops **Nepliget** or **Puttyus Utca.**

Car

Renting a car is not necessary to see the best sights of Budapest, though if you're touring from one city to the next, Budapest's city center is a little easier to navigate than the more medieval centers of other European cities. However, as in other cities, finding and keeping parking is expensive and a pain. The closer to the center, the more expensive the hourly rates are. When looking for parking, there are a number of park-and-ride (P+R) options near public transportation stations that will let you ditch the car for a few days for just a few euros a day. Erzsebet Tér P+R is your most central yet cost effective option.

GETTING AROUND

Budapest's public transportation system is easy to use. Trams, buses, and subways are all on the same ticketing system. Buy an individual **ticket** (340Ft) from machines and vendors usually found in every station. A booklet of **10 tickets** (2,800Ft) will save you money in a weekend unless you're getting around by bike.

Ticket checkers hang out near the validation machines and will check you if you don't validate a ticket. Ticket checkers here are more numerous than in any other European city I've seen. Trying to play the "dumb tourist" card does not work here! In Budapest, tickets do not include transfers at all except inside the metro system. That means if you need to change buses, you need two tickets. If you need to go on the metro and then a bus, again, it's two tickets.

Familiarize yourself with the primary stops and stations in the city in order to better know your way around. Start with: **Deak Ferenc Tér, Oktogon,** and **Blaha Lujza Tér.**

Metro

Budapest has a simple, four-line metro system. Visitors will most likely use the **yellow** (for the opera house, House of Terror, Széchenyi baths, and City Park), **red** (connecting Buda with Keleti train station), and **blue** (coming in from the airport and Nyugati train station) lines.

Bus

As the tram and metro networks are so easy to use, buses, while fully operational, take third place.

Tram

Over 30 tram lines lace the city, but there are just a few lines for you to get familiar with. **Lines 46** and **47** originate at Deak Ferenc Tér, running on Pest's inner ring road, past Váci Utca and the Grand Market Hall across the river to Gellért and the Citadel. **Lines 4** and **6** loop Pest's middle ring road, connecting major sights like Andrássy Út and Margit Island. **Line 2** runs north-south along the Pest side of the Danube, connecting the Grand Market Hall with the Parliament building.

Taxi

Always call for a cab to get a fair rate. Never flag down a taxi in Budapest as it's likely you'll get into an unlicensed taxi and the potential for getting ripped off is much higher. My favorite companies are **Radio** (+36 377 77 77) and **City Taxi** (+36 211 11 11).

Bicycle

Budapest is quite large, and having a bike makes it much more manageable to get across town. It opens up the city in a way that walking and using public transportation just don't. Budapest is a leader in bike paths throughout the city, and cars generally respect cyclists. But because it is such a large city, you'll also come across busy boulevards and fast traffic, so cyclists should use caution always and especially avoid riding down Rakoczi Utca in Pest, as there is no bike lane and the traffic is quite heavy. I recommend wearing a helmet if you plan on riding across town. **Yellow Zebra Bike Tours** and **Buda Bike** tour companies have bike rental options as well, with discounts for tour customers.

DAY TRIPS

Eger & the Valley of the Sirens

The pretty little town of Eger is famous for its 16th-century castle, but the real draw is the Valley of Sirens, a back holler in the hills of Hungary just outside of town. Local farmers and vintners have burrowed deep into the earth to create an elaborate network of wine cellars over hundreds of years. Today we can enjoy this intoxicating tasting experience, as these vineyards sell wine from each of the cellars. Pop in, strike up a conversation, have a snack, and toss back the glasses. This trip is best done over two days so you can have ample time to enjoy an afternoon out at the wine cellars. Ask at your hostel for the best option considering your time and itinerary.

Buses and trains leave often for Eger from

Budapest and take about two hours. Tourist bus connections to the Valley of Sirens leave from Eger's Dobo Square. Otherwise, it's about a 20-minute walk or 10-minute taxi ride (2,000Ft) from Eger's old town square.

Castles & Local Touring

For a supremely aggressive day of exploring greater Budapest, you can pound through three towns just northwest of Budapest and see the ruins of a castle. Well worth it for expert and efficient travelers who aren't scared of asking for help or directions.

Start your day with an early morning bus out to the town of **Esztergom** (1.25 hours via bus, 450Ft, buses leave from Arpad Hid Aitobusz station) to visit the beautiful basilica perched high on a hill overlooking the town. The basilica is free to visit. The crypts below are well worth the entry fee of 200Ft.

Head back to the bus station to continue onto the village of **Visegrad** on bus 880 (450Ft). You'll have to ask your bus driver to let you know when to get out. Pop into the **Hotel Visegrad** and ask for help calling a taxi to take you all the way up to some incredible ruins of a castle overlooking the bend in the Danube. The ruins of this castle on the hill are much more accessible than just about any other castle I've ever climbed around in. Just beyond the castle is a fun summer luge where you can buy a ticket for a ride down the course in your own little toboggan on wheels (450 Ft/run, open weekdays in good weather, 11:00-16:00, +36 26 397 397, bobozas.hu).

After the castle, return downhill to town via the path leading from the castle ruins. The signs and incline are easy enough to follow as long as it hasn't rained too much recently. Catch the bus (450Ft) on to the town of **Szentendre,** where you'll have a chance to explore the beautiful baroque old town center. You'll get off the bus on the big street that passes through the town. Work your way toward the river, explore the old town, and catch dinner before continuing back to Budapest via light rail from the station (450Ft). The train station is about a 15-minute walk south of the old town, and trains leave often for Budapest's light rail stops along the Danube river. Your best stop to get off is Margit Hid, near Margit Island, and then connect back into the center across the bridge via tram 6.

HELP!

Tourist Information Centers

Find the official Budapestinfo Point (daily 08:00-20:00) next door to the recommended Cserpes Tejivo Milk Bar:

Sütő Utca 2

+36 143 88 080

Pickpockets & Scams

Don't take unmarked cabs. They prey on wealthy, naïve tourists. Pickpocketing doesn't seem to be a major problem, but always have your wits about you, especially at busy bars. Anticipate your change when purchasing goods, because rather than getting a few dollars back, you'll be getting a few thousand forints, which can be overwhelming and difficult math. Don't be afraid to step aside and count your change before walking away—I've saved a substantial amount of money doing this and catching counting errors.

Emergencies

In an emergency, dial 112.

Hospital

FirstMed Center

Hattyú St 14

+36 06 1 224 9090

US Embassy

Szabadság Tér 12

+36 06 14 75 4400

DUBLIN

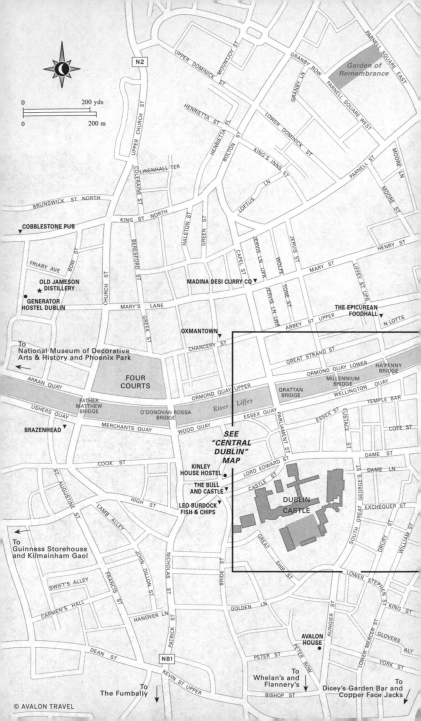

N2

0   200 yds

0   200 m

Garden of
Remembrance

UPPER DOMINICK ST

UPPER CHURCH ST

MOUNTJOY ST

GRANBY ROW

GRANBY LN

PARNELL SQUARE EAST

PARNELL SQUARE WEST

HENRIETTA ST PL

HENRIETTA ST

BOLTON ST

LOWER DOMINICK ST

KING'S INNS ST

PARNELL ST

MOORE LN

MOORE ST

COLERAINE TER

LOFTUS LN

HENRY ST

BRUNSWICK ST NORTH

KING ST NORTH

HALSTON ST

GREEN ST

JERVIS LN UPR

JERVIS ST

LIFFEY ST UPR

JERVIS LN LWR

▼ COBBLESTONE PUB

BOW ST

BERESFORD ST

CHURCH ST

CAPEL ST

WOLFE TONE ST

MARY ST

FRIARY AVE

OLD JAMESON
★ DISTILLERY

● GENERATOR
HOSTEL DUBLIN

MARY'S LANE

GREEK ST

MADINA DESI CURRY CO ▼

THE EPICUREAN
FOODHALL

ABBEY ST UPPER

N LOTTS

To
National Museum of Decorative
Arts & History and Phoenix Park

OXMANTOWN ◼

CHANCERY ST

GREAT STRAND ST

ORMOND QUAY LOWER

HA'PENNY
BRIDGE

ARRAN QUAY

FOUR
COURTS

ORMOND QUAY UPPER

MILLENNIUM
BRIDGE

GRATTAN
BRIDGE

WELLINGTON QUAY

TEMPLE BAR

River Liffey

FATHER
MATTHEW
BRIDGE

USHERS QUAY

O'DONOVAN ROSSA
BRIDGE

WOOD QUAY

ESSEX QUAY

PARLIAMENT ST

ESSEX ST

EUSTACE ST

COPE ST

BRAZENHEAD ▼

MERCHANTS QUAY

SEE
"CENTRAL
DUBLIN"
MAP

DAME ST

DAME LN

COOK ST

ST. AUGUSTINE ST

HIGH ST

LAMB ALLEY

KINLEY
HOUSE HOSTEL ●

THE BULL
AND CASTLE ▼

LEO BURDOCK
FISH & CHIPS ▼

LORD EDWARD ST

CASTLE ST

DUBLIN
CASTLE

SOUTH GREAT GEORGE'S ST

EXCHEQUER ST

DRURY ST

WILLIAM ST

To
Guinness Storehouse
and Kilmainham Gaol

JOHN DILLON ST

NICHOLAS ST

BRIDE ST

GREAT SHIP ST

SWIFT'S ALLEY

FRANCIS ST

CARMEN'S HALL

HANOVER LN

PATRICK ST

GOLDEN LN

AUNGIER ST

LOWER STEPHEN ST

KING ST

GLOVERS ALY

LOWER MERCER ST

DEAN ST

N81

KEVIN ST UPPER

PETER ST

PETER ROW

AVALON
HOUSE ●

YORK ST

To
The Fumbally

To
Whelan's and
Flannery's

BISHOP ST

To
Dicey's Garden Bar and
Copper Face Jacks

© AVALON TRAVEL

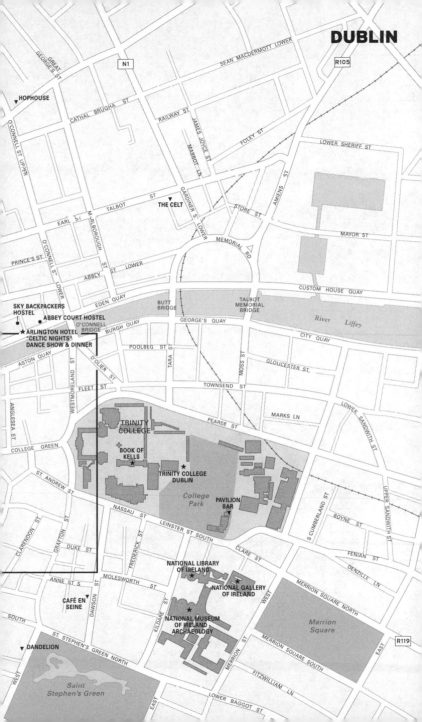

DUBLIN

N1

R105

HOPHOUSE

GREAT GEORGE'S ST

CATHAL BRUGHA ST

RAILWAY ST

JAMES JOYCE ST

FOLEY ST

SEAN MACDERMOTT LOWER

LOWER SHERIFF ST.

O'CONNELL ST UPPER

MARLBOROUGH ST

TALBOT ST

MABBOT LN

GARDINER'S LOWER

STORE ST

AMIENS ST

MAYOR ST

THE CELT

EARL ST

O'CONNELL ST LOWER

MEMORIAL RD

PRINCE'S ST. LOWER

ST. LOWER

ABBEY

CUSTOM HOUSE QUAY

EDEN QUAY

BUTT BRIDGE

TALBOT MEMORIAL BRIDGE

SKY BACKPACKERS HOSTEL

ABBEY COURT HOSTEL

O'CONNELL BRIDGE

BURGH QUAY

GEORGE'S QUAY

River Liffey

ARLINGTON HOTEL 'CELTIC NIGHTS' DANCE SHOW & DINNER

ASTON QUAY

WESTMORELAND ST

D'OLIER ST

POOLBEG ST

TARA ST

CITY QUAY

MOSS ST

GLOUCESTER ST.

FLEET ST

TOWNSEND ST

LOWER SANDWITH ST.

ANGLESEA ST

COLLEGE GREEN

PEARSE ST

MARKS LN

TRINITY COLLEGE

BOOK OF KELLS

ST. ANDREW ST

TRINITY COLLEGE DUBLIN

College Park

PAVILION BAR

S CUMBERLAND ST

BOYNE ST

UPPER SANDWITH ST.

CLARENDON ST

GRAFTON ST

DUKE ST

NASSAU ST

LEINSTER ST SOUTH

CLARE ST

FENIAN ST

DENZILLE LN

ANNE ST S

DAWSON ST

MOLESWORTH ST

FREDERICK ST

NATIONAL LIBRARY OF IRELAND

NATIONAL GALLERY OF IRELAND

WEST

MERRION SQUARE NORTH

CAFÉ EN SEINE

SOUTH

KILDARE ST

NATIONAL MUSEUM OF IRELAND ARCHAEOLOGY

Merrion Square

R119

DANDELION

ST. STEPHEN'S GREEN NORTH

MERRION ST

MERRION SQUARE SOUTH

EAST

WEST

Saint Stephen's Green

EAST

FITZWILLIAM LN

LOWER BAGGOT ST

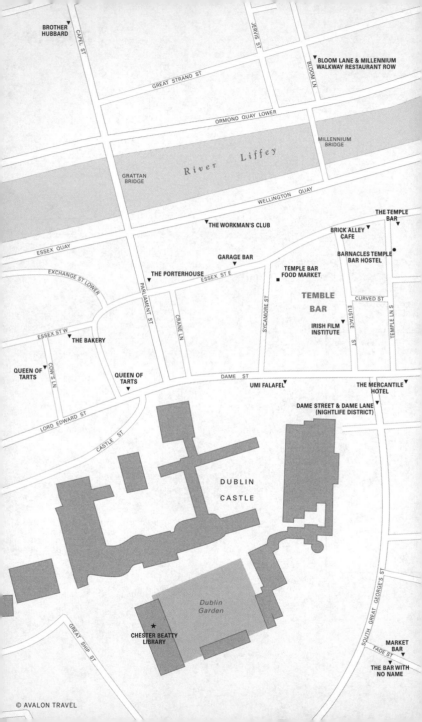

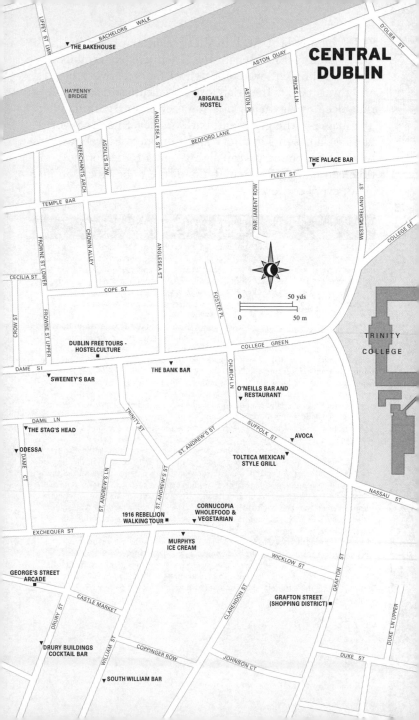

The modern and bustling capital of Ireland still retains the charm the Irish are so famous for. Dublin will welcome you with open arms, a hot tea, and a warm chat. The Irish love for culture and storytelling runs deep, with their pride for their country unmatched. The magic of the grain and barley is never far: The world-famous Jameson Distillery and Guinness Storehouse are some of the country's top sights, and a foot-tapping good time can be had for free at any of the pubs found on just about every corner.

DUBLIN 101

Dublin was founded as a Viking settlement in the 9th century and called Baile Atha Cliath (City of the Hurtled Ford). The Vikings laid an extensive network of underwater defenses navigable only for those who planted them, preventing enemy ships from coming up the river to the city. After some time, this settlement picked up another name, the one we're most familiar with: Dublin. Just behind where the Dublin Castle stands today was a dark eddy that formed at the crux of two intersecting rivers (*dubh* means black, *linn* means pool).

The city eventually became the second largest city of the British Empire in the 1600s and 1700s. After the devastating Great Hunger and London's oppressive colonial tactics, Dublin slid into decline throughout the 19th century, losing a full two-thirds of its population.

Seventy years later, in a glorious failure, a small band of students and intellectuals took up arms in 1916 and launched the Easter Rising, an attempt to win independence for the Republic of Ireland. In full war mode, England brought in thousands of troops and a battleship all the way up the River Liffey and began shelling the city of Dublin. The leaders of the operation took over a handful of municipal buildings and holed up for six days before all were captured and taken to Kilmainham Gaol prison. Most rebels were summarily executed by firing squad, a miscalculated move by the British, turning public opinion from general apathy to the side of the rebels.

Seeking peace, London offered a treaty of limited independence, making the Irish Free State still subject to the crown. The treaty split the opinion of the country in half. The pro-treaty side, supported by England, was content with taking a pragmatic step *toward* sovereignty—and peace. And the anti-treaty side wouldn't stop at anything short of home rule, full autonomy, and a united Republic of Ireland. The two opposing camps began fighting, kicking off the bloody and tragic Irish Civil War (1922-1923), pitting brothers against brothers and eventually bringing about the political lines of Ireland that we see today, with six counties in the north remaining loyal to the British crown. *The Wind That Shakes the Barley* (2006) is an excellent movie to watch to learn more about this heart-rending conflict.

During the 1990s and 2000s, Ireland entered a period of unprecedented economic growth, earning it the nickname the "Celtic Tiger." The good times didn't last though, as the economic crisis of 2008 hit the island particularly hard. But today, you'll find a city awakening once more from its slumber and charging into the 21st century with newfound confidence and optimism.

PLAN AHEAD

RESERVATIONS

Reserve hostel accommodations for St Paddy's day long in advance (at least three months ahead). It's also a good idea to plan ahead for a day outside of Dublin to the Cliffs of Moher and Howth.

Reservations are recommended for the following sights:
Guinness Storehouse (guinness-storehouse.com)
Jameson Distillery (bookings.jamesonwhiskey.com)

STUDENT DISCOUNTS

Student discounts are often available at Dublin's sights. Bring your student ID with you at all times.

LOCAL HAPPENINGS

St Patrick's Day

Americans love the St Paddy's Day traditions of shamrock-themed parties, wearing green, and drinking Guinness, but it's not until you travel to the country of this famous patron saint that you experience a real Irish celebration. While traditionally more of a religious holiday than its American celebration counterpart, the event has grown in leaps and bounds over the last few years as the enterprising Irish have seized this massive economic opportunity. The holiday has gone from a one-day celebration to a five-day festival filled with parades, street concerts, lectures, cultural events, and, of course, hitting the pubs. The holiday itself occurs annually on March 17, and most businesses will be closed. On each St Patrick's Day, the president, the archbishop of Ireland, and the head of the Irish military all attend St Mary's Pro Cathedral in Dublin for High Mass at 10:00. The Mass is held in Irish, and visitors receive blessed shamrocks to wear at the parade.

KNOW BEFORE YOU GO

KEY STATS & FIGURES

Currency:
Ireland uses the euro (€);
1 EUR = about 1.06 USD

Population:
530,000

National languages:
Irish, English

Oldest pub:
Brazenhead (open since 1198)

Famous Irishmen:
Bono, Oscar Wilde,
Colin Farrell, James Joyce

National dish:
Irish beef and Guinness stew

CALIBRATE YOUR BUDGET

TYPICAL PRICES FOR:

Hostel dorm bed:
€16

Two-course dinner:
€14

Pint of beer:
€5

Bicycle rental:
€12/day

Single bus ticket:
€1.60

MOVIES TO WATCH
P.S. I Love You, Once, The Wind That Shakes the Barley

THREE DAY ITINERARY

The city of Dublin is easy to walk across. This itinerary takes you to the top sights but leaves lots of time to explore the city's one-of-a-kind pub culture.

DAY 1: THANK GOODNESS FOR GUINNESS

MORNING

Start your day with a delicious, fresh pastry breakfast at the **Queen of Tarts** just off Temple Bar for a yummy Irish scone and jam. If you're hangry, the scrambled eggs with toast is superb.

After breakfast, walk a few blocks east down Dame Street to catch a free walking tour of the heart of Dublin with **Hostelculture,** meeting at 11:00 daily at **The Mercantile** pub. Pop in early for the free Wi-Fi and to get warm with a tea. The tour lasts about 3.5 hours and does an excellent job of orienting you to the city and culture.

AFTERNOON

If it's a nice day, walk to the **Guinness Storehouse,** about a 20-minute westerly walk from the city center. Otherwise, take one of the many city buses that run there from the center (123, 13, 40), west along Dame Street. Bus fare is €1.60.

Spend the afternoon in the storehouse, climbing up through the labyrinth of brewing science and delightful Guinness propaganda. Your entry ticket is also a voucher for a free pint, which you can redeem at numerous stations throughout the tour or at the top-floor Gravity Bar (last call at 17:00!), where you can enjoy a full 360-degree panorama while you sip away.

EVENING

Stop on your way back into town for a traditional Irish dinner at the city's oldest pub, **Brazenhead**, or at one of my favorite gastro pubs, **The Bull & Castle**. Both restaurants are on the Guinness Storehouse side of downtown, making for a convenient pit stop on the short walk back.

LATE

Commence the evening festivities by creating your own pub crawl from my recommended hot spots, starting at the famous **Temple Bar** and making your way to the nearby **Palace** pub, **O'Neill's,** and **The Porterhouse,** where the party goes late every night.

DAY 2: TRINITY COLLEGE & HOWTH

MORNING

Let yourself sleep in a bit to recover, and grab a hearty breakfast at **The Bakehouse**. Their strong coffee is a lifesaver. Consider taking one of their pastries or sandwiches for the road to keep you moving through lunch.

Cross the Liffey to meet at the front arch of **Trinity College** for a tour led by current students. Tours last about 30 minutes and leave about every half hour, with the first one of the day departing at 10:15 and the last one at 15:40 May through September. The €10 tour includes entry to see the **Book of Kells**.

AFTERNOON

Hop on the DART train at Tara Street station, just a block east from the O'Connell Street bridge, to head out to the coastal town of **Howth.** Spend the afternoon hiking, then relax for a bit at Howth's **Bloody Stream** pub. The trip to Howth takes about 40 minutes each way. The small town only takes 45 minutes to explore, and the hike takes about 1.5 hours.

EVENING

Once you're back in Dublin, head out for dinner. Try succulent pulled pork sandwiches at **South William Bar**, steaming tapas at **The Market Bar**, or burritos, Thai, sushi and more just north of the Millennium Bridge at **Millennium Walkway Restaurant Row.**

Alternatively, reserve ahead for the **Celtic Nights Dance Show & Dinner** at the Arlington Hotel, kicking off nightly at 20:30. Tap your feet along to their jigs as you sip a pint and enjoy a €34, three-course dinner.

LATE

Skip the touristy joints tonight and head out where the party always rages and the locals go till the wee hours. Walk south from Dame Street on South Great Georges Street for about 15 minutes to kick off with a couple pints at **Whelan's**, where *P.S. I Love You* was filmed. You may catch some live music there, as acts often start by 20:30. Continue warming up at **Flannery's**, and once you're in the dancing mood head to **Copper Face Jacks** and aim to close it down. All three venues are within easy walking distance of one another.

DAY 3: FAREWELL TO DUBLIN

MORNING

Break your fast at **Brick Alley Café,** located right on Temple Bar, for some coffee and pastries. Coffee and ice cream is a great combo for calming the stomach after a night out.

Walk over to spend a lazy morning exploring the **Grafton Street** shopping zone. Perhaps have a picnic snack in **St Stephen's Green**. There are a few top-class and free museums in the area: the **National Gallery**, the **National Museum of Archaeology,** and the **National Library** (closed Sun). Of the three, the National Gallery is my favorite, with an all-star cast of artists shown here, including Van Gogh, Rembrandt, and Caravaggio.

AFTERNOON

Take bus 37 or 39 from the southeast corner of Trinity College's campus toward the **Jameson Distillery**, getting off at Ushers Quay. Make sure to raise your hand when they ask for volunteers to join the tasting!

EVENING

For your last evening in town, grab some delicious beef and Guinness stew at the **Irish Film Institute** just around the corner from Temple Bar.

LATE

Make a crawl in the lane behind the **Mercantile Pub**. Start off with **Odessa**, continue onto **The Bar with No Name** and finish at **Sweeney's Bar.**

TOP NEIGHBORHOODS

The River Liffey runs straight through Dublin, cutting the city into north and south. The **South Bank** is home to most of Dublin's cultural and tourist sights, including Trinity College, the Grafton Street shopping district, the national museums, the Guinness Storehouse, and the **Temple Bar** neighborhood. The Temple Bar neighborhood is bordered by the River Liffey to the north, Dame Street to the south, Fishamble Street on the west, and Westmoreland Street to the east. It's world famous for its full lineup of more than two dozen bars, with most offering live music nearly every night. It's the most touristy part of Dublin, and pints here are the most expensive, running up to €7.

When it comes to the **North Side** of Dublin, most worthwhile sights, restaurants, and accommodations are within a few blocks of the river. You'll find a few recommended hostels, restaurants, and nightlife venues here, as well as the Jameson Distillery Tour and the grand boulevard of O'Connell Street.

TOP SIGHTS

Trinity College & Book of Kells

Ireland's oldest university was founded in 1592 by Queen Elizabeth I. It's still active today, and its claim to fame is the beautifully preserved "bog book," the Book of Kells, found inside the Trinity Old Library. This unique illuminated manuscript is one of the oldest in existence, and it illustrates each of the four gospels in beautiful, intricate Celtic weaves. A campus tour (€13, 30 minutes) includes entry into the library and viewing of the Book. Tours meet at Front Arch and depart about every 30 minutes. Entry to see the book without the student tour is €10.

Free, tour €13, May-Sept daily 10:15-15:40, Feb-April and Oct-Nov Sat-Sun only, no tours Dec-Jan, Book of Kells without tour €10, June-Sept Mon-Sat 09:00-18:00, Sun 09:30-18:00, Oct-May Mon-Sat 09:30-17:00, Sun 12:00-16:30, College Green, South Bank, tcd.ie

Guinness Storehouse

Tour the Guinness Storehouse to learn about the history and brewing process of one of the most recognizable brands of beer in the world. Follow an interactive virtual tour led by the grand master brewer himself, Fergal Murray. He first explains the four ingredients that go into the mix: water, hops, barley, and yeast. Continue upstairs to discover the tasting experience and a world of Guinness media and marketing materials (my favorites are the "Guinness Is Good for You" posters). Your entry ticket is also a voucher for a free pint of the black stuff once you reach the Gravity Bar at the top level. Sip it in while taking in Dublin's best 360-degree panorama. Alternatively, you can opt to redeem your drink voucher at one of the pour-your-own-pint stations on the third and fourth levels. You can also redeem your voucher for a soda or juice.

The storehouse is south of the River Liffey, a 20-minute walk from Dublin's city center. You can also take bus 123, 13, or 40, all of which run to Guinness Storehouse from the city center, west along Dame Street.

€16 for student over 18, €20 adult, €18 online, daily 09:30-17:00, July-Aug until 19:00, St James Gate, Greater Dublin, +353 (0)1 408 4800, guinness-storehouse.com

Chester Beatty Library

Chester Beatty was born in the United States with Irish heritage and became a powerful mining magnate. He began collecting as a young man and developed an impressive collection of everything from bottles to

manuscripts, including pieces of New Testament manuscripts dating back to before AD 200. He moved to Dublin in 1950 and was made an honorary citizen of Ireland by 1957, and he donated his entire collection to the state when he died in 1968. It's easy to spend two hours poring over the extensive collection, which features artifacts of all major world religions in the world, like early biblical manuscripts nearly 2,000 years old.

Nearby, you'll see **Dublin Castle**. You can tour the staterooms, but I wouldn't say they're worth the time on a short visit. The castle stood as a sign of oppression throughout history, occupied by whoever was controlling the local people. Today, it's where important state functions are held.

Free, Mon-Fri 10:00-17:00, Sat 11:00-17:00, Sun 13:00-17:00, closed Mon Oct-Apr, just behind Dublin Castle, South Bank, +353 (0)1 407 0750, cbl.ie

National Library

This library caters to those interested in Ireland's long roster of literary greats. You'll find in-depth exhibits of famous Irish authors like W B Yeats and James Joyce. The National Library is also charged with the collection and preservation of important Irish documents and records. Visitors can dig into some genetic lineage research via the extensive Irish parish registries, recording births, baptisms, marriages, and deaths. The library is worth a short visit to see the building, the neoclassical interior, and the handful of exhibits. It's possible to spend months here, researching to your heart's content.

Free, Mon-Wed 09:30-19:30, Thurs-Fri 09:30-16:30, Sat 09:30-12:30, Sun 13:00-16:30 (exhibits only), Kildare St, South Bank, +353 (0)1 603 0200, nli.ie

National Museum: Decorative Arts & History

This moderately sized museum is worth an hour. Housed in an old military barracks, it contains artifacts, art, historical pieces, and natural history from all throughout the ages, with a fascinating military history exhibit to boot. The museum displays a selection of objects that tell the story of Ireland, from prehistoric coins to a "decommissioned AK-47." Find it just north of the River Liffey, not far from the Jameson Distillery, Guinness Storehouse, and Phoenix Park. You could easily make a day of it by visiting all four sights together. To get here, take bus 25A or 25B to the Guinness Store stop.

Free, Tues-Sat 10:00-17:00, Sun 14:00-17:00, Blenburb St,

Greater Dublin, +353 (0)1 677 7444, museum.ie

National Museum of Archaeology

This interesting state-run museum features an extensive history of Dublin's Nordic ancestry on one main ground floor and a smaller upper floor. Take an hour to check out all the gold jewelry and fearsome-looking Viking weapons. Don't miss the Viking ship and bog books and mummies that have been discovered in recent years—the damp, grassy bogs preserve anything that falls into them.

Free, Tues-Sat 10:00-17:00, Sun 14:00-17:00, Kildare St, South Bank, +353 (0)1 677 7444, museum.ie

The National Gallery

This recently renovated art museum features a plethora of Irish masterpieces, as well as works of Monet, Caravaggio, Van Gogh, Titian, Poussin, and Rembrandt. I consider its one and a half floors of exhibits the perfect-sized bite of artistic culture to experience if feeling the effects of the night before.

Free, Mon-Sat 09:30-17:30, Thurs until 20:30, Sun 11:00-17:30, Merrion Square West Dublin, South Bank, +353 (0)1 661 5133, nationalgallery.ie

Jameson Distillery

If you're a whiskey lover, this is the place for you. While they don't actually distill the whiskey here anymore, the guided tour is a great way to learn the trade and sample some traditional Irish whiskey. It walks you through the distilling process and sheds some light on those sneaky angels taking their sharing during the aging process. Be sure to raise your hand when asked for volunteers to get in on a taste test—you won't be disappointed! The distillery is north of the River Liffey, on the western side of Dublin near Smithfield and just behind the Generator Hostel. To get here, take any bus going west along the river, alighting at Ushers Quay.

€15, €13.50 online booking, daily 09:30-18:30, last tour at 17:15, Bow St, Smithfield Village, Greater Dublin, +353 (0)1 807 2355, tours.jamesonwhiskey.com

Kilmainham Gaol

Dublin's active jail from 1796 until 1924, Kilmainham Gaol is on the far west side of town and worth the hike out to connect with the significant link of Irish nationalism—just about all leaders of the numerous Irish rebellions have been held in these cells at one point in time. The leaders of the Easter Rising in 1916 were brought here and summarily executed by firing squad, with one exception: Éamon de Valera was spared thanks to his

American citizenship. The jail itself was supposed to be an excellent architectural model of modern prisons, featuring a layout that maximized the number of prisoners that could be "humanely" kept, and minimizing the guards required to monitor all of them. Explore the small prison museum while waiting for your tour to kick off at the top of each hour. To get here, take bus 25A or 25B to Con Colbert Road, doubling back around the corner to the jail once you get off.

€7, entry price includes enjoyable hour-long tour of the complex, Apr-Sept daily 09:30-18:00, Oct-Mar Mon-Sat 09:30-17:30, Sun 10:00-18:00, last admission an hour before closing, Inchicore Rd, Greater Dublin, +353 (0)1 453 5984, heritageireland.ie/en/kilmainhamgaol

Celtic Nights Dance Show & Dinner

A Riverdance-style show that reflects Irish tradition and culture is a highlight for many visitors to Dublin. Fast-paced, costumed tap dancers stun audiences nightly at the famous Arlington Hotel dinner and dance show. To see the show, you now have to purchase a tasty, but pricey, three-course dinner. You'll be treated to numerous group and solo acts by dancers and musicians. Try not to let your jaw rest on the floor for too long as the performers pound through a litany of traditional and more modern Irish dance. Make—or avoid—eye contact with the dancers depending on whether or not you want to get dragged up to the stage and taught the basics for a song in front of the entire audience.

€34, hour-long show starts at 20:30, dinner seatings every half hour from 18:30, reservations recommended online, 23 Bachelors Walk, North Side, +353 (0)1 687 5200, arlington.ie

TOP EATS

Ireland has undertaken a transformative culinary renaissance, and I'm loving it! What used to be a country notorious for its bland food, and not much to eat besides potatoes, is now bursting with excellent restaurants, gastropubs, and cafés that take their trade seriously.

When it comes to traditional Irish food you've got a few staples. Fish-and-chips, of course, is a mainstay, but beef and Guinness stew (big cuts of meat and veggies in a thick, spiced stew), boxty dishes (savory potato pancakes usually wrapped around meat or veggies), and shepherd's pie (a filling of minced meat and veggies topped with mashed potatoes, usually served in a large ceramic bowl) are the comfort foods of Ireland. Look for them on the menu at any of the sit-down restaurants listed. Tip about 10 percent on your dinner tab.

Queen of Tarts

Queen of Tarts is probably the cutest little place in the city. A breakfast here feels like a drop into Alice's rabbit hole, and you're guaranteed one of the best biscuits you've ever had. They also have great egg dishes for a bigger brunch. Find another branch barely a block away at (4 Dame St).

Scones from €3, Mon-Fri 08:00-19:00, Sat 09:00-19:00, Sun 10:00-18:00, Cows Lane, +353 (0)1 633 4681, queenoftarts.ie

Avoca

Tucked in the basement of a housewares-slash-fashion store, this is a place that all divas are sure to love. The main attraction is down the staircase, though, where you can pop in and enjoy a wide array of fresh salads, super food wraps, and fresh sandwiches.

Plates and dishes from €4, Mon-Sat 09:30-18:00, Sun 11:00-18:00, 11-13 Suffolk St (just steps from the *Molly Malone* statue), South Bank, +353 (0)1 677 4215, avoca.ie/home

Epicurean Food Hall

If you're looking for a break from traditional Irish food, this is your one-stop shop for an international array of culinary choices. Stop in the food hall for everything from Italian sandwiches to a bowl of curry, but don't come expecting super-fresh food or super value: All food stalls have colluded to price their small plates at around €9 and their buffet plates at €10. Do a full lap of all your options and a close inspection of the food before you commit.

From €9, Mon-Sat 09:30-20:00, Sun 11:30-19:30, Lower Liffey St, North Side, +353 (0)1 878 8641

The Bakehouse

I love this funky 1960s-themed breakfast and lunch house, where they bake their own bread and pastries and compile delicious sandwiches throughout the day. I always go for the sandwiches on thickly sliced bread, but they've also got pies, salads, baked potatoes, and a whole range of filling breakfast dishes.

Breakfasts from €5, daily 10:00–18:00, 6 Bachelor's Walk, North Side, +353 (0)1 873 4279

The Bakery

Situated down a side street in Temple Bar, this place is an actual legit bakery, supplying many other pastry shops around town. Some of the freshest sandwiches I have ever had came from here, and make for a great picnic on your day trip out to Howth, or even for a quick lunch stop. Complete with a friendly staff, the Bakery is also friendly on the wallet.

Sandwiches from €4, Mon–Sat 08:00–17:00, Pudding Row 3, Temple Bar, +353 (0)1 672 9882

The Market Bar

This Spanish fusion restaurant in an expansive downtown warehouse has some of the best tapas this side of the Irish Sea. The *patatas bravas* (fried potatoes with a spicy ketchup sauce), chorizo salad, and chicken skewers are some of my favorites. The portions are generous and great to share, drawing families, young professionals, posh locals, and tourists alike to the Market Bar's renovated shabby chic interior. Make it before 19:00 to get in on their happy hour, which includes food and drink specials.

Dinner from €9, Mon–Thurs 10:30–23:30, Fri–Sat 10:30–00:30, Sun 12:00–21:00, 14 Fade St, South Bank, +353 (0)1 613 9094, marketbar.ie

The Bull & Castle

This is my favorite spot in town for high-quality pub grub. The steak sandwiches in this double-level restaurant are to die for. There's a fine dining restaurant downstairs, though I prefer the more casual bar upstairs, especially when a game is on. Though if a big game is on, you won't be finding a spot to sit, as it packs out with rowdy supporters.

Dinners from €11, daily 12:00–22:00, 5-7 Lord Edward St, Temple Bar, +353 (0)1 475 1122, bull-and-castle. fxbuckley.ie

Leo Burdock Fish & Chips

You've gotta have some Irish fish-and-chips while in town, and this is the place to go. No frills, great prices, and top-class fried goodness. Leo's is widely regarded as the best fish-and-chips joint in town, and who am I to disagree?

Plates from €7.50, daily 12:00–24:00, 2 Weburgh St, South Bank, +353 (0)1 454 0306, leoburdock.com

The Fumbally

A good example of the Irish food renaissance, the Fumbally ramps up the tastiness without the price gouging. Located about a 15-minute walk south of Temple Bar, it's a favorite for power lunchers and those who appreciate lean, fresh food like healthy sandwiches, freshly squeezed juices, and a wide array of salads and soups. Don't miss the pork sandwich, artfully assembled by bearded, aproned Irish hipsters.

Sandwiches from €5, Mon–Fri 08:00–17:00, Sat 10:00–17:00, Fumbally Ln, South Bank, +353 (0)1 529 8732, thefumbally.ie

South William Bar

This gastrobar offers a deceivingly simple menu of pork sandwiches, chicken wings, veggie nachos, and hot dogs. Take your pick of tasty fries with a selection of seasonings, like curry, garlic, and cheese; top them off with lime-, chili-, or rosemary-flavored salts; and dip them in sauces ranging from barbecue and chipotle to garlic and honey mustard. With so many choices, you might go mad, but it's well worth the risk. South William is a favorite spot to kick off the night, as you'll find a wide selection of trendy bars and venues in the immediate area.

Dinners from €8.50, Sun–Thurs 12:00–23:00, Fri–Sat 12:00–02:00, 52 S William St, South Bank, +353 (0)1 677 7007, southwilliam.ie

Irish Film Institute

Most famous for its festivals, the Irish Film Institute also contains a little hidden gem of a restaurant. The food isn't all that cheap, but it's not overpriced either, and this is a great spot to hit up when you don't feel like venturing too far from Temple Bar. The service is friendly and fast, and the menu features classics like beef and Guinness stew, fish-and-chips, and well-appointed burgers.

Dinner from €10, Mon-Thurs 11:00-22:30, Fri 11:00-23:00, Sat-Sun 12:00-23:00, 6 Eustace St, Temple Bar, +353 (0)1 679 3477, ifi.ie

Brick Alley Café

Just steps from the Temple Bar, the Brick Alley Café offers surprising value and quality in such a touristy district. This casual, cozy café offers strong coffee, hearty breakfast sandwiches on fresh baguettes, pancakes with maple syrup, and sugary treats like artisan hot chocolate and rich chocolate cake all day to keep you going. On nice days, grab one of the seats outside and take in the fun people-watching on the street. The service can be slow, but the great location and free Wi-Fi make for a clutch lunch stop. Lunch, dinner, and full vegetarian and gluten-free meals are available, too.

Pancakes from €4.90, Sun-Wed 09:00-22:00, Thurs 09:00-22:30, Fri-Sat 09:00-23:00, 25 East Essex St, Temple Bar, facebook.com/BrickAlleyCafe, +353 (0)1 679 3393

Tolteca Burritos

Chipotle wannabes are popping up all across Dublin, but I'm not complaining. Come out for some fresh Irish shredded beef or pork burritos. Tolteca is packed out at lunchtime with Trinity College students who appreciate the quality of ingredients as well as the prices. The line can get long, but it moves quickly, and the large space offers ample seating for the hungry crowds.

Burritos from €7, daily 11:00-22:00, till 23:00 on weekends, 21 Suffolk St, South Bank, +353 (0)1 677 9506, tolteca.ie

Murphy's Ice Cream

Ireland's most famous creamery, hailing all the way from Dingle, is taking the island by storm and has opened a second location in Dublin. Innovative flavors and quality ingredients make this some of the best ice cream you'll try on your trip. Go for the Caramelized Brown Bread, Spicy Cinnamon, or perhaps the Irish Coffee? Take me back!

Cups from €2.50, Mon-Sat 10:00-18:00, 27 Wicklow St, South Bank, +353 (0)86 031 0726, murphysicecream.ie

Cornucopia Wholefood & Vegetarian

Vegetarians, look no further than Cornucopia. I even find myself heading back for their vegetarian rice and curry dishes, but they've got much more, like enchiladas, salads, and bean dishes, all of which you can dish up just walking down the buffet line. Heads-up: The lines can get painfully long around lunch, when it feels like just about every young professional in town heads here for their generous portions and fair prices.

Dishes starting at €9, Mon-Tues 08:30-21:00, Wed-Sat 08:30-20:15, Sun 12:00-21:00, 19-20 Wicklow St, South Bank, +353 (0)1 677 7583, cornucopia.ie

Umi Falafel

I normally avoid recommending chains but am happy to make exceptions when they hit the spot! Umi Falafel is great for a quick, potentially healthy bite depending on your order. Find it right on Dame Street and head in for fresh falafel (of course) and also a wide range of Moroccan and Middle Eastern salads. It's a smoothly run operation: Order at the front and grab seats toward the back at this clean and bright fast-food joint.

Lunches from €7.50, daily 12:00-22:00, 13 Dame St, Temple Bar, +353 (0)1 670 6866, umifalafel.ie

Brother Hubbard

If you're on a diet, stay away from this place. This trendy Moroccan fusion restaurant has all you want for breakfast, like cinnamon rolls, brownies, delicious hot chocolate and coffee, and amazing breakfast dishes like eggs over beans with chorizo. I heard about their pork sandwiches and nearly fell off the chair when biting into the perfectly toasted bread. Their €30 set dinner menu takes you on a three-course culinary adventure through Morocco, featuring *kofta* (meatballs), spicy tagine (stew), couscous dishes, and more.

Brunch from €10, Mon-Fri 08:00-17:30, Sat-Sun 10:00-17:00, 153 Capel St, North Side, +353 (0)1 441 1112, brotherhubbard.ie

Hophouse

Head to the north side of O'Connell Street for a cozy little Asian spot with welcoming service and a friendly atmosphere. If you've never had either, try both the *bulgogi* (spiced and marinated beef grilled to perfection) and *bibimbap* (a festival of veggies and a meat on a bed of rice or noodles, topped with an egg) and prepare to get your socks knocked off.

Dinners from €13, Mon-Thurs 12:00-23:00, Fri-Sat 12:00-23:30, Sun 12:00-22:30, 160 Parnell St, North Side, +353 (0)1 872 8318, hophouse.ie

Madina Desi Curry Co

This is my favorite spot for Indian food in town. Most people don't stick around to eat in the modest restaurant, opting to take out their delicious budget meal. Get a plate of rice, tikka masala, and naan and you're good to go!

Curries from €8, daily 11:00-23:00, 60 Mary St, North Side, +353 (0)1 872 6007, madina.ie

Oxmantown

The best things in life are simple. So for lunch, what's better than a classically delicious sandwich and soup? Loved by locals, this place feels like it's about to get big, but just hasn't been discovered yet. I always go for the Ruby—thick pastrami and sauerkraut and a bit of spicy mustard. And the tomato soup warms you from the inside out. Limited seating inside this clean café encourages most diners to take the party outside, especially on nice days.

Sandwiches €5.50, Mon-Fri 07:30-16:00, 16 Mary's Abbey, North Side, +353 (0)1 804 7030, oxmantown.com

Bloom Lane & Millennium Walkway Restaurant Row

Just leading off to the north from the Millennium Bridge, you'll find a wonderful little lane with nearly a dozen choices for everything from a quick bite to a fancy sit-down dinner. Consider the following options: **Bar Italia,** a mod Italian restaurant and wine bar; **Enoteca Delle Langhe,** another Italian choice with wine and standard fare; **Cactus Jack's,** a sit-down Mexican restaurant with tapas options; **Koh Restaurant & Cocktail Bar,** a classy sit-in Asian fusion restaurant with discerning cocktail menu and cheaper takeaway option; and **Boojum,** with delicious Chipotle-style Tex-Mex burritos.

North Side

TOP NIGHTLIFE

Dublin is famous for its characteristic and upbeat nightlife, running the gamut from typical pubs and live music to rock bars and cocktail lounges to dance bars and clubs. The tourists flock to Temple Bar, while the locals avoid it, preferring to avoid the crowds and expensive pints—they prefer to enjoy a night out in the area south of Dame Street and at the pubs sprinkled throughout the city.

NIGHTLIFE DISTRICTS

The thing about Dublin nightlife is that you really can't go wrong no matter where you end up. There are so many pubs and bars around town that you'll often find the best parties simply by exploring on your own. There are a few things that you can count on in Dublin though, and they tend to break down by district.

Temple Bar

First off, Temple Bar is both a neighborhood in Dublin and an actual bar. "Bar" referred to the riverbank that used to come all the way to the street we call Temple Bar now, and the wealthy Temple merchant family owned this stretch of riverbank at one time. Here you'll find touristy bars and €6.50 pints, climbing

north as the clock strikes 23:00, pushing prices up to a whopping €7.50 per pint. The farther you walk from Temple Bar, the more the price of pints drops—about 10 cents per block. Farther out you can find local hangouts with substantially cheaper pints of Guinness.

Temple Bar

Dame Street & Dame Lane

Dame Street marks the southern border of Temple Bar. Just south of Dame Street is Dame Lane, a small back alley with half a dozen bars and pubs. This is a more local scene than what you'll find in the heart of Temple Bar. Continue south on Drury Street and South Williams Street to find classier, upscale bars, cafés, and restaurants.

South Bank

LGBT DUBLIN

While Ireland leans a bit socially conservative, the capital city of Dublin has had a gay scene that goes back for years. You'll find that hostels and restaurants are social and welcoming. For a good time, head to **The George** (89 S George St, +353 14 78 2983), Dublin's oldest gay pub, which draws a young and rowdy crowd. Drag shows and great music keep the party going late just about every night of the week! Gay Pride is towards the end of June each year (dublinpride.ie).

IRISH PUBS

A radio show once had a contest to see if anyone could walk across Dublin without passing by a pub. The winner called in and said "Any route works—you just have to go into each one!" Authentic Irish pubs are warm, cozy affairs, with amateur pickup bands playing traditional Irish music nearly every night. Head to the bar to grab your pint, and pull up a stool to strike up a conversation with your fellow imbibers.

The Temple Bar

If you're wondering what came first, the street or the bar, the answer is the street. An enterprising entrepreneur started a bar named after the street, and when the street rose in popularity as a destination for tourists the world over, it catapulted this corner bar to the stars. It's standing room only just about every night in the summer; come for the experience, because you aren't saving any money here. There's live music and a smoking patio out back. Check the website for scheduled music sessions.

Pints €7.50, 48 Temple Bar, Temple Bar, +353 (0)1 672 5286, thetemplebarpub.com

The Celt

The Celt's claim to fame is that it's one of the most authentically Irish pubs in Dublin, complete with a fireplace, Irish Republican flags, and lively trad sessions. Located a couple blocks east of O'Connell Street, this gem is safely tucked away from the tourist hordes.

Pints from €4.50, 81 Talbot St, North Side, +353 (0)1 878 8655, thecelt.ie

The Palace

Located at the end of Temple Bar, the Palace has always had a reputation as a literary pub. Its proximity to the *Irish Times* newspaper office made it a favorite of the likes of writers Patrick Kavanagh and Flann O'Brien. Nondescript and full of old-time locals, this is one of your more authentic options in Temple Bar.

Pints from €5, 21 Fleet St, Temple Bar, +353 (0)1 671 7388, thepalacebardublin.com

Brazenhead

This authentic Irish pub with stone walls claims to be the oldest pub in the city, dating all the way back to 1198, and I believe it. Stop by for the nightly live music, and also for a cozy, candlelit dinner in the evening. With a full dinner menu, the Brazenhead makes for a convenient stop on the way

back from the Guinness Storehouse. The beef and Guinness stew will keep you full for days! Don't forget to check out the hundreds of badges left by police officers and firefighters over the years, tacked onto the walls.

Pints from €5, 20 Lower Bridge St, South Bank, +353 (0)1 677 9549, brazenhead.com

The Stag's Head

The Stag's Head is right behind Sweeney's Bar and the Mercantile. Head upstairs and find a spot on their comfy red leather couch. Make some friends in this social and inviting pub.

Pints from €5, daily 10:30–01:00, 1 Dame Court, South Bank, +353 (0)1 679 3687

Cobblestone Pub

Widely regarded for having the best trad sessions in the city, the Cobblestone is your classic Irish pub with no-frills wooden interior and cozy, welcoming atmosphere. It draws local musicians and eager tourists. While a bit out of the way, and north of the river, it is in close proximity to the Jameson Distillery and the Generator Hostel, so keep it in mind if you're out that direction. Trad sessions don't usually kick off till around 20:00 or later. To get here, take a tram to the Smithfield stop.

Drinks from €5, Mon–Thurs 16:00–23:30, Fri–Sat 16:00–00:30, Sun 13:00–23:00, 77 King St N, Greater Dublin, +353 (0)1 872 1799

O'Neill's Bar and Restaurant

A few classic pubs in Dublin just feel like home as soon as you step inside. Come out for a pint, pub grub, or just some tea and head upstairs to find one of O'Neill's many cozy *snugs*—tiny walled-off booths typical to Irish pubs. Snugs were originally developed for women to enjoy their drinks in peace.

Pints from €5, daily 10:30–23:30, 2 Suffolk St, South Bank, +353 (0)1 679 3656, oneillsbar.com

BARS

The Mercantile

This hotel, restaurant, and bar right on the main drag of Dublin, Dame Street, is the meeting point for daily walking tours and nightly pub crawls put on by Hostelculture. The interior is richly decorated with textured ceilings and ornate ironwork, with three full bars done up in a kind of posh, old-world style. The open upper floor looks down onto the ground level. With quick and friendly service, the Mercantile is a great choice for an afternoon tea, after-work pint or to catch

ACT LIKE A LOCAL

The Trad

Traditional Irish music, or "trad," as it's called, is a mainstay of Irish culture. Locals grow up learning more than 400 traditional Irish songs with friends and family at the pub—which, in Ireland, really does mean "public house." Pubs are Ireland's "third space," where families enjoy spending time outside the home and workplace. In the countryside, it's quite normal to see entire communities hanging out in the pub enjoying dinner and listening to Celtic songs. The better the party vibe and atmosphere, the better the *craic* (enjoyment). Here's how to blend in with the locals and make the most of these Irish jam sessions.

Understand the trad. Traditional Irish music is kept alive by amateur musicians who aren't paid a thing besides a few pints of Guinness and the joy of playing the music of their forebears. Bands comprise any combination of the following instruments: the bodhran (pronounced BOH-run), the penny flute, the Irish pipes if you're lucky, and maybe a fiddle or two. You may even get a vocalist, which really completes the ensemble. Most every Irish person knows the words to every tune. Songs can be upbeat and happy, or they can be melancholy, about remembering the mass emigration from Ireland or battles in foreign lands, or about missing the motherland. When these morose ballads, or "laments," come on, hold your conversation out of respect for the musicians, especially if there's a vocalist. The scene is comparable to a pickup game of basketball: It never quite ends, and newcomers are always welcome, even if all they have is a pair of spoons. As a visitor, all you've got to do now is find your own little bar, pull up a stool, order a pint, and toast to the good life. *Slainte* ("To your health!"), my friends!

Sing along. Popular trad songs you'll hear at the pubs include "Galway Girl," "The Rocky Road to Dublin," "The Wild Rover," "Whiskey in the Jar," and "Molly Malone." Find lyrics online, and sing along!

Tap your foot. You may be tempted to clap along with the music because you're digging it just so much. If the musicians are on a fun riff, they'll continue, and before you know it, songs may flower into beautiful 20-minute runs. After a while, your arms get tired, you get thirsty, and you stop clapping to pick up your pint glass to take a sip. In the process, you completely deflate the energy of the song. So instead of clapping, tap your foot with the locals—or let out a little yelp if you're really impressed.

Buy a round. The Irish are all about pints with friends at the pub, and they've got the round system down to a science: Anytime you finish a pint, go around the circle for one person to get the group a round. It all operates on the assumption that once started, a circle of rounds must be completed. So when it comes to your turn, don't be running off to the loo!

the game on several large screens. The Mercantile's back door opens onto Dame Lane, where you'll find a whole slew of fun, casual bars to keep the night going late.

Pints around €5, 28 Dame St, +353 (0)1 670 7100, mercantile.ie

Drury Buildings Cocktail Bar

If the budget can handle €13 drinks, come out to the Drury Buildings Cocktail Bar and take a sip of their heavenly old-fashioned in a leafy multi-level and balconied floor plan complete with a budding urban garden.

While the old-fashioned is my go-to, they've got a quite a roster of creative and high-quality Prohibition-era cocktails, such as their sidecar and frothy whiskey sour, that make you feel like you've stepped back in time. Be prepared to wait a bit for your cocktails—they've gotta make it just right.

Cocktails from €13, daily 12:00-23:30, 55 Drury St, South Bank, +353 (0)1 960 2095, drurybuildings.com

Garage Bar

Take a load off on one of the Garage Bar's barrel stools and knock back drinks with a crowd that just doesn't really give a darn. This is Temple Bar's alternative bar, where they may well be playing *Star Wars Episode IV*. But you know what? It feels perfectly in place. Drinks here are the cheapest in this district.

Drinks from €4.50, Mon-Tues 17:00-24:00, Wed-Sun 17:00-02:30, Essex St East, Temple Bar, +353 (0)1 679 6543, garagebar.ie

The Bar with No Name

As with all things hipster, you can't quite have anything easy. In this case, try finding the bar with no name, also known as Snail Bar. Look for the wooden snail above its door, and climb the stairs into what feels like the city's biggest secret. The beer garden/smoking lounge is a favorite for everyone out back.

Pints from €5, Sun-Wed 12:30-23:30, Thurs 12:30-01:00, Fri-Sat 12:30-02:30, 3 Fade St, South Bank, +353 (0)1 648 0022, kellysdublin.com

The Bank Bar

The Bank Bar sports a spectacular interior in a renovated bank. I love this spot for the *craic*, especially when sports games are on. Gazing around the opulent golden architectural accents, I wonder if this is what Gatsby's world looked like.

Pints from €5.50, Mon-Thurs 11:00-00:30, Fri-Sat 11:00-01:30, Sun 11:00-24:00, 20 College Green, Temple Bar, +353 (0)1 677 0677, bankoncollegegreen.com

Sweeney's Bar

Probably my favorite bar in town, decked out with art nouveau-esque interior, yet packed out with Dublin's rasta and punk crew. Excellent live music goes down often both upstairs on the stage and downstairs in more of a concert type venue. Partiers spill

out onto Dame Lane, the back alley where everyone's having a smoke and checking out the vibe in each of the next-door bars.

Pints from €5, Sun-Tues 12:00-23:00, Wed-Sat 12:00-02:30, 32 Dame St, Temple Bar, +353 (0)1 635 0056, sweeneysdublin.ie

Whelan's

Made famous as a set in the tear-jerking *P.S. I Love You*, starring Gerard Butler, Whelan's is a great spot that doesn't rest on its laurels. You've got several rooms and bars to choose from, including a midsize concert venue frequently rocked out by resident and traveling bands alike. Check out the website, as some shows require a password or tickets ahead of time.

Pints from €5, Mon-Fri 14:30-02:30, Sat 17:00-02:30, Sun 17:00-01:30, 25 Wexford St, South Bank, +353 (0)1 478 0766, whelanslive.com

The Porterhouse

With two locations in Dublin, this chain pours only what they brew, so you won't find any Guinness here. With the excellent lineup of live music and the beautiful dark wood interior, you wouldn't even know that it's part of a larger chain. They feature live acts throughout the week. Find the second, less-interesting location alongside Trinity College (45 Nassau St).

Pints from €5, Mon-Wed 11:30-24:00, Thurs 11:30-01:00, Fri-Sat 11:30-02:00, Sun 12:30-24:00, 16 Parliament St, Temple Bar, +353 (0)1 679 8847, porterhousebrewco.com

The Workman's Club

Packed out with local students, this is Temple Bar's best spot to rock out to loud rock 'n' roll. Come out for the drink prices, and stick around if you don't mind the sticky, sweaty

college-dorm-party vibe. I also like the bar on the ground floor, Bison Bar, for a wee dram of whiskey on full-on leather saddles.

Pints from €4, daily 17:00–03:00, 10 Wellington Quay, Temple Bar, +353 (0)1 670 6692, theworkmansclub.com

Café en Seine
This is a strikingly beautiful renovated and decorated classic pub with delicious brunch options earlier in the day, tea for the afternoon, and serious parties each night. It's an excellent place for a drink underneath a turn of the 20th century art nouveau-style interior. A dance floor with a DJ kicks off on the weekends. Check out the posh whiskey bar next door, **37 Dawson Street,** too.

Drinks from €6, Mon-Tues 12:00-24:00, Wed-Sat 12:00–03:00, Sun 12:00-23:00, 40 Dawson St, South Bank, +353 (0)1 677 4567, cafeenseine.ie

Odessa
I love this little speakeasy-type cocktail lounge on the third and fourth floors of a building right behind Dame Lane. I dig the eclectic interior and retro '70s vibe. Climb the stairs to the top, order a drink, and enjoy sipping it on the rooftop patio, rubbing elbows with Dublin's socialites.

Drinks from €7, Mon-Thurs 12:00–00:30, Fri-Sat 12:00-02:30, Sun 12:00-24:00, 14 Dame Court, Temple Bar, +353 (0)1 670 3080, odessa.ie

Flannery's
If I know I'm going to be clubbing at either Dicey's or Copper Face Jacks, this is a requisite stop for the cheap drinks, fun vibe, and good chance of meeting people with the same agenda for the night.

Drinks from €4, daily 11:00–02:30, 6 Camden St Lower, South Bank, +353 (0)1 478 2238, flannerysdublin.com

The Pavilion
The student bar at Trinity College has cheap food and possibly the cheapest drinks in Dublin. Heads-up: The place packs out during Trinity exams; students go both before and after—first for confidence, and second to celebrate.

Drinks from €3.50, Mon–Sat 12:00-23:00, inside Trinity College, South Bank, +353 (0)1 608 1279, ducac.tcdlife.ie/pavilion

CLUBS
Dandelion
Clubs aren't cheap in Dublin, but they're certainly a great time, and this club is one of my favorites. Located just at the top of Grafton, Dandelion has a busy bar upstairs and pumping dance floor downstairs. Before heading in, know that they're heavy on the electronic. It's a good idea to check the program online to know what to expect.

MOLLY MALONE

You're sure to hear this popular song sharing the story of a 17th-century fishmonger who sold seafood by day and something else quite different by night:

Chorus:
Alive, alive oh,
Alive, alive oh,
Crying cockles and mussels,
Alive, alive oh.

Verse 1:
In Dublin's fair city,
Where the girls are so pretty,
I first set me eyes on sweet Molly Malone,
As she wheeled her wheelbarrow,
Through streets broad and narrow,
Cryin' "Cockles and mussels alive, alive oh!"

Chorus

Verse 2:
She was a fishmonger,
And sure it t'was no wonder,

As so was her Father and Mother before,
They each wheeled their barrows,
Through streets broad and narrow,
Crying "Cockles and mussels alive, alive oh!"

Chorus

Verse 3 (the sad verse):
She died of fever,
And no-one could save her,
And that was the end of sweet Molly Malone,
Now her ghost wheels her barrow,
Through streets broad and narrow,
Crying "Cockles and mussels alive, alive oh!"

Chorus

Covers €5-10 on the weekends, drinks around €7.50, 130-133 St Stephen's Green West, South Bank, +353 (0)1 476 0870, welovedandelion.com

Copper Face Jacks

Copper Face Jacks, aka Copper's, is a well-known sloppy meat market that draws nurses and firefighters whose shifts don't line up with the rest of ours. That means their parties go hard every night of the week in this large, double-floored dance venue. Dress to impress to give yourself a better chance at the door. Bouncers have been known to hold back the last person in a group to try to squeeze out an extra tenner.

Cover and drinks €10, 29 Harcourt St, South Bank, +353 (0)1 425 5300, copperfacejacks.ie

Dicey's Garden Bar

The crowd packs out Dicey's as a cheaper option to Copper's just down the street. You really can't complain about the €2 drinks every Sunday and Tuesday, but with them comes all the sloppiness of the crowd that is there for the same reason.

Drinks and cover usually around €5, daily 16:00-02:30,

21-25 Harcourt St, South Bank, +353 (0)1 478 4841, russellcourthotel.ie

PUB CRAWLS

Hostelculture Pub Crawl

The same company that runs daily walking tours through the city also offers a fun way to check out the town after the sun goes down: a pub crawl hitting up some of my favorite spots. This reasonably priced crawl includes a free half-pint and shots at each stop along the way.

€12, kicking off nightly at 20:00 at the Mercantile Pub, 28 Dame St, Temple Bar

Traditional Irish Musical Pub Crawl

For an immensely entertaining evening, join the trad music pub crawl. Each stop gives you not only the opportunity for another tasty pint of Guinness, but also another few songs and lessons put on by the Irish musicians, who double as your guides.

€12, Apr-Oct 19:30 nightly, meets at Oliver St John Gogarty Hostel's pub, 58 Fleet St, Temple Bar, book at discoverdublin.ie/musical-pub-crawl

TOP SHOPPING & MARKETS

Cute little boutiques are popping up all over Dublin, vending everything from black-and-white prints to lace and pottery.

SHOPPING DISTRICTS

Grafton Street

Grafton Street, leading from the corner of Trinity College's campus several blocks up to St Stephen's Green, is Dublin's main pedestrian shopping drag. You'll find everything from Diesel jeans to Starbucks coffee. While a bit mainstream, it's a one-stop shop for fashion, souvenirs, and food and coffee. Venture west a block or two and get lost in the lanes featuring endless options. Stephen's Green Shopping Centre at the top of the street has more stores and a food court upstairs.

South Bank

MARKETS

Georges Street Arcade

Probably the most beloved market amongst

locals and tourists alike, the Georges Street Arcade has it all. With over 50 shops and stalls inside an enclosed market, this place offers everything from vintage clothing, antiques, hairdressing, and music to art stalls, restaurants and cafés, and more.

Mon, Tues, Wed, Fri, and Sat 09:00-18:30, Thurs 09:00-20:00, Sun 12:00-18:30, off of S Great Georges St, South Bank, georgesstreetarcade.ie

Temple Bar Food Market

Right in the center of Dublin's party district, this small outdoor market is a foodie's paradise, with vendors selling a wide variety of items from all over the world, including cakes, sushi, waffles, Spanish tapas, French bread, German sausages, and delicious homemade chocolates.

Sat 10:00-16:30, 12 East Essex St, Temple Bar, templebar.ie

GUINNESS

ST. JAMES'S GATE BREWERY, DUBLIN

THE TEMPLE BAR

O'Reilly's
TRADITIONAL IRISH FOOD

TOBACCO

TOP PARKS & RECREATION

St Stephen's Green
St Stephen's Green is a beautiful manicured park in the heart of Dublin about two city blocks wide and two deep. Take a stroll over the bridges, through the trees, and past the landscaped shrubbery and statues. St Stephen's Green was turned from a private to a public park and has changed little in the last hundred years. Many original Georgian buildings still surround the park today.

Free, always open, South Bank

Phoenix Park
Spanning over 1,750 acres, this is the biggest gated city park in all of Europe. It is home to two herds of deer and the US Ambassador to Ireland (the mansion is right in the heart of the park). It's a great place to get away from the city without actually leaving it. Pack a picnic and relax in this inviting green escape. Explore miles of trails and fields and even the city **zoo** (€16.80, daily 09:30-15:00, +353 (0)1 474 8900). Phoenix Park was also the site of Pope John Paul II's visit in 1979, drawing more than one million faithful to a Mass and blessing with the late pope. The park is just about a thirty-minute walk west of the city center. To get here, take bus route 37 toward Blanchardstown Road South.

Free, always open, Greater Dublin

TOP TOURS

Hostelculture Free Walking Tour
Hostelculture offers daily free walking tours. I appreciate their entertaining approach to touring, with knowledgeable Irish guides. Count on consistency and a great intro to the city of Dublin over their three-hour tours. Hostelculture also offers a **Literary Walk** (free, Tues, Thurs, Sat, and Sun 14:30), a **Brew Legacy Tour** (free, Mon, Wed, Fri, and Sun 15:00), and a **Pub Crawl** (€12, nightly 20:00).

Free, daily 11:00 and 14:00, meet at the Mercantile pub, 28 Dame St, Temple Bar, +353 (0)83 117 1197, hostelculture.com/dublintours

Sandeman's New Europe Walking Tours
Sandeman's offers free walking tours to all of Dublin's most important sights. The casual tour lasts approximately 4.5 hours.

Just look for the guide in the red Sandeman T-shirt, and don't forget to tip for a job well done.

Free, 11:00 and 13:00 daily, meet at City Hall, Temple Bar, newdublintours.com

1916 Rebellion Walking Tour
For those interested in Ireland's tumultuous and complicated 20th-century history, this Easter Rising tour retraces the steps of those who brought the world's attention to the plight of Ireland. Kicking off in a typical pub, this tour starts with a rundown of the main players and timeline of the events, then takes you out to see the marks of the conflict still visible on the city today.

€12, meets Mon-Sat 11:30, Sun 13:00 at the International Bar, 23 Wicklow St, South Bank, +353 (0)868 583 847, 1916rising.com, lorcan@1916rising.com

TOP HOSTELS

Dublin has a wide selection of budget accommodations. They do fill up over popular periods like over St Patrick's week, New Year's, and Christmas, as well as during important sporting events. The annual international rugby tournament 6 Nations, happening each February and March, and other matches draw huge crowds to Dublin when the team is playing at home. Hostels are the first to get booked out. Once you know the dates of your visit, book ahead through each hostel's online booking system.

Barnacles Temple Bar Hostel
Literally next door to the famous Temple Bar, this is the place to stay in Dublin. This hostel has grown organically over time, slowly taking over the building to add more dorms and common rooms. A welcoming and friendly staff guarantees a wonderful time in the city, and they're happy to recommend sightseeing, activities, and nightlife options. Hang out in the common room to

get in on the relaxed, social backpacker vibe and make some friends. The stellar online reviews generate bookings fast and early, so make sure to reserve your spot ahead of time to join in on the party!

From €10, free Wi-Fi, free breakfast, common room, bunks and small private rooms available, 19 Temple Lane South, Temple Bar, +353 (0)1 671 6277, barnacles.ie, templebar@barnacles.ie

Abbey Court

Located on the north side of the River Liffey, Abbey Court is your best-located cheap option in town. The staff does their best to keep the place clean, but it's hard to stay up with the hundreds of guests staying here. There's a solid communal kitchen, a social lounge, and a new *shebeen* (speakeasy bar) out in the back in an old storage cellar. Each room in the place feels like it has just a couple too many beds, making space tight from the quad rooms on up to the large, 40+ bed snoring chambers.

From €15, 24-hour reception, free Wi-Fi, laundry, large bunk rooms, public kitchen, great storage, technology charging stations, private bar, food discounts at nearby restaurants, 29 Bachelors Walk, North Side, +353 (0)1 878 0700, abbey-court.com, info@abbey-court.com

Sky Backpackers Hostel

This is one of Dublin's newest hostels; look forward to an excellent location (just on the north side of the River Liffey), welcoming staff, and newly refurbished facilities. The brightly colored common room is great for the social atmosphere. The new paint job turns what is otherwise a junky alley into a welcoming oasis to escape the noise on Temple Bar.

Beds from €20, free Wi-Fi, common room, showers included, luggage storage available, activities and events organized often, and deals offered for visiting musicians, 4 Litton Ln, North Side, +353 (0)1 872 8389, skybackpackers.com, liffey@skybackpackers.com

Abigail's Hostel

Abigail's, popular among backpackers and school groups, is another of Dublin's superbly located large hostels. The breakfast and location (just south of the River Liffey in Temple Bar) are Abigail's two highlights. The slightly outdated rooms and overall cleanliness lag behind.

Beds from €14, free Wi-Fi, extensive free breakfast, showers included, 24-hour reception, adapters, towels and locks available for rent, common room, 7 Aston Quay, Temple Bar, +353 (0)1 677 9300, abigailshostel.com, stay@abigailshostel.com

Avalon House Hostel

Avalon is your true backpacker hostel, with all the charm and social atmosphere you could ask for. The price is right, and the welcoming staff is happy to recommend nearby restaurants and activities. They even go the extra mile of creating info sheets that are free for you to grab on arrival, with tips on food, sights, and nightlife. The hostel is just stumbling distance from some of Dublin's best bars and clubs, like Whelan's, Flannery's, and Copper Face Jacks. Avalon's sister hostel, **Kinlay House Hostel** (12 Lord Edward St, +353 (0)1 679 6644, kinlaydublin.ie, info@kinlaydublin.ie) is another good choice, offering the same experience and prices.

Beds from €12, free Wi-Fi, breakfast included, locks, towels, and adapters for hire, common rooms, free tours leaving daily from the lobby, free showers, 55 Aungier St (pronounced AN jer), South Bank, +353 (0)1 475 0001, Avalon-house.ie, info@avalon-house.ie

Generator Hostel

The Generator chain has found the right formula across its many locations in Europe. This branch is popular among American students for its new, large, bright, and institutional interior and its fast, free Wi-Fi. I love the hostel's bar and restaurant, open just about any time I need food! The drawback is its location in Smithfield, on the north side of River Liffey. It's about a 20-minute walk into central Dublin. Be attentive when walking these streets late at night (though the city is working hard to clean them up). To get here, take a tram to the Smithfield stop.

Beds from €18, free Wi-Fi, breakfast included, locks, towels and adapters for hire, female-only dorms available, comfy new beds, Greater Dublin, +353 (0)1 901 0222, generatorhostels.com/en/destinations/Dublin, dublin@generatorhostels.com

DUBLIN

GETTING THERE & AWAY

Since Ireland is an island, flying to Dublin is your best option if you're coming from outside the country. There is a ferry from mainland Europe and the UK; however, it's slow and doesn't save you money over the numerous cheap budget flights into Dublin.

Plane

All major airlines and budget airlines fly into **Dublin Airport** (DUB, dublinairport. com). All AerLingus flights arrive into the shiny new Terminal 2. All other flights use Terminal 1. Connections into the city center are quick and easy.

AirCoach, operating 24 hours a day, has buses running every 10 minutes during the day and less frequently at night. The connection into the center takes about 40 minutes (€7 one-way, €12 round-trip). There are numerous stops downtown, so ask which is closest to your accommodations as you purchase your ticket.

Dublin Bus's **Airlink**, bus 747, is convenient, and it's my usual choice at €6 each way. Monday-Saturday, the first bus is at 05:45, and then every 10 minutes until 19:40, when the buses come less frequently. On Sunday, the first bus is at 07:15.

You'll find the **taxi** stand just outside the arrivals hall. A cab from the airport to Temple Bar costs about €30, depending on the time of day and the traffic. Ask the driver for an approximate price before you get in, and be attentive that you're not taken on the "scenic route." I've not had the best of luck with drivers in this city. Cabbies will often offer to take you through the tunnel (a faster route saving about 10 minutes) for the cost of the toll fee (to airport: €10 Mon-Fri 16:00-19:00, €3 otherwise; from airport: €10 Mon-Fri 06:00-10:00, €3 otherwise), but unless you're in a hurry, it's not worth it. Or, skip the worry and use the free Wi-Fi at the airport to ping an **Uber**.

If you're flying RyanAir and forgot to print out your boarding pass, there are computers and printers located in both terminals. You can also use them to print directions to your accommodations upon arrival.

Train

Ireland has a convenient domestic network of train connections around the island by the **Iarnrod Eireann** (irishrail.ie) service.

Check the website for timetables and prices.

Dublin has two railway stations, which are important to note for travelers taking the train out of Dublin. **Dublin Heuston** serves all connections going west and south from Dublin (Galway, Cork, Dingle). It's on the west side of town, not far from the Guinness Storehouse and just south of the River Liffey and Phoenix Park. **Dublin Connolly** serves connections heading north (Belfast, Derry). The station is right next to the main bus station, north of the Customs House and the River Liffey.

Bus

Ireland has an extensive network of bus lines, with direct connections to most cities in Ireland. Do your research for timetables and prices on getthere.ie and book directly with the bus company offering the most convenient time and price. Major bus lines, including **GoBe** (gobe.ie), **Air Coach** (aircoach.ie), the national **Bus Eireann** (buseireann.ie), **CityLink** (citylink.ie), **Dublin Coach** (dublincoach.ie) and **Go Bus** (gobus. ie) all offer competitive pricing and free Wi-Fi on board.

Buses take 2.5+ hours to Galway, 3+ hours to Cork and 2.5+ hours up to Belfast. Find the main bus terminal, **Bus Aras,** directly behind the Customs House in downtown Dublin, just north of the River Liffey, east of O'Connell Street.

Car

Dublin is about 470 kilometers (7.5 hours) driving from Edinburgh and about 600 kilometers (9 hours) driving from London. Both routes include a ferry crossing. It's much easier and probably cheaper to fly into Dublin than to drive there.

GETTING AROUND

Dublin's relatively compact center makes it an easy city to walk across. For this reason, I've only provided public transportation connection information for sights farther from the center. That being said, Dublin's integrated public transportation makes it easy to get around town via bus and trams. If you're around for a few days and plan on taking the bus a few times, consider picking up a **Leap Card** (leapcard.ie, refundable €5 deposit), equivalent to London's Oyster Card. Tap in and out with your Leap Card on both buses and trams to receive slightly discounted fares. Individual tickets are nontransferable, so you must purchase another ticket each time you transfer.

Bus

It's easy to get around Dublin on the buses, and the drivers are generally nice and happy to help answer questions. Purchase your ticket as you board with exact change, telling the driver where you want to go (the machine just keeps the change if you overpay). If you overpay, you'll receive a "change ticket," which you then can take to the Dublin Bus office on O'Connell Street, where they'll give you your change—but it's hardly worth the time to do this. Break your bills ahead of time to have change on hand. Bus fare within greater Dublin is €1.60.

Look up routes on Google or through the nifty **Dublin Bus** app (available in the app store), which allows for dynamic route searches and shows you exactly where bus stops are located.

Tram

Dublin's tram system, **LUAS** (luas.ie), runs two disconnected lines that are convenient only if you find yourself near the tracks for accommodations or sightseeing. Purchase your ticket at the easy-to-use machines located at any station. Ticket prices are determined based on the number of zones you cross through. The **red line** connects the Connolly Train Station, the Busaras station, O'Connell Street, Jameson Distillery, and Phoenix Park on the north side of town before looping south past Heuston

train station. The **green line** picks up at St Stephen's Green and runs south.

Train

The **DART,** Dublin's regional commuter train service, is a convenient way to get outside the city for day trips to destinations like Dun Laoghaire and Howth. Connections for both leave from Tara Street station, near O'Connell Bridge. Buy tickets online or at the station from one of the ticket booths. Find more information at irishrail.ie.

Taxi

Taxis in Dublin are safe and registered. Make sure cabbies using their meter, and feel free to ask for an estimate before you get in. **Uber** and the Irish equivalent, **Hailo,** are both widely used.

Bicycle

Dublin is rated as one of the top 10 bike-friendly cities in the world. A public bike-rental service (dublinbikes.ie) gives you access to over 500 bikes and 15 stations across the city. Annual users get their subscription for €20, while visitors can opt into the three-day membership for €5. Membership gets you unlimited free 30-minute rides. After that, the service charges €0.50 for up to an hour, €1.50 for up to two hours, €3.50 for up to three hours, €6.50 for up to four hours, and €2 for each additional half hour. Leap-frogging from one station to the next, plugging in your older bike and taking a new one, is totally OK and an accepted use of the system. Purchase your pass at any of the stations that take credit cards and follow the on-screen directions.

DAY TRIPS

Howth & Coastal Hike

Originally founded by the Vikings a millennium ago, Howth is a small coastal town that has persevered as a fishing village and small port. The humble port gained notoriety in 1914, when 900 rifles were smuggled through it and used a couple years later during the failed Easter Rising and subsequent Irish Civil War. Take a half day to explore the port and enjoy the posh **farmers market** (Fri-Sun 9:00-18:00, better in the mornings) with blended juices and cutesy decorated muffins. You can also walk out on Howth's two piers, where some locals like to feed the seals. One of the piers is capped by a 200-year-old lighthouse.

For lunch, head to the **Bloody Stream** (desserts from €4.50, Mon-Thurs 12:00-23:30, Fri-Sat 12:00-02:30, Sun 12:00-01:30, Howth Railway Station, +353 (0)1 839 5076, bloodystream.ie), located right under the train station. Relax in front of the fire at this bar and restaurant, which serves a delicious homemade apple crumble, whiskey, and coffee that hits the spot on a typically drizzly day.

If it's not raining, take the challenging 1.5-hour-long hike out around the head of the rock. The hike offers stunning views of the rugged coastline and Dublin Harbor. It's a perfect substitute for those who don't have time to make it all the way out to the

Cliffs of Moher but still want to experience Ireland's natural beauty. Be sure to walk up to the "summit" parking lot, where you'll get some amazing views across Dublin Bay. On a clear day, you'll see the Bailey Lighthouse and even the dramatic Wicklow Mountains out in the distance to the south. Get started on the hike by following the street past the second pier and uphill along the coast before it leads you to the trailhead. Pick up a free map at the train station, or watch for displays of the limited hiking routes.

The suburban **DART** train from Dublin's Tara Street station makes the 30-minute, €3.15 transfer to Howth easy and cheap. Trains depart every 30 minutes. Ask for a town and trail map on arrival in Howth.

The Cliffs of Moher

For many people coming to Ireland, the Cliffs of Moher are at the top of their list. Packing them in in a day is a challenge, but just about everyone who visits says it's well worth the time out to the cliffs, which tower up to 700 feet above the water. Named after a fort that once perched at the south side of the cliffs, today they're one of Ireland's top tourist destinations, with over a million visiting each year. While it used to be free, the park now charges €6 a head to maintain the trails and the health of the park.

Start your experience at the visitors center, which shares background information on the cliffs and about the flora and fauna of this unique region through multimedia displays and interactive screens. A panoramic video mimics the view that the birds have over the steep drop, evoking butterflies in the stomach. You then leave the center and strike out in either of two directions for a stroll along the cliff face, seeing the rich green lawns abruptly drop straight to the sea far below. It's worth checking the forecast ahead of time, as limited visibility can really kill the experience, though the weather is nearly impossible to predict on the west coast of Ireland.

Numerous tour operators connect the Cliffs of Moher from Dublin city's center, leaving early in the morning and returning around dinnertime. The drive out from Dublin is across the entire country, and it lasts about three hours with some stops in between. Consider a tour with **PaddyWagon Tours** (€40, daily 08:00, meet on Suffolk Street at the *Molly Malone* statue, paddywagontours.com) or **Day Tours Ireland** (€45, daily 06:50, meet on Suffolk Street at the *Molly Malone* statue, daytours.ie/cliffs-of-moher).

HELP!

Tourist Information Centers

A heads-up to the smart tourist: Many enterprising companies have opened up storefronts on main tourist drags in Dublin like Grafton Street, Dame Street, and O'Connell. They've covered these storefronts with signs that say Tourist Information, portraying themselves as unbiased sources of information, but in fact they sell tours from only one brand or a certain set of hotels, for a commission. The only official tourist information office, **Visit Dublin** (25 Suffolk St) is located in the old stone St Andrew's church with the bronze *Molly Malone* statue pushing her wheelbarrow of cockles and mussels out front. The friendly staff is happy to help you plan your time in Dublin and for trips beyond the city.

Pickpockets & Scams

As in the rest of Western Europe, violent crime in Dublin is extremely low; however, purse snatching and pickpocketing do oc-

cur, so always be on your guard in crowded areas such as train stations and touristy destinations. ATM fraud is on the rise in Dublin. Thieves use "skimmers"—small electronic devices that can be attached to the outside of an ATM—to steal PIN codes. It's always important to check the ATM for any signs of tampering before using it. Certain parts of the far-north side of town can get a bit seedy later at night—but not to worry, I haven't recommended any sights in this area.

Emergencies
In an emergency, dial 999.

Hospital
St James's Hospital
James's St, Dublin 8
+353 (0)1 410 3000

US Embassy
42 Elgin Rd, Ballsbridge Dublin 4
+353 (0)1 668 9612

EDINBURGH

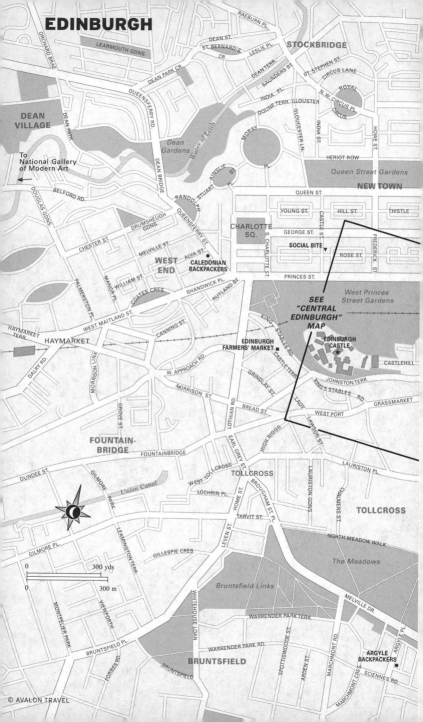

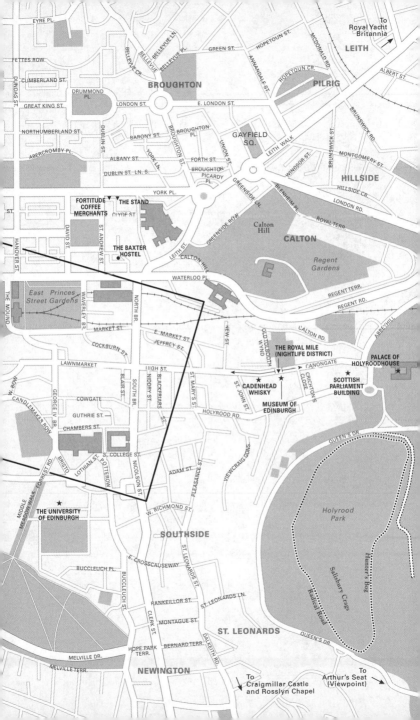

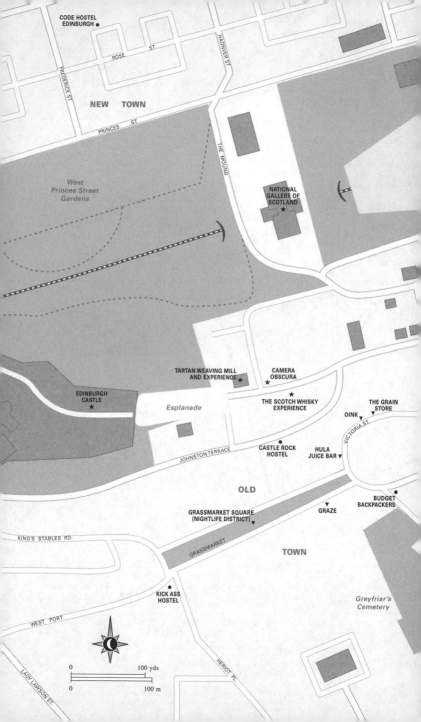

CODE HOSTEL
EDINBURGH ●

ROSE   ST.

FREDERICK ST.

HANOVER ST.

NEW TOWN

PRINCES   ST.

THE MOUND

*West
Princes Street
Gardens*

NATIONAL
GALLERY OF
SCOTLAND
★

TARTAN WEAVING MILL
AND EXPERIENCE ★

CAMERA
OBSCURA
★

THE SCOTCH WHISKY
EXPERIENCE ★

EDINBURGH
CASTLE
★

Esplanade

THE GRAIN
STORE

OINK ▾

VICTORIA ST.

JOHNSTON TERRACE

CASTLE ROCK
HOSTEL ●

HULA
JUICE BAR ▾

OLD

BUDGET
BACKPACKERS ●

GRASSMARKET SQUARE
(NIGHTLIFE DISTRICT) ▾

GRAZE ▾

KING'S STABLES RD.

GRASSMARKET

TOWN

*Greyfriar's
Cemetery*

KICK ASS
HOSTEL ●

WEST   PORT

HERIOT PL.

LADY LAWSON ST.

0   100 yds

0   100 m

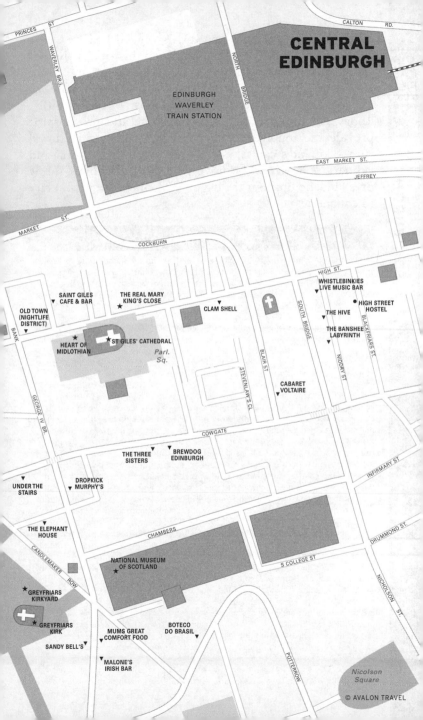

CENTRAL EDINBURGH

PRINCES ST.

WAVERLEY BR.

CALTON RD.

EDINBURGH WAVERLEY TRAIN STATION

NORTH BRIDGE

EAST MARKET ST.

JEFFREY

MARKET ST.

COCKBURN

HIGH ST.

SAINT GILES CAFE & BAR ▼

THE REAL MARY KING'S CLOSE ★

CLAM SHELL

WHISTLEBINKIES LIVE MUSIC BAR ▼

● HIGH STREET HOSTEL

OLD TOWN (NIGHTLIFE DISTRICT)

THE HIVE ▼

BANK

HEART OF MIDLOTHIAN ★

★ ST GILES' CATHEDRAL

Parl. Sq.

SOUTH BRIDGE

THE BANSHEE LABYRINTH ▼

BLACKFRIARS ST.

GEORGE IV BR.

STEVENLAW'S CL.

BLAIR ST.

CABARET VOLTAIRE

NIDDRY ST.

COWGATE

THE THREE SISTERS ▼

BREWDOG EDINBURGH ▼

INFIRMARY ST.

UNDER THE STAIRS ▼

DROPKICK MURPHY'S ▼

THE ELEPHANT HOUSE ▼

CHAMBERS

DRUMMOND ST.

CANDLEMAKER ROW

NATIONAL MUSEUM OF SCOTLAND ★

S COLLEGE ST.

NICHOLSON ST.

★ GREYFRIARS KIRKYARD

✚ GREYFRIARS KIRK ★

MUMS GREAT COMFORT FOOD ▼

BOTECO DO BRASIL ▼

SANDY BELL'S ▼

MALONE'S IRISH BAR ▼

POTTERROW

Nicolson Square

© AVALON TRAVEL

Edinburgh is renowned for its rugged beauty, Celtic roots, and gruesome medieval history. With its striking architecture and dramatic setting amid hills and cliffs that were carved by glaciers millions of years ago, it's one of Europe's most beautiful cities. Today, Edinburgh's solid volcanic stone and proud spirit provide the foundation for the city's compact medieval core. Scotland's capital is enjoying a full-on cultural and culinary renaissance. So leave your pants at home, throw on a kilt, and bust out the bagpipes: Edinburgh is your city to conquer!

EDINBURGH 101

The foundations of modern Edinburgh were established with a fort atop Castle Rock by an ancient Celtic tribe, the Gododdin, around AD 600, but evidence of settlement goes back much further than that, up to 3,000 years ago. Early settlers chose this strategic and easy-to-defend location quite deliberately. They named the fort Din Eidyn, and it kept the name until the English starting poking around in the 7th century. In 638, the Angles, the ancestors of the English we know today, invaded the fort and claimed control over the area for the next three hundred years, naming it "Eiden's Burgh," the word *burgh* meaning "fort." It wasn't until the 10th century that the Scots finally reclaimed Edinburgh as their own.

Over the centuries, Scotland battled England for independence and sovereignty. The struggle is depicted in the film *Braveheart,* which follows young William Wallace in the late 13th century as he tried to unite the Scots and defeat the intruders from the south. Utilizing skirmish and guerrilla tactics, Wallace led successful raids into the bordering region of England and battled the more numerous but less-nimble English armies. Wallace's good fortune ran out in 1298, when he lost the Battle of Falkirk. Barely escaping with his life, he lay low until being captured seven years later. He was subjected to the medieval punishment dished out to those charged with treason against the British crown: hanging, drawing, emasculation, and quartering. This brutal punishment involved being hanged to near death; being taken down while still alive to watch your guts get cut out and burned in front of you; and then having your genitals cut off, along with your arms and legs. Finally, your head was chopped off and your remains were displayed across the country to warn potential offenders just what happens to their kind when caught. Youch.

Things only settled down between Scotland and England around 1706, when the Acts of Union were passed. This led to the unification of England and Scotland into the Kingdom of Great Britain. At this point, Edinburgh, the capital of Scotland, was infamous for being a dark, filthy city. Edinburgh is credited with having the world's first tenements, where numerous families lived in single rooms. Bordered to the north by a lake, the city walls to the east and south, with the castle to the west, the old medieval town could not expand outward, only upward. As the city grew taller and taller, the streets grew darker and were covered in whatever would have gone down the nonexistent sewage system.

With the advent of industrialization and trade, Scotland began its steady rise into prosperity, gaining the nickname in the 18th century as the "Athens of the North" due to its classical architecture and its reputation for producing great minds, including Adam Smith, Joseph Black, and David Hume. Edinburgh came into its own as a center for intellectual and artistic thought. Also at this time, plans were drawn up for an expansion of the city just to the north of the Old Town. Once it was completed, anyone who could afford to move from the Old Town to this New Town did, leaving the filth and lower classes behind.

Today, Edinburgh is bustling with a renaissance of cuisine, culture, music, and live entertainment. It's a fascinating time to visit this vibrant northern capital.

PLAN AHEAD

RESERVATIONS

Reservations are required for **Real Mary King's Close** (realmarykingsclose.com).

Reservations are recommended for the following sights:

Scottish Parliament (scottish.parliament.uk)
Edinburgh Castle (edinburghcastle.gov.uk)

PASSES

While sightseeing in Edinburgh, you may be encouraged to buy the Scotland Explorer Pass. Note that out of more than 70 entries included in the pass, only 10 are actually in Edinburgh. For the visitor coming to see the city of Edinburgh and perhaps take a day trip to a castle outside of town, the pass just isn't worth the price tag.

LOCAL HAPPENINGS

Edinburgh Military Tattoo

Every August, more than 200,000 tourists and locals alike converge on the city of Edinburgh to observe the famous Military Tattoo. No, this isn't one giant inking session, but rather a massive concert repeated over about two weeks beginning in early August (Mon-Fri at 21:00, and twice on Sat, 19:30 and 22:30). Military bands perform in front of stadium seating erected in the Esplanade, the otherwise-nondescript parking lot just in front of Edinburgh Castle. With the dramatic backdrop of the crenellations of the castle, dozens of performing military bands are followed by the lilting serenades of a lone bagpiper, bringing on more than a few goosebumps for the finale. If you plan to visit at this time, book accommodations and tickets as far in advance as possible, as prices skyrocket and availability quickly becomes scarce.

KNOW BEFORE YOU GO

KEY STATS & FIGURES

Currency:
British pound (£);
£1 = about 1.50 USD

Population:
495,360

Language:
English with a killer accent

Top souvenirs:
Scotch whisky, anything plaid, a quaich (a small, traditional Scottish drinking vessel with two arms)

Weather:
generally chilly and damp; layer up!

Local dishes you've gotta try:
haggis and Scotch eggs

CALIBRATE YOUR BUDGET

TYPICAL PRICES FOR:

Hostel dorm bed:
£14

Two-course dinner:
£12

Pint of beer:
£4

Daily bicycle rental:
£20

Single bus pass:
£1.50

MOVIES TO WATCH
Braveheart, Trainspotting, Brave, The Illusionist, Skyfall

THREE DAY ITINERARY

Edinburgh is a compact and walkable city, with most of the major sights concentrated on the Royal Mile. This itinerary hits the top sights in and around town, with time left over for a taste or two of Scotch whisky.

DAY 1: OLD TOWN & EDINBURGH CASTLE

MORNING

Break your fast at one of the many cafés on the way up to the Edinburgh Castle. If you're a fan of smoothies and don't mind a light breakfast, go for **Hula Juice Bar**, at the near corner of Grassmarket Square.

Hike the hill and explore the ramparts of **Edinburgh Castle**, which opens at 09:30. Take advantage of the free, guided walks that head out about every 15 minutes. Two hours is plenty to explore the castle and take in the panoramic views.

AFTERNOON

Begin an easy stroll down the Royal Mile, Edinburgh's most famous promenade. Leaving the castle (the beginning of the Royal Mile), immediately on your left you'll find the **Camera Obscura** and the **Tartan Weaving Mill**. You can skip the Camera Obscura, but don't miss the weaving mill. Pop in to see the wide array of colors and uses of tartan material, but save your money for the less-touristy stores farther on down the road. If you love a drop of the good stuff, consider the **Scotch Whisky Experience** opposite the mill. Noon isn't too early for a drink, is it?

Continue a tipsy downhill stroll, and hang a tight right at the first roundabout to snag lunch on **Victoria Street** (nearly back to Hula Juice Bar) at **Oink,** where you'll find freshly made pork sandwiches for cheap. If pork ain't your thing, other good options nearby include the splurge-worthy **Grain Store** or the discreetly located **Under the Stairs** café.

Continue down the Royal Mile, dropping a little spittle on the **Heart of Midlothian**, popping into **St Giles' Cathedral**, and enjoying the bustling scene with shops, whisky tastings, and plaid to last a lifetime.

Toward the bottom of the mile, you've got several worthwhile spots, all of which are doable in short stops. First, hit the mecca for many whisky aficionados, **Cadenhead's Whisky Shop**. Don't miss the free, brief, and interesting **Museum of Edinburgh** or the groundbreaking **Scottish Parliament Building**.

LATE AFTERNOON

If it's a nice day, begin your climb up to **Arthur's Seat** for a beautiful sunset view over the town. In this panorama, you'll be able to see the whole of the route you took today, following the castle high on the hill opposite you down to the Palace of Holyroodhouse and parliament at the bottom.

EVENING

Regroup at your hostel and go out for dinner and drinks at the pubs and bars on **Cowgate**. Don't miss **BrewDog** or the **Three Sisters** for a good time. Just around the corner, **The Banshee Labyrinth** and **The Hive Nightclub** are also packed more often than not.

DAY 2: NEW TOWN

MORNING

Grab breakfast and delicious coffee at **Fortitude Coffee Merchants,** just beyond St Andrew Square. Then double back to the south side of the **Calton Hill** to begin your hike to the top—don't worry, it's not as intense as yesterday's! After summiting, you'll be rewarded with a view back to the Old Town, across the New Town, and all the way out to the bay and North Sea while getting up close views of the Parthenon-like National Monument of Scotland.

AFTERNOON

Take in the beautiful Georgian architecture and posh boulevards in the New Town. The two best shopping streets are **Princes Street** and **George Street.** Stop for lunch and coffee at the righteous **Social Bite** on Rose Street between the two main shopping boulevards. Or if it's a nice day, stop at **Cooperative Food Market** on Frederick Street for picnic supplies and post up on **Princes Street Gardens** for a broadside view of the castle and Old Town.

Continue west and a couple blocks north toward the **Dean Gardens** to wander along the **Water of Leith** to experience Edinburgh's natural beauty—it's hard to believe you're in the heart of the city in this leafy park with a ravine and river running through it. If you're interested in modern art, you can leave the path after less than a mile to find the **Scottish National Gallery of Modern Art.**

EVENING

Head back to the hostel to rest for a bit before another night out on the town. This time head up to the student district by the University of Edinburgh to find some entertaining venues and spots to grab a bite to eat—I love the Brazilian food at **Boteco do Brasil**. On a budget? Kebab and pizza-by-the-slice options abound in the neighborhood, especially on Teviot Place.

LATER

With over 30,000 students, the University of Edinburgh is plenty big enough to support a healthy nightlife scene in the surrounding area. Begin your night at **Malone's** and follow with **Sandy Bell's,** just across the street. Sandy Bell's has unforgettable traditional Scottish folk music seven nights a week.

DAY 3: DAY TRIP OPTIONS

Consider a full day trip out to **Loch Ness** (tours leave quite early and get back late: 07:30-20:30). Or stick closer to the city with this itinerary.

MORNING & AFTERNOON

Sleep off that hangover and get in a good breakfast, then tour the regional whisky distilleries with **Haggis Adventures**. If you're more into doing your own thing, drop south to see the **Rosslyn Chapel** and **Craigmillar Castle** to continue divining medieval Scotland.

EVENING

For classier nightlife than the student spots from the night before, spend your last evening getting started in **Grassmarket Square**, a plaza ringed by bars and restaurants located just in the shadow of the castle (on the south side). Follow the nightlife toward Haymarket Station to explore the **West End,** where you'll find bars popular with friendly locals rather than tourists.

TOP NEIGHBORHOODS

The modern city of Edinburgh huddles around its medieval core. You can't miss the castle high on the hill. Leading from the castle down to the Palace of Holyroodhouse is the **Royal Mile,** the heart of the **Old Town** neighborhood. The Royal Mile is where you'll find most of Edinburgh's noteworthy sights. Just below the castle is the **Grassmarket District**, a trendy nightlife and shopping district centered around Grassmarket Square.

Just north of the Old Town across the North Bridge and Waverly train station is the planned layout of the Georgian expansion, simply called the **New Town**. Dating back to the second half of the 18th century, the New Town was built so that the wealthy could

escape from the filthy and overcrowded medieval Old Town. Today, along with bigger avenues you'll find galleries, museums, posh shopping streets, and more upscale bars.

On the other side of the castle and hill just to the west is the **West End,** where you'll find Haymarket station, stadiums, tons of student housing, lively bars, and a bustling blue collar and student scene.

The University of Edinburgh is just to the south of the Old Town and borders the West End. In the **University District,** you can find exactly what you'd expect in any student neighborhood: cheap food, bars, entertainment venues, and bookshops.

TOP SIGHTS

Most of Edinburgh's top sights are located on the **Royal Mile,** the main tourist boulevard, which is full of shops and street performers. Five contiguous streets make up the mile: Castlehill, Laynmarket, High Street, Canongate, and Abbey Strand. The sights in this section are organized from the top of the hill at Edinburgh Castle down toward the Palace of Holyroodhouse.

Edinburgh Castle

Think *Lord of the Rings* meets *Braveheart*. This proud castle sits atop volcanic rock carved out by glaciers long ago, giving it perfect natural defenses: sheer cliffs along three sides and a long uphill trek to the front door, er, gate. The foundations of the castle were laid in the 9th century with Edinburgh's oldest building, St Margaret's Chapel, and primitive fortifications. Since then, numerous additions were made during the tenuous

centuries while England threatened the southern border of Scotland.

Frequent guided tours (included with admission) show you through numerous military museums and exhibits, the Scottish Crown Jewels (and a display demonstrating how they were found in the castle after being lost for nearly 200 years), the Scottish National War Memorial, and the ramparts of this fortress. Looking down the barrels of some serious cannons reminds visitors

of the very functional defensive purpose of this castle, even while taking in the dramatic panoramas of the city.

£16.50, Apr-Sept daily 09:30-18:00, Oct-Mar daily 09:30-17:00, last entry one hour before closing, Castlehill, Royal Mile, +44 (0)131 225 9846, edinburghcastle.gov.uk

Scotch Whisky Experience

Just outside the castle, take a barrel ride through this replica distillery to learn about the history, process, and regions of the world-renowned distillate that is Scotch whisky. The experience is just this side of a tourist trap, but this educational opportunity utilizes all your senses and gives you a chance to sip from what is said to be the world's largest collection of Scotch. Go for the Silver package or upgrade for the Gold tour to get an extra wee dram or two. Stopping in is worthwhile for both aficionados and those who have not yet developed their love for Scotch. The attached restaurant, Amber, is surprisingly good and much better than what you'd expect at such a tourist trap.

From £14.50, non-alcoholic drinks provided for those under 18, Apr-Aug daily 10:00-18:00, Sept-Mar daily 10:00-17:00, tours leaving on the hour, 354 Castlehill, Royal Mile, +44 (0)131 220 0441, scotchwhiskyexperience.co.uk

Tartan Weaving Mill

Pop into this cheesy, dusty warehouse stuffed full of just about everything you can smack a plaid pattern on. Converted from the water reservoir of the old town, it is now a painfully obvious tourist trap, but the displays and sheer choice of patterns are worth a gander. Dive deep into the warehouse to find a life-size timeline of old highland dress with some historical information breaking down the trends over the years. Save your money for cheaper shops off the main drag.

Free, daily 09:00-17:30, 555 Castlehill, Royal Mile, +44 (0)131 220 2477, royal-mile.com/interest/tartanweavingmill.html

Camera Obscura

The Camera Obscura is an interactive museum with exhibits about optical illusions, mirrors, and visual tricks. Because photography was pioneered in Edinburgh, it has a long history of optics, and Camera Obscura's main attraction is a live panorama of the city projected through a periscope downward inside the tower of the building of the museum onto a large viewing dish. Cool to see, but is it worth the 14 quid? That's your call.

£14 adult, £12 student, Apr-Jun daily 09:30-19:00, July-Aug daily 09:00-21:00, Sept-Oct daily 09:30-19:00, Nov-Mar daily 10:00-18:00, 549 Castlehill, Royal Mile, +44 (0)131 226 3709, camera-obscura.co.uk

Heart of Midlothian

It may surprise you to see locals spitting on this simple heart-shaped pattern of cobblestones as they pass, but this tradition goes way back to the 1300s. Then, the heart lay just outside the door to the Old Tollhouse, where taxes were collected and prisoners were held, tortured, and even executed. While the tax building is gone, pedestrians today express their discontent with the machine by donating a little spittle. Go on, hawk a loogie yourself.

Free, always open, northwest corner of St Giles' Cathedral, Royal Mile

St Giles' Cathedral

With its beautiful stained-glass windows and painted ceiling, St Giles is a fantastic display of high gothic architecture dating all the way back to 1385. St Giles was an ongoing project over the years, and you may notice the haphazard style from continuous improvements and additions. When entering, take in the main hall but be sure to make your way to the back and visit the spectacular Thistle Chapel, with its ornately wooden benches, bright stained-glass windows, and a heavenly network of ribbed vaults in the ceiling.

Free (£2 fee for photography), £3 suggested donation; May-Sept Mon-Fri 9:00-19:00, Sat 9:00-17:00, Sun 13:00-17:00; Oct-Apr Mon-Sat 09:00-17:00, Sun 13:00-17:00; High St, Royal Mile, +44 (0)131 225 9442, stgilescathedral.org.uk

The Real Mary King's Close

Beneath the Royal Mile, you'll find The Real Mary King's Close, an underground labyrinth of the tight alleyways and dank tenements of 16th-century Edinburgh. As the modern city has grown, builders have chopped off the tops of the old tenements and reused the largely untouched foundations, simply covering them over and leaving the old streets and rooms still accessible underneath the stately Royal Exchange building. Taking a walk through these streets is like hopping in a fun time machine back to Old Edinburgh. Your entry ticket comes along with a tour led by a costumed and in-character guide spinning a funny and dry yarn to help you bring these empty streets to life. Must book in advance.

£14 adult, £12.50 w/student ID, Apr-Oct daily 10:00-21:00;

A BRIEF HISTORY OF THE KILT

Kilts, which started emerging in the 1500s, were originally over 20 feet long and were wrapped around the torso, secured with a belt, and then draped over the shoulders. With time, the kilt evolved to be more of the skirt that we see today, with a separate piece for draping over the shoulders. The colors were a function of the dyes available in the region as well as the wealth of the person wearing it. Though we've been led to believe that nearly every family name has a "registered tartan" or plaid pattern, this was simply the genius strategy of a cunning businessman to sell more plaid to tourists. Early sporters of the garb were simply glad to have one to wear. So while it's fun to pick up some colors, be skeptical of sales clerks telling you, "Gonzalez? Yeah, we've got a pattern for that clan!"

Nov-Mar Sun-Thurs 10:00-17:00, Fri-Sat 10:00-21:00; 2 Warriston's Close, Royal Mile, +44 (0)845 070 6244, realmarykingsclose.com

Cadenhead's Whisky Shop

When it comes to Scotland, whisky is basically a requisite part of your visit, and Cadenhead's Whisky Shop is your classroom. Come out for an education in everything grain-mashed goodness. While they don't produce their own liquor, these guys go straight to the source and bottle their goods before the concoctions are watered down, colored, and prepared for mass distribution. This means their stuff is purer and stronger than what you'll find in any standard shop, and the decision about just how many drops to add to your dram is left to you. This small, intimate shop posts about new arrivals, classes, and tastings to their loyal followers throughout the week on their Facebook page. Tasty...

Free, bottles from £28, closed Sun, 172 Canongate, Royal Mile, +44 (0)131 556 5864, wmcadenhead.com with frequent updates to facebook.com/CHWSEdinburgh

Museum of Edinburgh

I enjoy city history museums to get a sense for the foundations of a city and what really put it on the map in the early days. This free museum is an excellent stop at the bottom of the Royal Mile. Check out their extensive and somewhat eclectic collection of artifacts and displays. You can see a model of Edinburgh's medieval Old Town as it would have looked in the 16th century, weapons used in World War I, trench artwork created by soldiers tinkering away on spent shells and ration cans, and even an original copy of the National Covenant—an important document that denounced the attempts of the Anglican church to incorporate the Scottish Presbyterian church way back in the 17th century—scrawled out and signed

on a sheep's hide. These displays (and the free bathroom) make this a convenient stop along the Royal Mile.

Free, Mon-Sat 10:00-17:00, Sun 12:00-17:00 during Aug only, 142 Canongate, Royal Mile, +44 (0)131 529 4143, edinburghmuseums.org.uk

Palace of Holyroodhouse

As Buckingham Palace is to England, so is Holyroodhouse to Scotland. Home of Mary Queen of Scots and built upon the ruins of an abbey, the palace was built by King David I in the 12th and 13th centuries. Today, it is still the official residence of the Queen of England on her visits to Edinburgh. Walk its halls and visit the many royal audience rooms, Mary Queen of Scots' chambers, and dining rooms of this fully functioning palace. The walls are decked out with priceless paintings, decorations, and tapestries, as any palace should be.

The palace does close down for several weeks each year in preparation for the queen's stay early on each summer, with the Royal Standard of the United Kingdom flying high when she is there. While visiting, take a minute and view Arthur's Seat through the windows just to the south; it is the highest peak of the group of hills you see.

£11.60, £10.60 student; Apr-Oct 09:30-18:00, last entry 16:30, Nov-Mar daily 09:30-16:30, last entry 15:15; Canongate, Royal Mile, +44 (0)131 556 5100, royalcollection.org.uk/visit/palaceofholyroodhouse

Scottish Parliament Building

Its modern steel and glass architecture makes the Scottish Parliament Building stand out along the backdrop of the Royal Mile and Holyroodhouse. After passing through some quick security, you can investigate a wonderful exhibit on the ground floor that displays the ins and outs of the Scottish legislative system and how it weaves culture and history within its modern framework of government and allegiance to the British crown—which is an important and very current discussion taking place in Scotland today.

Free, reserve guided tours online ahead of time, Mon, Fri, Sat 10:00-17:00, also Tues-Thurs 09:00-18:30 when in recess, last entry 30 minutes before closing, closed Sun, 2 Warriston's Close, Royal Mile, +44 (0)131 348 5200, visitscottishparliament.uk

University of Edinburgh

Both medieval and modern architecture surround this historic university located in the heart of the Old Town and just a few blocks from the castle. A stroll through the beautiful campus offers a chance to see one of the oldest universities in the world. Today, it's one of Scotland's most competitive universities, and I enjoy taking a walk through campus to see what UK college life is like. Just a couple hundred years ago, it was here that doctors of anatomy were charging £5 each to attend live dissections in their human anatomy courses, patronizing grave snatchers and serial killers to obtain their subjects.

Free, campus grounds always open, Old College, South Bridge, University District, +44 (0)131 650 1000, ed.ac.uk

National Museum of Scotland

This massive and newly renovated natural history museum takes up an entire block in Edinburgh's Old Town. Inside, find Dolly the Sheep (the world's first cloned animal, now stuffed) and a full-size *T. rex* skeleton, as well as displays on old Scottish artifacts, silversmithing, and world cultures. The diverse exhibits touch on the past and present of Scotland, from its people to the industrial transformation of the country, through a series of enthralling galleries.

Rotating exhibits present more personal facets of the country, like the Lewis Chessmen, a hand-carved ivory chess set dating back 800 years, or an in-depth look at the many lighthouses in Scotland, which have played an important role in this coastal country.

Free, daily 10:00-17:00, Chambers St, Old Town, +44 (0)300 123 6789, nms.ac.uk

Craigmillar Castle

Credited as one of the best-preserved medieval castles in Scotland, Craigmillar Castle was built around 1400 by Sir George Preston, and it provides visitors a chance to travel back to the 15th century via its complete ramparts and chambers. This large stone castle is famous for being the place where the assassination of Lord Danley, the unpopular husband of Mary, Queen of Scots, was planned. While it's not believed Queen Mary was privy to the scheme, it was hatched while she was staying here with her noble entourage. The offenders planned to blow up Lord Danley with two kegs of gunpowder stashed a floor under where he would be sleeping at the nearby church, Kirk O' Field. They lit off the kegs, and the body of Lord Danley was found a short distance away, half-dressed—meaning that somehow he knew of and had tried to escape the impending doom. It's not known whether the blast killed him or if he died by strangulation at the hands the queen's entourage when they found him still breathing. In this country, the truth is often stranger than fiction.

Today, a visit here lets you experience an impressive and well-preserved medieval fortress with many rooms, chambers, and ramparts, all without the hordes of tourists you'll see at the Edinburgh Castle. The castle is south of town. Take bus 3, 14, 29, or 30 from North Bridge and ask the bus driver to tell you where to get off for the castle.

£5.50; Apr-Sept daily 9:30-17:30; Oct-Mar Sat-Wed 09:30-16:00, closed Thurs-Fri; last entry 30 minutes before closing, Craigmillar Castle Rd, south of town, +44 (0)131 661 4445, visitscotland.com

Royal Yacht *Britannia*

The royal family's floating home for 40 years has been converted into a 412-foot exhibit, letting you stow away on the family's nautical travels. Start your visit in the command center (the bridge) and continue down five levels all the way into the engine room. Experience the decadent, gold-encrusted interiors, including the dining hall and royal staterooms—which have all the comforts of anything you'd expect on land. You can even see the crew quarters (not quite as fancy as those of the royal family). Take a pit stop for a snack and tea in the Tea Room, where sandwiches start from £5. At 2.5 miles from the city center it makes sense to take a bus (1, 11, 22, 34, or 35 from Waverley Bridge) to get here.

£14, £12.50 student, daily Apr-Sept daily 09:30-16:30, Oct daily 09:30-16:00, Nov-Mar daily 10:00-15:30, Ocean Terminal, Port of Leith, coastal suburb of Leith, +44 (0)131 555 5566, royalyachtbritannia.co.uk

EXTRA CREDIT
National Gallery of Scotland
This classic art museum spans the ages from gothic all the way to baroque, impressionism, and surrealism. You'll recognize names like Dalí and Duchamp, and will see pieces by less famous but no less fascinating Scottish artists covering just about all the genres and styles. Perched on the hill between the Old Town and New Town, it makes for a convenient—and free—stop between the two.

Free, daily 10:00-17:00, The Mound, New Town, +44 (0)131 624 6200, nationalgalleries.org

Scottish National Gallery of Modern Art
For a change, pop over to Edinburgh's modern art museum. Split across two neoclassical buildings, the interior exhibits are anything but. "Modern One" is the permanent exhibition, and "Modern Two" is where you'll find temporary exhibits featuring the likes of the great M. C. Escher.

Modern One free, Modern Two price varies, daily 10:00-17:00, 75 Belford Rd, New Town, +44 (0)131 624 6200, nationalgalleries.org

Greyfriars Kirk & Kirkyard
Greyfriars Kirk ("church" in Scotch Gaelic) is a beautiful old church just to the south of the Old Town, built out in the fields back in the day in the 17th century. It's the main church for central Edinburgh and is part of the Church of Scotland. The graveyard around the church is supposedly the most haunted part of the city, as it was a favorite hunting ground for grave snatchers and is the permanent home of many notable Scots. The most famous occupant, however, is a terrier named Bobby, who guarded his dead owner's grave for 14 years before his own death in 1855. A statue and bar commemorating the world's most loyal dog sits just outside the entrance to the graveyard closest to the church.

Free, daily 10:30-16:30 but may be closed for private events, Candlemaker Row, University District, +44 (0)131 664 4313, greyfriarskirk.com

Rosslyn Chapel
A hike out of town, but worth it for *Da Vinci Code* buffs, the Rosslyn Chapel dates all the way back to the 15th century. While the supposed connections with the freemasons and Knights of Templar are dubious, the chapel itself is beautiful and packed with intricate stonework, making for a great side trip out of the city to see the nearby countryside. Just beyond the church are the ruins of a 14th-century castle of the same name for you to explore. To get here, take bus 37 from North Bridge, which runs every 30 minutes and takes about half an hour.

Free, Mon-Sat 09:30-18:00, Sun 12:00-16:45, Chapel Loan, Roslin, +44 (0)131 440 2159, rosslynchapel.com

TOP EATS

Many of Edinburgh's most popular restaurants are clustered around Old Town's **Royal Mile** and New Town's **Princes Street.** On nice days, it's also pleasant to picnic at **West Princes Street Gardens.** Food is available nearby at the **Cooperative Food Market** (daily 07:00-23:00, 26-28 Frederick Street, +44 (0)131 220 0359).

The northern suburb of **Leith** is especially known for its fresh seafood restaurants. **South Edinburgh** has a variety of cheaper cafés and restaurants for budget-minded travelers. The neighborhood surrounding the **University of Edinburgh** is also full of cheap and ethnic food options, especially on Nicolson Street.

It's typical to round up to the nearest even number, or about 10 percent, on meals. If service is exceptional, feel free to head north to 15 percent.

Oink
This fast-casual food shop does one thing, and it does it well: steaming fresh pork sandwiches sourced from local farms in limited quantities. Pop in here to keep your energy level up on these long days of sightseeing. A second location at 82 Canongate on the Royal Mile ensures you're never far from a great pork sandwich.

Sandwiches from £2.95, Mon-Sat 11:00-17:30, Sun 11:00-17:00, 34 Victoria St, +44 (0)189 076 1355, oinkhogroast.co.uk

Saint Giles Café & Bar
When it comes to breakfast and lunch on the Royal Mile, Saint Giles Café & Bar is a favorite of mine, located at the top of Saint Giles Street and kitty-corner from the cathedral. Pop in here to get your day off on

HUNGRY FOR HAGGIS?

Scotland's national dish, haggis, is an interesting one, made of—if you really want to know—sheep's heart, liver, and lungs minced together with onions, oatmeal, and some seasoning; stuffed into a sleeve of stomach lining; and then simmered until cooked. It's usually dished up with *neeps* and *tatties*, or mashed turnips and potatoes. Scots love it, and for brave tourists, it's worth a try. Bobby's Bar, just outside Greyfriars Kirkyard, is a great place to sample it. Bon appétit!

the right foot with breakfast rolls and fresh pastries. The rustic interior is going to make you want to come back for tea or to hit the bar later on.

Scones from £1.50, daily 09:00-18:00, 8-10 St Giles St, Royal Mile, +44 (0)131 225 6267, saintgilescafebar.co.uk

The Grain Store

This is a splurge-worthy restaurant for those who want to check their Scottish cuisine box in style. With impeccable decor, swift service, and succulent main dishes, The Grain Store has established itself as the go-to restaurant for those who want to appreciate their saddle of lamb or venison and kale in a comfortable and classy setting.

Mains from £20, Mon-Fri 12:00-14:00, 18:00-22:00, Sat 12:00-15:00, 18:00-23:00, Sun 18:00-22:00, 30 Victoria St, Royal Mile, +44 (0)131 225 7635, grainstore-restaurant.co.uk

Under the Stairs

This discreet and somewhat difficult-to-find little joint serves up delicious entrées and expertly made cocktails like you'd expect at any hipster bar. It feels more like a tastefully decorated lounge and has become so popular it runs the risk of becoming mainstream. Until then, I'll keep coming back for their burgers and sweet potato wedges.

Beers from £4.50, cocktails from £7, daily 12:00-01:00, 3A Merchant St, Royal Mile, +44 (0)131 466 8550, underthestairs.org

Elephant House

Elephant House is a great place for reasonably priced panini, international foods, and hot drinks. This cozy café is located near Edinburgh University and provided the perfect ambience for J. K. Rowling to pen her first novels on those famous napkins, with the inspirational views of Edinburgh Castle through the window of the back room.

£11-16, Mon-Fri 08:00-22:00, Sat 09:00-23:00, Sun 09:00-22:00, 21 George IV Bridge, Royal Mile, +44 (0)131 220 5355, elephanthouse.biz

ClamShell

At this no-nonsense fast-food joint, they'll deep-fry almost anything, including pizza, ribs, haggis, and (my favorite) Mars bars! They also dish out some of the best fish-and-chips you'll find in all of Edinburgh. Order, then post up at the high-top bar along the wall inside or on the outdoor seating under the sun (if there is any) and enjoy.

£3-6, daily 11:00-01:00, 148 High St, Royal Mile, +44 (0)131 225 4338

Mums Great Comfort Food

The theme for this homey and slightly retro restaurant is "top nosh at half the cost," and it delivers just that in style. Mums uses all local ingredients and definitely doesn't hold back on the tasty calories, delivering all of the British classics we know and love—shepherd's pie, bangers and mash, fish-and-chips, and, of course, haggis.

Dishes from £7, Mon-Sat 09:00-22:00, Sun 10:00-22:00, 4a Forrest Rd, University District, monstermashcafe.co.uk, +44 (0)131 225 7069

Boteco do Brasil

As with any university district, you can count on finding cheap eats on the streets around the University of Edinburgh, and the Boteco do Brasil is one of my favorites, serving out delicious plates heaping with black beans, pork, beef, and burgers in a casual atmosphere with funky furniture and exposed brick walls. The friendly servers take their cocktails seriously—the *caipirinha* is almost as good as the ones back on Ipanema beach. Later on, space is made to turn the party up around 22:00 six nights a week, with students coming for their popular disco and salsa nights. There's nothing like a little slice of Rio across the street from Scotland's top educational institution.

Tapas from £5, burgers from £7, daily 11:00-03:00, 47 Lothian St, University District, +44 (0)131 220 4287, botecodobrasil.com

Hula Juice Bar

Your dear author isn't usually a juice bar kind of guy, but this one proudly breaks all the rules. Pop in for delicious healthy

smoothies with creative names like Whirling Dervish and Sunshine in a Cup, but get full on their tasty bagels stuffed with bacon and cheddar. Yes, there are vegetarian options.

Juices from £3.50, daily 08:00-19:00, 103-105 West Bow, Royal Mile, +44 (0)131 220 1121, hulajuicebar.co.uk

Graze on Grassmarket

The east side of Grassmarket Square seems to be on a health kick with Hula Juice Bar and this fresh entry, which pumps out sandwiches, wraps, salads, and baked potatoes stuffed with locally sourced ingredients to keep you going throughout the day. This small café is stripped down and simplified, with only a few seats for those who choose to stick around and have their takeout in.

Lunches from £3.50, Mon-Sat 07:30-18:00, Sun 11:00-16:00, 67 Grassmarket, Grassmarket District, +44 (0)131 629 4030, grazeongrassmarket.com

Fortitude Coffee Merchants

When it comes to breakfast in the New Town, I head to Fortitude Coffee Merchants for some of the best coffee in town. If you're a coffee snob at heart like me, you'll appreciate their quality beans and small-batch roasting—and you'll be in welcome company with the staff, who are happy to help you pick from their rotating roasts. While I wish they had a full kitchen, I'll settle for the locally sourced pastries and mini cakes. Fortitude offers just the right combination of caffeine and sugar for your climb to the top of nearby Calton Hill.

Coffee from £1.50, Mon-Fri 08:00-18:00, Sat 10:00-18:00, 3C York Place, New Town, +44 (0)131 557 3063, fortitudecoffee.com

Social Bite

I love it when good food made with local ingredients and sold at fair prices comes with a mission for social improvement. Social Bite makes excellent sandwiches, wraps, and soups in the New Town, offering both meat and vegetarian options, making it an excellent stop for a quick lunch. What's more, a quarter of their employees have a homelessness background, and Social Bite is helping them get on their feet. You can even buy an extra sandwich and drink to be redeemed later by a local homeless person—definitely something I can get behind.

Sandwiches from £3.95, Mon-Fri 07:00-15:00, 131 Rose St, New Town, +44 (0)131 220 8206, social-bite.co.uk

TOP NIGHTLIFE

Thanks to Edinburgh's compact city center, nightlife venues are never far from each other.

NIGHTLIFE DISTRICTS
Grassmarket Square

The Grassmarket district is one of the best places to hang around at night, as it offers some of Edinburgh's most authentic traditional bars, along with a happening nightlife. **Dropkick Murphy's** frequently offers live music in your quintessential Irish pub atmosphere.

Grassmarket District

Royal Mile

Nightlife on and near the Royal Mile is better than what you'd expect for such a touristy area. While certain places can be a bit generic and overpriced, I've listed some of my favorites to keep you from falling into the tourist traps. There are some incredible finds sprinkled throughout the neighborhood. You'll even find bars and clubs, like **Whistlebinkies** and the **The Banshee Labyrinth,** that are burrowed into old medieval cellars, making for a unique night underneath exposed brick arches dating back centuries.

Royal Mile

University District

This is where you'll find both the sloppy student hangouts and some notable exceptions—classy establishments with great food, fun vibes, and tasty drinks.

University District

Haymarket

The area surrounding the Haymarket train station has plenty of classic British-style pubs with heavy wooden interiors, bantering customers, numerous drafts on tap, and whiskies to pour. This area is more low key than the others, but it draws a higher ratio of locals than the touristy Royal Mile.

West End

BARS
Sandy Bell's

Sandy Bell's is an intimate bar that is bursting at the seams thanks to its popularity as one of Edinburgh's best traditional Gaelic music—or "trad"—bars. They keep it fresh with nightly rotating music, and in such an intimate little spot, you'll be part of the action before you know it. Sandy Bell's is your best bet if you want to catch some live Celtic jam sessions.

Pints from £3.50, Mon-Sat 12:00-01:00, Sun 12:30-24:00, 25 Forrest Rd, University District, +44 (0)131 225 2751, sandybellsedinburgh.co.uk

The Banshee Labyrinth

The Banshee Labyrinth is aptly named, as it is quite easy to get lost in this maze of cellars, bars, chill-out areas, movie theater (*The Departed* was showing the last time I popped in), and performance venue. Add the funky lighting, a little alcohol, and an inexplicable otherworldly haze that just seemed to float around this place (which must have been from smoke machines somewhere) and you feel like you could get lost forever. Come out for a good time, embrace the unexpected, and you never know what you'll discover in here. Check the website for upcoming events.

Drinks from £3.50, daily 19:00-03:00, 29 Niddry St, Royal Mile, +44 (0)131 558 8209, thebansheelabyrinth.com

Whistlebinkies Live Music Bar

This excellent pub right off the Royal Mile packs out the house with ales and a full bar to get the party going. The whole venue is oriented toward the stage, with musicians playing most nights, and varied enough to keep everyone happy. The layout is such that you can rage up close, dance in the middle, or keep a conversation going off to the side in the back.

Pricey drinks at £5, Sun-Thurs 17:00-03:00, Fri-Sat 13:00-03:00, 4-6 South Bridge, Royal Mile, +44 (0)131 557 5114, whistlebinkies.com

BrewDog

Although it's part of a chain, BrewDog is one of my favorite spots for a fresh artisanal pint in the shadow of the Royal Mile. Drop in to this welcoming, high-ceilinged hipster bar for a pint of their constantly rotating brews. Too many choices? The knowledgeable staff is happy to help narrow them down. While the beer is excellent, the pizzas are subpar, yet the jovial customers don't seem to mind.

Pints from £4, daily 12:00-01:00, 143 Cowgate, Royal Mile, +44 (0)131 220 6517, brewdog.com

Three Sisters

The highlight of this funky, unique venue is the large outdoor seating area, where big games are streamed live and the hen and stag parties (or bachelor and bachelorette parties, as they're known in the United States) get rowdy on the karaoke machine.

Drinks from £3.50, Mon-Fri 17:00-01:00, Sat-Sun 07:00-03:00, 139 Cowgate, Royal Mile, thethreesistersbar.co.uk

Malone's Irish Bar

Edinburgh, like just about every other city on the planet, has got to have its Irish bar, but this one is special thanks to the food and entertainment. Occupying what was a midsized, horseshoe-shaped theater, the bar now televises sporting events and features frequent live music acts. Hungry? The burgers and chips are unforgettable. If you like events, take a look at the program online for upcoming gigs.

Beers from £4, daily 12:00-01:00, 14 Forrest Rd, University District, +44 (0)131 226 5954, malonesedinburgh.com

Dropkick Murphy's

Known for its late nights and rowdy atmosphere, Dropkick Murphy's is tucked underneath the George IV Bridge. Find the bright green doors just a block off of Grassmarket Square and dive into the sloppy and friendly crowd.

Drinks from £4, Thurs-Tues 20:00-03:00, 7 Merchant St, Grassmarket District, +44 (0)131 225 2002, facebook.com/dropkickmurphys.edinburgh.1

LGBT EDINBURGH

Edinburgh is a progressive and welcoming city. Members of the LGBT community will have no problem getting along here, and there are numerous cafés, restaurants, and nightlife venues that cater to the gay scene. Most places center in what's known as the "Pink Triangle," just north of Calton Hill on the eastern edge of the New Town. **The Street** (2 Picardy Place, thestreetbaredinburgh.co.uk) is a popular bar that also offers food, and a DJ spins later in the night. Same goes for **Café Habana** (22 Greenside Place, facebook.com/habanaedinburgh). **Planet** (6 Baxter's Place, New Town, facebook.com/Planet-Bar-Edinburgh) is a smaller dance bar with drink deals and a DJ spinning nightly; it's popular among all partiers. **CC Blooms** (23 Greenside Place, New Town, ccbloomsedinburgh.com) is a tasty restaurant by day and a classy nightclub by night.

CLUBS

The clubs in town all seem to come with bouncers who like to dish out a hard time, and take a fiver for cover. Once in the door though, you're sure to have a blast.

Cabaret Voltaire

"Cab Vol," as the partiers call it, is one of Edinburgh's top clubs and is just off the Royal Mile. I love the grungy student-party-night-infused atmosphere in this club, which leaves pretentiousness in the dust in exchange for raucous live music and DJ acts. Be prepared for feisty bouncers, and just be happy to get in.

Cover around £6, Mon-Thurs 17:00-03:00, Fri-Sun 12:00-03:00, 36 Blair St, Royal Mile, +44 (0)131 247 4704, thecabaretvoltaire.com

The Hive Nightclub

This sweaty, cheap club packs out with a young crowd that appreciates the low prices and doesn't mind the sticky floor. No cover Thursdays and Sundays and student specials keep the crowds coming back. It's worth getting on the guest list on Fridays and Saturdays to avoid the line.

Cover around £3, drinks from £1, Sun-Thurs 22:00-03:00, Fri-Sat 21:00-03:00, 15 Niddry St, Royal Mile, +44 (0)131 556 0444, clubhive.co.uk

COMEDY SHOWS

The Stand

Known as Edinburgh's best comedy club, the subterranean Stand is so popular it often sells out, so it's best to book your tickets

online ahead of time. Formats most often have a rotation of five comedians over two hours but sometimes switch up for improv and solo act nights.

Tickets from £10, doors usually open at 19:30 and show starts at 21:00 but check schedule online, 5 York Place, New Town, +44 (0)131 558 7272, thestand.co.uk

PUB CRAWLS

New Edinburgh Pub Crawl

Hosted by the reliable crew at Sandeman's tours, the New Edinburgh Pub Crawl gives you a leg up in finding all the hidden nightlife gems Edinburgh has tucked away. You'll enjoy half-priced pints, three shooters, a dram of Scotch whisky, and drink deals in every pub you visit, ending with VIP entrance into Edinburgh's best nightclub. You'll also meet tons of travelers like yourself and make some great friends—at least for that night.

£15, nightly 20:00 at the Inn on the Mile, Royal Mile, newedinburghtours.com

Edinburgh Pub Crawl

Each pub crawl tries to outdo the others on the quantifiables (number of bars, clubs, free shots, etc etc), but sometimes you've just gotta go with the best vibe—and Edinburgh Pub Crawl has a great one. These guys have been showing people a great night out for years, and the groups of partiers are a ton of fun.

£10, nightly at 20:30 in front of St Giles' Cathedral, Royal Mile, edinburghpubcrawl.com

TOP SHOPPING & MARKETS

SHOPPING DISTRICTS

Royal Mile
Full of shops and street performers, the main tourist boulevard is a great place for souvenir shopping...kilts anyone? You'll find just about every Scottish knickknack and touristy souvenir you can imagine. In addition, there are many tiny alleyways or "closes," which branch off High Street with even more cafés, shops, and exhibits to explore.

Old Town

Princes & George Streets
This area is the Oxford Street of Edinburgh; come here to find all your top international name brands. While in the area, stop into Edinburgh's famous **Jenner's** (Mon-Fri 09:30-18:30, Sat 09:00-19:00, Sun 11:00-18:00, 48 Princes St, +44 (0)131 225 2442, houseoffraser.co.uk)**,** a beautiful Victorian-style department store built in 1938.

New Town

Grassmarket Square
Grassmarket (27-31 W Port, grassmarket. net) has many boutique fashion shops and vintage music and bookstores, along with trendy cafés and bars. Check out the website to explore in advance the places to visit.

Grassmarket District

Stockbridge
Visit this neighborhood if you're into secondhand clothing, unique jewelry, glassware, and independent art galleries. Many tea and coffee shops dot the area on the north side of the New Town, on **Kerr Street.** Stockbridge is a great place to get your shop on, enjoy an afternoon tea, and watch the world go by.

New Town

Bruntsfield Place & Morningside Road
While a bit south of town, this area has a young vibe, offering many boutique and vintage clothing stores, chocolatiers, and cafés. It also gets you out of the city center and into where the locals hang out, offering an untouristy experience you wouldn't get in the center.

South of University District (interesting until Cluny Ave)

MARKETS

Edinburgh Farmers' Market
Stock up on locally grown produce, organic beer, and fresh, seasonal fruits at the Edinburgh Farmers' Market. The market vendors assemble just off of Castle Terrace.

Sat 09:00-14:00, Castle Terrace, West End, edinburghfarmersmarket.com

TOP PARKS & RECREATION

Surrounded by dramatic geography, Edinburgh boasts some spectacular parks, hikes, and viewpoints that are worthwhile even on the shortest of visits.

PARKS

Meadows Park
Because of its proximity to the University of Edinburgh, students occupy the majority of this large, grassy, tree-filled park, making it a great place to people-watch or even chat up a few local students. Ask them about their university and their studies, or maybe they can recommend some places to go out at night. The park also makes for a great picnic spot and a cheap lunch.

Free, always open, University District

Holyrood Park
Holyrood Park, in the heart of Edinburgh, has been a royal park since the 12th century. You'll stumble upon many great sights while wandering the footpaths and craggy cliffs

of this local wilderness, such as the Palace of Holyroodhouse, the ruins of Holyrood Abbey, and the extinct volcano Arthur's Seat, Edinburgh's highest peak at 251 meters. The views are unbeatable, and the air is filled with the fresh smell of nature, making it the perfect place to spend a few hours.

Free, always open, end of Royal Mile

Dean Gardens & Water of Leith
Scotland's capital has beautiful parks and walkways, and this is one of my favorites. The Water of Leith is the river that borders the north side of the New Town; Dean Gardens is one of the most beautiful stretches, with a walkway along the river. Just steps into the park, the noises from the city fall away and you're back into Scotland's natural beauty.

Free, always open, New Town

West Princes Street Gardens

On a clear—and warm—day, one of my favorite things to do is to snag a sandwich or chips from one of the many eateries on the Princes Street strip and head to the park, where I can grab a bench and enjoy the view of the broad side of the Edinburgh Castle and the Royal Mile. The **Cooperative Food Market** (daily 07:00-23:00, 26-28 Frederick St, +44 (0)131 220 0359) is a great spot to pick up your supplies.

Free, always open

VIEWPOINTS

Arthur's Seat

A sweaty 45-minute climb up an extinct volcano in Holyrood Park provides wonderful views of Edinburgh, in particular the Edinburgh Castle, Palace of Holyroodhouse, Scottish Parliament, and Calton Hill.

Free, visit during daylight hours for best views, Holyrood Park, just south of the Palace of Holyroodhouse

Calton Hill

A 15-minute climb to the top of Calton Hill, located in the northeast section of the city center, will bring you to a beautiful World War I memorial, accompanied by panoramic views of downtown Edinburgh, Edinburgh Castle, and all the way out to the coast.

Free, visit during daylight hours for best views, 15 York Place, New Town

TOP TOURS

Excursion Scotland

Colin Mairs heads up this small tour company. If you're looking for a deep dive into everything Scotland, Colin's your man. A fun-loving, passionate Scot who often prefers to sport a kilt over trousers, Colin offers everything from half-day tours of Edinburgh's best sights to a weeklong, private custom tour of the entire country for small groups and families.

From £100, +44 (0)77 1623 2001, excursionscotland. wordpress.com, excursionscotland@gmail.com

Sandeman's New Edinburgh Free Walking Tours

A free walking tour with Sandeman's gives you the local's perspective of all the historic and not-so-historic sites of Edinburgh. These free, tip-based tours give you a brief introduction to the city, including its top sites and monuments, in the span of about 2.5 hours. While the walks do feel a bit scripted, the price is right for budget travelers: Tip what you feel the guide deserves.

Free, meets daily at 11:00 and 13:00 in front of the Starbucks on High St, +44 (0)305 105 0030, newedinburghtours.com

City of the Dead Ghost Tours

With Edinburgh's long history of resident body snatchers, serial killers, and crime, the ghost tour here is better than just about anywhere else in Europe. It's the city with one of the most fascinating—and bloody—walks, where you can pick up all sorts of ghoulish stories and freaky fun facts.

£10, tours nightly at 20:30 from Easter to Halloween, at 20:00 throughout winter, meet in front of St Giles' Cathedral, +44 (0)131 225 9044, cityofthedeadtours.com, info@cityofthedeadtours.com

Rabbie's Small Group Tours

Rabbie's is a Scottish tourism institution, offering 1- to 17-day excursions with a wide range of focus all around the country. From castles to whisky distributors, and from highlands to lakes (lochs in Scottish), Rabbie's local guides know exactly where to take you.

Day trips from £42, +44 (0)131 226 3133, rabbies.com, info@rabbies.com

Haggis Adventures

This is your fun backpacker option for day trips and longer ones around the country. With their "mad sexy" guides, you're sure to have a great time learning about Scottish history, food, and culture while touring the jaw-dropping Scottish countryside. The groups you'll tour with are one of the highlights. Check out the full lineup of trips and dates online. Group and student discounts available.

Trips from £50, +44 (0)131 557 9393, haggisadventures.com

TOP HOSTELS

Edinburgh has a slew of fun, social, and affordable backpacker hostels in or nearby the Old Town. They do their best to work within the older buildings that they've taken over. My favorite ones do it quite well, I like to think.

The Baxter Hostel

A brand-new entry into the Edinburgh backpacking scene, the midsized Baxter, with about 40 dorm beds, is following the trend of boutique hostels with a focus on comfortable rooms, friendly service, great location, and solid value. The interior feels retro chic, with clean industrial lines, custom fabricated steel and wood bunks, in dorms with exposed brick and wood-paneled walls. The enthusiasm carries over to the staff, who are happy to make recommendations on activities during your stay.

Dorms from £22, 24-hour reception, free Wi-Fi, full kitchen facilities, breakfast included, common room, linens included, 5 W Register St, New Town, +44 (0)131 503 1001, thebaxter.eu, info@thebaxter.eu

Code Hostel

This hostel in the New Town prides itself on keeping clean as well as on providing great service, value, and a fun, social atmosphere. The bunks packed into the rooms are unique in that you climb into a pod as in the airport hotels that you may have heard about in Japan. They're clearly economizing on space, but the privacy is nice as long as you're not claustrophobic. Each pod is equipped with plugs, USB ports, and reading lights.

Pod beds from £20, 24-hour reception, free maps, free Wi-Fi, breakfast included, towels available for rent, common room, 50 Rose St N Ln, New Town, +44 (0)131 659 9883, codehostel.com, hello@codehostel.com

Budget Backpackers

Voted #1 hostel in Scotland back in 2012, this place sports bright, clean rooms, friendly staff, funky decor, and a great location just off Grassmarket Square, barely a block away from the Royal Mile. Book early, as rooms fill up fast. En suite privates are also available if you'd prefer to skip the large dorms—the largest of which has 30 beds. The £5 nightly dinner is a great deal for those on a budget. Numerous common areas make this one of the more social hostels in town.

From £10.50, 24-hour reception, Internet available on PC (no Wi-Fi), common room, kitchen access, optional breakfast, pool table, towels for rent, 37-39 Cowgate, Grassmarket District, +44 (0)131 226 6351, budgetbackpackers.com, hi@budgetbackpackers.com

Caledonian Backpackers

This hostel was recommended to me by a local Edinburghian. I love it for the funky atmosphere with colorful designs coating the walls, as well as the on-site bar and café. The hostel also promotes a social atmosphere with its many common rooms and hangout spots. The rooms and facilities certainly aren't the cleanest I've found in Europe, but if you're not that picky, it'll do.

From £16, 24-hour reception, bar/café, free breakfast, free Wi-Fi, movie room, 3 Queensferry St, New Town, +44 (0)131 226 2939, caledonianbackpackers.com, reception@caledonianbackpackers.com

Castle Rock Hostel

This was voted as one of the top 10 hostels in the world back in 2010—and for good reason. With its high ceilings, old-fashioned furniture, fireplace, and stone-brick exterior, you really get to experience that "Scottish vibe." The rooms are clean, and it's the pickup location of the daily free walking tour of the city (enquire about it at the front desk on check-in).

From £11, free Wi-Fi, 24-hour reception, laundry (£3.50), breakfast (£1.80), bedside lockers, 15 Johnston Terrace, Royal Mile, +44 (0)131 225 9666, castlerockedinburgh.com, castlerock@macbackpackerstours.com

High Street Hostel

Find this gem of a hostel with welcoming staff and safe, secure rooms just downhill from the Royal Mile on Blackfriars Street. The

SHOULD WE STAY OR SHOULD WE GO? THE VOTE FOR INDEPENDENCE

Scotland was all over the news for their momentous vote on independence from London on September 18, 2014. The controversy really swirled around the pros and cons of being governed from outside their national border. While Scotland benefits quite a lot from being incorporated into England, many nationalists believe Scotland would be better off on its own.

Those in favor of independence lean on the vast oil fields in the North Sea. Scotland's GDP has grown faster than England's over the last few years, thanks to oil exports driving a healthy economy. Those in favor of independence highlighted the importance of home rule: to set priorities in foreign policy, the military, health care, and education in line for what's best for Scots and Scotland over anyone else.

Those who would have voted "no" point to things Scotland would have to sacrifice and the issues it would have to start from scratch on, like currency and health care. Those who voted against independence tended to be more conservative, opting for a system that may not be perfect but is definitely better with respect to security and general stability.

The counting went late into the night on September 18, but by the morning, it was clear that Scotland would remain in the union, at least for now. The final figures shook out to over 2 million no votes against about 1.6 million yes votes, with a remarkable 84 percent participation rate in the voting. Glasgow was the only council area to vote for full independence. Many don't consider this to be the end of the independence issue, but Scotland received accolades from all over the planet for their peaceful demonstration of the democratic process.

rooms are quiet even though you've got a ton of fun bars on the same street just steps away, you've got the best of both worlds.

Large dorms from £12, free Wi-Fi, 24-hour reception, breakfast (£2), luggage storage, lockers, 8 Blackfriars St, Royal Mile, +44 (0)131 557 3984, highstreethostel.com, reservations online

Kick Ass Hostel

With a name like this, it's gotta be good, and it is! New and brightly decorated, with an on-site bar and a social atmosphere, this is one of my favorite hostels in town. With a "Best New Hostel UK 2015" award under their belt, the team at Kick Ass Hostel is off to a great start. Take in an unobstructed view of the castle from the dorm windows and charge up with plugs next to every bed in the house.

Large dorms from £14, free Wi-Fi, 24-hour reception, on-site bar and drink specials, ping pong and pool tables, laundry

facilities, 2 W Port, Old Town, +44 (0)131 226 6351, kickasshostels.co.uk, reservations online

Argyle Backpackers

Located just across the meadows from the University of Edinburgh, this central hostel has been welcoming budget travelers for over 25 years. Choose from their cozy singles, double, triples, and four- and six-bed dorms, and feel at home in their welcoming common room and kitchen. The hostel is comfortable enough, but the Wi-Fi doesn't reach all rooms.

Dorms from £23, reception 09:00-22:00, check in after 14:00, three-night minimum stay in Aug and over New Year's, Wi-Fi in parts, luggage storage, kitchen access, common room, towels for rent, 14 Argyle Place, University District, +44 (0)131 667 9991, argyle-backpackers.com, reception@argyle-backpackers.com

TRANSPORTATION

GETTING THERE & AWAY

Plane

Edinburgh Airport (EDI, edinburghairport.com) is just 20 minutes from the center, and many of the budget airlines offer connections throughout the continent. A cab from the airport to the city center runs £25-30. Otherwise, the frequently leaving **Airlink 100** bus connects you to the Waverly Bridge Station for £4.50 each way in about half an hour. A **tram** system also connects

Edinburgh Airport with the city center (£5) in about 40 minutes, stopping throughout the New Town along the way.

Don't forget to consider **Glasgow Airport** (GLA, glasgowairport.com) as a secondary option. While it is about an hour away, and getting to Edinburgh takes two transfers on the train, there may be substantially cheaper connections.

Train

Edinburgh has two primary train stations, **Haymarket Station** and **Edinburgh Waverly Station,** located on either end of central Edinburgh, so it's important to confirm which one your train will arrive to or depart from.

To avoid the probable long lines at the bigger train station, Waverly, purchase your ticket in advance at virgintrainseastcoast. com. Direct express trains to London take about four hours and depart frequently.

Bus

National Express (nationalexpress.com) and **MegaBus** (megabus.com) offer dozens of national and international bus connections into Edinburgh, though the connection times, which can run over 10 hours from London, may bring many to consider the budget airline options. Reclining seats and Wi-Fi en route make the ride more bearable, and ticket prices (from £10) make it an attractive option for many on a tight budget.

Car

From London, the M6 leads you through the beautiful lake districts to Edinburgh in about 7.5 hours, assuming minimal traffic. Otherwise, consider the smaller A1 for more detours and stops along the way.

GETTING AROUND

Walking is the best way to explore the compact city of Edinburgh. It's only about a 20-minute walk across town. Walking will save you money and allow you to soak in every nook and cranny this city has to offer—there are tons of them. Just keep in mind that the steep slopes up to the Old Town can wind some folks.

Edinburgh's public transportation system consists of buses and a limited tram system that connects the airport with the city center, stopping in New Town along the way. There is no train or metro transportation within the city.

Bus

Buses are a handy way to visit some of the city's farther-flung sights. If you plan to utilize public transportation a lot, buy a **day ticket** (£3.50), which gives you 24-hour access to all buses and trams in Edinburgh—paying for itself by the third ride. Purchase your ticket either on board the bus or from a Lothian Bus Travel Shop. If you purchase your ticket on board, make sure you have the correct fare, as the driver will not have access to change. The same guidelines apply for a **single ticket** (£1.50).

Taxi

Edinburgh has classic black cabs, which you can flag down on the street or find at one of the numerous taxi stands. A downtown ride should run you no more than £15, but even then it's not cheap. **Uber** is also available in Edinburgh.

Car

Like just about every other medieval city of Europe, Edinburgh was built for pedestrians and horses and carts, not modern cars. Thanks to the public bus network, cars are not necessary to get around town, but they do provide some flexibility if you're considering heading into the Scottish countryside. If that's your plan, Edinburgh's **Park & Ride stations** (edinburgh.gov.uk/parkandride) let you park on the outskirts of the city for free and take public transportation into the city. You just need to pay for your bus ticket into town. Look up locations in Hermiston (open 24 hours), Ingliston (04:00-02:00), Sheriffhal (24 hours), and Straiton (24 hours) for options. All are free and open seven days a week.

Bicycle

Edinburgh is a cycling-friendly city with tons of bike lanes and more on the way. The city council is currently working to enact a public bike rental scheme as in Paris and London. In the meantime, find one of the numerous shops where you can rent a bike for around £12 per half day. These include **Cycle Scotland** (£20/day, 29 Blackfriars St, +44 (0)131 556 5560, cyclescotland.co.uk) in the Old Town and **Bike Trax** (£17/day, 11-13 Lochrin Pl, +44 (0)131 228 6633, biketrax. co.uk) in the West End. Get ready to sweat it out on the steep hills! If it starts raining, the cobblestones get slippery; I recommend parking the bike and walking.

DAY TRIPS

You've got a slew of day trips from Scotland's capital that will get you out into the rugged countryside and away from the big groups of tourists. The best way to do it is with a local guide on a fun group tour. Check out my recommended **tour companies** for options for whisky, visits to castles, hikes out in the countryside, and more. Prices run from £50 for the day, and options are available to keep you busy for weeks.

Glasgow

Just a one-hour train ride away, Scotland's biggest (and proudly patriotic) city is well within reach on a day trip from Edinburgh. With 100,000 more residents, Glasgow is Edinburgh's more industrial, grittier, hipster big sister, but is simultaneously refined with tons of museums and interesting sights. Attractions include the **University of Glasgow** (free, campus always open, about 1.5 miles west of the city center, gla.ac.uk), **Kelingrove Art Gallery and Museum** (free, Sun and Fri 11:00-17:00, Mon-Thurs and Sat 10:00-17:00, Argyle St, glasgowlife.org.uk), the **Gallery of Modern Art** (free, Sun and Fri 11:00-17:00, Mon-Thurs and Sat 10:00-17:00, Royal Exchange Square, glasgowlife.org.uk), and a bustling city center. For those interested in art nouveau (like I am), Glasgow was the home of Charles Mackintosh, the leader of the northern art nouveau. Mackintosh dabbled in everything from design and architecture to watercolor and furniture. You'll see a number of his works as you walk the streets, including the Glasgow School of Art and the *Glasgow Herald* newspaper offices.

Glasgow also has a raging nightlife scene that comes along with the big city feel you'll find here in the modern grid layout. The **West End** (around Byres Road) caters mostly to students thanks to its proximity to the university there. Otherwise, **Bell Street** and **Vincent Street** offer a string of great bars and clubs. Remember the early closing policies of Glasgow—midnight for bars, and 03:00 for clubs, so don't dilly-dally on your night out! If you've got a few extra days and prefer cities over natural beauty, Glasgow's definitely worth an overnight. Trains from Edinburgh take just over one hour for Glasgow and run about £15, with frequent departures.

Loch Ness

Everyone's heard of the legend of Nessie, the aquatic monster of Loch Ness. So, many want to take a day trip north to the lake to see if they can spot her themselves. It's doable in a day, but you'll be leaving early and getting back late, as it's a 3.5-hour straight drive each way. Your best bet is to link up with organized day trips that include fun guides and interesting stops along the way. I recommend **Haggis Adventures,** and their day trip starts at £65 for the 12-hour round-trip tour (haggisadventures.com).

HELP!

Tourist Information Centers

Find the main tourist information center just on the border of the New Town closest to the Old Town, at the top of the Princes Mall shopping center. Pop in here for pamphlets, maps, and souvenirs, but remember that a lot of the placement is paid for by the businesses.

Pickpockets & Scams

My best advice is to simply have your wits about you when walking the streets. Avoid sketchy neighborhoods, stay in well-lit, populated areas, keep your valuables close at hand, and never leave any belongings unattended. While extremely rare, pickpocketing and mugging can still occur if you follow these guidelines, but the chances will be greatly reduced if you use good old-fashioned common sense.

Emergency

In an emergency, dial 999.

Hospital

Royal Infirmary of Edinburgh

51 Little France Crescent

+44 (0)131 536 1000

US Consulate

3 Regent Terrace, Edinburgh EH7 5BW

+44 (0)131 556 8315

APPENDIX

FLYING TO EUROPE FROM THE UNITED STATES

Booking long-haul flights to Europe should be a two-part process: First, find your longer flight to the continent, then search for shorter flights into your destination of choice. If you're beginning your visit in Dublin or Venice, for example, search for direct flights to those cities, but also look into flights to **major transportation hubs** like London, Amsterdam, Frankfurt, and Paris. These airports offer many of the best connections to and from the States. If you're flying from the East Coast, you have additional direct flight options to cities like Madrid and Rome.

If you only frame your search by your desired trip starting point, search engines may get stuck on getting you to that destination on the same airline, skipping over good options. The more creative and flexible you are in your search, the more interesting opportunities you'll find. To promote tourism, airlines like Iceland Air even have deals that offer free multiple-day layovers in certain destinations.

CITY-HOPPING

With planes, trains, and buses, getting around Europe is easy. Each mode of transportation comes with pros and cons. Buses, for example, are often the cheapest option but take the most time. Weigh the value of your time in the destination against the money that you'll save by opting for the slower route.

FLYING

Budget airlines have opened up the continent to backpackers on a budget. Before the advent of cheap flights, a trip from Paris to Madrid would have been an uncomfortable 14-hour overnight train ride. Now, airlines like Ryanair and EasyJet offer a stripped down service for those who value low prices over comfort. While the days of $5 flights are long gone, you can still find deals to get around the continent for less than $100, as long as you know how to play the budget airline game.

Finding Cheap Flights

Let's help you get finding cheap flights down to a science. First, open up a series of web browser windows and conduct the same search across all these different websites:

- skyscanner.net
- cheapoair.com
- kayak.com
- momondo.com

Keep the search as flexible as possible across travel dates, travel times, and airports. Each search engine uses different algorithms to find results, so you may get back four different answers. Pay close attention to the following details:

- **Departure and arrival airports.** Many airlines use budget regional airports a couple hours outside a city. While this keeps costs down, it adds to your connection time and costs to travel into the city. Watch out for this in Paris and Barcelona in particular.

- **Baggage allowance.** Note how much it costs to check a bag. You are often given the choice between 15kg (33lb) and 20kg (44lb) for your checked bag. Pick the accurate one—you'll need to pay extra if you're over by even one kilo.

- **Departure time.** Cheap airlines save money by running super early and super late flights. Some flights leave so early that public transportation to the airport is not even running yet. If that's the case, factor in another €30-40 for a taxi!

Booking Cheap Flights

When you've selected your flight, book directly through the airline's website. This cuts out any middleman fees and potential system glitches, and puts you directly in touch with the airline.

The cheaper the airline, the more ads you'll have to click through and the more "options" you'll have to decline during the booking process. Ryanair offers you luggage, hotels, car rentals, airport transfers, and all sorts of other stuff you don't need or want. You'll have to scour each section to click the No Thank You box.

Be wary when it comes to the final checkout and payment. Before you click your final confirm, double-check the following elements:

- **Departure time.** It will be in 24-hour time! For reference: 09:00 = 9am, 19:00 = 7pm.

- **Departure date.** It will likely be in European format: February 7 is 07/02, not 02/07. Check the date visually on a calendar, or find it spelled out before purchasing.

- **Number of bags you'll need to check.** Pay to check a bag now so you don't need to do so later.

- **Departure and arrival airports.** Some cities have multiple airports, so always note the airport's full name. Also note necessary connection distances and costs.

- **Final price.** Make sure the price hasn't risen exorbitantly since your first search. Tally up the numbers and be sure you understand them. Always decline the option to be charged in US dollars, which is a scam to get you to pay a needless service.

Avoiding Hidden Costs

Extra fees add up. It is important to read and abide by the fine print in all materials relating to your budget flight. Watch out for and avoid these hidden costs:

- **Airport check-in fee.** If you don't check in online ahead of time, some airlines now charge a €40-plus penalty. To avoid this fee, pay attention to all emails you receive from your airline as your date of travel approaches.

- **Baggage checking and carry-on fees.** Checking a bag usually costs €35 for the first bag and €50 for a second. Certain airlines also charge for carry-on bags that are any larger than a medium-sized purse. If you're on a budget, pack light.

- **Boarding pass printing fee.** Print your boarding pass ahead of time, or keep it on your mobile device. Also note that some airports have printing stations that allow you to avoid this fee.

- **Heads-up:** Ryanair requires all non-EU passport holders to get their visa and passport checked before going through security. You need a stamp on your boarding pass clearing you through to your gate. Be sure to do this ahead of time to avoid missing your flight.

Budget Airlines by City

There are many budget airlines based in cities throughout Europe. Pay attention to which city acts as a hub for which airline and you'll generally find cheaper flights.

Amsterdam: Transavia

Barcelona & Madrid: EasyJet, Vueling

Berlin: Air Berlin

Budapest: Wizz Air

Dublin: Aer Lingus, Ryanair

DON'T BE PENNY WISE & POUND FOOLISH

I recently needed to get from Interlaken, Switzerland to Prague for my next WSA tour. My options were a €210 direct flight to Prague on Swissair at a comfortable hour or an earlier €120 flight with EasyJet/Wizz Air that connected through Rome. I jumped on the cheaper option. Here's how the associated costs shook out:

€55 Interlaken-Basel train (about €20 more than the connection would have been to Swissair's airport)

€32 to check my extra bag at the gate

€15 to check in at airport in Rome

€17 on food throughout the course of the day

€38 to check my second bag again

This all resulted in additional costs to the tune of at least €20 more for a less convenient flight. The more expensive flight would have wound up saving me money! Learn from my mistakes and do the math before booking.

TRANSIT TIMES

		Amsterdam	Barcelona	Berlin	Budapest	Dublin
Amsterdam	Bus	x	24	8	21.5	N/A
	Train	x	11.5	6.5	17.5	16.5
	Plane	x	2	1.5	2	1.5
Barcelona	Bus	24	x	33	N/A	N/A
	Train	11.5	x	19	28.5	21.5
	Plane	2	x	2.5	2.5	2.5
Berlin	Bus	8	33	x	15	N/A
	Train	6.5	19	x	12	24
	Plane	1.5	2.5	x	1.5	2
Budapest	Bus	21.5	N/A	15	x	N/A
	Train	17.5	28.5	12	x	N/A
	Plane	2	2.5	1.5	x	3
Dublin	Bus	N/A	N/A	N/A	N/A	x
	Train	16.5	21.5	24	N/A	x
	Plane	1.5	2.5	2	3	x
Edinburgh	Bus	N/A	N/A	N/A	N/A	10
	Train	10	15.5	22.5	N/A	9
	Plane	1.5	3	2	3	1
Florence	Bus	26	17	18.5	15	N/A
	Train	17.5	21.5	16	14	27
	Plane	2	1.5	2	1.5	3
London	Bus	12	27.5	20	16	14.5
	Train	5	11	18.5	19	10
	Plane	1	2.5	2	3	1
Madrid	Bus	27	9	N/A	N/A	N/A
	Train	21	3	25.5	26	N/A
	Plane	2.5	1.5	3	3.5	2.5
Paris	Bus	5	15.5	16	31	25
	Train	3.5	7	8.5	16	18
	Plane	1	1.5	2	2.5	1.5
Prague	Bus	14	10	4.5	10	N/A
	Train	14	24	4.5	7	N/A
	Plane	1.5	2.5	1	1	2.5
Rome	Bus	30	21.5	22	22.5	N/A
	Train	18	22.5	18	16.5	N/A
	Plane	2.5	1.5	2	1.5	3
Venice	Bus	27	23	16	10.5	N/A
	Train	16	22	16	11	N/A
	Plane	2	2	1.5	1.5	2.5

Use this chart to plan the best mode of transit between cities. Travel time (given in hours) is approximate.

Edinburgh	Florence	London	Madrid	Paris	Prague	Rome	Venice
N/A	26	12	27	5	14	30	27
10	17.5	5	21	3.5	14	18	16
1.5	1.5	1	2.5	1	1.5	2.5	2
N/A	17	27.5	9	15.5	10	21.5	23
15.5	21.5	11	3	7	24	22.5	22
2.5	1.5	2.5	1.5	1.5	2.5	1.5	2
N/A	18.5	20	N/A	16	4.5	22	16
22.5	16	18.5	25.5	8.5	4.5	18	16
2	2	2	3	2	1	2	1.5
N/A	15	16	N/A	31	10	22.5	10.5
N/A	14	19	26	16	7	16.5	11
3	1.5	3	3.5	2.5	1	1.5	1.5
10	N/A	14.5	N/A	25	N/A	N/A	N/A
9	27	10	N/A	18	N/A	N/A	N/A
1	3	1	2.5	1.5	2.5	3	2.5
x	N/A	8	N/A	N/A	N/A	N/A	N/A
x	N/A	4.5	N/A	7.5	N/A	N/A	N/A
x	3	1	3	2	2.5	3	2.5
N/A	x	29	26	18	14	4	4
N/A	x	16	26	10	14	1.5	3
3	x	2.5	2.5	2	1.5	1	1
8	29	x	29.5	7	17.5	33	30
4.5	16	x	20.5	2.5	17.5	17.5	16.5
1	2.5	x	2	1	2	2.5	2
N/A	26	29.5	x	16.5	N/A	31	31.5
N/A	26	20.5	x	25	26	25	25
3	2.5	2	x	5	3	2.5	2.5
N/A	18	7	16.5	x	15	21.5	19.5
7.5	10	2.5	25	x	17	11.15	14
2	2	1	5	x	2	2	2
N/A	14	7.5	N/A	15	x	20.5	14
N/A	14	17.5	26	17	x	17.5	12
2.5	1.5	2	3	2	x	2	1.5
N/A	4	33	31	21.5	20.5	x	7
N/A	1.5	17.5	25	11.5	17.5	x	3.5
3	1	2.5	2.5	2	2	x	1
N/A	4	30	31.5	19.5	14	7	x
N/A	3	16.5	25	14	12	3.5	x
2.5	1	2	2.5	2	1.5	1	x

Edinburgh & London: EasyJet

Paris: Air France

Prague: SmartWings, Czech Airlines

Rome, Florence, & Venice: Alitalia

Not-So-Budget Airlines

If you prefer convenience, comfortable seats, and free luggage allowance, budget airlines may not be for you. With these conventional airlines, you'll generally forgo the sneaky hidden costs for a little more up front: **British Airways, Lufthansa, Turkish Airlines, KLM,** and **Swissair.**

TRAINS

Trains are the middle ground between planes and buses for both cost and time en route. Do your search at **sbb.ch,** and book your tickets at local train stations. All of Europe is on the same nifty system, so you can buy train tickets for travel within Italy while you're still in Paris, for example.

Eurail Passes: Are They Worth It?

Everyone has heard of Eurail passes, but almost no one knows if one is right for them. I'd say they're a good option for the organized traveler who knows when and where they want to go. Eurail passes allow unlimited access to as many train rides in as many countries you decide for a flat rate (in a limited time period). Pass price depends on three factors:

- The number of countries in which it is valid

- The number of travel days included (5, 10, 20, unlimited)

- The window of dates during which the pass is valid (3 weeks, 6 weeks, 2 months)

Minimize each of these factors to get the best rate. Consider how much time you'll be spending in each country. If you'll be traveling in Italy, Spain, and France, with a side trip to Amsterdam, book the Eurail pass for three countries only, paying retail for the short trip to Amsterdam from Paris.

Visit eurail.com to view the available options. Personally, I prefer to do my timetable research online and then book my train tickets in person at any train station. This ensures that I receive all applicable discounts, and allows flexibility that I wouldn't get with the Eurail pass.

BUSES

While buses are generally slower than trains and planes, they're most likely your cheapest choice. I've found great bus connections to numerous cities departing daily across the continent. If you sign up for an overnight bus trip, pack some hefty sleeping pills and eye covers. Keep your valuables in a money belt and wear it into the bus so you're not showing everyone your valuables before you go to sleep. Buses are safe, but there are a lot of people getting on and off throughout the night.

Some of my favorite bus line websites are **eurolines.com, orangeways.com, berlinlinienbus.de,** and **studentagencybus.com.** Buses are more popular in Central and Eastern Europe, and provide a number of connections, some of which are as fast as some trains.

RIDE-SHARING

The sharing economy has grown into intercity drives across Europe. Luckily for us backpackers, there's a great website (carpooling.co.uk) where you can search for rides, post a needed ride, or jump on a trip last minute. This option has saved my hide more than once! Of course, safety is always in numbers, and trust your gut when it comes to meeting your driver and actually getting in the car.

CAR RENTAL

Renting a car can be expensive and frustrating. Planes, trains, and buses are often better choices. If you do want to rent a car, consider the following first:

- Most cars in Europe have manual transmissions.

- Parking is challenging and expensive and is regulated differently from one city to the next.

- Signage may not be in English.

- Those under age 25 are obligated to purchase more expensive insurance.

- Gas runs US$8-10 per gallon.

- Most cars are on diesel. Don't fill up the tank with standard gas, or you'll have to pay for a new engine!

- Read the fine print in the rental contract, keeping in mind accident insurance, when the car needs to be back, whether the tank needs to be full upon return, and if there is an additional cost for driving outside the country.

LOCAL TRANSPORTATION

Reading a bus or metro map can be like trying to understand a foreign language. But never fear! It's really simple once you get the hang of it. I've broken everything down for you. Google Maps has integrated just about all public transportation systems and can recommend directions.

TICKETS

Each city has its own system of ticket validation. I've outlined the exact process in each chapter, but the core concept is quite simple: After purchasing your ticket, you must validate it, or get a stamp on your ticket that shows what time you boarded the system. Tickets are generally time-based; validating starts the clock on your 30, 60, or 90 minutes of validity. You validate your ticket either onboard or beforehand at one of the validation machines on the platform. There are hefty fines if you get caught with an unvalidated ticket—but don't let police officers take you to an ATM and force you to withdraw cash. Instead, insist on a paper ticket.

Certain cities, like Budapest, offer multi-day transportation tickets that pay for themselves after a couple of rides. Some sightseeing packages include local transportation as well. Do your research ahead of time, or speak to an attendant at a major station on arrival to see what multi-day options are available.

METRO

As long as you know the name of your stop and can locate it on the metro map,

you won't have any problems reaching your destination. As you enter into the metro, you will see signs for northbound, southbound, eastbound, or westbound platforms. Metro maps are oriented north-south-east-west. On the map, simply locate what station you're currently in and the station you wish to travel to, and go to the platform that gets you in the right direction. If there isn't a direct line between the two stations on the map, you'll need to transfer at the point where the two lines intersect.

BUS & TRAM

Bus and tram maps follow the same basic format. Locate where you are (usually printed in boldface) in the list of stops on the map. Buses (or trams) will go to every destination listed *below* the stop you're at. Everything above the stop has already been visited. If your desired stop isn't below your current station, you've got to find the stop for buses going in the opposite direction.

UBER

Uber is active in a number of European cities, while in others, the taxi unions have blocked the company's access to the market. I mention whether Uber is active in each chapter.

ACCOMMODATIONS & FOOD

I rely almost exclusively on two websites to find my accommodations: **hostelwold.com** and **airbnb.com.** When using either one, do your research by neighborhood. Pick the best neighborhood for you and drill down to those streets to stay in the thick of it rather than commute.

HOSTELS

I love hostels for their social scene, organized activities, and fun atmosphere. While you'll save money staying in a hostel, you may sacrifice quality sleep. In bigger dorms, people come and go throughout the night and day. Bring a lock or leave your valuables at home.

Hostel Booking Tips
- Note the difference between professional photos and traveler shots. The traveler

shots show what the hostel is *really* like. The professional shots are the ones taken years ago when the hostel first opened.

- See what amenities are included. It may save you money to spring for the more expensive hostel if it includes towels, Wi-Fi, breakfast, etc.

- Read the reviews, and watch out for the fake ones that some hostels occasionally leave themselves.

AIRBNB

I use **airbnb.com** if I'm trying to stay in a quiet place with my own room. While this option lacks a social scene, I like having access to a kitchen, knowing that my valuables are secure, and getting to meet a local host who can recommend great bars, restaurants, and more. In certain cities like Paris, Airbnb can be an excellent value, while in cities like Prague and Budapest the value may be less: Hosts charge Western European rates when your money should go much further.

Airbnb Booking Tips

- Narrow your search by the type of accommodation you're comfortable with: entire apartment, private room, or shared room. A private room in a shared apartment will likely be cheaper than having an apartment to yourself.

- Airbnb.com no longer allows you to organize search results by price. You'll have to click through several pages to ensure you're getting the best deal.

- There are hidden fees! At first, you define your budget, but Airbnb has devised a slick system that rounds up and shows you nice options for a few euros more than what you input. Fees include cleaning fees, service fees, and additional guest fees (displayed rates are often for one occupant only). Double-check the final price before booking.

- Read between the lines and see if the apartment is just a money-maker for the owner, or if it's actually their home. Personally, I don't mind either way, but this is a factor for some travelers, depending on whether they want more or less interaction with their host. Read the reviews to anticipate whether the host's style will work for you.

- Pay attention to amenities. Are Wi-Fi and heating or air-conditioning included? Is the restroom private or shared?

- Check out the photos closely! Wide-angle lenses do wonders for the appearance of size of a room.

- Don't hesitate to ask your host about any special offers. It never hurts to ask.

FOOD

Remember that not every meal of your stay needs to be French, Czech, Spanish, etc. Consider treating yourself to one or two local meals and filling the rest of the gaps with cheaper alternatives. In notoriously expensive London, save by seeking out the city's excellent Indian food. Kebabs, sandwiches, and street food are cheap no matter where you go. Local supermarkets usually have everything you need for a relaxing picnic in the park.

Learn to recognize tourist traps. Don't eat at restaurants that are on the main square of any city. If the restaurants have neon lights and menus in 10 languages in the windows, it's safe to assume the locals don't go there. Get off the main drags and find where the locals eat, and you'll pay the locals'—not the tourists'—price.

MOBILE TECHNOLOGY

With the rise in mobile technologies, travelers can stay better connected than ever.

SMARTPHONES

A smartphone in your pocket—even if it's on Wi-Fi-only mode—has really changed the backpacker experience. I consider purchasing a local SIM card if I'm in any one country for more than a week. Otherwise, I rely on the free **Wi-Fi** at my hostel, restaurants, and bars.

I don't recommend purchasing **roaming plans** from your home provider for your entire time in Europe, as they're rarely a good deal. Many American providers are willing to temporarily suspend your account and drop the monthly price down to $10, effectively hibernating your plan until you return home.

Smartphones are a hot commodity, so keep them close. Consider finding a cheap phone to use while abroad. This way you stand to lose a lot less than your phone and everything on it while traveling.

European SIM Cards

You can purchase a European SIM card (the data chip within your phone) in the country you're visiting and top up as needed. With an unlocked smartphone, have the staff at the cell phone store plug in a SIM card. I've used **Vodafone** in most parts of Europe. SIM cards cost around €10 and come with €10 of credit. Opt for the pay-as-you-go plan, topping up by purchasing a scratch card from any convenience store. This method typically costs under €30 per month, whereas monthly plans can be upwards of €60 a month.

Apps

Your smartphone isn't just a camera for your trip abroad. Apps can go a long way toward enhancing your travel experience. **Skype** is a godsend for calling home easily and affordably. Pick a screen name for yourself and make a few practice calls before leaving home. **Facetime** is free while on Wi-Fi to others at home with an Apple device. See below for more of my favorite apps to use while traveling.

INTERNATIONAL CALLS

If dialing Europe from the United States, begin with the US international access code (011)—or, if you're dialing from a cell phone, replace the access code with a plus sign, which you get by holding down the 0. Next, dial the country code (each country has a specific one) of the country you're dialing. Next is a regional code, which is often a two-digit number, but sometimes is a single 0. Skip this when dialing internationally, but include it when dialing domestically. After the country code, the final phone number will be 9-10 digits.

CONVERTERS & ELECTRICAL ADAPTERS

Converters "convert" the electrical current so it doesn't blow out your electronics. Take a close look at whatever you're trying to plug in. If you see 110-220V, you *do not* need an electrical converter. If you only see 110V, you'll need a converter. In my experience, converters are not necessary for iPhones, MacBook Pros, and cameras (including SLRs).

Adapters "adapt" American plugs to physically fit into European outlets. You'll need a continental adapter (with two round prongs) for continental Europe and a British adapter (with three rectangular prongs) in England, Scotland, Ireland, and Wales. Adapters are cheap. Purchase them before your trip for convenience. It's also easy find adapters at local electronic stores all across Europe if you're in a pinch.

RESOURCES

TRANSPORTATION WEBSITES

Make use of helpful **flight search engines** (skyscanner.net, kayak.com, cheapoair.com, momondo.com), sites for booking **train travel** (sbb.ch) and **bus travel** (eurolines.com, orangeways.com, berlinlinienbus.de, and studentagencybus.com, renfe.com), and even a site for **ride-sharing** (carpooling.co.uk).

TRANSPORTATION APPS

Airline apps like EasyJet are streamlined so you can book a flight on the fly with just a few taps. Similarly**,** **iRail** and **SBB Trains** let you search the Eurail database for train timetables. Much like a flight search engine, they let you prioritize by number of stops and also show the route on a map so you can compare your most direct options.

Skyscanner

Global search engine that compares flights, though you can't use it to book directly.

Kayak

Impressively useful—and cheap—flight search engine. Use it for research, then book direct with the airline.

EasyJet

Book EasyJet flights directly.

Ryanair

Book Ryanair flights directly.

Aer Lingus

Book Aer Lingus flights directly.

iRail

Search the Eurail database for train timetables.

SBB Trains

Search the Eurail database for train timetables.

TripIt

Organize your flight travel, keeping confirmation numbers, rewards accounts, etc, handy.

ACCOMMODATIONS WEBSITES

I rely on two websites for booking accommodations: **airbnb.com** and **hostelworld. com.**

ACCOMMODATIONS APPS

Airbnb
Make apartment reservations on the fly.

Hostelworld
Search for sweet hostels.

APPS FOR KEEPING IN TOUCH

WhatsApp
Free messages-over-Wi-Fi service. Set up an account, and text away with any other friends who are also on the service.

Skype
Free and paid hybrid messaging and calling service that lets you video chat with fellow Skype users.

Facetime
Free while on Wi-Fi to others at home with an Apple device.

Facebook
Dial or video call friends around the world for free.

Snapchat
Send image and video updates available only temporarily.

Tinder
Let's face it: Meeting people has evolved in the digital age. Swipe from the comfort of your hostel bunk and set up dates with cute locals and fellow backpackers. Similar apps include **Happn** and **Bumble.**

TRAVEL APPS

Weekend Student Adventures
My own freemium app provides a ton of on-the-go tips and tricks for more than a dozen of my favorite cities.

Rick Steves' Europe Audio Guides
Free, informative travel listening. Search and download all the subjects on your destinations before you leave on your trip.

XE Currency
Keep track of fluctuating conversion rates.

Mint
Balance your budget while abroad.

USEFUL PHRASES

CATALAN

English	Catalan	Pronunciation
Hello.	Hola.	**oh**-lah
Excuse me.	Perdó.	pehr-**doh**
Do you speak English?	¿Parles anglès?	**pahr**-lahs ahn-**glays**
Yes.	Sí.	see
No.	No.	noh
Please.	Si us plau.	see oos plow
Thank you.	Gràcies.	**grah**-see-ahs
Goodbye.	Adéu.	ah-**day**-ooh
How much does it cost?	¿Quant és?	kwahn es
Where are the toilets?	¿On estan els serveis?	ohn an-**stahn** ehls sehr-**vays**
I'd like...	Voldria...	vool-**dree**-ah
...a room	una habitació	**ooh**-nah ah-bee-tah-see-**oh**
...a bed	un llit	un yeet
...a ticket	una entrada	oon-nah ahn-**trah**-dah
...a beer	una cervesa	**ooh**-nah sahr-**veh**-sah
...wine	vi	vee
Where is...	¿On està...	ohn ah-**stah**
...the train station?	l'estació de tren?	lah-stah-see-**yo** dah tren
...the bus station?	l'estació de bus?	las-stah-see-**yo** dah boos

CZECH

English	Czech	Pronunciation
Hello.	Dobrý den.	doh-**bree** den
Excuse me.	Promiňte.	**proh**-meen-tah
Do you speak English?	Mluvíte anglicky?	**mloo**-vee-teh **ahn**-glits-kee
Yes.	Ano.	**ah**-noh
No.	Ne.	neh
Please.	Prosím.	**pro**-seem
Thank you.	Děkuji.	**dyeh**-ku-yee
Goodbye.	Nashledanou.	**nah**-skleh-dah-now
How much does it cost?	Kolik to stojí?	**koh**-lek toh sto-**yee**
Where is the toilet?	Kde je záchod?	guh-**deh** yeh **zah**-hod
I'd like...	Rad(a) bych...	rahd bikh/**rah**-dah bikh
...a room	pokoj	**po**-koy
...a bed	postel	**pos**-tel
...a ticket	lístek	**lees**-tek
...a beer	pivo	**pee**-voh
...wine	vína.	**vee**-na
Where is...	Kde je...	guh-**deh** yeh
...the train station?	nádraží?	**nah**-drah-zee
...the bus station?	autobusové nádraží?	**ow**-toh-boo-soh-veh **nah**-drah-zee

APPENDIX

DUTCH

English	Dutch	Pronunciation
Hello.	Hallo.	**ha**-low
Excuse me.	Pardon	**par**-don
Do you speak English?	Spreekt u Engels?	spreekt oo **en**-gels
Yes.	Ja.	ya
No.	Nee	nay
Please.	Alsjeblieft.	alse-bleeft
Thank you.	Dank u wel	dahnk oo vehl
Goodbye.	Doei.	doo-ie
How much does it cost?	Wat kost het?	vaht kost het
Where is the toilet?	Waar is het toilet?	var ees heht **twah**-leht
I'd like...	Ik wil graag...	eek vil ghraagh
...a room	een kamer	ayn **kah**-mer
...a bed	een bed	ayn bed
...a ticket	een kaartje	ayn **kart**-yeh
...a beer	een biertje	ayn biert-je
...wine	wijn	vine
Where is	Waar is	var ees
...the train station?	het station	het **stash**-yun
...the bus station?	het bus station	het boos **stash**-yun

FRENCH

English	French	Pronunciation
Hello.	Bonjour.	bohn-**zhoor**
Excuse me.	Excusez-moi.	eggs-**cue**-say **mwah**
Do you speak English?	Parlez-vous anglais?	**par**-lay voo ahng-**lay**
Yes.	Oui.	wee
No.	Non.	nohn
Please.	S'il vous plait.	see voo play
Thank you.	Merci.	mehr-**see**
Goodbye.	Au revoir.	oh ruh-**vwah**
How much does it cost?	Combien?	cohm-bee-**ahn**
I'd like...	Je voudrais.	zhe **voo**-dray
...a room	une chambre	oon **shahm**-bre
...a bed	un lit	oon lee
...a ticket	un billet	oon **bee**-yay
...a beer	une bière	oone bee-**air**
...wine	vin	van
Where is	Ou est	oo ay
...the train station?	la gare	lah gar
...the bus station?	la gare routière	lah gar root-**yehr**

GERMAN

English	German	Pronunciation
Hello.	Guten Tag.	**goo**-ten tahg
Excuse me.	Entschuldigung.	en-**shool**-di-gung
Do you speak English?	Sprechen Sie Englisch?	**spree**-ken-zee eng-lish
Yes.	Ja.	ya
No.	Nein.	nine
Please.	Bitte.	**bee**-ta
Thank you.	Danke.	**dahn**-ke
Goodbye.	Auf Wiedersehen.	auf **vee**-der-zay-ehn
How much does it cost?	Wie viel kostet es?	vee feel **kost**-et es
Where is the toilet?	Wo sind die Toiletten?	voh zint dee toy-**leh**-tehn
I'd like...	Ich möchte...	eekh **mukh**-te
...a room	...ein Zimmer	ain **zim**-er
...a bed	...ein Bett	...ain bett
...a ticket	...eine Karte	ain **kar**-teh
...a beer	...ein Bier	...ain beer
...wine	...Wein	...vine
Where is	Wo ist	voh eest
...the train station?	...der Bahnhof	...der **bahn**-hof
...the bus station?	...der Busbahnhof	der **boos**-bahn-hof

HUNGARIAN

English	Hungarian	Pronunciation
Hello.	Szia.	**see**-yaw
Excuse me.	Bocsánat.	**boh**-chah-nawt
Do you speak English?	Beszész angolul?	**beh**-say-es **ahn**-go-lool
Yes.	Igen.	**ee**-gan
No.	Nem.	nem
Please.	Kérem.	**kay**-rehm
Thank you.	Köszönöm.	**koo**-sze-nem
Goodbye.	Viszlàt.	**vees**-lat
How much does it cost?	Mennyi?	**men**-yee
I'd like...	Kérnék/ Kérnénk.	**kayr**-nayk/**kayr**-naynk
...a room	...egy szobàt	...eidge **so**-bot
...a bed	...egy àgyat	eidge adg-yacht
...a ticket	...egy jegyet	eidge **yeg**-yet
...a beer	...egy sör	...eidge shohr
...wine	...bor	...bor
Where is	Hol van	hol van
...the train station?	...pàlyaudvar	**pah**-yood-var
...the bus station?	...buszpàlyaudvar	**boos**-pah-yood-var

ITALIAN

English	Italian	Pronunciation
Hello.	Buon giorno.	bwon **jor**-noh
Excuse me.	Permesso.	pear-**may**-soh
Do you speak English?	Lei parla inglese?	lay **par**-lah een-**gle**-zay
Yes.	Sì.	see
No.	No.	noh
Please.	Per favore.	pear fah-**vor**-ay
Thank you.	Grazie.	**grah**-zee-ay
Goodbye.	Ciao ciao.	chow chow
How much does it cost?	Quanto costa?	**kwan**-toh **koh**-stah
Where is the toilet?	Dove la toilette?	doh-**veh** lah twah-**leh**-tay?
I'd like...	Vorrei...	voh-**ray**
...a room	una camera	**oo**-nah **kam**-eh-rah
...a bed	un letto	un let-toh
...a ticket	un biglietto	oon bee-lee-**eh**-toh
...a beer	una birra	**oo**-nah bee-rah
...wine	vino	**vee**-noh
Where is	Dove...	do-vay
...the train station?	stazione	stah-zee-**oh**-nay
...the bus station?	stazione autobus	stah-zee-**oh**-nay **ow**-toh-boos

SPANISH

English	Spanish	Pronunciation
Hello.	Hola.	**oh**-lah
Excuse me.	Perdone.	pehr-**doh**-nay
Do you speak English?	¿Habla usted inglés?	**ah**-blah oo-**sted** een-**glays**
Yes.	Sí.	see
No.	No.	noh
Please.	Por favor.	por fah-**bor**
Thank you.	Gracias.	**grah**-thee-ahs
Goodbye.	Adiós.	ah-dee-**ohs**
How much does it cost?	¿Cuánto cuesta?	**kwan**-toh **kwest**-ah
Where are the toilets?	Dónde están los servicios?	**dohn**-day ay-**stahn** lohs sehr-**bee-**thee-ohs
I'd like...	Me gustaría...	may goo-stah-**ree**-ah
...a room	una habitación	**ooh**-nah ah-bee-tah-thee-**ohn**
...a bed	una cama	**ooh**-nah **kah**-mah
...a ticket	un billete	oon bee-**yeh**-tay
...a beer	una cerveza	**ooh**-nah ther-**beh**-thah
...wine	vino	**vee**-noh
Where is	Dónde está	**dohn**-day eh-**stah**
...the train station?	estación de tren	eh-stah-thee-**ohn** day tren
...the bus station?	estación de autobuses	eh-stah-thee-**ohn** day ow-tow-**boo**-sehs

PHOTO CREDITS

ACKNOWLEDGMENTS

This has been a huge project, and I couldn't have done it without my massive support network of close friends, excellent guides, and patient family who are all just as passionate about the redeeming value of travel as I am. Thanks to each of you from the bottom of my heart. Special thanks to: the Avalon Travel publishing team, Anne Jenkins, Jackie Steves, Rick Steves, Rhianne Taylor, Luke Watson, Bogi Palotas, Barbara Kiraly, Kevi Donat, Alexei Beck, Krista di Euleuterio, Giorgio di Laura, Asoka Esuruoso, Petr Zdenek, Sarka Hostinova, Arthur Bijlholt, Niki Harosi, Asoka Esuruoso, Taylor Smoot, Adi Hadzic, Dawid Kadziolka, Tessa Helber, Eric Miller, Stephen McPhilemy, Martina and Marco Zuccarello, Carlos and Jennifer Galvin, Jenna Laedtke, Christian Roberts, Matthew Jenks, and Mark Lambert.